Presented to:

Butler Area Public Library

In Memory of
Rex Clark

Donor
T.W. Phillips Gas & Oil Company-Butler

Auto Body
Repairing and Refinishing

William K. Toboldt
Member, Society of Automotive Engineers
Member, Automotive Rebuilders Association
Associate Member, Association of Diesel Specialists

Terry L. Richardson
Chair of Industrial Technologies
Northern State University
Aberdeen, South Dakota

Publisher
The Goodheart-Willcox Company, Inc.
Tinley Park, Illinois

William K. Toboldt

Member, Society of Automotive Engineers, Member, Automotive Rebuilders Association; Associate Member, Association of Diesel Specialists

Terry L. Richardson

Chair of Industrial Technologies, Northern State University, Aberdeen, South Dakota. Member, International Technology Education Association; Member, American Vocational Association; Member, Society of Plastics Engineers. Extensive background in plastics and other composites.

Important Safety Notice

The procedures recommended in this book are effective methods of performing auto body repair operations. This book also contains various safety procedures and cautions that must be followed to minimize risk of personal injury and part damage. These notices and cautions are not exhaustive. Those performing a given procedure or using a particular tool must first satisfy themselves that safety is not jeopardized.

Auto Body Repairing and Refinishing contains the most complete and accurate information available at the time of publication. Goodheart-Willcox cannot assume responsibility for any changes, errors, or omissions in this text. Always refer to the appropriate service manual for specific repair.

Library of Congress Catalog Number 99-17781
International Standard Book Number 1-56637-587-8

3 4 5 6 7 8 9 10   00   10 09 08 07 06 05

Library of Congress Cataloging in-Publication Data

Toboldt, William King.
   Auto body repairing and refinishing / by William K. Toboldt and Terry L. Richardson.
      p.   cm.
   Includes index.
   ISBN 1-56637-587-8
   1. Automobiles--Bodies--Maintenance and repair.
I. Richardson, Terry L.   II. Title.
TL255.T58 2000
629.2'6'0288--dc21   99-17781
                                           CIP

Introduction

In the past decade, there have been significant changes in the manufacture and design of vehicles. The growing use of polymers and metal alloys has radically changed the way vehicles are repaired. **Auto Body Repairing and Refinishing** has been extensively revised to include these changes. All phases of body repair, including repair of SMC plastic body panels, unibody and space frame construction, and high-strength steels, are discussed in this text.

The latest innovations and procedures for refinishing are also included in **Auto Body Repairing and Refinishing.** Numerous drawings and photographs are provided in each chapter to enhance the topics being discussed. Safe practices and techniques are stressed to ensure a safe work environment in the body shop.

Auto Body Repairing and Refinishing is intended to serve as an authoritative text for students and apprentices entering a career in the area of auto body repairing and refinishing. The text is organized so that the contents are presented in a logical order. It is well-suited for those people now engaged in auto body repair who want to increase their skills, and also for owners who wish to perform repair jobs that do not involve heavy structural work.

Each year, there are more cars on the road. As a result, there are more collisions, more wrecked vehicle bodies, and more damaged fender panels. This provides plenty of work for those who have auto body repair skills. A chapter on career opportunities is included to provide information on various areas of service in this growing field.

William K. Toboldt
Terry L. Richardson

Contents

Acknowledgements

The Authors and Publisher would like to thank the following companies, organizations, and agencies for their contributions to **Auto Body Repairing and Refinishing.**

Automatic Data Processing,
   Collision Service Division
Bee Line Co.
Binks
Black and Decker Co.
Blackhawk Automotive Inc.
Broncorp Mfg. Co.
Buick
Carborundum Abrasives Co.
Chevrolet
Chicago Pneumatic
Chrysler
Clements National Co.
Delta
DeVilbiss Company
DuPont Co.
Duz-mor
The Eastwood Company
John J. Fannon Co.
Ford
General Motors
Hobart Brothers Co.
Hunter Engineering
Justrite Mfg. Co.
Kent-Moore
Lenco, Inc.
Lincoln, A Pentair Company

Lisle Corp.
LORS Machinery, Inc.
MAC Tools
Mattson Spray Equipment, Inc.
Mitchell International
Nilfisk of America
Nissan
NORCO Industries, Inc.
Oatey
OTC Division of SPX Corporation
PBR Industries
Pull-it Corporation
Saturn
Seelye, Inc.
Smokeeter
Snap-on Tools Corp.
Solar Division of Century Mfg. Co.
Spartan International
Stewart-Warner Corp.
Tech-Cor, Inc.
3-M
Thornridge Motors
Toyota
VACO Products
Brian R. White Co.
Willson Safety Products
Monica Willson

I would like to dedicate this book to my father, who operated a body shop for more than forty years, and instilled a sense of pride of workmanship in me.

Terry L. Richardson

chapter 1

Body Shop Operations

After studying this chapter, you will be able to:

☐ Outline the history and development of the auto body.

☐ Describe the advantages and disadvantages of various types of business ownership.

☐ List several considerations that should be taken into account when planning a collision repair and refinishing shop.

Auto Body Origin

The first successful American automobile was built in 1893 by Charles and Frank Duryea, two bicycle mechanics from Springfield, Massachusetts. Early automobiles had wooden bodies that were almost identical to the horse-drawn vehicles of the time. By 1910, more than 600 companies were manufacturing automobiles in the United States. However, most of these companies were extremely small and never produced more than a few cars.

It is virtually impossible to determine when the first automobile collision occurred or estimate the number of motor vehicles in use by 1900. The first recorded automobile-related death occurred in New York in 1899. Although New York was the first state to require vehicle registration in 1901, compulsory registration laws did not go into effect in most states until 1903.

The demand for auto body repair did not develop until about 1910. By this time, fenders and partially enclosed bodies had begun to appear, and cars started to look less like horseless carriages. Although the first automobiles with closed bodies were built by the Fisher brothers in 1908, the design was not universally adopted until 1920.

By 1930, most vehicles were manufactured with the body built over a steel frame. The body and frame were nearly equal in mass (weight). The wood, fabric, glass, and sheet metal used to construct the body sometimes weighed more than the ladder-shaped frame. Body-over-frame construction was the standard for most manufacturers until the early 1980s.

Several foreign and domestic vehicles produced in the 1950s utilized a revolutionary design called **unibody** construction. In this design, the body and frame were manufactured as a single unit, and the body panels provided structural support. Unibody construction became common by 1980. Most automobiles manufactured today are unibody vehicles. It is anticipated that all future automobiles will be of the unibody design. See Chapter 3 for more information about body-over-frame and unibody construction.

Plastics have been used in automobile construction for many years. Although never produced, Henry Ford was planning a vehicle with a plastic body as early as 1941. In 1953, the first production sports car, the Chevrolet Corvette, was manufactured with a glass-reinforced plastic (composite) body.

Plastics have many unique properties. They are strong, light, and corrosion resistant. Additionally, they can be molded in a variety of complex shapes. By 1990, composite plastic panels were being used as structural panels in unibody vehicles. In addition to composite body panels, the 1990 Corvette had composite plastic rear leaf springs. The use of plastics in mechanical components, such as steering shafts, wheels, and engine blocks, is likely to increase as manufacturers look for ways to reduce vehicle weight.

Auto Body Operations

Today, there are approximately one hundred thousand auto body shops in the United States. With more than one hundred fifty million vehicles on the road each year, there will always be work for the body and paint shop.

In 1992, auto body repair and refinishing businesses earned an estimated twelve billion dollars. Over 58% of the vehicles on the road today have had auto body repairs.

There is no way to estimate the amount of auto bodywork accomplished by amateurs or hobbyists. Every town has someone doing ''backyard'' bodywork. This work may be to repair the family sedan or to restore a vintage vehicle.

There has been a shortage of trained collision repair technicians for several years. This shortage is expected to grow in the future. See Chapter 22 for more information on career opportunities.

Professional repair technicians must be well educated and highly skilled. As assembly processes and material technologies change, a thorough understanding of repair methods becomes critical. True professionals must keep up with advancements in the industry and participate in trade or professional associations. They must also confront the ethics and liabilities of operating a business and making repairs. Customers and insurance companies expect the technician to restore damaged vehicles to pre-accident condition. The shop owner and the technician may be legally liable for faulty repairs.

Professional Certification

Many shop owners expect their technicians to be professionally certified. The **National Institute for Automotive Service Excellence (ASE)** offers a certification program for the body and paint technician. For more information on ASE certification, write to the National Institute for Automotive Service Excellence, 1305 Dulles Technology Drive, Herndon, VA 22071-3145.

Educational courses, instructional literature, and certificates of achievement are available from the **Inter-Industry Conference on Auto Collision Repair (I-CAR)**. For more information about I-CAR courses and literature, write to I-CAR, Committee Handbook, 3701 Algonquin Road, Suite 400, Rolling Meadows, Illinois 60008.

Various automotive tool and equipment manufacturers also recognize the importance of professional certification. Many provide a license, certificate, or other credentials to verify minimum standards of technical knowledge.

Types of Ownership

There are three types of auto body shop ownership: proprietorships, partnerships, and corporations. Although body shops are occasionally classified by size, the terms large, medium, and small have only relative meaning. Proprietorships are often ''larger'' than partnerships or corporations.

Proprietorship

A **proprietorship** is a company or shop that is owned and operated by one person. This person is legally responsible (liable) for all aspects of the business. Most auto body shops fall into this category. Proprietorships can range in size from small, single-stall garages to large shops with multiple stalls and several employees, Figure 1-1.

Figure 1-1   This body shop is owned by one individual. This type of ownership is called a proprietorship.

Figure 1-2 A partnership is owned by two or more people.

Partnership

A *partnership* exists when two or more people share the legal responsibilities of operating a shop. As a proprietorship grows and expands, a partner is sometimes needed to help operate the business. See Figure 1-2.

Independent Shops. The term *independent shop* is used to describe both proprietorships and partnerships. This name stems from the characteristics of individual owners who desire some degree of independence when making business decisions.

It has become increasingly difficult for small independent shops to compete with large shops and franchised operations. The modern shop needs a computerized information system, dimensional diagnostic equipment, structural repair systems, and downdraft prep stations and spray booths. Large shops and franchised operations generally have the capital to invest in this technology, giving them a competitive advantage over many independent shops.

Independent shops may also find it difficult to take advantage of technical training. Many small shops must temporarily close to allow their employees to attend training sessions.

Corporation

A *corporation* is a business that has many owners. Shares of the corporation, which are called ownership stocks, are sold to raise capital for the business. Each share of stock entitles the stockholder to a voice in the corporation.

Unlike proprietorships and partnerships, stockholders cannot be made to pay for all of the corporation's debts. If a corporation does not have sufficient assets to

pay its debts, it may declare *bankruptcy*. When this occurs, the personal property (cars, home, land) of the stockholders is protected, but their investments (stocks) or loans to the corporation may be lost. Profitable corporations reward the stockholders for purchasing stocks by giving them part of the organization's profits. These rewards are called dividends.

Many new car dealers include a body shop as part of their service center. Many of these shops are part of a larger corporation. There are approximately 24,500 dealer-owned body shops in the United States. See Figure 1-3.

Planning Considerations

There are several important considerations that should be taken into account when planning an auto body shop, including location, appearance, construction costs, shop layout, rent costs, tax rates, and zoning ordinances.

Figure 1-3 This dealer-owned auto body service department is near a constant source of customers.

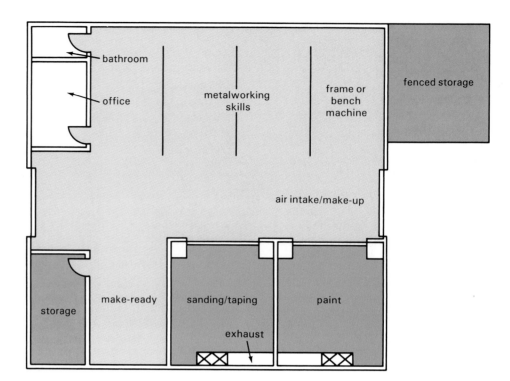

Figure 1-4 Most body shops contain several common elements. This shop has a dedicated stall for straightening equipment. Note the exhaust system in the sanding and painting areas.

Location

The location of a shop facility is extremely important for attracting customers. It does little good to advertise your business if it is difficult to reach. People must be able to find your business easily. A highly visible location on or near a major road is desirable. Auto body shops located in or close to new car dealerships have the advantage of being near a source of customers.

Appearance

The appearance of an auto body shop and its personnel is often more important to customers than location. A clean, well-kept facility with adequate parking will attract customers.

Neat, well-groomed personnel project an image of competence. Uniforms also help provide a professional appearance. A reputation as a dependable, competent, professional shop will keep customers coming back.

Construction Costs

The costs for constructing an auto body shop vary greatly. Construction costs will depend on property costs, building type and size, and local codes. Desirable commercial property in a high-traffic area is costly. Make certain that there is sufficient property for storage, parking, and expansion.

Shop Layout

Shop layout (floor plan) will vary with the type of ownership, the anticipated needs of the owners, and the physical size of the facility. As illustrated in Figure 1-4, there are six areas (zones) in a typical auto body shop, including:

- Office area.
- Storage area.
- Metalworking area.
- Sanding and taping area.
- Painting area.
- Make-ready area.

Office Area. A clean, well-equipped office area is an important part of any body shop. To maintain an efficient, profitable business, accurate records must be kept, and estimates must be carefully calculated.

In addition to miscellaneous supplies, the body shop office should be equipped with estimate forms, repair order forms, and a receipt book. These items are generally designed specifically for the auto body business.

Current shop publications, catalogs, manuals, and part price lists are essential for accurate ordering and proper repair procedures. The use of computers in the body shop continues to increase in popularity. Various programs are available that store and retrieve shop-related information. Estimates, part sources, and other data can be quickly retrieved using a computer system.

Storage Area. An important area that is often overlooked when planning shop layout is the storage area. Most body shops have an inventory of commonly used parts and supplies. Wiper blades, headlight lamps, mechanical fasteners, tape, solvents, sanding disks, etc., are generally stored inside the body shop. Exterior storage is required for larger parts and for vehicles awaiting repair. If necessary, the exterior storage area can be fenced for added security.

Metalworking Area. The metalworking area is where the vehicle's frame and body panels are repaired. The type of equipment in the metalworking area varies. Most shops are equipped with power tools, hand tools, air compressors, etc. Most large shops have frame straightening and wheel alignment equipment. Many small shops, however, do not have this type of equipment and must send straightening and alignment work to the larger facilities. Some shops have a wash stall to clean mud and debris from vehicles before the metalwork begins.

Sanding and Taping Area. The sanding and taping area is used when preparing a vehicle's surface for refinishing. Minor surface imperfections are sanded in this area, and the vehicle is wiped down with a surface preparation solvent. Emblems and other trim pieces are generally removed in the sanding and taping area. Because there are many solvents used in this area, adequate ventilation be must provided. The dust created when sanding old paint is a health hazard. Therefore, proper respiratory protection should be worn in the sanding and taping area.

Painting Area. A clean painting area (booth) is necessary for quality refinishing. A constant effort must be made to keep this area free of dust or other foreign materials that may contaminate freshly painted surfaces. Painting areas are often segregated from other areas of the shop to minimize the contaminates in the surrounding air. The paint booth is equipped with filters to assure that only clean, dust-free air is drawn into the area. A ventilation system pulls airborne paint to the outside of the booth, where another series of filters is generally used to remove paint particles before they are blown into the atmosphere.

Make-Ready Area. The make-ready area of the body shop is where masking tape is removed; parts are reinstalled; and windows, tires, interiors, and vinyl tops are cleaned. Compound polishing and hand rubbing are also done in this area. Minor repairs, such as installing glass, replacing lenses, and adjusting doors, are often performed in the make-ready area.

Other Shop Considerations

Many body shop owners find it more convenient to rent or lease a building than to buy one. One advantage to renting is that the shop owner does not have to make a large investment in property or real estate. It is also easier to relocate or quit a business if the building is rented.

Property tax, sales tax, and state tax must also be considered when deciding on a shop location. Communities and states vary on the methods of assessing taxes. Newly developed areas may have higher property taxes than older, well-established areas.

Most communities have *zoning ordinances* that limit the types of businesses allowed in a particular area or zone. In many cities, auto body shops are allowed only in commercial or industrial zones.

If necessary, a shop must acquire a sales tax permit number. In some states, wholesalers will not sell at wholesale prices unless a sales tax permit number is provided. Some states and communities require body shops to obtain a business or occupational license. Fire department permits are often required for businesses storing, using, or producing flammable or toxic materials.

If a shop employs one or more people, federal income tax, unemployment tax (most states), and Social Security tax must be deducted from the paychecks.

Summary

The first successful American automobile was built by Charles and Frank Duryea. Early automobiles had wooden bodies that were almost identical to horse-drawn carriages. The first automobile with a closed body was built by the Fisher Brothers in 1908. By 1910, partially enclosed bodies started to appear and the demand for body repair began to develop.

In 1930, almost all vehicles were built with a body-over-frame design. However, several vehicles were constructed in the 1950s using a unibody design. Although not common until the 1980s, most cars produced today are of unibody design.

Plastics have been used in automobile construction for many years. It is likely that the use of plastic composites will continue to grow as manufacturers try to reduce vehicle weight.

Today, there are approximately 100,000 body shops in the United States. There is currently a shortage of properly trained collision repair technicians.

Today's technician must be well trained. The National Institute for Automotive Service Excellence (ASE) offers a certification program for body and paint technicians. The Inter-Industry Conference on Auto Collision Repair (I-CAR) offers educational courses, instructional literature, and certificates of achievement. Various tool and equipment manufacturers also offer certification programs.

There are three types of body shop ownership: proprietorships, partnerships, and corporations. A proprietorship is a business that is owned by one person. In a partnership, business responsibilities are shared by more than one person. A corporation is a business that has many owners.

When planning a body shop, the location, appearance, construction costs, and layout must be taken into account. Tax rates and zoning ordinances must also be considered.

Know These Terms

Unibody, ASE, I-CAR, Proprietorship, Partnership, Independent shop, Corporation, Bankruptcy, Shop layout, Zoning ordinances.

Review Questions—Chapter 1

1. The first automobile manufactured in the United States had an enclosed steel body. True or False?

2. _____ designs first appeared in the 1950s.

3. There is a shortage of skilled auto body technicians. True or False?

4. The National Institute for _____ _____ _____ offers a certification program for the auto body technician.

5. A shop that is owned and operated by one person is called a _____.

6. Stockholders are responsible for all of a corporation's debts. True or False?

7. When planning an auto body shop, the owner must consider:
   a. appearance.
   b. costs.
   c. location.
   d. all of the above.

8. Shop layout will be the same for all auto body repair facilities. True or False?

9. List the six areas that should be included in the typical body shop.

10. _____ ordinances describe the types of businesses allowed in a particular area of the community.

Activities—Chapter 1

1. Visit a body shop in your area and ask the owner or manager for a tour of the facility. Take notes and sketch the shop layout. After your visit, write a short description of the shop. Compare your description to the information presented in this chapter.

2. Request auto body literature and information on collision repair courses from ICAR. When you receive these materials, place them in your classroom or shop so they can be used for reference.

3. Walk through your school shop and identify the major areas described in this chapter. Using a CAD program, prepare a drawing of the layout and label each area in the facility.

chapter 2

Body Shop Safety Practices

After studying this chapter, you will be able to:

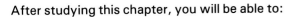

☐ Describe various safety practices that should be followed in the auto body shop.

☐ Explain the importance of the proper use and disposal of hazardous materials.

☐ Use personal protective wear correctly.

☐ Describe how to use the auto body tools and equipment safely.

Hazards in the Body Shop

Shop safety is everyone's responsibility. Most accidents in the auto body shop are caused by careless acts or unsafe working conditions. Approximately 10% of shop accidents are caused by physical or environmental deficiencies, such as poor housekeeping, insufficient guarding, defective equipment, improper working conditions, or improper dress. The remaining 90% are due to unsafe work practices, carelessness, and disobeying rules or procedures.

One of the basic safety rules in any shop involves the proper conduct of individual employees. Running, practical jokes, and horseplay must be prohibited in the shop. This type of behavior invariably results in accidents and distracts other shop personnel from their work.

The auto body shop must be well lighted. Proper lighting prevents eye strain and reduces the possibility of accidents caused by poor illumination. Adequate lighting is essential when doing bodywork and painting.

Due to the nature of the work, the body shop has a tendency to become more cluttered than other types of repair facilities. Pay special attention to keeping the aisles clean and free from obstructions. This may be a difficult task in the auto body shop, because various panels and parts are often removed so that other components can be easily reached. In such cases, place removed parts against the wall or in designated storage areas. A dirty, cluttered work area is not only dangerous, but contributes to poor craftsmanship. The shop floor should be kept clean and free from oil, grease, and solvents. Spills or drips on the floor should be cleaned up immediately. Special compounds are available for absorbing oil and cleaning such spots. Personnel and customers can slip and fall on dirty, oily, or greasy floors. For this reason, signs should be posted to warn visitors that the work areas of the body shop are for personnel only.

Numerous electrical outlets should be provided throughout the shop, so that there is no need to have extension cords running across the shop floor. Refer to page 17 for additional information on the proper use of portable electric tools.

There is a great possibility of cuts, bruises, and pulled muscles in the auto body shop because the body technician often works with sharp, heavy sheet metal parts. Always wear gloves to protect your hands. When lifting heavy items, keep your back straight and lift with your legs.

Everyone in the shop should know how to provide first aid. All accidents and injuries must be reported to the supervisor. Keep emergency numbers posted near each telephone in the shop.

HAZARDOUS SUBSTANCES FOUND IN THE BODY SHOP			
Material	Health Hazards	Material	Health Hazards
Acetone	Flammable; Explosive; Skin irritant; Moderate narcosis from inhalation; Permanent liver and kidney damage	Hydrogen	Flammable; Explosive
Acrylic (finish)	Flammable; Explosive; Narcosis from inhalation; Skin irritant	Lacquer thinner	Flammable; Explosive; Skin irritant; Moderate narcosis from inhalation; Permanent liver and kidney damage
Alkyd (finish)	Flammable; Explosive; Narcosis from inhalation; Skin irritant	Lead	Poison; Respiratory and nerve damage
Aluminum	Lung damage	Methanol	Flammable; Vapor harmful; May be fatal or cause blindness
Asbestos	Respiratory diseases; Carcinogenic	Methyl ethyl ketone	Slightly toxic; Effects disappear after 48 hours
Carbon fibers	Skin and respiratory system irritant	Nitrocellulose lacquer	Flammable; Explosive; Respiratory problems
Carbon monoxide	Asphyxia; Headache; Nausea	Polyester (resin)	Flammable; Explosive; Resporatory problems; Toxic danger from inhalation of styrene monomers; Highly reactive catalyst may cause irreversible liver damage
Cobalt	Skin irritant; Possible lung disease	Polyoxithane (finish)	Flammable; Explosive; Respiratory problems; Nervous system damage
Cyclohexane	Flammable; Inhalation causes liver and kidney damage	Polyurethane (finish)	Flammable solvents; Isocyanates cause respiratory problems, flu-like symptoms, Kidney and liver damage; Carcinogenic
Cyclohexanone	Flammable; Inhaled and absorbed; Possible organ damage	Sulfuric acid	Skin, lung, and eye damage
Epoxy	Flammable; Highly irritating to eyes; Absorbed through skin and respiratory tract; Carcinogenic	Toluene	Similar to benzene; Possible liver damage
Ethylene dichloride	Flammable; Anesthetic and narcotic; Possible nerve damage; Inhaled	Vinyl chloride	Carcinogenic
Ethylene glycol (antifreeze)	Liquid; Gas poisonous if taken internally; Moderately toxic	Zinc	Flu-like symptoms
Glass fibers	Skin irritant; Causes respiratory discomfort	Zinc Chromate (primer)	Flammable solvents; Flu-like symptoms

Figure 2-1   Many hazardous substances are encountered in the auto body shop.

Persons with a history of bronchitis, asthma, or skin problems may be at risk in the auto body environment. Allergic reactions can develop from exposure to many materials (dusts, vapors, fumes, etc.) found in the shop. Skin sensitization can result in rashes, hives, swelling, blistering, or scaling. Respiratory sensitization can result in coughing, shortness of breath, or other symptoms.

Safe Handling of Materials

There are many potentially dangerous materials encountered in the auto body shop. These materials can cause bodily harm and property damage if improperly handled. Always follow the manufacturer's suggestions when working with any material.

Hazardous Materials

Hazardous materials include any material that can cause serious physical harm or pose a risk to the environment. *Hazardous substances* are a subset of hazardous materials. These substances pose a threat to waterways and the environment. A list of several hazardous substances found in auto body shops is shown in Figure 2-1.

The terms hazardous materials and hazardous substances have specific legal meanings. These materials are identified and regulated by the United States Environmental Protection Agency (EPA). There are many laws designed to protect people from the careless use of hazardous materials. You can be prosecuted if any of these laws are broken in your shop. Check state and local laws governing the use and disposal of hazardous materials.

There are four types of hazardous materials found in the body shop:

☐ Flammable materials: easily catch on fire or explode.

☐ Corrosive materials: dissolve metals and damage skin.

☐ Reactive materials: become unstable and likely to burn, explode, or give off toxic fumes.

☐ Toxic materials: cause illness or death from contact, ingestion, or inhalation.

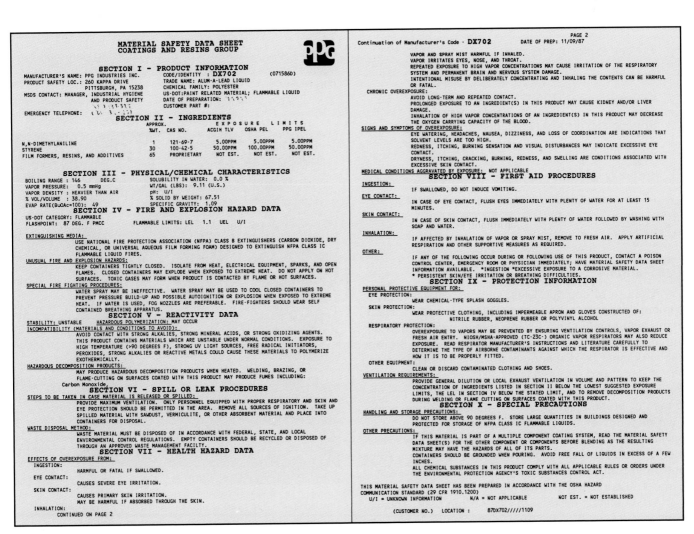

Figure 2-2 Typical material safety data sheet (MSDS). Material safety data sheets must be obtained for all paints and chemicals used in the body shop.

WARNING: Always read product labels and warnings and follow the manufacturer's suggestions. Protect yourself and your co-workers from potential hazards!

Right-to-Know

Right-to-Know laws require employers to inform their employees about the hazardous materials used in the shop and teach them to take the proper safety precautions when using these products. Every employer must make certain that hazardous materials are properly labeled. They must document the fact that their personnel have been trained in the safe use and handling of hazardous materials and keep accurate records of hazardous chemical accidents. Employers are also responsible for keeping up-to-date *material safety data sheets* (MSDS). These sheets are available from paint and chemical manufacturers for every substance they produce. Each MSDS should contain nine sections:

☐ Chemical identification.

☐ Hazardous ingredients.

☐ Physical data.

☐ Fire and explosion data.

☐ Health hazards.

☐ Reactivity data.

☐ Storage and disposal procedures.

☐ Spills and leaks.

☐ Protective equipment.

All personnel should occasionally review MSDS information. A sample MSDS for polyester resin is shown in Figure 2-2.

Fire Dangers

The use of combustibles, such as volatile organic compounds, presents fire and explosion hazards. Flammable and combustible liquids should be stored in approved containers, cabinets, or storage rooms. Storage cabinets must be distinctly marked ''Flammable–Keep Fire Away.'' Bulk storage and transfer containers must have grounding and bond wire connections to prevent sparks of static electricity from causing an explosion. Two methods of transferring liquids from a drum to a portable safety can are shown in Figure 2-3. Always remember to replace the caps or lids on all containers. Rags and other combustible materials should be disposed of in a metal receptacle with a lid, Figure 2-4.

When plastic parts burn, they often melt. This results in the spread of the fire. Some plastics emit large amounts of smoke while burning. See Chapter 9 for more information on the characteristics of plastics.

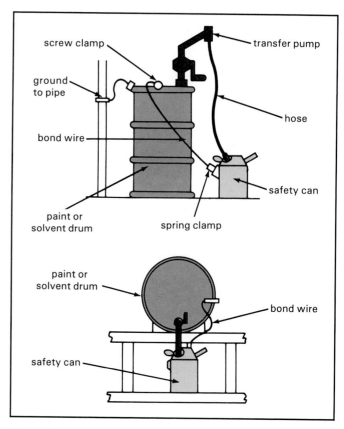

Figure 2-3 Two methods of transferring flammable liquids from a drum to a portable safety can. (Du Pont Co.)

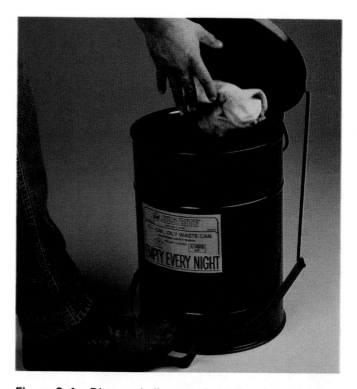

Figure 2-4 Dirty and oily rags should be placed in specially designed cans to prevent ignition of waste from spontaneous combustion or outside sources. (Justrite Mfg. Co.)

The danger of fire is always present when welding and grinding equipment are used. Smoking and unprotected flames should never be permitted in the shop. Warning signs should be prominently displayed throughout the facility, Figure 2-5.

Everyone working in the shop should be familiar with the location and use of fire extinguishers. It is the responsibility of the shop owner or manager to inspect fire extinguishers regularly. As a rule, extinguishers should be checked monthly.

Portable fire extinguishers are generally effective for small fires. Dry chemical-type extinguishers leave a residue when used and, therefore, make cleanup difficult. Additionally, dry-type extinguishers can destroy delicate electrical equipment and damage certain finishes. Carbon dioxide and halogenated hydrocarbon (Halon 1211) extinguishers eliminate these problems. Multiclass B-C extinguishers are desirable in the body shop. Choosing the right extinguisher is extremely important. Seek advice from your local fire department and fire insurance carrier on the selection of proper types and sizes. See Figure 2-6.

Depending on the nature of a collision, a vehicle's electrical wiring may be damaged. If this occurs, there is a strong possibility of an electrical short. Therefore, it is always a good policy to disconnect the battery as soon as any vehicle is brought into a shop. This practice greatly reduces the possibility of electrical fires.

All exits in the shop must be plainly marked "EXIT" with letters not less than 6 in. in height.

Hazardous Wastes

Hazardous wastes are discarded materials that pose a risk to humans or the environment. The EPA has established rules that prohibit washing most chemicals down waste drains, dumping them on the ground, burning them, or throwing them out with other refuse. Product warning labels and MSDS are important sources of information on how to dispose of hazardous products. Contact your local wastewater and sewage treatment office or your state hazardous waste management agency for more information on hazardous wastes. A complete list of hazardous wastes can be obtained from the EPA and is published in the Code of Federal Regulations.

Figure 2-5 No smoking signs should be posted throughout the shop.

Control of Hazardous Wastes

All body shops generate considerable wastes. Paints, thinners, catalysts, solvents, sanding residues, cleaners, and metal preparation chemicals are all considered to be hazardous materials. When the technician disposes of these materials, they become hazardous wastes. It is the owner's responsibility to identify hazardous wastes and document proper disposal.

Recycling and proper disposal are the only two legal methods for eliminating of hazardous wastes. The *Resource Conservation and Recovery Act* (RCRA) was passed to enable the EPA to control and manage hazardous waste generators. There are three categories of hazardous waste generators:

☐ Conditionally exempt waste generators: Produce under 100 kilograms of hazardous waste per month.

☐ Small quantity waste generators: Produce 100 to 1000 kilograms of hazardous waste per month.

☐ Large quantity waste generators: Produce more than 1000 kilograms of hazardous waste per month.

Most auto body shops fall into the conditionally exempt generator category. If you generate fewer than 100 kilograms (about 220 pounds or 25 gallons) of hazardous waste and not more than 1 kilogram (about 2 pounds) of acutely hazardous waste per month, you are a conditionally exempt generator and federal hazardous waste laws require you to do the following:

☐ Identify all hazardous wastes generated.

☐ Send hazardous wastes to an appropriate waste facility or approved landfill.

☐ Dispose of waste before accumulating more than 1000 kilograms of hazardous waste on your property.

Proper hazardous waste management involves good housekeeping. Always use materials as many times as possible before discarding them. This will help reduce the amount of waste produced by your shop. When discarding waste, treat it to reduce potential hazards. If possible, recycle or reclaim all hazardous wastes. Remember not to mix nonhazardous wastes with hazardous wastes. Doing so will make recycling more difficult and disposal more expensive.

If a waste hauler is called to dispose of hazardous wastes, make certain it is from a reputable company. Contact your state or local hazardous management agency to verify the company's credentials. The shop owner is responsible for the safe disposal of hazardous wastes even after they are hauled away! If a hazardous waste spill does occur, contact the National Response Center by calling 1-800-424-8802. A fine of $10,000 and/or a year in jail may result from the failure to report spills.

Some auto body shops are equipped with solvent recovery systems. Used thinners and reducers are placed in specially designed solvent recycling equipment, Figure 2-7. These devices filter out paint vehicles so that thinner can be reused as a solvent or cleaner.

Handling Volatiles

As previously mentioned, volatile organic compounds create fire and explosion hazards. Volatile chemicals readily evaporate into the air. Organic compounds contain carbon and hydrogen (better know as hydrocarbons) and are extremely flammable. Most organic compounds are insoluble in water. Therefore, water is an ineffective fire extiguisher when dealing with these compounds. Common organic compounds found in the body shop include solvents, thinners, primers, topcoats, adhesives, hardeners, fillers, and various additives.

Some states have adopted tough regulations for the use of volatile organic compounds (VOC). When *volatile organic compounds* are released into the atmosphere during refinishing and subsequent drying, they react with other compounds and sunlight to form ozone. *Ozone* is the primary component of smog. Check your city and state for VOC limits.

Waterborne paints and high-volume, low-pressure (HVLP) spray equipment are effective ways to deal with the VOC issue. Auto body technicians can expect to use

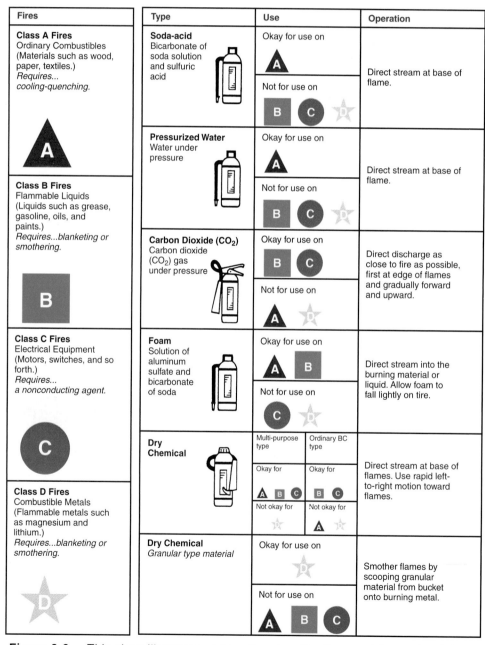

Figure 2-6. This chart illustrates various fire classifications and fire extinguisher types. Always use an extinguisher designed for electrical and chemical fires in the body shop.

Additional protection is warranted when working with chemicals, welders, grinders, drills, or performing other "chip removal" operations. Goggles are effective against airborne debris. Metal shavings and dust particles can be blown great distances with compressed air. Contact lenses should never be worn if you are exposed to chemical liquids, dusts, or vapors. Severe eye damage may result if these materials become trapped under the lenses. Fine particles can enter tiny openings and ducts located in and around the eyes. Examples of typical protective eye wear are shown in Figure 2-8.

Grinders can be very dangerous. Grinding wheels and disks can disintegrate, injuring the operator or others near the machine. The arc produced during many welding procedures can severely burn the eyes. Therefore, a welding helmet equipped with a protective lens or protective goggles must be worn when welding, Figure 2-9.

Figure 2-7 This solvent recycling (recovery) unit removes paint vehicles from used thinners. The 5-gallon model is the most popular size for body shop applications. (PBR Industries)

more waterborne paints and paint compositions that are in compliance with VOC regulations. (See Chapter 15 on use of refinishing materials.) HVLP spray paint systems also help reduce the amount of volatile organic compounds introduced into the air. See Chapters 16 and 17 for more information on the use of refinishing materials and equipment. Eventually, it is possible that only licensed professionals will be able to obtain many of the materials needed for auto bodywork and painting.

Use of Protective Wear and Equipment

Protective wear and equipment should be used to guard against the hazards in the shop environment. Prevention is the best defense against injury. Personal protective wear falls into three broad categories: face protection, body protection, and respiratory protection.

Face Protection

The face and eyes should be protected at all times when working in the auto body shop. A *face shield* or *safety glasses* should be worn to protect the eyes.

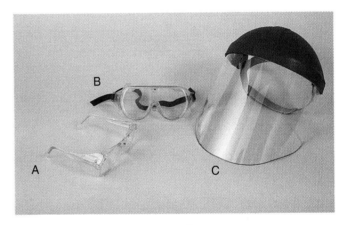

Figure 2-8 Examples of protective eye wear. A—Safety glasses with side shields. B—Safety goggles. C—Safety face shield. (Binks)

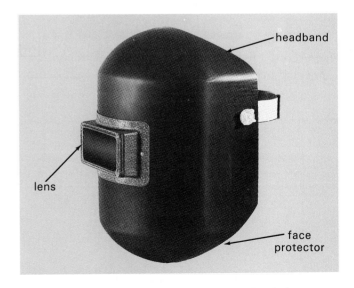

Figure 2-9 One type of protective welding helmet. The helmet shields the face from hot sparks, and the lens protects the eyes from harmful welding arcs.

When working with chemicals and other materials that can cause eye damage, it is essential that an *eye bath* or wash system be provided in the shop. An inexpensive water bath system, such as the one shown in Figure 2-10 can be attached to standard fixtures.

The ears should be protected when grinding, pounding, or working in areas where *noise intensity* may exceed allowable limits. Depending upon intensity, frequency, and duration, noise at a level of 85 dB can lead to hearing loss. Permissible noise exposure levels are shown in Figure 2-11. Excessive and extended noise can affect hearing. Damage frequently occurs gradually and may not be noticeable until it becomes severe. Common protective ear wear is shown in Figure 2-12.

Body Protection

Various types of protective hand wear are shown in Figure 2-13. *Barrier creams* may provide some protection and soothe the skin, but they should never be used as a substitute for gloves. *Nitrile gloves* are commonly used when working with paints, solvents, catalysts, and fillers. Leather gloves offer protection from hot sparks and molten metal when welding or cutting. To minimize the possibility of absorbing hazardous materials into the

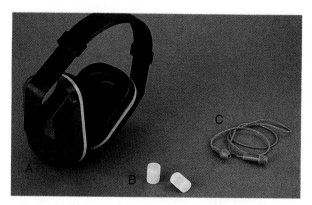

Figure 2-12 Ear protection should be worn to guard against the harmful effects of noise. A–Ear muffs. B and C–Canal cups.

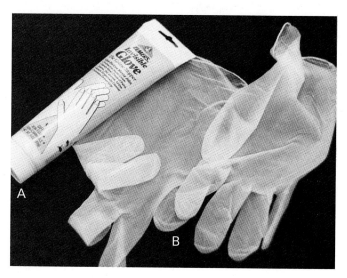

Figure 2-13 Hand protection. A–Hand cream. B–Nitrile gloves.

Figure 2-10 This eye bath system can be connected to a standard faucet.

PERMISSIBLE NOISE EXPOSURES	
Duration Per Day in Hours	Sound Level–dB–Slow Response
8	85
6	92
4	95
3	97
2	100
1 ½	102
1	105
½	110
¼ or Less	115

Figure 2-11 Permissible noise exposures levels.

body, always wash hands thoroughly before rubbing your eyes or eating.

Because auto body personnel must work on concrete floors for long periods of time and risk having objects fall on their feet, well-constructed, metal-toed *safety shoes* should be worn.

Most auto body personnel prefer to wear long-sleeve shirts and long pants. These items permit adequate mobility and provide protection against abrasion and chemicals. Plastic aprons or jackets can be worn when working with chemicals. *Jump suits* or *coveralls* are favored in the painting area. These specially made, lint-free garments resist paint absorption, provide full-body protection, and may be worn over other clothing, Figure 2-14. A leather jacket and leggings or spats should be used for protection when welding, Figure 2-15.

Care must be taken when working around engines or other rotating equipment. Loose clothing can become entangled in moving parts. Neckties should always be

Figure 2-14 This painter is wearing protective coveralls and rubber gloves.

Figure 2-15 Welders should wear a protective welding jacket, gloves, and spats. The jacket, gloves, and spats are often made of leather.

tucked in the shirt, and long sleeves should be buttoned at the cuff. Jewelry should never be worn in the shop area. Always wear caps without brims. A protruding brim can be caught in a rotating part and pulled into a machine. A *hard hat* can help protect the head from abrasions, hot sparks, and chemical sprays.

Respiratory Protection

Ventilation or exhaust fans are not sufficient to protect the auto body technician worker from airborne hazards encountered in the shop. *Carbon monoxide* is a deadly gas, which is created by the incomplete burning of fuel. Even a small amount of carbon monoxide can be fatal. Auto exhaust and space heaters are two common sources of carbon monoxide. Never operate an engine in an enclosed area without proper ventilation. A mechanical ventilation system that is attached to a vehicle's exhaust pipe is the most effective. This type of system forces the exhaust directly to the outside of the shop.

In some shop areas (painting, sanding), an appropriate respirator should be worn. There are three basic types of respirators: air-purifying respirators, atmosphere-supplied respirators, and self-contained respirators. All respirators should be approved by the National Institute for Occupational Safety and Health (NIOSH).

Air-Purifying Respirators

Air-purifying respirators are used to clean or purify the surrounding air. Contaminated air is purified by chemicals in a canister. *Canisters* are designed to remove specific vapors and gases. Care must be taken to select the correct type of canister. The most popular respirators are particulate filter or particulate cartridge types. They provide adequate protection against most particulates and do not restrict movement. Filters and cartridges must be replaced regularly. It is important to note that air-purifying respirators do not filter out all fumes and vapors.

Atmosphere-Supplied Respirators

If air quality becomes too hazardous or if there is a lack of oxygen, *atmosphere-supplied respirators* must be used. These systems employ a blower or a special compressor to supply outside air to a face mask or hood.

Self-Contained Respirators

Self-contained respirators are rarely used in the auto body shop. Nevertheless, compressed air (cylinder), self-contained equipment provides excellent protection and added mobility over atmosphere-supplied respirators. Examples of typical respirators are shown in Figure 2-16.

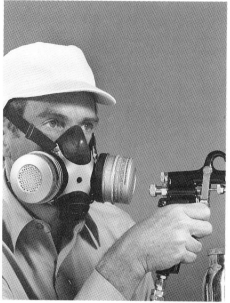

A   B

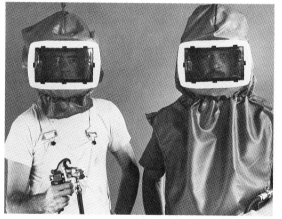

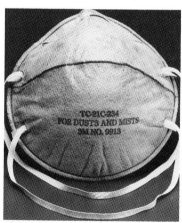

C   D

Figure 2-16 Respirators should be worn to protect against harmful airborne contaminants. A–Air-purifying respirator. B–Atmosphere-supplied respirator. C–Hood respirator. D–Dust/mist respirator. (Binks, 3-M)

Safe Use and Care of Tools and Equipment

Never use shop tools or equipment without a thorough understanding of the proper operating techniques and safety precautions. Always follow the manufacturers' safety recommendations.

Large equipment, such as compressors, paint guns, vacuum cleaners, solvent recovery systems, and welders, is generally provided by the shop owner. Safety precautions concerning specific tools and equipment will be discussed in greater detail as they are introduced in later chapters.

Auto body repair work is frequently performed with the car raised on jacks, lifts, or stands. Make sure all lifting equipment is in safe operating condition and capable of supporting the vehicle at hand. If a floor jack is used, see that the handle does not protrude into an area where it could cause someone to trip. Jack stands must be used when working under vehicles. If lifts are used,

make certain that hoist plates and lift points are properly positioned to prevent damage to unibody or frame components. Make certain all locking devices are engaged before working under any vehicle.

Periodically check the condition of the chains, hooks, and pins on frame and panel straightening equipment. Leaky hydraulic (oil) and pneumatic tools should be repaired immediately. Oil spills can cause extremely slippery floor conditions. Jacks that prematurely or unexpectedly release or bleed off fluids (oil or air) are extremely dangerous.

Clean, dry compressed air is necessary to power pneumatic tools. Any compressed air used for cleaning purposes should be set at a pressure below 30 psi. High-pressure compressed air can blow particles at such a high speed that they will puncture the skin. Air guns should be equipped with a pressure relief nozzle to prevent accidental injection of air into the skin. Compressed air blown through the skin or other body openings can cause serious injury or even death.

Make sure that all portable electric tools are grounded with a third wire (except fully insulated tools) and that the power cords on portable tools are in good condition. Plugs with missing grounding prongs must be repaired immediately. Without the grounding prong, there is a greater possibility of electrical shock. Only authorized personnel should make electrical repairs.

Machine guards are used to prevent personnel from coming into contact with moving parts, such as grinding wheels, cutters, and gears. They also protect the operator from kickbacks and from particles being thrown out of a machine. An unguarded machine is a serious hazard.

Guards on grinding wheels are designed to protect the operator if centrifugal force causes the wheel to fly apart. It is advisable to stand to one side when starting a bench grinder. Anyone standing in line with the rotating grinding wheel can be severely injured if the wheel breaks apart. Never use the side surfaces of a grinding wheel unless the wheel is specifically designed to take such strains.

Auto body personnel usually purchase their own hand tools. Technicians generally take better care of personal tools. Always select the correct tool for the job. High-quality tools will usually last a lifetime. Tools should be kept clean and stored properly. Some body shops provide employees with a tool allowance, which can be used to purchase special tools and replace broken or worn tools. Other shops provide employees with expensive tools and specialized equipment. Defective tools and equipment should be removed from service immediately.

Summary

Shop safety is everyone's responsibility. Most accidents are caused by carelessness and unsafe working conditions. Running and horseplay should never be allowed in the shop. Proper lighting is essential for body shop safety. The shop should be kept clean and free from obstructions. Clean grease and oil spills as soon as they occur.

There are many potentially dangerous materials used in the body shop. Hazardous materials can cause serious physical or environmental harm. Therefore, there are many laws governing the use of hazardous materials. The four types of hazardous materials found in the body shop include flammable materials, corrosive materials, reactive materials, and toxic materials. Right-to-Know laws require employers to teach employees to safely handle the hazardous materials used in the shop. Material safety data sheets contain information on the dangers of hazardous materials. The use of combustibles and volatile chemicals creates fire and explosion hazards. Flammable and combustible liquids should be stored in approved containers. Rags and other combustible materials should be disposed of in metal containers

with lids. Everyone in the shop should be familiar with the use of fire extinguishers.

When hazardous materials are discarded, they become hazardous wastes. Hazardous wastes must be disposed of properly. Shop owners are responsible for the proper disposal of hazardous wastes.

Protective gear should be worn in the body shop. Safety glasses and face shields provide eye and face protection. Goggles are recommended when working with chemicals or performing chip removal operations. All shops should be equipped with an eye bath system. The ears should be protected when working in areas where noise intensity may exceed allowable limits. Gloves should be worn to protect the hands. Metal-toed shoes should be worn to protect feet and toes from falling objects. Long-sleeve shirts and long pants are generally worn in the body shop. Loose clothing can become entangled in rotating machinery. Never wear jewelry in the shop.

An appropriate respirator should be worn to protect the technician from airborne hazards in the shop. When using tools and equipment, follow all manufacturers' safety recommendations.

Know These Terms

Hazardous materials, Hazardous substances, Right-to-Know law, Material safety data sheets, Hazardous wastes, Resource Conservation and Recovery Act, Volatile organic compounds, Ozone, Face shield, Safety glasses, Eye bath, Noise intensity, Barrier creams, Nitrile gloves, Safety shoes, Jump suits, Coveralls, Hard hat, Carbon monoxide, Air-purifying respirators, Canisters, Atmosphere-supplied respirators, Self-contained respirators, Machine guards.

Review Questions–Chapter 2

1. Most shop accidents are caused by defective equipment. True or False?

2. A dirty, cluttered shop contributes to poor _____.

3. Emergency numbers should be posted next to each _____ in the shop.

4. _____ _____ include any material that can cause physical or environmental harm.

5. Right-to-Know laws require employers to inform technicians about the hazardous materials used in the body shop. True or False?

6. Material safety data sheets should be reviewed by all shop employees. True or False?

7. To prevent a fire or explosion, bulk storage tanks must be _____.

8. Burning plastic often _____, which results in the spread of the fire.

9. Multiclass B-C extinguishers are preferred in the body shop. True or False?

10. Hazardous _____ are discarded materials that pose a risk to humans or the environment.

11. Most auto body shops are:
    a. small quantity waste generators.
    b. large quantity waste generators.
    c. conditionally exempt waste generators.
    d. none of the above.

12. A body shop owner is responsible for the proper disposal of hazardous wastes even after they are hauled away. True or False?

13. _____ compounds contain carbon and hydrogen.

14. Volatile organic compounds react with other compounds and sunlight to form _____.

15. Safety glasses offer sufficient protection when working with chemicals. True or False?

16. A noise level of 85 dB can cause hearing loss. True or False?

17. _____ _____ are often worn in the paint area because they are lint free and resist paint absorption.

18. A deadly gas created by the incomplete burning of fuel is:
    a. oxygen.
    b. carbon dioxide.
    c. carbon monoxide.
    d. none of the above.

19. Air-purifying respirators are rarely used in the auto body shop. True or False?

20. When compressed air is used for cleaning purposes, it should be at a pressure below _____ psi.

21. Grounding is not necessary if electric tools are used in dry areas. True or False?

22. Machine _____ protect personnel from moving parts and should never be removed.

23. The side surfaces of all grinding wheels can be used to sharpen equipment. True or False?

Activities–Chapter 2

1. Walk through your shop and identify safety hazards. The work area should be clean and the equipment should be in proper condition. Make sure that fire extinguishers are the correct type for use in the shop and that they have an adequate charge.

2. Write to several refinishing material manufacturers and ask them to send you material safety data sheets (MSDS) for their products. Place the MSDS in a three-ring binder and use them for reference when working in the shop.

3. Identify the hazardous wastes generated in your shop. Write to the appropriate environmental agency in your area and ask for information on hazardous waste disposal in your community.

chapter 3

Auto Body Construction

After studying this chapter, you will be able to:

☐ Classify vehicles by body style and structural design.

☐ Describe the major automobile frame designs.

☐ Discuss the differences between body-over-frame construction and unibody construction.

☐ List several materials used in the manufacture of modern automobile bodies.

☐ Describe the various assembly and joining techniques used in today's vehicles.

Automobile Classifications

Many methods are used to classify automobiles. Some of the classification methods are arbitrary. For example, automobiles that are more than 15 years old are often referred to as **early-model vehicles.** Vehicles manufactured in the last fifteen years are classified as **late-model vehicles.** Most vehicle classifications, however, are more objective. For example, automobiles are often categorized as either foreign or domestic. At one time, vehicles engineered in North America were considered to be **domestic,** and vehicles engineered outside of North America were considered **foreign.** This method of classifying vehicles has changed dramatically. Today, many foreign auto companies are producing vehicles (or components) in the United States. Additionally, several domestic automobile manufacturers are producing vehicles and components in foreign countries. According to government regulations, any vehicle that has at least 75% of its parts manufactured in the United States is considered to be domestic. For example, the 1993 Mazda 626 sedan was engineered in Japan, but 75% of its parts were manufactured in the United States. Therefore, this vehicle is classified as a domestic automobile.

Another criterion used to classify vehicles is the position of the engine. Longitudinal engines, transverse engines, and rear engines are common. **Longitudinal engines** are positioned so the engine's crankshaft is perpendicular to the vehicle's axles. **Transverse engines** are positioned with the crankshaft parallel to the axles. **Rear-engines** are generally mounted directly above or slightly in front of the vehicle's rear axle. See Figure 3-1.

Power train configurations are often used to classify vehicles. Front-, rear-, and four-wheel drive vehicles are primary examples of this type of classification. Generally, rear-wheel drive vehicles are equipped with longitudinal or rear engines, and front-wheel drive vehicles are equipped with transverse engines.

Body styles are also taken into account when classifying vehicles. The terms sedan, station wagon, hatchback (lift-back), coupe, and convertible are common automobile body style classifications. Although commonly used for passenger transportation, vans, minivans, sport-utility vehicles, and pickup trucks are not included in automobile classifications. These vehicles are generally categorized as trucks. See Figure 3-2.

Automobile Construction Materials

To reduce the total mass (weight) of the automobile, high-strength steels, aluminum, and plastic composites are used in automobile construction. If the proposed **Corporate Average Fuel Economy** (CAFE) of 40 mpg is to be realized by the year 2000, the physical size of the automobile may continue to decrease and the use of lightweight materials may increase.

Steel

There are two broad categories of steels: carbon steels and alloy steel. All *carbon steels* are composed of carbon and iron. Carbon steel may also contain small amounts of certain alloying elements, such as sulfur and tungsten. Carbon is the primary strengthening agent in this type of steel. Other names for carbon steel include *mild steel* and *straight steel.* Depending on the carbon content of the steel, carbon steel is commonly classified as high-carbon steel, medium-carbon steel, or low-carbon steel. *High-carbon steels* contain more than .50% carbon, *medium-carbon steels* contain between .35% and 0.5% carbon, and *low-carbon steels* contain between .05% and .35% carbon. Until 1985, most vehicle bodies were made from low-carbon steels. Because of their low carbon content, these steels are easily welded and repaired.

Alloy steel is made by adding relatively large quantities of alloying elements (chromium, tungsten, etc.) to carbon steel to produce certain properties. The type of alloying elements depends on the desired characteristics of the alloy. For example, tungsten is commonly added to steel to produce a strong, abrasion-resistant alloy.

The Society of Automotive Engineers (SAE) and the American Iron and Steel Institute (AISI) have developed a system of number designations, which is based on a steel's alloying elements or carbon content. A Unified

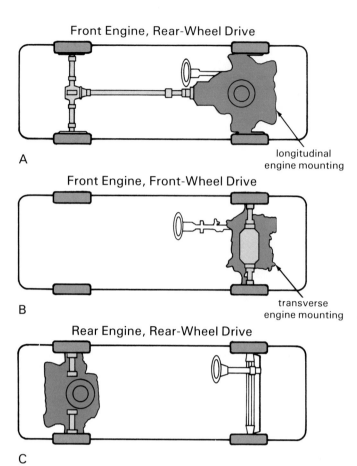

Figure 3-1   Vehicles are often classified by engine position. A–Longitudinal engine. B–Transverse engine. C–Rear engine.

Numbering System (UNS) has also been developed by the SAE and American Society for Testing Materials (ASTM).

Steel is currently the most common material used in auto body construction. High-strength steel unibody construction has replaced the mild steel body-over-frame construction used for most early-model vehicles, Figure 3-3. The auto body technician must take special precautions when working with high-strength steels. Improper repair techniques can cause these materials to lose their desirable properties.

High-strength steels (HSS) are used extensively for structural components in modern unibody and space frame vehicles.

High-strength Steels can be divided into two categories: high-strength, low-alloy steel and ultra high-strength steel.

High-strength, low-alloy steels (HSLA) can have a yield strength of up to 100,000 psi. These steels are stronger and more corrosion resistant than carbon steels. HSLA steels are primarily used in structural applications where weldability is important. The low carbon and alloy contents of these steels increase weldability. In modern unibody construction, high-strength, low-alloy

Figure 3-2 Body styles are taken into account when classifying vehicles.
A–Sedan. B–Coupe. C–Convertible. D–Mini-van. E–Sport-utility vehicle.
F–Pickup truck.

steels are used for front and rear rails, rocker panels, bumper reinforcements, door hinges, and lock pillars. High-strength steels should never be welded using conventional gas welding techniques. Many should not be heated above 700 °F (370 °C). Prolonged heating results in lower strength.

Ultra high-strength steels (UHSS) are extremely strong and have a yield strength that exceeds 150,000 psi. *Tool steels* and other steels with high concentrations of alloying elements are considered ultra high-strength steels. *Martensitic steels,* which are formed by heating and quickly quenching various steels, also fall into this category. Ultra high-strength steels are used in key structural components, hinges, bumper reinforcements, and mechanical components. Be certain to check the manufacturer's specifications for the location of ultra high-strength steel parts. Because UHSS becomes extremely hard and brittle when worked or heated, damaged UHSS components should never be repaired.

Aluminum

Aluminum use has also grown rapidly in the last two decades. Aluminum is light, strong, and corrosion resistant. In 1991, the world's first all-aluminum production car, the Acura NSX, was manufactured.

Figure 3-3 Early-model vehicles had mild-steel, body-over-frame construction. (Buick)

Plastic Composites

Plastic composites are used for body panels on several late-model vehicles. According to industry experts, the extensive use of plastic composites will continue to grow. By using composites, the total number of body parts can be reduced. This will result in significant construction changes. Plastic composites will be covered in detail in Chapter 9.

Auto Body Construction/Structural Designs

There are three principal types of auto body construction used today:

☐ Body-over-frame construction.

☐ Unibody construction.

☐ Space frame construction.

Body-over-frame construction was the primary manufacturing technique prior to 1980. Since that time, unibody construction has been used extensively. About 95% of all passenger cars on the road today are manufactured with unibody construction. Space frame construction, which evolved from unibody construction, consists of a specially designed frame that is covered with plastic body panels.

Auto body personnel must be able to make repairs on all types of automobiles. Repair procedures will vary with the type of construction. With minor damage, such as a dented panel, the procedures are the same for both body-over-frame and unibody construction. Panel replacement is generally easier in body-over-frame vehicles than in unibody vehicles, because the body panels are not load bearing in body-over-frame designs. If the frame is damaged on a body-over-frame vehicle, it must be straightened before performing additional work. When repairing a unibody or space frame vehicle, it must be treated as a single unit because the outer body panels add to the structural integrity of the vehicle.

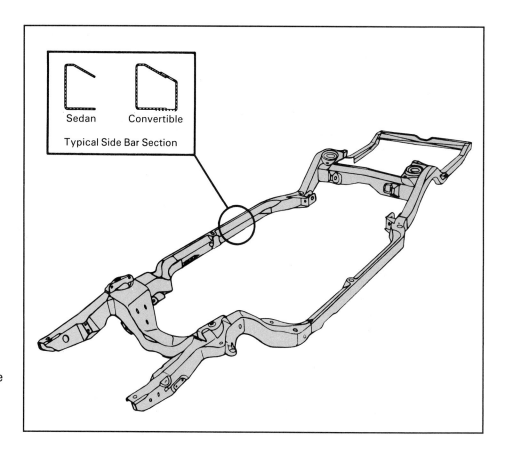

Sedan   Convertible

Typical Side Bar Section

Figure 3-4 Conventional frame construction. The car body is attached to this perimeter-type frame.

Body-Over-Frame Construction

In conventional **body-over-frame construction**, the automobile's body is bolted to a separate frame, Figure 3-4. Over the years, there have been four basic frame designs: ladder frames, X-frames, platform frames, and perimeter frames. See Figure 3-5.

Ladder frames were common in the 1950s. In this design, the frame rails were nearly straight. Several crossmembers were used to stiffen the frame structure. **X-frames** were commonly used on large American cars. This frame design does not rely on the floor pan (underbody area) for torsional rigidity.

Platform frames consist of a floor pan and a central tunnel that runs down the middle to provide strength. This type of frame was used on the Volkswagen Beetle. **Perimeter frames** were used for many years. They are still used for most vans and pickup trucks.

Rubber mounts and pads are used to hold a vehicle's body to the frame. These mounts help reduce the transmission of vibration and noise into the car.

Unibody Construction

In **unibody construction** (unitized body construction), Figure 3-6, individual metal parts are welded together to make up the body assembly and to provide overall body rigidity through an integral, welded-steel construction. A unibody vehicle does not have a separate frame; the body and frame are one piece. A light, strong vehicle is produced with this type of construction.

To add strength in strategic areas of the **floor pan** (underbody area) on a unibody vehicle, box- or channel-like reinforcements called **submembers** are welded to the floor. Power train and suspension systems are generally mounted on these reinforcements.

In some unibody designs, a subframe is used to increase strength. The **subframe** consists of a pair of short rails that is fastened to the car. The subframe is often referred to as the "sub." See Figure 3-7.

If a collision results in damage to one section of a unibody vehicle, other areas are likely to be affected. Stiff unibody designs tend to conduct energy from the point of impact to other portions of the assembly. This may result in misalignment and damage in areas far from the impact. Because there is no heavy frame to effectively push against, pulling techniques are used to repair most unitized bodies. See Chapter 10 for detailed information on repairing unibody damage.

Unibody Sections

A unibody assembly is composed of three major sections: the **doghouse** (front end or front clip), the **greenhouse** (passenger section), and the **rear clip** (rear

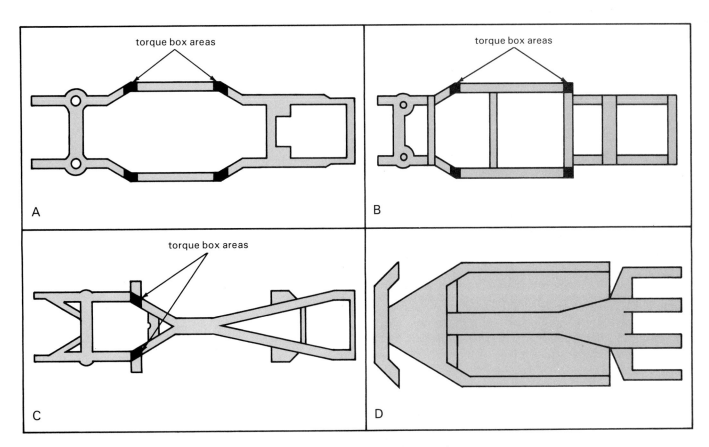

Figure 3-5 Conventional frame designs. A–Perimeter frame. B–Ladder frame. C–X-frame. D–Platform frame.

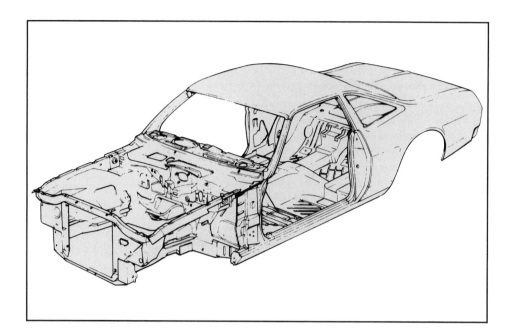

Figure 3-6 Typical unibody vehicle. Note the absence of a separate frame.

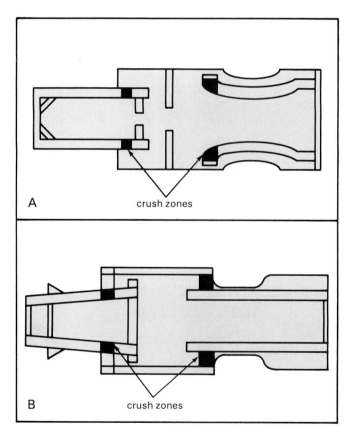

Figure 3-7 Unibody construction designs. A–Unibody construction with subframe welded to the body. This configuration is used on many late-model vehicles. B–Unibody construction with a bolt-on subframe.

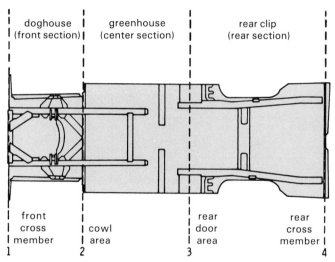

doghouse (front section) greenhouse (center section) rear clip (rear section)

front cross member cowl area rear door area rear cross member

1 2 3 4

Figure 3-8 A unitized body is composed of three major sections: doghouse, greenhouse, and rear clip. (Blackhawk Automotive Inc.)

which is used to locate various automobile components. The hot line is linked to other salvage yards that are tied into the network.

Space Frame Construction

Space frame construction is a variation of unitized body construction. In this type of assembly, molded plastic panels are bonded (with adhesive or mechanical fasteners) to a specially designed space frame. The plastic panels add to the structural integrity of the vehicle. See Figure 3-9.

Figure 3-10 shows a robotic arm applying adhesive to the composite body panels. After the adhesive is applied, the panels are placed on the space frame. The frame contains several mill and drill pads, which serve as

section), Figure 3-8. These section names are used extensively by personnel in body shops and salvage yards to identify the various sections of a vehicle's structure. Most salvage yards have a special telephone hot line,

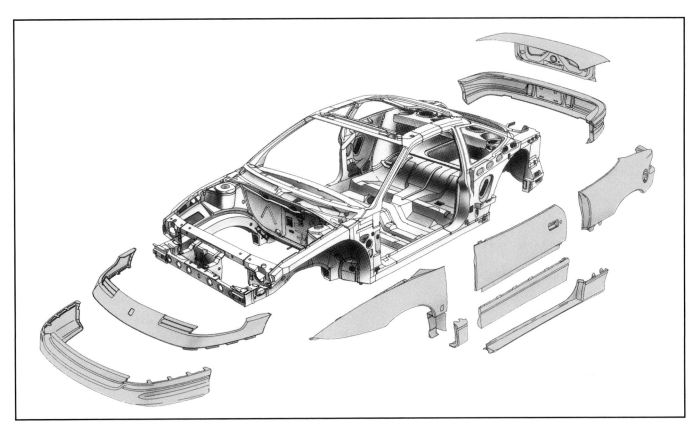

Figure 3-9 A typical space frame and plastic body panels. (Saturn)

locators or reference points when installing the plastic panels. The panels are often held in place with mechanical fasteners while the adhesive cures. When cured, the adhesive provides a strong structural bond. See Chapter 11 for additional information on space frame construction.

Crush Zones

To reduce passenger compartment vibration and absorb energy from impact, torque boxes or crush zones are used in many vehicles. *Torque box* designs allow some twisting to occur in strategically placed areas on the vehicle's frame or rails.

Crush zones, which are generally located on a vehicle's front and rear rails, can be identified by crinkled (pleated), dimpled, or convoluted areas. Some crush zones simply consist of a series of strategically placed holes or slots that allow the rails to collapse on impact. Crush zone and torque box placement on unibody and body-over-frame cars is shown in Figures 3-5 and 3-7.

Body Terminology and Construction

Auto body technicians must be familiar with the proper names of various automobile components. They must also know how each component is constructed. This information will make disassembly and reassembly

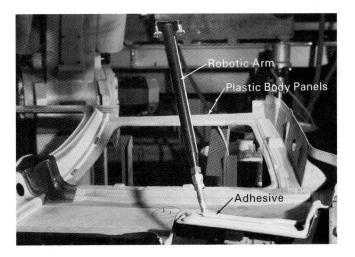

Figure 3-10 During manufacture, a robotic arm is used to apply adhesive to plastic body panels. (Saturn)

much easier. It will also save time and minimize errors when ordering and estimating.

Many of the common terms used to identify individual parts of an automobile are shown in Figure 3-11. Some of these terms date back to the days of horse-drawn coaches. These terms may vary with the manufacturer.

Each year, automobile companies produce *shop manuals* for the cars that they manufacture. These

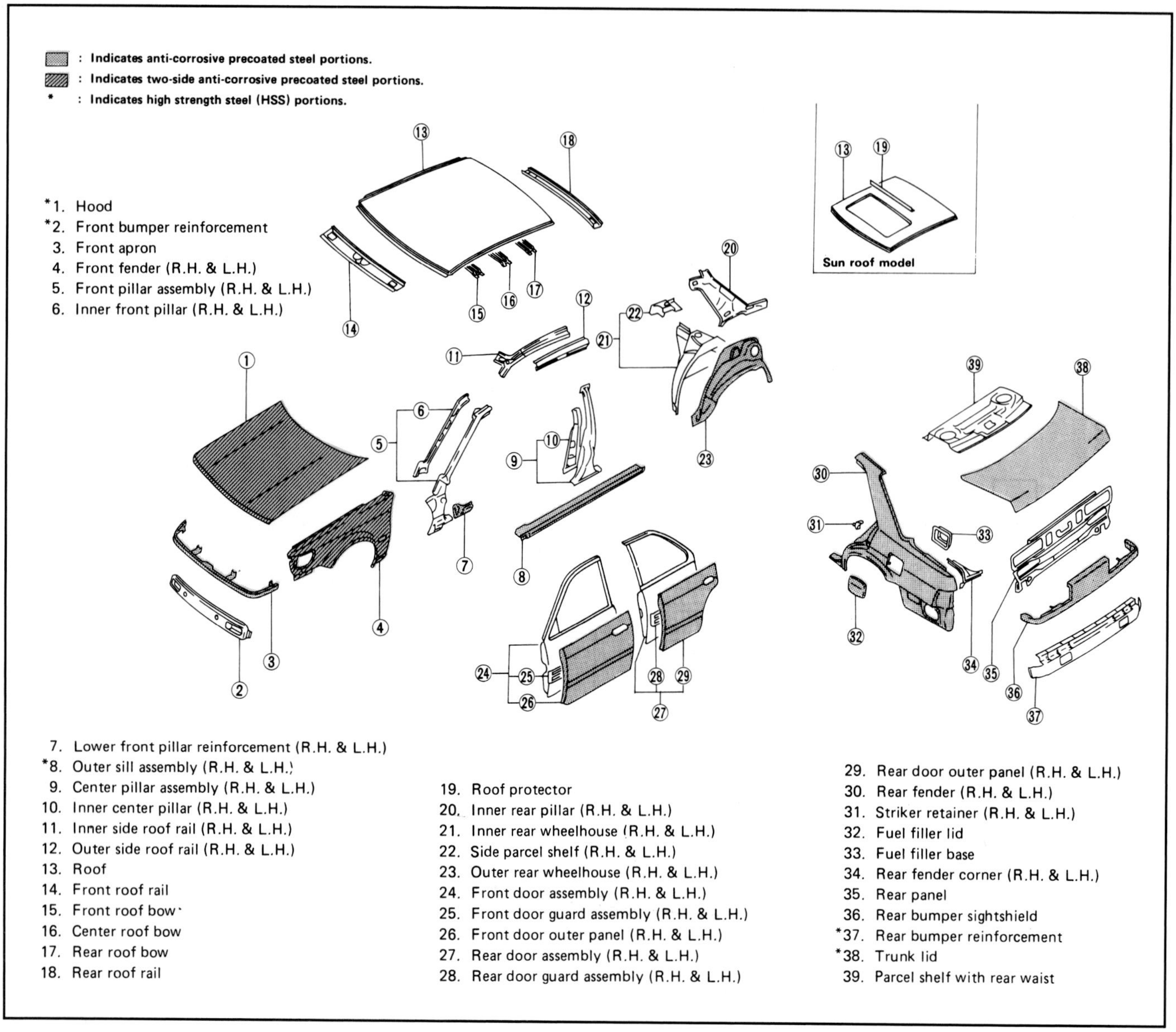

■ : Indicates anti-corrosive precoated steel portions.
▨ : Indicates two-side anti-corrosive precoated steel portions.
* : Indicates high strength steel (HSS) portions.

Sun roof model

*1. Hood
*2. Front bumper reinforcement
 3. Front apron
 4. Front fender (R.H. & L.H.)
 5. Front pillar assembly (R.H. & L.H.)
 6. Inner front pillar (R.H. & L.H.)

 7. Lower front pillar reinforcement (R.H. & L.H.)
*8. Outer sill assembly (R.H. & L.H.)
 9. Center pillar assembly (R.H. & L.H.)
10. Inner center pillar (R.H. & L.H.)
11. Inner side roof rail (R.H. & L.H.)
12. Outer side roof rail (R.H. & L.H.)
13. Roof
14. Front roof rail
15. Front roof bow
16. Center roof bow
17. Rear roof bow
18. Rear roof rail

19. Roof protector
20. Inner rear pillar (R.H. & L.H.)
21. Inner rear wheelhouse (R.H. & L.H.)
22. Side parcel shelf (R.H. & L.H.)
23. Outer rear wheelhouse (R.H. & L.H.)
24. Front door assembly (R.H. & L.H.)
25. Front door guard assembly (R.H. & L.H.)
26. Front door outer panel (R.H. & L.H.)
27. Rear door assembly (R.H. & L.H.)
28. Rear door guard assembly (R.H. & L.H.)

29. Rear door outer panel (R.H. & L.H.)
30. Rear fender (R.H. & L.H.)
31. Striker retainer (R.H. & L.H.)
32. Fuel filler lid
33. Fuel filler base
34. Rear fender corner (R.H. & L.H.)
35. Rear panel
36. Rear bumper sightshield
*37. Rear bumper reinforcement
*38. Trunk lid
39. Parcel shelf with rear waist

Figure 3-11   Common terms used to identify the individual body parts of an automobile. (Nissan)

manuals are important sources of information on the terminology, construction, and repair techniques for specific vehicles. There are also numerous independent publications that contain similar data. Popular magazines and commercially available collision manuals are valuable sources of information. A page from a commercial manual is shown in Figure 3-12. If there is any question about correctly identifying a vehicle's make, body type, year, paint color, etc., check the *vehicle identification number* (VIN), the *paint code plate,* or the *body code plate.* These plates can be found in various places on the automobile. Refer to the appropriate owner's manual for the plate locations. The owner's manual also contains the information necessary to interpret the numbers on the plates, Figure 3-13.

Shop manuals contain many detailed assembly drawings. These drawings should be used by the auto body technician to ensure proper assembly procedures.

Typical locations and names for the underbody components of a unibody vehicle are shown in Figure 3-14. The rear section of a hatchback vehicle is shown in Figure 3-15. Note the names of the different panels and the locations of the seams. Construction techniques will vary with make, model, and year of manufacture. See Chapters 11, 12, and 13 for more information on the illustrations and terminology used to identify various assemblies and parts.

Assembly and Joining Techniques

Modern vehicles are manufactured using a number of assembly techniques. Before repairs can be properly made, it is essential that the technician thoroughly understands how the vehicle is fabricated. Many repairs require the removal, repair, or replacement of entire body sections.

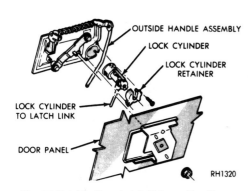

Fig. 17 Outside Door Latch Release Handle

FRONT DOOR LATCH

FRONT DOOR LATCH REMOVAL (FIG. 18)

(1) Remove door trim panel and water shield as necessary to gain access to door latch.
(2) Disconnect all linkage rods from latch.
(3) Disconnect power door lock actuator wire connector.
(4) Remove screws holding latch to door end frame.
(5) Separate door latch from door.

FRONT DOOR LATCH INSTALLATION

Reverse the preceding operation.

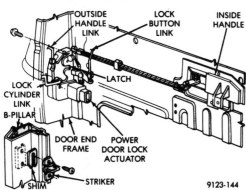

Fig. 18 Front Door Latch

FRONT DOOR SIDE VIEW MIRROR

FRONT DOOR SIDE VIEW MIRROR REMOVAL (FIG. 19)

(1) Remove door trim panel and water shield as necessary to gain access to side view mirror.
(2) Disconnect power side view mirror wire connector, if equipped.
(3) Remove nuts holding side view mirror to door frame.

(4) Separate mirror from door.

FRONT DOOR SIDE VIEW MIRROR INSTALLATION

Reverse the preceding operation.

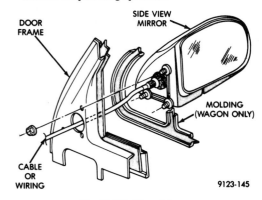

Fig. 19 Side View Mirror

FRONT DOOR GLASS

FRONT DOOR GLASS REMOVAL (FIG. 20)

(1) Remove front door trim panel and water shield.
(2) Raise glass to align attaching nuts to access holes in inner door panel.
(3) Remove nuts holding door glass to window regulator lift plate.
(4) Separate glass from lift plate.
(5) Lift glass upward through opening at top of door.

FRONT DOOR GLASS INSTALLATION

Reverse the preceding operation. To align glass, install attaching nuts hand tight allowing glass to slide on lift plate. Raise glass to full up position. Secure glass attaching nuts.

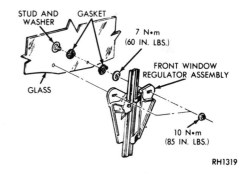

Fig. 20 Front Door Glass

Figure 3-12 Typical page from an auto body repair manual. (Chrysler)

There are two basic categories or types of automotive assemblies: stationary assemblies and movable assemblies. **Stationary assemblies** are permanent and cannot be moved. Stationary assemblies include the roof, cowl, quarter panels, rocker panels, underbody sections, pillars, inner panels, and other reinforcing components. **Movable assemblies** are often attached with hinges and, therefore, can be moved. Movable assemblies include doors, trunk lids, tailgates, hoods, and other components.

Joining Techniques

The techniques for joining sections and components together can be grouped into three broad categories: mechanical joining, adhesive joining, and welding (cohesive joining).

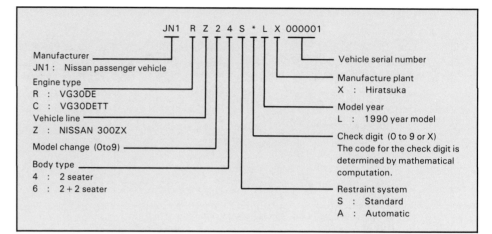

Figure 3-13 Vehicle identification numbers are used to identify vehicle options, year, manufacturer, division, series, engine size, and body code. (Nissan)

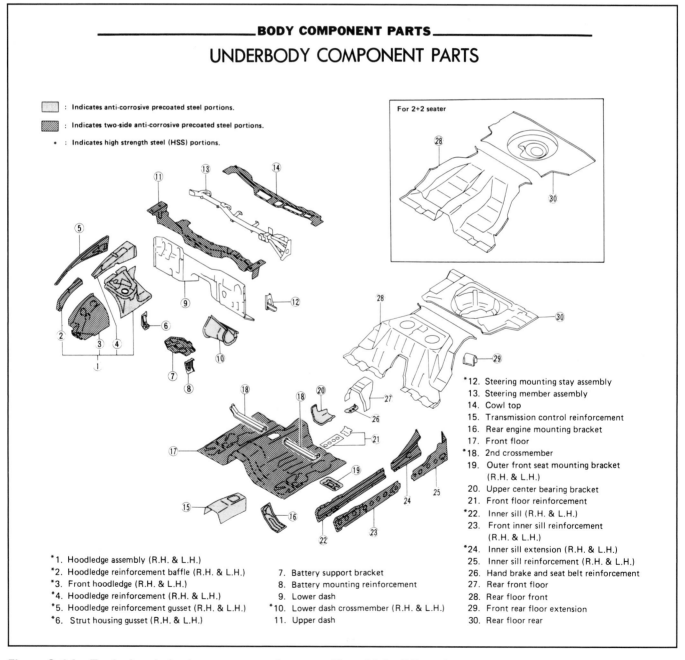

Figure 3-14 Typical underbody components for a specific vehicle. (Nissan)

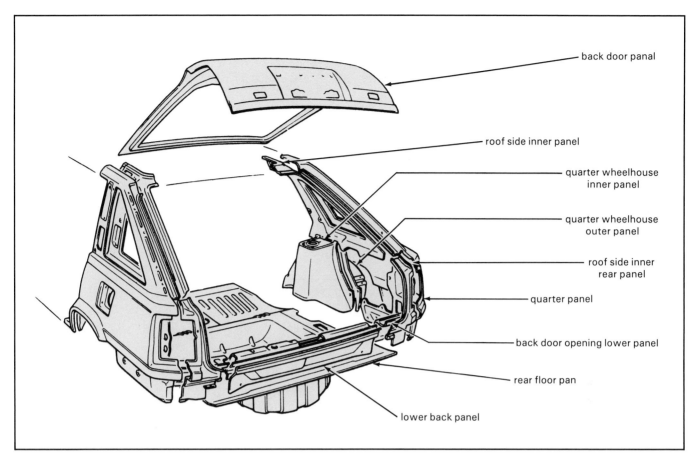

back door panal

roof side inner panel

quarter wheelhouse
inner panel

quarter wheelhouse
outer panel

roof side inner
rear panel

quarter panel

back door opening lower panel

rear floor pan

lower back panel

Figure 3-15 The rear section of a unibody vehicle. (Toyota)

Mechanical Joining

Mechanical joining techniques include assemblies or components that are made by bending metal to form joints. Lids or tops on food and beverage bottles are familiar examples of this technique. Some door components and engine compartment pieces are assembled in this way.

The term *friction fit* is sometimes used to describe a number of pressure-tight joints used in stationary and movable assemblies. Pressure-tight joints do not need mechanical fasteners. **Press fits** and **snap fits** are two types of pressure-tight joints commonly used in auto body construction.

Press fitting implies that an *interference* (negative allowance) is used to insure a tight joint between two parts. Force is required to fit parts together in this type of joint. Studs, bearing races, and shafts commonly use press-fit joints.

In snap-fit joints, parts are forced over a lip or into an undercut retaining ring. Snap-fit joints are commonly used for latches, dome lenses, and instrument panels.

Mechanical fasteners, such as screws, nuts, bolts, rivets, and spring clips, are commonly used in automobile assembly. These fasteners allow for convenient adjustment and replacement of assemblies or components. Mechanical fasteners are commonly used to attach trim moldings to body panels. See Figure 3-16.

Adhesive Joining

Adhesive joining continues to gain popularity in automobile construction. Adhesives, which are available in the form of tapes, films, pastes, and liquids, have a number of advantages over other joining methods. During manufacture, components may be quickly assembled using adhesives. Unlike many mechanical fastening methods, holes are not required for adhesive joints. Adhesives offer excellent bond strength in metal-to-metal, metal-to-glass, and plastic-to-metal assemblies. Adhesive joints seal against moisture, dust, and air. (See sealing and caulking in Chapter 8). Additionally, adhesives do not rust and are resistant to corrosive environments. Inner panels and reinforcing panels are often fastened with adhesives. Adhesive joining techniques are also used for attaching exterior moldings, overlays, and interior mirrors.

On some vehicles, door skins and other body components are attached with adhesives. Structural adhesives are commonly used in conjunction with welds. Some manufacturers apply adhesives to pinch weld seams. This adds strength and torsional rigidity, while providing noise and corrosion protection. Torsional rigidity refers to the resistance to twisting or wrenching of a unitized body or panel. Adhesive joints are commonly stronger than joints secured with mechanical fasteners or spot welds. Adhesive-weld bonds are used on seams around doors, outer rocker panels, and roof side rails.

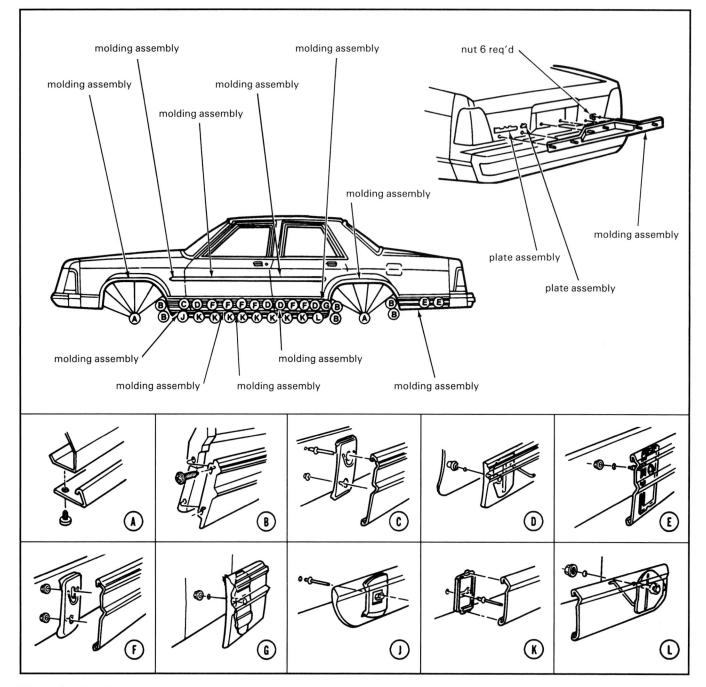

Figure 3-16   Typical clips used to secure exterior moldings. (Ford)

The use of structural adhesives (commonly known as epoxies) will continue to grow as manufacturers seek to improve assembly methods, reduce weight (mass), and add strength and rigidity to vehicles. In adhesive bonds, there is no mingling of molecules between workpieces. The adhesive holds the pieces together by surface attachment (adhesion).

Some plastics (thermoplastics) can be joined by *cohesive* bonding. In this procedure, solvents are used to chemically melt the surfaces together. Therefore, there is mingling of the molecules between parts. Plastic repair is discussed in Chapter 8.

Welding

Welding is a method of melting and fusing two pieces of material together to form a permanent joint.

Considerable skill is required to make high-quality welds. Many hours of training and practice are essential before attempting critical repairs to underbodies and panels. Faulty welding techniques may endanger the lives of customers or result in steering problems, accelerated rusting, and excessive tire wear. Welding will be covered in detail in Chapter 6.

Disassembly

Disassembling an automobile body may seem very complicated. It is best to think of disassembly as a series of small steps. To facilitate reassembly, use a marking pen to label part locations during disassembly. It is important to place identification tags on electrical wires. This procedure is essential if wires are not color coded. It also saves time during reassembly and helps prevent damage to electrical components.

Group related parts together so that they can be easily reassembled. Some technicians put bolts, nuts, shims, washers, and screws in labeled cans. Others put screws and bolts back into their holes. Masking tape is commonly used to hold fasteners, shims, screws, etc., in place so that shop personnel will know exactly how everything should be reassembled.

Summary

Automobiles can be classified by engine position, power train configuration, and body style. Typical body styles include sedans, hardtops, station wagons, and hatchbacks.

There are many materials used to produce modern automobiles. To reduce the total mass of the automobile, aluminum, high-strength steels, and plastics are now being used extensively in automobile construction.

The three types of auto body construction used today include body-over-frame construction, unibody construction, and space frame construction. The auto body is bolted to a separate frame in body-over-frame construction. In unibody construction, metal body parts are welded together to form an integral assembly. A unibody vehicle does not have a separate frame. Space frame construction is a variation of unibody construction. In this design, molded sheets of plastic are fastened to a specially designed frame. The plastic panels add to the structural integrity of the vehicle. Crush zones and torque boxes are designed into frames and rails to help reduce passenger compartment vibration and absorb energy from impact.

The auto body technician must be familiar with various automobile components. Automobile manufacturers and numerous independent companies produce shop manuals, which are excellent sources of information on terminology, construction, and installation techniques. These manuals contain detailed assembly drawings, which are used to guarantee proper part locations and assembly procedures.

When disassembling an auto body, think of the task as a series of small steps. Label part locations with a marker and tag electrical wires for easy reassembly.

Know These Terms

Early-model vehicles, Late-model vehicles, Domestic, Foreign, Longitudinal engines, Transverse engines, Rear-engines, Corporate Average Fuel Economy, High-strength steel, Aluminum, Plastic composites, Body-over-frame construction, Ladder frames, X-frames, Perimeter frames, Platform frames, Unibody construction, Floor pan, Submembers, Subframe, Doghouse, Greenhouse, Rear clip, Space frame, Torque box, Crush zones, Shop manuals, Vehicle identification number, Paint code plate, Body code plate, Stationary assembles, Movable assembles, Mechanical joining, Press fits, Snap fits, Mechanical fasteners, Adhesive joining, Welding.

Review Questions – Chapter 3

1. List several criteria used to classify automobiles.

2. A _____ engine is positioned so that the engine's crankshaft is perpendicular to the vehicle's axles.

3. Rear engines are used in most front-wheel drive vehicles. True or False?

4. High-strength steels, aluminum, and plastics are used in automobile construction to reduce _____.

5. Improper repair techniques can cause high-strength steel to lose its desirable properties. True or False?

6. By using plastic composites, manufacturers can _____ the total number of body parts.

7. List the three types of auto body construction commonly used today.

8. Ladder frames are still used for most vans and pickup trucks. True or False?

9. List the major differences between unibody construction and conventional body-over-frame construction.

10. In a unibody vehicle, the power train and suspension components are attached to _____ on the floor pan.

11. In space frame construction, _____ panels are bonded to a specially designed frame.

12. Torque boxes and crush zones reduce passenger compartment _____ and absorb _____ from an impact.

13. Crush zones are only used on unibody vehicles. True or False?

14. Shop _____ are important sources of information on auto body repair.

15. Information on the make, body style, year, and paint color of a specific car can be found on the _____ _____ _____.

16. Hoods and trunk lids are stationary assemblies. True or False?

17. Welding is the most common mechanical joining technique used in the auto body shop. True or False?

18. Adhesives are available as:
    a. liquids.
    b. tapes.
    c. films.
    d. all of the above.

19. _____ is a method of fusing two pieces of metal together.

20. When disassembling damaged components, they should be _____ to ease installation.

Activities—Chapter 3

1. Collect several manufacturer's sales brochures and group vehicles based on one or more of the classifications described in this chapter. Arrange pictures of vehicles with similar designs together on a poster board. Label the pictures based on the classifications used to group them.

2. If you have access to a video camera, visit a local dealership and record vehicles with various body styles, power train configurations, and engine positions. Show the video to your classmates and explain the differences between the vehicles in the video.

3. Write to several automobile manufacturers and request collision manuals. Store the manuals you receive in your school shop and use them for reference as necessary.

chapter 4

Body Shop
Hand Tools

After studying this chapter, you will be able to:

☐ Explain why having a large assortment of general-purpose hand tools is important.

☐ Explain the importance of owning high-quality tools.

☐ Differentiate between general-purpose tools, specialty tools, and shop tools.

☐ Identify body hammers, slide hammers, dollies, spoons, and other auto body tools.

Tools of the Trade

Professional auto body technicians use a large assortment of hand tools. It is important to purchase high-quality tools. Quality tools will last a lifetime if properly used, cleaned, and stored. Many hand tools are essential for proper repair and craftsmanship. Others, although not necessary, are tremendous time savers.

The number of tools needed to make all types of automobile repairs requires a substantial investment. Therefore, many shop owners prefer to send some repair work to *specialty shops.* These shops specialize in frame straightening, wheel alignment, upholstering, custom painting, etc. By sending specialized work out, the shop owner is not required to invest in the equipment needed to perform such services.

Auto body technicians should be thoroughly familiar with the hand tools found in the body shop. Tools used in the shop can be divided into four broad categories: general-purpose tools, auto body repair tools, specialty tools, and shop tools. Although it is not practical to describe all of the hand tools used in the auto body repair shop, we will cover the most common tools in this chapter. Power tools will be discussed in Chapter 5.

General-Purpose Tools

General-purpose tools are common to any shop that performs automotive service or repair. These tools include wrenches, screwdrivers, pliers, saws, files, hammers, punches, chisels, measuring instruments, and miscellaneous other tools. In addition to auto repair, general-purpose tools are useful for many other jobs, including shop maintenance and equipment repair.

WARNING: Many technicians are injured each year from the improper use of hand tools. Tools should be used only for their intended purpose. Always make certain that tools are kept in proper working condition.

Wrenches

Several types of **wrenches** are used to turn various fasteners. Wrenches are designed to fit over a fastener (bolt or nut) or into a socket head (hex, Torx®, etc.). Therefore, both metric and customary nominal wrench sizes must be slightly larger than the heads of the fasteners (smaller for socket head fasteners). Open-end, box-end, combination, adjustable, socket, torque, pipe, hex, and Torx® wrenches are commonly used in the body shop.

WARNING: Never place an extension on a wrench or hit it with another tool. Metric and customary wrenches are not interchangeable. To prevent injury, use a pulling action when possible. Keep wrenches clean and replace bent or damaged wrenches.

An *open-end wrench* has two flat sides that grip the flat sides of a fastener. Open-end wrenches are used primarily to hold bolts or nuts during disassembly. They are utilized when there is insufficient clearance to use a socket wrench or a box-end wrench. Offset angles of 10° to 60° and turning angles of 15° to 80° allow fasteners to be turned in recessed or confined areas. The wrench must fit securely on the nut or bolt to prevent slipping or rounding of the fastener's corners. See Figure 4-1.

Box-end wrenches completely surround the head of the fastener and have 6 or 12 contact points. Because all flat surfaces on a fastener are gripped when using a box-end wrench, the chance of slipping or rounding is greatly reduced. A 12 point box-end wrench can be swung in an arc of about 15°.

Combination wrenches offer the advantages of both open-end wrenches and box-end wrenches. Combination wrenches are open on one end and closed (boxed) on the other. See Figure 4-2. The closed end of the combination wrench should be used whenever possible.

Adjustable wrenches have one fixed jaw and one movable jaw. The movable jaw can be adjusted to fit various sizes of nuts and bolts. Like open-end wrenches, adjustable wrenches grip two flat sides of a fastener.

When used with too much force, the jaws of the adjustable wrench tend to spread apart and slip. By pulling on the handle of the wrench, force is placed on the fixed jaw and spreading is minimized. Pulling on the wrench also helps prevent skinned knuckles and provides better control over the tool. A pushing action may be required when disassembling components or when tightening fasteners with left-hand threads.

A *socket wrench* consists of a drive handle and a detachable socket. There are several different styles of *drive handles* used to hold and drive the sockets. Breaker bars (break overs or power handles) are used when great turning force is necessary. Removing large, heavily corroded fasteners on bumpers or frame extensions is a typical application for these tools. *Speed handles* (speeders) are designed to turn fasteners quickly. These wrenches are popular in auto body shops because of their long shank length and the speed with which fasteners may be removed or tightened. Speed handles are designed for light torque applications. Various attachments permit use on hex head self-tapping screws and machine bolts or nuts. Phillips, Torx®, hex, square, and other screw head drive accessories are used with speed handles.

The most popular drive handle is the *ratchet handle.* This type of handle allows a nut or bolt to be turned in a restricted area without removing the wrench from the fastener. To prevent damage to the ratchet mechanism, a breaker bar should be used when removing stubborn fasteners. Various drive handles are shown in Figure 4-3.

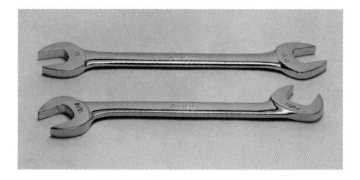

Figure 4-1 Open-end wrenches. Note that the offset is greater on the bottom wrench to assist in turning obstructed fasteners. (Snap-on Tools Corp.)

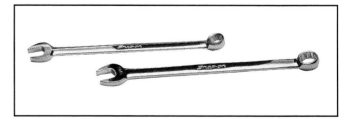

Figure 4-2 Combination wrenches share traits with both open-end wrenches and box-end wrenches. (Snap-on Tools Corp.)

A

B

C

D

Figure 4-3 Various drive handle designs. A–Ratchet. B–Speed handle. C–Breaker Bar. D–T-handle.

Drive handles come in different drive sizes, including 1/4 in., 3/8 in., and 1/2 in. drives. Drive size represents the size of the square lug that the socket fits on. The 1/2 in. drive wrenches and sockets are much stronger than the smaller sizes.

The *sockets* have six or twelve contact points and are designed to fit securely over the heads of nuts and bolts, Figure 4-4. Sockets can be purchased in standard and deep-well configurations. Deep-well sockets can be used to reach nuts that are attached to long bolts or threaded studs.

Torque wrenches are used with standard sockets when nuts and bolts must be tightened to exact torque specifications. The amount of torque applied to a fastener is measured in pound-feet, pound-inches, or newton-meters, Figure 4-5.

Pipe wrenches are seldom used in the auto body shop. These wrenches are designed with an adjustable jaw and a fixed jaw. Both jaws have serrated teeth on their faces to securely hold cylindrical objects. Pipe wrenches are sometimes used to remove damaged studs, hold tie rods, and set up hydraulic pulling equipment.

Hex wrenches (Allen wrenches) are used to remove or tighten mechanical fasteners with hexagon socket heads. *Torx®* wrenches are used to remove or tighten fasteners with six-point, star-shaped socket heads. Torx® screws and hex screws are often used to fasten interior and exterior trim. Both Torx® and hex wrenches are sold in sets with L-shaped and/or T-shaped handles. They are available in a variety of lengths and sizes. See Figure 4-6.

Screwdrivers

A variety of **screwdrivers** are needed in the auto body shop. The size of a screwdriver is determined by the length of its shank and the size of its head. Screwdrivers

are available in several styles, including straight shank (round or square shank) and offset shank designs.

Tip Design

Screwdrivers are classified according to the shape of their tips. The tip of the screwdriver must fit the screw head properly. If the tip is worn or if it is the wrong size,

Figure 4-4 Sockets are available in a variety of styles and configurations. Note the deep-well sockets at the top of the photograph.

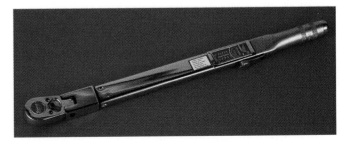

Figure 4-5 This torque wrench displays torque in a small window on its handle. (Snap-on Tools Corp.)

it may damage the screw or jump out of the screw slot. Common screwdriver types include:

- ☐ Standard screwdrivers.
- ☐ Phillips screwdrivers.
- ☐ Pozidriv® screwdrivers.
- ☐ Reed and Prince screwdrivers.
- ☐ Clutch-head screwdrivers.
- ☐ Torx® screwdrivers.

Standard screwdrivers have a straight, flat blade (tip) and are used on screws with slotted heads. They have been in common use for many years. *Phillips screwdrivers* have a four-pronged tip, which fits the four surfaces in heads of Phillips screws. Phillips-head fasteners are widely used on automotive trim and molding. All shops should be equipped with several sizes of Phillips screwdrivers.

Pozidriv® screwdrivers should not be confused with Phillips screwdrivers. Although they have similar tip designs, the tip of the Pozidriv® is much flatter. *Reed and Prince screwdrivers* are also similar to Phillips screwdrivers. However, the tips of Reed and Prince screwdrivers are much more pointed than the tips of Phillips screwdrivers.

Clutch-head screwdrivers come in two styles: the older G-style, which is sometimes called the figure-eight or the butterfly, and the newer A-style. The A-style head, which has an hourglass shape, is commonly used by General Motors. *Torx® screwdrivers* have six-point, star-shaped tips. This configuration continues to gain popularity in the automotive industry. Torx-head drivers and fasteners provide excellent torque and minimize slipping. Some Torx® screwdrivers have a small hole in the end of their heads. This hole enables the drivers to fit over the peg in the center of tamper-resistant Torx® screws. Various screwdriver configurations are shown in Figure 4-7.

Pliers

Pliers are designed for gripping objects and should never be used as substitutes for wrenches. They are available in a variety of shapes, sizes, and configurations. Some pliers have special crimping, cutting, or stripping edges in addition to (or instead of) conventional jaws.

Combination pliers (slip-joint pliers) are commonly used in the auto body shop. They have a notched, flat jaw and may also have a built-in wire cutter. A slip joint allows for two different jaw openings.

Adjustable-joint pliers (interlocking-grip pliers) have long handles and allow for a wide range of jaw adjustments. These pliers are sometimes called Channellock® pliers because of the interlocking channel that keeps the jaws in alignment during adjustment. See Figure 4-8. Large adjustable-joint pliers, which are commonly called water pump pliers, are ideal for heavy-duty work, such as bending sheet metal. The term water pump pliers stems from a time when this tool was used to tighten water pump seals.

Locking-jaw pliers (Vise-grip® pliers) are equipped with a mechanism that locks the tool's jaws in a desired position. Once the jaws are locked in place, they can be released by pulling or squeezing a release lever. Locking-jaw pliers are used for holding metal pieces together while forming, riveting, or welding.

Figure 4-6   Hex and Torx® wrenches are available in several styles. The tools with the L-shaped handles are designed for use in confined spaces. (Snap-on Tools Corp.)

DRIVER CONFIGURATIONS				
⊖	✦	⬡	⬡	✦
Slotted	Phillips®	Torx®	Hex	Pozidriv®
◖	⊗	◼	⊗	✚
Clutch	Eaton Tamper-Proof	Robertson	Torx® Tamper-Proof	Reed-Prince

Figure 4-7   There are many driver configurations used in the auto body shop. Some of the common configurations are illustrated above. (MAC Tools)

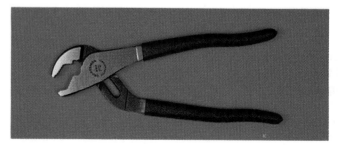

Figure 4-8   Adjustable-joint pliers are used for many jobs in the auto body shop.

Needle-nose pliers have long tapered jaws and are used for holding small wires, clips, pins, or other objects. See Figure 4-9.

Hacksaws

Hacksaws are frequently used in the auto body shop. They consist of a frame, handle, and saw blade. Hacksaw blades are made from high speed steel and are available in standard lengths of 8 in., 10 in., and 12 in. Most blades are 0.50 in. wide and 0.025 in. thick. The spacing of the blade's teeth is called the *pitch.* Common pitches for hacksaw blades are 14, 18, 24, and 32 teeth per inch. Hacksaws are commonly used for cutting small metal parts.

General-Purpose Files

The three **general-purpose files** commonly used in the auto body shop include the flat file, the round file, and the half-round file. These files are generally used to remove burrs and sharp edges from metal parts. Files are sold in many lengths and are available in four different cuts (filing surface configurations): single cut, double cut, curved-tooth cut, and rasp cut. See Figure 4-10.

Most body shops will have a flat, 10 in., double-cut file for general filing of steel and aluminum. Curved-tooth files are commonly used on lead, aluminum, and plastic. Rasps are very course and are generally used for wood removal.

Round or rat-tail files are used to file small radii or to enlarge small holes. Half-round files can be used for flat filing or for shaping large radii and holes.

There is always danger of injury from the pointed tang on the end of the file. Therefore, files should never be used without protective handles. Because they are made of hardened steel, files are extremely brittle. Never use them as pry bars or hit them with a hammer. Small pieces of metal may fly off the file and cause severe injury.

General-Purpose Hammers

Although there are many hammers used in the auto body shop, only **general-purpose hammers** are discussed in this section. Body hammers will be discussed later in this chapter. The three types of general-purpose hammers used in the body shop include hard-faced hammers, soft-faced hammers, and sledge hammers.

Hard-faced hammers have steel heads and are categorized by head weight (mass). The hardened surfaces of these hammers are brittle and should never be struck together. Small pieces of steel may fly off the hammer and cause injury. Care must be taken to ensure that the hammer head is securely attached to the handle. One commonly used hard-faced hammer is the *ball peen hammer.* It is used to form heads on rivets, bend or flatten metal parts, and strike blows when removing stubborn components.

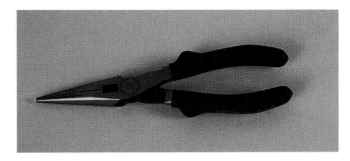

Figure 4-9 Needle-nose pliers are used to hold small objects.

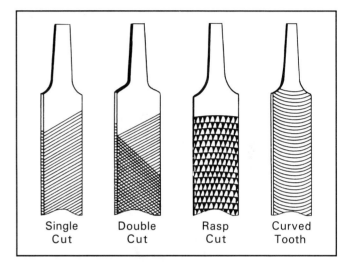

Single Cut   Double Cut   Rasp Cut   Curved Tooth

Figure 4-10 Files are manufactured with various cutting surfaces. Each surface is designed for specific tasks.

Soft-faced hammers are generally made of plastic, rubber, lead, leather, or wood. These hammers are used to minimize damage to the surfaces being struck. A sharp blow with a soft-faced hammer will generally dislodge a stubborn bolt without damaging the bolt head or the threads.

A *sledge hammer* (maul, hand drilling, or engineer hammer) is sometimes used during the initial stages of straightening heavy metal pieces. A hammer with a 12 in. long handle and a 3 lb. head is preferred for most auto body applications. See Figure 4-11.

Chisels and Punches

Chisels and punches are available in a variety of shapes and sizes. See Figure 4-12. They have many applications in the auto body shop. When punch or chisel heads become mushroomed and flared, the tools should be discarded or reground. If the flared end of a chisel (or punch) is hit with a hammer, small pieces of steel may fly off and cause injury.

Flat chisels (cold chisels) are designed for shearing steel. They are commonly used to cut off bolt heads,

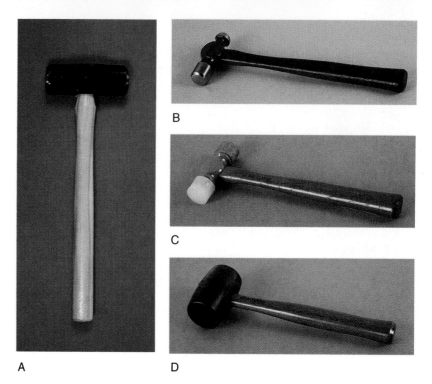

Figure 4-11 Various hammers. A–Sledge. B–Ball peen. C–Plastic tipped. D–Rubber mallet.

A   D

Figure 4-12 Chisels are often available in sets. (Snap-on Tools Corp.)

remove rivets, separate welds, and cut sheet metal. **Pin punches** have long straight shafts and flat tips. They are used to drive out pins and stubborn bolts.

Drift punches (starter punches) have long tapered shafts with flat tips and are used to align holes. They are valuable during the assembly of body components. **Center punches** have pointed, tapered shafts and are commonly used to make "starting dents" for drilling.

Measuring Tools

Several measuring tools are used to measure repair areas and to align body parts. Instruments graduated in metric units and U.S. customary units are needed in the auto body shop.

Tape measures with retractable blades are extremely useful. They can be used to check frame or unibody alignment and measure metal or plastic repair patches. See Figure 4-13. A meter stick with millimeter increments is a popular, inexpensive measuring tool. Dial or digital calipers or micrometers are used for precision measurements in the shop.

A **slide caliper rule** is also useful in the body shop. It can be used for measuring inside or outside dimensions and the depth of holes.

Miscellaneous General-Purpose Tools

Every auto body technician should have a large assortment of miscellaneous hand tools. Although many are not used regularly, it is important that they are available when needed.

Metal snips (metal shears) are used to cut sheet metal. These scissor-like tools are made in several designs. Tin snips are single-action snips used to cut thin metals. Compound lever-action snips are used to achieve more leverage when cutting hard, heavy-gauge sheet metal. Compound lever-action snips, commonly called "aviation snips," have narrow, serrated, offset blades. The offset blades are designed to allow the cut material to pass beneath the operator's hand. Aviation snips are available with jaws that are designed to cut straight, to the left, or to the right. See Figure 4-14.

A **scratch awl** has a long tapered blade, which comes to a point on the end. Scratch awls are useful for marking (scratching) and piercing sheet metal.

Pop rivet guns are designed to place rivets into blind holes. A blind hole is not accessible from the back side of the repair. Special rivets and threaded inserts are also available for use in blind holes. When the handles of a rivet gun are drawn together, the clinching mandrel

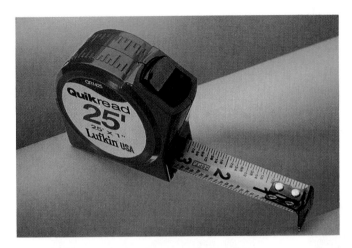

Figure 4-13 A metal tape measure with a retractable blade is very useful in the body shop.

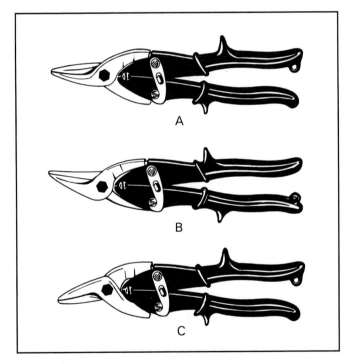

Figure 4-14 Aviation snips are designed to cut straight (A), to the left (B), or to the right (C). The correct tool should be used for each application. (Snap-on Tools Corp.)

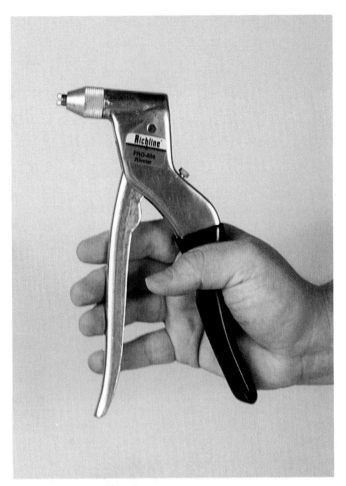

Figure 4-15 Pop rivet guns are used to set rivets in blind holes.

Scrapers and *brushes* are useful for removing gaskets, paint, dirt, and rust. Flexible wire scrapers and blade scrapers are used to remove paint and undercoating. Specially designed scraper handles that hold a single-edged razor blade are used to remove window stickers or other foreign materials from glass. Putty knife scrapers are used for scraping and for spreading body fillers and glazing putty. Brushes are used for many cleaning tasks in the shop. The type of brush used depends on the application. For example, a brush with wire bristles is often used to remove rust and other stubborn materials. See Figure 4-16.

Auto Body Repair Tools

Auto body repair tools are designed for specific auto body repair tasks. Many of these tools are too specialized to be very useful for other types of repair. You should have a thorough understanding of how and when to use each tool before attempting to perform auto body repairs. Common auto body repair tools include body hammers, dollies, spoons, picks, pullers, body files, squeegees, and spreaders.

causes the rivet to spread on the underside of the joint (hole). Body shops use rivets for permanent repairs and as temporary fasteners. Rivets are commonly used to hold panels in place during welding operations. There are several styles and sizes of rivets. The most popular rivet sizes used in the auto body shop are 1/8 in. and 3/16 in. See Figure 4-15.

Utility knives and pocket knives are useful for cutting or trimming tape, upholstery fabrics, and other materials. Many utility knives have retractable blades.

Figure 4-16 Various types of putty knives, scrapers, and brushes are used in the auto body shop. (Snap-on Tools Corp.)

Body Hammers

Although there are many varieties of *body hammers* available, most technicians find that six types are used most often, including the bumping hammer, dinging hammer, pick hammer, finishing hammer, shrinking hammer, and mallet. Selecting the right hammer for the job is extremely important.

Body hammers can have round, square, or pointed heads. The face of the hammer head can be flat, serrated, or slightly crowned (curved). Some body hammers have soft heads or faces. Handle lengths vary from 12 in. to 17 in.

WARNING: Never use a body hammer to pound nails, drive chisels, or strike hardened objects. Striking a hard surface can cause metal fragments to fly from the hammer, resulting in serious injury.

Bumping hammers are probably the most frequently used hammers in the body shop. These hammers may have round or square faces and flat or crowned striking surfaces. Bumping hammers are normally used in conjunction with dolly blocks to "bump" out large dents. This step in repairing body damage is referred to as metal bumping.

Dinging hammers are used to remove small dents from sheet metal. The face of the dinging hammer may be round or square, with a pointed or peen-shaped striking surface. The round face is used for general dinging, and the square face is used when working close to a bead or a bend. The proper technique for using a dinging hammer is covered in detail in Chapter 6.

Pick hammers (combination hammers) are used to remove small dents that would be difficult to remove with a bumping hammer. The most popular pick hammer has a round, smooth face on one end of its head and a pointed shank on the other. The smooth face is used to bring down high spots from a damaged panel. The pick end is used to push up small dents from the underside of the damaged surface. Only light blows are used when striking with the pick (pointed) end. Generally, a pick hammer is used without a dolly. See Figure 4-17.

Figure 4-17 A pick hammer is used to remove small dents.

Finishing hammers are used to achieve the final shape of a damaged panel (metal finishing). Finishing hammers and bumping hammers have similar shapes, but finishing hammers are considerably lighter. The finishing hammer's face is crowned. The striking force should be concentrated on the high spot of the face. Finishing hammers are normally used in conjunction with metal files to prepare body panels for filling and priming. See Chapter 7 for information on straightening.

Shrinking hammers are similar to finishing hammers, but they have serrated or corrugated faces (waffle-like pattern). These hammers are used to help shrink stretched sheet metal. The small serrations on the hammer's face cause metal to gather as it is struck, creating a shrinking effect. This process is sometimes called cold shrinking. A shrinking hammer should only be used with a conventional dolly. Dollies are discussed later in this chapter.

Mallets are hammers with heads (or replaceable faces) made of wood, rubber, leather, lead, plastic, or other soft materials. They can be used to gently bump sheet metal without damaging painted surfaces. A mallet can sometimes be used to straighten chrome trim without marring the finish.

Dollies

Dollies are available in a variety of shapes and sizes. Each shape is intended to be used for specific dents and metal contours. See Figure 4-18. The work surface on most dollies is smooth. A dolly is held against the back of a dent, while the front of the dent is tapped with a dinging hammer. Dollies are sometimes used to bump up low spots. Hammering techniques using dollies are described in Chapter 7. The six most popular dolly shapes include:

☐ *Toe dollies* (used for dinging flat surfaces with low crowns).

☐ *Heel dollies* (used in sharp corners and on wide radii).

☐ *General-purpose dollies* (contain many of the crown shapes needed for general repair).

☐ *Comma wedge dollies* (have a single thin blade to help force up dents from behind curved reinforcements).

☐ *Anvil dollies* (have an oval shape and are designed to fit against outside curves or contours).

☐ *Shrinking dollies* (have serrated faces and are used for cold shrinking).

The serrated pattern on the face of the shrinking dolly creates a series of peaks and valleys in the work surface, thereby decreasing the surface area of the metal. Cold shrinking will be covered in Chapter 7.

Spoons

Spoons are special types of dollies. They have long handles and are designed to reach into areas where obstacles prevent the use of conventional dollies and hammers. See Figure 4-19.

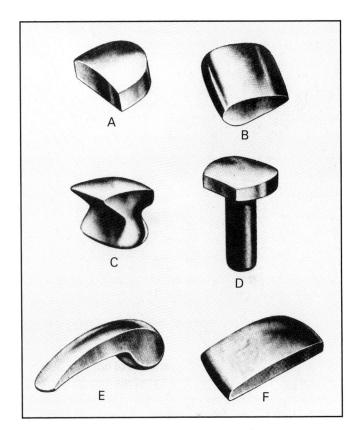

Figure 4-18 An assortment of dolly blocks is necessary for efficient bodywork. A–Heel dolly. B–Utility dolly. C–General-purpose dolly. D–Mushroom dolly. E–Comma wedge dolly. F–Toe dolly.

Figure 4-19 When space prohibits the use of dollies, spoons can be used to help remove damage.

Spoons come in a variety of shapes and sizes. They are used to pry out dents and to spread out hammer blows. They are also useful for reforming sharp crowns on fenders and other body parts. See Figure 4-20. The seven most popular spoon types include:

☐ *Spoon dollies* (have long handles to reach deep pockets in doors and panels).

☐ *Light dinging spoons* (hammering is done on top of these spoons to smooth and level ridges; never use for prying).

☐ *Surfacing spoons* (used for spring hammering, slapping, prying, and as a backup tool for dinging operations).

☐ *Inside high-crown spoons* (have a shallow curve to reach into grooves behind inner construction on doors, hoods, and other panels).

☐ *Inside medium-crown spoons* (used as pry bars or backup tools).

☐ *Inside heavy-duty spoons* (serve as heavy-duty prying, driving, or backup tools).

☐ *Bumping files* (have spoon-like shape and serrated surfaces to slap down and shrink high spots).

WARNING: Bumping files are not designed to be hit with a hammer. They are made from hardened steel and, therefore, may shatter if struck with another hard object.

Picks

Picks are used to push against low spots located in confined spaces. They are designed to push up low areas that cannot be reached with a pick hammer. Most pick tools have pointed ends and U-shaped handles.

Pullers

Pullers are tools used to pull out dents. They are commonly used when it is not possible or desirable to reach a dent from behind. There are three general types of pullers: dent pullers, pull rods, and suction pullers. See Figure 4-21.

Dent pullers are commonly called slide hammers or snatch hammers. These tools consist of a sliding weight that is mounted on a shaft, Figure 4-22. To use a dent puller, holes are drilled in a dented area. Screw or hook devices, which are attached to the dent puller, are placed in the holes. Repeated blows with the sliding weight pull the dent out. After the dent has been removed, the holes are filled with body filler. Holes are not necessary if specially designed pulling attachments are welded or glued to the dented area.

Pull rods (rod pullers) are used like dent pullers. They simply consist of a rod with a hook on one end and a handle on the other. To use these tools, holes must be drilled in the dented area. The pull rod hook is then inserted in one of the holes, and a pulling force is applied to the rod. If necessary, several pull rods can be used at one time. A hammer is often used to tap lightly around the dented area as the pulling force is applied, Figure 4-23. Pull rods and dent pullers usually leave a raised rim around each hole. These raised areas must be hammered down before the holes can be filled.

Suction cup pullers are used to pull out large, shallow dents. They consist of a rubber suction cup and a

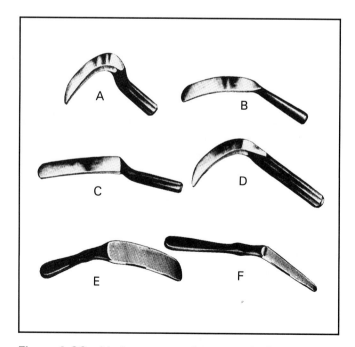

Figure 4-20 Various types of spoons. A—Short elbow spoon. B—Curved spoon. C—Offset straight spoon. D—Long elbow spoon. E—Curved flat spoon. F—Flat top spoon.

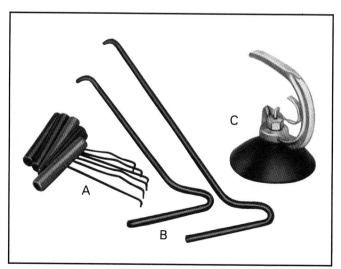

Figure 4-21 Several types of pullers are used in the body shop. A—Pull rods. B—Picks. C—Suction tool. (Snap-on Tools Corp.)

Figure 4-22 This dent puller has several attachments. (Snap-on Tools Corp.)

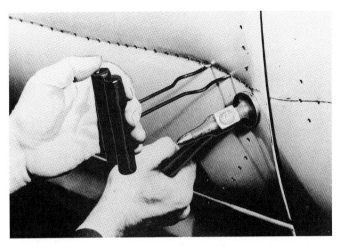

Figure 4-23 Pull rods are used to pull out dents. Note that two pull rods and a hammer are being used to remove this dent.

pulling handle. Slide hammers or jacks can be used with suction cup pullers. If there is a crease in the metal around the dented area, some hammer and dolly work will be necessary to repair the damaged section. If the dent has not been ''locked in'' by a crease, it may be removed with a suction cup puller without damaging the paint.

Files

Many *files* are used during finishing operations. The files used for bodywork are usually single-cut and come in a variety of shapes and sizes. Most have curved teeth to allow for better cutting and easier cleaning. All files are designed to be used with a handle or holder. Files work on the same principle as wood planes. Material is removed from high spots by the cutting teeth. This reveals the low spots that should be raised or pulled out. The five types of files used for auto bodywork include reveal files, body files, speed files, short block files, and surform files.

Reveal files are used to shape tight curves or rounded panels. These curved files are designed to be pulled (not pushed) across the work surfaces. The file's teeth will cut off the high spots and ''reveal'' the low areas.

Body files can be purchased in flat or half-round shapes. Flat files are often placed in a flexible file holder.

An adjustable turnbuckle on the holder allows the files to be bowed into a convex (curved out) or concave (curved in) shape. Curved files are always attached to a fixed holder. All body files are designed to be pushed across the work surface in the direction of the cutting teeth.

Speed files (flat boys) are long, rigid, wood or metal sandpaper holders. As these files are pushed across the work surface, the abrasive action of the sandpaper will reveal both high and low spots. The length of the speed file helps to detect and minimize waves (uneven areas) in damaged panels. *Short block files* are similar to speed files, but are much shorter. These short sandpaper holders are commonly used to sand repair areas to assure a smooth, flat surface.

The *surform file* (surface forming file) is a special file that was originally manufactured by the Stanley Tool Company. This type of file is also known as a grater file because of its similarity to a kitchen cheese grater. Flat and semi-curved shapes are most popular styles of surform files. Surform files are used to shape body filler before it has fully hardened. The body filler shavings fall through the openings behind the rasp-like teeth of the grater file.

Squeegees and Spreaders

Squeegees and spreaders are used to smooth and spread materials during the finishing phases of auto body repair.

Squeegees are rectangular pieces of plastic or rubber that are used to apply glazing putty or plastic body filler. The squeegee action helps to force tiny air bubbles out of the filler material. Since squeegees are semi-flexible, they are ideal for spreading plastic fillers over flat or concave surfaces.

Spreaders are made of rigid, rectangular pieces of plastic. They are used to spread body filler over dented areas. The filler is spread in a manner similar to using a trowel to smooth and spread concrete. Large putty knives with flexible blades can be used as spreaders.

A **solder paddle** is made of wood (maple) and is designed for applying body solder. A torch is used to keep the solder in a plastic condition, while the solder paddle is used to spread the solder into low areas on a damaged panel. After cooling, body files are used to shape and smooth the soldered area.

Specialty Tools

Auto body technicians must have a number of speciality tools to keep up with ever-changing automotive designs. Some tools are used to remove mechanical fasteners, while others are needed to install various components. Most specialty tools have only one or two specific applications. Although it is not possible to list all the specialty tools used in a typical body shop, the most popular tools will be covered in the following sections. Specialty tools can be grouped into three general categories: window tools, door tools, and miscellaneous tools.

Window Tools

Window and windshield replacement is part of most body shop operations. Several special **window tools** are required to properly remove and install glass.

Wire cutters are used to cut the adhesive caulk that holds windshields in place. These tools simply consist of a piece of piano wire that is attached to two handles. The wire is wrapped around the caulk and simply pulled through the adhesive material.

Cold knife cutters are also popular for cutting windshield adhesives. A cold knife cutter simply consists of a short, curved cutting blade mounted in a handle. The cutting blade is used to cut through the adhesive windshield caulk. Electric and pneumatic knives are also used for this purpose.

A *caulking gun* is necessary when applying a bead of adhesive to a window frame (pinch weld flange) before reinstalling the windshield. Caulking guns hold adhesive caulk cartridges and force the adhesive out as needed. *Suction cups* are used when holding and positioning windshield glass. Windshield locking or lacing tools are used to install a locking cord in the rubber gasket channel on some windshields. A window clip remover, which is designed for closing window retaining clips, is shown in Figure 4-24.

Door Tools

There are a number of special **door tools** used to remove door trim and handles. Various mechanical clips are used to secure door handles. Special tools are needed to remove or install these clips. Door handle tools come in a variety of styles.

Trim pad removal tools are designed to assist in removing the various mechanical fasteners used to attach upholstery panels and trim pieces to the door. These tools help prevent clip and trim damage.

A door hinge wrench, which is designed to access hinge bolts, is shown in Figure 4-25.

Miscellaneous Specialty Tools

There are many specialty tools used on the bodies and chassis of automobiles. Few body shops will have all the specialty tools necessary to perform every type of repair. Some body shops do not repair upholstery, align

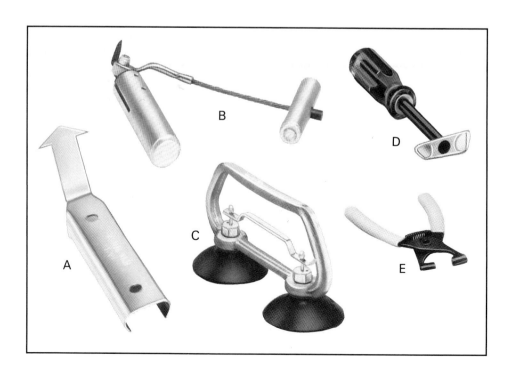

Figure 4-24 Typical window tools. A–Mold release tool. B–Windshield removal tool (cold knife). C–Suction cups. D–Windshield locking tool. E–Window clip remover. (Snap-on Tools Corp.)

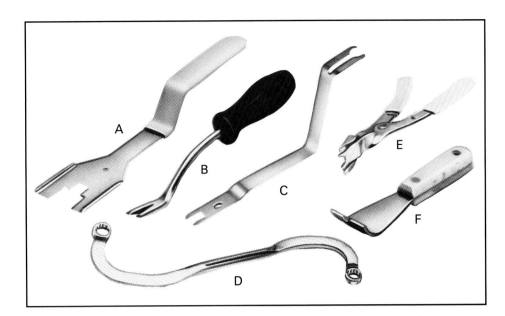

Figure 4-25 Door tools. A–Door handle tool. B–Trim pad remover. C–Door handle tool. D–Door hinge wrench. E–Clip removal tool. F–Universal trim/seal tool. (Snap-on Tools Corp.)

wheels, or do unibody and frame straightening. Some specialty tools, such as spanner sockets, upholstery ring pliers, and clip removal tools are used by most body shops.

Spanner sockets are designed to aid in the removal of antennas, mirrors, and radio trim nuts. The number of prongs on the socket depends on the type of bezel nut used. Most spanner sockets have 2, 3, or 4 prongs. The diameter of spanner sockets varies from 1/4 in. to 1 in. Metric sizes are also available.

Upholstery ring pliers (hog ring pliers) are used to crimp the C-shaped mechanical fasteners used to hold upholstery in place.

Clip removal tools are used to remove the clips that secure trim pieces. Many have tapered forks that slide under the clips. This prevents damage to the trim and the clips.

Shop Tools

Tools that the shop owner normally provides are often referred to as *shop tools.* Many of these tools are too expensive for individual employees to purchase or are not used enough to warrant individual ownership. Shop tools are shared by all employees. These tools may include C-clamps, tap and die sets, bench vises, brooms, tape and paper dispensers, jack stands, creepers, stools, and miscellaneous service tools. Some shops provide each worker with rubberized fabric seat and fender covers to protect the customers' cars from accidental scratches or stains.

C-Clamps

C-clamps are used to hold parts together during assembly. They come in a variety of sizes and are available in two basic styles. In one style, the screw threads are shielded for protection from welding sparks and other damage. The screw threads are not protected in the other style.

Tap and Die Sets

Taps and dies are available in numerous sizes and thread types. Both customary and metric sizes are needed in the body shop. Taps are used to cut internal threads in holes. Dies are used to cut external threads on the surface of a bolt or rod. Taps and dies are commonly used to restore damaged threads.

Bench Vises

There are various types of *bench vises* used in the auto body shop. Most have serrated jaw inserts for greater gripping power. They are used when filing, sawing, chiseling, or bending metal parts. Heavy hammering should not be done on a bench vise. When securing delicate parts in a vise, soft jaw covers can be used to prevent damage. These covers are often made of wood, plastic, rubber, or brass.

Brooms and Brushes

Brooms and *brushes* are useful for keeping work areas safe and clean. Because much of the dirt and dust found in the body shop is fine, a medium to fine bristle push broom should be used. A floor squeegee is also valuable when cleaning wash areas.

Tape and Paper Dispensers

To assist in quality masking, a *tape and paper dispenser* is commonly used in the body shop. Some dispensers automatically apply tape to the edges of the masking paper. This saves time and increases productivity.

Jack Stands

Jack stands are mechanical devices that are used to safely support a vehicle after it has been lifted off the floor. A technician should never work under a vehicle that is supported only by a hydraulic or pneumatic jack. See Figure 4-26.

Creepers and Stools

Creepers are devices that allow workers to roll under a vehicle while lying on their back or stomach. A creeper essentially consists of a flat board that is mounted on

Figure 4-26 Typical jack stands. Never work under a vehicle supported only by a hydraulic or pneumatic jack. (Lincoln, A Pentair Company)

caster-type wheels. Never leave a creeper on the floor unattended. Workers may accidentally step on the device and fall. *Stools* allow technicians to work while sitting rather than kneeling. Many stools are equipped with caster-type wheels. See Figure 4-27.

Miscellaneous Service Tools

Miscellaneous service tools include the instruments used to adjust brakes, clean battery terminals, dispense grease, check antifreeze, adjust headlights, check air pressure, and bend exhaust pipes. Although most of these tools are used for services not normally performed in a body shop, they are convenient for general repair.

Summary

There are many types of hand tools used in the auto body shop. The correct use, care, and storage of these tools is very important. High-quality tools will last a lifetime if properly maintained.

To hold down the cost of equipment, many shop owners send work to specialty shops. These shops specialize in frame straightening, upholstering, etc.

Auto body technicians must be familiar with the basic hand tools found in the shop. General-purpose tools are common to any shop that performs automotive repair and maintenance. They include wrenches, screwdrivers, pliers, saws, files, and hammers.

Auto body repair tools are designed for specific body repair tasks. Auto body repair tools include body hammers, dollies, spoons, picks, pullers, files, squeegees, and spreaders.

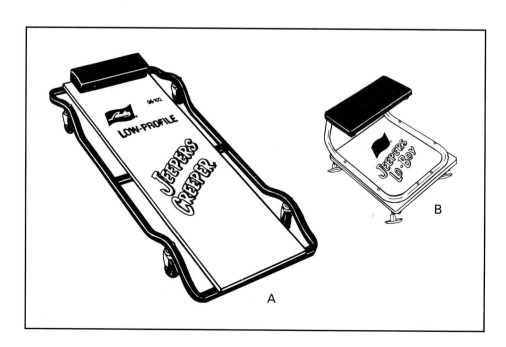

Figure 4-27 Creepers (A) and stools (B) are used when working under a vehicle or on low panel surfaces. (Lisle Corp.)

Specialty tools generally have one or two specific applications. Commonly used specialty tools include window/windshield installation tools, door handle tools, and trim tools. Miscellaneous specialty tools include spanner sockets, upholstery ring pliers, and clip removal tools.

Tools that a shop owner provides are called shop tools. Common shop tools include C-clamps, tap and die sets, bench vises, brooms, jack stands, creepers, and stools.

Know These Terms

Specialty shops, General-purpose tools, Wrenches, Screwdrivers, Pliers, Hacksaws, General-purpose files, General-purpose hammers, Hard-faced hammers, Soft-faced hammers, Flat chisels, Pin punches, Center punches, Drift punches, Tape measures, Slide caliper rule, Metal snips, Scratch awls, Pop rivet guns, Utility knives, Scrapers, Brushes, Body hammers, Dollies, Spoons, Picks, Pullers, Files, Reveal files, Body files, Speed Files, Surform file, Squeegees, Spreaders, Solder paddle, Window tools, Door tools, Spanner sockets, Upholstery ring pliers, Clip removal tools, Shop tools, C-clamps, Taps and dies, Bench vises, Jack stands, Creepers, Stools.

Review Questions--Chapter 4

1. High-quality tools will last a lifetime if properly _____, _____, and _____.

2. Shop owners can hold down equipment costs by sending some work out to _____ _____.

3. The tools used in the auto body shop can be divided into four broad categories. Name them.

4. What type of wrench should be used whenever possible?
   a. Open-end wrench.
   b. Adjustable wrench.
   c. Box-end wrench.
   d. None of the above.

5. The advantage of a ratchet is that it can be turned in confined areas without removing the wrench from the fastener. True or False?

6. What type of wrench is used when a fastener must be tightened to exact specifications?
   a. Pipe wrench.
   b. Torque wrench.
   c. Hex wrench.
   d. Socket wrench.

7. Screwdrivers are classified according to the shape of their _____.

8. _____ screwdrivers have straight, flat blades and are used on screws with slotted heads.

9. Describe the differences between the Phillips, Reed and Prince, and Pozidriv® screwdrivers.

10. Pliers can be used to loosen a bolt when a wrench is not available. True or False?

11. The _____ _____ hammer is a hard-faced hammer that is commonly used in the auto body shop.

12. The heads of soft-faced hammers can be made of _____, _____, _____, _____, or _____.

13. The tool commonly used to help align holes in body components is the:
    a. center punch.
    b. pin punch.
    c. drift punch.
    d. all of the above.

14. A body hammer should be used to drive a chisel. True or False?

15. _____ hammers are used to remove small dents from body panels.

16. Pullers are used when the back of the damaged area cannot be reached. True or False?

17. Files should always be mounted in a _____ or _____.

18. Squeegees and spreaders can be used to apply _____ _____.

19. Most specialty tools have only a few applications. True or False?

20. Soft _____ _____ can be used with a bench vise to prevent damage to delicate parts.

21. A technician can safely work under a vehicle supported by a hydraulic jack. True or False?

Activities–Chapter 4

1. Request product catalogs from several tool manufacturers. Review the material in the catalogs and identify the tools used in your shop. The catalogs can be used for reference in the shop or the classroom.

2. Identify the various types of hammers, dollies, spoons, pullers, and other auto body repair tools found in your shop.

3. Examine the tools in your shop to make sure they are in proper condition. Check for loose handles, dull blades, bent shafts, etc. Write a short report summarizing your findings and submit it to your instructor.

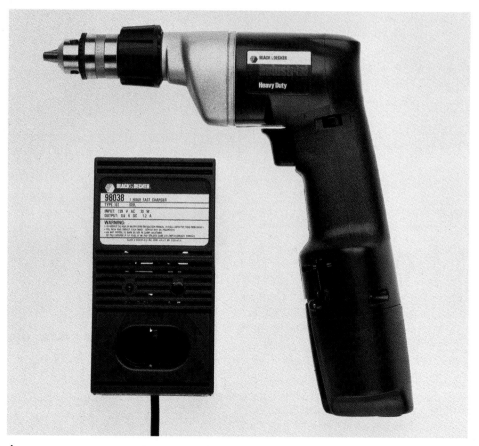

A

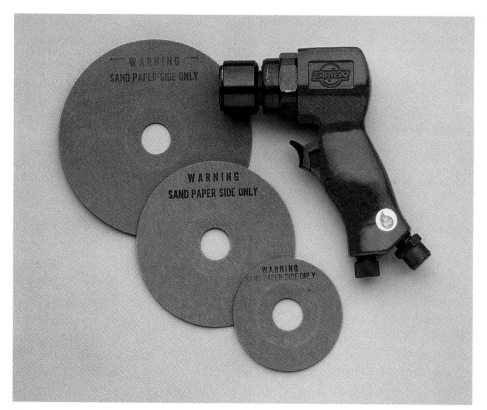

B

A variety of power tools are frequently used in the body shop.
A–Rechargeable electric tool. B–Typical pneumatic tool.
(Black and Decker, The Eastwood Co.)

chapter 5

Body Shop Power Tools and Equipment

After studying this chapter, you will be able to:

☐ Cite the advantages of using power tools in the auto body shop.

☐ Differentiate between power tools and power equipment.

☐ Explain the differences between electric, pneumatic, and hydraulic power tools and equipment.

☐ Explain the safety procedures that should be followed when using power tools and equipment.

☐ Identify the power tools commonly used in the body shop.

Introduction

Today's auto body shop must be equipped with both hand tools and power tools. Power tools and other pieces of power equipment are essential if a body shop is to be profitable. Power tools allow the body technician to complete repair work quickly and, therefore, help reduce labor costs. Labor costs are a significant part of any estimate or repair bill.

The tools covered in this chapter fall into three categories: electric tools, hydraulic tools, and pneumatic tools. Specific applications of power tools will be described in later chapters.

The distinction between power tools and power equipment is generally one of size. Power equipment is too large to be held or used by hand. Most power equipment cannot be moved easily and may be bolted to a bench or to the floor.

Electric Tools

Electric tools operate on electrical power. Impact wrenches, sanders, polishers, grinders, drills, screwdrivers, and welders are typical examples of the electric tools used in the body shop. See Chapter 6 for information on welding equipment. Although there are pneumatic equivalents for almost every electric tool used in the shop, some tools are only available as electrically powered models. These tools include bench grinders, drill presses, vacuum cleaners, heat guns, infrared dryers, air compressors, power washers, and various cordless tools.

WARNING: To prevent electrocution, never stand on a wet floor when using electric tools. Always repair tools immediately if they operate hot or if you notice electrical arcing.

There are many **cordless tools** used in the auto body shop. The term cordless simply implies that a battery (cell) has been used as the power supply instead of a wall outlet. Cordless tools do not require power cords. The portability of cordless tools and the absence of power cords makes them convenient. However, these tools require frequent recharging and have a much shorter service life than conventional electric tools. The cordless tools commonly used in the body shop include drills, screwdrivers, orbital sanders, and vacuum cleaners, Figure 5-1.

Pneumatic Tools

Pneumatic tools are powered by compressed air and are used extensively in the body shop. These tools have replaced comparable electric models for many applications. Pneumatic tools are preferred by many auto body technicians because:

☐ Compressed air is readily available in the shop.

☐ The possibility of fire or explosion is reduced because pneumatic tools do not produce electric sparks.

☐ The possibility of electric shock is reduced because there are no electrical connections.

☐ Pneumatic tools are lighter and smaller than comparable electric models.

☐ Repeated overloading and stalling will not damage or overheat pneumatic tools.

☐ Pneumatic tools consist of fewer parts and, therefore, are generally cheaper to purchase and service than their electric equivalents.

☐ Pneumatic tools run cooler than electric tools.

☐ Pneumatic tools have variable speed and torque adjustments.

Dry, clean air is essential for the proper operation of pneumatic tools. Moisture and dirt will cause the tools to lose efficiency and wear out prematurely. An air transformer can be used to filter dirt and moisture from the air.

All air-powered tools and equipment should be oiled frequently. A lubricator can be used on the air systems that power pneumatic tools (except blowguns, sandblasters, and spray guns). Always follow the manufacturer's recommendations on the care and maintenance of air-powered tools.

Figure 5-1 Cordless drills are commonly used in the body shop.

A short **leader hose** (whip hose) with quick coupler connections is recommended for use with pneumatic tools. The short leader hose permits greater movement and flexibility when using the tool. Quick couplers allow tools to be easily connected and disconnected. These connections permit twisting and turning of the hose and tool. Therefore, hoses are less likely to become twisted and tangled when a leader hose is used.

WARNING: Always wear a face shield or safety goggles when working with compressed air or using pneumatic tools.

Typical pneumatic tools include: sanders, grinders, impact chisels, impact wrenches, drills, floor jacks, spray guns, blowguns, ratchet wrenches, screwdrivers, polisher/buffers, sandblasters, and nibblers.

Hydraulic Tools

Hydraulic tools depend on fluid pressure for proper operation. These tools are equipped with a pump system that forces hydraulic fluid into a cylinder. The pressurized fluid can either push or pull a ram in the cylinder. Hydraulic pumps can be operated manually (by hand) or by a motor. **Air-over-hydraulic systems** utilize a pneumatic motor to drive the hydraulic pump. **Electric-over-hydraulic systems** utilize an electric motor to drive the pump. Pneumatic and electric motors are used when large amounts of hydraulic fluid must be pumped (large cylinder) or when great force is required to accomplish a job. In some repair work, auto body technicians prefer manually operated pumps, which allow them to ''feel'' the pressure or action of the pump when applying force.

The hydraulic tools and equipment discussed in this chapter include: lifts, jacks, presses, cranes, and body-frame straighteners.

Power Tool Hazards

Working with power tools creates several risks for body shop personnel. The use of pneumatic, hydraulic, and electric power tools presents potential hazards from pressurized fluids and electric current. All personnel must use power tools properly. Always wear protective gear. Follow the manufacturer's recommended procedures for use and care of all tools and equipment.

When working with electric tools, make sure that power cords are as short as possible. Extension cords must be large enough (correct gauge) to carry the current being drawn by the tool. Use the table in Figure 5-2 to determine the minimum wire gauge necessary for the length of cord used and the amount of current drawn by a tool. For example, if a 50 ft. extension cord is used with a grinder or other electrical tool that draws 5 amps of current, the extension cord must be at least 18 gauge. Always plug an extension cord and a tool together before inserting the extension cord into an electrical outlet.

Many electric tools are made with plastic housings. These tools are often referred to as *double-insulated tools.* Double-insulated tools have two-prong plugs and do not require separate grounding. Tools with three-prong plugs must be grounded. Grounding helps to prevent the operator from accidental electrical shock. Never use an adaptor that converts three-prong plugs to two-prong plugs. This will interrupt the ground continuity and increase the risk of electric shock. Some building codes require ground fault interrupters (GFI) for the electrical outlets used in body shops. Ground fault interrupters are fast-operating circuit breakers that interrupt the flow of current to ground. They do not, however, protect in the event of line-to-line contact.

Working for long periods with vibrating tools can affect the blood vessels in the hands. Damage to the circulatory system in the hands can lead to traumatic vasospastic disease (TVD). This disease causes all or parts of the fingers to turn white when cold and may affect gripping ability.

When there is little relief from repetitive motion, body technicians can develop cumulative-trauma disorders, such as carpal-tunnel syndrome. Carpal-tunnel syndrome is caused by the narrowing of the carpal tunnel in the wrist. As the tunnel narrows, pressure on the median nerve produces numbness, pain, and weakness in the hands and fingers. Carpal-tunnel syndrome is a crippling occupational hazard.

Tools of the Trade

The following sections contain information on several power tools that are commonly used in the auto body shop. These tools are powered electrically, pneumatically, or hydraulically. Many of the tools are available as both electric and pneumatic models. Hydraulic tools often utilize electric or pneumatic systems to produce fluid pressure. As previously mentioned, pneumatic tools are preferred over comparable electric tools for most body shop applications.

Impact Wrenches

Impact wrenches are available in several sizes. The most popular size has a 1/2 in. square drive lug. These wrenches are used to drive impact sockets when loosening or tightening nuts and bolts.

Pneumatic impact wrenches are generally preferred over electric models because they are lighter, more compact, and can produce varying speed and torque settings. See Figure 5-3. A regulator, which is built into the tool, allows for adjustments in speed and torque. Nevertheless, do not rely on an impact wrench to accurately apply the desired amount of torque to a bolt or nut. Final tightening should be done with a torque wrench.

Only use specially designed impact sockets with impact wrenches, Figure 5-4. Impact sockets are stronger than the sockets and attachments used for ordinary hand tools. Standard sockets may crack or shatter if used with an impact wrench.

Power Ratchets

Power ratchets are not as heavy-duty as impact wrenches and are usually equipped with a 1/4 in. or 3/8 in. drive lug. Power ratchets are similar in shape to hand

Based on current equivalent to 150% of full load of tool and a loss in voltage of not over 5 volts. This table is for 115-volt tools. For 220-volt tools, use wire size corresponding to an extension length of one-half the contemplated length.						
Full-load ampere rating (on nameplate)	0– 2.00	2.10– 3.4	3.5– 5.00	5.10– 7.0	7.10– 12	12.1– 16.0
Ext. Cable Length	Wire size (B & S gauge)					
25 ft.	18	18	18	18	16	14
50 ft.	18	18	18	16	14	12
75 ft.	18	18	16	14	12	10
100 ft.	18	16	14	12	10	8
200 ft.	16	14	12	10	8	6
300 ft.	14	12	10	8	6	4
400 ft.	12	10	8	6	4	4
500 ft.	12	10	8	6	4	2
600 ft.	10	8	6	4	2	2
800 ft.	10	8	6	4	2	1
1000 ft.	8	6	4	2	1	0
Note–If voltage is already low at the source (outlet), have voltage increased to standard, or use a much larger cable than listed in order to prevent any further loss in voltage.						

Figure 5-2 Recommended wire sizes for various cable lengths and ampere ratings.

Figure 5-3 High-output impact wrenches are commonly used in the body shop.

Figure 5-4 Impact sockets are much stronger than conventional sockets. (Snap-on Tools Corp.)

ratchets, Figure 5-5. These wrenches are used extensively to quickly remove or install nuts and bolts. Standard sockets and attachments can be used with power ratchets.

Nibblers

Pneumatic and electric *nibblers* utilize a scissor-like action to cut through metal. A moving center blade travels up and down between two stationary blades. See Figure 5-6. The term nibbler was derived from the jaw-like movement of the blade.

Sanders

Sanders are often classified according to the abrasive action or movement of their sanding surface. There are six basic types of sanders: disk sanders, orbital sanders, dual-action sanders, straight-line sanders, reciprocating sanders, and continuous sanders.

Disk sanders are commonly used to remove paint and locate low spots in panels. The sanding surface of a disk sander moves in a rotary or circular pattern. See Figure 5-7.

On most surfaces, a conventional, flat abrasive disk is used. On curved surfaces, a cone-shaped, tube-shaped, or curved abrasive is placed on an appropriate mandrel. See Chapter 7 for more information on using disk sanders.

The sanding surface of an *orbital sander* (oscillating sanders) moves in an oval or circular pattern. Orbital sanders are commonly called vibrator, pad, or jitterbug sanders. They are used primarily for finish sanding and feathering, Figure 5-8. *Feathering* involves tapering the paint surfaces surrounding the edges of a damaged area. This practice eliminates the ridge or edge between the original paint and bare metal. For best results, only apply light pressure when using an orbital sander.

Dual-action sanders combine the merits of disk sanders and orbital sanders. See Figure 5-9. These sanders can remove materials quickly for high-speed grinding, but can also be used for feathering and finishing.

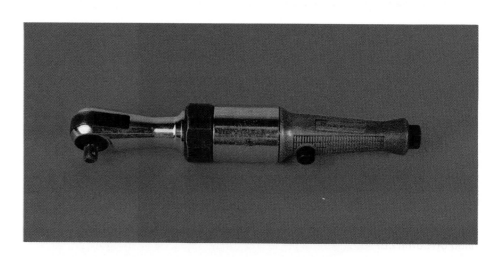

Figure 5-5 High-torque, pneumatic ratchet wrench quickly removes nuts and bolts.

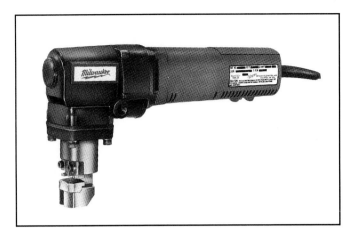

Figure 5-6 An electric nibbler cuts without deforming the metal. (Snap-on Tools Corp.)

Figure 5-8 An orbital sander is commonly used for finish sanding and feathering. (The Eastwood Co.)

Figure 5-7 This technician is using a disk sander to locate low spots on a damaged panel.

Figure 5-9 Dual-action sanders have many applications in the body shop. (The Eastwood Co.)

Straight-line sanders, Figure 5-10, are sometimes known as in-line, long board, or speed sanders. The sanding surface of straight-line sanders moves back and forth in a straight line. The sanding surface on a *reciprocating sander* is designed to reciprocate (move in small circles) while moving in a straight line. Reciprocating sanders and straight-line sanders are used mainly for sanding large areas. The large pad area of these sanders helps to smooth out high spots and wavy areas.

Continuous sanders (belt sanders) utilize an abrasive belt to remove paint and to sand body filler. These sanders are generally used on flat surfaces, but can be used on some curved areas by using the toe of the tool.

Most continuous sanders are equipped with a dust collector attachment. This feature greatly reduces the chances of breathing irritating or hazardous dusts from fillers and fiberglass. See Figure 5-11.

Always keep the sander moving in a back-and-forth motion. The large surface area of the abrasive belt will quickly reveal high and low spots. Avoid ridges, trim pieces, or other projections when using any type of sander.

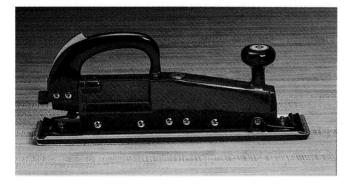

Figure 5-10   Straight line sanders are used to sand large, relatively flat areas. (The Eastwood Co.)

Figure 5-11   A belt sander can be used on both flat and curved surfaces. Some belt sanders have the added advantage of a bag attachment, which traps sanding dust. (Bosch)

WARNING: Always wear protective gear when using sanders. The sanding disk is similar to a saw blade. Any contact can cause serious injury. Always wear eye protection when using any power tool or performing chip removal operations (sanding, grinding, polishing, drilling, air blowing, cutting, etc.).

Although sanders are available in both electric and pneumatic models, many technicians prefer air-powered sanders because they are durable, safe, and easy to handle. See Figure 5-12. To reduce the risk of electrocution, use pneumatic sanders when wet sanding is necessary.

Buffers

Buffers (polishers) resemble disk sanders, but are designed to run at a higher speed. A polishing bonnet (pad) is used to buff the final coat of paint. A mild abra-

Figure 5-12   This pneumatic disk sander is equipped with a vacuum system, which removes nuisance and toxic dusts. (Nilfisk of America)

sive (machining compound) or polish may be applied to the surface prior to buffing. This will generally provide a high luster (shine) to the finish.

Old finishes can sometimes be renewed using a buffer. The polishing action of the bonnet removes old paint oxides and brightens metallic particles. Some electric polishers are equipped with a slow-speed switch, which allows them to be used with abrasive disks.

Like electric buffers, pneumatic models are used primarily for compounding and polishing of the final painted surface. However, grinding can also be done with these tools because pneumatic buffers operate at various speeds. A lamb's wool bonnet is preferred for all polishing and waxing operations. See Figure 5-13.

Grinders

Portable grinders are available in both pneumatic and electric models. Vertical grinders are designed for heavy-duty grinding, deburring, and smoothing of welds. A cut-off grinder is used to cut through sheet metal, bolts, and clamps. Waste and metal warpage is minimized when using a cut-off grinder. Although it is difficult to cut small radii with a grinder, many auto body technicians prefer an abrasive cutting method to flame cutting or pneumatic chiseling when removing panels. Always remember to wear eye protection when using sanders or grinders.

Pneumatic grinders have replaced electric models in many applications. See Figure 5-14. Although air grinders perform the same tasks as electric grinders, they do not overheat with prolonged use. Because they provide excellent speed control, pneumatic grinders are easier to handle than electric models.

Figure 5-13 This pneumatic polisher is equipped with a wool polishing bonnet. (Chicago Pneumatic)

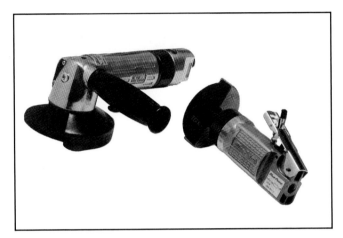

Figure 5-14 A–Pneumatic grinder. B–Pneumatic cut-off grinder.

Bench Grinders

A **bench grinder** is generally bolted to a workbench and driven by an electric motor. This type of grinder is classified by wheel diameter. Most bench grinders used in body shops have 6 in. or 8 in. diameter wheels. Although some grinders may be used with wire wheels to remove rust, scale, and paint, most are used to sharpen tools or to grind sharp edges from metal pieces, Figure 5-15. Special wheels are used for nonferrous metals, such as aluminum, copper, and brass. Never grind aluminum, on grinding wheels designed to be used for steel. Aluminum particles will clog the abrasive surface of the wheel.

Drills

Electric and pneumatic **drills** are classified by chuck capacity (1/4, 3/8, or 1/2 in.), motor size (amperes), and configuration. Most shops buy variable-speed, reversible drills. A chuck key is used to tighten drill bits or other attachments in the chuck.

Wire brush attachments are sometimes used with a drill to remove paint, scale, and rust from cracks or irregular surfaces. Always wear eye protection when operating any tool that creates chips.

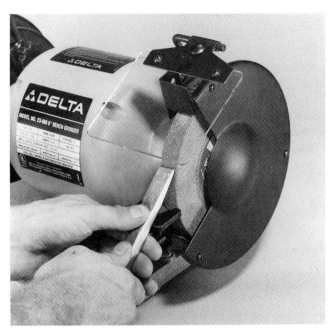

Figure 5-15 This type of bench-mounted grinder is commonly used to sharpen tools. (Delta)

Drill Presses

Floor- and bench-mounted, electric **drill presses** are used to drill holes in various objects. The tool's rigid frame and platform allow the operator to support the workpiece during drilling, Figure 5-16. Variable speed adjustments accommodate a variety of materials and hole sizes. A drill press with a 1/2 in. chuck capacity is sufficient for most auto body applications.

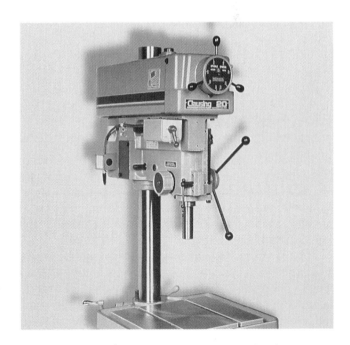

Figure 5-16 A floor-mounted drill press is often used to drill holes in metal.

Screwdrivers

Many electric **screwdrivers** resemble conventional, pistol-style drills. These screwdrivers are equipped with specially designed chucks that hold short screwdriver blades. Variable and reversible speeds allow screws to be quickly tightened or removed. Some cordless (battery operated) screwdrivers usually have a straight-grip, which is similar to that of a conventional screwdriver. See Figure 5-17.

Pneumatic screwdrivers are comparable to their electric counterparts and resemble the cordless electric models. They provide excellent torque and speed control.

Vacuum Cleaners

All auto body shops should have a portable **vacuum cleaner.** Canister and drum types are used to clean glass, dirt, and other debris from interiors. Most vehicles are cleaned prior to painting. This reduces the chance of getting dirt into the fresh paint. Additionally, customers appreciate receiving a clean car after the repair work has been completed.

Heat Guns and Infrared Dryers

Heat guns are similar to hand-held hair driers. Air is heated as it is forced over electrical heating elements in the gun. Caution must be observed when using heat guns to prevent fires and burns. Air temperatures can exceed 1200 °F (880 °C). Heat guns are used to soften plastics, dry paint, cure fillers, and remove stickers or pin stripes. See Figure 5-18.

Portable **infrared dryers** are used in many shops to speed the drying or curing of paints. Electrical heating elements (rods or bulbs) in these dryers emit radiant energy.

Figure 5-17   One type of cordless screwdriver.

Figure 5-18   Heat guns are often available in kits that contain various accessories. (Black and Decker Co.)

Air Compressors

An **air compressor** is an absolute necessity in the body shop. Compressed air is used to power pneumatic tools, clean various components, and apply paint. See Figure 5-19. Air compressors draw air from the atmosphere, compress it, and force it into a storage tank. A preset pressure switch is used to turn the electric compressor motor on and off.

Air compressors generate a great deal of heat. Therefore, it is important to have adequate ventilation around air-cooled compressors to help dissipate this heat. When hot compressed air reaches the comparatively cool storage tank and lines, the moisture in the air will condense. Tanks and lines must be opened daily to drain out moisture. Automatic drain valves may be installed to eliminate the need to drain the tank and the lines.

There are two basic types of compressors: single-stage compressors and double-stage compressors. A single-stage compressor uses one or more pistons to compress air to about 100 psi (690 kPa). At pressures above 100 psi, single-stage compressors are very inefficient.

Double-stage compressors utilize at least two cylinders of unequal size. Air is compressed in a large cylinder at an intermediate pressure. It is then passed to a smaller cylinder where it is compressed further and forced into the storage tank. Double-stage compressors are more efficient than single-stage models in the 100 psi to 200 psi range. Most air tools require between 100 psi and 125 psi (690 kPa and 865 kPa) of air pressure to operate properly. Therefore, a double-stage compressor is generally used to power these tools. For additional information on air compressors, see Chapter 16.

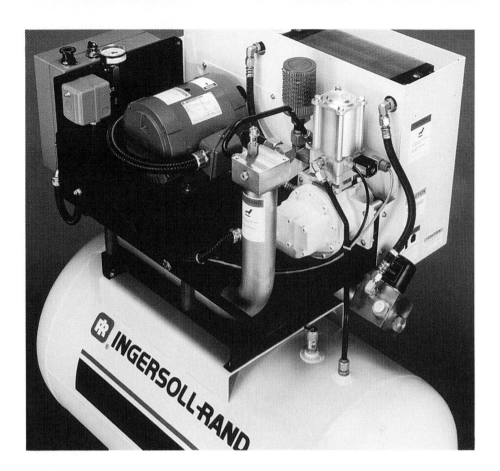

Figure 5-19 Air compressor and storage tank. (Ingersoll-Rand)

Power Washers

Power washers are frequently used when preparing vehicles for repair. Stubborn debris (mud, insects, grease, etc.) can be removed from the undercarriage, engine compartment, and damaged areas with the high-pressure spray from a power washer.

Reciprocating Saws

Reciprocating saws have small metal cutting blades that move in and out. These saws are excellent for cutting sheet metal. The saw produces a small kerf (slot) and creates very little metal distortion. Small arcs and straight lines are easy to cut with reciprocating saws.

Paint Shakers

Paint shakers are used to thoroughly mix paint. It is difficult and time-consuming to completely mix modern paints without a paint shaker. Metallic particles in some paints quickly settle to the bottom of the paint vehicle. Although paint shakers are usually powered by an electric motor, pneumatic models are available.

Spray Guns

Spray guns are the most commonly used pneumatic tools in the auto body shop. There are three types of spray guns used for refinishing: suction-cup guns; pressure-pot guns; and high-volume, low-pressure guns (HVLP).

Suction-cup guns (siphon-cup guns) are generally equipped with a one quart paint cup, Figure 5-20. As air passes through the gun, paint is drawn from the cup and atomized out through the mix cap. Small airbrush-type spray guns are of the suction type. They may be used for simple touch-up or custom finishing.

Figure 5-20 Suction-cup guns are commonly used in the body shop. (The Eastwood Co.)

Pressure-pot guns are used for relatively large jobs. Several quarts of paint can be placed in the pot at one time. Compressed air forces the paint through a hose to the spray gun. A paint hose and an air hose are needed with this gun. See Figure 5-21.

High-volume, low-pressure guns are similar to suction-type guns, Figure 5-22. However, a high volume of low pressure air is used to atomize the paint in high-volume, low-pressure (HVLP) systems. HVLP systems help to improve shop air quality by significantly reducing overspray.

See Chapter 17 for more information on the operation and care of spray equipment.

Blowguns

Blowguns use blasts of compressed air to help clean and dry work surfaces. Use only venturi (vented-tip) guns for cleaning purposes. These blowguns are approved by the Occupational Safety and Health Administration (OSHA). If the tip of a venturi gun contacts the skin or other obstructions, air pressure is bled out of the vents on the side of the gun's head. This safety feature eliminates most potential hazards. See Figure 5-23.

Always wear eye protection when working with compressed air. Small particles can be blown into the eyes. To reduce the amount of dust blown into the air, a vacuum cleaner should be used instead of a blowgun whenever possible.

Impact Chisels

Pneumatic impact chisels (air hammers) are used with a variety of attachments to cut rivets, punch holes, and shear sheet metal, Figure 5-24. The tool creates a hammering, reciprocating action on the chisel bits. Air

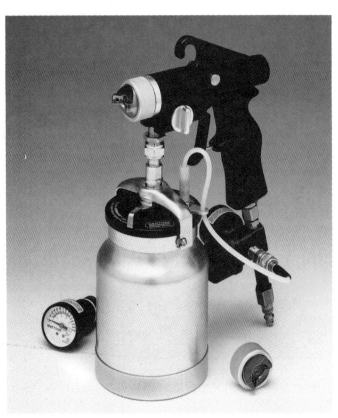

Figure 5-22 Although the HVLP spray gun resembles a conventional suction-cup spray gun, it produces much less overspray. (Mattson Spray Equipment, Inc.)

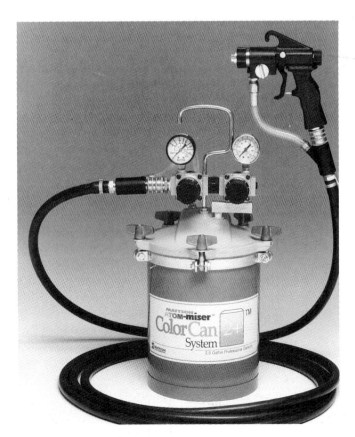

Figure 5-21 One type of pressure-pot gun. In this system, the paint hose is housed in the air hose. (Mattson Spray Equipment, Inc.)

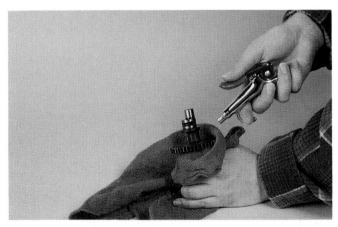

Figure 5-23 This technician is using a vented-tip blowgun to clean and dry parts.

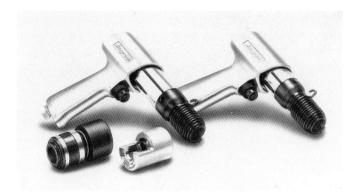

Figure 5-24 Pneumatic impact chisels with safety retainers. (Snap-on Tools Corp.)

chisels are equipped with a safety retainer that firmly locks the bits into the tool. Remember to keep the chisel bits properly sharpened and discard chipped or cracked bits, Figure 5-25.

Sandblasters

Sandblasters are devices that shoot a high-pressure stream of air and abrasive particles (sand or other abrasives) to remove paint and rust. See Figure 5-26. Sandblasting should be done outdoors whenever possible. Care must be taken to protect glass, plastics, and other parts from the abrasive blast. After blasting, prime bare metal immediately to prevent rust.

Lifts

Lifts are hydraulic mechanisms that are designed to raise a vehicle off the floor, allowing the technician to inspect and/or work under it. Lifting a vehicle a few inches off the shop floor may provide a more comfortable work level when making body repairs. This will greatly reduce fatigue. Lift-locking devices must be engaged before working under a vehicle.

Single- and double-post lift designs are popular in the auto body shop. Four-post designs are satisfactory for some mechanical work, but they limit access to the vehicle's sides.

Figure 5-26 Sandblasters are used to remove rust and paint from various components. This particular blaster is equipped with a dead-man valve, which stops the flow of the abrasive particles when its handle is released. (The Eastwood Co.)

Lift pads must be carefully positioned under the car at designated lift points on the frame or suspension. Carefully follow the manufacturer's operating and maintenance instructions when operating a lift.

Jacks

There are five basic types of hydraulic *jacks:* floor jacks, end lift jacks, bottle jacks, body jacks, and power jacks. All of these jacks can be operated with a manual pump.

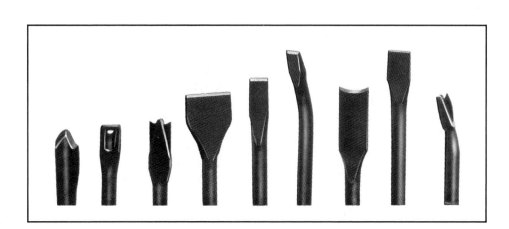

Figure 5-25 Typical cutting chisel bits. Note that only the tips of the bits are shown. (Snap-on Tools Corp.)

Never work under a vehicle that is supported only by a jack. Use safety stands. Always alert others when a vehicle is about to be lowered.

Floor jacks (service jacks) are commonly used in the body shop. These jacks are mounted on four wheels for easy maneuverability. The pumping action of the jack's handle forces a hydraulic piston or ram to raise the jack saddle. See Figure 5-27. Always make certain that the jack saddle is placed under a proper lift point on the vehicle. The lifting capacity of floor jacks ranges from 1-1/2 tons to 5 tons.

Any jack that leaks down under pressure or will not fully extend or retract should be repaired immediately. Leaky seals, contaminants in the hydraulic oil, or a defective check valve may be the cause. Have a reputable service center repair hydraulic tools and equipment.

Bottle jacks (hand jacks) are small, hydraulic, tube- or bottle-shaped tools. They are used to lift portions of a vehicle, assist in frame and body repairs, and a variety of other jobs. Bottle jacks used in the body shop range in capacity from 1 ton to 10 tons. See Figure 5-28.

Bumper jacks (end lift jacks) are popular for lifting vehicles by the front or rear end. These jacks employ a hydraulic cylinder to lift the front or rear end of the vehicle. Always be certain that a vehicle's bumpers or frame can support the lifting action. Hand-pump bumper jacks are common in the body shop.

Hydraulic body jacks are small portable tools that use a mechanical pump to push or pull damaged sheet metal back into place. They can also be used to repair certain types of frame damage. A wide range of attachments are manufactured for use with body jacks. The attachments can be purchased individually or as part of a body repair kit. See Figure 5-29.

Figure 5-28   Typical hydraulic bottle jack. (Lincoln, A Pentair Company)

Figure 5-27   Hydraulic service jack. This jack has a lifting capacity of 4 tons. (Snap-on Tools Corp.)

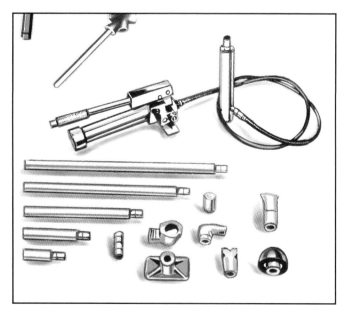

Figure 5-29   A body jack kit with hydraulic unit and attachments. (Snap-on Tools Corp.)

When a panel is dented, the force required to restore the panel to its original shape must be equal to (or greater than) the force that caused the damage. If two tons of force pushed a panel in, at least two tons of force will be required to push or pull the damage out. Although pulling a dent out is preferable, there are times where pushing can't be avoided. Body jacks range from 2 tons to 10 tons in capacity.

Hydraulic tools can be dangerous. Follow the manufacturer's recommendations for the use and maintenance of jacks and accessories. Always protect the ram (plunger), extension pipes, and other attachments. Avoid kinking or smashing flexible hydraulic hoses.

Although *power jacks* are portable, they are generally larger than body jacks. Most power jacks utilize an air-over-hydraulic system. The technician simply presses a treadle (foot pedal) to activate the jack. Power jacks are used for heavy body repair and frame straightening. They range in capacity from 4 tons to 50 tons. When using power jacks, be careful not to overwork an area. Overworking can cause metal fatigue and failure.

Hydraulic Presses

Hydraulic presses are used for pressing, straightening, assembling, and disassembling various components. A press typically consists of a hydraulic jack that is held overhead in a heavy frame. Manual, air-over-hydraulic, and electric-over-hydraulic models are available. Press capacities vary from 10 tons to 50 tons. A variety of attachments and accessories are available for most presses.

Always wear eye protection when operating a hydraulic press. Make certain that workpieces are securely held in place. Operators and observers should take the necessary precautions to prevent injury if the ram should slip off the work.

Cranes

Many body shops may have a portable **crane**, which can be used to lift or move heavy objects. Portable cranes are often used to lift engines from vehicles. Hydraulic and electric cranes are popular in the auto body shop.

Frame-and-Panel Straighteners

Frame-and-panel straighteners can be grouped into two general categories: portable straighteners and stationary straighteners. Frame-and-panel straighteners are sometimes called *frame-and-panel pullers* or *jacks.* Most frame-and-panel straighteners are hydraulically operated.

It is important to remember that all frame or underbody alignment must be accomplished before repairing outer panels or other sheet metal parts. The use of hydraulic equipment and check gauges to realign body and underbody parts is discussed in Chapters 7 and 10.

Portable frame-and-panel straighteners are used primarily to repair damaged sheet metal and correct slight frame damage. Although they are less expensive than stationary units, most portable straighteners can only make one pull at a time. Portable units come with a variety of attachments. Most use a 10 ton hydraulic jack for pulling and ram action. Most body shops have a portable straightening unit. See Figure 5-30. Larger shops may also have a separate frame and underbody straightener.

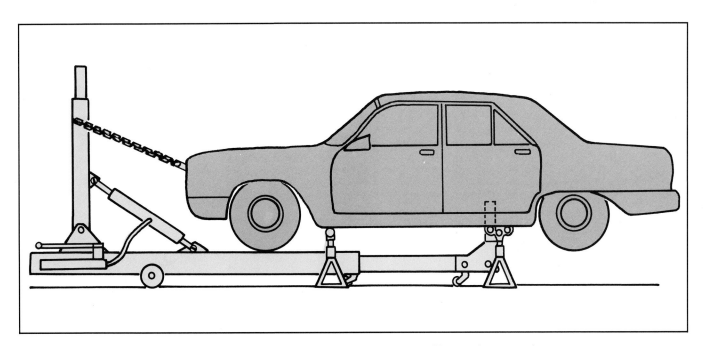

Figure 5-30   This portable unit is being used to repair front-end damage. Note safety stands. (Blackhawk Automotive Inc.)

Stationary frame-and-panel straighteners can pull and push in several directions at the same time. These units are used to correct severe damage. Stationary frame-and-panel straighteners are more expensive and require more space than portable units.

There are several styles of frame-and-panel straightening systems used today. *In-floor systems* have anchoring locations set in the shop floor. Rails or anchor-pots are built into the floor. When not in use, these areas can be used for other shop operations. See Figures 5-31 and 5-32.

Rack systems are designed with several pulling towers or arms attached to a strong rack. A vehicle is placed on the rack, and pulls are made on the vehicle from various towers.

Bench systems are available as either portable or stationary systems. They typically have a heavy beam frame upon which various measuring and pulling fixtures can be attached. Multiple pulls and alignment measurements can be made at one time on bench systems. See Figure 5-33. Some bench systems are used in conjunction with in-floor systems.

Figure 5-31 Typical in-floor rail system. Note that several pulls can be made simultaneously with this system. (Blackhawk Automotive Inc.)

Figure 5-32 An in-floor pot system being used to pull out damage.

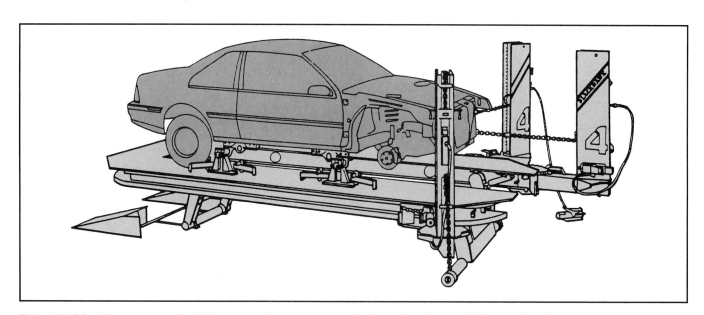

Figure 5-33 Bench-type straightening systems are popular for unibody repair. The vehicle is held at the rail pinch welds. Several pulls can be made at one time with bench systems. (Blackhawk Automotive Inc.)

Summary

Many power tools are used in the body shop. Electric tools operate on electrical power. Typical electric tools include drills, grinders, welders, and air compressors. Cordless tools utilize a battery for a power supply.

Pneumatic tools are powered by compressed air. Many technicians prefer air-powered tools to comparable electric models. Dry, clean air is required for the proper operation of pneumatic tools. A short leader hose with quick coupler connections is commonly used with pneumatic tools.

Hydraulic tools depend on fluid pressure for proper operation. Hydraulic pumps can be operated manually, electrically, or pneumatically. Typical hydraulic tools include jacks, presses, and straighteners.

Working with power tools can be hazardous. The use of pneumatic, hydraulic, and electric power tools presents potential hazards from compressed air, pressurized fluids, and electric current. Always wear protective gear and follow the manufacturers' recommendations when using power tools.

Know These Terms

Electric tools, Cordless tools, Pneumatic tools, Leader hose, Hydraulic tools, Air-over-hydraulic systems, Electric-over-hydraulic systems, Impact wrenches, Power ratchets, Nibblers, Disk sanders, Dual-action sanders, Orbital sanders, Feathering, Reciprocating sanders, Continuous sanders, Buffers, Portable grinders, Bench grinder, Drills, Drill press, Screwdrivers, Vacuum cleaner, Heat guns, Infrared dryers, Air compressor, Power washers, Paint shakers, Reciprocating saws, Spray guns, Blowguns, Pneumatic impact chisels, Sandblasters, Lifts, Jacks, Hydraulic presses, Crane, Frame-and-panel straighteners.

Review Questions–Chapter 5

1. Because power tools help technicians accomplish repair work quickly, they also help reduce _____ costs.

2. Power tools are generally larger than power equipment. True or False?

3. Most electric tools have _____ equivalents.

4. A _____ _____ tool has a plastic housing and a two-prong plug.

5. Pneumatic tools are powered by:
   a. compressed air.
   b. water.
   c. electricity.
   d. oil.

6. _____ and _____ can damage pneumatic tools.

7. Hydraulic tools are equipped with a pump that forces _____ into a cylinder.

8. An air-over-hydraulic system utilizes a(n) _____ motor.

9. Pneumatic tools are often preferred over comparable electric models. True or False?

10. Impact wrenches must be used with special impact sockets. True or False?

11. A _____ uses scissor-like action to cut through metal.

12. Sanders are classified by the _____ of their sanding surfaces.

13. A typical sander found in the body shop is the:
    a. disk sander.
    b. reciprocating sander.
    c. continuous sander.
    d. all of the above.

14. _____ sanders are used for feathering.

15. Although buffers resemble disk sanders, they run at a _____ _____.

16. _____ protection should always be worn when using grinders.

17. Most shops utilize _____-_____, _____ drills.

18. Pneumatic screwdrivers provide excellent _____ and _____ control.

19. An air compressor's tanks and lines must be drained of excess _____ daily.

20. Double-stage compressors use one piston to compress air. True or False?

21. Reciprocating saws create very little metal distortion. True or False?

22. Suction-cup spray guns can hold several quarts of paint at one time. True or False?

23. _____ shoot a stream of abrasive particles at high pressures.

24. When using a lift, pads must be positioned under the vehicle at designated _____ _____.

25. It is safe to work under a vehicle that is supported by a floor jack. True or False?

26. _____ frame-and-panel straighteners can be used to pull and push in several directions at the same time.

Activities—Chapter 5

1. Study the power tools in your school shop. Make a list of the tools and list several applications for each tool.

2. Make a warning sign advising fellow students of the dangers associated with using power tools. Ask your instructor to display your sign in the classroom.

3. Disassemble a typical suction cup spray gun. Carefully mount the various parts of the gun on a board. Label each part and ask your instructor to display your project in the classroom.

4. Using the chart in Figure 5-2, determine the wire gauge necessary to power various electrical tools in your shop. Assume that you will be using a 50 ft. extension cord.

5. Demonstrate the proper way to use impact wrenches, nibblers, sanders, and other power tools found in your shop. Remember to wear appropriate safety equipment.

chapter 6

Welding Practices

After studying this chapter, you will be able to:

☐ Explain the basic principles that lead to high-quality welds.

☐ Cite several applications for oxyacetylene welding techniques.

☐ Operate plasma arc cutting equipment.

☐ Explain how to use various types of arc welding equipment.

☐ Explain the major differences between brazing and soldering.

☐ Describe various techniques used to cut sheet metal components.

Welding Principles

There are many **welding** processes used to repair automobile body and frame damage, Figure 6-1. In order to produce strong, high-quality welds, it is essential that certain basic principles be understood, including compatibility, distortion, and contamination. These principles apply to all of the welding processes covered in this chapter and can be applied to both ferrous and nonferrous metals. Iron and its alloys are classified as ferrous metals. Metals with no iron or insignificant amounts of iron are called nonferrous metals. Aluminum, brass, and copper are common examples of nonferrous metals.

It is difficult to identify different types of steel with the human eye. Most bare steels look alike. A steel's atomic structure and crystalline grain pattern determine its physical properties, such as hardness, strength, brittleness, and malleability.

During forming (bending, stamping, forging, etc.), the crystalline grain structure of metal is forced into various new positions. When the grain structure becomes misaligned, grain movement is impeded and the metal becomes stronger. A similar condition occurs when metal is bent in a collision. Mechanical working, either wanted or unwanted, strengthens metals.

Various elements are added to pure metal, such as iron, to strengthen it. Carbon or other alloying elements have different dimensions than iron and, therefore, impede movement of the crystalline grains. See Chapter 7 for more information on the properties of metals.

Figure 6-1   This technician is using a welder to repair a unibody vehicle.

Figure 6-2   This technician is welding a repair panel in place. The replacement panel and the welding electrode must be compatible with the base metal. (The Eastwood Co.)

By definition, welding is the process of fusing one material with another through the application of energy, such as heat. *Fusibility* is the measure of a material's ability to join another while in a liquid state. In addition to metals, many thermoplastics can be welded. A hot gas torch is commonly used to weld plastic materials. For more information on welding plastics, see Chapter 9.

Compatibility

Compatibility (weldability) is an important consideration when welding different materials together. Any metal can be welded to another metal with modern techniques. However, this does not mean that the weld will have usable properties. Compatibility refers to the ease with which a weld is made and the soundness of the finished joint and surrounding area. Poor compatibility may cause cracking of the weld and the heat-affected zone, porosity, and weld embrittlement. Heating high-strength, low-alloy steels and ultra high-strength steels is likely to cause the heat-affected zone to go through a molecular restructuring similar to that which occurs during quench-hardening. The heat will cause the steel to become hard and brittle.

A satisfactory weld cannot be made between dissimilar materials unless they have metallurgical (or chemical) solubility. Care must be taken to select welding rods or wire (metallic or plastics) that is compatible with the material being welded. The chemical composition of the base materials and filler rod (if used) is the primary factor that controls compatibility. This is true for both metals and plastics. See Figure 6-2.

Distortion

Distortion occurs when materials buckle or bend and do not return to their original shape. When excessive heat is applied to most materials, they expand. Expansion is a major cause of distortion in the auto body repair shop. Large, flat panels have a tendency to distort when heated. Panels can be so badly distorted by the heat generated during the welding process that they must be replaced.

Any technique that reduces heat buildup also reduces stresses in materials. By reducing stresses, the tendency to distort is minimized. *Stitch welding* can be used to reduce distortion. This process limits heat buildup by utilizing a series of short overlapping welds, Figure 6-3. Spot welds can also be utilized to limit heat buildup. Spot welding techniques are discussed later in this chapter.

Controlled heating and cooling techniques, such as heat treating and tempering, are used to relieve the stresses caused by welding and cutting. Controlled heating techniques are also used to shrink metal. See Chapter 7 for more information on shrinking techniques.

To prevent panels from bending or buckling when exposed to heat, they should be clamped in position before welding. After clamping the panels, tack weld them together at regular intervals. *Tack welds* are small, temporary welds that hold parts in place during final welding operations. See Figure 6-4.

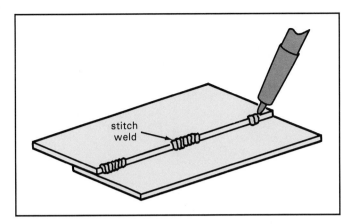

Figure 6-3 Stitch welds are used to prevent distortion by limiting heat buildup.

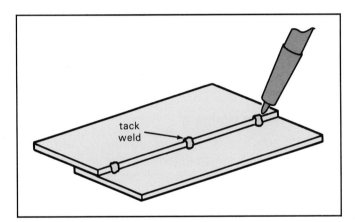

Figure 6-4 Tack welds are used to hold components in place during final welding procedures.

Contamination

Contamination is one of the leading causes of weld failure. The area to be welded must be free of paint, rust, and other contaminates. *Impurities* can contaminate a weld and substantially weaken a joint.

General Welding Safety

It is important to recognize the potential hazards associated with welding. Always use protective gear recommended to protect the eyes, skin, and respiratory system.

Anytime that metal is heated, fumes are produced. Most of these fumes are hazardous to the environment and are toxic to humans! Always work in a well-ventilated area or use an appropriate exhaust system.

Eye protection is essential when welding. Ultraviolet radiation and sparks or splatters produced during welding and cutting operations can cause burns. Gloves, face shields, long-sleeve shirts, and head wear will provide some protection, Figure 6-5. Always warn your fel-

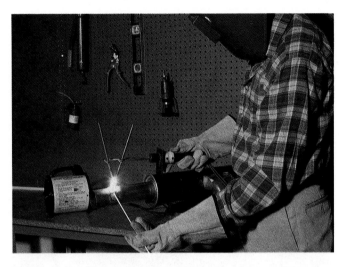

Figure 6-5 This technician is wearing appropriate protective equipment. Note the welding helmet and the leather gloves. (The Eastwood Co.)

low workers before using welding equipment. Ultraviolet radiation and hot metal splatters can harm bystanders.

Because welding operations require heat, there is a constant danger of fire. Many fires are caused by careless workers. Never weld, heat, or cut metal near solvents or other combustible materials. Don't forget to protect fuel lines, brake lines, fuel tank, plastic parts, upholstery, etc., from sparks and heat.

When using oxyacetylene techniques, special care must be taken when handling the regulators and pressurized gas cylinders. Cylinders must always be securely fastened to the wall or an appropriate hand cart. A broken valve can cause a cylinder to be propelled like a rocket! Leaks from valves, joints, hoses, and regulators add to the risk of fire and explosion. Never use acetylene at a gauge pressure above 15 psi (103 kPa). Exceeding this pressure may cause the gas to explode and burn.

There is always the possibility of electrocution when using electricity. Arc welding and plasma cutting equipment are powered by electrical energy. Always follow the manufacturers' instructions and make certain that cables, clamps, and handles are in proper operating condition. Check for loose connections and cracks or breaks in the cable insulation.

Joint Types

An important part of the welding preparation process is selecting the proper type of joint. Joint selection and preparation depends on the type and thickness of the material to be welded, joint access, and the desired strength and appearance of the joint. Joint types used in the body shop include butt joints, tee joints, lap joints, edge joints, and corner joints. Butt joints and lap joints are the most common of the welded joints. See Figure 6-6.

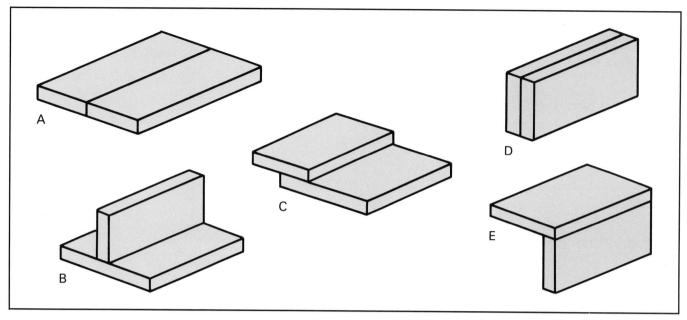

Figure 6-6   Various welded joints used in the body shop. A–Butt joint. B–Tee joint. C–Lap joint. D–Edge joint. E–Corner joint.

Butt joints are formed when two panels are "butted" together and welded to form a continuous seam. These joints are used when panels are replaced in sections on side members and frame rails. Reinforcing patches are commonly spot welded or tack welded behind a butt joint to add support and strength.

Tee joints are made when two pieces of material are welded together with their surfaces at right angles to each other. A tee joint can be used to fasten panels, liners, and reinforcing pieces together.

The lap joint is probably the most common joint used in the body shop. It is easy to fabricate and weld. The lap design helps to distribute the weld area and add strength to the welded joint. Replacement panels, rails, pillars, and stiffeners are commonly lap welded. Lap and flange (metal folds over edge of second piece) joints should not be used to assemble more than two pieces.

Edge and corner joints are similar to tee and lap joints. It is common for two metal edges to come together in a parallel fashion. Edge and corner joints are commonly encountered when attaching panels to door frames and reinforcing members to panels.

Welding Techniques

There are four basic welding techniques used in auto body shops: oxyacetylene welding, electric arc welding (arc, MIG, and spot welding), hot gas welding, and low temperature welding (brazing and soldering).

In professional shops today, metal inert gas welding (MIG) and compression resistance spot welding have replaced oxyacetylene and stick welding for most collision repair procedures.

Oxyacetylene Welding

In the auto body shop, *oxyacetylene welding* equipment is used as a source of heat for welding, soldering, brazing, straightening, and shrinking. However, the applications for oxyacetylene welding techniques have declined as the use of high-strength steels has increased. Heat distortion and strength reduction are difficult to control when using oxyacetylene equipment. Additionally, oxyacetylene welding heats a large zone and burns off the protective zinc-rich coatings used in many modern vehicles.

If high-strength steel must be heated, *temperature-indicating crayons* (temp-sticks) should be used to monitor the temperature of the steel. A temp-stick with a reading of 1000 °F (520 °C) is appropriate for use with most high-strength steels. The markings from this stick, which are made across the weld area, will disappear as the metal reaches 1000 °F (520 °C). This will serve as a warning that the high-strength steel is approaching the critical temperature. Above this temperature, the grain structure of steel will begin to oxidize and disintegrate. Heat distortion or warpage is more difficult to control on low-crown dents than on other types of damage. Automobile manufacturers do not recommend the use of oxyacetylene techniques for the repair of late-model vehicles.

Oxyacetylene techniques are used primarily to repair older body-over-frame vehicles. Oxyacetylene welding equipment utilizes a mixture of oxygen and acetylene to produce an intensely hot flame that melts metals and fuses them together. As acetylene gas burns in oxygen, it can produce a flame with temperatures of more than 6000 °F (3120 °C). Flame temperatures depend on the percentages of oxygen and acetylene coming out of the torch (blowpipe).

When welding two pieces of metal together, the edges are melted with the flame and the molten metals flow together. In most cases, welding (filler) rod is added to help strengthen the joint.

Electric Arc Welding

There are three basic electric arc welding processes used in the auto body shop:

☐ Arc welding.

☐ Metal inert gas welding.

☐ Spot welding.

Arc Welding

Conventional **arc welding** (stick welding) utilizes low-voltage, high-current electricity that flows between an **electrode** and a grounded workpiece to produce a weld. When the electrode and the workpiece are separated a short distance, an arc is formed. Current continues to flow through the arc, causing the metal and the electrode to melt. Temperatures as high as 6300 °F (3482 °C) are produced by this method. The electrode, commonly called a rod or a stick, is coated with a chemical that serves as a flux and provides a gaseous shield around the molten pool during welding. The electrode is used to maintain the arc and to supply the metal needed to fill or reinforce any gap separating metal joints. See Figure 6-7. There are many different types, sizes, and compositions of welding electrodes. The AWS 6012, which is 7/32 in. in diameter, is commonly used when welding mild steel. The AC electric welder has been most popular for auto body use. Current (amperage) is controlled by a rheostat or by plug-in jacks.

As previously mentioned, arc welding equipment presents a potential electrical hazard. All cables should be examined periodically to make sure that the insulation is in good condition. Always follow the manufacturer's safety procedures.

When arc welding, wear a special helmet to protect your eyes from the light of the arc. Warn others to move away from your work area or erect a shield to protect customers and co-workers from possible eye or skin damage. Ultraviolet radiation can penetrate light-weight clothing. Protective clothing, such as leather gloves and aprons, should be worn to prevent injury from sparks (splatter), ultraviolet radiation, and heat. Make certain that sparks do not fall on flammable materials. Be careful when welding near brake, fuel, or air conditioning lines. Fuel tanks and storage batteries also present hazards.

Arc welding is not recommended for welding the high-strength, low-alloy (HSLA) steels used for floor pan subassemblies, pillars, brackets, stiffeners, and other reinforcements in late-model vehicles. Like oxyacetylene welding, this process produces intense heat and may cause permanent embrittlement and loss of strength. Nevertheless, not all components in unibody construc-

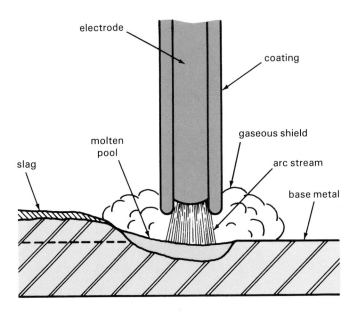

Figure 6-7 Close-up showing electric arc welding procedure.

tion are made of HSLA steel. Some outer panels of late-model vehicles and the frames and bodies of early-model vehicles are constructed from mild steel. There is less concern with warpage and loss of strength when welding mild steel.

Arc Welding Techniques. To start the weld, move the electrode toward the work as shown in Figure 6-8A. As soon as the electrode touches the surface of the work, withdraw it to achieve the desired arc length. This method of beginning or striking an arc is sometimes called the **tapping technique.** Another common method of striking an arc is to move the electrode at an angle to the work surface. The electrode will scratch across the work and form the arc. This is called the **surface-scratching method.** See Figure 6-8B. When the arc is formed, withdraw the electrode to establish the proper arc length. Beginners commonly fuse (weld) the electrode to the work surface. If this occurs, quickly twist the electrode holder to free the electrode. If this does not free the electrode, release it from the holder, shut off the welder, and carefully remove the electrode from the work surface.

Arc welding takes a great deal of skill. Keep the electrode moving (normally from left to right) steadily while running a bead. Watch the appearance of the molten pool as it solidifies behind the arc. There should be a steady humming noise as the arc is held at a constant distance from the work. Most welds are made by moving the electrode in a straight continuous line. Welds made in this single direction of travel are called **stringer beads.** If a wider bead is needed, the electrode can be moved back and forth in a weaving motion. The bead produced with this procedure is called a **weave bead.**

Heat settings affect the weld as much as the rate of travel and rod selection. Too little heat will result in beads that are too high and have little penetration. Too much heat will burn holes in light metals or produce a flat, porous weld. The bead will generally be undercut (melted below the surface of the base metal) if too much heat is used.

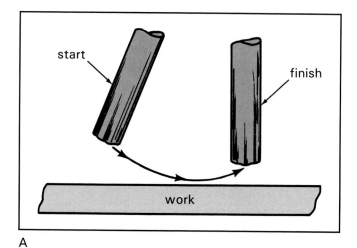

start

finish

work

A

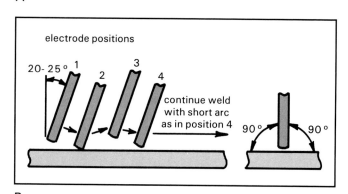

electrode positions

20- 25° 1   2   3   4

continue weld with short arc as in position 4

90°   90°

B

Figure 6-8 A–One method of striking an arc is to move the electrode downward and vertically. As soon as the electrode touches the surface of the work, withdraw it to the correct length of arc. B–In this method of striking an arc, the electrode is moved across the surface of the work in a scratching motion.

Metal Inert Gas (MIG) Welding

Metal inert gas (MIG) welding is sometimes called wire welding or **gas metal arc welding** (GMAW). This welding process is the only recommended welding procedure for structural repairs on unibody vehicles. MIG welding equipment utilizes a continuous wire as a filler electrode. A cover gas (carbon dioxide, argon, helium) is used to prevent air from contacting the weld. There is little slag formation and no residual flux, which is common in arc "stick" welding. The concentrated heat from the MIG arc leaves a narrow heat-affected zone. MIG welding equipment has replaced conventional "stick" arc welders in most body shops.

MIG Welding Equipment.   Most shops prefer self-contained, 208/240 volt, continuous-duty welders. Polarity switches are provided on some machines. Numerous features, models, and accessories are available to accommodate most shop requirements. Self-contained units allow for greater flexibility. Although they are relatively inexpensive, short-duty welders that operate on 120 volts are not recommended for body shop use.

There are several wire diameters, compositions, and types available. Most shops use AWS ER70S-6 wire for panel welds. This is a solid, mild steel wire that provides strong, porosity-free welds. AWS ER80S-D2A is a solid steel wire that can be used for welding structural members. An aluminum hard wire (AWS ER4043) is sometimes used for aluminum welds. Although aluminum is light and corrosion resistant, costs have prevented the extensive use of this metal for auto body applications. The Acura NSX is currently the only production car that features all-aluminum construction.

The MIG welding gun is generally held about 3/8 in. (10 mm) from the work surface. When welding, cover gases shield the arc from the atmosphere. This helps prevent oxidation of the molten metal in the weld. A gas cup is attached to the end of the gun to help direct the cover gases. Mixed gas (75% argon, 25% carbon dioxide) is commonly used for (steel) auto body repair. See Figure 6-9. The term MIG originated when the gases used for

Figure 6-9   MIG process parameters.

MIG PROCESS PARAMETERS				
Steel Material		.030 In. Diameter Wire	Short-Arc Mode	
Thickness	Gas	Amperes	Wire Speed	Volts
22 Ga.	CO_2	40-55	90-100	16-17
20 Ga.	CO_2	50-60	120-135	17-18
18 Ga.	CO_2	70-80	150-175	18-19
16 Ga.	CO_2	90-110	220-250	19-20
14 Ga.	CO_2	120-130	250-340	20-21
22 Ga.	75 Ar-25 CO_2	40-55	90-100	15-16
20 Ga.	75 Ar-25 CO_2	50-60	120-135	15-16
18 Ga.	75 Ar-25 CO_2	70-80	150-175	16-17
16 Ga.	75 Ar-25 CO_2	90-110	220-250	17-18
14 Ga.	75 Ar-25 CO_2	120-130	250-340	17-18

shielding the molten metal pool were inert (argon and helium). Although it is not technically an inert gas, carbon dioxide is used as a shielding gas in many shops. Carbon dioxide is cheaper, heavier, and requires a higher voltage setting than argon. This heavy gas covers the weld pool well. Carbon dioxide works well when welding steel and, because it requires a higher voltage setting, it offers excellent penetration of heavy gauge metals. Pure argon is used when welding aluminum.

MIG Welding Techniques. When MIG welding, the operator sets the voltage range, gas flow rate, and wire feed speed. Typically, the gun (wire) is connected to the positive terminal of the DC welder. This arrangement is referred to as *reverse polarity.* Reverse polarity provides greater penetration and a flatter bead than straight polarity. A straight polarity arrangement can be used to help reduce penetration and splatter when welding thin gauge metals. In straight polarity, the gun (wire) is connected to the negative terminal of the welder.

The gas flow rate is usually set at about 15 cubic feet per hour (420 liters per hour) for high-strength, low-alloy steel. The flow rate should be doubled when using argon for welding aluminum.

The welder's amperage is determined by the arc and the consumption of the filler wire. A hot arc is generated between the base metal and the wire. The arc melts the wire and the base metal, creating the weld. See Figure 6-10. Many prefer holding the gun at about a 15° angle and welding from right to left (forward).

Strong welds with good penetration can be made if the wire feed and travel are controlled properly. Welding speed is determined by metal thickness and voltage setting. Bead width and penetration depth can be increased by slowing gun travel and increasing voltage. If the wire speed is too slow, a popping sound will be heard. Examples of good and bad welds are shown in Figure 6-11.

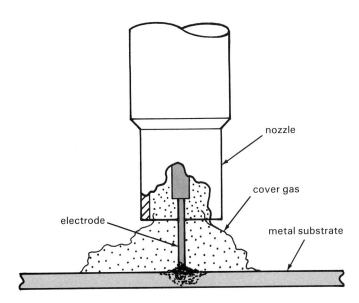

Figure 6-10 Gas metal arc welding of two metal pieces.

MIG welding presents the same dangers as stick arc welding: intense heat, sparks, fumes, and harmful light rays. Always use protective gear when welding.

If carbon dioxide is used as a shield gas, make certain that the amount of gas in the surrounding air does not increase beyond acceptable limits. The use of any cover gas can result in oxygen displacement. Do not work in unventilated, confined areas. Wear supplied air breathing equipment when entering a space that is filled with an inert gas or carbon dioxide. Deadly phosgene gas and other toxic gases may be present if the welded parts were cleaned with chlorinated hydrocarbon solvents!

Spot Welding

Instead of using a continuous weld to join two pieces of sheet metal together, *spot welds* (two-sided) are often utilized. Spot welds are confined to very small areas and, therefore, limit heat buildup. Spot welding techniques can be used to successfully join thin HSLA steels with good weld strength and minimal distortion. Automobile manufacturers make extensive use of spot welding on their assembly lines. Most auto body repair shops use spot welding procedures for collision damage repair. See Figure 6-12. There are three basic types of spot welding techniques:

☐ Arc spot welding.

☐ Resistance spot welding.

☐ MIG spot welding.

Arc Spot Welding. *Arc spot welding* is similar to arc welding. A special electrode holder and welding rod are used to create this type of weld. The operator simply places the gun-type electrode holder over the spot to be welded and pushes the handle forward. Once the arc starts, the trigger is pulled to begin the automatic welding cycle. It is important to maintain a constant pressure on the holder to help assure proper penetration. This process produces a slight hump at each weld. The spot welding cycle can be repeated as many times as necessary. Generally, spot welds are placed about one inch apart.

Arc spot welding is used primarily in areas that are not accessible with resistance spot welders. This process is also used to tack panels in position prior to MIG welding procedures.

Low, medium, and high amperage power settings are used to control penetration and allow for different gauges of metal. Proper grounding and joint preparation are critical for uniform penetration and high-quality welds. Rust, dirt, undercoating, and paint must be removed from the areas to be welded to guarantee proper fusion.

Resistance Spot Welding. There are two basic types of resistance spot welding: compression resistance spot welding (squeeze-type) and panel spot welding. Neither of these welding operations requires a filler

GOOD Proper Current, Voltage, & Speed	BAD Welding Current Too Low	BAD Welding Current Too High	BAD Arc Too Long (Voltage Too High)	BAD Welding Speed Too Fast	BAD Welding Speed Too Slow
Cross-section Weld Bead	*Cross-section Weld Bead*	*Cross-section Weld Bead*	*Cross-section Weld Bead*	*Cross-section Weld Bead*	*Cross-section Weld Bead*
Face Weld Bead	*Face Weld Bead*	*Face Weld Bead*	*Face Weld Bead*	*Face Weld Bead*	*Face Weld Bead*
A smooth, regular, well formed bead.	Excessive piling up of weld metal.	Excessive spatter to be cleaned off.	Bead very irregular with poor penetration.	Bead too small, with contour irregular.	Excessive piling up of weld metal.
No undercutting, overlapping or piling up.	Overlapping bead has poor penetration.	Undercutting along edges weakens joint.	Weld metal not properly shielded.	Not enough weld metal in the cross section.	Overlapping without penetration at edges.
Uniform in cross section.	Slow up progress.	Irregular deposit.	An inefficient weld.	Weld not strong enough.	Too much time consumed.
Excellent weld at minimum material and labor cost.	Wasted electrodes and productive time.	Wasted electrodes and productive time.	Wasted electrodes and productive time	Wasted electrodes and productive time.	Wasted electrodes and productive time.

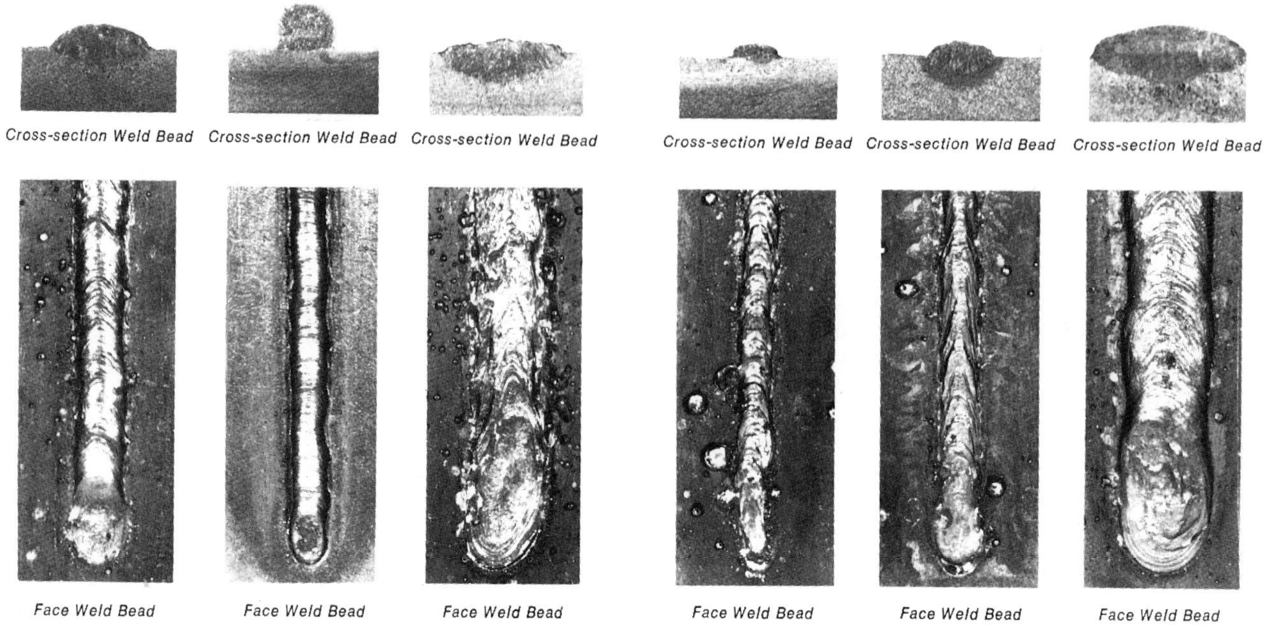

Figure 6-11   Examples of good and bad welds. (Hobart Brothers Co.)

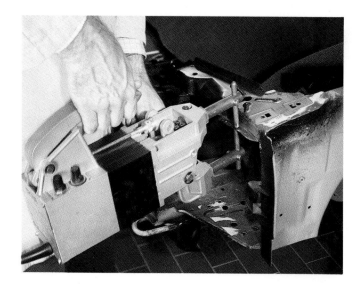

Figure 6-12   One type of spot welder commonly used in the body shop. (LORS Machinery, Inc.)

rod: the metal surfaces to be joined are simply fused together. To use resistance spot welds effectively, joint areas must be clean and there must not be an air gap between the workpieces.

When *compression resistance spot welding*, the metal joint is gripped between the welder's electrodes and a clamping force is applied to help produce the spot weld, Figure 6-13. When the switch is activated, the welder automatically completes the weld cycle. High-amperage, low-voltage current passes between the electrodes to generate heat. The heat is sufficient to form the weld by melting the metal at the points of electrode contact, Figure 6-14. The compression resistance weld process creates a two-sided spot weld. (It should not be confused with one-sided spot welding that was commonly used for many years.) Two-sided welds produce reliable, strong joints.

Compression resistance welding equipment may be spring loaded or pneumatically assisted. To consistently

Figure 6-13 This technician is using a compression resistance spot welder to repair this vehicle. (LORS Machinery, Inc.)

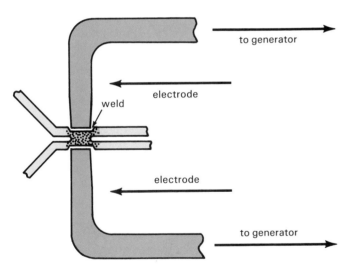

Figure 6-14 Schematic drawing of resistance spot welding operation.

make high-quality welds for unibody repair, a force-multiplying mechanism is essential. Manual grip pressure is generally not sufficient when welding unibody structures. Additionally, compression resistance equipment must also be capable of varying (adjusting) current and weld time (dwell) to allow for different metal gauges.

Access to both sides of a panel is necessary when using a compression resistance spot welder. Contamination (paint, rust) or air gaps between surfaces will cause poor current flow and, consequently, will result in a poor weld. Most car manufacturers recommend placing about

10% more repair spot welds than factory welds, Figure 6-15. Factory welds are made with larger electrodes (6-9 mm in diameter), more clamping force, and more electrical current than repair shop welds. Therefore, factory welds are generally stronger than those made in the repair shop.

There are several advantages to compression resistance spot welding. Little smoke is generated, and filler electrodes are not used in this process. Also, spot welds duplicate factory welds with little or no grinding. Good and bad spot welds are illustrated in Figure 6-16.

Panel Spot Welding. *Panel spot welders* (panel spotters) are used in body shops to weld patches and replacement panels in place, Figure 6-17. Panel spot welders produce a one-sided weld. Therefore, car manufacturer's do not recommend this procedure for use on structural components.

Replacement panels or patches should be clamped or tack welded in position before applying panel spot welds. Remember, as with any spot welding operation, it is important that matching parts be clean and firmly held together. The panel spot welder's two electrodes are pressed firmly against the outer panel to be welded. When the weld button is depressed, the welder automatically completes the welding cycle. The resistant heat generated at the two electrodes produces two welds each time the welder is used.

Although the panel spot welder is not recommended for making structural welds, it may be used in places not accessible by other means. Panel spot welders are also used to install studs or pins when removing dents, Figure 6-18. The studs are welded into the low portions of the damaged area and are used as pulling points when removing the dent. See Chapter 6 for more information on metal straightening.

MIG Spot Welding. Although spot welds can be produced with MIG welding equipment, the results are not entirely satisfactory. Nevertheless, this technique is

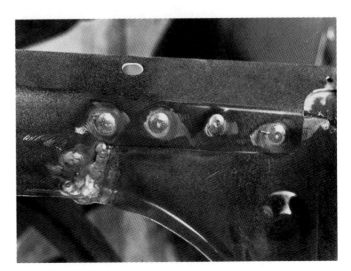

Figure 6-15 Repair spot welds should be closer together than factory spot welds.

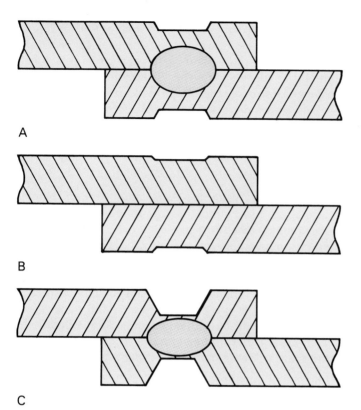

Figure 6-18 Studs being spot welded to panel. A special head attachment is placed on both guns and a small metal stud is inserted into the attachment. (Lenco)

Figure 6-16 Spot welds. A–Good weld. B–Not enough heat. C–Too much force.

Figure 6-17 Typical panel spot welder. (Lenco)

often used to tack panels in place before welding with continuous MIG welds or compression resistance spot welds. In order to perform *MIG spot welding*, the welder must be equipped with a spot timer. This feature adjusts the timed pulses that burn through the outer work surface and penetrate the inner work surface. The weld cycle is repeated each time the trigger is pulled and

released. A special gun nozzle is used to correctly position the wire electrode above the work surface. This nozzle is held directly against the work surface until the weld cycle has been completed.

Plug Welding. *Plug welding* is similar to spot welding. To apply this type of weld, a hole must be drilled or punched through one of the panels to be joined. The two panels are then clamped together, Figure 6-19, and the MIG welder is used to fill the hole with a molten pool. Plug welding provides excellent penetration. Sufficient strength is achieved for use on structural members. To limit heat buildup, welds should be staggered and adjacent welds should be allowed to cool before placing additional welds. Plug welds can be ground flush, allowing fast, easy finishing, Figure 6-20.

Hot Gas Welding

Plastics are used extensively in late model vehicles. Air or inert gas, which is heated by a specially designed torch, is used to melt and fuse some thermoplastics and plastic filler rods together. This process is called *hot gas welding.* It is important to note that not all plastics can be welded in this way. For more information on hot gas welding, see Chapter 8.

Low-Temperature Welding (Soldering and Brazing)

Brazing and soldering are often referred to as low-temperature welding procedures. However, neither is a true welding process, because the base materials are not actually melted together. There is no fusion between the

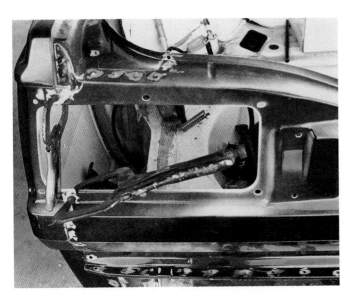

Figure 6-19 Replacement panel is aligned and clamped prior to welding.

Figure 6-20 Completed welds are ready for grinding, polishing, and painting.

workpieces and the filler rod (if used). Brazing utilizes brass filler rods that melt above 840 °F (450 °C). Most brass rods melt at about 1600 °F (870 °C). Soldering is a process using filler rods that melt at temperatures below 840 °F (450 °C).

Brazing

Brazing is a process in which a brass filler rod is used to join metal together. Brazing equipment and procedures are similar to those used for oxyacetylene welding. When brazing, however, the metals being joined do not melt. The brass acts as an adhesive to hold the pieces together. In order to achieve sufficient joint strength, a wide lap joint is commonly used. Brazing should never be used for repairing critical suspension or structural parts. Do not braze any body components other than those brazed at the factory.

Before brazing, clean the metal joints thoroughly. If the surface is not clean, the brazing material will ball up

and will not stick to the joint properly. A carburizing flame (flame feather about 2 times longer than flame cone) is used for brazing. This type of flame has a relatively low temperature, and, therefore, the danger of warping or damaging the base metal is minimized.

When brazing, the torch tip should be held at about a 45 ° angle. Do not hold the torch as close to the work as when welding. Once a section of the work is heated to a dull red, melt a flux-coated rod onto the hot metal. The molten brazing material will flow back through the joint as a result of capillary action (like ink being drawn up by blotting paper). Melt temperature is controlled by torch tip movement. A very common mistake is to overheat the work surface. After brazing, a fine, white, powdery material (zinc from brass rod) will be left on both sides of the joint. Once the joint is cooled, the flux must be thoroughly scrubbed from the weld area with a wire brush and water. Paint will not adhere to flux! After the flux has been removed, sanders can be used to level off the joint.

NOTE: If flux-coated rods are not used, paste or powder flux must be applied before brazing. Flux is needed to help clean the base metal for better adhesion. It also serves as a protective cover to help prevent oxidation of the joint.

Soldering

Solder is used primarily as a filler and should not be used to join panels. **Soldering** is a slow, difficult process, which requires a great deal of skill. When soldering, the base metal is heated enough to allow the solder to melt and make the adhesive bond. An oxyacetylene torch is commonly used as a heat source. Aluminum, stainless steel and some die cast metals (zinc alloyed) can be soldered. Soldering is covered in detail in Chapter 7.

Cutting Techniques

There are several techniques commonly used to cut metal in the body shop, including oxyacetylene cutting and plasma arc cutting.

Never perform cutting operations without the proper protective wear. Although plasma arc cutting procedures produce fewer sparks (hot slag), less smoke, and lower levels of ultraviolet radiation, protective wear is essential. The zinc metals used extensively in primers and galvanized coatings produce toxic fumes. Always work in a well-ventilated area. Do not inhale the fumes.

Oxyacetylene Cutting

An oxyacetylene torch can be used to quickly cut mild steel sheet metal. The material to be cut is heated with an acetylene flame until it is bright red and starts to melt. Then, a jet of oxygen is directed toward the preheated area. The oxygen quickly burns a narrow slit through the metal. Remember, heating sheet metal on late-model vehicles may result in considerable warpage and changes in the material's crystalline grain structure. Care must be taken to prevent underbody structural members from becoming hard and brittle. Abrasive wheels, nibblers, and plasma arc cutters are preferred for cutting high-strength steels.

Plasma Arc Cutting

Plasma arc cutting has replaced oxyacetylene cutting for most auto body repair applications. This method is preferred by most auto body technicians for cutting sheet metal. It makes clean, smooth, fast cuts without destroying the properties of high-strength steel. In plasma arc cutting, hot (ionized) gas heats the metal. The molten metal is blown away by nitrogen or compressed air. See Figure 6-21.

When cutting thin metal, place the cutting nozzle directly on a conductive part of the work. Press the torch switch to begin the plasma arc. Slowly drag the torch across the work surface. A clean, smooth cut should result. If the cut is not completely through the metal, reduce the cutting nozzle travel.

Figure 6-21 Example of using a plasma cutting torch on auto body sheet metal. (Solar Division of Century Mfg. Co.)

Summary

Several basic concepts must be understood in order to produce strong welds. These concepts include compatibility, distortion, and contamination. Joint types and welding techniques are also important considerations when welding body components.

Oxyacetylene welding equipment is used in the auto body shop as a source of heat for welding, cutting, brazing, soldering, and shrinking. However, the applications for oxyacetylene welding techniques have declined as the use of high-strength steel has increased. Heat distortion and strength reduction can occur when high-strength steel is subjected to the heat produced by oxyacetylene equipment.

Conventional arc welding utilizes low-voltage, high-current electricity, which flows between an electrode and a grounded workpiece. Like oxyacetylene welding, conventional arc welding procedures produce intense heat and may permanently damage high-strength steels.

Metal inert gas welding (MIG) is the only process recommended for repairing high-strength steel components. MIG welding equipment utilizes a continuous wire as a filler electrode. When welding, a hot arc is formed between the base metal and the filler wire. The arc melts the base metal and the filler wire, creating the weld. Cover gasses are used to shield the arc from the atmosphere.

As the name implies, spot welding is a technique that fuses metal together in very small areas or "spots." This technique can be used successfully on high-strength steels. Arc spot welders utilize a special welding rod to create the weld. Generally, arc spot welding is used on seams that are not accessible with resistance spot welders.

There are two types of resistance spot welding techniques: Compression resistance spot welding and panel spot welding. When performing compression resistance spot welding, a force is applied by the welder's electrodes. Current passing through the electrodes generates heat to produce the weld. Although panel spot welders produce two welds each time they are activated, they only produce one-sided welds.

MIG welders can be used to produce spot welds to tack panels in place before applying a continuous weld. MIG spot welds are not satisfactory for general repairs.

Plug welds are similar to spot welds. However, a hole is drilled through the outer panel of the joint to accept the weld. A MIG welder is used to fill the hole with a molten pool. Plug welding provides excellent penetration and strength.

Hot gas welding is used to seal and join plastic composites, which are used extensively on late-model vehicles.

Brazing and soldering are often referred to as low-temperature welding procedures. However, they are not true welding processes because there is no melting of the work surfaces. When brazing, brass filler rod is used to join metal together. Soldering, on the other hand, is primarily to fill damaged areas and not as a method of joining panels.

When cutting with oxyacetylene equipment, the material to be cut is heated with an acetylene flame and then cut away with a blast of oxygen. Plasma arc cutting has replaced oxyacetylene cutting for most body repair applications. Plasma arc cutting provides fast, clean, smooth cuts without destroying the properties of high-strength steels.

Know These Terms

Welding, Fusibility, Compatibility, Distortion, Stitch welding, Tack welds, Contamination, Impurities, Oxyacetylene welding, Temperature-indicating crayons, Arc welding, Electrode, Tapping technique, Surface-scratching method, Stringer beads, Weave bead, Metal inert gas welding, Gas metal arc welding, Reverse polarity, Spot welds, Arc spot welding, Compression resistance spot welding, Panel spot welders, MIG spot welding, Plug welding, Hot gas welding, Brazing, Soldering, Plasma arc cutting.

Review Questions—Chapter 6

1. _____ is the measure of a material's ability to join with another material while they are in the molten state.

2. Satisfactory weld joints cannot be achieved if the base materials are compatible. True or False?

3. When excessive heat is applied to most materials, they tend to _____.

4. A _____ _____ is a small, temporary weld used to hold panels in place while a continuous weld is made.

5. Stitch welding can be used to limit heat buildup. True or False?

6. Rust and paint in the area of a weld can lead to a weak joint. True or False?

7. Most fumes produced when heating metals are _____ to humans.

8. Ultraviolet radiation is produced during the welding process. True or False?

9. When welding, care must be taken to protect:
   a. fuel lines.
   b. plastic components.
   c. brake lines.
   d. all of the above.

10. The weld joint types commonly used in the body shop include:
    a. tee joints.
    b. lap joints.
    c. butt joints.
    d. all of the above.

11. Oxyacetylene welding equipment can be used when straightening and shrinking metal. True or False?

12. Auto manufacturers recommend the use of oxyacetylene welding techniques for repairs on late-model, unibody vehicles. True or False?

13. Arc welding equipment utilizes low-voltage, high-current electricity that flows between an _____ and a grounded workpiece.

14. Arc welding is often called _____ welding.

15. MIG welding is the only procedure recommended for structural repairs on unibody vehicles. True or False?

16. When MIG welding, a _____ _____ is used to protect the arc from the atmosphere.

17. Carbon dioxide is an inert gas. True or False?

18. The MIG welding gun is typically connected to the _____ terminal of the DC welder.

19. Automobile manufacturers use _____ welds extensively on the assembly line.

20. An arc spot welder is used in areas that are not accessible to resistance spot welders. True or False?

21. A filler rod is used when compression resistance spot welding. True or False?

22. Panel spot welders produce a _____-_____ weld.

23. A MIG welder can be used to produce spot welds. True or False?

24. When _____ welding, a hole is drilled in one of the panels to be joined and the hole is filled with a molten pool.

25. Hot _____ is used to weld plastic materials together.

26. Low-temperature welding procedures fuse the base metals together. True or False?

27. _____ is a process in which a brass filler is used to join metal together.

28. Soldering can be used to join panels together. True or False?

29. Oxyacetylene cutting is recommended when working with high-strength steel. True or False?

30. _____ _____ cutting makes clean, smooth cuts without destroying the properties of high-strength steel.

Activities—Chapter 6

1. Make a sketch of the various weld joints encountered in the body shop. Under each sketch, list the area(s) where the joint is commonly used.

2. Inspect the welding equipment in your shop. Use the owner's manual to identify all of the controls, jacks, leads, etc.

3. Using equipment available in your shop, practice welding various pieces of scrap metal. Try to produce several of the joints described in this chapter.

chapter 7

Simplified Metal Straightening

After studying this chapter, you will be able to:

☐ Describe the properties of metal that must be taken into account when straightening damaged steel components.

☐ Explain the differences between mild steel and high-strength steel.

☐ Analyze metal damage and discuss the differences between direct, indirect, major, and minor damage.

☐ Describe the various tools and procedures used to straighten sheet metal.

☐ Explain the basic procedures for cold shrinking, kinking, and heat shrinking.

☐ Describe the differences between open-coat and closed-coat abrasives.

Fundamentals of Metallurgy

Metal straightening requires more skill than any other task in the auto body repair shop. To straighten damaged metal components properly, the auto body technician must understand some of the basic properties of metals. When a body panel is stamped in a press at the factory, residual stresses are left in the metal panel. In some parts, these stresses are so great that they cause the metal to stretch (strain). The stretched areas can often be identified by wavy lines in the metal. In some cases, the lines look similar to the branches of a tree. Stretched areas are commonly found on compound curves, inner panels, and various reinforcements.

The curvature of a panel is called the **crown**. A low crown has little curvature and is structurally weak. Most roofs are low-crown panels. Pulling is always the best method for straightening metal parts. This is particularly true with low-crown panels. A high crown has a high degree of curvature and is relatively strong. Fenders and door panels are often produced with both high- and low-crown areas. This combination of curves adds strength to the panels. Inside or reverse crowns are areas where the manufacturer has stretched the metal into complicated curves. These areas have very high stress concentrations. Areas around taillights, air vents, and some hood and fender designs commonly have inside or reverse crowns.

When a body panel is damaged, additional stresses are created in the damaged area. It is often necessary to release some of these stresses during the repair process. Heat is commonly used to release stresses when straightening steel panels. Anytime that heat is applied (torch, grinder, etc.) to metal, oxidization, expansion, and structural changes can occur. Color can often be used to roughly estimate the temperature of steel. Steel will change to a blue color at about 600 °F (315 °C). The steel's color will fade to a dull red at about 900 °F (480 °C). Use extreme care when utilizing heat to release stresses. HSLA steels lose strength when heated above 1000 °F (520 °C). This is why oxyacetylene welding techniques are not recommended for use on HSLA steel parts. Never heat door beams or bumper reinforcements. Spot welding, plug welding, or MIG welding is preferred for high-strength steel repair.

The property that allows metal to be shaped is called **plasticity**. Plasticity is required if sheet metal is to be formed into fenders, hoods, or other components. The use of force (compressive or tensile) to change the shape of metal is called **plastic deformation**.

Malleability is the property that allows metal deformation under compression. Deformation under compression is called **upsetting**. **Ductility** is the property that permits metal deformation under tension. Deformation under tension is called **stretching**.

All materials have some degree of elasticity. The term **elasticity** refers to a material's ability to be stretched and then return to its original shape. Rubber has good elasticity. When materials are stretched beyond a certain point, however, they will not return to their original shape. This point is called the **elastic limit**. Whenever metal is stretched beyond its elastic limit, permanent stresses occur and the material takes a permanent set. Permanent stresses cause the metal to become stiffer and harder in the stretched areas. This is known as **work hardening**. If several sharp bends (stretches) are made in sheet metal (or wire), the material around the bends will become hard and brittle. Work hardening also occurs when damaged metal is straightened or stretched back into shape. Working metal without applying heat is called **cold working**.

When a material is not stretched beyond its elastic limit, **elastic deformation** occurs. If a dent is the result of elastic deformation, it will spring back to its original shape when the stresses are released, Figure 7-1. Permanent stresses in the form of ridges or buckles often cause elastic stresses. Before the elastic stresses will spring back into shape, the permanent stresses must be removed. When repairing a dented panel, it may be tempting to strike the center of the damaged area with a hammer. Although this will force a large portion of the damaged metal back into its original position, it may cause additional damage to the panel. Always remove permanent stresses before attempting to repair elastic deformation.

Types of Metals

Mild steel (low carbon) has been used to make body panels and structural components for many years. This material is not affected by working, welding, and heat shrinking. As manufacturers strive to produce more fuel-efficient vehicles, however, the use of stronger, lighter materials continues to grow. Composite plastics, aluminum, and high-strength steels are commonly used in the construction of the modern auto body. The use of these materials has had a tremendous impact on auto body repair techniques.

High-strength, low-alloy steel (HSLA) has replaced mild steel for many exterior body panel applications. HSLA is also used for structural components, such as front and rear rails, rocker panels, door hinges, pillars, and other reinforcements. HSLA has two to three times the yield strength of mild steel. Yield strength is the stress required to produce a certain amount of permanent strain (elongation) in a piece of steel. Since HSLA is stronger than mild steel, thinner, lighter sections of this material can be used to produce a structurally sound vehicle. Unfortunately, HSLA is more brittle than mild steel. Instead of stretching or deforming smoothly, it tends to kink and crack.

High-strength steels (HSS) include a number of different types of high tensile strength steels. Tensile strength is the metal's ability to withstand being pulled apart. HSS is often used for suspension components, door side guards, and bumper reinforcements. *Ultra high-strength steel* (UHSS) may have a tensile strength that is almost ten times that of mild steel. UHSS is used for door beams, bumper reinforcements, hinges, and other structural components.

Internal stresses in high-strength steels are commonly relieved by applying a pulling force or by spring hammering. Spring hammering is a process that involves lightly striking the ridge of a dent with a bumping hammer while holding a spoon firmly against the back of the damaged area. The pressure and rebound energy from the spoon helps to straighten the dent. The vibrations from the light hammer blows help to relieve pressure by rearranging the molecular structure of the metal.

As previously mentioned, heat causes high-strength steels to lose their strength. If high-strength steel (HSLA and HSS) must be heated, use a carburizing flame and do not heat the metal to temperatures above 1000 °F (520 °C). Excessive pounding or working will

Figure 7-1   This panel will spring back into shape when the stresses are released.

cause high-strength steel to become brittle and crack. Cracked high-strength steel components must be replaced. Ultra high-strength steels must never be welded or heated. Damaged UHSS parts should be replaced. See Chapter 6 for more information on heating high-strength steels.

Metal Damage

The terms *kink* and *bend* are sometimes misused when referring to auto body damage. A bend is any change in a part from its original shape. When a bend is straightened, there will be no permanent deformation in the damaged area. A kink, on the other hand, is a bend of more than 90° in a distance of less than 3 mm. After straightening a kink, there will be permanent metal deformation. Cracks and tears commonly occur when straightening kinked areas. If a structural component is kinked, it should be replaced.

When metal is bent into a sharp ridge, the outer surface of the ridge is *stretched* and the inner surface of the ridge is *upset.* Stretched areas are lengthened, and upset areas are shortened (compressed). To remove the damage, force must be applied at the bend area. See Figure 7-2.

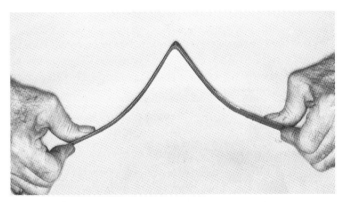

A

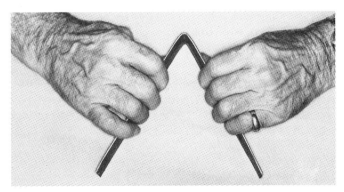

B

Figure 7-2 A–Simply pulling on the ends of a sharp ridge will not remove the damage. B–Force must be applied at the bend area to remove the ridge.

Types of Damage

Before beginning any repair procedure, it is essential to analyze the damaged area. Damage will fall into two or more of the following categories:

☐ Direct damage.

☐ Indirect damage.

☐ Minor damage.

☐ Major damage.

Direct Damage

Direct damage is the result of direct contact with an object. Holes, tears, gouges, and scratches are typical examples of direct damage. Generally, only about 10% of total collision damage is direct damage.

Indirect Damage

Indirect damage is the result of direct damage. When an impact causes a hole in a panel (direct damage), buckles in other areas of the panel generally occur. These buckles (pressure ridges) are typical examples of indirect damage. A front-end collision may result in direct damage to the front of a vehicle, but indirect damage may occur in the underbody and the rear panels. About 90% of all collision damage is indirect damage.

Minor Damage

Minor damage involves repairs that require relatively little time and skill to complete. Therefore, the cost of repairing minor damage is generally low. A simple dent in the door panel of a late-model vehicle is considered minor damage.

Major Damage

Major damage requires more time, equipment, and skill to repair than minor damage. This type of damage includes severely bent body panels and damaged frame or underbody components. Repairing major damage generally involves replacing body panels and straightening structural parts. If the damage is extremely severe, a decision must be made to determine if the repair is warranted. If the repair estimate exceeds the replacement value of the vehicle (similar make, year, etc.), the repair may not be made. See Chapter 21 for more information on estimating repair costs.

Assessing Damage

The auto body technician must carefully assess all damage before attempting to make repairs. It is important to know how the vehicle is constructed in order to determine the correct repair procedures. Carefully inspect and measure the vehicle to determine if the damage is restricted to the body panels. Check for both direct and indirect damage.

A metal ruler can be used to help determine the extent of panel damage. Hold the ruler against the damaged panel and observe its reflection in the paint. The ruler's reflection will be distorted in the damaged areas, Figure 7-3.

Carefully study the damaged area to locate the point of impact. This will help you determine the best procedure to follow when removing the damage. If the wrong procedure is used, additional work will often be required to complete the straightening operation. The wrong repair procedure can actually cause further damage.

To keep straightening work to a minimum, damage should be removed in reverse order–the damage that occurs last should be removed first. Damage does not occur instantaneously, but progresses from the moment of impact until the vehicle comes to rest. After the initial contact (direct damage), the damage spreads in a series of ridges (indirect damage). These ridges become deeper and more sharply bent as they spread from the point of initial contact.

The technician must study the damage to determine where the panel was struck first and which ridges were formed last. The ridges that were formed last must be removed first. As the ridges are removed, the metal that is merely flexed (elastic deformation) out of position will spring back into place.

The simplest form of damage occurs when a part is struck by a direct blow. The damage illustrated in Figure 7-4 was caused by a direct push from the bumper guard of another vehicle. The force of impact was centered at ''B,'' and the deepest ridge is at ''A.'' Note that the ridge at ''A'' is farthest from ''B'' and should be removed first. As this ridge is removed, the entire damaged area will

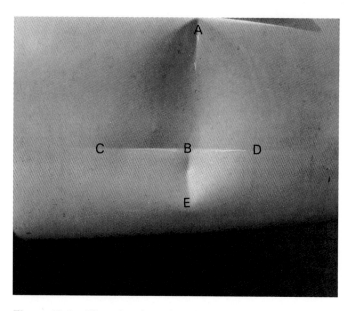

Figure 7-4   The simplest dent is made when a panel is struck by a direct blow.

tend to spring back into place. If, on the other hand, the technician works on area ''B'' first, the ridge at ''A'' will not spring out. The crease ''C-D'' is not a ridge and, therefore, will flex back into shape when ''A'' is removed. Remember that the straightening process should start at the farthest edge of the damage, not at the center.

The most complicated damage results when a vehicle is struck by a series of blows that superimpose one set of wrinkles and dents on another. This type of damage occurs when a car rolls over several times, Figure 7-5.

Basic Straightening Techniques

There are a number of techniques used when repairing body damage. The technique or combination of techniques utilized will depend largely on the age of the damaged vehicle, the location of the damage, and the wishes of the customer. A customer with a new car may insist on the most expensive repair techniques. Owners of older automobiles or vehicles being reconditioned for resale often request the most inexpensive techniques. Some damage is difficult to access and requires special repair techniques. These techniques are generally time-consuming and, therefore, greatly increase repair costs.

Before straightening procedures are started, dirt, wax, grease, and undercoating should be removed from the damaged area. Dirt and wax will quickly dull or fill abrasive disks. Undercoating interferes with hammer-and-dolly work. Heat is sometimes used to aid in the removal of undercoating.

There are several tools and techniques used to straighten metal in the body shop, including vacuum cup pullers, pull rods, slide hammers, pull tabs, picks, bumping spoons, power rams (jacks), hammers, dollies, pick

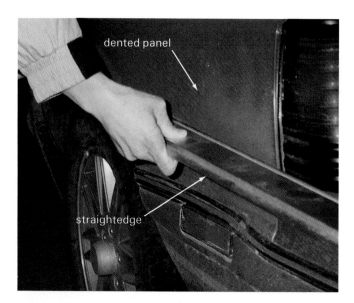

Figure 7-3   The reflection of a straightedge in a damaged panel can be used to detect irregularities (waves or dents).

Figure 7-5 When a car rolls over, a complicated series of dents is formed.

hammers, and files. When metal is stretched, various shrinking techniques can be used to return it to its original size and shape. Filling is an important part of panel repair and is covered in Chapter 8. Panel replacement is detailed in Chapter 11.

Vacuum Cup Pullers

If a metal panel has not been bent beyond its elastic limit (no ridges or creases), a **vacuum cup puller** can often be used to remove the damage. The surface of the damaged panel must be clean, and the puller's vacuum cup(s) should be wet to assure the best vacuum grip on the damaged surface. The puller is simply attached to the lowest portion of the dented area. A steady pull on the tool should cause the metal to ''pop'' back into its original position. Vacuum cup pullers are not effective if the damaged area has been buckled or kinked. Additionally, this procedure will not work on high- or reverse-crown surfaces.

Pull Rods and Slide Hammers

When removing ridges and creases from auto body panels, a considerable amount of time is often spent removing interior trim and upholstery to access the back of the panel. Repair work is often complicated when damage is located in areas where braces and other structural members prevent the use of conventional dolly and hammer techniques.

On many jobs, the use of **pull rods** eliminates the need to remove upholstery or interior trim. Pull rods allow the repair work to be performed from the outside of the damaged panel. Before using the rods, a number of holes are drilled in the deepest part (creased area) of the damaged area. These holes should be spaced about 1/4 in. (6 mm) apart. The damage is then worked up gradually by inserting the hooked ends of the pull rods into the holes and pulling on the handles. Depending upon the type of damage, several pull rods may be used at one time. In

Figure 7-6, two pull rods and a hammer are used to remove a dent. Tapping around the outside of the damage helps to release some of the stresses introduced during impact. The rods should be pulled at a right angle to the surface of the panel. Never pry on the rods.

A **slide hammer** can also be used to repair damaged panels from the outside. This tool is generally used for deeper, more complicated damage. Before using the slide hammer, holes are drilled in the damaged area. Hook or screw attachments, which are connected to the hammer, are placed in the holes. The dent is pulled out as the hammer's sliding weight is struck against its handle. Be careful when using a slide hammer. The hook or screw can be pulled out of the hole if excessive force is used.

When using pull rods or slide hammers, light reflections from the surface of the paint will help to uncover low spots. To take full advantage of this technique, place a light at an angle to the damaged area. In a final check, use a body file to locate low spots.

In Figure 7-7, a technician is using a modification of a pull rod system. In this setup, a chain attachment is bolted to the damaged area and a pulling force is applied with the mechanical advantage of a pipe handle. After dents and creases have been removed with pull rods or slide hammers, the holes must be filled.

Pull Tabs

Like pull rods, **pull tabs** are used to repair damaged panels from the outside. When using pull tabs, however, there is no need to drill holes in damaged areas. The pull tabs are attached to the low areas of a dent with a panel spot welder, Figure 7-8. The points of attachment should be clean and free from paint to ensure complete adhesion. Some pull tabs have sharp points, which are designed to penetrate the paint film to provide proper

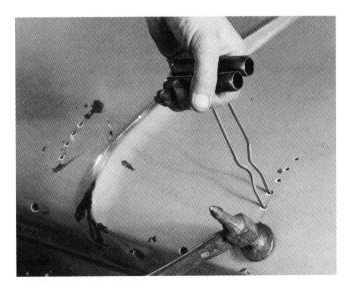

Figure 7-6 As a pulling force is exerted on the pull rods (hooked in the holes), a hammer is used to force the ridge back into place.

Figure 7-7   This technician is using a pulling force to remove damage.

Figure 7-9   This technician is using a slide hammer to pull out the damaged area.

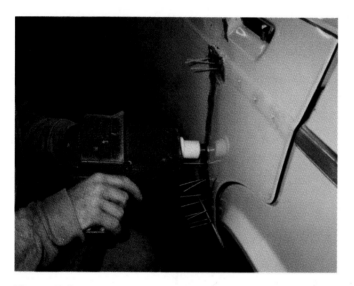

Figure 7-8   Attaching pull tabs to a damaged area.

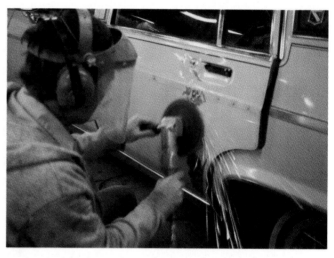

Figure 7-10   After the pull tabs are twisted off, the repair is ground smooth.

electrical contact. Once the tabs have been attached, a slide hammer can be used to pull the dent out. See Figure 7-9. A pull plate is commonly used to link several tabs together when large areas must be pulled out. Once the proper contour of the panel has been restored, the tabs can be twisted off and the damaged area can be ground smooth, Figure 7-10.

Picks

Picks are used to pry out damaged areas. They are also used to push up low areas that cannot be reached with a hammer. Picks are commonly inserted through access holes in doors and reinforcing panels. Drain holes are commonly used for this purpose. If a sufficient number of access holes are not provided, it may be necessary to drill or punch holes in the bottom edge of a damaged panel, Figure 7-11.

Figure 7-11   Using a pick tool to remove a dent from a door panel.

Picks can also be used to aid in the installation and alignment of body panels. These long, thin tools are used to hold panels in position during assembly.

Spoons

There are several types of spoons used to straighten damaged metal panels. Heavy **bumping spoons** are often used as pry bars. They are particularly helpful when working on doors or trunk lids where the back of the damaged area is obstructed by strengthening braces, Figure 7-12. Heavy bumping spoons can also be used as dollies when obstructions prevent the use of conventional dollies. See Figure 7-13.

Light bumping spoons are designed to spread hammer blows over a wide area. They are placed on top of ridges and struck with a hammer. By spreading hammer blows over a large area, the possibility of marring painted surfaces is reduced.

Unless bumping spoons are being used for prying, they should be held loosely in the hand. When using these spoons as dollies, the hand should serve only as a guide or positioner.

A slapping file is a surfacing spoon that is used to "slap" down high ridges and buckles in low-crown panels. Like bumping spoons, slapping spoons should be held loosely in the hand.

Power Rams

A considerable amount of force is required to repair extensive collision damage. If a panel is pushed in by two tons of force, an equal force must be applied to pull the damage out. Therefore, **power rams** (hydraulic body jacks) are often used to correct severe damage.

Power rams are available in a variety of sizes. Rams are commonly used to pull out dents and to realign pillars. See Figure 7-14. **Spread rams** are commonly used to spread components in confined areas. A spread ram has two jaws that are forced apart when the tool is activated. See Figure 7-15.

Numerous attachments and accessories are available to accommodate a wide range of pulling situations. Prior to using a power ram, pull tabs are often welded to the damaged area. Chains and clamps are used to attach the ram to the tabs. After the damage is pulled out, the tabs are simply twisted off.

Pull plates are used with a ram when large areas must be pulled out. These plates are bolted to the damaged panel before the pull is made. After the damaged area is pulled out, the bolt holes must be welded shut.

Some power rams can be modified so that a pulling force is applied from two directions. This action is similar to pulling on the edges of a bed sheet to remove wrinkles. See Figure 7-16.

Figure 7-12 One method of using a spoon is as a pry bar. It can also be used as a dolly in restricted areas.

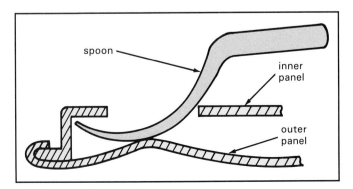

Figure 7-13 This spoon is being used to straighten a panel in an area that is not accessible with a dolly.

Figure 7-14 A power ram is being used in a simple pushing operation.

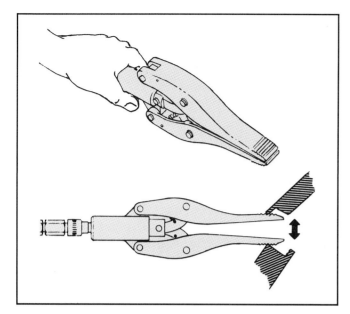

Figure 7-15 A typical spread ram. (NORCO Industries, Inc.)

Figure 7-16 Using a power ram to correct damage to a roof panel.

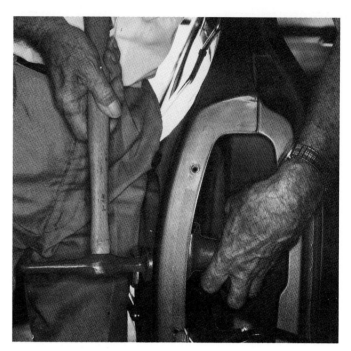

Figure 7-17 The dolly is held on one side of the panel where it acts as an anvil. The opposite side of the panel is struck with the hammer.

Hammers and Dollies

The most frequently used tools in the body shop are the body hammer and the dolly, Figure 7-17. They are commonly used for roughing and bumping operations.

When *roughing* damaged areas, a hammer or dolly is used to drive damaged metal back into its original shape. Considerable skill is involved in this process. Care must be taken to prevent over-correcting or stretching the damaged metal. High spots are often more difficult to remove than low spots. Nevertheless, a few strategic blows will quickly complete most roughing operations. Power rams can also be used during the roughing phase.

After the roughing phase has been completed, the bumping phase begins. *Bumping* is the process of smoothing the damaged area further. A number of tools can be used during the bumping phase, including dollies, hammers, pry bars, pull rods, spoons, and picks. Highly skilled technicians often combine roughing and bumping operations.

Care should be taken when selecting the dollies and hammers used during the bumping operation. A dolly with the correct crown on its working face will result in a better and faster repair. Never use the flat surface of a dolly on the concave side of a crowned panel. The curve of the dolly should always have a smaller radius than the concave side of the panel being straightened. See Figure 7-18. Similarly, when selecting a hammer, the radius of its face should always be less than the radius of the concave side of the damaged panel, Figure 7-19. If a hammer with a flat face is used on a concave panel, it will nick the surface of the panel. The flat face of a hammer should only be used on convex surfaces.

Body hammers must be used carefully. Heavy blows tend to stretch metal panels. The face of the body hammer must strike the panel squarely. If the edge of the hammer strikes the panel, a nick will be made in the panel's surface.

When driving nails with a claw hammer, a considerable amount of force and follow-through is used. When using a body hammer, follow-through is not recommended. Instead, a light slapping action should be used to prevent the metal from stretching and thinning. The body hammer should be gripped loosely and close to the end of the handle. It should be swung with the wrist, not the elbow.

The process of using a body hammer and a dolly to remove minor dents is commonly called *dinging.* Generally, a body technician strikes about 100 blows per minute during dinging operations. This number will vary with the technician's style and the complexity of the straightening job.

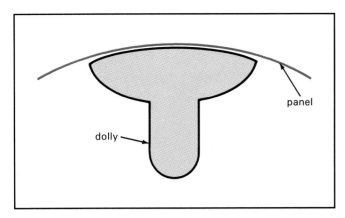

Figure 7-18 The arc of the dolly block should coincide with the contour of the body panel.

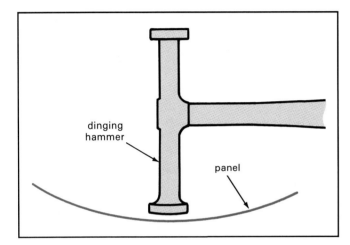

Figure 7-19 Use the curved face of the hammer on a concave surface to avoid making small dents and nicks in the surface.

Figure 7-20 The dolly must be held firmly against the surface of the metal.

The dolly should be held firmly against one side of the damaged panel, Figure 7-20. As the damaged area is hit with the hammer, the dolly is driven away from the panel. However, it returns immediately due to the pressure of the technician's hand. As previously mentioned, the dolly should conform to the curve of the panel. The curve of the dolly should never be less than the curve of the panel. Dollies with a straight working surface are used along the edge of straight molding.

Figure 7-21 shows the dinging operation in its simplest form. The dolly is held against one side of the dent, while hammer blows are directed against the rim of the dent.

On-the-dolly dinging occurs when the dolly is held directly under the area being struck by the hammer, Figure 7-22. This operation causes the dented metal to be smoothed between the working faces of the dolly and

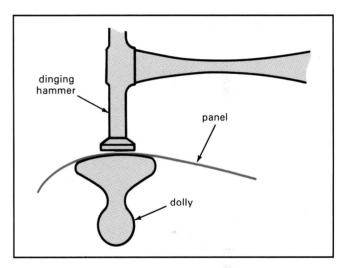

Figure 7-21 Simplest form of ding work. Note that the radius of the dolly block face is less than the basic curve of the body.

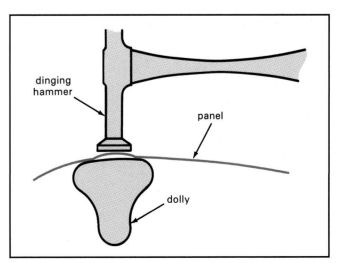

Figure 7-22 On-the-dolly dinging. The dolly is held directly under the area being struck by the hammer.

the hammer. Each blow of the hammer forms a smooth spot on the panel. The size of the spot depends on the crown of the hammer. As the dolly is moved along the surface of the panel, successive hammer blows leave a series of overlapping spots on the panel. Additional rows are dinged next to the initial row until the panel is straight. As a result of the dinging operation, the repaired area will be covered with parallel rows of flat spots.

The condition illustrated in Figure 7-23 is known as *off-the-dolly dinging.* In this arrangement, the hammer drives one area of the damaged panel down, while the reaction of the dolly drives an adjacent area up.

Files and Pick Hammers

During the final stages of bumping, *files* and *pick hammers* are used to raise low spots. It takes considerable practice and skill to remove dents without leaving low spots or high spots. If a panel appears to be smooth, run your hand over the work surface in an effort to locate low areas. Fine irregularities cannot be determined as accurately by feel as they can by reflection. Irregularities can often be located by changing the position of trouble lights.

When the panel appears to be perfectly smooth, draw a body file lightly over the surface to locate high and low spots on body panels. When using a body file, push it diagonally across the work surface, Figure 7-24. Pushing the file straight forward tends to cut a groove in the panel. Place only enough pressure on the file to prevent chattering. Heavy pressure will cause the file's teeth to dig into the metal rather than cut through it.

At the start of each file stroke, the teeth at the front end of the file do the cutting. As the stroke progresses, the cutting action moves toward the heel or rear of the file. Consequently, each of the file's teeth is used at some point during the stroke. File strokes should be long and smooth, not short and choppy.

Always start filing on an undamaged section and work into the damaged area. Normally, the file should be stroked in the general direction of the flattest crown on the panel. Because a crown may extend in several directions, filing should be shifted to create a criss-cross pattern over the damaged area. This pattern will help to reveal low spots that were not detected during initial filing. If a flexible file holder is used, it should be adjusted to conform to the contour of the panel. Areas that are not touched by the file are generally low and will have to be raised. High spots must be hammered down.

A pick hammer is normally used to raise low spots or small dents that have been revealed after a surface has been filed. See Figure 7-25. The fine, pointed end of the pick hammer is used on small dents, and the rounded end is used on larger dents. The technician simply strikes the dent with the point of the pick hammer. Care must be taken to limit the force of the blow. Excess force can raise too much metal and create additional damage.

After the low and high spots are located and removed, a disk sander is commonly used to remove scratches and tool marks from the panel. Experienced auto body technicians use a disk sander or a reciprocating sander instead of a body file to help reveal high and low spots.

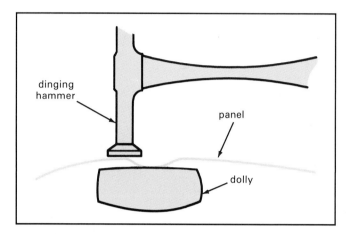

Figure 7-23 Off-the-dolly dinging. The dolly is held directly under the dent, but the hammer blows are directed against the edge of the dent.

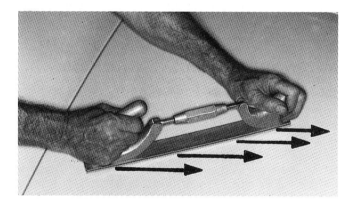

Figure 7-24 When using a body file, it should be pushed diagonally across the work surface.

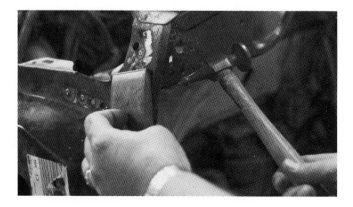

Figure 7-25 Using a pick hammer to remove small dents.

Shrinking

In many cases, sheet metal will stretch as a result of a collision. Dolly and hammer work can also stretch sheet metal. When stretching occurs, metal tends to bulge, Figure 7-26. When metal stretches and bulges, it is often necessary to shrink it to its original size and shape.

Cold Shrinking. *Cold shrinking* techniques can be used on all metals. *Shrinking hammers* and *shrinking dollies* are designed to reduce the surface area of metal without using heat. These tools have small cross-grooves milled into their faces, Figure 7-27. The cross-grooves (serrations) are quite deep and mark the stretched metal with a series of square dents. These dents tend to gather the metal, reducing the surface area.

A shrinking hammer is used with a conventional dolly. Care must be taken so that the full face of the hammer strikes the surface of the panel. When using a shrinking hammer, square marks (dents) are made on the front side of the damaged panel.

A shrinking dolly is used with a conventional hammer. When using a shrinking dolly, square marks will occur on the back side of the damaged panel. Shrinking dollies and shrinking hammers should never be used together.

Kinking. *Kinking* is a variation of cold shrinking. Although this method does not actually shrink the metal, it lowers the stretched portion slightly below the surrounding surface. Kinking is accomplished by using a pick hammer and a dolly to create a series of pleats (kinks) in the bulged area. The kinked area is then filled, smoothed, sanded, and primed.

Heat Shrinking. Although *heat shrinking* works well on mild steel and aluminum, it is not recommended for high-strength steel panels. Work must be completed quickly when heat shrinking. Do not attempt to heat shrink a panel until the surface has been worked and is relatively smooth. Remove all finishes (primer, paint, etc.) before starting the shrinking process. The five basic steps for heat shrinking are as follows:

1. Heat a small area of the stretched metal with an oxy-acetylene torch until it is cherry red. The first spot heated should be located in the center of the stretched area. This spot will usually bulge up because the top of the metal is heated first.

2. Quickly tap the center of the bulge several times to drive it down. This must be accomplished while the center is still red-hot.

3. Bring the dolly up under the work and strike the ridges flat. Strike hammer blows around the perimeter of the spot while holding the dolly directly beneath the hammer. See Figure 7-28.

4. Once the metal has lost all of its reddish color, quench the heated area with a water-soaked rag or sponge. *Quenching* is the process of quickly cooling hot metal. The rapid cooling causes the metal to harden and shrink. If metal is quenched when it is too hot, it may crystallize and become brittle.

5. Repeat steps 1-4 until the bulge begins to assume its original shape and contour. Follow the sequence illustrated in Figure 7-29.

The size of the heated spots depends on the location of the bulged surface. On surfaces with compound curves, the spots should not exceed 1/4 in. (6 mm)

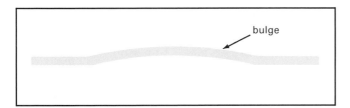

Figure 7-26 Hot and cold working may cause sheet metal to stretch and bulge.

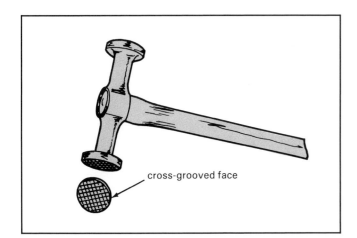

Figure 7-27 The face of a hammer used for shrinking metal. Note that face is cross-grooved.

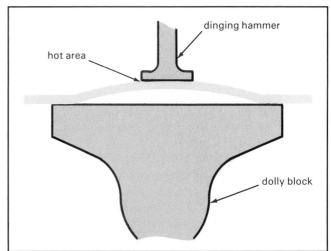

Figure 7-28 After heating the bulged area, the surface is worked with a hammer and dolly.

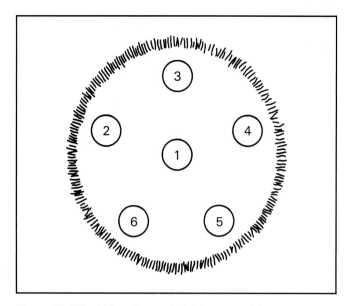

Figure 7-29 When heat shrinking metal, heat a spot at the center of the bulge and continue as shown by the numbered spots.

diameter. On flat (low-crown) surfaces, 1/2 in. (12 mm) diameter spots are used. Larger heat spots can be used in cases of excessive bulge, but the spots should never exceed 3/4 in. (20 mm) diameter. Heating larger areas may cause the panel to warp (become wavy and irregular). Care should be taken to prevent overheating or melting the metal surfaces.

If possible, two technicians should perform shrinking operations: one can apply the heat, and the other can work the metal with the hammer and dolly.

Because metal expands when it is hot, the surface may be slightly bulged even after the last spot is hammered and quenched. It is very important to allow the metal to cool thoroughly before any final work is attempted. If additional high spots are discovered, heat shrinking can be resumed.

It is important to remember that auto body sheet metal loses its temper or ''spring'' when it is heated to a cherry red. By heating small spots, the natural spring and resiliency of the metal is retained around each spot.

Most body panels have at least a slight curve. Therefore, excessive shrinking will cause the curve to flatten out and may cause buckles to appear elsewhere in the panel. Flattened areas must be reshaped with a hammer and dolly. When shrinking long, narrow areas, start at either end, not in the center.

Shrinking aluminum is very similar to shrinking steel. However, aluminum absorbs heat much more rapidly than steel and does not change color when heated. It also cools faster than steel. Extreme care must be taken to avoid burning through aluminum panels. As soon as the surface starts to blister at the point of flame contact, the flame must be removed and hammering must be done quickly. Hot aluminum should be tapped very lightly to prevent additional stretching.

Paintless Dent Removal

Paintless dent removal involves the use of specially designed picks and spoons to remove minor dents. This method is often used to remove minor dings from doors and fenders, as well as hail damage. It is less costly than other techniques and results in a quality job with no concern for matching paint.

Most dents are accessible through inner panels. In some cases, however, small holes must be drilled in the edges of doors or other inner panels to access the dents. These holes are then plugged after the work is complete. It may take more than fifty pressure pries to properly raise a dent. The technician must use light reflection to aid the progress of each pry. If the repair is completed properly, no sanding, filling, or refinishing is needed. The area is simply cleaned and polished. This process is labor intensive, and charges are usually made by the dent. A dent the size of a quarter may take 20–30 minutes to remove, and the technician may charge 30–40 dollars per hour.

Sanding Metal Surfaces

After a damaged area has been returned to its correct shape, it must be cleaned and sanded to ensure that fillers and primers will adhere properly. A disk sander is commonly used to remove small pits, scratches, and hammer marks before fillers or primers are applied. The sander can also be used to feather (taper) the surrounding surfaces so that they will blend with the repaired area.

See Chapters 16 and 17 for more information on refinishing materials and techniques.

Selecting the Correct Abrasive

The quality of the final finish is largely dependent on the proper selection and use of abrasives. The correct use of abrasives also minimizes finishing time.

The term *coated abrasives* refers to most abrasives used for automobile refinishing. Although there are many types of coated abrasives, all consist of a combination of abrasive grains, backing materials, and bonding agents. Typical examples of coated abrasives include sandpaper, waterproof paper, grinding disks, grinding combs, and grinding belts.

Aluminum oxide and *silicon carbide* abrasives are commonly used in the auto body shop. Some authorities recommend silicon carbide (black color) abrasives for finishing primer-surfacer coats. These abrasive crystals fracture during use and continually provide a sharp cutting edge. Aluminum oxide (reddish-brown color), on the other hand, is extremely tough. It is highly resistant to fracturing and capable of penetrating hard surfaces without dulling. Because of these properties, aluminum oxide is often preferred for metal finishing. Although the term sandpaper is frequently used when referring to abrasives, it is not entirely accurate. Sand is no longer used as an abrasive grain.

The two products most frequently used for bonding abrasive grains to backing materials are glue and resin. Organic glue is used to bond aluminum oxide grains to a non-waterproof backing material. Resin is used to bond silicon carbide to a waterproof backing material. Glued abrasives are less resistant to frictional heat than resin-bonded abrasives. Paper, cloth, screen, and fiber are commonly used as backing materials.

Abrasive Surface Types

Abrasives are manufactured in two surface types: open coat and closed coat, Figure 7-30.

The abrasive grains on **open-coat abrasives** are widely separated. There is a noticeable space between individual particles. The backing material is only 60% to 70% covered with abrasive grains. Open-coat abrasive grades range from #16 grit to #300 grit. The #16 grit

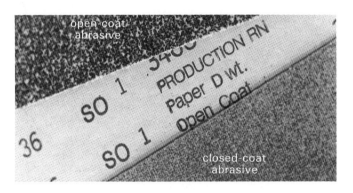

Figure 7-30 Example of open-coat abrasive and closed-coat abrasive.

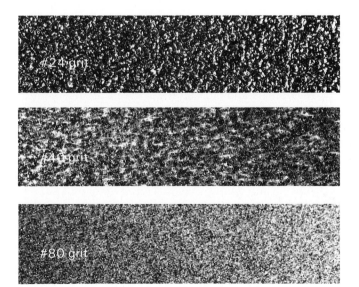

Figure 7-31 Various abrasive grit sizes.

abrasive has coarse, heavy grains. Higher grade abrasives have finer grains. See Figure 7-31. Fine grains are generally more closely spaced than coarse grains. Commonly used aluminum oxide grades include #16, #24, #36, and #50 grit. Open-coat abrasives are designed for removing paint and for cutting down welds or other coarse materials that tend to clog or adhere to the abrasive grains.

The abrasive grains on **closed-coat abrasives** are as close together as possible. The backing material is 90% covered with grains. Closed-coat abrasives are available in grades from #16 grit to #320 grit. These abrasives are used to sand materials that produce very fine particles. As a rule, fine particles do not clog the abrasive grains.

Choosing the Proper Grade

An abrasive's grade is generally marked on its backing material. Although coarse grades cut quickly, they produce deep surface scratches. Fine grades produce smooth surfaces, but they remove material very slowly. Therefore, a coarse grade, open-coat paper is recommended for removing paint and eliminating tool marks made during straightening operations. After the paint has been removed, the contour restored, and the heavy tool marks eliminated, a closed-coat, fine-grade abrasive can be used to provide surface smoothness. An extremely fine abrasive, usually #80 to #320 grit, is used for feathering and final smoothing. Undercoats and some color coats are sanded to achieve the desired surface smoothness. This type of sanding can be done with or without water. Although dry sanding produces a relatively smooth surface, wet sanding results in a much smoother surface. Abrasive paper for wet-sanding is available in grades ranging from #60 grit to #1200 grit. Those ranging from #600 to #1200 grit are most popular for wet sanding undercoats and color coats. Hand-sanding and wet-sanding techniques will be discussed further in Chapter 18.

Disk Sanders

The **disk sander** is used for virtually all types of sanding, from the heavy sanding required to cut down welds to the light sanding necessary to feather painted surfaces. In some designs, a screw is used to attach an abrasive disk to a soft, motor-driven pad. In other designs, the abrasive disk's backing material is coated with a pressure-sensitive adhesive that bonds to a soft, motor-driven pad. In either case, the disk's soft backing pad and the fact that it rotates permit its use on many different surface contours.

Open-coat disks are used to cut down welds and to sand paint. At times, even open-coat disks will load up or become impacted with filler and paint. This condition can usually be prevented by stopping the sander from time to time and striking the disk sharply with a metal bar. This will loosen the material adhering to the abrasive grains so that they will cut again. Specially designed disk cleaning bars are also available for this purpose. These eraser-like bars are held against the rotating disk to help clean the clogged abrasives.

Using the Disk Sander

When using the disk sander for filing purposes, it should be moved across the surface so that the grit marks bridge (do not touch) the low spots. Sufficient pressure should be applied to cause the disk pad to flex slightly. About 1/3 of the disk's cutting surface should be used. Never use the disk in a flat position. During the side-to-side strokes, the sander should be tilted so that alternate sides of the disk are used. Moving the sander in this way will create a criss-cross swirl pattern.

When removing paint, the sander should not be tilted as much as when using it for filing purposes. Therefore, more disk area is used. See Figure 7-32. A #16 grit, open-coat disk is often used for paint removal. Finer grades are used for the final sanding. Loose metal or dirt on the sanding area will cause scratches. A worn or loaded disk can also cause scratches. Failure to cross-sand, especially when changing from a coarse grit to a fine grit, is another cause of troublesome scratches. Cross-sanding under a strong, direct light will help the technician detect sanding imperfections.

When the outer edge of an abrasive disk becomes worn and will not cut, the worn area can be trimmed off and the disk can be mounted on a smaller pad. The sanding pad should always be the same size as the abrasive disk. A special machine for cutting abrasive disks is shown in Figure 7-33.

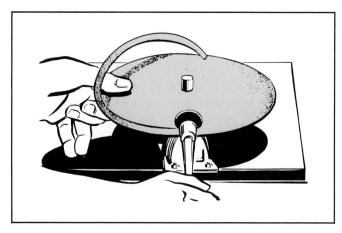

Figure 7-33 After considerable use, the outer edge of the abrasive disk can be cut off and the remainder of the disk can be installed on a smaller pad.

When using a disk sander near a bead, there is a possibility of cutting into the bead. To prevent this, it is advisable to sand such areas by hand.

Burned spots may result if the sander is held in one spot for too long. Excessive disk pressure and worn or glazed (clogged) disks can also cause burned spots. These spots can be prevented by maintaining a fast working rhythm and applying only light pressure on the disk. Using the proper disk grade will also help prevent burned spots.

Summary

The auto body technician must understand the basic properties of metals in order to repair damaged metal components properly. The property of metal that allows it to be shaped is called plasticity. Plastic deformation occurs when a force is used to change the shape of metal. Malleability is the property that permits deformation under compression. Ductility is the property that permits deformation under tension. A material's ability to be stretched is called elasticity. When a material is stretched beyond its elastic limit, it will not return to its original shape.

Mild steels and high-strength steels are used in the manufacture of the modern automobile. Unlike mild steels, high-strength steels lose their desirable properties when heated above 1000 °F. Additionally, excessive working of high-strength steels will cause them to become brittle.

All collision damage will fall into two or more of the following categories: direct damage, indirect damage, minor damage, and major damage. Direct damage is the result of direct contact with an object. Indirect damage results from direct damage. Minor damage requires little time and skill to complete. Major damage, on the other hand, generally involves replacing entire body panels and straightening structural components.

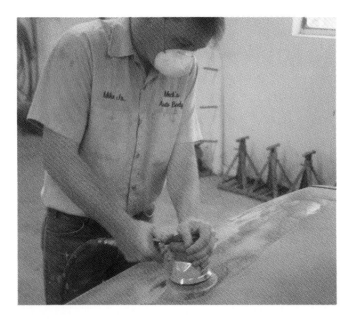

Figure 7-32 This technician is using a disk sander to remove paint.

There are several techniques for repairing auto body damage. The techniques used will depend on the age of the damaged vehicle, the location of the damage, and the wishes of the owner.

Vacuum cup pullers, pull rods, slide hammers, pull tabs, picks, spoons, rams, dollies, pick hammers, and files are all used to straighten damaged metal.

If metal is stretched, shrinking may be necessary to return it to its original size and shape. Cold shrinking techniques can be used on all metals. Heat shrinking should only be used on mild steel and aluminum. When heat shrinking a surface, care must be taken to prevent overheating.

After a damaged panel has been straightened, it must be sanded to assure that fillers and primers will adhere to the metal surface.

Aluminum oxide and silicon carbide abrasives are commonly used for auto body applications. Abrasives are available with two surface types: open coat and closed coat. The grains on open-coat abrasives are widely separated. Open-coat abrasives are designed for cutting coarse materials that tend to clog the abrasive grains. The abrasive grains in closed-coat abrasives are close together. Closed-coat abrasives are used to sand materials that produce fine particles and do not clog the grains.

A disk sander is used for many types of sanding in the body shop. The sander should be held at a slight angle so that only a portion of the sanding disk surface is used. Never use the disk in the flat position. Holding the sander in one spot for too long can cause burned spots on the metal.

Know These Terms

Crown, Plasticity, Plastic deformation, Malleability, Upsetting, Ductility, Stretching, Elasticity, Elastic limit, Work hardening, Cold working, Elastic deformation, Kink, Bend, Direct damage, Indirect damage, Minor damage, Major damage, Vacuum cup puller, Pull rods, Slide hammer, Pull tabs, Picks, Bumping spoons, Power rams, Spread rams, Roughing, Bumping, Dinging, Off-the-dolly dinging, On-the-dolly dinging, Pick hammers, Files, Cold shrinking, Shrinking hammers, Shrinking dollies, Kinking, Heat shrinking, Quenching, Coated abrasives, Aluminum oxide, Silicon carbide, Open-coat abrasives, Closed-coat abrasives, Disk sander.

Review Questions—Chapter 7

1. When a metal panel is damaged, _____ are often created in the damaged area.

2. Color is often used to estimate the temperature of steel. True or False?

3. High-strength, low-alloy steels lose strength when heated above _____ °F.

4. The property that permits deformation under compression is called:
   a. plasticity.
   b. malleability.
   c. elasticity.
   d. none of the above.

5. When metal is stretched beyond its _____ _____, it will not return to its original shape.

6. Permanent stresses often cause elastic stresses. True or False?

7. Permanent stresses should always be removed _____.

8. _____ _____ can occur when metal is stretched and straightened during the repair process.

9. Mild steel is more brittle than high-strength, low-alloy steel. True or False?

10. A _____ is a sharp bend that results in permanent metal deformation.

11. Holes, tears, gouges, and scratches are typical examples of _____ damage.

12. When removing dents, the damage at the point of initial contact should be removed _____.

13. The techniques used to repair a damaged vehicle will depend on:
    a. the wishes of the vehicle's owner.
    b. the age of the vehicle.
    c. the location of the damage.
    d. all of the above.

14. Before performing straightening procedures, _____, _____, _____, and _____ should be removed from damaged areas.

15. A vacuum puller should be used on a panel that is bent beyond its elastic limit. True or False?

16. The curvature of a panel is called the:
    a. bow.
    b. crown.
    c. hill.
    d. none of the above.

17. When using pull rods, all work can be done from the _____ of the damaged panel.

18. Before using pull tabs, holes must be drilled in damaged panels. True or False?

19. A _____ _____ can be used to spread hammer blows over a wide area.

20. Power rams are used to correct severe collision damage. True or False?

21. The working face of the dolly should have a _____ radius than the surface being straightened.

22. On-the-dolly dinging smooths damaged metal between the faces of the dolly and the hammer. True or False?

23. Heavy on-the-dolly dinging tends to make damaged panels _____.

24. _____ _____ and _____ are used to raise low spots during the final stages of bumping.

25. A shrinking hammer should be used with a _____ dolly.

26. Kinking does not actually shrink metal. True or False?

27. _____ shrinking is not recommended for high-strength, low-alloy steel panels.

28. When heat shrinking, the bulged area should be quenched when the steel is red hot. True or False?

29. Heating large areas can cause _____.

30. Excessive shrinking will cause curved areas to:
    a. bulge.
    b. burn.
    c. flatten out.
    d. none of the above.

31. Aluminum turns bright red when heated to temperatures above 900 °F. True or False?

32. After straightening a damaged panel, a _____ sander is often used to remove scratches and hammer marks.

33. Aluminum oxide and silicon carbide abrasive materials are commonly used in the body shop. True or False?

34. Open-coat abrasives are used when sanding coarse materials that tend to _____ the abrasive grit.

35. Cross-sanding with a disk sander will cause deep scratches. True or False?

Activities—Chapter 7

1. Bend a strip of sheet metal without forming a permanent kink and note what happens when you release the strip. Next, bend the same strip so that a kink is formed. Note that the sheet metal will not return to its original shape when the stresses are released. Using the procedure outlined above, demonstrate the difference between elastic and permanent stresses to your classmates.

2. Visit a body shop and take pictures of several damaged vehicles. Mount the pictures on a poster board and identify direct, indirect, major, and minor damage. Display your project in the shop or classroom.

3. Practice using a hammer and dolly on a discarded sheet metal body panel. Be sure to attempt both on-the-dolly and off-the-dolly dinging techniques.

4. Mount several pieces of abrasive paper to a poster board. Label the material as open-coat or closed-coat and identify the abrasive grades. List several applications for each piece of abrasive.

chapter 8

Simplified Metal Repairs

After studying this chapter, you will be able to:

☐ Differentiate between spot putties, glazing putties, and body fillers.

☐ Describe the proper filling techniques used to repair various types of damage.

☐ Identify the safety precautions that should be taken when working with lead-based products.

☐ Evaluate various types of corrosion damage and determine the best method of repair.

☐ Cite several advances that have been made in area of corrosion protection.

Types of Filler Materials

Before applying primer to a panel, all imperfections should be removed. Although metal straightening techniques are used to remove most damage, it is generally necessary to fill low spots or other small flaws. It is virtually impossible to eliminate all dents, pits, and hammer marks without utilizing filler materials. The three basic filler materials used in the body shop include:

☐ Spot putties.

☐ Glazing putties.

☐ Body fillers.

Note: Several of the chemicals used during filling operations can damage automotive finishes. Additionally, a great deal of dust is created when sanding filler materials. Therefore, it is advisable to cover or mask surrounding areas. A sheet of plastic can be used to protect vinyl tops, interiors, and engine compartments.

Spot Putty

When repairing small, shallow imperfections on paint films and primers, *spot putties* are often used. Spot putties are generally made of the same basic materials as primer-surfacers, but have a high concentration of solids (90%). These putties have the consistency of toothpaste. Some manufacturers recommend one type of spot putty for lacquers and another type for enamels.

Spot putty should be applied with a putty knife. Two or more thin coats of putty are better than one thick coat.

As the solvents in the putty evaporate, thick layers tend to shrink more than thin layers. This may cause cracking, separation, and poor adhesion. Most spot putties cure (harden) in approximately 30 minutes. After the putty is dry, it can be sanded, primed, and painted with a color topcoat. Because spot putties are solvent-based, solvents in the topcoat may cause the putty to soften. This can cause stains in the topcoat.

Glazing Putty

The term *glazing putty* is sometimes used to distinguish between polyester or epoxy resin-based putties and solvent-based spot putties. Glazing putties must be thoroughly mixed with a hardener (catalyst) before being applied. A putty knife is used to apply these putties over small imperfections. Like spot putties, most glazing putties will cure in about 30 minutes. After the putty has hardened, it can be sanded and finished.

In many applications, glazing putties are preferred to spot putties because they do not bleed, lift, or soften when topcoats are applied. Glazing putties contain 80% solids.

Body Fillers

Filling techniques have always been used in the auto body repair industry. Body fillers are commonly used in areas where dents are difficult to remove, such as in sections that are impossible to reach with a hammer, spoon, or dolly. Even when pull rods are used, some filling may be required. Nevertheless, body fillers should only be used when warranted. Filling should not be a substitute for professional metalworking processes. Fillers are often misused by technicians with little regard for professional reputation or first-rate work.

A damaged area must be cleaned to bare metal before applying any type of filler. See Figure 8-1. If necessary, an octagonal disk can be used to remove paint, rust, and oxides from low spots and inside curves. Octagonal disks are made by cutting worn disks into the proper shape, Figure 8-2.

There are two basic types of *body fillers* used today: solder fillers and plastic fillers.

Solder Fillers

Solder is an alloy of tin and lead. Solder alloys containing 70% lead were originally used for auto body repair. Consequently, the terms *lead* and *leading* have become associated with this filler. When applied properly, solder bonds very well to sheet metal and will not crack, peel, or flake. Additionally, a limited amount of hammer and dolly work can be performed after the solder has been applied.

WARNING: Precautions should be taken when using any compound that contains lead. To prevent inhaling smoke and sanding dust from lead-based products, always wear an approved respirator when working with these materials. Lead can accumulate in the body and cause various nervous system disorders, paralysis, and death. Never smoke or eat while working with lead products.

Solder filling is a slow, expensive process that requires considerable skill. Although solder is no longer used by automobile manufacturers, it is still preferred by some auto body personnel. Restoring classic automo-

Figure 8-1   Before applying plastic filler to a car body, the damaged area should be cleaned to bare metal.

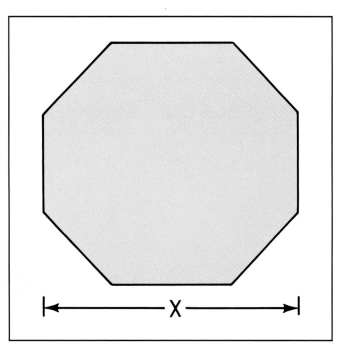

Figure 8-2   Template for use in cutting abrasive disks to be used on rough surfaces. Dimension X is 5 1/2 in. for 7 in. disks and 7 in. for 9 in. disks.

biles, performing custom work, filling weld seams and windshield posts, and forming edges on panels and doors are the most common applications of solder filling.

Filling Dents with Solder

After cleaning the area to be soldered, brush a tin-based soldering paste (mixture of acid, ground lead, and tin) that contains flux on the area. Use a heavily carburizing oxyacetylene flame to heat the base metal and the paste/flux. This process is called *tinning*. Tinning will help the solder adhere to the base metal. If necessary, an acid-based solder can be used instead of soldering paste to tin the surface, Figure 8-3. Melt the solder onto the damaged area. While the solder is soft, use a heavy rag to wipe excess material from the center of the dent outward. The area should have a bright, shiny appearance, Figure 8-4.

As solder (usually in bar form) is melted onto the tinned area, a wooden paddle (spatula) is used to spread and level the soft material, Figure 8-5. Solder is added until the area is filled. It requires a great deal of skill to add solder while working the soft, hot material with the wooden paddle. Only apply enough heat to keep the solder plastic, but not molten.

Once the solder has cooled, water should be used to neutralize and clean the repair. A metal body file and a sanding board can be used to smooth and level the filled area. The repair should be cleaned with bare-metal cleaner/etcher before it is primed. If the repaired area is not cleaned properly, residual acid will eventually cause the finish to blister.

Plastic Filler

Most shops now use plastic materials to fill low spots and other imperfections. **Plastic fillers** have replaced lead in most facilities. Plastic fillers have the

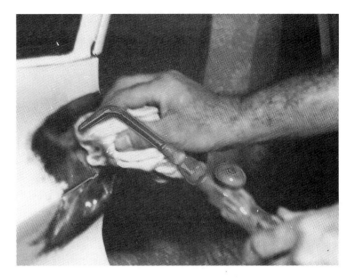

Figure 8-4   A clean cloth or steel wool can be used to spread solder over the surface being tinned.

A

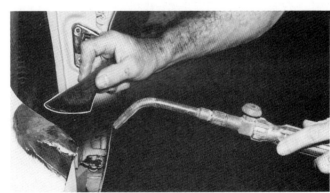

B

Figure 8-5   A–Melting solder on tinned surface. B–Spreading soft solder over the surface with a wooden paddle.

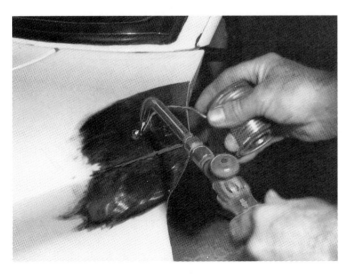

Figure 8-3   Using acid core solder and a torch to tin an area before filling with solder.

consistency of putty and are often packaged in plastic bags or metal cans, Figure 8-6. Several companies sell dispensing devices to facilitate the use of these materials. See Figure 8-7. There are two types of plastic fillers used in repair work:

☐ Polyester resin-based filler.

☐ Epoxy resin-based filler.

Both polyester and epoxy fillers require the use of a chemical hardener (catalyst), which must be thoroughly mixed with the resin-based filler. Talc is the most common filler in the resin base, but glass fibers, clay, glass beads, aluminum flakes, and other materials are also used.

Polyester resin-based fillers are the most common plastic fillers used in the body shop. They are considered to be general-purpose fillers. Polyester fillers are gener-

ally applied with a putty knife and can be worked for approximately 10 minutes before they begin to harden.

A thin (low viscosity) polyester filler (Featherfill) is available that can be sprayed onto a damaged panel. It is a combination surfacer and plastic filler. Like other plastic fillers, a catalyst must be mixed with this material before it is sprayed on the repair area.

Epoxy resin-based fillers are generally stronger and more expensive than polyester fillers. They bond well to both steel and aluminum. Depending on the manufacturer, the working time for epoxy fillers varies from 5 minutes to 1 hour.

Filling Dents with Plastic Filler

Before applying a plastic filler, the area to be repaired must be sanded to bare metal. A coarse abrasive, such as a #24 open grit, should be used to roughen the surface slightly, providing a good bonding surface for the filler. Additionally, the surfaces surrounding the damaged area should be cleaned with a grease and wax remover. If the surrounding surfaces must be feathered, a #80 grit abrasive should be used to taper back the paint.

Always mix fillers according to the manufacturer's instructions. In most cases, two materials are provided: a filler resin and a hardener (catalyst), Figure 8-8. The materials should be mixed together with a putty knife. Always knead the mixture instead of stirring it. Kneading will help to prevent air bubbles, which cause pinholes in the applied filler. Most technicians prefer to mix the ingredients on a sheet of glass, a polyethylene board, or a plastic-covered piece of cardboard, Figure 8-9.

After the filler is properly mixed, it can be applied to the damaged surface with a plastic spreader or a wide putty knife. See Figure 8-10. Apply the mixture to the work area with a downward-sideways motion to force out air bubbles. Use long, unidirectional strokes. Direction changes may lift the filler applied during previous strokes. If the damaged areas are very deep, it is advisable to apply several thin layers of filler. Do not spread

Figure 8-6 Body filler can be purchased in metal cans. (Oatey)

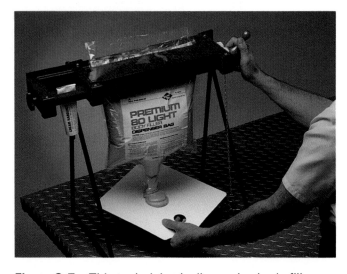

Figure 8-7 This technician is dispensing body filler from a bag-type dispenser onto a plastic mixing board. (Oatey)

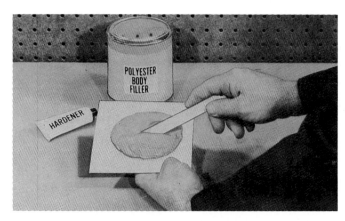

Figure 8-8 Follow manufacturer's instructions and mix only enough body filler to re-establish the original surface contour.

Figure 8-9 This technician is mixing body filler on a polyethylene-covered board. (Oatey)

Figure 8-10 Body filler is commonly applied with a plastic spreader.

filler over paint. It will not adhere properly and will eventually peel. Plastic fillers should never be used in areas where flexing may occur or where strength is required. If an area must be filled to an exposed edge or lip, solder should be used at the edge. Do not use plastic fillers to form an edge.

All resin-based plastic fillers will shrink slightly as they cure. Be sure to allow sufficient time for each layer to harden before subsequent layers are applied. The term *kicks over* is sometimes used to indicate that the mixture has hardened. Although hardening times vary, most fillers form a firm bond with the base metal in 10 to 15 minutes. Clean unused filler from the mixing board and spreader tool before it hardens. Some technicians use a disposable paper cover on the mixing board to simplify cleaning tasks.

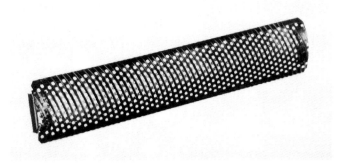

Figure 8-11 A surform file is used to remove partially cured filler. (Oatey)

After the filler has cured for about 5 minutes, a surform file can be used to shape and smooth the filled area, Figure 8-11. The filler should be easily worked or ''grated.'' If the filler sets for too long, it will be too hard to shape with a surform file. When this occurs, the file will leave white streaks in the filler. A body file may be required to shape hardened filler. Remember, the surform file is a fairly crude tool and should only be used to obtain general surface contour.

The actual curing time of any filler will depend on the age of the resin and hardener, the temperature and humidity in the shop, and thickness of the filler layers. Too much hardener will speed curing time, but may result in a porous, poorly bonded repair. As a rule, more catalyst can be used when applying a thin layer of filler than when applying a thick layer. Heat from the chemical reaction of the catalyst is more quickly dissipated in thin layers. Although heat lamps can be used to speed curing, care must be taken to prevent overheating. Overheating can result in porosity, poor bond strength, and blistering.

After achieving the general contour with a surform file, a sanding block or reciprocating sander should be used to smooth the filled area and blend it with the surrounding contour. The sanding block is essential for removing high spots. Rough sanding should be done using a #40 grit abrasive and long, crisscrossed strokes. Finish sanding may be done with a sanding block or an orbital sander, beginning with a #180 grit abrasive and progressing to a #280 grit abrasive. The finished area should be cleaned and primed immediately after sanding to prevent moisture from penetrating the filler and oxidizing the base metal. Most fillers are hygroscopic and porous, which means they will absorb moisture. If moisture is allowed to permeate the filler layer, the metal surface under the filler will rust and the filler-to-metal bond will deteriorate.

Repairing Rusted Areas

Unfortunately, automobiles do not last forever. Even with the most aggressive anti-rust treatments, metal is constantly attacked by corrosive elements.

When oxygen, water, and corrosive chemicals, such as salt, combine with steel, rust (iron oxide) is formed. Moisture and mud often get stuck in confined areas. Spaces between fenders and inner panels or spots where accessories are attached (mirrors, brackets, trim moldings, etc.) are potential problem areas. As drain plugs in rocker panels, doors, and other areas become clogged, dirt and moisture collect. This keeps the metal wet and promotes corrosion. Corrosion destroys more vehicles each year than accidents.

In recent years, vehicle manufacturers have made significant advances in the fight against rust. The use of galvanized steel, undercoatings, zinc-rich primers, anti-corrosion coatings, and various sealants has increased dramatically. A cathodic electrodeposition coating process known as *E-coat* produces a tough epoxy primer. New and better anti-corrosion materials are placed on the market each year. Additionally, plastics and other rust-resistant materials have been used in the manufacture of the automobile. Many of the moldings used on today's vehicles are attached with adhesives rather than metal clips. Clips generally require holes for attachment. These holes create potential spots for rust (oxidation).

Very few parts on late-model vehicles are without some form of zinc protection. To prevent rust, many interior surfaces are coated with zinc-rich coatings and most joints are sealed. Zinc helps protect steel by sealing it from the corrosive elements in the environment. When zinc coatings are applied, the zinc, rather than the steel, is attacked by the corrosive elements (sacrificial corrosion). Zinc-rich coatings also protect metals from galvanic (electro-chemical) action. Galvanic action occurs when dissimilar metals contact each other. This contact causes corrosion to form between the metals. For example, when steel bolts are used to secure an aluminum panel, corrosion will occur between the bolts and the panel. Unless the materials are given a protective coating, there will be degradation of both the fastener and the surrounding panel.

There are two basic types of rust damage commonly encountered in the body shop: outside surface rust and inside rust-out.

Outside Surface Rust

Outside surface rust begins from the outside of a panel. It usually starts in areas where paint is chipped and scratched or where moldings and accessories are attached. Surface rust is more easily detected and repaired than rust that begins on the inside of a panel. See Figure 8-12.

There are several methods used to remove surface rust. Chemical rust removers and metal conditioners deep clean and etch the metal. Sanding or sandblasting rusted areas to bare metal is also common. This method helps to reveal weak spots in the metal.

When auto bodies are stripped to bare metal, rust will form quickly. In order to prevent the formation of rust, the metal should be chemically cleaned and immediately primed. Metal conditioners (deactivating agents) and rust inhibitors can be applied before priming to help neutralize rust and provide better adhesion of the primer. Rust inhibitors are sometimes called *conversion coatings*. These inhibitors form a zinc phosphate coating that chemically bonds to metal.

Inside Rust-Out

Rust-out occurs when rust is allowed to eat through a metal panel, Figure 8-13. Most rust-out progresses from the inside of a panel and often goes undetected until it penetrates the outside surface. This condition is more

Figure 8-12 This surface rust resulted from scratches in the surface of the paint.

Figure 8-13 This panel has rust-out.

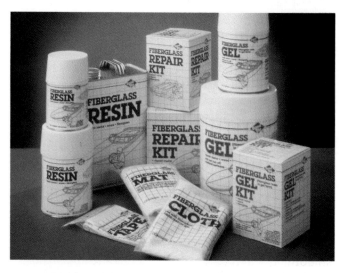

Figure 8-14 Resin and glass reinforcing materials are commonly sold in kits. (Oatey)

costly to repair than outside surface rust. It is always best to remove panels or doors with inside rust-out. This will provide for better access, diagnosis, and treatment of the damaged area.

Depending on the extent of the damage, several procedures can be utilized to repair rust-out areas, including replacement; cutting and patching; and the use of fiberglass fillers, fiberglass mats, or foam fillers. Fiberglass repair kits are available for the repair of rust-out areas. See Figure 8-14.

Replacement

If panels or components are severely rusted, new parts may be needed. In some cases, replacement "skins" can be purchased and placed over a damaged panel. Before installing a new skin, always remove as much of the rusted area as possible and treat the remaining material with metal conditioner and rust inhibitor. Undercoat the inside of the replacement panel and place it in proper alignment. After the replacement panel is welded in place and the joints are ground down, the panel should be sanded and primed. Undercoating should then be applied to the inside of the repair to retard the reoccurrence of rust.

Cut and Patch

If rust is limited to one section of a panel, the rusted area can be removed and replaced with a metal patch. The area around the damage should be sanded to bare metal, and the rusted section should be cut back to solid metal. A sheet metal patch is placed over the cut section and welded in place with a MIG welder. After welding, the weld joints are ground smooth. Body filler (metal or plastic) can be used to complete the finish contour of the patch.

Fiberglass Fillers

If rust-out is minor, **epoxy fiberglass fillers** can be used to repair the damage. Fiberglass fillers have short strands of glass fiber in an epoxy resin system. The glass fibers do not absorb moisture and are considered waterproof. Additionally, the fibers help to reinforce the repair and bridge small gaps in the metal. Regular body fillers should not be used to repair rust-out. These materials usually contain talc or clay and, therefore, tend to absorb moisture.

Before filling a damaged area, it must be thoroughly cleaned and treated with metal conditioner and inhibitor. Like other body fillers, fiberglass fillers are mixed with a hardener and applied with a putty knife. It is important that the filler penetrates to the inside of the panel. This will assure that the filler is firmly locked in place. After smoothing and finishing the filled area, the back of the repair should be treated with rust inhibitor and undercoating.

A belt sander with a vacuum attachment is often used when finishing fiberglass fillers. The vacuum will collect much of the resin and fiber dust created during the sanding process.

Fiberglass Mat or Patch

If there are numerous holes in a panel or if the metal is weak and easily gives when pressed, a fiberglass mat or cloth patch can be used to repair the damaged area. Before applying a patch, the damaged surface must be sanded and prepared in the usual manner to remove rust, dirt, and paint, Figure 8-15. To ensure proper adhesion of the epoxy resin-soaked patches, a series of small holes should be drilled through the metal in the damaged area. The fiberglass cloth or mat should be large enough to lap about 2 in. (50 mm) over the damaged area. See Figure 8-16. If the rusted area is depressed below the surrounding surface, several layers of cloth or mat can be applied. These patches should be cut in progressively larger sizes, so each succeeding patch will overlap the preceding one.

Before applying a fiberglass patch, the resin system (epoxy) must be catalyzed and the patch must be

Figure 8-15 Prior to the application of fiberglass cloth, the damaged area is sanded and warmed with heat lamps.

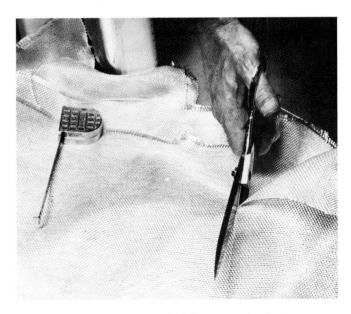

Figure 8-16 Fiberglass cloth is cut to size before being applied to the rusted area.

impregnated with the resin, Figure 8-17. Follow the manufacturer's instructions for mixing the resin. Care must be taken to use the correct proportions. Use personal protective wear and work in a well-ventilated area.

After the patches are saturated with the resin, they are applied to the rusted area, Figure 8-18. A spreader should be used to press out air bubbles and smooth each succeeding layer. A specially grooved brayer is sometimes used to help smooth the resin-saturated reinforcement. This tool is similar to a small paint roller. A heat lamp can be used to speed the curing time. See Figure 8-19.

On vertical surfaces or in areas where there is considerable damage, an alternate patching method can be used. In this method, a wetting coat of resin is applied directly to the damaged area. Then the resin-soaked patches are built up (in reverse order) on a supporting board, such as a thin piece of cardboard. Polyethylene, Mylar, or plastic food wrap is used to cover the support-

ing board, preventing the resin from adhering to the cardboard. The supporting board is firmly pressed into position over the damaged area. Masking tape can be used to temporarily hold the supporting board and patch in place. After the patch has hardened, the supporting board can be easily removed. The resin system will not adhere to the covered board.

After the resin has hardened, the patched area can be sanded and a thin coat of body filler can be applied over the repair to help fill minor imperfections. The area is then ready for final sanding and finishing. If the inside of the patch is accessible, it should be covered with undercoating.

Many technicians use an alternate method to repair rust-out areas. After the damaged area has been carefully cleaned and the inhibitor has been applied, structural adhesive is used to bond a small metal patch to the back of the rusted area. Once the adhesive has cured, the remaining depression is filled with an epoxy-based filler.

Foam Fillers

Two types of foam fillers can be used to repair rust-out. **Syntactic foams** are resin and catalyst systems that contain small glass or plastic spheres. These foams are used to fill rusted areas in door sills and rocker panels. Because of the large number of spheres, these putty-like materials have good compressive strength.

The second type of foam filler is also a two-part resin system. This filler is available in small kits. Upon mixing, the material immediately begins to expand. After it expands, it is forced into the cavity and allowed to cure (harden). When the filler has cured, it is generally sanded with a #36 grit paper. The foam filler should be about 1/4 in. (6 mm) below the adjoining metal, and body filler should be applied over the foam. Normal procedures are followed for shaping and finishing the body filler.

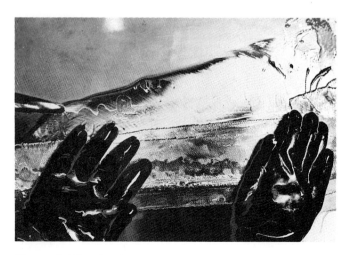

Figure 8-17 Before applying fiberglass patches, they are saturated with epoxy resin and hardener.

Figure 8-18 Applying the fiberglass patches to the rusted area.

Figure 8-19 Heat lamps can be used to speed drying time. After the patch has dried, it can be sanded and painted in the usual manner.

Restoring Corrosion Protection

There have been considerable gains in the durability and quality of automobile bodies in recent years. Some of these gains can be attributed to better design, the use of corrosion-resistant materials, and the application of corrosion protection products. Many decorative parts, such as moldings and name plates, are simply attached by adhesives. Aluminum, plastic, and bimetal parts are also used. Zinc-rich preprimers are often applied in areas where corrosion is most likely to occur. The entire body is generally coated with a corrosion resistant primer (zinc phosphate), Figure 8-20. This can be accomplished by spraying the primer onto the body or by submerging the body in a tank of the solution. Many joints are coated with sealants, and exposed surfaces are coated with wax or petroleum-based compounds, Figure 8-21. These compounds help to prevent corrosion, seal cracks, and deaden sound.

In the automotive service field, auto dealers and specialists are offering corrosion protection (rustproofing), undercoating, sound deadening, and upholstery and paint protection services. See Figure 8-22.

It is the technician's responsibility to restore corrosion protection when making auto body repairs.

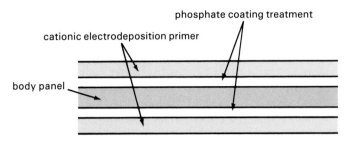

Figure 8-20 Many primers provide excellent corrosion protection. Note that both sides of this body panel are coated with a cationic electrodeposition primer and a phosphate treatment. (Nissan)

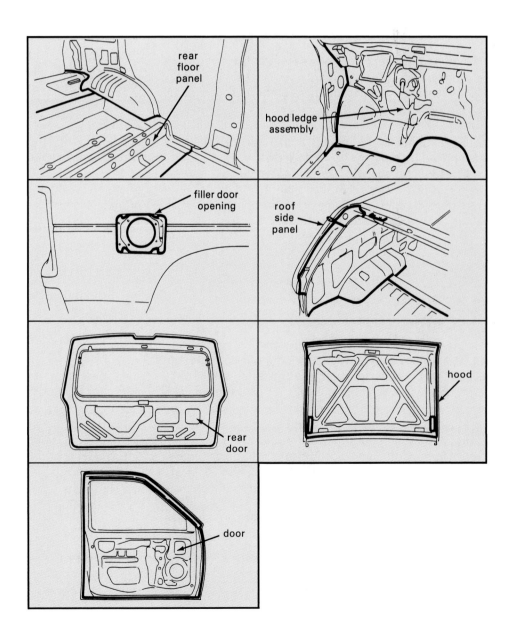

Figure 8-21 Typical body sealer locations. (Nissan)

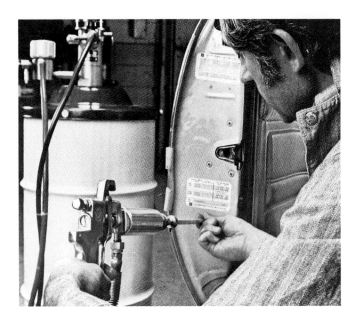

Figure 8-22 This technician is using special equipment to apply rustproofing and sound deadening material to the interior of a door. (Stewart-Warner Corp.)

Self-etching primers may be used in areas away from welded joints. These primers contain an agent that "bites" into the metal for improved adhesion. *Two-component epoxy primers* offer superior adhesion and protection. Zinc-rich *weld-through primers* should be applied to all joints before welding. These primers help prevent galvanic corrosion in the joints.

Because of the wide variety of anticorrosion compounds, body sealers, antirust agents, and other metal treatment products available, it is essential to carefully follow the manufacturer's instructions for application or use. See Chapters 7 and 10 for additional information on corrosion protection.

Summary

The three general types of filler materials used in the body shop are spot putties, glazing putties, and body fillers. Spot putties are used when repairing small, shallow imperfections. These solvent-based putties may be softened by the solvents in topcoats. Glazing putties, on the other hand, are polyester or epoxy resin-based materials. They do not soften when topcoats are applied.

Fillers are commonly used in areas where damage is difficult to remove. Solder fillers and plastic fillers are both used in the shop. Body fillers should not be used as substitutes for professional metalworking processes.

Solder filler is an alloy of tin and lead. It bonds well to metal and does not crack, peel, or flake. Although solder is no longer used in the manufacture of automobiles, it is still preferred by some body shop personnel. Safety precautions must be taken when working with any lead-based product.

Plastic fillers have replaced lead solder in most body shops. Both polyester and epoxy resin-based fillers are used. These fillers require the use of a chemical hardener. Plastic fillers should never be used in areas where flexing may occur or where strength is required.

When oxygen, water, and corrosive chemicals combine with steel, rust is formed. There are two basic types of rust damage: outside surface rust and inside rust-out. As the name implies, outside surface rust begins on the outside of a panel. This type of rust is more easily detected and repaired than rust that begins on the inside of a panel. Inside rust-out, on the other hand, generally starts on the inside of a panel. Rust-out is generally more difficult to repair than surface rust.

The techniques used to repair rust-out include panel replacement; cutting and patching; and the use of fiberglass fillers, fiberglass mats, or foam fillers. The technique used depends on the extent of the rust damage.

After making auto body repairs, it is the technician's responsibility to restore proper corrosion protection. Self-etching primers, epoxy primers, and weld-through primers are commonly used to restore protection to the damaged sections.

Know These Terms

Spot putties, Glazing putty, Body fillers, Solder, Lead, Leading, Tinning, Plastic fillers, Kicks over, E-coat, Outside surface rust, Conversion coatings, Rust-out, Epoxy fiberglass fillers, Syntactic foams, Self-etching primers, Two-component epoxy primers, Weld-through primers.

Review Questions–Chapter 8

1. Spot putties tend to _____ when topcoats are applied.

2. Glazing putties must be mixed with a catalyst before being applied. True or False?

3. Body fillers are used in sections where damage is easy to remove. True or False?

4. Solder body filler is an alloy of _____ and _____.

5. Solder filler has a tendency to:
   a. crack.
   b. flake.
   c. peel.
   d. none of the above.

6. _____ is a process used to prepare base metal for solder.

7. A wooden paddle is used to spread soft solder. True or False?

8. Plastic fillers have replaced solder fillers in many body shops. True or False?

9. Plastic fillers require the use of a chemical _____.

10. Epoxy resin-based fillers are considered to be general purpose fillers.

11. Plastic fillers can be applied directly over painted surfaces. True or False?

12. Before a plastic filler is fully cured, a _____ file can be used to obtain general surface contour.

13. The curing time of plastic fillers depends on:
    a. humidity.
    b. thickness.
    c. temperature.
    d. all of the above.

14. _____ is formed when oxygen, water, and corrosive chemicals combine with steel.

15. Zinc-rich coatings are used to protect late model vehicles from corrosion. True or False?

16. _____ rust usually begins in areas where paint is chipped or scratched.

17. Rust-out generally progresses from the _____ of a panel.

18. Fiberglass body fillers are commonly used to repair rust-out. True or False?

19. Syntactic _____ contain small glass or plastic spheres.

20. It is the responsibility of the auto body technician to restore corrosion protection to damaged areas. True or False?

Activities—Chapter 8

1. If you have access to a video camera, visit a local body shop and film a body technician applying filler. Show the video to your classmates and describe the application procedure to them. Be sure to emphasize the importance of proper surface preparation.

2. Examine several vehicles for signs of surface rust or rust through, and make a list of your findings. Study the list to determine which areas of a vehicle are most likely to experience rust damage.

3. Mix a small amount of body filler with the recommended quantity of hardener. Use a plastic spreader or putty knife to apply the filler to a scrap piece of metal. Make sure that the putty is the right consistency, that it cures properly, and that it adheres well to the metal surface.

Engineers in the automotive field are constantly working to develop new applications for plastic materials. (G.E. Plastics)

chapter 9

Simplified Plastic Repairs

After studying this chapter, you will be able to:

☐ Explain why plastics are being used extensively in the modern automobile.

☐ Differentiate between thermoset materials and thermoplastic materials.

☐ Describe the methods used to identify plastic materials.

☐ Explain the various techniques used to repair plastic components.

Use of Plastics

Plastics are being used extensively in all automobiles. More than 90% of the interior components in a modern automobile are made of some type of plastic. The use of plastics for exterior components continues to grow. Exterior applications of plastic materials include body panels, bumper and fender extensions, soft fascias, fender aprons and skirts, fan shrouds, grilles, trim pieces, fuel tanks, and many other components.

There are a number of reasons for the extensive use of plastics in the modern automobile:

☐ Plastics have less mass (weight) than steel.

☐ Plastics do not rust or corrode.

☐ Plastics can be formed into complicated, compound curves.

☐ Plastics can be flexible or rigid.

☐ Plastics can be produced in a variety of colors.

☐ Plastics have a high strength-to-mass (weight) ratio. Many plastics (composites) are actually stronger than the steels they replaced.

☐ Plastics are easily processed into parts and require little or no post-processing.

As manufacturers strive to reduce vehicle weight and improve fuel efficiency, the use of plastics will continue to grow. Researchers have estimated that every 100 lb. reduced from a 2500 lb. automobile will produce a fuel savings of 0.3 miles per gallon. Additionally, the energy resource requirements per pound of most plastics are only half those of steel or aluminum.

Composites

The term *composite* is used to describe any plastic that is formed by combining two or more materials, such as a polymer resin (matrix) and a reinforcement material.

Fibrous composites are composed of fiber reinforcements in a resin base. These materials are commonly referred to as reinforced plastics or fiber reinforced plastics (FRP). In this text, the term *fiberglass* will be used when referring to any material that consists of a thermoset resin and fibrous glass reinforcements. Two common thermoset resins used in fiberglass systems are polyester resins and epoxy resins.

Fiberglass is often sold in the form of fibrous mats. *Fibrous mats* consist of nondirectional strands of chopped glass that are held together by a resinous binder. A *surfacing mat* or *veil* is a very thin fibrous mat that is used as the top or outermost layer when making repairs. Woven *fiberglass cloth* is relatively heavy and provides the greatest physical strength of all the fibrous mats.

Laminar composites are composed of layers of reinforcing materials that are held together by a resin matrix. This type of composite material will be used extensively in future automobile designs. Compression molding processes permit special layering of the reinforcing materials and the resin to produce dense, strong, paintable material.

Manufacturers have experienced difficulty in using plastics for the rear quarter panels of unibody vehicles. In unibody construction, these panels are important structural components. However, composite thermoset *sheet molding compounds* (SMC) are now being used in the manufacture of rear quarter panels and other structural components. These laminar composites are currently the only plastic materials that meet the stiffness requirements for structural applications and provide a class-A surface that is capable of withstanding E-coat baking techniques. In addition to structural components, sheet molding compounds are being used for hoods, doors, lift gates, roof panels, and removable hard tops.

Sheet molding compounds are precombined sheets of resin, reinforcements, fillers, and other additives. Because these materials are in sheet form, they are easily adapted to mass production techniques. Parts are formed by molding the sheets between two heated dies (molds).

Reaction injection molding (RIM) and *reinforced reaction injection molding* (RRIM) processes involve injecting reactive polyurethane (PU), polyurea, or dicyclopentadiene (DCPD) resin into a mold that contains a preformed glass mat. In some processes, the reinforcing fibers are mixed directly with the resin before it is injected into the mold. The Pontiac Fiero had both polyurethane and polyurea RIM doors.

It is important to note that although SMC, RIM, and RRIM refer to materials and manufacturing processes, they do not identify specific plastics or composites.

Composite Bodies

Entire vehicle bodies have been made of composites. Fiberglass bodies are the most common. Fiberglass bodies have been used on a variety of limited-production vehicles, such as sports cars, racing cars, dune buggies, recreational vehicles, and trucks.

Currently, the major disadvantage to using composite fiberglass is that the manufacturing process is too slow. Sheet metal parts can be rapidly stamped and fabricated. Fiberglass, on the other hand, is sprayed into a mold or laid up by hand. Consequently, steel continues to be more economical than fiberglass composites in the manufacture of automobile bodies.

Several vehicles are currently being manufactured with SMC panels that are attached to a *space frame*. Adhesives and/or mechanical fasteners are used to secure the panels to the frame. A typical space frame is illustrated in Figure 9-1. The space frame and the exterior plastic panels provide the structural integrity for the vehicle.

The front fenders and rear quarter panels on the Saturn automobile are molded of a polyphenylene-ether/polyamide (PPE/PA) blend. The door panels are molded of a rigid blend of acrylonitrile butadiene styrene/polycarbonate (ABS/PC). See Figure 9-2. These panels are attached to the vehicle's frame with adhesives and mechanical fasteners. The typical composite components on a vehicle with metal body panels are illustrated in Figure 9-3.

The use of exterior composite body parts on American vehicles is expected to double in the next 10 years. The use of plastic composites has had many implications for the auto body repair business.

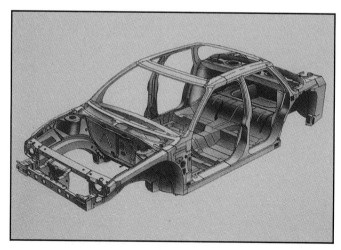

Figure 9-1   Typical space frame. (Saturn)

Chapter 9 Simplified Plastic Repairs 109

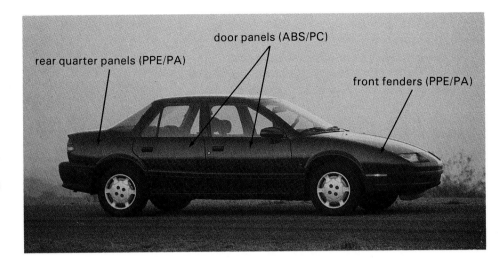

Figure 9-2 Plastic composites are used for the front fenders, door panels and rear quarter panels on this vehicle. (Saturn)

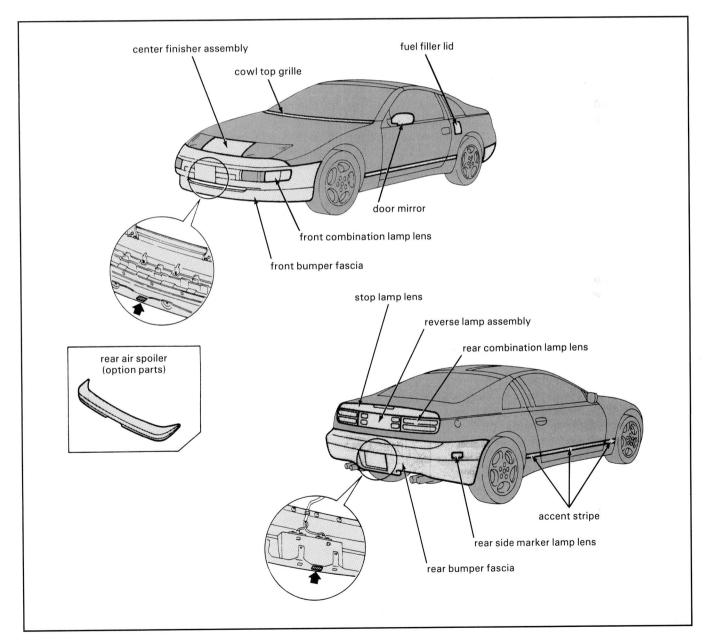

Figure 9-3 Location of plastic parts on a specific vehicle. Arrows in enlarged areas indicate the location of the ISO symbols that identify the type of plastic used. (Nissan)

Families of Plastics

There are two basic families of plastics: thermoplastics and thermosetting plastics (thermosets). Each family contains various types of plastics.

Thermoplastics

Thermoplastic materials become soft when heated and hard when cooled. Thermoplastics react like wax when exposed to heat. Polyethylene, polyamide, acrylic, polystyrene, and polyvinyl chloride are common thermoplastic materials. Soft interior panels, bumper covers, fluid reservoirs, fans, shrouds, and many other parts are made of thermoplastic materials.

Thermoplastic materials are used because they can be rapidly molded into a variety of complex shapes. Thermoplastic materials are commonly extruded (polyamide tubing), reaction-injection molded (bumper fascia), injection molded (cowl vents), vacuum formed (duct halves), or blow-extruded (fluid reservoirs).

Thermosetting Plastics

Thermosetting plastics (thermosets) cannot be softened after they are initially formed. Raw thermosetting material is heated (or catalyzed) and formed into a desired shape. Once this type of plastic has set, it cannot be reformed. Applying additional heat will result in material degradation. Forming thermosetting plastics can be compared to baking a cake or boiling an egg.

Thermosetting plastics are stronger and have a higher service temperature than thermoplastics. Thermosetting materials cannot be bonded with cohesive methods. Adhesive bonding techniques must be used when repairing thermosetting plastics.

Polyester, epoxy, and polyurethane are familiar thermosets. Common applications of thermosetting materials include exterior body panels, filler panels, bumper covers, exterior and interior trim panels, and knobs.

Identifying Plastics

In order to repair damaged plastic parts correctly, the auto body technician must be able to identify various families and types of plastics. All technicians should study a text on industrial plastics.

There are five broad methods used to distinguish between various types of plastics. Plastics can be identified by: trade names and abbreviations, application and method of fabrication, effects of heat, effects of solvents, and relative density.

Trade Names and Abbreviations

Many plastic and resin names are difficult to spell and pronounce. Therefore, common names and trade names are often used to identify plastics and manufacturers. Abbreviations are commonly used to identify plastics and elastomers. The term *elastomer* is used to describe any rubber-like material. By definition an elastomer is a material that can be stretched to at least twice its original length (at room temperature) and return to its original size when released. Many manufacturers imprint the ISO (International Organization for Standardization) abbreviation for a specific plastic or elastomer on the underside of a plastic component. ISO abbreviations for common plastics are shown in Figure 9-4.

Method of Fabrication and Application

The method of fabrication and product application are important clues when attempting to identify plastics. Thermoplastics are commonly extruded, reaction-injection molded, injection molded, vacuum formed, or blow-extruded. Polyethylene (PE) is a thermoplastic material that is used extensively to produce containers (tanks, bottles, etc.). Polyethylene (PE), polypropylene (PP), polytetrafluoroethylene (PTFE), polyacetal (POM), and polyamide (PA) have a waxy feel not found in most plastics. Acrylics (PMMA), polystyrenes (PS), and polycarbonates (PC) are commonly used when transparency is needed. Acrylic lacquers and enamels have replaced most cellulosic finishes as a durable exterior coating on automobiles.

Thermosetting plastic parts are usually compression molded, cast, or laminated. Polyester (UP) and epoxy (EP) resins are commonly used in the body shop. Alkyd resins have been popular for many years as finishing resins. Epoxy resins and, to a lesser extent, phenolic (PF) resins are used as tough, durable coatings. Polyurethane enamels are used as clear top coats and as original finishes on trucks and heavy equipment.

Effects of Heat

An electric soldering gun can be used to determine if a material is a thermoset or a thermoplastic. The hot tip of the gun will sink into thermoplastic materials. Thermosets, however, will remain hard when touched with the gun.

The burning of a sample piece of plastic in an open flame may provide further clues. Polystyrene or plastics containing polystyrene will burn with black (carbon) smoke. Polyethylene burns with a clear, blue flame and will produce flaming, molten drips. Polyvinyl chloride burns with a blue-green flame. A burn test chart for selected plastics is shown Figure 9-5. When heated, many plastics give off distinctive odors. Caution: do not inhale smoke or fumes from burning plastics.

Identification is not always an easy task. Some plastics are available as both a thermoplastic and a thermoset. For example, unsaturated polyester (UP) is a thermoset, but saturated polyester is a thermoplastic. Polyurethanes (PU) are available as hard, tough

PLASTIC MATERIALS USED IN AUTOMOBILES				
ISO Abbreviation	Material	Common/Trade Name	Applications	Repair Selection
ABS	Acrylonitrile-Butadiene-Styrene	Cycolac, Lustran	Interior/exterior trim, grilles, garnish molding, louvers, outside mirrors	S, W, AB, FGB
ASA	Acrylonitrile-Styrene-Acrylate	Luran, Geloy	Exterior trim	S, W, AB, FGB
EPS	(Expandable) Polystyrene	Styrofoam	Headlining, thermal insulation	S, AB
FRP	Fibrous Glass Reinforced Plastics	Fiberglass	Body filler, body accessories, headlamp covers	FGB, AB
HDPE	High-density Polyethylene	Marlex, Dylan	Fuel tanks, wash tanks	W, AB
LDPE	Low-density Polyethylene	Marlex, Dylan	Housings, expansion tanks	W, AB
PA	Polyamide	Nylon	Gears, clips, housings, hub caps, pipes, fans	AB, W
PBT	Polybutylene Terephthalate	Ealox, Celanex	Bearings, headlamp bodies, radiator grilles	A B
PC	Polycarbonate	Lexan	Covers, knobs, housings, lenses, instrument panels	S, AB, FGB
PE	Polyethylene (expanded)	Marlex, Dylan	Paneling for doors, head and arm rests, sun visors, shelves, consoles	W, AB
PE	Polyethylene (molded)	Marlex, Dylan	Fender skirt, interior trim, spoiler, sill cover	W, AB
PMMA	Polymethyl Methacrylate	Plexiglas, Lucite	Tail light lens, instrument lens	S, AB
POM	Polyacetal	Celcon	Gears, window lift mechanisms, clips, bushings, handles, antenna holders, exterior trim	AB, FGB
PP	Polypropylene	Profax, Marlex, Azdel	Ducts, covers, moldings, boot carpeting, interior trim, scuff plate, coolant tank	W, AB, FGB
PPO	Polyphenylene Oxide	Noryl	Pump impellers, housings, bezel grilles	FGB, W, S
PS	Polystyrene (molded)	Luxtrex, Dylan, Styron	Electrical parts, instrument panels, housings	S, AB, FGB
PUR	Polyurethane Rubber (thermosetting)	Bayflex (RIM, RRIM)	Foam seats and arm rests, dashboards, bumpers, moldings	AB, W
PVC	Polyvinyl Chloride (plasticized)	Geon, Vinylite, "Vinyl"	Seat covers, exterior trim, artificial leather, tops, safety pad	S, AB, W
SAN	Styrene-Acrylonitrile	Lustran, Tyril, Foracryl	Headlamp bodies, interior/exterior light covers, gauge lenses	S, W
SMC	Sheet Molding Compound	Fiberglass	Body panels, spoilers	FGB, AB
TPUR	Polyurethane Rubber	Pellethane, Estane	Bumper cover, gravel deflector, soft filler panel	AB, W
UP	Polyester (unsaturated)	SMC, Selectron	Body filler, base resin for some SMC	FGB, AB

AB = Adhesive bonding (polyurethane, epoxy, anerobic)   W = Welding (hot-gas, airless, heated tool)
FGB = Fibrous glass bonding (polyurethane, epoxy, polyester)   S = Solvent bonding

Figure 9-4 Abbreviations for plastic materials commonly used in automobiles.

BURN TEST CHART	
To conduct burn test, apply flame to the material	Type of Plastic Material
No smoke, blue flame, candle wax odor.	Polyethlene (PE)
No smoke, orange flame, acid odor.	Polypropylene (PP)
Black sooty smoke hangs in the air, sweet odor.	Acrylonitrile Butadiene Styrene (ABS)
Self extinguishing. Won't flame.	Polyvinyl Chloride (PVC)
Black smoke. Sputtering effect.	Polyurethane (TPUR)

Figure 9-5 Burn test chart for selected plastics. (Seelye, Inc.)

thermosetting plastics and as either thermosetting or thermoplastic elastomers (PUR or TPE).

Today, plastics are often blended to change or improve their properties. A *plastic alloy* is formed when two or more different polymers are physically mixed together. *Polyblends* are plastics that have been modified by the addition of an elastomer. Burn or odor tests are of little help in identifying blended materials.

Effects of Solvents

Solvents can be used in the identification and repair of plastic materials. Thermoplastic materials (except for PE, PP, POM, PA, and PTFE) are soluble at room temperature. Therefore, certain solvents will cause these materials to melt. Thermosetting plastics, on the other hand, are solvent resistant and will not melt when exposed to solvents. The chemical *ethylene dichloride* is commonly used as a solvent to cement acrylic, polycarbonate, and polystyrene plastic joints.

Relative Density

A plastic's relative density is the relationship between the density of the plastic and the density of water. Water, which serves as a reference, has a density of 1.0. The relative densities of polyethylene and polypropylene range from 0.91 to 0.97. Because these materials have a lower relative density than water, they will float. All other plastic materials have a relative density that is greater than 1.0 and will sink in water unless they are produced in cellular form. Polystyrene, polyvinyl chloride and polyurethane are commonly made into cellular (foam or expanded) parts.

Repairing Plastic Materials/Components

There are five different methods used to repair plastics: cohesive bonding, adhesive bonding, welding, mechanical fastening, and patching and filling.

The auto body technician must determine which method is best for the job at hand. Badly torn or damaged parts are generally replaced. In conspicuous areas or on new vehicles, customers often insist on new parts, even if the damage is relatively minor. However, some customers may wish to have plastic parts repaired if it is the most economical method. Additionally, if the replacement parts are no longer available, damaged components must be repaired.

Regardless of the repair method used, it is essential to properly clean and prepare the damaged surfaces. Soap and water can be used to clean away road debris. *Isopropyl alcohol* (95%) should then be used to clean all joint areas. This alcohol will dissolve grease, oil, and wax, but will not harm paint finishes or plastic surfaces. Prep-Sol, Acryli-Clean, or a general purpose adhesive and wax remover can also be used for this purpose. Cleaning will help assure strong cohesive or adhesive bonds. Grinding, sanding, or trimming may be required before performing welding, adhesive bonding, or patching and filling operations. All plastic surfaces must be thoroughly dry before any adhesive repair is attempted. Moisture will cause a poor bond.

Cohesive Bonding

Cohesive bonding is commonly used to repair thermoplastic materials. In this process, *solvent cements* are used to melt plastic materials together. See Figure 9-6. Most solvent cements have the viscosity of water. *Bodied cements*, however, are solvent cements that are composed of solvents and a small quantity of compatible plastics. These thick (syrupy) cements melt the mating pieces and help fill small gaps along the joint by leaving a thin film on the joint area.

PMMC, PS, PVC, and ABS are easily solvent cemented. The joints are simply wet with the solvent and held together until the solvent evaporates. Apply only enough cement to wet the joint area. Excess solvent cement may run and attack other surfaces. Only light pressure is needed to hold the pieces together. The solvent will quickly attack the joint surfaces and evaporate. Most joints set in about ten minutes and dry in one hour. Because cohesive bonds provide only about 75% of original joint strength, scrap pieces are sometimes cemented on the back or underside of a repair to add strength. Cohesive bonds can also be made by allowing solvent to flow into crack joints by capillary action. Small brushes and syringes are handy cementing tools.

As previously mentioned, not all thermoplastic materials can be solvent cemented. Polyethylene, polypropylene, and polyacetals cannot be dissolved with solvents.

Adhesive Bonding

Adhesive bonding techniques are generally used to join materials that cannot be solvent cemented, such as thermosetting plastics. Adhesives can also be used to

COMMON SOLVENT CEMENTS FOR THERMOPLASTICS	
Plastics	Solvent
[ABS] Acrylonitrile-Butadiene-Styrene	Methyl ethyl ketone Methyl isobutyl ketone Methylene chloride
[PMMA] Acrylic	Ethylene dichloride Methylene chloride Vinyl trichloride
[PA] Polyamide	Aqueous phenol Calcium chloride in alcohol
[PC] Polycarbonate	Ethylene dichloride Methylene chloride
[PPO] Polyphenylene oxide	Chloroform Ethylene dichloride Methylene chloride Toluene
[PS] Polystyrene	Ethylene dichloride Methyl ethyl ketone Methylene chloride Toluene
[PVC] Polyvinyl chloride and copolymers	Acetone Cyclohexane Methyl ethyl ketone Tetrahydrofuran
[SAN] Styrene-Acrylonitrile	Methylene chloride Trichloroethylene

Figure 9-6 Common solvent cements used for thermoplastics.

repair thermoplastic materials. Before bonding, joint areas must be clean and as stress free as possible. Heating thermoplastic joints slightly with a heat gun or torch may help to release stresses in the materials. In thermosetting materials, a small hole can be drilled at the end of a crack to help release stresses. Adhesives rely on adhesion to the plastic pieces for bond strength. A clean, dry, slightly rough surface provides the best adhesion. Passing the part through a hot oxidizing flame for a few seconds makes the surface of polyethylenes, polypropylenes, polyacetals, and polyamides more receptive to adhesives. The flame will help to oxidize and roughen the plastic without causing distortion. Use caution to prevent overheating and melting the plastic. Sanding may also roughen the surface for better adhesion. An adhesion promoter should be used on TPO, PP, PE, and on blends containing these materials. *Adhesion promoters* are chemicals that react with the plastic surface and the adhesive to provide superior adhesion.

Epoxy and Polyester Adhesives

Two-part epoxies or polyester adhesives are often used for rigid plastic repairs. These adhesives are commonly used with reinforcing materials (glass mat, cloth,

or tape) to attain greater strength. Epoxy resins are commonly used for SMC repairs because they offer excellent adhesion and are compatible with other resin systems. Polyester resin systems are not recommended for SMC repairs.

For flexible plastic panels, such as bumper covers and dash pads, two-part thermosetting polyurethane (PUR) adhesives are commonly used. These materials, which are often called *structural adhesives*, are available in both room-temperature and elevated-temperature curing formulas. Polyurethanes are the most versatile adhesives for bonding plastics.

After cleaning the damaged area, a torch can be used on punctured or torn thermoplastic materials to improve adhesion. If possible, tape the back of the joint together to maintain the proper alignment. To help ensure the best possible joint, grind a slight bevel on the damaged edges and feather the painted surfaces around the damage. Remove all sanding dust and, if necessary, apply a coat of adhesion promoter to the joint. Thoroughly mix the two-part adhesive and apply a thin coat to the damaged area with a squeegee. Polyurethane repairs must not overlap painted areas. Structural adhesives will begin to set in about two minutes. Therefore, the work must be completed quickly. Clean the squeegee and the mixing board immediately after applying the adhesive. Heat the adhesive for about 15 minutes with a heat lamp to speed the cure. At room temperature, the adhesive may require more than an hour to fully cure. If additional coats of adhesive are needed, sand the repair with #280 grit paper and repeat the application process.

After the adhesive has completely cured, the entire piece can be sanded with #400 grit paper and the surface can be coated with an appropriate finish. Flex-Tex is a commercial material designed to retexture panels, vinyl tops, padded dashes, etc. *Flex-additives* should be added to color topcoats (enamel, lacquer, acrylic, etc.) and clearcoats before they are applied to plastic panels. These additives will make the topcoats flexible.

WARNING: Most flexible paints and flex additives contain isocyanates. Wear a high-quality respirator when using these materials.

Adhesive joining techniques and plastic welding techniques can be used on thermoplastic polyurethane (TPUR) parts. Most dash pads and padded instrument panels are made of polyvinyl-clad polyurethane foam. Therefore, they can be repaired with airless welding techniques or with adhesives.

Trim Cements and Silicone Adhesives

Trim cements are used to repair torn vinyl (PVC) trim and upholstery. These adhesive cements, which are available in squeeze tubes, have the consistency of grease and remain flexible when dry. Since they are solvent based, trim cements dry quickly. Precautions should be taken to prevent these cements from contacting painted surfaces. The solvents in trim cements may attack paint finishes. **Silicone adhesives** are similar to trim cements. Slight tears in vinyl tops can be repaired with this type of adhesive. Be careful to apply the silicone only to the underside of the vinyl fabric. Wipe excess adhesive from the surface immediately. Allow 48 hours for silicone adhesives to cure.

Liquid Vinyls

Liquid vinyl (polyvinyl chloride) is sometimes used to repair holes or tears in polyvinyl tops and upholstery. All vinyl repairs should begin with a thorough cleaning. A special vinyl cleaner must be used to remove all wax and oil from the damaged area.

Solvent-based liquid vinyls (organosols) are available in cans and squeeze tubes. These clear liquids are applied to the underside of the fabric or used to fill small holes. If necessary, pigments can be added to aid in color matching. Allow 24 hours for solvents to evaporate before repainting the repair area.

Heat-cured liquid vinyls (plastisols) have the consistency of toothpaste and are used to fill and repair holes. Heat-cured liquid vinyl is placed in the damaged area, and a silicone-treated graining paper is positioned over the repair. A heat iron, which is placed on top of the graining paper, is used to cure the liquid vinyl. After the vinyl has cured, the graining paper can be removed from the repair. Graining papers are available in numerous patterns. Every attempt should be made to select a graining paper that matches the grain pattern of the damaged vinyl.

Although vinyl repair products can be tinted to match most surfaces, it is sometimes necessary to paint the entire repair area. Aerosol cans of vinyl repair paint are commonly used for this purpose. This material actually permeates the vinyl and will not crack or chip. Additionally, vinyl repair paints will not hide the original texture of the vinyl. Vinyl door trim, dashboards, and seat covers are often repainted with this product.

For more information on vinyl top repair and replacement, see Chapter 12. Woodgrain overlay and vinyl molding are discussed in Chapter 20.

Hot Glue Guns

Hot glue guns are used for a variety of plastic repairs. An adhesive stick is simply melted in the pistol grip-type gun. The molten adhesive is forced out of the gun's nozzle and onto the joint. Both flexible and rigid adhesives can be used in hot glue guns. Preheating the joint surface will ensure maximum adhesion. Full joint strength is achieved when the adhesive cools.

Cyanoacrylate Systems

Two-part **cyanoacrylate adhesive systems** are commonly used to join various small parts. These adhesives, which are sometimes called super glues, are available in various viscosities to help fill voids and irregular joints. Cyanoacrylate systems are not effective on all plastics. As a rule, these systems work best on hard plastics or on those that can be solvent cemented.

Welding Plastics

Most thermoplastic materials can be welded. However, before any weld repair is made, the damaged surfaces must be properly cleaned and beveled. Both sides of a repair should be welded whenever possible. Backing patches should be used to provide additional support to the damaged area. Backing patches consist of small pieces of plastic, which are simply welded or adhered to the back side of the damaged area. In all types of plastic welding, a compatible filler rod is used to help reinforce the welded joint. It is important to note that thermoplastics do not melt or flow like metals. When heated, these plastics have the consistency of chewing gum. Therefore, special techniques must be used when welding plastics.

When repairing a cracked plastic part, Figure 9-7, grind a "V" groove (20° taper) about 2/3 of the way through the material along the crack. After grinding, make a continuous weld along the groove. See Figure 9-8. To minimize distortion, it may be necessary to tack weld the ends of the crack or hold the plastic piece in position with a screwdriver while welding. After the weld has cooled, it should be smoothed with a disc sander, primed, and sprayed with an appropriate paint formulation. A repaired plastic part is shown in Figure 9-9.

There are two basic types of plastics welding used in the body shop: hot-gas welding and airless welding (heated tool welding).

Figure 9-7 This cracked plastic part can be repaired. (Brian R. White Co.)

Hot-Gas Welding

Hot-gas welding procedures utilize heated air or nitrogen to help fuse plastic materials together. Nitrogen is preferred because it reduces the oxidization of plastic surfaces. The gas is heated as it passes through an electric welding gun. As the hot gas is discharged from the gun, it heats the joint surfaces (substrate), the gun tip, and the filler rod. The heat from the gun and pressure on the filler rod work together to fuse the rod and the joint surfaces together. Note that the filler rod is held at 90° to the joint, Figure 9-10.

Conventional hot-gas welding guns can be fitted with a speed tip, which increases welding speed by preheating the filler rod and the joint surfaces, Figure 9-11. Speed tips have two openings: one for the filler rod and one for the hot gas that preheats the joint area. Once the weld is started, the filler rod is automatically drawn into the tip.

Figure 9-10 This technician is welding a crack in a bumper. (Brian R. White Co.)

Figure 9-8 A weld is placed along the crack. (Brian R. White Co.)

Figure 9-11 This hot air welder is equipped with a speed tip. (Brian R. White Co.)

Figure 9-9 Repaired plastic part. (Brian R. White Co.)

Weld penetration for hot-gas welding is controlled by regulating the rate of gas flow (about 2-3 psi) and the speed of gun travel. Gas pressure is used to control the weld temperature. Reducing gas pressure will increase weld temperature, while increasing gas pressure will lower weld temperature. Weld temperatures vary from about 500 °F (260 °C) for ABS to 575 °F (300 °C) for PP and TPUR. If gun movement is too slow or weld temperature is too high, the plastic may char and distort. Properly applied welds can exceed 85% of the tensile strength of the parent material. Basically, the same types of welds are performed in plastic welding as in metal welding. See Figure 9-12. Examples of good and bad welds are shown in Figure 9-13.

In addition to welding, a hot air welding gun can be used to activate adhesive when applying protective moldings. See Figure 9-14.

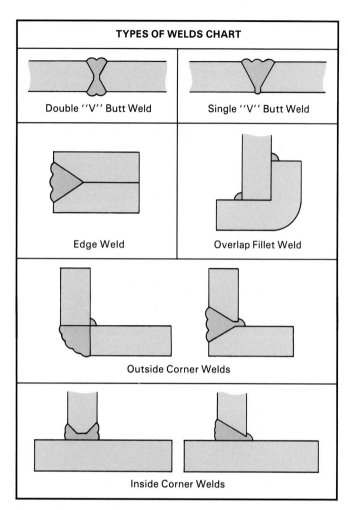

TYPES OF WELDS CHART

Double "V" Butt Weld | Single "V" Butt Weld

Edge Weld | Overlap Fillet Weld

Outside Corner Welds

Inside Corner Welds

Figure 9-12 Various types of welds can be created with plastic welding equipment. (Seelye, Inc.)

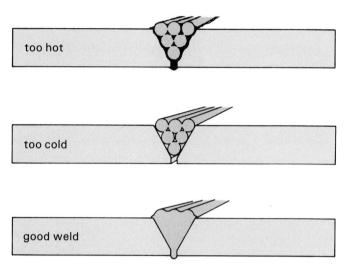

too hot

too cold

good weld

Figure 9-13 Weld quality is affected by heat. (Seelye, Inc.)

Figure 9-14 This technician is using a heat gun to activate adhesive on protective molding. (Brian R. White Co.)

Airless Welding

Airless welding techniques are easier to master than hot-gas welding techniques. Before using an airless welder, clean and grind the damaged surface as described in the previous section. Set the electrically heated welding gun to the proper temperature and select a compatible rod. The 1/8 in. (3 mm) rod is fed into the melt tube of the gun, and the hot tip or shoe of the gun is placed on the joint. A slight pressure on the filler rod will force it into the joint, which has been heated by the shoe. After the weld is complete, it can be smoothed with the gun's shoe. Heated gas is not used in this technique. Only the molten rod and hot gun shoe are used to create the weld.

Soldering irons or other heated tools are sometimes used to repair small parts. These heated tools are used to soften plastic surfaces and fuse joints together.

Mechanical Fasteners

There are a variety of mechanical fasteners used to make selected repairs on both thermosetting and thermoplastic materials. Self-threading screws, nuts and bolts, thread, and rivets are sometimes used to make temporary or inexpensive repairs. Fabrics and thin plastics are commonly sewn with a needle and thread. Inconspicuous repairs can be held together with blind rivets. To add strength in critical areas, adhesives are often used in conjunction with fasteners. Sheet metal or scrap plastic pieces can also be used with mechanical fasteners to help reinforce damaged areas.

Patch-and-Fill Repair Techniques

Plastics can often be repaired by patch-and-fill techniques. An epoxy adhesive and several pieces of wire, glass fiber, or string can be used to repair plastic gears, tubing, rods, grilles, etc., Figure 9-15. Patch-and-fill techniques can also be used to repair fiberglass or SMC panels and other composite components.

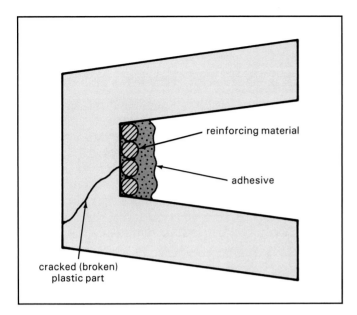

Figure 9-15 Patch-and-fill technique being used to repair a broken grille part. This method is preferred for grille repairs because solvents may loosen the bright metal (metalized) or painted finish.

A key to all plastic repairs is cleanliness. The quality of any repair depends on the strength of the bond. Proper adhesion will not take place if the bonding surfaces are dirty or contaminated.

WARNING: Most patch-and-fill procedures require the use of resins, fillers, or hardeners. Always observe the following safety precautions when working with these materials:

☐ Wear safety goggles and neoprene (rubber) gloves when working with resins, fillers, and hardeners. Although skin cream should never be used as a substitute for gloves, it can help prevent irritation to exposed areas. If resin contacts the skin, wash the affected areas immediately with soap and water.

☐ Keep all sparks and flames away from the work area. All resin systems and solvents are highly flammable.

☐ Be sure the work area is well ventilated. Many solvents and resin systems create toxic fumes.

☐ Do not allow mixed resin or other catalyzed materials to stand in the shop for extended lengths of time. Make certain that resin systems are disposed of properly. Chemical action may result in rapid heat buildup and, therefore, may pose a fire hazard. For more information on the proper disposal of hazardous materials, see Chapter 1.

☐ When grinding or sanding resin repair areas, wear a respirator mask to avoid inhaling resin and fibrous dust. Inhaling fibrous dust can lead to silicosis, a serious lung disease. A vacuum system can be attached to some power sanders to help remove sanding dust.

☐ Wear a disposable shop coat to keep dust and fibers from becoming embedded in clothing.

☐ Follow the resin manufacturer's recommended safety procedures and precautions.

Keep all resin system containers closed and store them in a cool place. Resin systems (can or cartridge) have a storage or shelf life. Therefore, they must be consumed before their expiration date. Refrigeration can extend the useful life of a resin system by six months to a year. A resin system must be allowed to return to room temperature before it is used. Never return catalyzed or unused filler or resin to the stock container. Mask or cover surrounding areas to prevent spilling resin or filler on paint and trim.

Repairing Scratches

Minor scratches that do not penetrate the paint film can be repaired by simply cleaning the damaged area and filling the scratch with touch-up paint.

Scratches that extend through the paint film should be carefully cleaned and hand sanded with #400 grit sandpaper. Always feather the damaged area. Care must be taken to avoid cutting into the glass reinforcement. If glass reinforcements are cut, a two-part epoxy body filler can be used to fill and level the damaged area. Do not use body fillers that are designed for sheet metal. After the damage is filled, the repair area can be primed and painted with an appropriate finishing system.

Repairing Cracked or Split Panels

Fiberglass and SMC body panels have a high resistance to impact. In many minor accidents, these panels are not damaged. If damage does occur, it is generally localized because the force of impact is not transmitted through the composite panels. Indirect damage, which is common in vehicles with metal bodies, rarely occurs in composite bodies. However, because SMC panels tend to recover from collisions, they often hide structural damage to the space frame or other components.

When a fiberglass or SMC panel is cracked or split, the broken portions of the panel must be removed and the damaged area must been cleaned. A hacksaw blade can be used to cut along the break line. If the crack is not severe, grind a "V" groove (20° bevel) about 2/3 of the way through the panel along the entire crack, Figure 9-16. For more severe damage, remove all cracked and fractured material along the break and bevel the break edge to a 20° taper on the inside and the outside of the

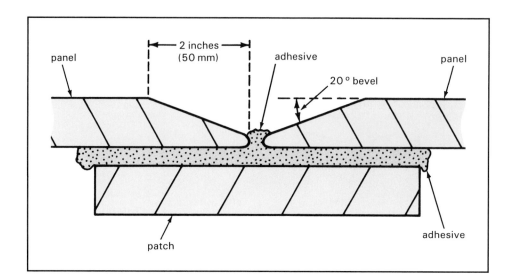

Figure 9-16 Repair of a cracked or split panel. Note that a backing patch is used to reinforce the repair.

joint. This will provide better patch adhesion. To help relieve stresses and prevent fractures from continuing, drill a small hole at the end of the crack. Use C-clamps or other suitable tools to bring the surfaces on each side of the break into proper alignment. Remove all paint and primer to expose the plastic material for about 3 in. (76 mm) on each side of the crack and scuff the area around the crack with #80 grit abrasive paper. This will ensure a good bonding surface.

If necessary, a backing or bonding patch can be cut from a scrap SMC panel. If scrap pieces are not available, several alternate layers of cloth and adhesive (resin) can be used to fabricate a backing patch. Cut three pieces of fiberglass cloth, tape, or mat that are large enough to overlap the repair area by about 2 in. (50 mm). Apply an adhesive resin mixture to each layer of cloth and to the inner surface of repair area. A serrated roller can be used to help spread the resin, force out air bubbles, and fully wet the reinforcement cloth.

It is often helpful to place the adhesive-saturated cloth on a piece of cardboard that is covered with polyethylene film. This cardboard can then be used to hold the resin-soaked patches in position over the damaged area. Press the saturated cloth and the supporting board against the back of the crack. Make sure the cloth is in full contact with scuffed area and that it extends about 2 in. (50 mm) beyond the break. Masking tape can be used to hold the supporting board and patch in place.

Once the adhesive has cured at 200 °F (93 °C) for 45 minutes, the supporting board can be removed and structural filler can be applied to the outside of the crack. The filler should never overlap the primer or the paint. After the filler has hardened, it should be leveled and smoothed with a sander or a body file. Body filler can then be used to fill minor imperfections.

At the present time, General Motors has approved only two adhesives for SMC repairs. *Ashland Pliogrip* and *Lord Fusor* body panel repair adhesives are recommended for bonding panels to space frames. Only Lord Fusor is recommended for patch repairs. Do not use polyester fillers for SMC repairs. Polyester resin systems do not provide adequate adhesion. In time, adhesion will be lost and the repair will fail. Panel bonding adhesives, which are formulated to attach structural panels to space frames, can also be used to secure patches. Patching adhesives, however, should never be used to attach structural panels to a space frame.

Panel and patching adhesives are available in cartridges designed to fit mechanical or pneumatic applicator guns. These guns have specially designed mixing tubes or nozzles. Remember, once two-part adhesives are mixed, they must be used immediately or discarded.

Repairing Holes

The first step in repairing holes in composite panels is to remove all broken or splintered material from the inside and the outside of the hole and to clean the damaged area. Remove all paint and primer with #80 grit abrasive paper to expose the plastic material 3 in. (76 mm) beyond the damaged area. To provide a good bonding surface, be certain to scuff the inner (back) surface of the damaged area with #80 grit abrasive and bevel the outside edge of the hole to a 20 ° taper. The inner edge of the hole can also be beveled slightly.

It is best to use a scrap piece of SMC for a backing patch when repairing holes. If scrap pieces are unavailable, it will be necessary to fabricate a backing patch as previously described. If the damage is inaccessible from the back side, drill a small hole in the center of the backing patch and attach a wire through the hole. Apply a 1/2 in. (13 mm) bead of an appropriate adhesive around the edge of the patch. Place the patch through the hole in the panel and pull it up against the panel with the wire. Twist the wire around a wooden stick to help hold the patch in place. Make certain that the patch is in full contact with the scuffed area surrounding the hole. When the patch is positioned correctly, heat cure the adhesive at about 200 °F (93 °C) for 45 minutes.

After the adhesive has cured, apply additional adhesive to the hole depression and place several layers of glass mat in the depression. Make certain that these layers are fully saturated with adhesive and in complete contact with the patch and panel. These layers of glass mat must fully contact the scuffed area surrounding the hole. See Figure 9-17.

To help spread and wet the glass reinforcement, place a piece of waxed paper or polyethylene film over the repair area. Using a brayer, roll over the covered patch area to fully wet and evenly spread the glass mat. The wax paper will not stick to the patch, and the brayer roller will not require cleaning.

Note: If necessary, immediately clean the adhesive from brayers, squeegees, and other tools. Once the adhesive has cured, it is virtually impossible to remove.

When the adhesive has cured and the surface is cool, sand the repair area with a disk sander and an #80 grit abrasive disk.

After sanding, it may be necessary to spread another layer of adhesive over the repair area to fill low spots. Leave a sufficient mound of adhesive to allow for grinding and smoothing after the material has hardened. As previously mentioned, waxed paper or polyethylene film can be taped over the patch, and a squeegee or brayer can be used to smooth the adhesive. Heat cure the patch for about 25 minutes. Excessive heat may cause the resin to crack and the material to distort.

When the patch has fully hardened, sand down the excess material with #80 grit abrasive on a sanding block, reciprocating sander, or belt sander. Finish sanding with #280 grit abrasive. After sanding, a polyester primer should be applied to the repair area.

Mold Core Method-Repairing Curved Sections

The **mold core method** is commonly used to repair curved or irregularly shaped sections. Additionally, flat backing patches are easily produced with this technique.

The mold core method can be used on both metal and plastic components.

A new or used panel that is similar in shape to the one being repaired is needed to help form a thin core of resin and glass cloth. This panel is referred to as the mold panel. The core is formed and secured to the damaged section as follows:

1. Carefully cover the appropriate area of the mold panel with a layer of polyethylene film (0.10 mm). Make certain that the film completely covers the area to prevent the resin from contacting the finish.

2. Securely tape the polyethylene film in place. It may be necessary to use double-faced tape to hold the film in concave areas. See Figure 9-18.

3. Cut several pieces of glass mat or veil (thin glass mat) into 4-6 in. (102-152 mm) squares. Single layers of mat can be used to make small or flat cores (backing patches).

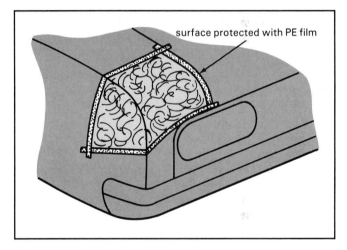

Figure 9-18 The first step in the mold core method is to cover the mold panel with polyethylene film.

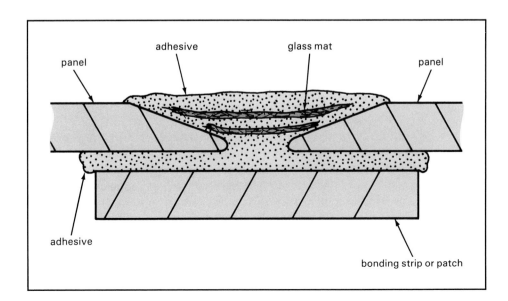

Figure 9-17 Repair of a hole. This technique is also used for panel sectioning or replacement.

4. Coat the polyethylene film-covered mold panel with an appropriate resin system.

5. Apply overlapping pieces of glass reinforcement and squeegee, brush, or roll the catalyzed resin into each piece. See Figure 9-19.

6. Apply an additional coating of resin and make certain all mat reinforcement is saturated.

7. After allowing the core to cure, carefully remove it from the mold panel. The polyethylene film will protect the mold panel, and the core will release from the film.

8. Trim the core to the desired size.

9. Clean and bevel the damaged panel in preparation to receive the core.

10. Apply an adhesive resin to the core and fit it into place on the damaged section. Hold the core securely in place until the adhesive cures. See Figure 9-20.

11. Use additional structural adhesive and glass mat to fill the damaged area.

12. Sand and shape the repair area in preparation for final finishing.

Sectioning

In many cases, it is not cost effective or possible to replace an entire damaged panel. For example, the roof panel overlaps the side and door surround panels on most vehicles. If the side panels are damaged, *sectioning* (splicing) is required unless the entire roof panel is replaced. In some trucks, vans, and sport cars, there are no visible seams between panels and other body components. In these vehicles, panel replacement requires the use of sectioning techniques.

In order to section panels properly, the technician must know how the panels are attached to the frame and where mill-and-drill pads are located. *Mill-and-drill pads* are used to help align the panels and hold them in place. Sectioning of SMC panels should be done between mill-and-drill pad locations.

After determining where a panel is to be sectioned, the mill-and-drill pad fasteners are removed and the damaged area is cut away. A pneumatic cutter with a radial blade or a mini air saw is commonly used to cut through SMC materials. Before the damaged section is removed, the adhesive bond lines must be broken away from the steel frame. Use a heat gun to help weaken the adhesive. After the damaged section is removed, the heat gun can be used to remove excess adhesive. Sand the remaining adhesive or fibers to remove them from the steel structure. Before applying a new section, repair damaged steel and restore corrosion protection. See Chapter 10 for information on correcting body and structural damage.

Before applying adhesive, the new panel should be trial fit. The joint areas on both the original panel and the

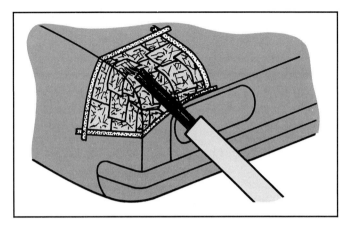

Figure 9-19 Adhesive is applied to the mat reinforcement with a small brush.

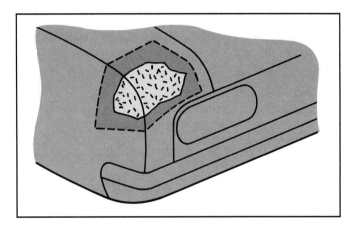

Figure 9-20 Hold the patch (core) in place until adhesive has cured.

replacement section should be beveled to a 20° taper as described in the section on repairing a hole. A 1/2 in. (13 mm) gap should exist between the original panel and the replacement section.

Bonding strips or backer plates should be placed behind the joint areas to help reinforce the repair. If necessary, the bonding strips can be cut from an old SMC panel. Apply structural adhesive to the bonding strips and clamp them to the back side of the existing panel. Allow the adhesive to heat cure.

Apply a generous amount of adhesive to the back side of the new section and to the factory bond lines, including the mill-and-drill pads. A 1/2 in. (13 mm) bead will make a sound bond and seal the repair properly. Place the new panel on the space frame and, if necessary, secure the panel with mechanical fasteners.

Heat cure the joint areas per the adhesive manufacturer's recommendations. Once the resin has cured, fill the spliced areas with matting and adhesive as previously described. When the adhesive has dried, sand the patch and fill the imperfections with additional adhesive. Complete the repair using conventional finishing procedures.

Panel Replacement

When making composite repairs, the structural integrity of unibody panels must be restored. If there is any doubt that sectioning techniques will not restore rigidity and strength, the entire damaged panel should be replaced.

The first step in replacing a panel is to remove the internal trim from the damaged section. After removing the trim, many of the mill-and-drill pads will be visible. Some internal reinforcements may have to be removed for full access to the damaged panel.

Some SMC panels are simply bolted to the space frame. In many designs, however, adhesives are used to bond the panels to the doors and the frame. When panels are bonded with adhesives, a heat gun and flat pneumatic chisel are used to separate the seams and remove the panels from the attachment points. After the panels are removed, old adhesive can be removed from the space frame with a heat gun and a putty knife. To ensure proper panel adhesion, sand and clean all joint areas. Remember to prime and restore corrosion protection to the steel frame before applying the new panel.

Make certain that the new panel fits the space frame properly and, if necessary, replace reinforcing panels. Apply panel adhesive to duplicate the factory bond lines. Adhesive should be applied to the panel, the mill-and-drill pads, and any bonding strips. After the adhesive has been applied, place the panel on the frame. The mill-and-drill pads will help to align the panel while the adhesive cures. The panel should be resting on the pads, and the adhesive should fill any gaps between the pads and the panel. Follow the adhesive manufacturer's instructions.

Summary

Plastics are used extensively in the automobile. As manufacturers work to reduce vehicle weight and improve fuel efficiency, the use of plastics will continue to grow.

Composites are plastics that are formed by combining two or more materials. Fibrous composites are plastics that consist of fiber reinforcements in a resin base. Laminar composites consist of layers of reinforcing materials held together by a resin matrix. Sheet molding compounds are laminar composites that are strong enough to be used for the rear quarter panels in unibody vehicles.

Many vehicle bodies are made of composite materials. Fiberglass is the most common material used for this purpose. Several vehicles are currently being manufactured with composite panels that are attached to a space frame. The use of composite body parts on domestic vehicles is expected to double in the next 10 years.

Thermoplastic materials repeatedly become soft when heated and hard when cooled. Thermosetting plastics, on the other hand, cannot be softened after they are initially formed. Thermosetting plastics are stronger and have a higher service temperature than thermoplastics.

To repair plastic parts correctly, the auto body technician must identify various types of plastics. Plastics can be identified by trade names and abbreviations, applications, method of fabrication, effects of heat, effects of solvents, and relative density.

There are five methods used to repair plastics, including cohesive bonding, adhesive bonding, welding, mechanical fastening, and patching and filling. Regardless of the method used, the damaged area must be prepared properly before the repair is made.

In the cohesive bonding process, solvent cements are used to melt plastic materials together. Adhesive bonding techniques are used to join pieces that cannot be solvent cemented.

Most thermoplastics can be welded. There are two types of plastics welding: hot-gas welding and airless welding. Hot-gas welding techniques utilize heated air or nitrogen to help fuse plastics together. Airless welders only use the molten welding rod and the hot shoe of the gun to produce a weld.

Mechanical fasteners are commonly used to make temporary or inexpensive plastic repairs. These fasteners include screws, nuts, bolts, thread, and rivets.

Patch-and-fill techniques are commonly used to repair plastics. Epoxy adhesive and several pieces of wire, fiber, or string can be used to repair scratches, holes, etc. The mold core method is often used to repair curved or irregularly shaped panels. In this method, a core of resin and glass cloth is made to bridge the damaged area.

In some cases, it is not desirable to replace an entire damaged panel. The process of replacing only the damaged portion of a panel is called sectioning. When sectioning a unibody panel, the structural integrity of the panel must be restored. If sectioning will not restore rigidity and strength, the entire panel must be replaced.

Know These Terms

Composite, Fibrous composites, Fiberglass, Fibrous mats, Surfacing mat, Veil, Fiberglass cloth, Laminar composites, Sheet molding compounds, Reaction injection molding, Reinforced reaction injection molding, Space frame, Thermoplastic, Thermosetting plastics, Elastomer, Plastic alloy, Polyblends, Ethylene dichloride, Isopropyl alcohol, Cohesive bonding, Solvent cements, Bodied cements, Adhesive bonding, Adhesion promoters, Structural adhesive, Flex-additives, Trim cement, Silicone adhesives, Liquid vinyl, Hot glue guns, Cyanoacrylate adhesive systems, Ashland Pliogrip, Lord Fusor, Mold core method, Sectioning, Mill-and-drill pads, Bonding strips.

Review Questions–Chapter 9

1. Less than 50% of the interior components in a modern automobile are made of plastic. True or False?

2. Plastics are used extensively in the automobile because they:
   a. are lighter than steel.
   b. do not rust or corrode.
   c. can be formed into compound curves.
   d. all of the above.

3. Composites are formed by combining _____ or more materials.

4. _____ composites are composed of layers of reinforcing materials held together by a resin matrix.

5. In addition to hoods, doors, and roof panels, sheet molding compounds are often used for structural components. True or False?

6. Reaction injection molded components are always made of polyurethane. True or False?

7. The most common composite used for automotive bodies is _____.

8. Sheet molded compounds are usually attached to a vehicle's _____.

9. Thermoplastic materials have a higher service temperature than thermosets. True or False?

10. A plastic can be identified by its:
    a. color.
    b. relative density.
    c. weight.
    d. none of the above.

11. An _____ is a material that can be stretched to at least twice its original length and return to its original size when released.

12. A soldering gun can be used to determine whether a material is a _____ or a _____.

13. Polyurethanes are available in both thermosetting and thermoplastic forms. True or False?

14. Most _____ materials are soluble at room temperatures.

15. Solvent cements are commonly used in the adhesive bonding process. True or False?

16. Thermosetting polyurethane is used to repair _____ plastic panels.

17. Small tears in vinyl tops and upholstery can be repaired with:
    a. trim cements.
    b. silicone adhesives.
    c. liquid vinyls.
    d. all of the above.

18. Most thermosetting plastics can be welded. True or False?

19. Hot-gas welders use heated air or _____ to help fuse plastic materials together.

20. When using a hot air welder, the weld temperature is controlled by the speed of gun travel. True or False?

21. Patch-and-fill techniques utilize an _____ _____ and several pieces of wire, glass fiber, or string to repair plastic parts.

22. Scratches that do not penetrate the paint film can be filled with touch-up paint. True or False?

23. Because SMC panels tend to recover from impact, they often hide _____ damage.

24. A backing patch should never be used when repairing a crack in a SMC panel. True or False?

25. _____ fillers should never be used for SMC repairs.

26. Structural panels should never be attached with patching adhesives. True or False?

27. Before repairing a hole in a SMC panel, broken and splintered material should be _____.

28. The mold core method is used to repair _____ or irregularly shaped sections.

29. The process of replacing a portion of a damaged panel is called:
    a. piecing.
    b. sectioning.
    c. trimming.
    d. all of the above.

30. Mill-and-drill pads are used to help align SMC panels. True or False?

Activities–Chapter 9

1. Test several scrap pieces of plastic with a soldering iron to determine if they are thermosets or thermoplastics.

2. Draw a side view of a late-model automobile and label the plastic components using the information and abbreviations found in Figure 9-4.

3. Perform a burn test on several scrap pieces of plastic material. Use the chart in Figure 9-3 to help identify the plastics.

4. Using the processes outlined in this chapter, practice welding scrap pieces of plastic together. If possible, try to form several of the joints shown in Figure 9-12.

chapter 10

Body and Structural Alignment

After studying this chapter, you will be able to:

☐ Describe the methods used to determine the extent of damage to body-over-frame and unibody vehicles.

☐ Explain why indirect damage is common in unibody vehicles.

☐ Explain how to check frame and body alignment.

☐ Describe several types of body and frame straighteners.

☐ Discuss the safety procedures that should be followed when working with body or frame alignment equipment.

Introduction

Experienced auto body technicians know that the careful inspection of a damaged vehicle is essential. An accurate assessment of the damage will save time, increase profits, and reduce the chances of making costly errors or uncovering hidden damage during the repair process. A careful inspection is the first step in providing the customer with a quality repair and restoring the vehicle's safety features.

Major damage may require frame, suspension, and underbody repairs. Special tools and equipment are often needed to correct this type of damage. A high degree of skill and technical knowledge is necessary to make most major auto body repairs.

Alignment is a general term used to refer to the arrangement of a vehicle's basic structural components in relation to each other. Alignment also refers to the arrangement of the various body panels and suspension components.

Misalignment of the frame or the underbody will make it difficult to straighten or align body components. Many mechanical components, such as suspension, steering, engine, and differential parts, are mounted directly to body members. Failure to detect underbody damage will cause repair and alignment problems.

There are three basic steps that should be followed when repairing major damage:

1. Carefully inspect and analyze the damage.

2. Determine a plan of action or a general sequence of repair.

3. Repair the damage.

Analysis of Damage

Knowledge about a vehicle's construction, the point and direction of impact, and the type of damage (buckles, tears, etc.) will help you to establish a repair plan.

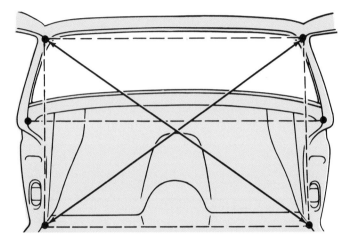

Figure 10-1 Typical points within the body that should be measured when checking for misalignment. This measuring technique is called X-checking.

Although a visual inspection of the damaged area will reveal most of the essential information, additional inspections must be made to accurately analyze damage on late-model vehicles. Because most vehicle bodies are symmetrical (the right and left halves are identical), taking measurements and comparing them to corresponding dimensions on the opposite side of the vehicle will help to reveal damage. This technique is sometimes referred to as **X-checking**. See Figure 10-1. The spacing between doors and adjacent panels should be the same on both sides of the vehicle. See Figure 10-2.

In many cases, damage is so extensive that a vehicle's major structural members are bent. When this occurs, the entire vehicle is distorted. This type of damage is more complex than simple dents to body panels. When structural damage is suspected, the dimensions between several major control points (reference points) should be compared with the manufacturer's specifications, Figure 10-3. Any deviation from the specifications may indicate major damage.

Body-Over-Frame Damage

There are four major control points on body-over-frame vehicles. These points are located on the front crossmember, the cowl crossmember, the rear door area crossmember, and the rear crossmember. The control points serve as reference points when checking frame dimensions. Several reference points on a body-over-frame design are illustrated in Figure 10-4.

Extensive body-over-frame damage may include sidesway, sag, mash, diamond, twist, or a combination of these conditions.

Figure 10-2 Spacing between doors and adjacent panels should be the same on both sides of a vehicle.

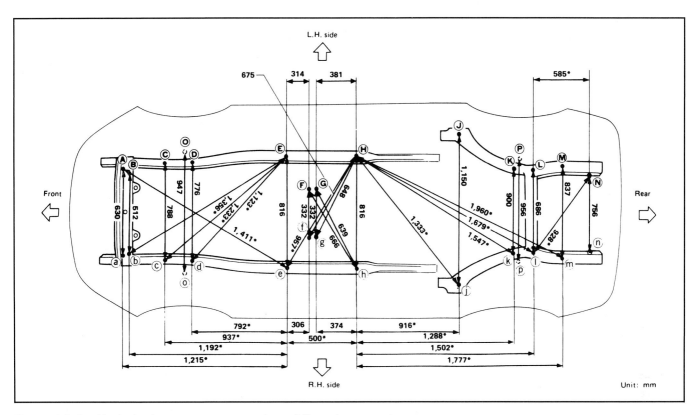

Figure 10-3 Underbody measurement points. (Nissan)

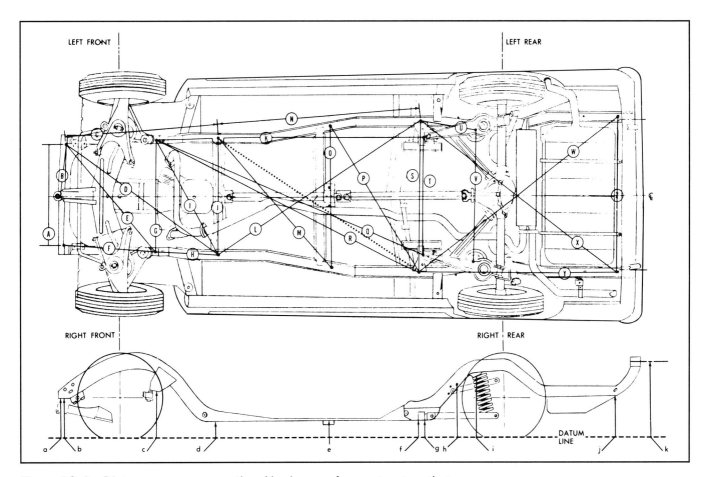

Figure 10-4 Distances on a conventional body-over-frame structure that should be checked for misalignment.

Sidesway or *sway* collision damage occurs when an impact to the side of a vehicle causes the frame to bend or wrinkle. See Figure 10-5. Sidesway damage may cause the gaps around the doors to be narrow on the side of impact and wide on the opposite side of the vehicle. A typical setup for correcting sidesway damage is shown in Figure 10-6.

Sag damage is caused by an impact to the front or rear of a vehicle, Figure 10-7. When sag damage occurs, a portion of the frame is forced downward. Sag may cause the gaps around the doors to be narrow at the top and wide at the bottom. A typical setup for correcting sag damage is shown in Figure 10-8.

Mash occurs when a front or rear impact shortens a section of the frame. This type of damage is generally restricted to the front end and the cowl section or to the rear end and back-window area. See Figure 10-9. If a frontal impact is severe, the bumper will be pushed back into the grille and radiator section. The hood and fenders are likely to be distorted or pushed into the top cowling and the front doors. Mash may cause the damaged portion of the frame to buckle or wrinkle.

Diamond damage occurs when an impact to the front or rear corner of a vehicle forces the frame out of square, Figure 10-10. This type of damage may cause buckles in body panels and a general misalignment around the hood and trunk.

Twist occurs when a vehicle strikes a curb or bank at a high speed. The impact causes one corner of the frame to bend up and the opposite corner to bend down, Figure 10-11. This type of damage may cause the hood, deck lid, and doors to bind.

Unibody Damage

In a unibody vehicle, the body panels are an integral part of the structural assembly. A typical unibody design showing important structural components is illustrated in Figure 10-12.

Since the body panels and the structural members of a unibody vehicle behave as a single unit, the shock of a collision is absorbed by a large portion of the body. Consequently, *indirect damage* is common in unibody

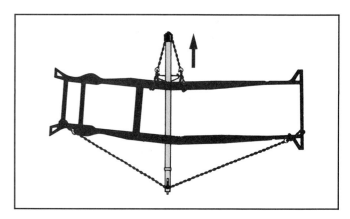

Figure 10-6 Typical equipment setup for correcting sidesway damage.

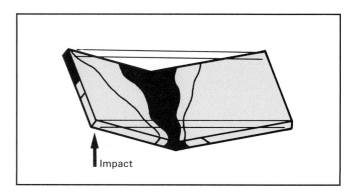

Figure 10-7 Sag damage.

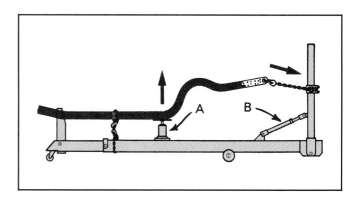

Figure 10-8 Setup for correcting a sag condition in a vehicle's frame.

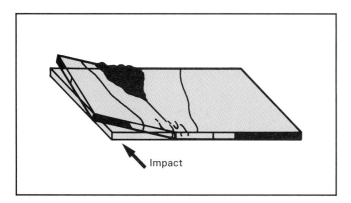

Figure 10-5 Sidesway damage.

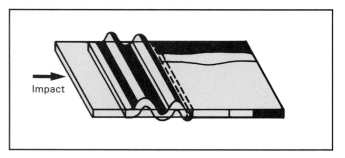

Figure 10-9 Mash damage.

vehicles. To improve passenger safety and reduce indirect damage, many late-model vehicles are engineered to absorb considerable impact. A great deal of attention has been given to finding ways to strengthen panels and

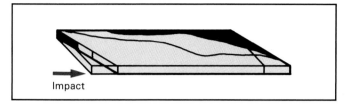

Figure 10-10 Diamond damage.

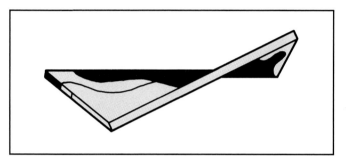

Figure 10-11 Twist damage.

reduce the damaging effects of a collision. Doors are strengthened with steel reinforcing beams, Figure 10-13. Bumpers are equipped with gas or hydraulic energy-absorbing units, Figure 10-14. Some bumper designs utilize rubber pads to help absorb energy. Energy absorbing bumper fascia and guards are also used.

Specially engineered *crush zones* are built into unibody vehicles. These areas (front end and rear end) are designed to collapse and absorb energy in the event of a collision. Because the crush zones are constructed of thin pieces of sheet metal, considerable damage is expected in these areas. This damage may require repair to numerous components and the replacement or sectioning of the crush zone.

Both unibody and body-over-frame vehicles utilize torque boxes. These boxes allow the front and rear sections of the vehicle to move up and down (twist) to absorb road vibrations or impact shocks. Torque boxes help to reduce the shock transferred to the passenger compartment.

Unibody vehicles experience the same types of damage as body-over-frame vehicles–sidesway, sag, mash, diamond, and twist. Because unibodies and space frames are designed to absorb and disperse impact energy, damage generally occurs in a planned sequence. This sequence may include bending, crushing, collapsing, widening, and twisting. These terms are often used

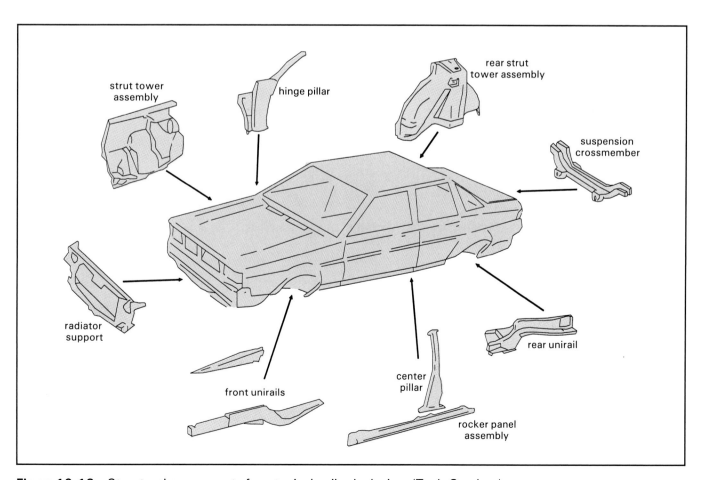

Figure 10-12 Structural components for a typical unibody design. (Tech-Cor, Inc.)

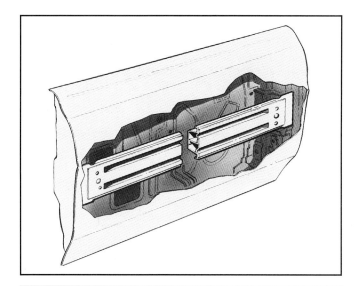

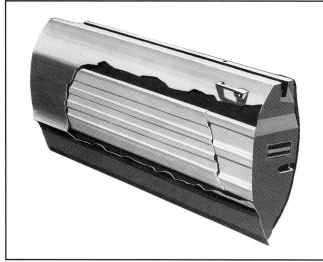

Figure 10-13   Steel reinforcing beams inside doors provide side impact protection on late-model cars. (Ford, Chrysler)

to distinguish unibody damage from body-over-frame damage. See Figure 10-15.

When mash damage occurs from a front-end impact, the stub frame or crush zone and suspension members will bend first. The next areas to bend and absorb energy are the dash cowl and the floor pan. The impact will cause the sheet metal in these areas to crush or collapse and shorten. Wrinkles in the floor pan and other components commonly occur. This damage may resemble ''accordion bellows.'' As mash damage continues, the passenger compartment is designed to distort outward or widen. This action dissipates the impact energy.

Reinforcing door beams, pillars, and structural sills are designed to protect the passenger compartment during sidesway damage. These components transfer impact energy to the opposite side of the vehicle and allow the structure to open, dissipating energy. Sidesway damage often results in the widening of the passenger compartment on the side opposite the impact.

Twisting of unibody vehicles is similar to the twist damage that occurs in conventional body-over-frame designs. Diamond damage rarely occurs on unitized vehicles. When diamond damage does occur, the vehicle is generally beyond economical repair.

Checking Body and Frame Alignment

To accurately assess collision damage, precise underbody measurements must be taken and compared to the manufacturer's specifications. Generally, underbody alignment must be within 1/16 in. (1.5 mm) of the specifications. There are three broad classes of measurement systems used to check body and frame alignment: gauge measuring systems, universal measuring systems, and dedicated fixture measuring systems. These systems are used to check measurements before, during, and after the repair process.

Figure 10-14   One type of energy absorbing bumper. The energy absorber units, which are mounted between the bumper and the stub frame, are similar to conventional shock absorbers. Upon impact, they absorb some of the energy and then return the bumper to its original position.

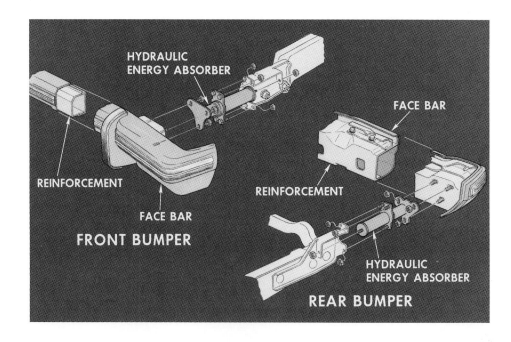

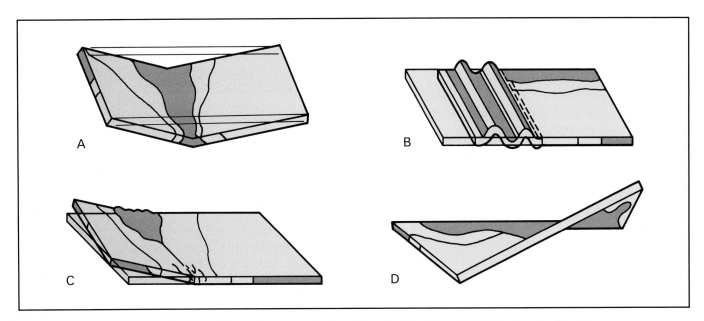

Figure 10-15 Typical unibody collision damage. A–Bending. B–Crushing. C–Widening. D–Twisting. (Blackhawk Automotive Inc.)

Gauge Measuring Systems. The four basic types of gauge measuring systems used in the body shop include tram gauges, tracking gauges, self-centering gauges, and centerline strut gauges.

Tram gauges are used to check for damage that would cause frame or body racking and shortness. They are also used to check the progress of straightening procedures. Tram gauges are designed to verify dimensions between two reference points. The tram is named after the trammel, which is a compass that consists of a beam and two sliding adjustable parts. A steel tape measure can be used to set the tram gauge pins to the manufacturer's specification. Additionally, millimeter scales, which are located on the beam of most tram gauges, can be used to set the gauge pins.

Tram gauges are designed to check one measurement at a time. Dimensions are generally verified between control points. Most control points are actually holes in the vehicle's structure. Gauge pins should be placed in the center of these holes. In Figure 10-16, several dimensions are shown on a horizontal plane that is parallel to the underbody of the vehicle. These dimensions can be easily verified with a tram gauge. The gauge must be held parallel to the plane of the underbody when checking dimensions.

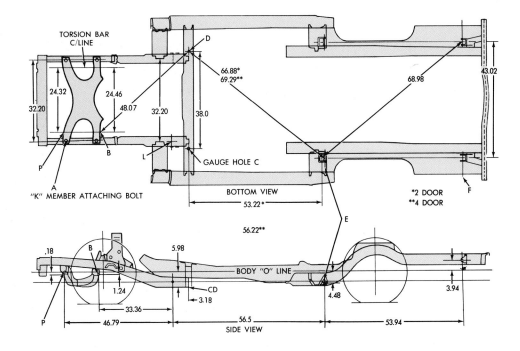

Figure 10-16 A tram gauge can be used to check the dimensions in this illustration. All diagonal dimensions are of equal distance to the (corresponding) matching reference points, unless otherwise specified. Specifications also show differences in the vertical height of the reference points.

If tram gauges are not available, adequate measurements can be made using the following procedure:

1. Place the vehicle on a clean, level floor. The floor must be level because measurements are given with a tolerance of 1/16 in. (1.5 mm). Ideally, measurements should be made with the vehicle on a straightening rack. Straightening racks will be covered in detail later in this chapter.

2. Select several points along one side of the vehicle and carefully transfer them to the floor with a plumb bob. Locate the corresponding points along the opposite side of the vehicle and transfer them to the floor.

3. Carefully measure the vertical distance from the floor to the check points on the vehicle.

4. Move the car away from the marks on the floor and measure the distance between the points, Figure 10-17. Corresponding measurements should be the same (within tolerance). Most manufacturers specify underbody dimensions in metric units. Therefore, a high-quality metric measuring tape is vital for taking accurate measurements.

5. To isolate certain conditions of misalignment, it may be necessary to set up diagonal check points to cover areas other than those shown in Figure 10-17. If additional points are selected, be sure that they are symmetrically opposite.

In addition to checking the structural components for misalignment, the body should be checked by measuring and comparing diagonals as illustrated in Figure 10-18. Tram gauges make it easy to establish dimensions around components and to check contours by comparing measurements from one side of the vehicle to the other.

Figure 10-18 A tram gauge can also be used to check the alignment of body panels. (Pull-it Corporation)

Tracking gauges are used to detect misalignment of front and rear wheels. These gauges are similar to tram gauges. A long beam with three adjustable tracking gauge pins is held against wheels to check critical measurements. These measurements, which are taken at the front and rear wheels, are compared from side to side and from front to back. Strut damage and diamond damage often cause tracking problems. See Figure 10-19. The condition that occurs when the rear wheels do not follow the front wheels correctly is commonly called *dog tracking*.

Self-centering gauges are designed to show general misalignment; they do not provide actual measurements or verify specific dimensions. They are called self-centering gauges because as one side of the gauge is moved, the other side automatically moves. This keeps a sighting

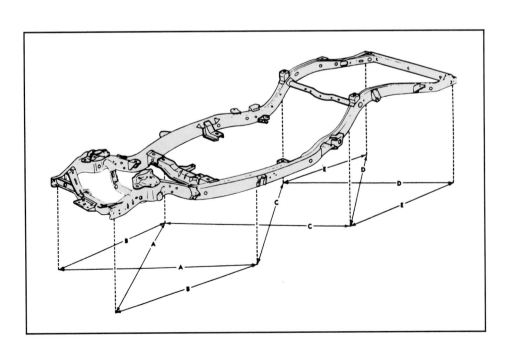

Figure 10-17 Another method of checking for misalignment in body-over-frame and unibody construction. A plumb line is used to project points from the frame (or unibody) to the floor. The distances between these points are then measured.

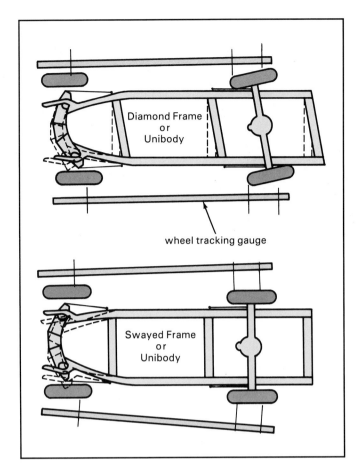

Figure 10-19 Common types of frame damage may be found using a wheel-tracking gauge. (Blackhawk Automotive Inc.)

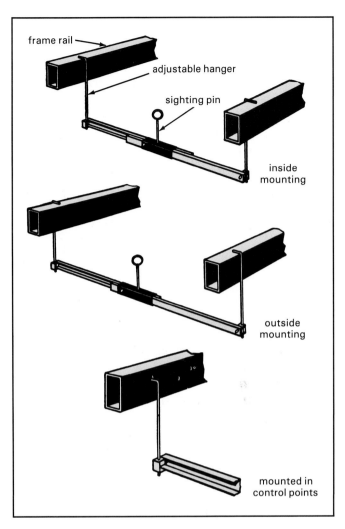

Figure 10-20 Methods of attaching self-centering gauges when checking for misalignment.

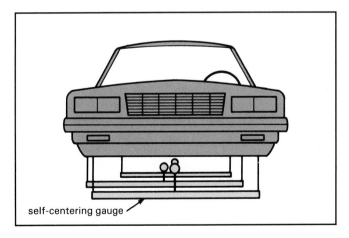

Figure 10-21 Pins on gauges will not be in alignment if the frame or unibody is bent.

pin (bullseye), which is used as an alignment device, centered on the gauge at all times.

Various mounting brackets are used to attach the gauges to a vehicle. Most gauges utilize mounting rods or pegs that are placed in reference holes or control points specified by the manufacturer. The gauges simply hang from these control points on the rods or pegs. See Figure 10-20. Self-centering gauges should be suspended in three or four control points along the frame or unibody. The technician must sight down the self-centering gauges to determine if all pins are in the center of the vehicle and if they are aligned properly. Misalignment is present if the pins are not aligned or centered, Figure 10-21.

Self-centering gauges can be used to quickly reveal twist, sidesway, sag, or diamond damage by detecting variations in the vehicle's datum plane, center plane, and zero planes. The ***datum plane*** is an imaginary horizontal line or plane of reference that is parallel to the bottom of the vehicle. It may be helpful to think of the datum plane as a table top that is located under the car. All height dimensions are taken from this plane.

The datum plane can be divided into two equal portions by an imaginary centerline or ***center plane.*** The center plane runs lengthwise along the datum plane and provides a reference point for taking width dimensions.

The ***zero planes*** divide the datum plane into three sections: the front section, center section, and rear section. In Figure 10-22, the datum, center, and zero planes are shown.

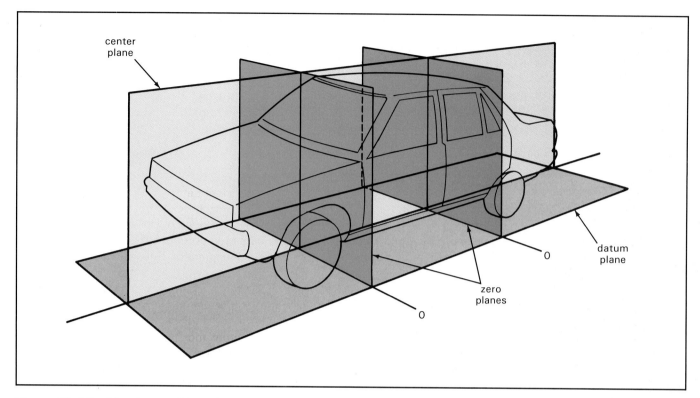

Figure 10-22   The three vehicle planes are used for reference when checking for structural damage.

It is not practical to provide measurement specifications between all points on a vehicle. Therefore, manufacturers often use the center plane and the datum plane as reference points for various dimensions. Measurements from both the datum plane and the center plane will be required to properly assess a damaged vehicle.

When the self-centering gauges are hung from the vehicle, the plane along the top of the gauges serves as the datum plane. If all gauge beams are level and the sighting pins are aligned, the vehicle is properly aligned, Figure 10-23.

The center section of a vehicle is deliberately designed to withstand impact. Therefore, the zero planes that cut through the cowl and rear door areas can be used as reference planes when checking alignment.

A *centerline strut gauge* is used to detect misalignment of strut towers in relation to the center plane and the datum plane. Strut gauges consist of upper and lower horizontal bars that are held together by left and right vertical bars. Some strut gauges have adjustable mounting stands, while others are mounted to measuring benches and/or fixture systems. The lower horizontal bar is set at the datum plane height. The upper horizontal bar is usually calibrated from the center out and has two adjustable pointers. These pointers are used to measure and compare the strut tower measurements and alignment with the factory specifications. It is essential that body dimension manuals be consulted when checking strut tower alignment. These manuals will provide the information necessary to determine whether the towers

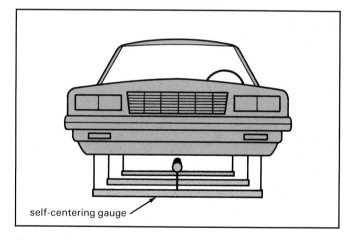

Figure 10-23   Gauges will be in alignment if the frame or unibody is not damaged.

are symmetrical or asymmetrical. The tops of symmetrical towers should be an equal distance from the vehicle's centerline. If necessary, centerline strut gauges can also be used to detect misalignment of other components.

Universal Measuring Systems.   The major advantage of *universal measuring systems* is that they can measure most or all of a vehicle's control points at one time. These systems are light and adjustable. They are used to check the distances between control points. Universal measuring systems fall into two categories: mechanical measuring systems, and laser measuring systems.

Mechanical measuring systems utilize a precision bridge (beam) and a series of tram-like adjustable pointers to verify dimensions. These instruments can be free standing or they can be attached to the vehicle. The system's pointers are set to the manufacturer's horizontal and vertical specifications, and the bridge fixture is placed on the vehicle's datum plane. If all pointers align with the corresponding control points, the vehicle is in alignment. Any control points that do not line up can be easily detected by the technician. Both upper and lower body reference points can be measured using these systems. See Figure 10-24.

Laser measuring systems utilize one or more light beams to measure alignment. These systems are adjusted to the height of the datum plane. Once mirrored and transparent (calibrated) scales are attached to various control points on the vehicle, measurements of the entire body and underbody are made. A laser (light) beam is projected on measuring scales or deflected (mirror reflection) from one or more control points to take several measurements at the same time. Although laser systems are strictly measuring devices, they permit instantaneous readings during straightening operations. Some laser measuring systems are capable of checking body, strut, and wheel alignment.

Dedicated Fixture Systems. Dedicated fixture systems consist of a heavily constructed bench or frame and a variety of fixtures. Some fixtures are bolted to the vehicle at specified suspension or bumper mountings. Fixtures with pins are designed to fit into control point holes. Long strut fixtures are attached to the strut towers. Several different fixture sets must be available to check the alignment of various vehicles. Dedicated fixture systems are used to "gauge" the position of control points rather than measure the distance between them. It is important to note that many dedicated fixture systems are equipped with power rams, which are used to straighten the damaged vehicle. There are two basic types of dedicated fixture systems: frame systems and bench systems.

Dedicated *frame systems* are composed of a heavy frame assembly upon which various attachments are mounted. These attachments, which include a variety of jigs, probes, and other devices, are designed to match a manufacturer's control points. If the control points on a vehicle do not align properly with the measuring attachments, the damaged components or sections must be pulled into proper alignment. See Figure 10-25.

Bench systems consist of a heavy bench and movable jigs that are fitted with numerous fixtures. These fixtures are designed to correspond to a specific vehicle's control point locations and often bolt to suspension and bumper mountings. If a vehicle does not align properly with the fixtures, it is damaged and must be repaired. Bench systems require matched sets of fixtures for various vehicle constructions. Therefore, these systems are too expensive for most small body shops. See Figures 10-26 and 10-27.

Determining the Repair Procedure

After carefully analyzing a damaged vehicle, the technician must decide on an appropriate repair procedure. The method and sequence of repair is planned in this step. The repair sequence depends on the extent and

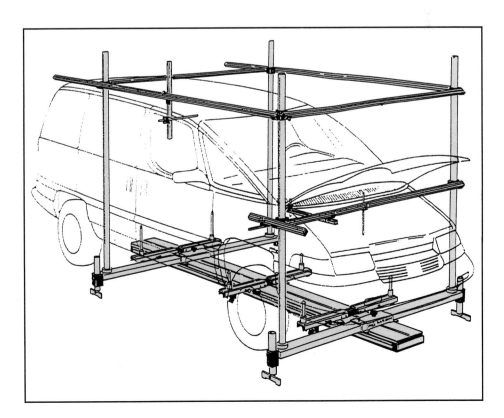

Figure 10-24 Mechanical measuring system. Several reference points can be measured at once when using this system. (Blackhawk Automotive Inc.)

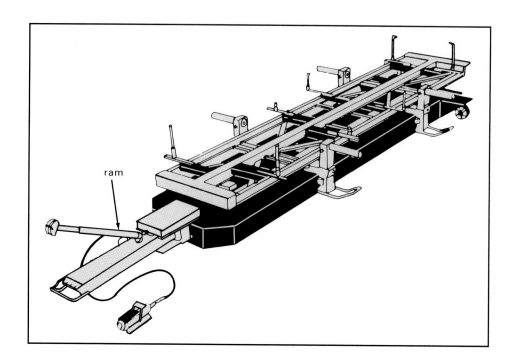

Figure 10-25 One type of dedicated frame system. This system is equipped with a power ram.

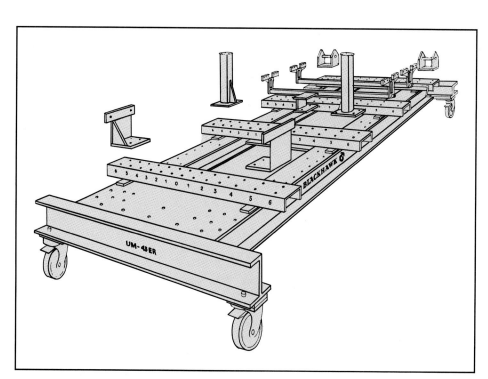

Figure 10-26 This heavy-duty bench-type measuring system is equipped with several fixed measuring and anchoring devices. (Blackhawk Automotive Inc.)

location of the damage. Structural (frame) damage must be straightened before attempting to work on body sheet metal. In order to access structural members, various components and trim pieces may require disassembly or removal. Mechanical components are normally repaired before any bodywork is performed.

If necessary, the repair procedure should include the ordering of repair parts and supplies. It is important to have these items available when needed. Repair work can be impeded if the proper repair parts are not available. A detailed repair procedure will help reduce wasted effort and eliminate substandard repairs.

Repairing Damage

After analyzing a damaged vehicle and establishing an appropriate repair procedure, the actual repair process can begin. It is the responsibility of the technician to restore the vehicle to its original shape and condition. To accomplish this, it is necessary to know how much the individual members of the body and/or frame must be straightened. This can only be determined by taking accurate measurements and comparing them to the manufacturer's specifications. Special tools are used to check for frame and underbody damage. Remember that

Figure 10-27 A vehicle mounted on a bench-type measuring system. (Blackhawk Automotive Inc.)

all structural and mechanical damage must be repaired before sheet metal repairs can be made.

In the event of extensive collision damage, major underbody repairs may be required to re-establish proper alignment. In most cases, power straightening equipment is used to correct extensive damage. This equipment can be used to perform a variety of controlled pushing and pulling operations. Most power straightening equipment is equipped with accurate frame and leveling gauges.

Body and Frame Alignment Systems

CAUTION: A great deal of care is required when straightening unibody vehicles. The metal in the subframe and underbody of a unibody vehicle is considerably lighter than the metal used in a conventional frame. It is important to remember that unibody vehicles do not have conventional frames from which to push or pull. These vehicles must be securely fastened to the straightening equipment (or the floor). Also remember to properly distribute the pulling and anchoring force during straightening procedures. Unibody vehicles can be anchored at the pinch weld flanges. See Figure 10-28. Anchor points on vehicles with space frame construction include the lower rail hem flanges and rear suspension brackets. Pinch weld areas should never be used as anchor points on space frames, because the metal in these areas is not strong enough to secure the vehicle during straightening operations. Additionally, the damaged areas of unibody vehicles should be pulled back into position without applying heat if possible. In the case of sharp bends or ruptured welds, it may be necessary to use heat. Remember that HSLA steels can be weakened by heating. Refer to Chapters 5 and 6 for more information on repairing high-strength steels.

Figure 10-28 A clamping device is used to hold the pinch weld area securely to a straightening bench.

There are three basic types of alignment systems used for body and frame repair: portable systems, stationary rack systems, and rail or floor systems.

Portable Alignment Systems. *Portable alignment systems* are designed for correcting slight frame and body damage. Many of these units are only able to pull in one direction at a time. Portable units can be moved from job to job and can be stored when not in use.

When using a portable system for body and frame repair, the damaged vehicle is commonly placed on safety stands and the equipment is moved to the desired position.

Most portable alignment systems consist of a vertical mast that is attached (hinged) to a heavy, horizontal main frame. Once the horizontal frame is secured to the underbody with clamps, pulling chains can be attached to the mast and to the impact area with clamps or bolts. See Figure 10-29. A hydraulic jack system is used to pull on the chain, Figure 10-30.

Figure 10-29 Clamp attachments are used to secure pulling chains to the damaged section of this vehicle. (Chief Automotive Systems, Inc.)

Figure 10-30 Using a portable puller to correct damage.

Stationary Rack Systems. *Stationary rack systems* can be used to repair extensive collision damage. These systems provide an accurate base from which measurements can be taken to determine the extent of damage. The racks are usually constructed of heavy steel members. Most stationary rack systems are about 18 in. (450 mm) above the floor. Some units tilt so that the damaged vehicle can be driven or pulled onto the racks. The vehicle is fastened to the racks with chains and clamps. Most stationary rack systems have hydraulic pulling (power) towers mounted to the racks, Figure 10-31.

In Figure 10-32, a unibody vehicle is securely held to the rack at the pinch welds, while hydraulic power is used to pull components back into position. Note the adjustable pulling towers.

Figure 10-33 illustrates an alternate method of anchoring a vehicle to a rack. Note the round bar that is placed across the rack and the heavy chain used to

Figure 10-31 A vehicle with extensive rear-end damage is mounted to this stationary rack system. Note hydraulic pulling towers at the rear of the vehicle.

hydraulic pulling towers

rack

Figure 10-32 This stationary rack system is being used to repair front-end damage. Note that the vehicle is secured at the pinch welds. (Blackhawk Automotive Inc.)

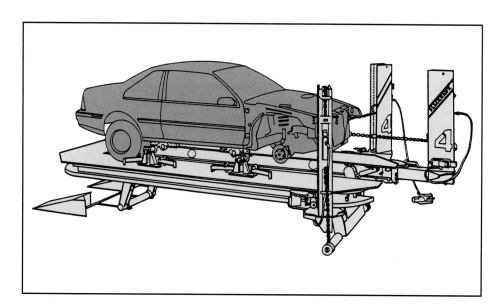

secure the body to the rack. In some systems, electric-over-hydraulic power is used to make several pulls at one time. See Figure 10-34.

The vehicle shown in Figure 10-35 was struck on the side, damaging the top, door pillars, floor pan, rocker panel, and side bar. Note the rig used to pull the roof and door pillar into alignment. Figure 10-36 shows a correction being made to a damaged rear fender panel.

Rail Systems. *Rail systems* (in-floor systems) consist of specially designed steel members that are set into the shop floor. These members provide a firm anchorage for the pushing and pulling equipment used when repairing body or frame damage.

Figure 10-33 Alternate method of anchoring a car to the rack. (Bee Line Co.)

Figure 10-35 Preparing to straighten a roof panel and a door pillar on a rack-type system. (Bee Line Co.)

Figure 10-34 This rack system is set up to make four pulls. Note that the pulling towers can be moved to any position around the vehicle. (Duz-mor)

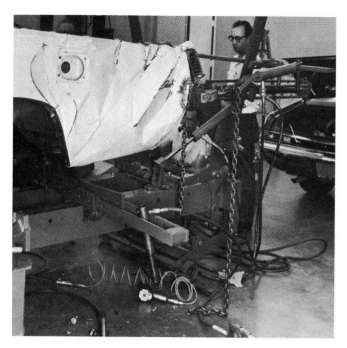

Figure 10-36 Pulling a rear panel to obtain the original contour. (Bee Line Co.)

It is possible to push, pull, and anchor from any point around the vehicle when using rail systems. Force can be exerted upward, to the side, or downward as desired. Additionally, straightening forces can be applied in several directions at the same time.

When using a rail system to correct damage, the vehicle is placed on safety stands so the extent of the damage can be accurately gauged. The stands also place the vehicle at a convenient working height.

Since any pulling or pushing force will have an opposite reaction on the anchoring system, it is very important to anchor the vehicle to the base properly. Anchoring at or near the safety stands is recommended whenever possible. Placing the anchors close to the stands prevents the undamaged portions of the vehicle from being bent downward. The pulling forces are applied by 10 ton hydraulic rams. See Figure 10-37.

Figure 10-38 shows four different pulls being made on a car that was struck in the left rear fender. Note that three of the pulls are horizontal. The hydraulic ram attached to the right corner of the trunk opening is pulling at an upward angle. The forces can be applied simultaneously or independently.

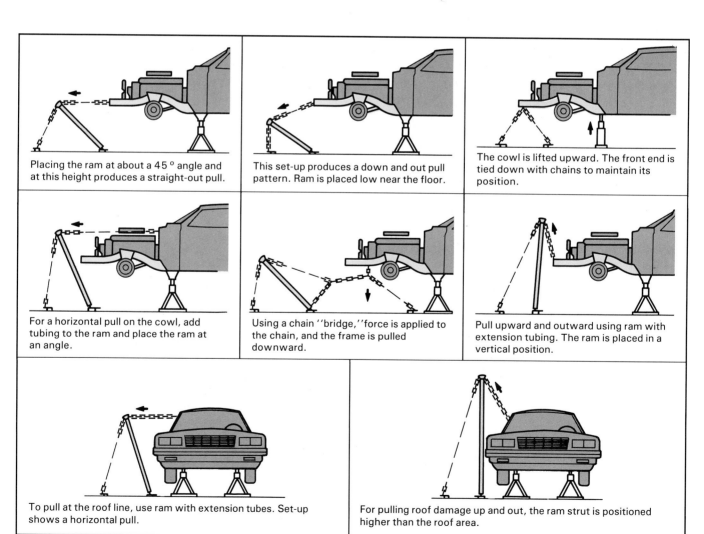

Placing the ram at about a 45° angle and at this height produces a straight-out pull.

This set-up produces a down and out pull pattern. Ram is placed low near the floor.

The cowl is lifted upward. The front end is tied down with chains to maintain its position.

For a horizontal pull on the cowl, add tubing to the ram and place the ram at an angle.

Using a chain ''bridge,'' force is applied to the chain, and the frame is pulled downward.

Pull upward and outward using ram with extension tubing. The ram is placed in a vertical position.

To pull at the roof line, use ram with extension tubes. Set-up shows a horizontal pull.

For pulling roof damage up and out, the ram strut is positioned higher than the roof area.

Figure 10-37 Basic hydraulic ram hookups for straightening various types of damage.

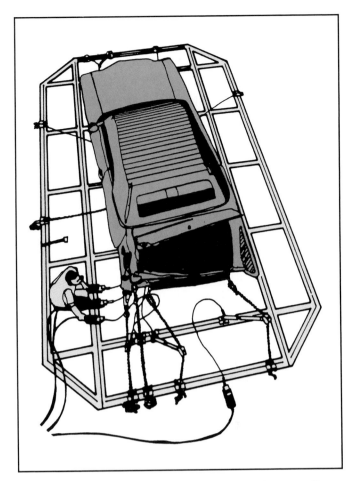

Figure 10-38 Typical rail setup. Four different pulls are made to straighten the rear-end damage on this vehicle. (Blackhawk Automotive Inc.)

Figure 10-39 Rail setup for correcting front-end damage using two hydraulic rams. Note the direction of the pulls.

Figure 10-39 shows a car with heavy damage to the right front corner. Note that self-centering gauges are attached to the underside of the car. The vehicle is anchored with the help of a round bar that runs from one side of the car to the other. To straighten the damage, two pulls are made. One is a direct, forward pull; the other is to the side and slightly downward.

Above-the-floor rail systems do not require concrete installation. They simply consist of a low-profile platform that sits on top of a concrete floor. The platform is bolted to the floor and can be moved if necessary. The system performs the same operations as the in-floor system. A typical above-the-floor system is shown in Figure 10-40.

A variation of the rail system is the *pot system* (pad system). This type of system utilizes portable hydraulic units that are anchored to attachment holes in the floor. These units can be moved to numerous positions. Figure

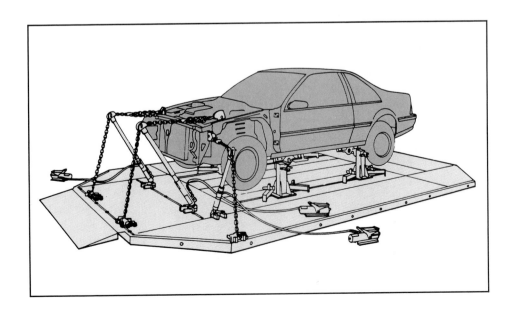

Figure 10-40 Above-the-floor system that is set up to make three pulls. (Blackhawk Automotive Inc.)

10-41 shows two pulls being made on the front end of a vehicle. Note the additional holes in the floor around the vehicle.

The major advantage of in-floor rail and pot systems is that the pulling equipment can be removed, and the space can be used for other work.

Safety Precautions

There are several safety precautions that should be followed when using straightening and alignment equipment:

☐ Follow the manufacturer's instructions for the proper use of all straightening equipment.

☐ Use the grade and type of chain recommended for the equipment.

☐ Never pull chains around sharp corners. Chain links will nick or crack and may eventually break.

☐ Do not bolt chains together. The bolt may not be strong enough to withstand the forces exerted on the chain.

☐ Cover the chain with a tarpaulin or other heavy material. When a chain breaks, the ends fly with a whip-like action that can cause severe injury.

☐ Always anchor the vehicle securely before making a pull.

☐ Make certain that the chains and pulling attachments are secure and that anchor bolts, pinch weld clamps, or other clamps are tight. See Figure 10-42.

☐ When hooking a chain into an anchor, remember that the anchor, ram foot, and attachment point on the vehicle must be in a straight line in the direction of the pull.

☐ Never use a service jack to support a vehicle while working on or under it. Always use safety stands.

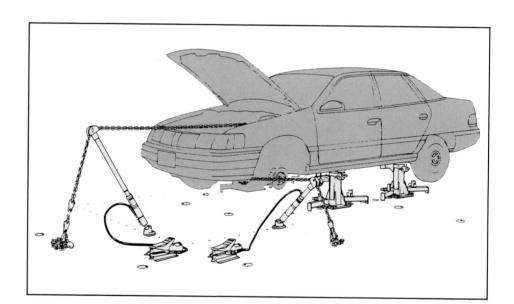

Figure 10-41 Pulls are being made from attachments (pots) in the shop floor. (Blackhawk Automotive Inc.)

Figure 10-42 Before using power straightening equipment, make sure that clamp attachments and anchors are installed properly.

☐ When making side pulls, remember to provide counter supports to prevent pulling the vehicle off of the alignment benches.

☐ When using a portable body-and-frame straightener, both the holding chain and the pulling chain should be attached to the pivot arm at the same location. This will prevent the straightener from tipping while the pull is being made.

☐ When attaching a pulling chain to a vehicle, use short pieces of angle iron or wood blocks to pad the corners where the chain wraps around the frame or other components.

☐ Never heat chains. High temperatures will weaken chains.

☐ Carefully measure repair progress to prevent overpulling. Overpulling may not be correctable!

☐ Be sure to restore structural integrity when making repairs. Remember, the customer is relying on the auto body technician to restore the damaged vehicle to its original condition.

Summary

The careful inspection of a damaged vehicle is the first step in providing the customer with a quality repair. Major damage may require frame, suspension, and underbody repairs. A high degree of skill is necessary to make most major auto body repairs.

The term alignment is used to refer to the arrangement of a vehicle's basic structural components in relation to each other. Misalignment of a vehicle's frame or underbody will make it difficult to straighten or align many body components.

There are several techniques used to analyze collision damage. X-checking is a process in which measurements are taken and compared from one side of a vehicle to the other. Special measuring tools are also used to assess damage. When structural damage is suspected, distance between major control points should be compared to manufacturer's specifications.

Severe body-over-frame damage includes twist, sidesway, mash, diamond, and sag. Indirect damage is common in unibody vehicles because the body panels and structural members in these vehicles act as a single unit. Additionally, crush zones are built into unibody vehicles to absorb impact energy. Nevertheless, the unibody vehicle experiences the same types of damage as the body-over-frame vehicle—twist, sidesway, mash, diamond, and sag. The terms bending, crushing, collapsing, widening, and twisting are sometimes used to describe unibody damage.

To accurately assess collision damage, precise underbody measurements must be taken and compared to the manufacturer's specifications. There are three broad classes of measurement systems used in the body shop: gauge measuring systems, universal measuring systems, and dedicated fixture measuring systems.

The four types of gauge measuring systems used in the body shop include tram gauges, tracking gauges, self-centering gauges, and centerline strut gauges. Tram gauges are used to take measurements between reference points. Tracking gauges detect misalignment of the front and rear wheels. Self-centering gauges are designed to show misalignment of the body or frame. Centerline strut gauges are used to detect misalignment of the strut towers.

Universal measuring systems are also used to assess collision damage. These systems can measure all or most of a vehicle's control points at one time. Universal measuring systems are divided into two categories: mechanical measuring systems and laser measuring systems. Mechanical systems utilize a bridge and several adjustable pointers to take measurements. Laser systems utilize light beams to take measurements.

There are two basic types of dedicated fixture systems: frame systems and bench systems. Frame systems consist of a heavy frame assembly upon which various attachments are mounted. Bench systems are movable jigs that are fitted with numerous fixtures. Dedicated systems gauge rather than measure the distance between control points.

After analyzing the damage, the technician must decide on a repair procedure. This procedure depends on the extent and location of the damage. Structural damage must be repaired before straightening sheet metal body panels.

After the repair procedure has been chosen, the vehicle can be repaired. The three alignment systems used for body and frame repair are the portable system, the stationary rack system, and the rail system. Portable systems are designed for correcting slight frame and sheet metal damage. Stationary systems can be used to repair extensive damage. Rail systems can also be used to repair extensive damage.

Know These Terms

Alignment, X-checking, Sidesway, Sag, Mash, Diamond, Twist, Indirect damage, Crush zones, Tram gauges, Tracking gauges, Dog tracking, Self-centering gauges, Datum plane, Center plane, Zero planes, Centerline strut gauge, Universal measuring systems, Mechanical measuring systems, Laser measuring systems, Frame systems, Bench systems, Portable alignment systems, Stationary rack systems, Rail systems, Pot system.

Review Questions—Chapter 10

1. A careful inspection is the first step in providing a quality auto body repair. True or False?

2. Major damage may require:
   a. underbody repairs.
   b. frame repairs.
   c. suspension repairs.
   d. all of the above.

3. _____ refers to the arrangement of a vehicle's basic structural components in relation to each other.

4. Taking measurements and comparing them from side to side is called _____.

5. Typical body-over-frame damage includes:
   a. sidesway.
   b. widening.
   c. cracking.
   d. all of the above.

6. Sag is caused by an impact to the side of a vehicle. True or False?

7. _____ occurs when a front or rear impact shortens a section of the frame.

8. Unibody damage is often described by the terms bending, crushing, collapsing, widening, and twisting. True or False?

9. To accurately assess collision damage, underbody measurements must be compared to the _____ _____.

10. Tram gauges are designed to take measurements between two reference points. True or False?

11. Tracking gauges are used to check for misalignment of the front and rear:
    a. frame rails.
    b. fenders.
    c. wheels.
    d. all of the above.

12. Self-centering gauges are equipped with _____ pins.

13. The datum plane is a vertical line that runs through the center of the vehicle. True or False?

14. The zero planes divide the _____ plane into three sections.

15. Zero planes can be used as reference points when taking alignment readings. True or False?

16. A centerline strut gauge is used to check for misalignment of the _____ _____.

17. _____ measuring systems can measure most of a vehicle's control points at one time.

18. When using a mechanical measuring system, the bridge is placed on the vehicle's _____ plane.

19. Laser measuring systems utilize _____ beams to measure alignment.

20. Dedicated fixture systems are used to measure the distance between control points. True or False?

21. The procedure used to repair a vehicle depends on the _____ and _____ of the damage.

22. Before repairing damage, the technician must determine how much the damaged members of the body and/or frame must be straightened. True or False?

23. Unibody vehicles must be securely fastened to the _____ _____ or the _____ before pulling out damaged components.

24. Portable alignment systems are designed for correcting extensive frame or underbody damage. True or False?

25. Straightening forces can be applied in several directions at the same time when using rail systems. True or False?

Activities—Chapter 10

1. Use X-checking techniques to check a damaged vehicle for misalignment. Make a sketch of the vehicle and record the results of your measurements on the sketch.

2. Study several damaged vehicles and identify sidesway, sag, mash, diamond, and twist damage. Take pictures of the vehicles observed. Mount the pictures on a poster board and label them according to the type of damage shown.

3. Using a tram gauge or a measuring tape, compare a vehicle's underbody dimensions to the manufacturer's specifications. If the dimensions are not within tolerance, determine how much the vehicle must be straightened to correct the misalignment.

4. Study the body and frame alignment equipment in your shop. Make a warning sign listing the safety precautions that should be followed when using the equipment. Ask your instructor to display the sign in an appropriate area.

# chapter 11

Replacing Panels, Hoods, Doors, and Fenders

After studying this chapter, you will be able to:

☐ Explain various methods used to replace damaged body panels.

☐ Describe the precautions that must be taken when sectioning structural components.

☐ Adjust and align bumpers, hoods, deck lids, fenders, and doors.

☐ Explain the procedures for adjusting rubber stops, hinges, and striker plates.

Panel Replacement

Outer body panels can be repaired after a vehicle's underbody/frame and inner body panels have been straightened. In many cases, damage to the outer body panels can be repaired using hammer-and-dolly techniques or other straightening methods. In some cases, however, considerable time can be saved by removing an entire damaged panel and installing a new one or by cutting out the damaged area and inserting a salvaged (used) section.

The decision of whether to repair or replace a damaged panel depends on the extent and location of the damage. It is often less expensive to replace a panel than to repair it. In order to make an appropriate decision, accurate estimates of the time and material required to both repair and replace a damaged panel are essential. The ability to make these estimates can only be gained through experience.

Replacing a Complete Panel

Severely damaged panels are often replaced. Typical *replacement panels* are shown in Figure 11-1. Before a damaged panel is replaced, it should be roughly shaped to its original contour and alignment. This will help to ensure that the inner panels and other components are in the approximate position to receive the replacement panel. If necessary, the damaged panel can be checked by comparing it with the corresponding panel on the opposite side of the vehicle. Measuring gauges can also be used to check for proper alignment.

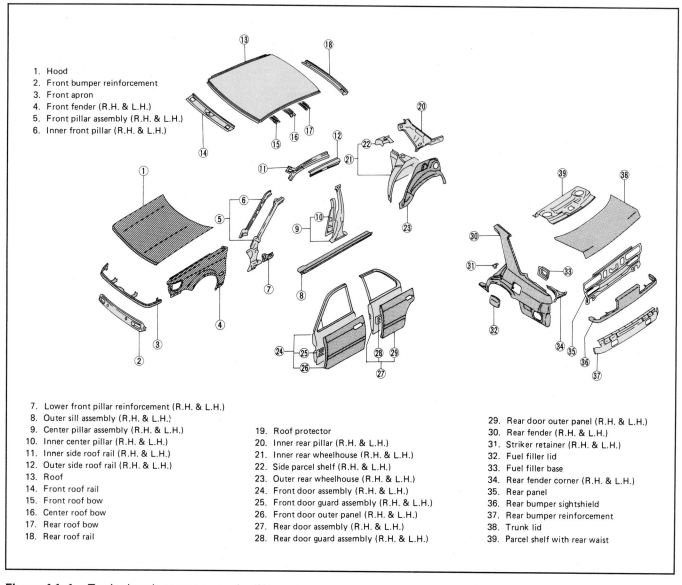

1. Hood
2. Front bumper reinforcement
3. Front apron
4. Front fender (R.H. & L.H.)
5. Front pillar assembly (R.H. & L.H.)
6. Inner front pillar (R.H. & L.H.)

7. Lower front pillar reinforcement (R.H. & L.H.)
8. Outer sill assembly (R.H. & L.H.)
9. Center pillar assembly (R.H. & L.H.)
10. Inner center pillar (R.H. & L.H.)
11. Inner side roof rail (R.H. & L.H.)
12. Outer side roof rail (R.H. & L.H.)
13. Roof
14. Front roof rail
15. Front roof bow
16. Center roof bow
17. Rear roof bow
18. Rear roof rail

19. Roof protector
20. Inner rear pillar (R.H. & L.H.)
21. Inner rear wheelhouse (R.H. & L.H.)
22. Side parcel shelf (R.H. & L.H.)
23. Outer rear wheelhouse (R.H. & L.H.)
24. Front door assembly (R.H. & L.H.)
25. Front door guard assembly (R.H. & L.H.)
26. Front door outer panel (R.H. & L.H.)
27. Rear door assembly (R.H. & L.H.)
28. Rear door guard assembly (R.H. & L.H.)

29. Rear door outer panel (R.H. & L.H.)
30. Rear fender (R.H. & L.H.)
31. Striker retainer (R.H. & L.H.)
32. Fuel filler lid
33. Fuel filler base
34. Rear fender corner (R.H. & L.H.)
35. Rear panel
36. Rear bumper sightshield
37. Rear bumper reinforcement
38. Trunk lid
39. Parcel shelf with rear waist

Figure 11-1   Typical replacement panels. (Nissan)

After roughly shaping the damaged panel, it can be removed. When removing a panel, it may be necessary to remove the bolts that secure it to the rest of the structure. In most cases, it is also necessary to cut through spot welds. Many technicians use a drill and a ***spot cutter bit*** to cut through the welds (nuggets). A ***clamp saw*** can also be used to cut through spot welds. This type of saw only cuts through the top layer of material. See Figure 11-2. Panel designs and weld locations vary among manufacturers. Collision manuals contain panel design and weld location diagrams for specific vehicles.

After removing the damaged outer panel, carefully check the inner panel. If necessary, the inner panel should be straightened or replaced. The new outer panel should be placed on the vehicle and held in position with vice-grip pliers, C-clamps, or mechanical fasteners (screws). When the panel is aligned properly, it can be bolted or spot welded in place. If spot welds are used, start the welds at the center of the panel and proceed

toward one end. Then repeat this procedure for the other half of the panel. In order to reduce distortion, place the spot welds at 3 or 4 in. (100 mm) intervals. This procedure will help keep metal temperatures to a minimum. After the panel is welded in place, additional welds can be made between the initial welds to help secure the panel.

Replacing a Partial Panel

In many cases, it is desirable to replace only the damaged area of a fender or panel. This type of repair is called ***sectioning***. As previously mentioned, the decision of whether to replace or repair a panel depends on the time required to straighten the damaged area. The decision also depends on the price and availability of a replacement panel and the cost of labor. It is important to note that many replacement parts—even new parts—require straightening before installation.

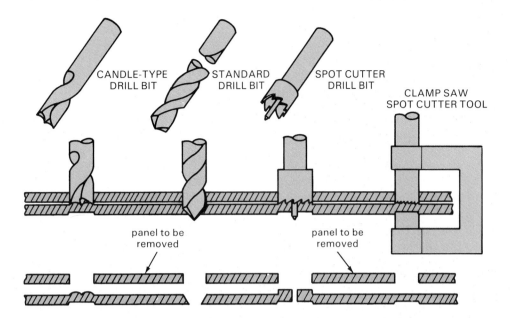

Figure 11-2   Various bits and cutters can be used to drill through spot welds.

The first step in sectioning a panel is to straighten the damaged area so that it is aligned with the surrounding surface. Make sure the areas adjacent to the damage are not out of proper contour. Measure the damaged area carefully and transfer the measurements to the replacement panel. If possible, plan the repair so that joints occur at edges, under ridges, or under trim pieces. It is generally advisable to cut the replacement panel about 2 in. (50 mm) larger than the damaged area. This will allow a minimum of a 1 in. (25 mm) overlap joint and will ensure a strong overlap joint. It will also provide some leeway for error and for trimming damaged edges. If necessary, a 2 in. (50 mm) overlap joint can be used to provide greater strength. After transferring the measurements, scribe lines where the replacement panel is to be cut.

Cut the replacement panel along the scribed lines to obtain the desired size and shape. There are several methods that can be used to cut the panel. The use of pneumatic cutters, plasma torches, nibblers, and abrasive wheels was discussed in previous chapters.

Position the replacement panel over the damaged area and outline the panel with a scribe or a piece of chalk. Cut out the damaged area at least 1 in. (25 mm) inside of the scribed lines. See Figure 11-3A. Trim the replacement panel to fit along edges and around other stopping points.

After the damaged area has been cut away and the replacement panel has been trimmed properly, temporarily clamp or screw the replacement panel in position. Never install replacement panels when a vehicle is supported by jacks or jack stands. The stresses caused by lifting the vehicle can be transferred to the panel. When the vehicle is removed from the jack and the stresses are relieved, the panel will distort.

After carefully checking for proper alignment and fit, remove the screws and the panel. Sand all paint from the joint areas on both the damaged panel and the

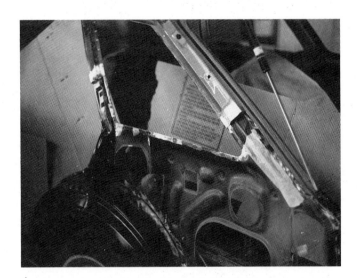

A

B

Figure 11-3   A–The damaged panel has been removed from this vehicle. B–A replacement panel is welded into place.

replacement panel. Apply rust inhibitors and sound deadeners to the back of both panels to prevent rust and reduce sound transfer. Keep these materials away from the joint areas.

Reinstall the replacement panel with screws or clamps, and spot weld the lap joints. See Figure 11-3B. In Figure 11-4, pinch welds around a replacement panel are being spot welded. A continuous MIG weld must be made along some joints to provide the required strength. Remember, special care must be taken when sectioning or welding high-strength steel components. Sectioning structural components is covered in detail later in this chapter. After the joints are welded, the screws or clamps should be removed. A disk sander can be used to smooth out the welds and the joint seams. After sanding, body filler is applied to complete the smoothing operation.

An alternate method for joining panels involves using a special **pneumatic flange tool** or a **panel crimper.** These tools form an offset crimp or a "step" along the joint edge on either the replacement panel or the damaged panel. The crimp permits a "no-bump" lap joint, which provides for a flush, professional joint.

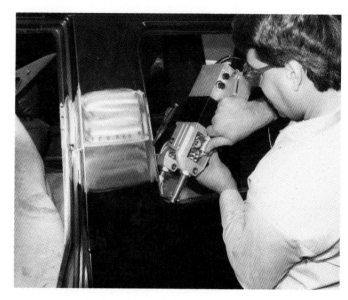

Figure 11-4 This technician is spot welding the pinch seams on a replacement panel. Note the spot welded lap joint and the sanded surface on the panel. (LORS Machinery, Inc.)

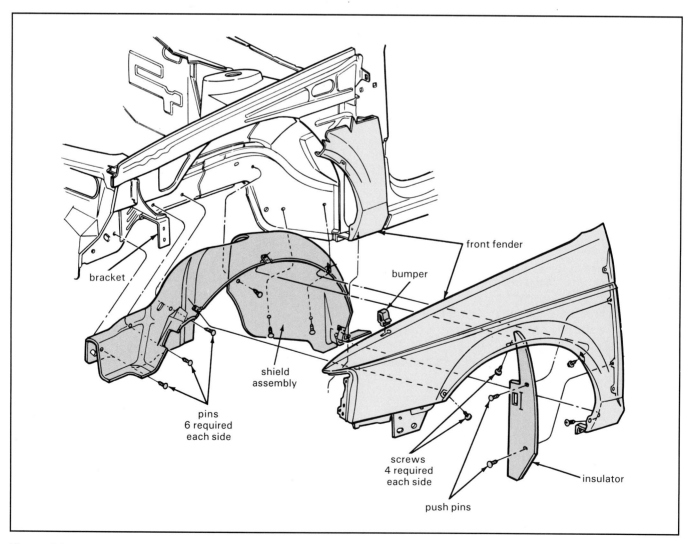

Figure 11-5 Typical fender attachment points. (Ford)

Front Fender Panel Replacement

On many vehicles, the front fender panels are bolted to the rest of the structure, Figure 11-5. All wiring must be disconnected from the fenders before they are removed from the vehicle. On some models, headlamps, parking lamps, and side-markers must be removed before the fender can be removed.

Before discarding the old fender, make a paper pattern of emblem, molding, and hole locations. The pattern is used to transfer these locations to the new fender. This technique can be used when replacing any body panel. If a pattern is not made, molding and hole locations can be transferred from the corresponding fender on the opposite side of the vehicle.

The installation of a new fender is not difficult if the rest of the body has not been damaged. The alignment of a new front fender is simplified if its holes are elongated, Figure 11-6. The elongated holes allow the panel to be shifted during installation to achieve the proper alignment.

Rear (Fender) Panel Replacement

Before replacing a rear panel (structural or non-structural), all other structural damage must be repaired. In modern unibody designs, the rear fender panels are often important structural members. Therefore, it is

essential to follow the manufacturer's recommendations when repairing or replacing these panels. A repaired structural member must be as strong as it was before the collision. Some manufacturers do not allow cutting or sectioning of structural panels.

Replacing a rear panel begins by carefully determining where to make the joints. It may not be practical or desirable to remove a rear panel at all of the factory seams. If the entire panel has not been damaged, it may be quicker and easier to replace only the damaged portion of the panel as described previously.

Most rear fenders (rear quarter panels) are fastened with spot welds, Figure 11-7. A spot cutter bit or a clamp saw can be used to cut through the welds. Although a plasma torch can be used to quickly cut through a variety of welds, it is difficult to control. Grinders are sometimes used to remove continuous welds and stitch welds. The use of plasma torches and grinders is not recommended when removing structural panels. After the welds are cut, a pneumatic chisel can be used to separate the damaged fender from the rest of the structure.

The replacement panel should be positioned correctly and secured with clamps and/or screws. When the panel is aligned correctly, it can be removed and prepared for permanent installation. Remove the primer along all joint areas and apply a weld-through primer. If necessary, replace undercoating, insulation, and sound

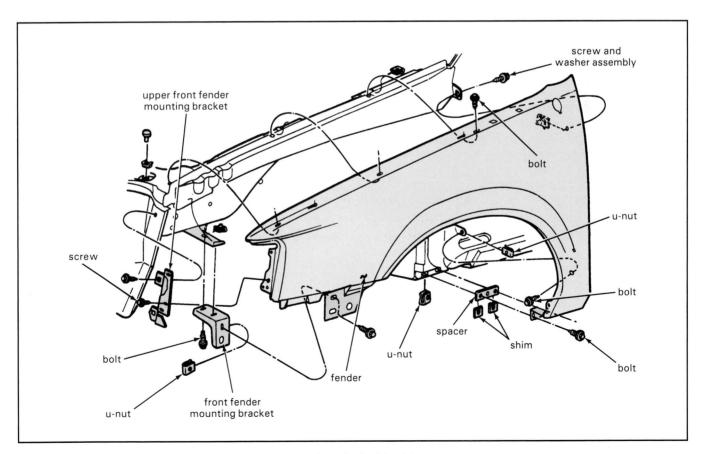

Figure 11-6 Note that many of the attachment points (holes) in this fender are elongated. (Ford)

Figure 11-7   This joint on a replacement panel is being spot welded. (LORS Machinery, Inc.)

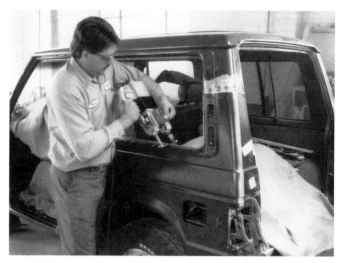

Figure 11-8   This technician is securing a new rear panel with spot welds. (LORS Machinery, Inc.)

deadening pads. Body sealer should be applied around the perimeter of the panel (joint area). After preparing the panel properly, it can be repositioned and clamped or screwed in place. The panel must be precisely positioned before welding. Check body lines, gaps, and joints for alignment. The panel can be spot welded or continuous welded as described in Chapter 6. Figure 11-8 shows a technician installing a new rear fender.

Door Panel Replacement

A severely damaged outer door panel is generally replaced if the inner panel can be repaired. Outer door panels are commonly called **door skins** or *skins*.

To replace a door skin, remove the door from the vehicle and take off the exterior moldings and hardware. It is generally not necessary to remove the window regulator, remote control mechanism, lock mechanism, or window runs.

Place the door on a flat surface so that the bottom edge of the door extends over the edge of the surface. Remove the **hem flange** with a grinder and remove the damaged door skin. See Figure 11-9. If necessary, repair any damage to the inner panel. Before installing the new door skin, apply sealers and sound deadeners to the back of the panel. The internal door mechanisms may obstruct portions of the replacement panel after the skin is installed.

On adhesive-bonded door skins, a strong, two-part polyurethane adhesive is used to secure the skin. Clean and prime the hem flange and the inner flange before installing the skin. Correctly position the new skin over the door frame and apply the adhesive to the flanges. Bend the hem flange over the inner panel flange with a hammer and a dolly. This will create a **hem seam**. A special pneumatic **hemming tool** can also be used to create the seam. Use extreme care to prevent deforming the new skin when making the hem seam.

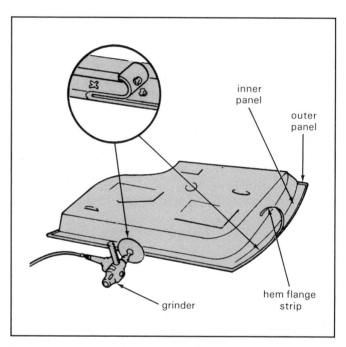

Figure 11-9   Before removing a damaged door skin, the hem flange must be removed.

The procedure for replacing welded door skins is similar to the procedure for replacing adhesive-bonded skins. After removing the damaged door skin, apply weld-through primer to the flange area. Replace sound deadener pads (silencers) and apply sealer to the back of the new skin. Carefully align the skin and clamp it in position. Bend the hem flange over the inner flange. After bending, the hem seam can be spot welded or plug welded. Make certain that the welds penetrate to the inner panel or frame of the door.

After installing the new skin, prime and paint the exterior surface of the panel and attach all trim and hardware.

Top Panel Replacement

In some cases, the entire top panel of a vehicle must be replaced. Before replacing a top panel, it is important to verify that the basic body dimensions are within tolerance. These dimensions can be checked by taking triangular measurements as shown in Figure 11-10. If necessary, the new top panel can be used as a template to check for body distortion. Place the new panel over the damaged area before removing the damaged top panel. This will help determine if the structural components (pillars) and other panels are aligned properly. Structural misalignment must be repaired before replacing the top panel.

After making sure that the body is properly aligned, reposition the replacement panel over the damaged top and scribe a line along the edges of the panel. Remove the replacement panel and cut the old roof along the scribed lines. An abrasive grinding wheel is commonly used to cut through areas where the top is attached to the windshield pillars, center pillars, and rear pillars. The joints in these areas are MIG welded or arc-brazed at the factory. After removing the damaged top panel, align the new panel on the body and secure it with an occasional tack weld. Depending on the design, both butt joints and lap joints can be used when installing top panels. After the panel is tacked in position, check it again for proper alignment and MIG weld all joints. Remember, if a continuous weld is required, a series of connecting or overlapping stitch welds will help prevent heat distortion.

Sectioning Structural Components

Because much of a vehicle's body strength is provided by the rocker panels, pillars, rails, and floor pans, careful attention must be given when sectioning these components. Improper sectioning techniques will jeopardize the **structural integrity** of the vehicle.

Rocker panels, pillars, and body rails are constructed as **closed sections.** These components are often fabricated from two or more pieces. See Figure 11-11. Floor pans and trunk floors, on the other hand, are made of a single layer of metal.

Sectioning techniques for rocker panels, pillars, and rails are similar. A metal saw or an abrasive cutting disk is used to remove the damaged section. If possible, avoid cutting into anchor points or inner reinforcements. Suspension, seat belt, and shoulder belt anchor points should not be disturbed. They provide excellent points of measurement or reference. If the inner reinforcement layer of a pillar, rocker panel, or rail is not damaged, the outer layer can generally be replaced.

Sectioning Rocker Panels

When sectioning rocker panels, butt joints and **metal inserts** are used to help strengthen and secure the repair. If only the outer rocker panel skin is removed, the metal inserts can be plug welded in place before the new skin is installed. Be certain that the inserts allow the rocker panel skin to be positioned properly. When sectioning closed rocker panels, the inserts telescope (slide) into the joint areas. Once the inserts and the sectioned piece are in place, they can be secured temporarily with sheet metal screws. The screws will pull the inserts securely against the inside of the joints. Clean the joint edges and remove all burrs before welding. A weak joint will result if the pieces are not properly fused together. Plug weld both sides of each joint as illustrated in Figure 11-12. Finish the repair by MIG welding the butt joint. A small gap in the joint will ensure that the welds penetrate the inserts.

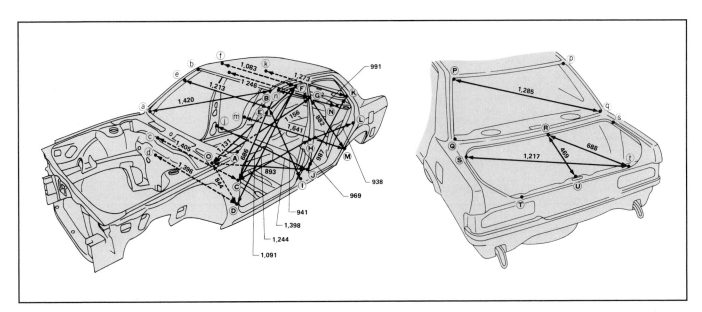

Figure 11-10   Vertical, horizontal, and diagonal measurements should be taken when checking for misalignment. The dimensions in this illustration are given in millimeters. (Nissan)

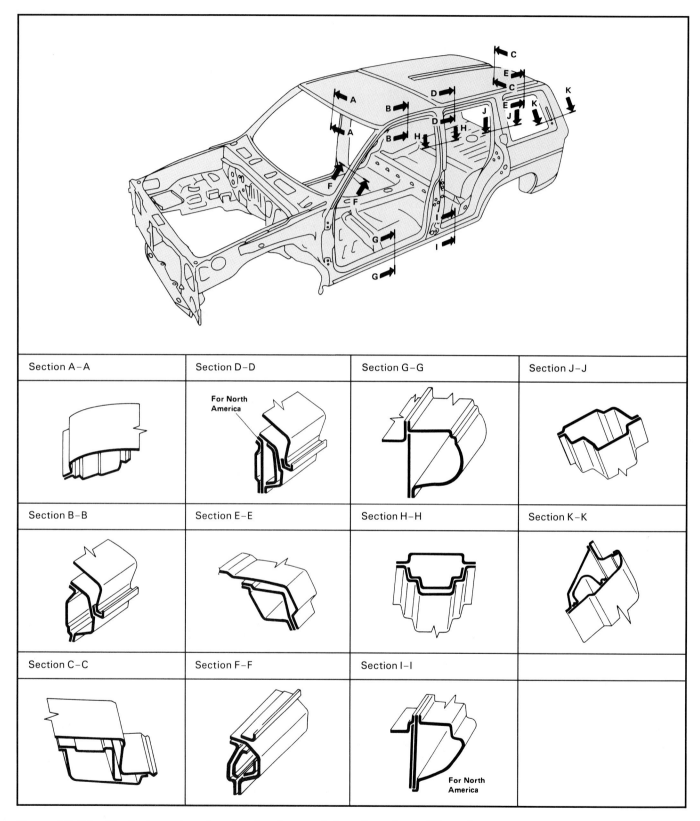

Figure 11-11   Typical construction details of several closed sections. (Nissan)

When using salvaged parts, make certain that all weld cuts are trimmed. Heat damage and corrosion will jeopardize the structural strength of the component.

When it is impossible to place an insert in a rocker panel or when only the outer section of a panel is re-placed, lap or offset butt joints are commonly used. See Figure 11-13. Screws or clamps can be used to hold the pieces in place during welding. It is advisable to treat the joint area with an antirust compound before and after welding. Self-etching primers or weld-through primers

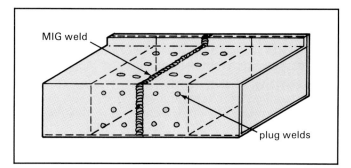

Figure 11-12 A butt joint and an insert are commonly used when sectioning structural components. Note the plug welds and the continuous MIG weld.

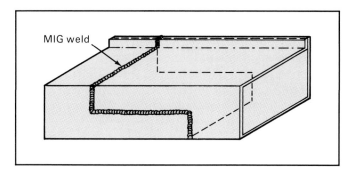

Figure 11-13 Offset butt joints are used when an insert cannot be used.

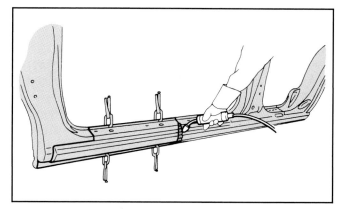

Figure 11-14 The outer sill is clamped in place during welding. (Nissan)

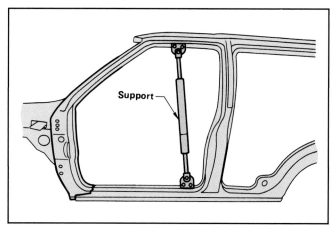

Figure 11-15 The roof should be supported before removing a damaged pillar. (Nissan)

are often used to provide a protective zinc coating in the weld zone. Short (1 in.) stitch MIG welds should be used to secure the joint. Overlapping welds are then used to fill and complete the joint. See Figure 11-14. Resistance spot welds can be used on some rocker panel flanges. Make certain that adequate penetration is made when applying spot welds.

Sectioning Pillars

As previously mentioned, sectioning techniques for forward (windshield or A-pillars), center (B-pillars), and rear pillars are similar to those used for rocker panels. Before removing a damaged pillar, support the roof to prevent additional damage, Figure 11-15. If possible, leave the factory joints when removing the damaged sections. Inserts and butt joints can be used to achieve strength when sectioning pillars. Offset butt joints can also be used.

The pillars in some late-model vehicles are filled with **polyurethane foam.** The foam adds strength, rigidity, and sound insulation. Special, two-part, foam-in-place kits are used to refill the pillar cavities. Some replacement pillars come with the foam already in place.

Little or none of the center pillar is exposed in late-model vehicles. Therefore, damage to this component is often overlooked during initial inspections. The center pillar adds rigidity to the body and functions as a lock and

hinge pillar. In some models, it also helps to support the roof. Offset butt, butt, and lap joints are commonly used when repairing center and rear pillars. Inserts can be added to increase strength and rigidity in the joints. If side damage is severe, the rocker panel and the center pillar can often be replaced as a unit.

Full-Body Sectioning

Full-body sectioning is performed when the rear portion of a vehicle has sustained severe damage. In this procedure, a salvaged rear half is joined to the undamaged front half. Severe damage to the front portion of a vehicle is generally beyond economical repair.

Floor pans and trunk floors must be sectioned with extreme care. Errors in this process may result in costly repairs and a hazardous (unsafe) vehicle. Never cut through reinforcements or anchor points when removing damaged sections. Label all mechanical and electrical connections for easy identification during reassembly. Remove the fuel tank when working on the trunk floor.

Lap joints or reinforced lap joints are used when sectioning floors. The rear section of the floor should overlap the front section. The sectioned pieces are temporarily held together with sheet metal screws. See Figure 11-16. All joints should be treated with antirust compounds before and after welding. Zinc-rich weld-through primers are a popular means controlling corrosion in weld joints.

When the sections are aligned properly, the lap joint (2 in. [50 mm]) should be plug welded. A stitch weld can then be made along the top and bottom side of the joint to secure the lap joint. The top joint is completed by overlapping and filling in between the stitch welds. To strengthen critical sections, sheet metal **reinforcement pieces** can be welded in place along the joint.

After the welds have been made, the joint areas should be cleaned, coated with rust-inhibitor, and primed. Seam sealer should be used along the joint before the topcoat is applied.

Replacing Sound-Deadening Materials

Various **sound-deadening materials** are used in most vehicles. A plastic-like material about 1/8 in. (3 mm) thick is frequently used on the inside surfaces of trunk cavities, door skins, or other panels. As previously mentioned, these materials must be removed before panel repairs are made. Repaired surfaces should be treated and painted before new sound-deadening materials are applied.

Replacement sound-deadening pads are often used. They are sold in tile-like squares and in rolls. Most sound-deadening pads are backed with a pressure-sensitive adhesive, which is covered by a peel-off backing. If necessary, a heat gun can be used to soften and shape the pads to ease installation.

Aligning and Adjusting Body Components

It is important for hoods, deck lids, bumpers, and other body components to fit properly. Unless correctly aligned, hoods, doors, and deck lids will not close properly. They may also leak, squeak, or rattle. Improper alignment of fenders and other components will cause an unsatisfactory appearance.

If panels (fenders, hood, cowl, doors, etc.) are not in proper alignment, adjustments must be made. While alignment procedures vary among manufacturers, most panels can be adjusted by one or more of the following: slotted holes, caged plate assemblies (floating anchor), adjustable stops, or shims. If necessary, hinges can be bent to achieve proper alignment.

Remember, before removing a hood, door, or deck lid, mark the hinge positions with a pen or a scribe. This will make it easier to reinstall the components.

Hinges and caged plate assemblies are usually manufactured with elongated holes that permit adjustment. **Caged plate assemblies** are used on the inside of doors or door pillars. A sheet metal "cage" is spot welded to the inside of the door or the pillar. This cage holds a threaded (tapped) plate, which accepts hinge bolts, striker bolts, etc. The plate is moved in the cage during adjustment. See Figure 11-17.

The position of latches and some panels can be adjusted by adding or removing shims. Hoods and some doors have adjustable stops, which help to align and hold the components in place. If there is insufficient adjustment, brackets, hinge arms, or attachment points can be bent to achieve proper alignment. Bending should only be attempted if all other alignment methods fail.

For correct installation of hoods, doors, and deck lids, the **clearance** between these panels and adjacent panels should be equal on both sides of the vehicle, Figure 11-18. Clearance between panels should generally be about 5/32 in. (4 mm). Gaps between fenders and

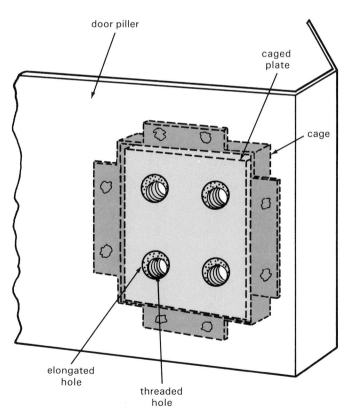

Figure 11-17 Typical caged plate assembly. The plate is pulled against the outer panel when the bolts are tightened.

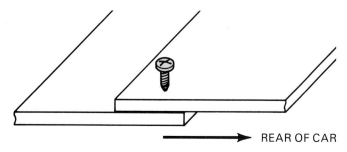

REAR OF CAR

Figure 11-16 A lap joint is temporarily held together with mechanical fasteners before welds are made.

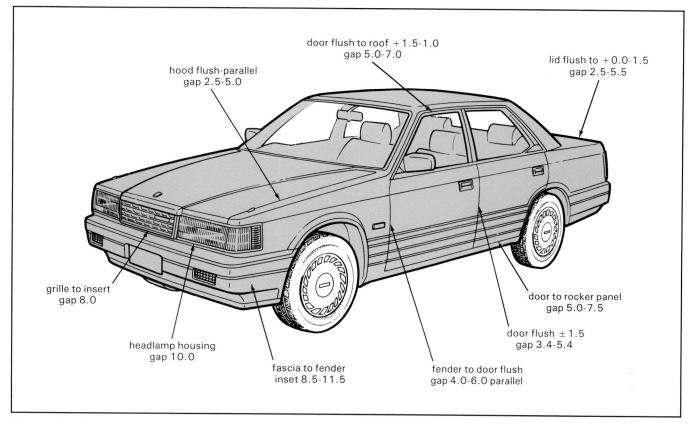

Figure 11-18   Typical body component clearances.

doors should be less then 1/4 in. (6 mm). The surface of each panel should be flush with the adjacent panels or the cowling. Always use care when aligning components. Painted edges can be accidentally chipped when shifting a component. Some shops place a layer of masking tape along cowl, fender, or door edges before making adjustments. This practice provides limited protection against chipping.

Bumper Adjustments

Prior to 1972, most bumpers were simply bolted to the frame using several bumper braces (irons). These bumpers were designed to protect the vehicle from front and rear damage. Modern bumpers (impact-absorbing bumpers), on the other hand, are designed to absorb energy from impact and to help protect the vehicle's occupants from injury.

If necessary, most damaged metal bumpers (steel or aluminum) can be straightened. Painted metal bumpers are sometimes straightened in a hydraulic press, and small dents are filled with an appropriate filler. Chrome-plated bumpers, on the other hand, are often replaced with new or reconditioned components. Specialty shops straighten and rechrome many automotive parts. The minor repair of polyurethane-covered bumpers was discussed in Chapter 9.

Some vehicles have ***adjusting slots*** on the mounting brackets and the bumper shock absorbers. Cars with

metal and rubber impact-absorbing isolators have both adjusting slots and shear bolts. Impact-absorbing bumpers must be adjusted for safety protection and proper appearance. See Figure 11-19.

Bumper adjustment is normally a two-person job. One person holds the bumper in place, while the other person tightens the bolts. When initially installing the bumper, tighten the bolts partially to allow for adjustment. Check each corner to make sure that alignment, clearance, and height are equal. There should be an even gap around the top edge of the bumper when it is properly aligned. Once the bumper is properly adjusted, completely tighten all of the bolts. After the bolts are tightened, recheck the alignment. In some cases, the alignment will change as the bolts are tightened.

Hood Adjustments

Because hoods are relatively large, misalignment is quite obvious. The spacing along the front of the hood, the fenders, and the cowl must be even. Adjustments can be made at the hinges, the adjustable stops, and the hood latch.

Slots in the hinges permit the hood to be moved back and forth and from right to left. Before adjusting a hood, scribe a reference line along the edge of each hinge flange. Loosen the hinge-to-hood bolts and shift the hood from the scribed line as required. The rear height of a hood can be adjusted using shims that fit between the

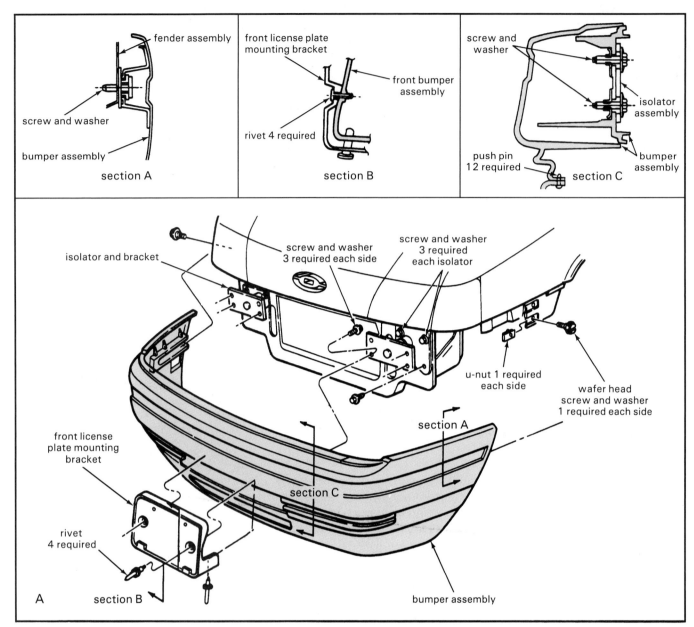

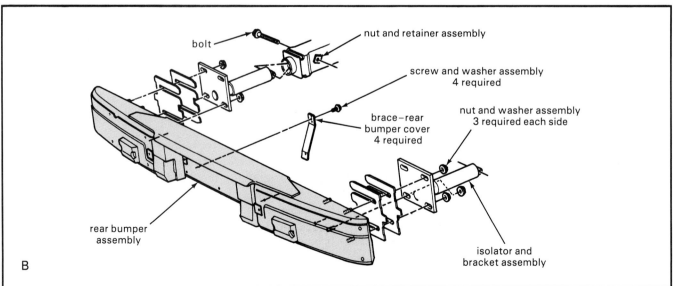

Figure 11-19 A–Typical front bumper assembly. B–One type of rear bumper assembly. (Ford)

hood and the hinge. Removing or adding *shims* will shift the rear of the hood up or down. If the rear of the hood flutters, there may not be enough tension at the rear portion of the hinge. To increase tension, add shims or washers between the hood and the front hinge bolts. The torsion bars, hood springs, or gas-filled lift assemblies may require adjustment or replacement if they do not hold the hood open.

Some hood hinges are welded to the cowl. If these hinges are bent or damaged, they must be replaced. The procedure for replacing welded hood hinges is similar to the procedure for replacing welded door hinges.

Adjustable *rubber stops* are used to make minor alignment adjustments and to keep the hood from fluttering or squeaking. The front height of the hood is determined by the position of two adjustable rubber stops, Figure 11-20. If the hood latch is improperly adjusted, the front of the hood may not contact these stops. Be careful when adjusting rubber stops. If the stops are set too high, the hood or the hinges may be bent out of shape. Always lower the hood carefully when making any adjustment.

On most hoods, the hinges are located at cowl and the latch assembly is attached to the radiator core support. In a few hood designs, the hinges are attached to the radiator support and the latch is located on the cowl. All hoods have a latch assembly, a safety catch, and a striker bar. Both the latch assembly and the striker bar (underside of hood) are adjustable. The adjustment procedure for most latch assemblies and striker bars is to loosen the striker bar mounting bolts until they are finger tight. Slowly close the hood, making certain that the striker bar enters the latch. As the bar enters the latch, it should shift into the correct position. Open the hood carefully and tighten all of the bolts. If the hood must be slammed to latch, slightly raise the latch assembly or lower the striker bar until the hood closes properly.

Deck Lid Adjustments

Although deck lids (trunk compartment lids) fit like most hoods, they must seal properly around the trunk opening. A weatherstrip is used around the trunk opening to prevent air, dirt, and water from entering the trunk compartment. Some deck lids have adjustable hinges and torsion bars, while others have welded hinges and springs or gas-filled lift assemblies.

The three major points of adjustment for deck lids include the hinges, the torsion bars, and the latch.

To adjust the deck lid forward or backward and from side to side in the trunk opening, loosen the hinge bolts and shift the lid into the proper position. Up or down deck lid adjustment is made by using shims between the deck lid and the hinges. To raise the front edge of the lid, place shims between lid and forward portion of one or both hinges. To lower the front edge of the lid, place the shim(s) between the lid and the back (rearward) portion of one or both hinges. On models with welded hinges or

Figure 11-20 Adjustable hood stop.

on designs that do not permit sufficient shim or hole adjustment, the hinges may be bent slightly to achieve proper alignment.

Torsion bars are designed to hold the deck lid open. These bars are twisted when the lid is closed, providing the spring tension necessary to ''pop'' the lid open when the latch is released. If the lid does not remain open, both torsion bars may need adjustment. This is done by moving the torsion bar ends to different holes or slots in the hinge support brackets. See Figure 11-21.

WARNING: Use extreme care when moving torsion bars. They are usually under tension and may spring loose, causing injury.

The latch and striker assemblies can be used to make minor deck lid adjustments. Adjustable rubber stops are used on a few deck lid designs. Adjustments to these assemblies are similar to adjustments made to hood latches and rubber stops.

Fender Adjustments

On most vehicles, only the front fenders are adjustable. The front section of most fenders is bolted to the radiator core support. Several bolts are used to hold the inner and outer fender panels together. Bolts at the upper and lower portion of the cowl hold the fenders in alignment. As previously mentioned, most bolt holes (fender and bracket) are slotted to allow for adjustment. See Figure 11-22.

If there is insufficient (slot) adjustment in fenders, door hinges, radiator core supports, etc., it is sometimes necessary to make adjustments to the front door and the front fender at the same time. A fender can be shifted forward or backward to increase or reduce the amount of

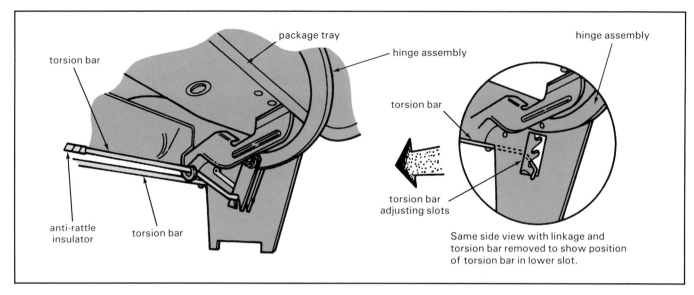

Figure 11-21 Torsion bars are often used to hold deck lids open. The tension can be adjusted by moving the end of the bar to a different slot. (Ford)

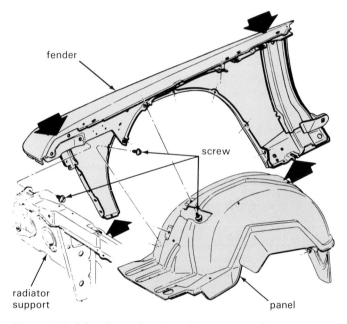

Figure 11-22 Front fender adjustment points for one particular vehicle.

clearance between the door and an adjacent fender. All fender bolts and cap screws must be loose when adjusting a fender. It may be necessary to push the radiator core support forward when making adjustments. This support holds the hood lock brace and the radiator components in place. It also holds the fenders apart. In modern unibody construction, some components of the radiator support are welded together to increase body strength.   After loosening the support bolts and the fender bolts, push the support forward with a power jack. A wooden spreader can be placed on the cowl as the jack pushes on the support. The wooden spreader is simply a board that helps distribute the force being

exerted against the cowl and reduces the possibility of denting or scratching the painted cowl surface. When the fender is properly positioned, tighten the fender bolts and cap screws. After the bolts have been tightened, recheck the alignment.

Shims can be added or removed as needed for minor fender alignment. In-and-out adjustment of the lower rear edge of the fender is accomplished by adding shims at the fender-to-cowl attaching bolts. If the front end of the fender is too high or too low, spacing will be uneven between the fender and door. When this occurs, it is necessary to add or remove shims at the front support locations. Before adding or removing shims at the front supports, the lower rear attachment bolts and the inner panel bolts must be loosened.

Door Adjustments

It is important to adjust doors properly. When doors are not adjusted correctly, they are difficult to close and may rattle or leak.

When doors are properly adjusted, the clearance on the bottom edge should be about 1/4 in. (6 mm). The surrounding frame gap should be about 5/32 in. (4 mm).

Front and rear doors are adjusted in a similar fashion. Both are held in the body opening by hinges and latches. Latches hold on to a striker bolt or plate, which is located on a pillar (or the cowl). Weatherstrips are used around the doors to prevent water, air, and dust from entering the passenger compartment. They also help prevent rattles from metal-to-metal contact.

Because rear quarter panels or fenders are not adjustable, the rear doors (on four-door models) should be adjusted first. Hardtop doors should be adjusted to fit the body contours. The unframed glass can then be adjusted until it rests against the soft rubber gasket at the top of the door opening. Use caution when adjusting hardtop doors. The glass in these doors is not protected by a frame and may be easily broken.

Hinges can be bolted or welded to either the door, the cowl, or the pillar. Most doors can be adjusted at the hinges. Some hinge bolts are only accessible with a specially shaped wrench.

It is sometimes advisable to remove the striker plate or bolt when adjusting doors. This reduces interference when attempting to center the door in the body opening.

If doors and bolted hinges are to be removed from the pillars (or cowling), mark the original hinge locations on the door and the hinge pillar. On bodies equipped with electrically operated windows, the interior door trim assembly and the water deflector must be removed. Disconnect the wiring from the motor. Remove the conduit from the door and the wiring harness from between the door panels. With the door properly supported, remove the bolts securing the upper and lower hinges and remove the door from the body. To reinstall the door,

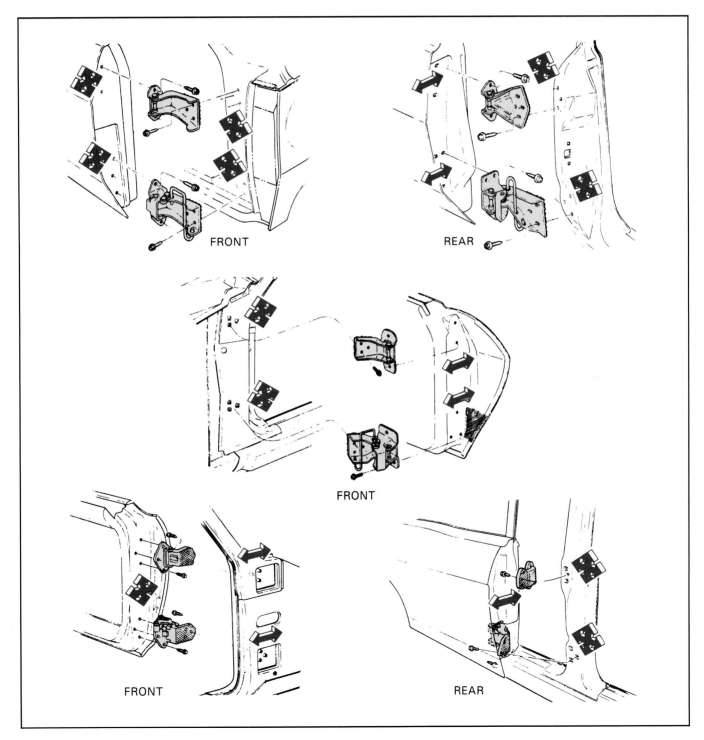

Figure 11-23 Typical front and rear door hinge installation. (Ford)

reverse this procedure. It is good practice to clean off old sealing compound at the hinge attaching areas and to apply a coat of body sealer to hinge straps. A hydraulic floor jack can be used to support the door and aid in adjustments. Align the hinge straps with the scribe marks on the pillar or cowl and tighten the hinge bolts. After the bolts are tightened, recheck the door for proper alignment.

In-and-out adjustments are usually provided on the door hinge. Fore-and-aft and up-and-down adjustments are made at the body pillars or at the cowl. When performing in-and-out or fore-and-aft adjustments, adjust one hinge at a time so that the up-and-down adjustment is maintained. To help prevent wind noise between the front fender and the door, it is best to adjust the leading edge of the door so that it is positioned slightly below the edge of the fender. Shims can be used to move the door in or out as desired. See Figure 11-23.

A hinge pin allows the removal of a door with welded hinges. In some cases, the hinges or attachment points on the cowling or pillars can be bent slightly to provide adjustment. A floor jack can be used to help lift a sagging door. If necessary, a power ram can be used to push the cowl or pillar slightly. A block of wood can be placed near the hinge, and the door can be forced partially closed. This may bend the hinges in the desired manner, allowing proper alignment.

If welded hinges must be removed, remove the retaining rings or pins from the lower and upper hinge pins. Disengage the door hold-open spring by prying upward against the spring.

WARNING: Cover the hinge with a towel to prevent injury when the spring is released.

Drive a wedge between head of the hinge pin and the hinge. This will raise the pin enough to force the shoulder out of the hinge. Support the door at the rear edge, remove the loosened hinge pins, and remove the door. Mark the outline of the hinge on the door by drilling a few small holes around the perimeter of the welded hinge. Center punch the spot welds, Figure 11-24, and drill a 1/8 in. (3 mm) hole through each weld. These holes can then be used as pilot holes when drilling through the hinges with a spot cutter bit. A spot cutter bit only penetrates the hinge base, not the door. If necessary, a grinder can be used to cut through continuous welds on hinge straps. Be careful to cut only through the welds and not the door or the body. After the welds are cut, the hinge can be removed from the door.

The hinge location should be ground smooth to remove metal burrs or old welds. After grinding, a new hinge strap can be installed. Sheet metal screws or tack welds can be used to temporarily hold the hinge strap in place until a continuous MIG weld is made around the strap.

Before removing body side hinge straps, make certain the hinge position is clearly marked (drill holes if necessary). Remove the hinge straps as previously described. Once the old hinges are removed, grind the hinge locations smooth. Tack weld the new hinges in place and gently rehang the door to make certain that the hinge straps are aligned properly. If the alignment is correct, remove the door and complete the MIG welds around hinge straps. It is best to refinish the repair area before installing the door. With the door in place, install the hinge pins and retaining rings. A special spring compressing tool may be used to reinstall the hinge spring.

Striker Adjustments

The *striker pin* (bolt) can be adjusted laterally (in and out) and vertically (up and down), as well as fore and aft. A caged plate moves with the striker until it is tight.

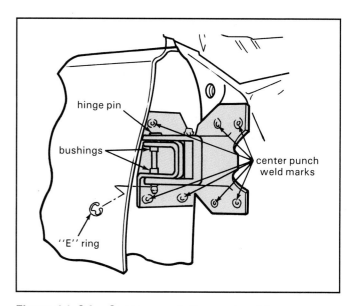

Figure 11-24 Center punch the spot welds before drilling pilot holes.

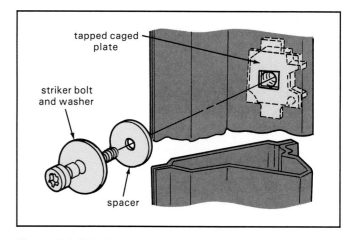

Figure 11-25 Typical door striker assembly. Note that the caged plate assembly is shown.

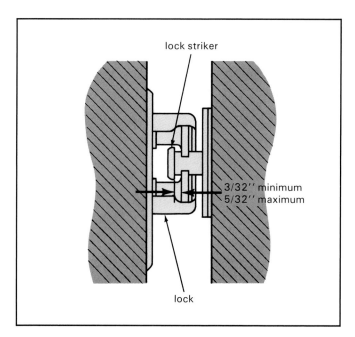

Figure 11-26 Proper door lock striker adjustment for a specific vehicle. (Ford)

When adjusting the striker, it should be shimmed to achieve the proper clearance as shown in Figure 11-25. Fore-and-aft adjustment is made by adding or removing shims between the striker and the post. Move the striker assembly laterally to provide a flush fit at the door and the pillar or quarter panel. When adjusted properly, the striker should lift the door slightly. However, the striker should never be used to correct door sag. A properly adjusted striker is illustrated in Figure 11-26.

The door latch assembly is designed to allow the door to be opened, closed, and locked. A mechanical or an electronic locking device is attached to the door latch. The latch assembly is generally not adjustable. See Chapter 12 for information on servicing latches.

Summary

Panels that are severely damaged are often replaced. The decision of whether to repair or replace a panel depends on the extent and the location of the damage. It is often less expensive to replace a panel than to repair it.

When a complete panel is replaced, the damaged panel should be roughly shaped before it is removed. This will ensure that the inner panels are in approximate position to receive the replacement panel. In some cases, only the damaged portion of a panel is replaced. This type of repair is called sectioning.

On many vehicles, the front fenders are bolted to the rest of the structure. All wiring must be disconnected before removing a fender from a vehicle. Installing a new front fender is not difficult if the rest of the body is undamaged.

Rear fenders are generally welded to the body structure. The rear fenders on modern vehicles must be repaired carefully to restore a vehicle's structural integrity. Always follow the manufacturer's recommendations when repairing or replacing structural panels.

A severely damaged door panel is often replaced if the inner panel is not extensively damaged. Outer door panels are called door skins.

In some cases, the entire top panel of a vehicle is replaced. Before removing the damaged panel, use the replacement panel as a template to check for distortion. Structural misalignment must be repaired before replacing the top panel.

Much of a vehicle's body strength is provided by the floor pan, rocker panels, pillars, and rails. Therefore, care must be taken when sectioning these components. Improper sectioning techniques will jeopardize the structural integrity of the vehicle.

After panels are replaced, sound deadening insulation must be restored. Repaired surfaces should be treated and painted before new sound deadening materials are applied.

Unless correctly aligned, hoods, deck lids, and doors will not close properly. Additionally, they may leak, squeak, or rattle. Improper fender alignment will cause an unsatisfactory appearance. When panels are not aligned properly, they must be adjusted. Adjustment procedures vary among manufacturers. However, most panels have slotted holes, caged plate assemblies, adjustable stops, or shims to aid in adjustment. If necessary, hinges can be bent to achieve proper alignment.

Know These Terms

Replacement panels, Spot cutter bit, Clamp saw, Sectioning, Pneumatic flange tool, Panel crimper, Door skins, Hem flange, Hem seam, Hemming tool, Structural integrity, Closed sections, Metal inserts, Polyurethane foam, Full-body sectioning, Reinforcement pieces, Sound-deadening materials, Caged plate assemblies, Clearance, Adjusting slots, Shims, Rubber stops, Torsion bars, Striker pin.

Review Questions–Chapter 11

1. It is always less expensive to repair a panel than to replace it. True or False?

2. To prevent _____ when replacing a panel, spot welds should initially be placed at 3-4 in. intervals.

3. Replacing only the damaged area of a panel is called _____.

4. Before removing a damaged panel, it should be roughly shaped so that the inner panels are in position to receive the new panel. True or False?

5. When sectioning, the replacement panel should be approximately _____ in. larger than the damaged area.
    a. 1
    b. 6
    c. 2
    d. 8

6. The front fenders on many vehicles are _____ to the rest of the body structure.

7. A grinder should be used to remove welds on structural panels. True or False?

8. Most rear fenders are _____ to the body structure.

9. The _____ fenders on many unibody vehicles add to the structural integrity of the vehicle.

10. The outer panel on a door is called the:
    a. cover.
    b. skin.
    c. wrapper.
    d. none of the above.

11. A damaged top panel should always be replaced before repairing structural misalignment. True or False?

12. Improper sectioning of rocker panels, pillars, rails and floor plans may jeopardize the _____ _____ of a vehicle.

13. A metal _____ is used when sectioning rocker panels to help strengthen the repair.

14. When sectioning pillars, the damaged components should be removed at the factory joints. True or False?

15. The pillars in many late-model vehicles are filled with:
    a. fiberglass beads.
    b. polyurethane foam.
    c. compressed air.
    d. none of the above.

16. Full-body sectioning is performed when the front portion of a vehicle is severely damaged. True or False?

17. When sectioning a trunk floor, the _____ _____ must be removed.

18. Repaired surfaces should be treated and _____ before sound deadening materials are applied.

19. Improperly aligned hoods, doors, or deck lids will often _____, _____ or _____.

20. Before removing a hood, the hinge positions should be marked with a scribe. True or False?

21. Bumpers on late-model vehicles are designed to _____ energy.

22. It is hard to determine if a hood is misaligned. True or False?

23. Hoods are generally adjusted at the:
    a. hinges.
    b. adjustable stops.
    c. latch.
    d. all of the above.

24. _____ is used around trunk openings to prevent the entry of air, dirt, and water.

25. Torsion bars are not adjustable. True or False?

26. The _____ fenders are adjustable on most vehicles.

27. The rear doors on four-door vehicles should be adjusted _____.

28. The striker plate should never be removed when making door adjustments. True or False?

29. In-and-out adjustments are generally made at the door _____.

30. Extreme care must be taken when adjusting welded hinges. True or False?

Activities—Chapter 11

1. Contact either a body shop or an insurance adjuster and explain that you are a student gathering information for a class. Obtain the cost of an OEM (Original Equipment Manufacturer) replacement left front fender for a three-year-old automobile (your choice of make and model). Also obtain the cost of an aftermarket (third-party) replacement. Next, contact a salvage yard and obtain the cost for the same part salvaged from a wrecked vehicle. Compare the costs and show the results of your research on a horizontal bar graph. For extra credit, write a short report on the reasons for and against using each type of part (this may take some more research).

2. Use a video camera to record the steps involved in removing a damaged door skin and installing a new one. Narrate the work, step-by-step, and show the finished video to the class.

3. Measure the gap between hood and fender of a car, on both sides, at the front edge of the hood. If the gaps are not of equal size, determine how much adjustment will be needed. (Subtract the smaller number from the larger, then divide by 2. This is the amount the hood must move toward the side with the larger gap.) Make the adjustment and re-measure. Continue to adjust until the gaps are equal in width.

chapter 12

Repairing and Replacing Miscellaneous Components

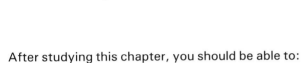

After studying this chapter, you should be able to:

☐ Explain the installation procedures for various types of automotive trim.

☐ Repair holes and tears in automotive carpet.

☐ Differentiate between cloth headlining and molded headlining.

☐ Describe the techniques for repairing and replacing vinyl roof coverings.

☐ Locate and repair leaks in sealers and weatherstripping.

Introduction

After repairing sheet metal or plastic panels, the auto body technician must repair or replace trim, glass, weatherstripping, carpet, vinyl tops, insulation, and other miscellaneous items.

The repair and replacement processes for any component will vary with the make, model, and year of the vehicle at hand. Therefore, only general suggestions can be given in this chapter.

Much of the work performed on components other than the chassis and the body panels is service or maintenance oriented. The technician should check window regulators, locks, latches, etc., for proper operation. Lubricating and cooling fluids should be restored to their proper level. Safety and emission features must be repaired before returning a vehicle to the customer.

Preventive measures must be taken in the body shop. Every effort should be made to avoid causing additional damage when making repairs. Upholstery, carpet, and other components should be covered to protect them from grease, solvents, and overspray. When pushing out damaged areas, do not place the body jack against trim, step plates, carpet, etc. Protect finished panels and other components from being scratched by sharp objects or damaged by heat, sparks, or solvents.

Trim

Interior and exterior automotive *trim* is used to add strength, insulate, identify a model, deaden sound, conceal joints, finish or protect edges, and beautify. Interior trim pieces are sometimes called *garnish moldings.* Exterior trim pieces that accent glass openings are called *reveal moldings.* The terms garnish and reveal are used loosely by manufacturers. A few manufacturers refer to both inner and outer moldings as garnish moldings or simply as moldings.

Automotive trim is made from a variety of materials, including stainless steel, aluminum, plastic, metal, rubber, and fabric.

Stainless steel is very durable and can be polished to a high-gloss finish. Drip rail moldings, wheel opening moldings, side moldings, and reveal moldings are often made of stainless steel. Exterior trim moldings are sometimes referred to as ''chrome.'' This term stems from a time when nearly all trim moldings were made of chrome-plated steel.

Aluminum trim has replaced many chrome-plated steel and stainless steel trim parts. Aluminum is lighter and less expensive than steel. It can be die-cast into emblems, letters, and doorknobs; stamped into step plates and raised moldings; and extruded into side moldings and other components. Additionally, aluminum can be polished to a chrome-like finish.

Plastics are now being used extensively in the manufacture of automotive trim. There are several advantages to using plastics for trim pieces, including the following:

- Plastics can be made into flexible parts.
- Plastics can be molded into various shapes.
- Plastics are lighter than most metals.
- Plastics will not rust.
- Plastics can be molded in nearly any color.

Additionally, plastics can be made to simulate chrome-plated items. Some plastics are molded into soft

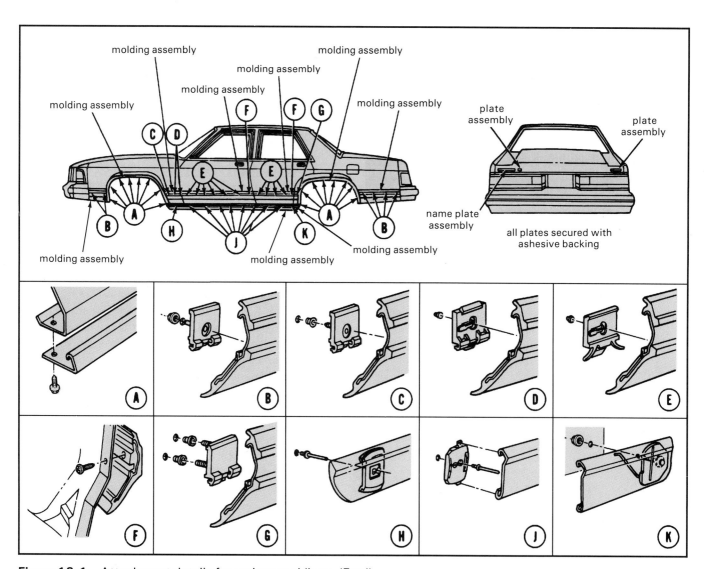

Figure 12-1   Attachment details for various moldings. (Ford)

(cellular or rubber-like material) trim panels, while others are formed into grilles, bumpers, knobs, and moldings. **Wood-grain transfer films** are used to simulate wood. They are often used on the sides of mini-vans and station wagons. **Decals** (decalcomanias) and **accent stripes** are used on many vehicles to add a decorative, customized look. See Chapter 20 for more information on custom work.

Screws, bolts, retaining clips, molded studs, retainer inserts, and adhesives are commonly used to attach trim pieces to body panels. Some trim pieces are self-locking and are designed to snap-fit when forced into position. See Figure 12-1.

It is often necessary to remove exterior and/or interior trim when repairing panels, replacing glass, or working on door mechanisms. Repairing trim pieces is generally difficult and time consuming. Therefore, most damaged trim pieces are replaced.

Exterior Trim

Many auto body repairs require the replacement of **exterior trim pieces.** After body repairs have been made, it is advisable to carefully mark the location of exterior trim pieces that require the drilling of holes. The holes should be drilled before the paint is applied. This will prevent marring of the final finish. *Paper templates* can be used to transfer the location of trim pieces from an old panel to a new panel.

Moldings must be installed accurately. Carefully lay out each molding location. A measuring rule, tape measure, or magnetic tape can be used to help determine the proper location. A vehicle should be parked on a level surface when measuring and marking trim locations. Many moldings follow ridge lines on fenders and other panels. If necessary, the location of trim pieces can be compared from one side of the vehicle to the other. Masking tape or a marking pen can be used to mark the molding position. Care should be taken when using masking tape. Fresh paint can be damaged when the tape is removed. Do not permanently install clips and moldings until after final finish has cured for at least 24 hours.

When replacing **adhesive-backed moldings,** the surface of the panel must be free of dirt, oil, wax, and silicone. Thoroughly clean the area with water and detergent to remove dirt and road grime. A cloth dampened with enamel thinner can be used to remove waxes and silicones. Prep-Sol, Acryli-Clean, or a general-purpose adhesive and wax remover can also be used for this task. The panel surface should be at least 70 °F (20 °C) to ensure proper adhesion.

To install adhesive-backed molding, peel about 10 in. (300 mm) of the protective backing from the molding and align it with the marks on the panel. Begin at an edge joint and press the molding gently against the panel. Repeat this process for the remaining molding. After the molding is applied, firmly press it against the body panel.

If necessary, a brayer can be used to help press the molding against the panel. It may take several days for the molding's adhesive to develop full bond strength.

Vinyl or plastic door moldings should be beveled at 45° and cut about 1/8 in. (2 mm) from the edge of the panel. This will allow for adequate clearance and prevent the end of the molding from catching on objects. Fender moldings should also be cut about 1/8 in. (2 mm) from the edge of the panel.

Track moldings, which consist of a metal track and a plastic insert, are used on some vehicles. See Figure 12-2. Some metal tracks have adhesive backings; others are riveted in place. If adhesive-backed tracks are to be installed, follow the preparation procedure outlined previously. To install rivet-on tracks, drill the rivet holes with the track in position. Place one rivet about 3/4 in. from each end of the track. Be sure to leave sufficient clearance on both ends of the track for end caps or spears. After attaching the track to the body, place the molding in the track and install the end caps (or spears).

Exterior Handles

Three basic types of **exterior door handles** have been used on the automobile: lift-bar handles, pull-out handles, and push-button handles. Screws are commonly used to attach all three types. Some pull-out handles use nuts (on handle studs) to fasten the handle to the latch mechanism. See Figure 12-3. Push-button handles are commonly secured with a metal retaining clip.

Most cars do not have handle mechanisms for the trunk or the hatch. Key- and/or power-operated **latch assemblies** are generally used on these components. The switch for power-operated latch assemblies is commonly located on the dash, in the storage compartment (glove box), or on the floor next to the driver's seat. An

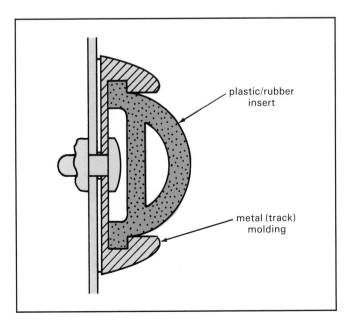

Figure 12-2 Typical track molding detail.

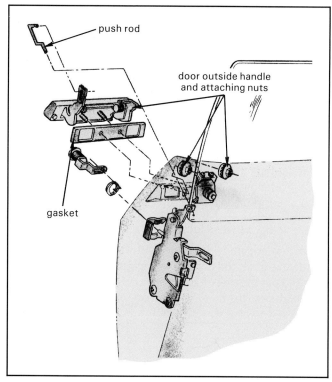

A

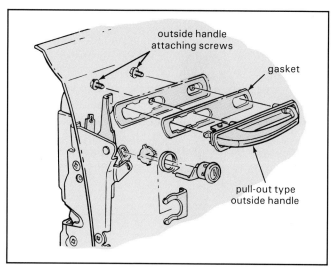

B

Figure 12-3   Exterior door handles. A–Lift-bar handle. B–Pull-out handle.

electric solenoid is often used to trigger power-operated latch assemblies. This solenoid is bolted to the inside of the hatch door or deck lid and is connected to the latch assembly with a control rod.

Exterior Locks

There are many types of locking mechanisms used on automobiles. In this text, the word *lock* is used to describe the mechanisms that prevent a latch assembly from operating. Locks may include mechanical stops, keyed cylinders, or electronic systems. The word lock is commonly used in technical literature to refer to the entire latch assembly. See Figure 12-4.

Exterior locks can be operated mechanically or electrically. These locks are used on front doors and on trunk lids or hatches. Rear doors are not equipped with exterior locks.

The *lock cylinder* is operated with a key in mechanical lock systems. A spring *retaining clip* is normally used to secure the cylinder to the door panel. See Figure 12-5. The clip can be removed by sliding it forward with the blade of a screwdriver. Most retaining clips are accessed through a large access hole in the door's inner panel. On some models, it is necessary to remove the window glass in order to access the retaining clip. A gasket seal is commonly used between the lock cylinder and door skin to keep moisture and dust from entering the door from around the cylinder. *Extension rods* or arms are used to connect the cylinder to the locking mechanism on the door latch assembly. Always make certain that the extension rod engages with the latch assembly properly and that the latch assembly and cylinder are lubricated. Lock cylinders are commonly lubricated with graphite.

When a new lock cylinder is installed, its tumblers must be set to match the tumblers in the original cylinder. If this is not done, the new cylinder will not operate with the same key as the original cylinder.

Keyless lock systems are becoming increasingly popular. In a typical system, a five-button key pad is located on the driver's door. When the proper combination (a predetermined sequence of digits) is entered into the keypad, an electrically operated locking mechanism

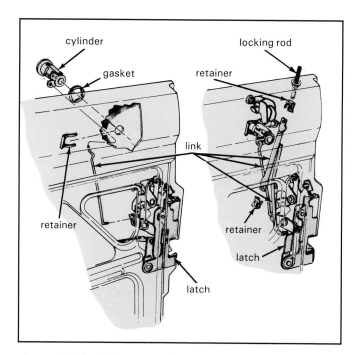

Figure 12-4   This type of door lock is used on many vehicles. (Chrysler)

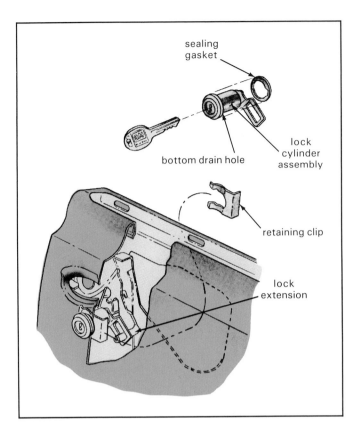

Figure 12-5 Typical lock cylinder assembly. Note the retainer, which is used to hold the cylinder in place. (General Motors)

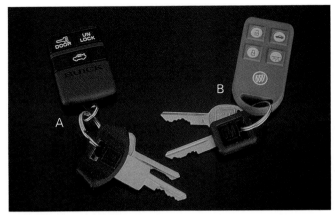

Figure 12-6 Keyless lock transmitters are common on many late-model vehicles. A–Transmitter operates door locks. B–Transmitter operates door locks, activates interior lights, and releases trunk lid.

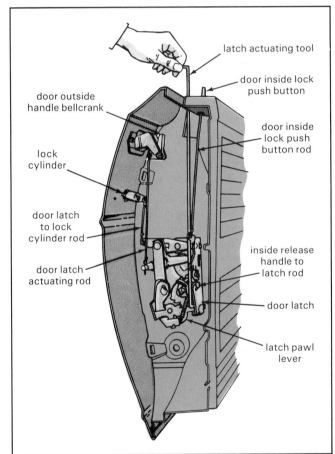

Figure 12-7 Using a special lock-out tool to release a door latch. (Chrysler)

(solenoid and relay) will release. Some keyless lock systems can be programmed to turn on the interior lights or unlock all of the doors when a specific code is entered.

The most popular keyless lock systems are the ***transmitter/receiver lock systems.*** In these systems, a signal is sent from a small, key ring transmitter to a receiver located in the door. When the receiver receives the signal, it activates the locking mechanism and unlocks the driver's door. Some systems are designed to activate the interior lights and release the trunk lid. See Figure 12-6. Most transmitters have a range of approximately 30 ft. (10 m). Low transmitter voltage is a common problem with these systems. The battery in the transmitter should be replaced regularly.

Emergency Opening Procedures.   If a door latch is inoperative or the keys are lost, various ***lock-out tools*** can be used to open the door. A piece of 1/8 in. (3 mm) welding rod can sometimes be used to reach interior lock buttons or door handles. The rod is simply pushed between the weatherstripping and the glass or between the weatherstripping and the door opening. A piece of wire or a narrow metal band (strip) can often be used to reach the latch assembly or locking pawl lever. See Figure 12-7. The pawl lever is the pivoted tongue or sliding bolt on the lock cylinder. Although doors with power locks can be opened in a similar manner, care must be taken to prevent pulling off or loosening electrical connections.

Interior Trim

Interior trim includes all the components and hardware that make up the interior of a vehicle, including vinyl- or fabric-covered trim panels, seats, visors, armrests, kick panels, and headliners. The pillar trim (the fabric, vinyl, or molded plastic panel that covers the center post), parcel shelf, floor covering, floor console, dash, floor-pan insulators, and garnish moldings are also considered interior trim components.

Interior trim hardware includes side mirror controls, door and window handles, lock buttons, seat belts, clothes hangers, dome lights, rearview mirrors, and scuff (step) plates. Scuff plates are the metal or plastic plates that cover the door sill openings.

Interior Handles

Before removing a door's interior trim assembly, it is generally necessary to remove the mirror controls, lock buttons, and inside door and window handles. Special tools are needed to remove retaining clips from handles and to remove bezel nuts from some mirror controls.

Many door and window handles are held in place with a retaining clip. In some cases, the clip is exposed when the armrest is removed. In many cases, however, it is hidden by the base of the handle. Hidden clips are disengaged by depressing the door trim assembly and inserting a forked tool between the handle and the bearing plate. See Figure 12-8. The **bearing plate** (escutcheon plate) is a plastic spacer that reduces friction between the door handle and the trim panel. This helps to prevent damage from the continuous use of the handle.

Some handles are held in place with a screw. Although the screw is exposed in a few designs, it is hidden by a cover plate in most cases. The cover plate is generally held in place by short tabs. Some cover plates are cemented in place. These plates must be pried loose to access the screw and must be recemented when reinstalled.

On late-model vehicles, pull-type handles are generally used as interior door handles. All mechanical-type door handles rely on a *control mechanism* to operate the door latch assembly. See Figure 12-9. The control mechanism is attached to the door with screws, bolts, or rivets. It is connected to the latch assembly with extension rods or links.

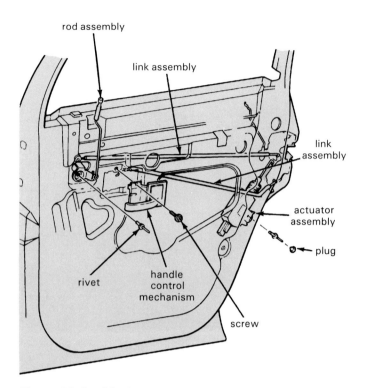

Figure 12-9 Mechanical door handle control mechanism and related assemblies. (Ford)

Interior Locks

Interior locks can be powered mechanically or electrically. A mechanical knob or button is commonly used for interior locks. The knob is attached to a rod, which is connected to the lock portion of the latch assembly. Pushing or pulling the knob activates or deactivates the lock portion of the latch. *Power lock systems* are equipped with electric solenoids, which push or pull a rod that is attached to the locking mechanism. There are numerous combinations of locking features available on late-model vehicles equipped with power locks. On most models, the driver's lock switch can be used to control all door locks.

Interior Door Trim Assemblies

The procedures for removing **interior door trim assemblies** vary. See Figure 12-10. In some cases, armrests must be removed before the door trim assembly can be removed. Some armrests are attached to doors with screws that are located on the underside of the armrest. In many designs, however, the armrest is an integral part of the door trim panel.

There are two basic types of door trim assemblies used in vehicles today: one-piece trim assemblies and two-piece trim assemblies, Figure 12-11. A one-piece trim assembly generally hangs over the top of the door's inner panel and is secured to the door with clips or other mechanical fasteners.

A two-piece trim assembly consists of an upper section and a lower section. The upper section hangs over

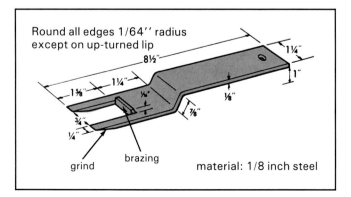

Figure 12-8 Detail of a tool for removing door and window regulator handles.

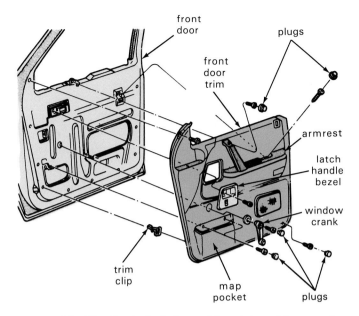

Figure 12-10 Exploded view of front door trim panel and related hardware. (Chrysler)

the top of the door's inner panel and is fastened with trim clips and screws. The lower section of the assembly is generally secured with clips and screws.

On doors with electric switches or courtesy lights in the interior trim assemblies, the wiring harnesses must be disconnected before removing the trim assemblies.

Before installing a door trim assembly, carefully seal the **water/air shield** (water dam or water deflector) to the door with adhesive and/or tape. This shield helps to keep dust, moisture, and air from entering the door. Place a small quantity of sealer over the retaining clips to seal them when they are pushed into the door. It is good practice to apply sealer around the window regulator shaft and other holes before applying the door trim assembly. See Figure 12-12.

Seats

Seats are generally removed when repairing a vehicle's top or side panels. Seats are also removed when they require repair. The methods for attaching seats vary among manufacturers. Some front seats are simply bolted into a reinforcement in the floor pan from the interior of the vehicle. Others are bolted through the floor pan from the exterior.

Front seats are adjustable and have a mechanical or electrically powered track mechanism. **Manually operated seats** are easily repaired. A jammed track mechanism or a disconnected adjusting bar (and/or spring) is common in these systems.

Power seats are more complex than manually operated seats. Four-way and six-way power seat mechanisms are driven through gear boxes and flexible drive cables by electric motors.

To remove a power seat from a vehicle, use the *control switch* to raise the seat and move it to the rearmost position. Then, remove front and rear attaching bolts from the seat track. Once these bolts are removed and all electrical connections are disconnected, the seat can be removed. Be certain to note if spacers are used between the seat bracket and the floor pan. These spacers are used to adjust the seat and must be replaced when reinstalling the seat.

Maintenance and troubleshooting procedures for power seats will vary. Never operate a seat motor without a load. The motor may turn at an excessive speed and damage may occur. The frictional surfaces of power seat

Figure 12-11 A—One-piece door trim assembly. B—Two-piece door trim assembly.

A

B

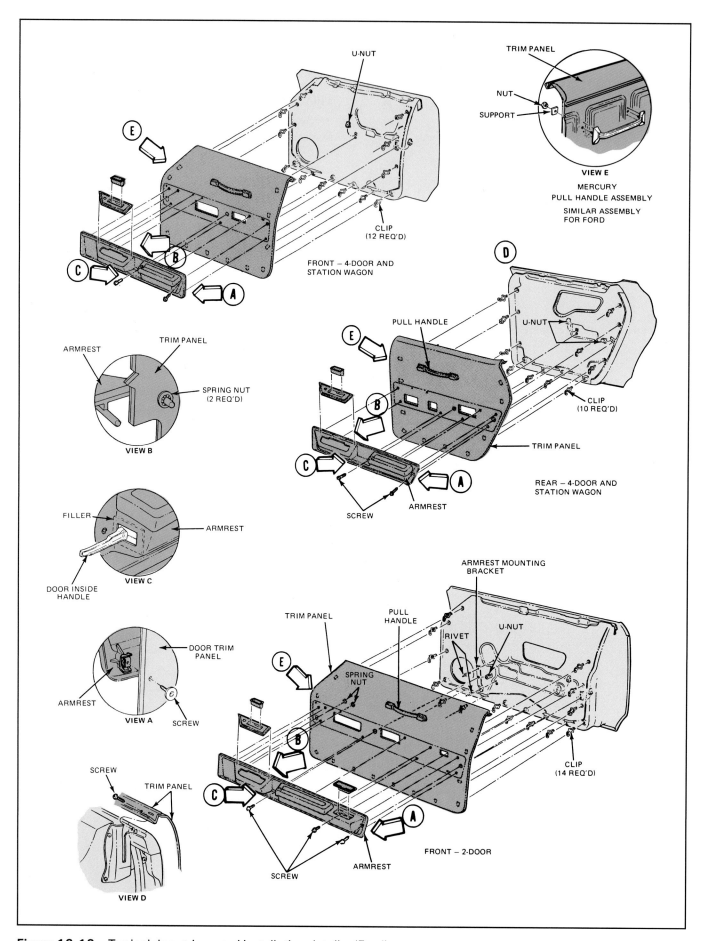

Figure 12-12   Typical door trim panel installation details. (Ford)

transmissions can generally be lubricated with the type of lubricant used on brake mechanisms. Frictional surfaces include gears, gear shafts, thrust washers, drive cables, and adjuster tracks. See Figure 12-13. Check the appropriate service manual for specific lubricating instructions.

If horizontal operation is not smooth, check for a lack of lubrication on the adjuster shoes and channels. Check the adjuster horizontal gear for proper adjustment. It may be too tight in the gear rack. Similarly, the adjuster shoes may be too tight in the upper channel. If there is looseness in the horizontal operation, the horizontal actuator may be incorrectly adjusted. Make certain that all drive cables are connected properly. If the adjusters will not operate vertically or horizontally, check the operation of the solenoid in the seat transmission.

Rear seats are not adjustable. In some models, it is necessary to remove the rear trim panels before removing the rear seat. The *rear seat cushion* is generally removed by pushing in and upward on the lower edge of the cushion. This action disengages the cushion from the retainers on the floor pan. Once the seat cushion is disengaged from the retainers, it can be removed. In some designs, the cushion is bolted to the floor pan.

The *rear back rest* (vertical portion of the rear seat) is generally fastened to hanger brackets on the back panel and held to the floor pan with a bolt. Once the bottom fastener is released, the back rest can be lifted from the hanger brackets.

Although small tears in vinyl fabrics can be fixed in the body shop, most upholstery repairs are done in upholstery specialty shops. See Chapter 8 for information on repairing plastics.

Carpet

Carpets are produced in one or two pieces. In most sedans, *two-piece carpets* are used. In these designs, one piece of carpet is positioned in the front of the passenger compartment and another is positioned in the rear. *One-piece carpets* are common in two-door vehicles. Some door panels have carpeted scuff plates, which match the floor carpeting. See Figure 12-14.

Cuts, tears, and burns in a carpet can generally be repaired. Trim cement is often used to mend cuts and tears. A piece of canvas material can be cemented to the back of a tear to reinforce the damaged area. Thread can also be used to add strength to the repair.

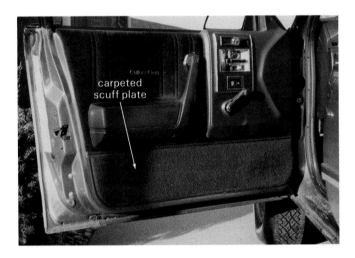

Figure 12-14   The carpeted scuff plate on this door panel matches the floor carpet.

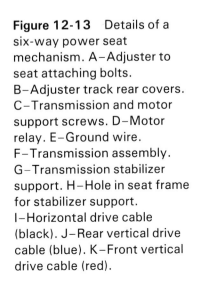

Figure 12-13   Details of a six-way power seat mechanism. A–Adjuster to seat attaching bolts. B–Adjuster track rear covers. C–Transmission and motor support screws. D–Motor relay. E–Ground wire. F–Transmission assembly. G–Transmission stabilizer support. H–Hole in seat frame for stabilizer support. I–Horizontal drive cable (black). J–Rear vertical drive cable (blue). K–Front vertical drive cable (red).

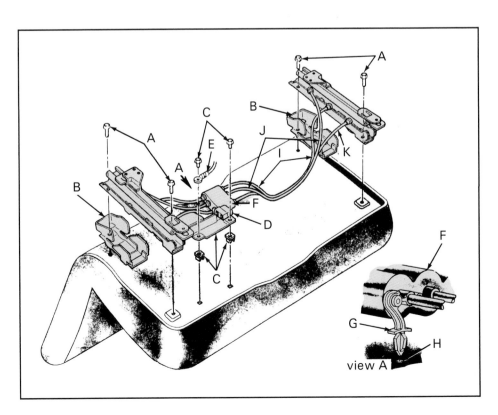

Small burns or holes can be patched with a plug of the original carpet. Select an inconspicuous place to remove a small carpet plug. Carpet that extends under seats or trim pieces can be used for this purpose. Place the carpet on the end grain of a block of wood and punch (round punch) out a plug of the carpet. Repeat this process to punch out the area around the burn or hole. Cement a canvas reinforcing patch over the back of the repair area. Then cement the carpet plug in the hole.

It may be necessary to comb the plug's pile so that it blends evenly with the adjacent carpet. Badly worn or damaged carpets must be replaced.

Headlining

Headlining is used to cover the passenger side of the roof panel, hide electrical wires, and provide insulation. There are two basic types of headlining: cloth or coated-fabric headlining and molded (formed) headlining.

Cloth Headlining.   Cloth headlining is soft and flexible. In some cases, the headlining is held in position with *support rods.* These rods, which span the roof area, are supported along the roof rails. The support rods slip into small pockets in the headlining called *listings*. Because they are not all the same length, most support rods are color coded to aid in installation. See Figure 12-15. In other designs, *retaining strips* are sewn into the headlining. These strips are attached to T-slots on the inner roof panel. The dome lamp base, sun visor brackets, coat hooks, shoulder strap retainer covers (pillar covers), and

garnish moldings also help to hold the headlining in place. These items must be removed before the headlining is removed. Trim cement is used to help secure the lining around openings.

Molded/Formed Headlining.   Many late-model station wagons, mini-vans, and sedans use headlinings made of molded hardboard. The hardboard is covered with foam and a cloth or vinyl facing. Clips and tabs are used along the roof rails to help hold the molded headlining in place. See Figure 12-16. Be careful to avoid bending or creasing molded headlining during removal or installation.

Restraint Systems

Federal safety standards have had a large impact on automobile design and repair processes. Seat belts, double-latch doors, head and neck restraints, interior padding, safety glass, pop-out windshields, collapsible steering wheels, and many other safety features are now standard on many vehicles.

Safety belts have been mandatory on all automobiles manufactured since 1968, with single-unit, combined lap and shoulder belts standard since 1983. Seat belts that the occupants must fasten are considered *active restraints.*

Passive restraints do not require action from the occupants to make them functional. A 1990 federal ruling, which is supported by the National Highway Traffic

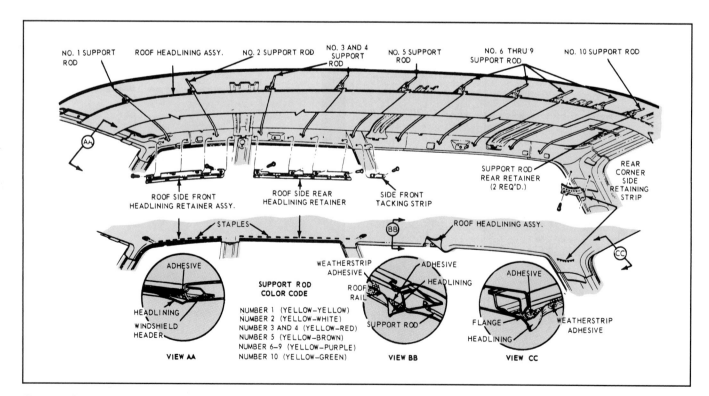

Figure 12-15   Support rods are used to secure this headlining. Note that the rods are color coded. (Ford)

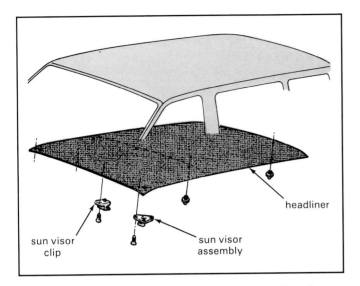

Figure 12-16 Molded headlining. This headliner is held to the roof panel with moldings, sun visor clips, and other miscellaneous fasteners. (Chrysler)

Safety Administration (NHTSA), required all manufacturers to install passive restraints in their automobiles. By 1996, light trucks and vans were also required to conform to this ruling. Manufacturers responded by providing motorized seat belts (front only) or air bags (driver side and front passenger side). Some manufacturers offer both systems. A built-in child seat is offered in some late-model vehicles. This seat is an integral part of the rear seat cushion.

Seat Belts

Nonmotorized *seat belts* are found in most vehicles. These are active restraint systems that require the occupants to fasten the lap belt into the buckle latch assembly. A warning light and an audible signal are often used to remind front-seat passengers to fasten their seat belts when the ignition switch is turned to the ''on'' position.

All lap and shoulder belts (active or passive) are made of fabric webbing. They should be inspected for cuts, frayed edges, and broken threads. The latch and retractor assemblies should also be checked for damage.

Lap and shoulder belts should allow limited movement by occupants and should retract when disconnected. Upon sudden deceleration, an emergency locking device in the retractor assembly securely holds the lap and shoulder belt in position.

Motorized Seat Belts

A *motorized seat belt system* is designed to automatically apply the shoulder belts to the front-seat passengers. These systems operate only when the ignition switch is in the ''on'' position. Door-jamb switches signal a control module to cycle drive motors, which move the belts along overhead tracks, Figure 12-17.

The overhead tracks and the drive motors are often damaged in rollover or side collisions. Most manufacturers recommend that these components be replaced rather than repaired.

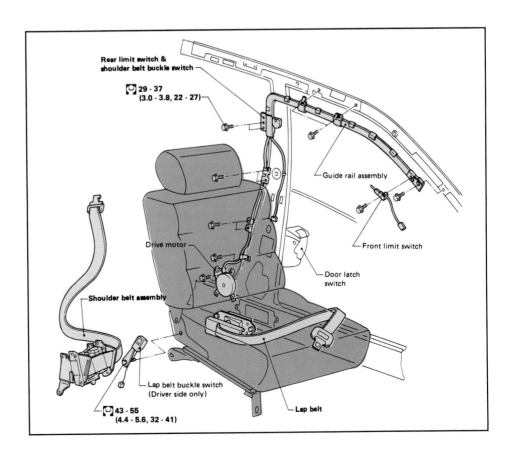

Figure 12-17 Motorized seat belt system. Note the drive motor and the rail assembly. (Nissan)

If a motorized seat belt system does not work, check the fuse, the wiring, and the voltage at the drive motors. See Chapter 14 for more information on testing electrical components.

Air Bags

Air bag systems are designed to deploy when a vehicle is involved in a severe frontal collision. When a frontal collision occurs, impact sensors signal a control module to ignite sodium azide pellets that are located in the *inflator modules.* The inflator modules, which are mounted in the steering wheel assembly and, in most cases, in the dash on the passenger side, also contain the air bags. As the pellets burn, they produce a large quantity of nitrogen gas that rapidly inflates the air bags. Some vehicles are equipped with side air bags, which are located in the door panels or the front seat. These air bags are designed to deploy in the event of a side impact.

Air bag deployment can also occur if impact sensors are accidentally bumped during the repair process or if an unwanted electrical charge or short occurs in the system. Therefore, it is best to disarm the air bag system before making repairs. This will prevent unintentional deployment. Although most manufacturers recommend simply disconnecting the battery (remove the negative cable first; then remove the positive cable), some require

additional steps to disable the system's energy reserve module. The *energy reserve module* serves as an alternate source of power if battery voltage is lost during a collision. Refer to an appropriate service manual for instructions on disarming specific air bag systems. See Figure 12-18.

Most air bag systems have *self-diagnostic capabilities.* Electronic scan tools can be used to retrieve trouble codes from the control module in these systems. The trouble codes can be used to identify problems in the system. Never try to troubleshoot an air bag system with conventional test equipment. Incorrect testing procedures may activate the system. Many components in an air bag system cannot be serviced. If deployment has occurred, the inflator module must be replaced. Additionally, many manufacturers recommend that the impact sensors be replaced following deployment. Using damaged or faulty components may lead to unprovoked system activation. Carefully follow the manufacturer's diagnostic, installation, and service instructions. See Figure 12-19.

After air bag deployment, the interior of the vehicle must be cleaned of *sodium hydroxide powder.* This powder, which is produced when the sodium azide pellets are activated, may irritate the skin, eyes, nose, and throat. Wear rubber gloves and safety glasses when removing the powder or handling a deployed air bag.

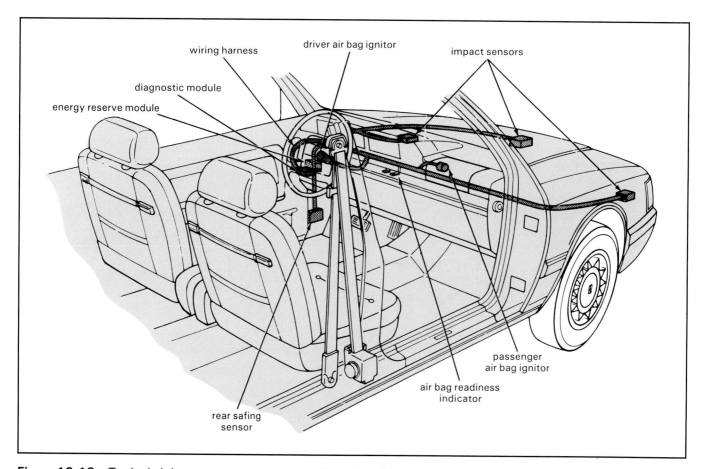

Figure 12-18   Typical air bag system components. Note that this system is equipped with a passenger-side air bag. (Ford)

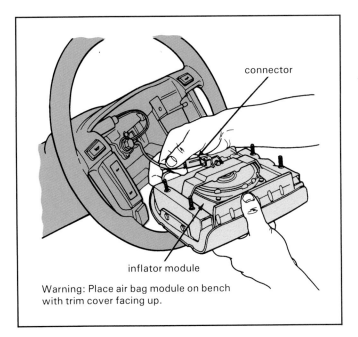

Warning: Place air bag module on bench with trim cover facing up.

Figure 12-19 The inflator module must be handled carefully during installation. (Chrysler)

Vinyl Roof Repair and Replacement

There are two basic types of vinyl roof coverings: vinyl-coated fabric coverings and spray-on vinyl coverings. The types of vinyl used for these coverings varies among manufacturers.

When servicing roof coverings, the technician must determine the extent of the damage and decide how to proceed with repair or replacement. Environmental exposure can cause vinyl tops to crack, peel, discolor, and shrink. As *plasticizers* (softening additives) are released from the vinyl, it may shrink and become brittle. It is always more economical to repair a small tear than to

replace a vinyl top. Nevertheless, the customer must be satisfied with the decision to repair the top. If the customer desires, a specially formulated dye or paint can be used to change the color of a vinyl roof covering.

Vinyl-Coated Fabric Coverings

Vinyl-coated fabrics (polyvinyl chloride) have frequently been used to fully or partially cover roof panels. On most models, the fabric is cemented directly to the panel. On some models, however, a foam-rubber pad is used between the fabric and the roof panel. Various mechanical fasteners and moldings help to hold this type of covering in place. In addition to being decorative, vinyl roof coverings provide thermal insulation and sound insulation.

Vinyl-coated fabric roof repairs fall into four categories: minor repairs, major repairs, partial removal, and replacement. Before starting any repair, carefully clean the vinyl roof with an appropriate cleaner. Use a scrub brush to remove all of the dirt that is embedded in the grain.

Minor Repairs

Minor vinyl-coated fabric repairs include mending scuffs and surface cuts. To repair scuffs, connect a heat-controlled soldering iron and set the temperature to about 225 °F (106 °C). Clean the iron's tip thoroughly with an abrasive pad. Using short, overlapping strokes, lightly slide the soldering iron over the scuff marks until the frayed vinyl has fused into the surrounding surface.

If the scuff marks are deep enough to expose the cloth backing, the damaged area must be filled with vinyl. This can be accomplished by using the hot tip of the soldering iron to strip off a small quantity of vinyl from a piece of scrap material, Figure 12-20. Carefully fill the scuffed area with the vinyl using short, overlapping strokes.

Figure 12-20 Vinyl-coated fabric repair. A–Vinyl is stripped from scrap piece of fabric. B–Scuffed area is filled with stripped vinyl.

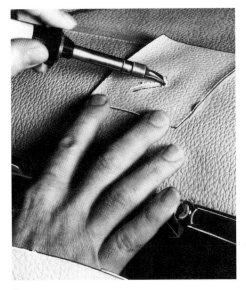

A

B

The **grain pattern** in the vinyl can be restored by carefully etching the pattern into the repair with the sharp tip of the soldering iron. The gloss created by the repair process can be removed by spraying the area with liquid vinyl. **Liquid vinyl** (organosol) is a specially formulated paint that consists of vinyl in an organic solvent. A vinyl coating is left on the painted surface once the solvents evaporate.

To repair minor cuts (6 mm or less), slide the heated tip of the soldering iron across the cut until it is covered with vinyl. Smooth out the surface of the repair with the iron and use the tip to produce the desired grain pattern. If necessary, spray the repair area with liquid vinyl to eliminate the gloss around the repair.

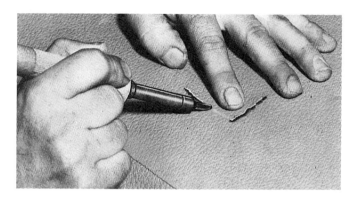

Figure 12-22   A soldering iron can be used to fuse a damaged area in vinyl.

Major Repairs

Major vinyl-coated fabric repairs include mending tears, bubbles, wrinkles, gaps, and seams, Figure 12-21. If a vinyl-coated fabric covering is torn and loose, apply a light coat of adhesive to secure the fabric to the roof panel. It may be necessary to cut off frayed fabric edges. Do not use cement if the damage is over a padded area.

After the damaged fabric has been glued to the top panel, a soldering iron can be used to complete the repair. Starting at the center of the tear, slide the iron across the damaged surface with short, light strokes, Figure 12-22. Continue this procedure until the tear is covered with vinyl. To restore the grain pattern, etch the surface of the repair with the hot tip of the soldering iron. The shine can be eliminated by spraying the repair area with liquid vinyl.

Severely damaged areas may require the application of **liquid vinyl patching compound.** This viscous vinyl is applied to the damaged area with a small paint brush or trowel (pallet) and is carefully worked under the loose edges of the tear. Several coats of vinyl may be required to fill the damaged area properly. Allow 10-15 minutes between coats. A heat gun can be used to speed the drying process. The tip of a soldering iron can be used to etch the grain pattern into the repair.

A special patching compound (plastisol) is also available for repairing vinyl. Like other patching com-

pounds, this material is applied with a small brush or trowel. However, this compound will not air dry and requires the application of heat (heat gun or iron) for proper curing. A special **silicone-treated graining paper** is used to create the final grain pattern in this type of repair. The graining paper is pressed against the final application of vinyl compound. A heat gun or a household flat iron is then used for the final cure. The graining paper can be removed after the patched area has completely cooled.

Repairing Bubbles.   Bubbles that are caused by trapped air can be corrected by removing the air with a hypodermic needle, Figure 12-23. It may be necessary to reactivate the adhesive under the vinyl after the air bubbles have been removed. This is done by applying heat to the vinyl surface with a heat gun. Hold the gun about 12 in. (300 mm) from the surface to prevent overheating and discoloration. A moist rag and an electric household iron can also be used to activate the adhesive. Place the rag over the bubble area and use the iron to generate hot water and steam on the vinyl surface. The moist rag helps to prevent the iron from overheating the vinyl.

Repairing Wrinkles.   Wrinkles in vinyl-coated fabrics usually have small, radial folds with an excess of slack material that cannot be displaced without rearranging the fabric. Small wrinkles can often be removed with

Figure 12-21   The major cuts shown in these photographs are repairable.

A

B

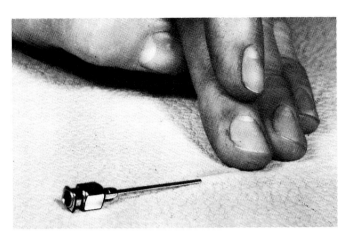

Figure 12-23 Using a hypodermic needle to remove the air from a bubble in vinyl.

a household iron and a moist rag. The heat from the iron softens the fabric and reactivates the adhesive. If this method fails, the fabric around the wrinkle must be removed and reglued as follows:

1. Remove moldings and ornamentation in the immediate area around the wrinkle.

2. Pull the vinyl material free from the roof panel up to the bonded seam or approximately 10 in. (300 mm) beyond the wrinkle. Only loosen the material on one side of the wrinkle and test to see if it can be stretched or pulled flat.

3. Thoroughly clean old adhesive from the surface of the roof panel.

4. Apply a thin film of adhesive to the vinyl material and along the drip rail flanges or the edges of the roof. Note: The drip rail flanges are located along the roof directly above the door openings. These flanges help direct runoff from rain and prevent water from running into the passenger compartment when the door is open.

5. Allow the adhesive to air dry for several seconds.

6. Grasp the vinyl material firmly and draw it tightly against the roof panel until the wrinkles disappear, Figure 12-24. If necessary, fabric pliers can be used to pull the material.

7. Fold the excess vinyl material under the drip rail flange and secure it with the flange moldings.

8. Secure the front edge of the material with drive nails (if originally used) or molding clips. It is a good idea to apply sealer over the drive nails or clips to prevent possible water leaks and rust damage.

9. Replace the moldings as required.

Repairing Gaps along Moldings. In some cases, vinyl top fabric is too short to be concealed under the roof molding. With age, vinyl fabric tends to shrink and the

adhesive may no longer be able to hold the material securely. This may cause gaps to occur along moldings. Gaps can sometimes be corrected by adjusting the molding or by stretching the fabric. If it is necessary to stretch the fabric, use *pop rivets* or *drive nails* to prevent it from slipping back to its former position. The application of heat may aid in the stretching process by softening the vinyl material. It is sometimes necessary to loosen the fabric from the roof (approximately 5 in. or 150 mm) before stretching. After stretching, the fabric must be reglued.

Repairing Bonded Seams. A soldering iron that is equipped with a curved tip can be used to mend separated bonded seams. Slowly move the tip of the iron across the underside of the seam, and immediately press the seam together. Hold the material securely with your fingers. Reverse the soldering iron and place the tip on the outer edge of the seam, Figure 12-25. Slowly move the tip along the outer edge of the seam and press the seam down into position. This will bond and seal the seam joint. If the seam is torn and separated from shrinkage, the top must be replaced.

Partial Fabric Removal

When repairing a roof panel, it may be necessary to peel the vinyl-coated fabric covering away from the repair area. After removing the fabric, make certain that it

Figure 12-24 Correcting wrinkles at the front corner of a vinyl top.

Figure 12-25 Applying heat to the edge of a bonded seam. By reversing the tip of the iron, heat can first be applied to the underside of the seam.

is protected from heat and mechanical abuse. Place several rags in the fold areas to prevent creases from forming. After the repairs are made, re-apply the fabric as previously described. Remember to apply rust inhibitors and primers to the repair area before re-applying the fabric.

Replacement of Top Fabric

When a fabric roof is severely damaged, it must generally be replaced. Moldings, emblems, and other mechanical fasteners must be removed before removing the fabric. If necessary, a heat gun and a scraper can then be used to remove the damaged fabric. Although it is not necessary to remove all traces of the old adhesive before installing the new top fabric, make certain that all lumps of adhesive are removed from the roof panel. Xylol or other adhesive solvents can be used to smooth and level the old adhesive.

After removing the damaged top and cleaning the roof panel, lay the new fabric top on the roof. Check to make sure that the new top will fit properly and allow the folds and wrinkles to relax. It is best if the temperature exceeds 70 °F (20 °C) during installation. After the wrinkles have relaxed, fold the fabric lengthwise at the center and carefully measure the fabric and the roof panel. Mark the centerline on the fabric (backside) and on the roof panel with a marking pen.

Be certain that all painted areas are masked and protected before applying vinyl top adhesive. Adhesive should be applied to half of the roof panel. Follow the manufacturer's recommendations when applying the adhesive. Align the centerline marks on the roof and the fabric. Carefully place the fabric over the adhesive. A brayer (roller) and a heat gun can be used to smooth out wrinkles and air bubbles. After the wrinkles have been removed, repeat the installation procedure described above for the other half of the top.

After both sides of the top have been thoroughly fitted, apply cement around the window openings. It may be necessary to make *relief notches* at the corners of the top material to allow the fabric to achieve a continuous bond. Fabric pliers can be used to help pull the fabric tight. A putty knife can be used to work the material into or around window openings. Drive nails, clips, and moldings can be installed to help hold the fabric in place. It may be necessary to trim excess fabric from along the belt line or other moldings. *Belt line* is a general term used when describing the position of a vehicle's components. It grew from a reference to the human center or belt line. Horizontal moldings, crowns, or other components located around the center of the vehicle are on the belt line. The roof panel and all windows are above the belt line.

Spray-On Roof Coverings

Spray-on roof coverings are becoming increasingly popular. Spray-on coverings can be applied faster and more economically than fabric-type coverings. These coverings are available in numerous colors. Before applying a spray-on covering, make certain that the roof is clean and sanded and that all bare spots are primed. *Simulated seam tape* can be used to provide the appearance of seams. To use this tape, carefully measure and mark the location of simulated seams. Apply the tape along the marks. Use firm pressure on the tape to ensure proper adhesion. Before applying the roof covering, carefully mask the vehicle. It is advisable to practice applying the spray-on covering on a scrap piece of metal to adjust the viscosity and the application pressure. After making the necessary viscosity and pressure adjustments, apply the spray-on covering to the roof panel. One wet coat followed by two texturing coats is normally sufficient. Allow flash time between coats. *Flash time* is the time needed for the solvents in the finish to evaporate. The coated surface loses its wet, high-gloss appearance when adequate flash time has been allowed. This will help ensure good adhesion and coverage. It will also help to prevent runs. Allow the finish to dry thoroughly before removing the masking tape.

A similar procedure is used when applying *vinyl paint* to restore color to top fabrics. The old top must be thoroughly cleaned before the vinyl paint is applied. Use an appropriate solvent, such as Prep-Sol, to remove all traces of wax and polish. Remove all moldings and emblems and mask the glass and body panels. Three coats of vinyl paint are generally required to produce a satisfactory finish. Although the finish will dry in about 30 minutes, the masking should not be removed for at least 4 hours.

Convertible Tops and Sunroofs

There are several convertible top and sunroof systems on the market. System operation and maintenance will vary among manufacturers. It is best to consult service manuals before making adjustments or major repairs.

Repairing and Replacing Convertible Top Fabric

The repair and installation of *convertible top fabric* is commonly done by upholstery and convertible top specialists. Early-model tops were made of treated canvas. Few are likely to be in service today. Replacement tops and late-model tops are made of synthetic fabric and vinyl.

Because convertible tops are tightly stretched over a number of *roof bows* and *rails,* tears must be carefully reinforced with a backing patch and sewn together. This type of repair is not very attractive. Consequently, torn tops are commonly replaced. Some early-model tops are no longer available and must be custom made. Be certain to save the old top for use as a pattern. The old top may also help when making repairs or adjustments to rails, bows, or other mechanisms. Repairing or replacing convertible top fabric is a very time-consuming task.

Manual Convertible Top Operation

Manual convertible top systems have been popular for many years. These systems are generally less costly to manufacture and require less service than power systems. Manual top systems utilize springs to assist in raising and lowering the mechanical lift assembly. These springs are under compression when the top is up and under tension when the top is down. A locking mechanism, which secures the top in the up position, is located on the front roof rail. Many systems are equipped with an aligning mechanism, which is positioned on the windshield header.

If it becomes necessary to repair a manual convertible top system, the rear seat and other interior trim must generally be removed. Do not detach the mechanical lift assembly if the springs are under tension or compression. Most systems have several adjusting points on the lift assembly. In addition to adjusting the lift assembly, it may be necessary to make minor adjustments to doors, door glass, or other components to achieve proper top alignment.

Electric Convertible Top Operation

Most late-model vehicles use a 12-volt electric motor to drive a gear assembly. Drive cables transfer power from a gear reduction assembly to an actuator assembly that raises and lowers the convertible top. If an *electric convertible top* is inoperative, make certain that power is reaching the relay and the motor. Disconnect the drive cables from the actuator assembly. If the motor operates the cables freely, check the top actuator assembly and the rail mechanism for proper operation. Remember to lubricate cables and moving joints. Dirty or damaged cables are common problems in electrically powered systems. Clean or replace the cables as necessary.

Hydraulic-Electric Convertible Top Operation

Hydraulic-electric convertible tops are found on many early-model vehicles. These systems consist of a 12-volt reversible motor, a rotor-type pump, two hydraulic lift cylinders, and upper and lower hydraulic hose assemblies. These components are installed behind the rear seat, Figure 12-26.

When the control switch is moved to the ''up'' position, the motor and pump assembly forces hydraulic fluid through the hoses to the lower ends of the lift cylinders. The fluid pushes the piston rods upward, raising the top. The fluid in the top of the cylinders returns to the pump and is recirculated to the bottom of the cylinders.

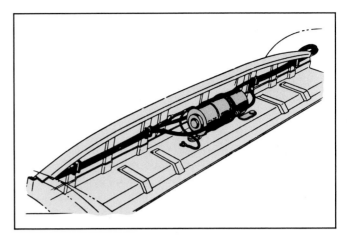

Figure 12-26   A hydraulic-electric motor and pump assembly for a convertible top.

When the control switch is moved to the ''down'' position, the motor and pump assembly operates in the reverse direction. The hydraulic fluid is forced through the hoses to the top of the cylinders. The fluid forces the piston rod and cylinders downward, lowering the top. The fluid in the bottom of the cylinder returns to the pump and is recirculated to the top of the cylinder.

If there is a failure in the hydraulic-electric system and the cause is not evident, the mechanical operation of the top should be checked. If the top assembly seems to bind, disconnect the top lift cylinder piston rods from the top linkage and manually raise and lower the top. The top should travel through its cycle without binding. If binding is noted when the top is being locked at the header, check the alignment of the door windows, ventilators, and rear quarter windows in relation to the side roof-rail weatherstripping. If the problem continues after mechanical adjustments have been made, the hydraulic-electric system should be checked. A failure in the electrical system may be caused by a low battery, broken wire, loose connection, faulty component, or short circuit.

To check the hydraulic fluid level, slowly remove the filler plug from the fluid reservoir with a standard screwdriver. The fluid level should be within 1/4 in. (6 mm) of the lower edge of the filler plug hole. If the fluid level is low, the reservoir should be filled.

To fill and bleed the reservoir, a filler plug adapter can be made by drilling a 1/4 in. (6 mm) hole through the center of a spare filler plug. Install a 2 in. (12 mm) length of metal tubing into the center of the filler plug and solder the tubing on both sides of the plug to form an airtight connection.

Place the top in the raised position and remove the folding top compartment bag from the rear seat back panel. If necessary, remove the pump and water shield.

Place absorbent rags below the reservoir at the filler plug and slowly remove the filler plug from the reservoir. Install the filler plug adapter in the reservoir and attach a 4 in. (100 mm) length of rubber tubing or hose to the adapter.

Place the opposite end of the hose in a container of hydraulic brake fluid, Figure 12-27. Note: The container should be placed in the rear compartment below the level of the fluid in the reservoir. Sufficient fluid must be available in the container to prevent drawing air into the hydraulic system.

Operate the top to the down position. After the top is fully lowered, continue to operate the motor and pump assembly for about 20 seconds or until the noise level of the pump is noticeably reduced. A reduction in pump noise level indicates that the hydraulic system is filling with fluid. Operate the top several times or until the operation is consistently smooth in both the up and down cycles.

With the top in the down position, remove the filler plug tubing and the filler plug adapter from the reservoir. Check the level of fluid in the reservoir and reinstall the original filler plug.

Manual Sunroof Operation

Sunroof panels can be made of metal, plastic, or tinted glass. The operation of manual sunroofs varies. In some designs, the roof slides on a simple track assembly and can be locked in the closed (forward) position. In other models, a mechanical crank system is used to move the sunroof. Some glass or plastic sunroofs do not slide back and forth (fixed-glass panel). In these designs, the sunroof is generally hinged so the panel can be raised. See Figure 12-28. Many of these panels can be removed from the roof opening and stored until needed.

Electric Sunroof Operation

On some vehicles, the sunroof panel is actuated by a two-way electric motor located in the center of the windshield header area. See Figure 12-29. The motor turns a drive assembly, which powers an output shaft. The shaft extends up into the cable drive housing. A pinion on the end of the output shaft drives flexible cables that are attached to the roof panel.

When the control switch is moved to the ''open'' position, the roof panel retracts down and rearward. It travels on guide rails from the flush, roof-mounted position into a storage space between the headlining and the stationary roof panel.

When the control switch is moved to the ''close'' position, the roof panel moves forward on the guide rails. Near the end of the forward travel, the rear portion of the panel moves upward on two ramps. This action positions the panel flush with the roof and seals it in the roof opening.

If the sunroof is not operating, check for tripped breakers or blown fuses. Remove the switch and check it for continuity. There should be continuity between the terminals in both switch positions (forward and backward). See Chapter 14 for more information on testing electrical components. Check the motor and cable

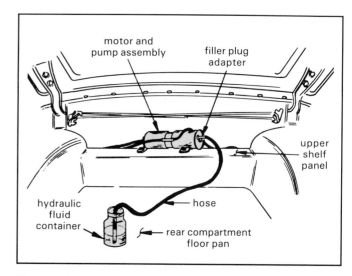

Figure 12-27 Typical setup for bleeding the hydraulic system.

Figure 12-28 This sunroof is hinged and can be raised at the rear.

assemblies as described in the section on electrically controlled convertible tops. Remember to lubricate the cables during replacement or reinstallation. It is not necessary to lubricate the top surface of the guide rail covers or the slide tracks.

During regular maintenance, check to see that drain holes are open and free of foreign materials. Close the roof panel and, if necessary, adjust the ramps until the proper closing action is obtained.

Insulation

Interior and exterior *insulation* is commonly applied to muffle excessive noise, reduce vibration, and provide thermal insulation.

A plastic insulation or *undercoating* is applied to the underside of vehicles and to the inside of fenders, doors, and quarter panels. The term undercoating should not be

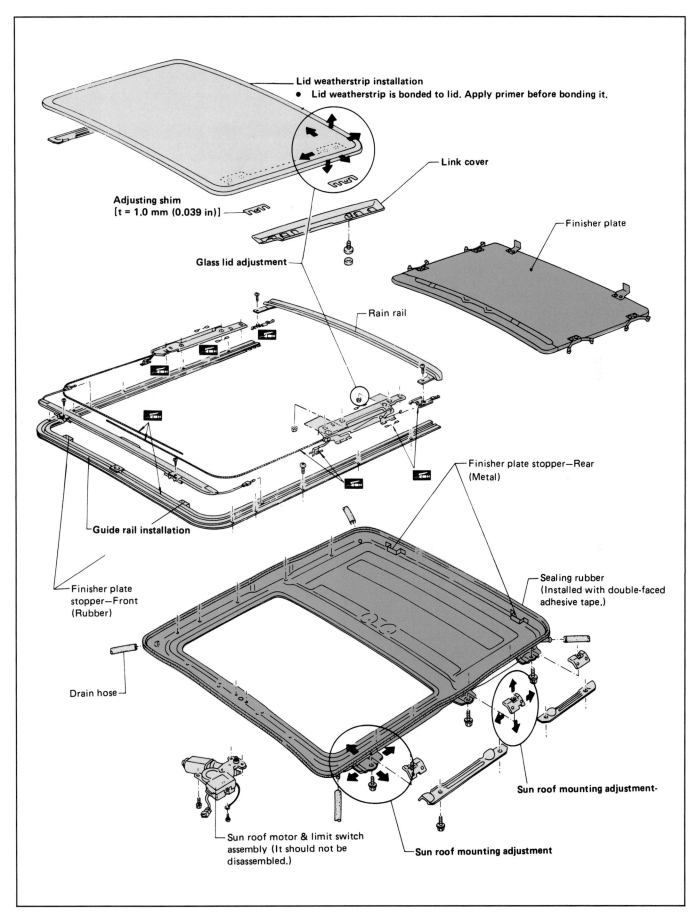

Figure 12-29   Details of an electric sunroof for a specific vehicle.
Note the areas that require lubrication. (Nissan)

confused with the asphaltic undercoats used on early-model vehicles. This tar-like material provided little rust protection. Modern undercoating materials contain anti-corrosion agents that prevent rust. These viscous materials are applied with specially designed pneumatic spray guns. This thin coating of undercoating absorbs sound and provides protection against rust. It also prevents dust and moisture from entering through body seams.

Fibrous pads (resinated fiber, fiberglass, etc.) are used on the inside of the hood, trunk, roof, and some sections of the floor pan to help deaden sound and provide thermal insulation. In the hood and trunk, adhesive cements and mechanical clips are used to hold the pads in place. On the floor pan and roof panel, adhesive cements are used to secure the insulation pads.

Floor pan insulation is needed to protect the passenger compartment floor from the hot exhaust system and from harsh environments. Make certain that the correct type of insulation is used in areas that are exposed to extreme heat. Never place electric cables or harnesses under insulator pads. See Figure 12-30.

Weatherstripping/Sealers

Weatherstripping and ***sealers*** are used to prevent air, dust, and water from entering a vehicle. Weatherstripping is used between movable and stationary parts, such as deck lids and trunk openings, Figure 12-31. Sealers are used on stationary joints to stop dust, air, and water leaks. They also help prevent rust from occurring in joints. Sealers come in several forms. The form used depends on the intended application. Polyurethane adhesive and butyl-rubber sealers are sometimes used around glass and body seams. Silicone-based sealants should not be used for auto body repairs because they are difficult to paint. Heavy-bodied caulking sealers can

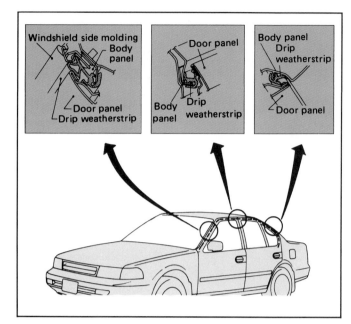

A

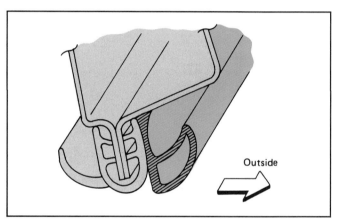

B

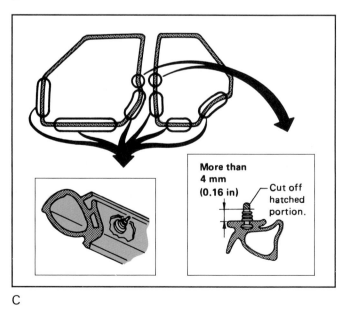

C

Figure 12-31 Typical weatherstripping locations. A—Drip weatherstripping. B—Body side welt weatherstripping. C—Door weatherstripping. (Nissan)

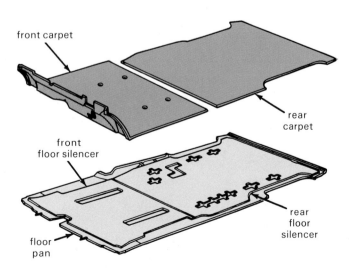

Figure 12-30 Floor carpet and silencer pads help deaden sound and provide thermal insulation. (Chrysler)

be purchased in cartridge form and applied with a caulking gun. They are also available in "rope" form and can be applied by hand. Spray or brush-type undercoatings may also be used to seal small seams and provide anti-corrosion protection. Always follow the manufacturer's instructions when applying sealers.

When repairing a vehicle, it is important to repair or replace all damaged weatherstripping and sealers. Since most weatherstripping is made of rubber-like compounds, it is susceptible to wear, damage, and deterioration. A special rubber/vinyl protectant can be applied to reduce deterioration from chemical and ultraviolet light exposure.

Locating Leaks

Worn, damaged, or improperly installed weatherstripping and sealers may lead to air, dust, noise, and water leaks. Many leaks are difficult to locate. There are several methods used to find leaks around weatherstripping and sealed joints, including:

☐ Spraying the joint with water.

☐ Driving on a dusty road.

☐ Directing a beam of light on the joint.

☐ Directing compressed air on the joint.

☐ Directing an aerosol can of talc on the joint.

☐ Using an ultrasonic leak detector.

Before testing for leaks, it is sometimes advisable to remove the interior trim from the area around the leak. It should be emphasized that the actual leak may be some distance from where it appears in the interior. After removing trim items, the location of most leaks will be more readily evident.

Look for the Obvious

When checking for leaks, always check for the most probable sources before performing complex tests. Check to see that the doors and trunk lid close properly. Study the weatherstripping and seals around windows for signs of damage. Make sure the water/air deflector on the inner panel of the door is not torn or loose.

There are many plugs and grommets used in the floor pans, trunk floors, and dash panels to keep out dust and water. These items should be inspected carefully to make sure that they are installed properly and are in good condition. Dust and water leaks often leave a trail of dust or silt from their point of entrance.

Locating Leaks with Water

After removing the interior trim in the general area of a leak, spray the area with a stream of water. A garden hose without a nozzle should be held about 10 in. (250

mm) from the area of the suspected leak. An assistant on the inside of the vehicle should be able to locate the spot where the water is entering.

It is important to keep *drain holes* open so water that seeps past the windows will not collect between inner and outer panels. Drain holes are located along the lower edges of doors, rocker panels, and quarter panels. The construction of drain hole systems varies. See Figures 12-32 and 12-33. Some vehicles are equipped with drain hole *sealing strips* that prevent dust from entering the drain holes, but allow water to drain. These strips are commonly held in place with retainers. If necessary, the strips can be removed for inspection.

Locating Leaks on a Dusty Road

As a vehicle moves forward, a slight vacuum is created in the passenger compartment. Cracks in seals, gaps between openings, and partially open windows allow air and dirt to be drawn into the vehicle. Leaks are sometimes found by observers as a vehicle is driven down a dusty road. However, dust entering through the

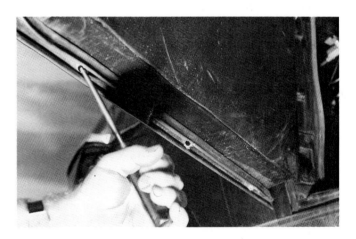

Figure 12-32 This technician is opening drain holes on the lower edge of the door. (Ford)

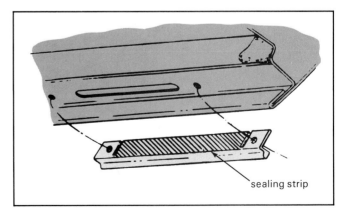

Figure 12-33 Drain hole opening sealing strips prevent dirt and moisture from entering the drain holes. (Chevrolet)

trunk, quarter panels, or rocker panels is difficult to detect. Dust that enters through these areas often travels a lengthy route before exiting through the interior trim.

Locating Leaks with Light

Some leaks can be located by moving a bright light around the general area of the leak while an observer watches for the light from the inside of the vehicle. Because light does not bend, this method will only work when the source of leakage is in a straight line to the interior of the vehicle.

Locating Leaks with Compressed Air

Compressed air can be used to simulate highway speeds when trying to detect sources of wind noise. Wind noises are commonly generated around doors, vents, and glass. Loose moldings, misaligned joints, and small leaks are the most common causes of wind noise. When the source of noise is discovered, place tape over the noise-generating area and retest for noise. If the noise stops, the area should be repaired.

Air escaping from the passenger compartment can also cause noise. Air conditioning systems and incoming air slightly pressurize the passenger compartment. Carpenter's chalk can be rubbed on weatherstripping to check for leaks. When the door is closed and opened, there should be an unbroken chalk mark along the area where the weatherstripping contacts the door frame. To help locate leaks, compressed air can be directed around the weatherstripping. The chalk dust will be disturbed by air traveling through leaking weatherstripping.

A soap-and-water solution is often applied around the exterior of glass seals or weatherstripping to help detect leaks. Compressed air is directed around the seals or the weatherstripping from the inside of the vehicle. Leaks around glass seals will cause the solution to bubble or lather. Leaks around weatherstripping will produce a lather trail. When using compressed air to check for leaks, pressure should not exceed 10 psi (70 kPa).

Locating Leaks with Aerosol Talc

Aerosol cans of talc can be used to help locate leaks around weatherstripping. A pressurized stream of talc is directed on the weatherstripping in the area around the suspected leak. A trail of talc dust will be present on sections of the weatherstripping that are not sealing properly.

Locating Leaks with an Ultrasonic Detector

A special ultrasonic detector can be used to locate leaks. Before using the detector, a tone generator is placed inside the vehicle. This generator produces inaudible, high-frequency sounds. The detector meters

the sounds produced by the generator. Problem areas can be easily located by observing the signal strength indicated on the detector's meter. The signal will grow stronger as the detector is moved closer to the leak. See Figure 12-34.

Glass and Body Sealers

A flexible sealer is often used to repair leaks. It is also used to fill small spaces between parts, spot welded joints, and gaps around clip holes. Sealing products are available in squeeze tubes and caulking cartridges. They are also available in the form of caulking cords, foam tapes, and pressure-sensitive tapes.

Leaks around gasket-held glass are generally repaired with a bedding or sealing compound that remains flexible after curing. The gap between the gasket and the glass (or the gasket and the body panel) must be clean

Figure 12-34 Using an ultrasonic tester to check for leaks. (Ford)

and dry. The sealer should be forced between the gasket and the glass or the panel. Excess sealer can be removed with solvent or enamel thinner. Butyl sealers are commonly used on windshield and taillight leaks.

Leaks around adhesive-held glass are repaired with special liquid butyl or polyurethane adhesive sealers. To ensure a good bond between old and new adhesive sealants and to allow room for moldings, clean the repair area and remove excess old adhesive. Use a solvent to remove all traces of oil from the old adhesive and apply an adhesive primer. After about five minutes, apply the adhesive sealer evenly with a putty knife. Once the sealer has cured, the trim can be reinstalled and the excess sealer can be removed.

Weatherstripping Repair

When weatherstripping becomes loose or damaged, leaks often occur. On most vehicles, the weatherstripping used around doors and deck lids is cemented in place. When this type of weatherstripping becomes loose, it can be recemented. Replacement weatherstripping may be secured with screws, clips, or cement. Some weatherstripping is designed to slip over flanges. On some body styles, the weatherstripping is attached to the stationary portion of the body. In others, it is attached to the door (or deck lid). On some models, the weatherstripping is used around the body openings and on portions of the doors.

To check for the correct positioning of the weatherstripping around the perimeter of door and deck lid openings, place a 0.020 in. (0.5 mm) feeler gauge or card between the weatherstripping and the door or lid. If there is little or no resistance when withdrawing the gauge, the weatherstripping may need to be replaced. It may be possible to close or tighten the seal by cementing a thin (1 mm) strip of cellular rubber under the weatherstripping. Because most door edges, trunk edges, and openings are manufactured with a slight crown or taper, moving the weatherstripping closer to the edge of these panels can also help reduce the gap. When the gap is reduced, the weatherstripping will often create the desired seal.

Some manufacturers use nylon retainers to secure the weatherstripping on both front and rear doors. These retainers are an integral part of the weatherstripping. Serrations on the retainers hold them securely in holes along the perimeter of the door. On framed doors (hardtop doors), nylon retainers are used below the belt line only.

Weatherstripping adhesive is used to secure the weatherstripping around the upper door frame (above the belt line). In some cases, the adhesive is used in conjunction with retainer clips or with weatherstripping that is forced over flanges or into channels.

A special tool is used to disengage weatherstripping retainers from door panels, Figure 12-35. This tool permits the removal of the retainers without damaging their serrations. If the retainers are not damaged during removal, the weatherstripping can be reinstalled.

To install weatherstripping on framed doors, apply a bead of adhesive to the weatherstripping seating area on the upper and lower areas of the door. On vehicles with gasket-type weatherstripping, carefully place the stripping over the flange or install the retainer clips. Install the lower half of the weatherstripping first. Observe the factory-installed joint locations. Be careful not to stretch or pucker the weatherstripping during installation. Stretching the weatherstripping may cause it to shrink or retract later and result in gaps and leaks.

When installing weatherstripping on most *door openings,* begin at the hinge face near the belt line. Work fasteners into holes or force the weatherstripping over the metal flange around the door opening. Silicone lubricant is sometimes used to help lubricate the exterior of the weatherstrip. This reduces friction between the door and the weatherstrip.

Weatherstripping on the doors of hardtop and convertible vehicles is attached in a different manner. The interior trim panel must be removed to gain access to the weatherstripping retainer fasteners in these vehicles.

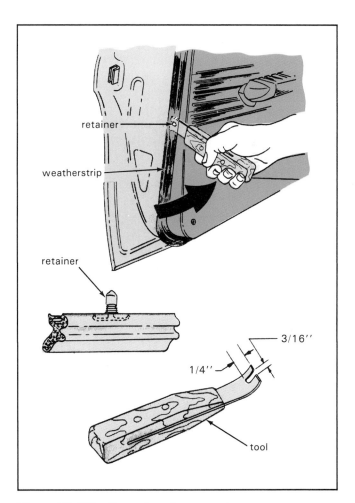

Figure 12-35 Procedure for removing weatherstripping from a specific vehicle. (General Motors)

Remove screws or use a flat blade tool to break the adhesive bond and/or plastic clips holding the weatherstripping in place. Be sure to remove all old weatherstripping particles before installing the new weatherstripping.

Various methods are used to attach weatherstripping to the roof rail. Metal and plastic retainer strips are commonly held by mechanical fasteners. Some weatherstripping is forced over a weld flange and secured by friction, cement, or plastic clips. Carefully observe the design of each model and follow the manufacturer's installation instructions.

Outer-belt weatherstripping is located between the door panel and the window glass. It helps to prevent dirt, air, and moisture from entering the door cavity. To replace the outer-belt weatherstripping, remove the interior trim panel and the water/air shield. Then remove the fasteners that hold the weatherstripping in place and remove the weatherstripping, Figure 10-36. Position the new weatherstripping properly and secure it with the appropriate fasteners. On some models, the outer-belt weatherstripping is an integral part of an exterior metal molding.

In some models, a window track, which is generally held in place by mechanical fasteners, serves as a weatherstripping. To remove this type of weatherstripping, detach the glass from the lift plate and rest it on the bottom of the door. Remove the weatherstripping attaching screws or clips and remove the old weatherstripping. To install the new weatherstripping, slip it into place and secure it with mechanical fasteners or clips (depending upon make and model). Attach the window to the lift plate and roll the window up and down to test for a proper seal. Do not forget to replace the water/air shield before replacing the interior trim panel.

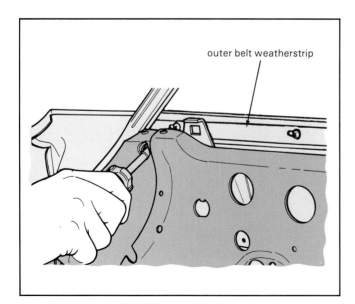

Figure 12-36 The door trim assembly must be removed before removing outer-belt weatherstripping. (Chrysler)

Know These Terms

Trim, Garnish moldings, Reveal moldings, Woodgrain transfer films, Decals, Accent stripes, Exterior trim pieces, Adhesive-backed moldings, Track moldings, Exterior door handles, Latch assemblies, Lock, Exterior locks, Lock cylinder, Retaining clip, Extension rods, Keyless lock systems, Transmitter/receiver lock systems, Lock-out tools, Interior trim, Bearing plate, Interior locks, Interior door trim assemblies, Water/air shield, Manually operated seats, Power seats, Carpets, Headlining, Support rods, Listings, Retaining strips, Active restraints, Passive restraints, Seat belts, Motorized seat belt system, Air bag systems, Energy reserve module, Sodium hydroxide powder, Plasticizers, Vinyl-coated fabrics, Grain pattern, Liquid vinyl, Liquid vinyl patching compound, Silicone-treated graining paper, Belt line, Spray-on roof coverings, Simulated seam tape, Flash time, Vinyl paint, Convertible top fabric, Manual convertible top systems, Electric convertible top, Hydraulic-electric convertible tops, Sun roof panels, Insulation, Undercoating, Fibrous pads, Weatherstripping, Sealers, Drain holes, Sealing strips, Outer-belt weatherstripping.

Summary

Trim, glass, weatherstripping, carpet, vinyl tops, insulation, and other items must be repaired or replaced after repairing metal and plastic body panels. Repair procedures will vary with the make, model, and age of the vehicle at hand.

Interior and exterior trim is used to add strength, insulate, identify, deaden sound, etc. Interior trim pieces are often called garnish moldings. Exterior trim pieces that accent glass openings are called reveal moldings.

When installing exterior trim pieces (moldings), paper templates can be used to help transfer the location of the trim from an old panel to a new panel. A measuring rule, tape measure, or magnetic tape can also be used to help determine the proper molding location. Never install clips or moldings until the final finish has cured properly. Before installing adhesive-backed moldings, clean dirt, oil, wax, and silicones from the surface of the panel. Track moldings are used on some vehicles.

Lift-bar, pull-out, and push-button exterior door handles are commonly used. These handles are linked to a latch assembly. Most cars do not have handles on the trunk lid or hatch.

A lock is a mechanism that prevents a latch assembly from operating. Exterior locks can be operated manually or electronically. If a door latch is inoperative, various lock-out tools can be used to open the door.

Interior trim includes all the components and hardware that make up the interior of a vehicle. Before a door's interior trim assembly can be removed, mirror controls, lock buttons, and door and window handles must be removed. The procedures for removing interior door trim assemblies vary. When installing a door trim assembly, make sure the water/air shield is secured properly. Additionally, sealer should be placed around the retaining clips before they are pushed into the door.

Seats are often removed when repairs are made to top or side panels. They are also removed when they require service. Some seats are bolted to the floor pan from the interior of the vehicle, while others are bolted through the floor pan from the exterior of the vehicle. Both manually operated and power seats are available.

Carpets are available in one- and two-piece designs. Most tears, cuts, and burns in carpet can be repaired. Headlining is used to cover the occupant side of the roof panel, hide electrical wires, and provide insulation. There are two types: cloth headlining and molded headlining.

Active and passive restraint systems are used in late-model vehicles. Active restraints require action from the occupants to make them functional. Conventional seat belts are active restraints. Passive restraints require no action from the occupant. Motorized seat belts and air bag systems are typical passive restraint systems. Always follow the manufactures recommendations when servicing restraint systems.

There are two basic types of vinyl roof coverings, vinyl-coated fabric coverings and spray-on coverings. The procedure for repairing coverings depends on the type used and the extent of the damage. Small scuffs and cuts can generally be repaired. In some cases, however, the entire covering must be replaced. When repairing roof panels, it is often necessary to remove the vinyl-coated fabric covering in the damaged area.

Operation, service, and maintenance of convertible tops and sunroofs will vary among manufacturers. Consult an appropriate service manual before making adjustments or major repairs. The repair and installation of convertible top fabric is generally done by upholstery specialists. Manual, electric, and hydraulic-electric convertible top systems are common. Sunroof panels are generally made of plastic, metal, or tinted glass. Both manual and electric sunroofs are used on late-model vehicles.

Interior and exterior insulation is used to muffle noise, reduce vibration, and provide thermal insulation. Weatherstripping and sealers are used to prevent air, dust, and water from entering a vehicle. When repairing a vehicle, it is important to repair or replace damaged insulation, weatherstripping, and sealer.

Worn, damaged, or improperly installed weatherstripping may lead to leaks. They can be located by spraying the area of the leak with water; driving on a dusty road; using an ultrasonic leak detector; or directing light, compressed air, or aerosol talc on the leak area.

In some cases, flexible glass and body sealers can be used to repair leaks. Damaged weatherstripping can often be recemented. If weatherstripping does not seal properly, a thin piece of cellular rubber can be placed under the weatherstripping to achieve the desired seal. In some cases, repositioning the weatherstripping will improve the seal.

Review Questions–Chapter 12

1. Interior and exterior trim is used to:
   a. add strength.
   b. deaden sound.
   c. protect edges.
   d. all of the above.

2. Exterior trim pieces that accent glass openings are commonly called _____ moldings.

3. Automotive trim can be made of plastic. True or False?

4. It is generally easier to repair damaged trim than to replace it. True or False?

5. Paper _____ can be used to transfer the location of trim pieces from one panel to another.

6. Masking tape should never be used to mark molding positions. True or False?

7. When replacing adhesive-backed moldings, the panel surface should be at least _____ °F.

8. Exterior door handles are commonly secured with screws. True or False?

9. An electric _____ is often used to operate the latch assembly on hatches and trunks.

10. A _____ is a mechanism that prevents a latch assembly from operating.

11. Rear doors are often equipped with exterior locks. True or False?

12. A _____ _____ is used to secure lock cylinder to a door panel.

13. To prevent water and dust from entering a door from around a lock cylinder, manufacturers use a:
    a. gasket seal.
    b. washer.
    c. butyl sealant.
    d. none to the above.

14. _____ rods are used to connect the lock cylinder to the locking mechanism.

15. Lock-out tools can be used to open a trunk if the latch assembly is inoperative. True or False?

16. Interior trim includes the:
    a. seats.
    b. headliner.
    c. carpet.
    d. all of the above.

17. A _____ plate is a plastic spacer that reduces friction between a door handle and a trim panel.

18. Mechanical-type interior door handles rely on a _____ _____ to operate the door latch assembly.

19. Power lock systems use a hydraulic solenoid to activate the locking mechanism. True or False?

20. In some door trim assemblies, the _____ _____ is an integral part of the panel.

21. The _____/_____ _____ keeps dust, moisture, and air from entering the door.

22. Seats are often removed when repairing a damaged top panel. True or False?

23. Most upholstery repairs are done in the body shop. True or False?

24. _____-_____ carpets are used in most sedans.

25. _____ cement is commonly used to repair cuts and tears in carpet.

26. Headlining is used to:
    a. cover the passenger side of the roof panel.
    b. provide insulation.
    c. hide electrical wires.
    d. all of the above.

27. Passive restraint systems must be applied by a vehicle's occupants. True or False?

28. Seat belts should be inspected for:
    a. cuts.
    b. broken threads.
    c. frayed edges.
    d. all of the above.

29. Air bag deployment can occur if the _____ _____ are accidentally bumped during the repair process.

30. Disconnecting the negative battery cable is a sure way to disable all air bag systems. True or False?

31. After deployment, the air bag inflator module can generally be reused. True or False?

32. Vinyl-coated fabrics are always cemented directly to the roof panel. True or False?

33. Before starting any vinyl roof repair, the damaged area should be _____.

34. A _____ _____ is often used when mending scuffs and cuts in vinyl-coated fabric roof covering.

35. _____ _____ is a specially formulated paint that consists of vinyl in an organic solvent.

36. Wrinkles in vinyl-coated fabrics are not repairable. True or False?

37. Vinyl-coated fabric roof covering is often removed when repairing a damaged _____ _____.

38. When replacing a vinyl-coated fabric roof, all traces of old adhesive must be removed. True or False?

39. _____ _____ is a term used when describing the general location of a vehicle's components.

40. _____ _____ provides the appearance of seams when using spray-on roof coverings.

41. Flash time is the time needed for _____ in a finish to evaporate.

42. Convertible top fabric is commonly repaired in the body shop. True or False?

43. Hydraulic-electric convertible tops are found on most late-model vehicles. True or False?

44. Some manual sunroofs slide on a _____ assembly.

45. Insulation is used in vehicles to:
    a. muffle noise.
    b. prevent rust.
    c. protect paint.
    d. none of the above.

46. _____ is used between movable and stationary parts to prevent air, dust, and water from entering a vehicle.

47. Leaks in weatherstripping and sealers can be located by:
    a. probing weatherstripping or sealer with a screwdriver.
    b. using an ultrasonic leak detector.
    c. directing a high-pressure stream of water directly on weatherstripping or sealed joint.
    d. all of the above.

48. Drain holes are located along the top edge of doors and rocker panels. True or False?

49. When using compressed air to check for weatherstripping leaks, the pressure should not exceed _____ psi.

50. Weatherstripping is always attached to the stationary portion of the auto body. True or False?

Activities–Chapter 12

1. Demonstrate the use of a soldering iron to repair two kinds of minor damage (scuff and a small cut) on a piece of vinyl top material. Also show how a small quantity of vinyl can be transferred to fill a hole or deep scuff by using a soldering iron to melt it from the surface of a scrap piece of material.

2. Assume that the weatherstripping around the trunk of your car, or a car in the school shop, must be replaced. Measure the existing weatherstripping to determine the amount needed, then check a collision manual or other source (such as a dealership parts department or auto parts store) to determine what the material will cost.

chapter 13

Glass Service and Replacement

After studying this chapter, you will be able to:

☐ Differentiate between laminated glass and tempered glass.

☐ Explain various installation procedures for fixed glass.

☐ Describe the techniques used to polish glass and attach a rearview mirror to a windshield.

☐ Explain various installation and adjustment procedures for movable glass.

Introduction

For greater design flexibility and increased visibility, manufacturers are using a great deal of glass in late-model vehicles. Glass is frequently broken during a collision. Glass can also be broken from the strain produced when a vehicle's body twists. To prevent damage, glass should be removed before major auto body repairs are started. Consequently, auto body technicians must be familiar with several methods of glass removal and installation. Windshield installation details for a specific vehicle are illustrated in Figure 13-1.

Automotive glass is generally described as being either fixed or movable. **Fixed glass** is not designed to move. Windshields and rear windows are common examples of fixed glass. Some hatch, opera, vent, and side windows are also fixed. Generally speaking, the installation procedures for windshields and back windows on late-model cars are similar. **Movable glass** is designed to be moved up and down or to be opened and closed. Common examples of movable glass include door windows and rear side windows.

Types of Glass

There are two types of glass used in automobiles: laminated glass and tempered glass. See Figure 13-2. Both types are considered to be safety glass because they do not shatter as easily as conventional glass.

During the 1980s, automakers began using thinner glass in an attempt to cut the weight of their vehicles. During this period, glass was reduced from 5 mm thick

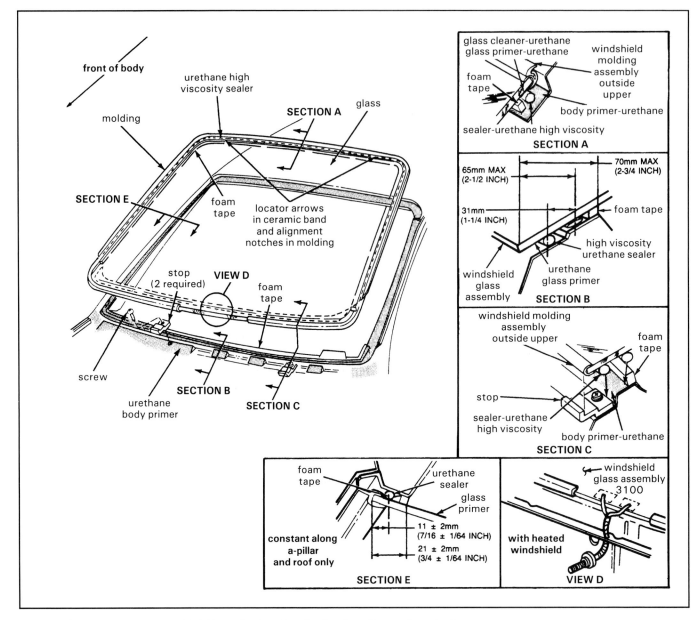

Figure 13-1 Typical windshield installation details. In view D, an electrical connection is illustrated. (Ford)

Figure 13-2 This late-model vehicle is equipped with both laminated glass and tempered glass. (Buick)

to 4 mm thick. By 1991, however, manufacturers were again using glass that was 5 mm thick. The thicker glass helps to provide the occupants with a more luxurious ride by reducing road noise.

Laminated Glass

Laminated glass is constructed with one or more layers of plastic sandwiched between two layers of glass. If laminated glass is broken, the plastic laminate layer will hold the shattered pieces of glass in place. This helps to prevent injury from sharp glass pieces. See Figure 13-3. **Antilacerative glass** is a form of laminated glass that has an additional layer of plastic on the occupant's side. Windshields are made from laminated glass or antilacerative glass.

Tempered Glass

Tempered glass consists of a single layer of glass that is about 1/4 in. (5 mm) thick. This type of glass is produced using a special heat-treating process called tempering. During this process, the glass is heated and then cooled rapidly. The rapid cooling causes the glass to compress and shrink. Tempered glass is harder and will withstand greater impact than laminated glass. After the tempering process, the glass cannot be cut, ground, or drilled. When tempered glass breaks, it shatters into small, granular pieces. Cracked tempered glass is impossible to see through. Therefore, tempered glass is used in all glass applications except windshields. See Figure 13-4.

Figure 13-3 Although this windshield is damaged, the shattered pieces are held in place by the plastic laminate.

Figure 13-4 Tempered glass shatters into small pieces when broken. (Monica Willson)

Tinted and Shaded Glass. Windshields are commonly tinted or shaded. Tinted or shaded glass is recommended for vehicles with air conditioning because it helps to keep the passenger compartment cool. **Tinted glass** is available in both laminated and tempered forms. Various color tints can be added to the glass or the laminate layer to provide the desired tint. Metallic particles are sometimes used to tint the glass or the laminate. **Shaded glass** has a dark, transparent band along its top edge. This band is recommended to help lessen glare and reduce eye strain. In some cases, glass is tinted *and* shaded.

Tinted or shaded tempered side glass is used on some vehicles. However, visibility must not be reduced by the glass. Rear glass should never be shaded. Some automobile dealers and glass shops can install a tinted plastic film to the interior of existing windows. There are also spray products available that can be used for tinting windows. In many states, the density or darkness of tinting material is regulated.

Antenna and Defroster Circuits

When antenna and/or defroster circuits are on or in fixed glass, extreme care must be taken when removing and installing the glass. On some windshields, the **antenna wire circuit** is either placed between the layers of glass or printed on the interior surface of the glass. Rear glass may have both an antenna and a defroster circuit. **Defroster circuits** often consist of narrow bands of a conductive coating that are printed on the interior surface of the glass. The coating consists of metallic powders, which are baked on the glass during the tempering process. When a small current is passed through the conductive metallic coating, heat is produced. The technician must use great care to prevent any damage to the thin coating or delicate wires. Damage will generally make the antenna or defroster circuit inoperable!

Replacing Fixed Glass

Rubber *gaskets* were used extensively to secure fixed glass on early-model vehicles. Windshields and rear windows on most late-model vehicles are held in position with *adhesive compounds* and, to a certain extent, reveal and garnish moldings. Fixed glass serves as a structural member on many late-model vehicles. Therefore, the technician must install this glass properly to maintain the structural integrity of these vehicles.

Before removing fixed glass, place protective coverings around the work area and remove all trim and hardware from around the glass. Reveal and garnish moldings, antenna and defroster connecters, windshield wiper arms, and rearview mirrors must be removed. If the glass is to be reinstalled, tape the electrical leads from the antenna and/or defroster circuits to the inside surface of the glass. This will help to protect them during handling.

Various retaining clips, which are attached to the gasket or the body, are used to secure reveal moldings on older vehicles. Some (mostly lower) reveal moldings are locked into a channel on the gasket. Screws are commonly used to secure garnish moldings. Over the years, numerous tools have been designed to remove moldings and retaining clips. See Figure 13-5. Use great care to prevent damage when removing molding.

WARNING: Glass can be easily broken during the repair process. Therefore, it is important to wear safety glasses and other protective gear when installing or removing glass.

Gasket-Type Glass Installation

As previously mentioned, fixed glass is held in position with rubber gaskets on many older vehicles. Some models use a rubber *locking strip* or *locking cord* to secure the glass in the gasket. This strip fits into the gasket groove between the glass and pinch-weld flange. Once the locking strip is removed, the glass can be replaced without removing the gasket from the body opening. A sealer is commonly applied to the gasket before the glass is replaced. Liquid soap is often used to assist in the reinstallation of the locking strip.

In many cases, the glass and the gasket can be removed as a unit. Removing the glass *and* the gasket from the window opening is generally a two person job. The locking strip must be pulled out before removing the glass and gasket from the window opening. A putty knife or other tool can be used to carefully pry the lip of the gasket from the pinch-weld flange on the inside and outside of the vehicle. Do not allow metal tools to touch the glass! A slight outward pressure on the glass will assist in forcing the gasket's lip over the flange. It is best to start at the top of the gasket and work down along each edge. Remember to protect the edges of the glass at all times. After the glass has been removed from the vehicle, tape the gasket in place and store the glass in a protected area until it is to be reinstalled.

Before reinstalling gasket-held glass, make certain that the pinch-weld flange is clean and smooth. If PVC or butyl tape is to be used, apply sheet metal primer to the flange. Then apply the tape to the flange. Insert a strong cord in the pinch-weld channel of the gasket, Figure 13-6. Overlap the cord about 12 in. (300 mm) at the lower center of the glass. Tape the ends of the cord to the glass as shown in Figure 13-7. Lubricate the channel with liquid soap and place the glass (and gasket) in the window opening. The bottom channel of the gasket should be placed over the pinch-weld flange with the cord ends extending toward the outside of the glass. Push in on the glass and pull out on the cord. As the cord is withdrawn, the gasket will be pulled over the pinch-weld flange, Figure 13-8. A hard wooden stick is sometimes used to assist in forming the gasket seal. After the gasket is in place over the pinch-weld flange, the locking strip can be reinstalled in the gasket.

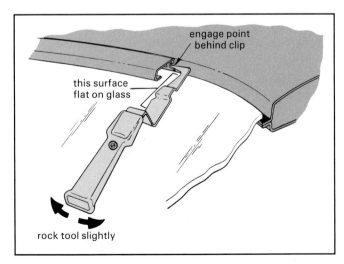

Figure 13-5   One type of tool used to disengage retaining clips.

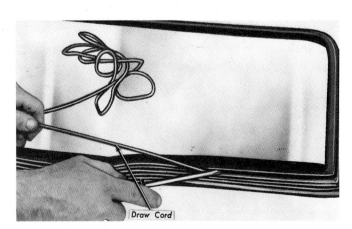

Figure 13-6   Installing a draw cord prior to the installation of gasket-held glass. (Ford)

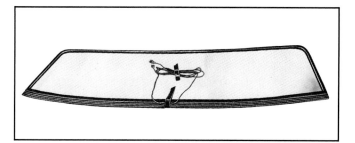

Figure 13-7 After the cord is installed, the ends are taped to the glass.

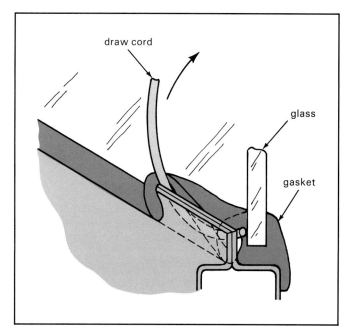

Figure 13-8 A cord is used to help slip the gasket's lip over the pinch-weld flange.

Adhesive Installations

On most vehicles, windshields, back windows, and some quarter windows are bonded to the body opening with adhesives. Polysulfide, polyurethane, and butyl adhesives have been used for this purpose. **Butyl** or **polyurethane adhesive** and **butyl tape** are commonly used together to bond windows. Never use butyl tape alone to secure a windshield. It has no structural bonding properties. Always check to make certain that the adhesive used will not damage the butyl tape or the plastic layer in the glass.

There are four basic tools used to remove adhesive-bonded glass from a window opening: hot knives, cold knives, vibrating knives, and music wire.

A **hot knife** is often used to remove glass that is secured with tough adhesive. The knife is heated to 750 °F (400 °C) to help soften the adhesive. This makes cutting easier. See Figure 13-9.

A **cold knife** can be used to cut through all types of adhesives, Figure 13-10. However, greater force is

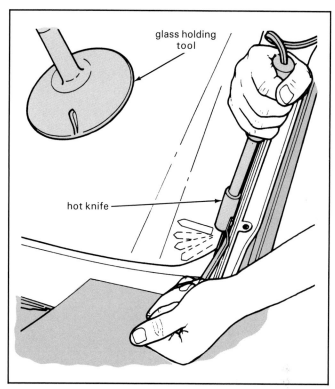

Figure 13-9 A hot knife is often used to cut through polyurethane adhesive. (Ford)

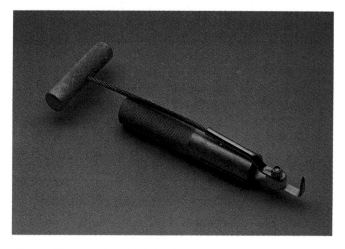

Figure 13-10 A cold knife is commonly used to cut through window adhesives. (The Eastwood Co.)

needed to pull a cold knife through the adhesive than a hot knife. The blades on both hot and cold knives must be clean and sharp.

A **vibrating knife** (electric or pneumatic) can also be used when removing adhesive-bonded glass. As previously mentioned, many modern vehicles depend on the glass and adhesive to help provide structural strength. Tough polyurethane adhesives are commonly used on these vehicles. The vibrating knife's rapidly moving blade gently cuts through polyurethane adhesives. See Figure 13-11.

Figure 13-11 This technician is using a pneumatic vibrating knife to cut through windshield adhesive.

Figure 13-12 Adhesive material can be cut with the aid of a piece of steel music wire.

Another technique for cutting through adhesives involves the use of steel *music wire* and two wood handles. To use this technique, attach one end of a 2 ft. (800 mm) piece of music wire to a wood handle. Cut a slot in the window adhesive with a cold knife and insert the other end of the wire through the slot. After the wire is pushed through the slot, tie it to the other handle.

With the help of an assistant, carefully pull the wire back and forth to cut through the adhesive material around the perimeter of the glass, Figure 13-12. Keep tension on the wire throughout the cutting operation to prevent it from kinking and breaking. After cutting through the adhesive material, lift the glass from the window opening.

A variation of the music-wire technique can be performed by one person. Insert one end of a piece of wire through the adhesive material at inside upper edge of the glass, and insert the other end of wire at the inside lower edge of the glass. Attach a handle to each wire end from outside of the body. Pull the wire back and forth to cut through the adhesive material. See Figure 13-13.

If the glass is to be reinstalled, place it on a protected bench or in an appropriate holding fixture. Remove the old adhesive compound from the windshield with a razor blade. If necessary, remove the remaining traces of adhesive compound with thinner. See Figure 13-14. When cleaning laminated glass, avoid contacting the edge of the plastic laminate material with volatile cleaner. Contact may cause discoloration and deterioration of the plastic laminate. Petroleum-based solvents should not be used to clean glass. The presence of an oily film will prevent the adhesive compound from adhering properly.

Replacing a windshield, rear glass, or fixed side window requires either partial or complete replacement of the adhesive material. Complete replacement of the adhesive is known as the *extended method* or the *full cut-*

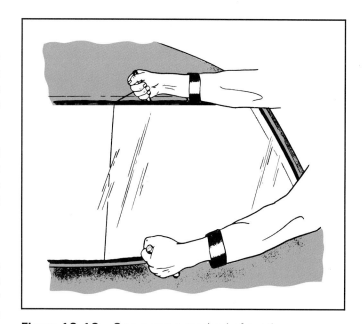

Figure 13-13 One-person method of cutting adhesive material.

out method. See Figure 13-15. Partial replacement of the adhesive is referred to as the *short method* or the *partial cut-out method*, Figure 13-16.

Extended Method of Glass Installation. When the butyl tape and the adhesive around a window must be replaced, the extended method of installing glass must be used. When performing the extended method, all of the old adhesive material must be removed from the pinch-weld flange before the new window is installed. If the original glass is to be reinstalled, apply masking tape over each side edge of glass and onto the adjacent body panels before it is removed. Cut the tape between the

Figure 13-14 This technician is cleaning the adhesive from a windshield.

glass and the body and remove the glass from the opening. The tape will be used to help align the glass during installation. See Figure 13-17.

Scrape the old adhesive material from around the window opening with a sharp scraper or chisel. Although it is not necessary to remove all traces of adhesive material, there should not be any mounds or loose pieces.

Inspect the reveal molding clips. If the upper end of a clip is bent away from the body metal more than 1/32 in. (0.8 mm), replace or re-form the clip.

If plastic or rubber **stops** (check blocks or spacers) were removed when removing the original glass, re-attach them to the window opening pinch-weld flanges. The stops should be positioned to provide equal support and spacing around the perimeter of the glass. If necessary, reinstall the **lower glass supports** at the bottom

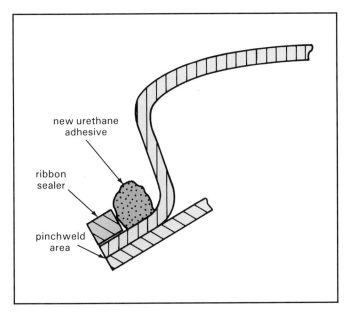

Figure 13-15 Extended method of installing glass showing the new adhesive and ribbon sealer on the pinch-weld flange.

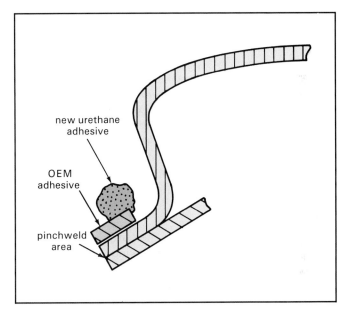

Figure 13-16 Short method of installing glass showing new adhesive placed on the original adhesive.

Figure 13-17 If a window is to be reinstalled, masking tape should be placed over the edge of the glass and the A-pillar. This tape can be used to help realign the window during installation.

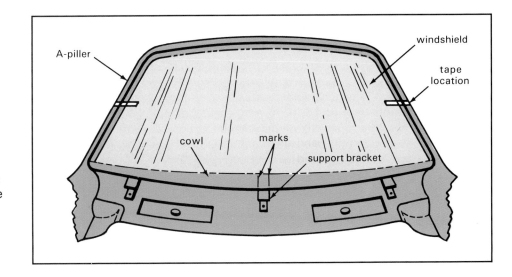

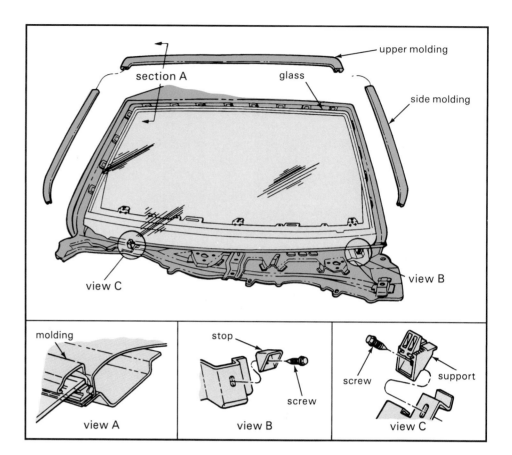

Figure 13-18 Typical windshield installation detail showing seal, stops, and molding. (Ford)

edge of the window opening, Figure 13-18. Usually, it is not necessary to remove rubber stops or supports when removing a windshield.

With the aid of a helper, lift the glass into position. With one hand on each side of the glass, hold the window at about 60 ° to the opening and carefully place the bottom of the glass on the lower glass supports. See Figure 13-19. While one person holds the glass in this position, the other can reach one arm around the body pillar and support the glass. This operation can then be repeated by the second person so that both installers have one arm on each side of the body pillars. If the original windshield is being reinstalled, the tape guides should be used to help align the glass. When installing back windows, it may be necessary to use suction cups to position the glass in the opening. In some designs, the rear glass is removed and installed from the inside of the vehicle.

After positioning the glass, check the relationship between the glass and the pinch-weld flange. The overlap of the pinch-weld flange should be equal around the perimeter of the opening (3/16 in. [5 mm] minimum). The overlap across the top of the windshield can be corrected by repositioning the lower glass supports. Overlap across the top of a back window can be adjusted by shimming or shaving the lower supports.

Check the relationship between the glass contour and the body opening contour. The gap between the glass and the pinch-weld flange should be between 1/8 in. (3 mm) and 1/4 in. (6 mm). If the gap is incorrect, it can be corrected by repositioning the spacers, applying

Figure 13-19 These technicians are positioning a windshield in the body opening.

more adhesive during installation, reworking the pinch-weld flange, or selecting another piece of glass.

After the final adjustments have been made and the glass is in the correct position, apply strips of masking tape over each side edge of the glass and onto the adjacent body panels. This tape will be used to align the glass during the final phases of installation. If the original windshield is being reinstalled, this tape should already be in place.

Cut the masking tape between the glass and the body panels and remove the glass from opening. After the glass is removed, apply masking tape around the inner surface of the glass (1/4-1/2 in. [6-12 mm] in from the outer edge). On windshields, apply the tape to the top and the sides only. Do not use tape across the bottom. After installation, the tape will be removed to give the adhesive a smooth, even edge.

Thoroughly clean the surface of the glass where the adhesive will be applied. Isopropyl alcohol is commonly used for this purpose. Using a dauber or a brush, apply **polyurethane primer** (blackout primer) to the areas where the adhesive will be applied.

Apply butyl tape adhesive to the inside edge of the pinch-weld flange, Figure 13-20. This will create a temporary seal and hold the glass in place while the polyurethane adhesive cures. Do not stretch the tape adhesive during installation. A 45° joint should be made when splicing or ending the tape adhesive.

After the tape is in place, apply a continuous bead of polyurethane adhesive around the inside edge of the glass or the perimeter of the pinch-weld flange, Figure 13-21. This bead should be about 3/8 in. (9 mm) high and 3/16 in. (5 mm) wide. Most auto body technicians prefer to place the adhesive directly on the pinch-weld flange. See Figure 13-22. This helps to prevent contact with the adhesive when handling the glass. Additionally, excess adhesive is more easily removed when it is applied in this way. Any polyurethane adhesive that is squeezed out from around the edges of the glass can be removed with a knife blade and a cloth. New windshields have a black **ceramic mask** baked directly on the perimeter of the glass. This mask will help obscure the view of the black polyurethane adhesive and the butyl tape.

If there are antenna leads in the glass, do not apply adhesive to the area around the leads. A special **filler strip,** which is provided in most installation kits, should be used in the antenna lead area. Make certain that adhesive is applied at the ends of the butyl tape to ensure a proper seal.

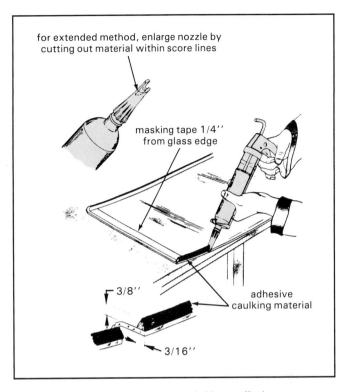

for extended method, enlarge nozzle by cutting out material within score lines

masking tape 1/4'' from glass edge

3/8''

3/16''

adhesive caulking material

Figure 13-21   Adhesive material is applied to the perimeter of the glass.

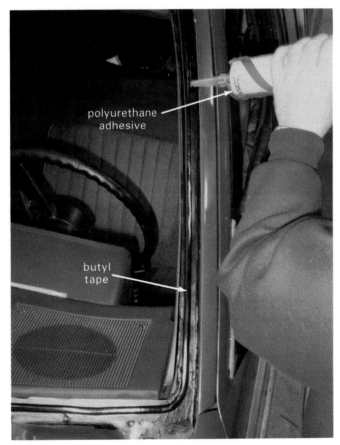

polyurethane adhesive

butyl tape

Figure 13-22   This technician is applying polyurethane adhesive directly to the pinch-weld flange.

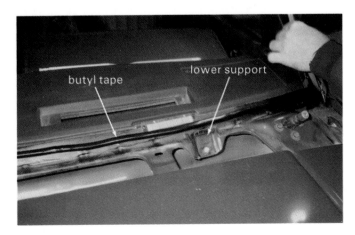

butyl tape

lower support

Figure 13-20   New butyl tape is installed along the pinch-weld flange on this vehicle.

Since polyurethane adhesive begins to cure in approximately 15 minutes, the glass must be installed quickly. With the help of another person, carefully position glass in the opening. Use the tape guides that were previously applied to help align the glass. Guide the lower edge of the glass onto the lower supports. Avoid smearing the fresh adhesive. After making sure that the glass is properly aligned, gently apply pressure on the glass to "wet out" the adhesive material. This will ensure that the adhesive bond is made to the glass and the body opening. If poor contact is noted between the glass and the butyl tape, apply more pressure to the areas that are not sealed properly. The bond width should be a minimum of 1/4 in. (6 mm). Dull spots indicate areas where the glass is not contacting the tape properly. After the desired bond is achieved, technicians commonly apply additional polyurethane adhesive around the top and sides of the glass and the pinch-weld area. This is done to eliminate any chance of leakage. A wooden paddle is sometimes used to force the adhesive between the glass and the joint area and to provide a smooth channel for moisture to run off. Any lumps of adhesive can create dams, which trap and hold water. Excess adhesive can be removed with a sharp knife and a cloth.

After the glass is installed, test it for leaks with a spray of cold water. Do not direct a strong stream of water at the fresh adhesive material. If leaks are found, paddle in extra adhesive at the leak point.

Before the adhesive hardens, work the moldings into position. See Figure 13-23. Remove all masking tape and other protective covers from the glass and the body panels. Clean the glass with an appropriate cleaner.

Owners should be warned to limit driving until the adhesive has cured. Polyurethane adhesives generally require about 48 hours to fully cure. Some of the new polyurethanes cure in only six hours. Always caution customers about curing time. Avoid slamming doors with the windows up and driving on rough roads until the adhesive has cured.

Short Method of Glass Installation. The short or partial cut-out method of glass installation can be used if, after the original glass is removed, the adhesive material on the pinch-weld flanges can serve as a base for the replacement glass. If there is a sound base of material on the pinch-weld flange, only new polyurethane adhesive is required to ensure adequate bonding strength. If there is a substantial loss of adhesive material or if the material does not adhere properly to the pinch-weld flange, the opening must be reworked and the extended replacement method must be used. Whenever in doubt, the extended method should be used.

Note: Polyurethane adhesives do not adhere well to old, cured adhesives. Since the structural strength of many vehicles depends on a sound adhesive bond between the glass and body, it is often advisable to remove all old material and use the extended method of glass installation. Additionally, many technicians prefer to use the extended method of installation because butyl adhesives hold the glass in position until the polyurethane adhesives cure. This allows the customer to take the vehicle immediately.

If the short method will be used to install glass, hold the wire or knife close to the inside plane of the old window during removal. This will prevent cutting an excessive amount of adhesive from the pinch-weld flange. Before installing new glass (or reinstalling original window), inspect the reveal molding retaining clips. Replace or reshape clips that are bent away from the body more than 1/32 in. (0.8 mm).

Position the glass in the opening. If new glass is being installed, check the relationship of the glass to the adhesive material on the pinch-weld flange. Gaps in excess of 1/8 in. (3 mm) must be corrected by shimming or by applying more adhesive material.

When the glass is properly positioned, apply masking tape over each side edge of glass and onto the adjacent body panels. During the final installation, this tape will be used to help align the glass.

Cut the alignment tape between the glass and the body and remove the glass from the opening. To speed clean up and give the adhesive a smooth, clean edge, apply masking tape across the top and down each side of the inside surface of the glass. The tape should be placed 1/4-1/2 in. (6-12 mm) in from the edge of the glass. Make certain that all stops and spacers are properly positioned. See Figure 13-24.

Clean the surface of the glass where the adhesive will be applied (edge of inside surface) and dry it with a clean cloth. Apply polyurethane primer to the clean surface according to the manufacturer's instructions. Apply a smooth, continuous bead of polyurethane adhesive (about 3/16 in. or 5 mm in diameter) along the perimeter of the pinch-weld flange.

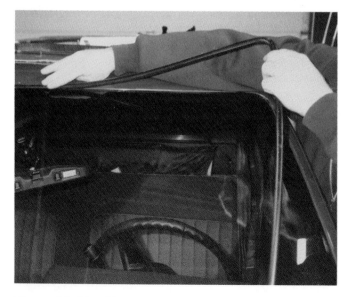

Figure 13-23 The molding must be installed before the adhesive begins to cure.

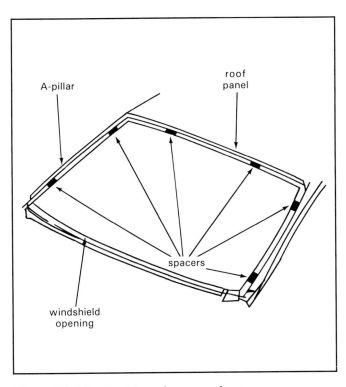

Figure 13-24 Position of spacers for a specific vehicle. (Chrysler)

With the help of an assistant, lift the glass into the opening. Carry the glass with one hand on the inside of the glass and one hand on the outside of the glass. Hold the glass in the vertical position directly in front of the window opening. While one person holds glass in position, the other can reach one arm around the body and support the glass from behind the roof pillar. After the glass is supported properly, the second installer can reach around the roof pillar in the same manner. On back glass and some windshield installations, it is necessary to use **suction cups** to position the glass in the opening.

Center the glass in the opening and place it on the lower supports. Use the tape guides that were previously installed to align the glass. Press firmly on the glass to ''wet out'' and ''set'' the adhesive material. Use care to avoid pushing the adhesive out from between the glass and the pinch-weld flanges. This will cause appearance problems and leaks.

After the glass has been installed, test it for leaks and complete the installation as described in the section on the extended method of glass installation.

Installation procedures for quarter window glass and rear windows are similar to those for windshields. Rear window installation details for a specific vehicle are shown in Figure 13-25.

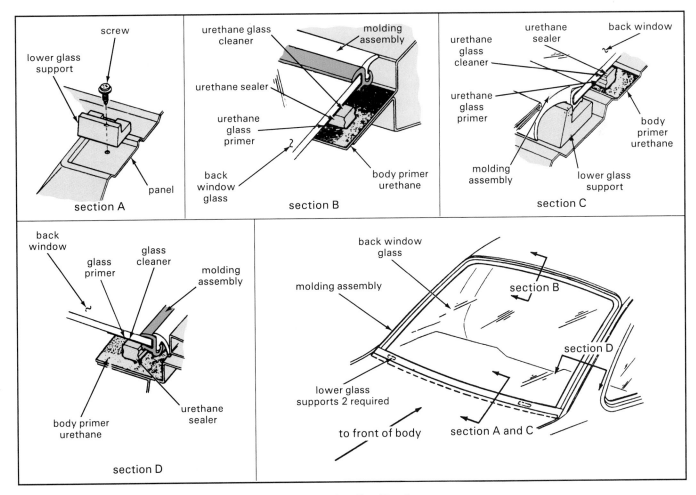

Figure 13-25 Rear window removal and installation details. (Ford)

Bonding a Rearview Mirror to Glass

To bond a rearview mirror to a windshield, carefully clean the glass in the area of attachment. The use of a scouring cleanser followed by isopropyl alcohol or a glass cleaning solution is preferred. On the outside of the glass, measure and mark the desired position of the mirror support with tape or a marking pen. Sand the bonding surface of the support and clean it with isopropyl alcohol. Apply **adhesive primer/hardener** on the mirror support and on the glass where it is to be placed. Allow primer to dry for a few minutes.

Apply two drops of **mirror bracket adhesive** (polyvinyl butyral, acrylic, methyl acrylic ester, etc.) to the mirror support. Spread the adhesive over the surface of the support and immediately press the support against the marked location on the windshield. Hold the support in position for about one minute. Allow the adhesive to cure for 10 minutes before installing the mirror on the support.

If a mirror support must be removed from a windshield, heat the glass with a heat gun to help soften the adhesive. A sharp blow to the end of a putty knife will generally break the adhesive bond between the glass and mirror support. New supports and replacement glass with the support already attached are available.

Glass Polishing and Chip Removal

Minor scratches on laminated glass can be removed by polishing the glass with a special compound. A low-speed polisher (600-1300 rpm) is used with a wool-felt polishing pad that is about 3 in. (75 mm) in diameter and 2 in. (50 mm) thick. Commercial polishes, such as **cerium-oxide powder**, are available for polishing glass.

Mix a small quantity of the polish with water to obtain a creamy consistency. Use a crayon or a marking pen to draw a circle around the scratches in the glass. This circle will act as a guide when polishing. Draw on the side of the glass that is opposite the scratches. Dip the polishing pad in the polish and apply it to the glass with moderate, steady pressure. Use less pressure on the outer edges of the scratched area. Do not hold tool in one spot for an extended period of time. See Figure 13-26.

Chips and pits on a windshield can be filled by applying a special **plastic-resin mixture.** After the resin is applied, a **vacuum patch** is placed over the repair area to withdraw all air and ensure that all voids are filled with the resin. After curing, the patch is removed and the repair area is polished. This procedure cannot be used to repair or stop cracks in glass.

Replacing and Adjusting Movable Glass

As previously mentioned, movable glass can be raised and lowered or moved in some way. Adjustments are often required to eliminate rattles and leaks in movable glass. Improperly adjusted windows will not operate correctly.

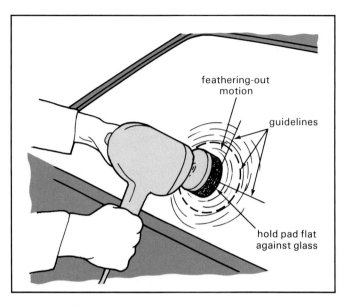

Figure 13-26   Minor scratches can be removed from windshield glass with a low-speed polisher.

Although it is not practical to describe all movable glass removal and installation procedures in this chapter, repair procedures for typical applications will be covered. All procedures should be studied for their similarities and their differences. There will be variations in the repair procedures for different models produced by the same manufacturer.

To install most door, vent, and movable quarter glass, the door trim assembly and the air/water shield must be removed. It may not be necessary to remove the door trim assembly when installing some types of fixed or swing-out glass.

Door Styles

There are two basic door styles used on automobiles: framed doors and hardtop doors. Many vans and sedans have **framed doors**. In this design, the door frame surrounds and supports the glass. **Hardtop doors** do not have a frame around the glass. In this design, the glass rests against the top and sides of the door opening or the quarter glass frame and the weatherstripping. When the window is fully raised, a soft gasket protects the window around the door opening. The glass in hardtop doors requires more adjustments than the glass in framed doors.

Framed or hardtop tailgates are used in station wagons, hatchbacks, and minivans. The glass in these tailgates can be either fixed or movable. Poor closing, leaks, and rattles are common problems with tailgates.

There are four styles of tailgates:

☐ *Lift-gates* (swing up).

☐ *Drop-gates* (swing down).

☐ *Dual-action tailgates* (drop or swing open).

☐ *Three-way tailgates* (drop and swing open).

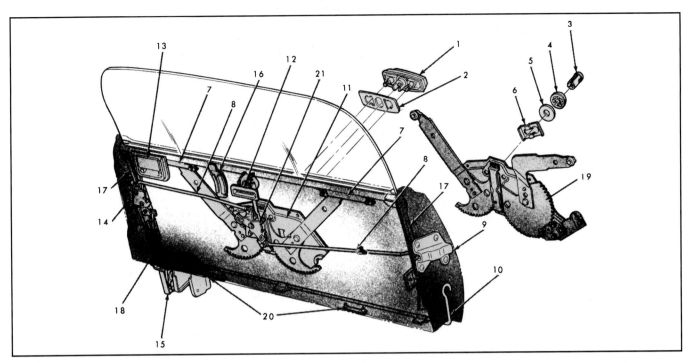

Figure 13-27 Dual-action tailgate hardware. 1–Outside handle. 2–Gasket. 3–Lock cylinder. 4–Electric feed block. 5–Gasket. 6–Lock cylinder retainer. 7–Lift channel cam. 8–Remote control connecting rod. 9–Left upper lock and hinge. 10–Torque rod. 11–Regulator, manual. 12–Inside remote gate handle. 13–Inside door handle and cable. 14–Right upper lock. 15–Right lower lock. 16–Glass stabilizer. 17–Lower glass run channels. 18–Glass block-out rod. 19–Regulator, electrical. 20–Sealing strip. 21–Remote control assembly (gate operation).

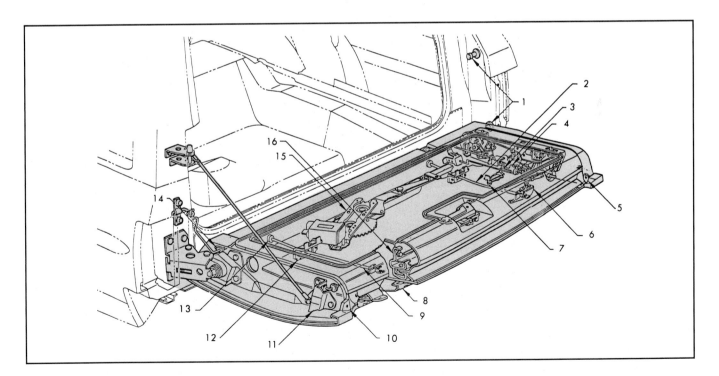

Figure 13-28 Three-way tailgate. 1–Striker, tailgate lock upper right side. 2–Tube assembly, tailgate window guide. 3–Rod assembly, tailgate lock cylinder-to-lock. 4–Rod assembly, tailgate lock-to-power actuator. 5–Weatherstrip assembly. 6–Handle assembly, tailgate outside. 7–Lock cylinder assembly. 8–Sealing strip assembly. 9–Tube assembly, tailgate window guide. 10–Weatherstrip assembly. 11–Lock assembly, tailgate upper hinge left side. 12–Plate assembly, tailgate window left side. 13–Bumper, tailgate window down stop. 14–Grommet, torque rod. 15–Regulator assembly, tailgate window electric. 16–Retainer assembly, tailgate belt trim support.

Examples of the typical components for a dual-action tailgate and three-way tailgate are shown in Figures 13-27 and 13-28.

Regulators

All movable door glass requires a mechanism that allows it to be moved up and down. This mechanism is called a *regulator*. In some van, truck, and car side windows, a regulator or cam mechanism allows the glass to be opened outward a limited distance at the rear of the window opening. In some sunroof windows, the regulator will run the glass backward and forward.

Regulators can be manually operated or power operated. Gears, cams, counterbalance springs, and electric drives (which use a flexible steel tape or band) are used in some regulator designs. See Figure 13-29.

The regulator mechanism and associated parts are bolted, riveted, or spot-welded to the inner door panel. Rivets and spot-welds must be drilled out when removing these components. On some models, it is possible to remove the regulator without removing the glass from the door. If this is done, be certain to carefully support the glass in the up position.

In most cases, the glass and the *lift channel* (sash channel) must be removed before removing the regulator. The lift channel can be removed from the regulator by lowering the glass until the channel screws or clips are accessible through *access holes* in the door panel. After the screws or clips are removed, the glass and channel can be lifted out of the door. In some designs, it may also be necessary to remove up-stops and belt trim support retainers (stabilizers) before removing the channel from the regulator. *Up-stops* limit the upward travel of the lift channel. The *belt trim support retainers* hold the glass in position and prevent it from wobbling. It is important to note that the lift channel is not a permanent part of the regulator itself.

On framed doors, the run channel must be removed or loosened before attempting to remove the glass and the lift channel. After removing the run channel, the glass and lift channel can be removed from the regulator by

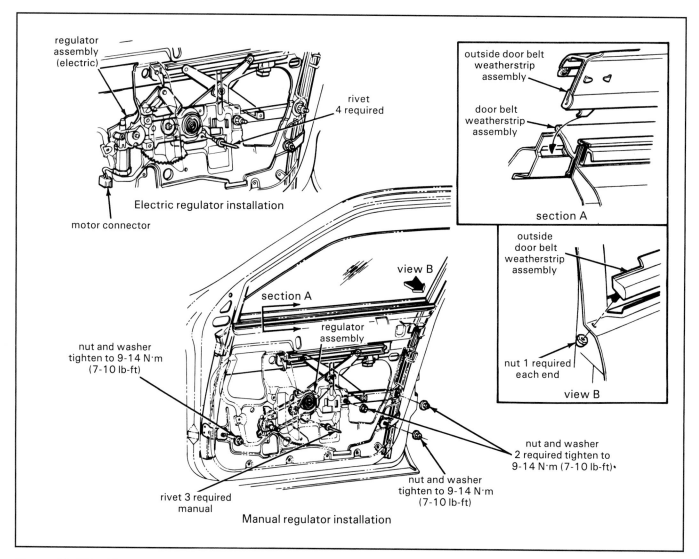

Figure 13-29 Manual and electric regulator installation details for a specific vehicle. (Ford)

lifting it up and tilting it slightly inward. Once the glass has been removed, the regulator can be removed through an access hole in the door.

Quarter glass regulator mechanisms are similar to door regulators. Some move up and down. Others have curved guides that are positioned at an angle to permit the glass to be moved up and down in a curved path. See Figure 13-30.

Power window systems use an electric, reversing motor to operate the regulator mechanism. System designs vary among manufacturers. Refer to an appropriate service manual for information on specific systems. See Figure 13-31.

Although power window systems vary, troubleshooting techniques and repair procedures are similar for all designs. Use caution when servicing regulators equipped with counterbalance springs. On some models, these springs must be released before working on the regulator mechanism.

If none of the windows operate, the trouble may be caused by a short or open in the power feed circuit. When this occurs, check the feed connection to power harness for cuts or abrasions. Check the feed circuit for continuity and verify the proper operation of the ignition relay. The ignition switch must be in the ''on'' position to operate most power equipment.

If a window operates in one direction only, check the switch. If it operates sluggishly, check the regulator and window channels (runs) for excessive friction. If necessary, lubricate the regulator and the runs with an appropriate silicone lubricant. If the motor runs but the window does not move, make sure the motor is attached to the regulator coupling. For more information on troubleshooting electrical circuits and components, see Chapter 14.

Movable Glass Installation

Movable glass is commonly secured in the regulator mechanism with channels, adhesives, and mechanical fasteners.

Before replacing glass that is held in place by a U-shaped channel, remove all debris from the channel. In some designs, rubber spacers or sealer tape is used to hold the glass in the channel. The tape or the spacers are placed on the lower edge of the replacement glass, and the glass is forced into the channel. If necessary, a rubber mallet can be used to tap the channel onto the glass. A tight friction fit holds the glass securely in the channel. Do not let metal contact the glass at any time. If the glass is too loose, additional tape can be used or the channel can be squeezed together slightly.

In many late-model vehicles, clips or stays are used to position the replacement glass, and epoxy adhesive is used to secure the glass in the channel. Silicone adhesive sealant is then used to fill gaps and voids on the inside and outside of the channel.

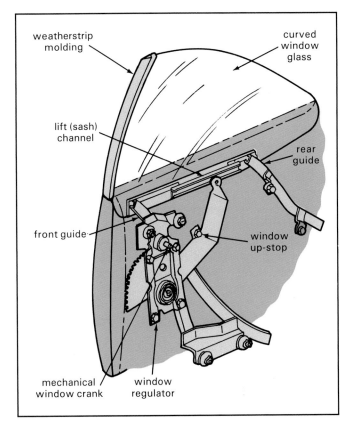

Figure 13-30 Typical curved quarter window with regulator assembly.

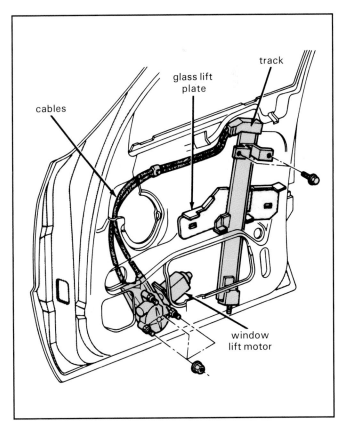

Figure 13-31 Front door with power window regulator. (Chrysler)

Bolt-through glass is held to the regulator mechanism with mechanical fasteners, such as bolts or rivets. These fasteners pass directly through holes in the glass and secure it to the lift bracket. Plastic or rubber bushings are commonly placed in the holes to prevent metal parts from directly contacting the glass. The fasteners must be installed carefully. Figure 13-32 identifies typical bolt-through window components and their assembly sequence. Specified installation torque is about 72 ft.lbs./in. (98 N•m).

Caution: In some designs, the stabilizer guide, shown at 14 in Figure 13-32, is riveted to the glass during production. When servicing this guide, a special hand rivet tool must be used. If the hand rivet tool is not available, the stabilizer guide can be bolted to the glass. Special bushings, bolts, and nuts are required for bolt-on installation. Rivet bushings and retainers must not be used when installing the guide with bolt-on hardware. Using rivet bushings and retainers with bolts may cause the glass to break when tightening the nuts.

Adjusting Regulators

Regulators must be adjusted properly so that the movable door glass operates and seals correctly. Regulator adjustments may include adjusting the pivot guide tracks, guide brackets, up-stops, and retainers (stabilizers when used). The front door glass should be adjusted before the rear door glass on four-door hardtop models.

Rubber runs on framed doors and gaskets on hardtop models may be lubricated with silicone spray, which will ease the operation of the glass and prevent squeaks. Silicone will not harm the rubber.

If door glass tips or binds, check the adjustment of the lower lift channel. Also, make sure that the cam rollers and the guide assembly are engaged. The cam adjustments allow the glass to be tilted. Depending on the design, one or two lift arms are used to raise the lift channel. If two arms are used, the second arm helps prevent the lift channel from tipping or jamming. Window up-stops are located on the lift channel cam. These stops limit the upward travel of the lift channel (and glass). Note: If glass in a hardtop door does not fit properly after regulator adjustments are made, the door may require repositioning.

Know These Terms

Fixed glass, Movable glass, Laminated glass, Anti-lacerative glass, Tempered glass, Tinted glass, Shaded glass, Antenna wire circuit, Defroster circuits, Gaskets, Adhesive compounds, Locking strip, Locking cord, Butyl adhesive, Polyurethane adhesive, Butyl tape, Hot knife, Cold knife, Vibrating knife, Music wire, Extended method, Full cut-out method, Short method, Partial cut-out method, Lower glass supports, Stops, Polyurethane primer, Ceramic mask, Filler strip, Suction cups, Adhe-

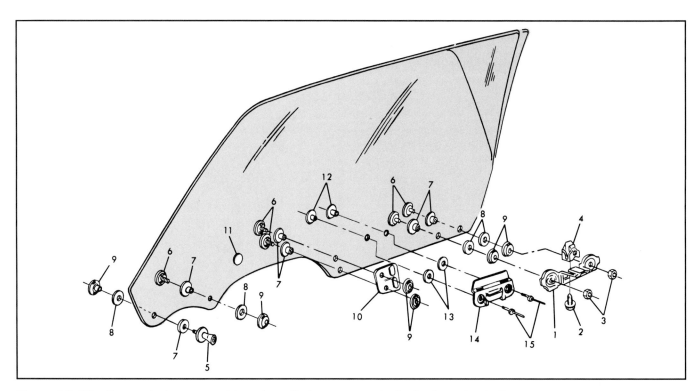

Figure 13-32 Door window assembly as installed on one particular body style. 1—Rear up-stop support. 2—Rear up-stop screw. 3—Rear up-stop support to glass nuts. 4—Rear up-stop. 5—Front up-stop. 6—Spanner bolt. 7—Bushing. 8—Washer. 9—Spanner nut. 10—Spacer. 11—Stabilizer button. 12—Rivet bushing. 13—Rivet retainer. 14—Stabilizer guide. 15—Rivet.

sive primer/hardener, Mirror bracket adhesive, Cerium-oxide powder, Plastic-resin mixture, Vacuum patch, Framed doors, Hardtop doors, Regulator, Lift channel, Access holes, Up-stops, Belt trim support retainers, Bolt-through glass.

Summary

Glass is frequently broken during a collision. To prevent damage during major auto body repairs, glass should be removed before repairs are started. Automotive glass is generally described as fixed or movable. Fixed glass does not move. Movable glass, on the other hand, can be moved up and down or opened and closed.

Both laminated glass and tempered glass are used in automobiles. Laminated glass consists of one or more layers of plastic sandwiched between two pieces of glass. Tempered glass is a single layer of glass that is subjected to a special heat-treating process.

In many cases, glass is tinted or shaded to help keep a vehicle's passenger compartment cool and to reduce eyestrain. Some glass can be tinted and shaded. Visibility must never be reduced by tinting or shading.

Many fixed glass panels are equipped with antenna or defroster circuits. Special precautions must be taken when installing or removing panels equipped with these circuits.

Rubber gaskets were used extensively to secure glass on early-model vehicles. To remove gasket-type glass, a putty knife is used to pry the lip of the gasket from the pinch-weld flange. When installing gasket-type glass, a cord, which is placed in the gasket's channel, is used to pull the gasket over the pinch-weld flange.

On late-model vehicles, adhesive compounds are generally used to hold the glass in position. A hot knife, cold knife, vibrating knife, or music wire can be used to remove adhesive-bonded glass from a window opening. The extended method of glass installation requires the complete removal and replacement of the window adhesive (butyl tape and polyurethane adhesive). The short method of glass installation involves the partial replacement of the adhesive.

A special mirror support adhesive should be used to bond a rearview mirror support to a windshield. Allow the adhesive to cure for 10 minutes before installing the mirror on the support. Minor scratches on glass can be removed using a low-speed polisher, a felt polishing pad, and a commercial glass polish. Small chips in glass can often be filled with a plastic-resin mixture.

It is often necessary to remove the interior door trim assembly and the air/water shield when replacing movable glass. There are two door styles used on automobiles: framed doors and hardtop doors. Regulators are the mechanisms in doors that allow glass to be moved up or down. Regulators can be manually operated or power operated. The regulator is generally bolted, riveted, or spot-welded to the inner door panel. Quarter glass mech-

anisms are similar to door regulators. They allow quarter glass to be moved up and down. Movable glass is commonly secured in the regulator mechanism with channels, adhesives, and mechanical fasteners. After movable glass is installed, regulators must be adjusted so that the glass seals and operates correctly.

Review Questions—Chapter 13

1. Automotive glass is often removed before major auto body repairs are made. True or False?

2. _____ glass is not designed to move.

3. _____ consists of a layer of plastic sandwiched between two pieces of glass.
   a. Tempered glass.
   b. Laminated glass.
   c. Shaded glass.
   d. None of the above.

4. When tempered glass breaks, it shatters into _____, granular pieces.

5. Tempered glass is commonly used for windshields. True or False?

6. Tinted glass and shaded glass are often used in air-conditioned vehicles to help keep the passenger compartment _____.

7. _____ circuits consist of bands of a conductive coating that are painted on glass.

8. Gasket-type windshield installations are commonly used on late-model vehicles. True or False?

9. Fixed glass can be held in position with:
   a. adhesives.
   b. reveal and garnish moldings.
   c. rubber gaskets.
   d. all of the above.

10. In gasket-type glass installations, the lip of the gasket fits over the _____-_____ flange.

11. Polyurethane adhesive and _____ tape are commonly used to bond fixed glass.

12. Adhesive-bonded glass can be removed by cutting the adhesive with a piece of music wire. True or False?

13. Volatile cleaners may cause discoloration if they contact the edge of _____ glass.

14. The short method of installing glass is used when:
   a. only the butyl tape requires replacement.
   b. only the polyurethane adhesive requires replacement.
   c. both butyl tape and polyurethane adhesive require replacement.
   d. none of the above.

15. Plastic or rubber _____ are used to provide equal support and spacing around the perimeter of adhesive-bonded glass.

16. Butyl tape should be installed to:
   a. window glass.
   b. pinch-weld flanges.
   c. both the pinch-weld flange and the glass.
   d. none of the above.

17. To help obscure the view of polyurethane adhesive and butyl tape, many new windshields have a _____ _____ baked on the perimeter of the glass.

18. To prevent leaks, extra adhesive should be applied in areas adjacent to antenna leads. True or False?

19. Polyurethane adhesives begin to set in approximately:
   a. 15 minutes.
   b. 5 minutes.
   c. 45 minutes.
   d. none of the above.

20. In some cases, polyurethane adhesives do not adhere well to old, cured adhesives. True or False?

21. Masking tape is commonly used to help align glass during installation. True or False?

22. Before bonding a rearview mirror support to a windshield, the area of attachment must be _____.

23. After attaching a rearview mirror support, the mirror can be installed immediately. True or False?

24. Minor scratches in most windshields can be repaired by _____ the glass with a special compound.

25. _____-_____ powder is commonly used to remove scratches from glass.

26. Small chips and pits on a windshield cannot be repaired. True or False?

27. _____ glass can be adjusted to eliminate rattles and leaks.

28. Hardtop doors are equipped with a frame that surrounds the window glass. True or False?

29. The mechanism that allows glass to be moved up and down is called a:
   a. support bracket.
   b. stabilizer.
   c. regulator.
   d. none of the above.

30. _____ _____ limit the upward travel of the lift channel.

31. Movable glass is often secured by:
   a. channels.
   b. adhesives.
   c. mechanical fasteners.
   d. all of the above.

32. Movable glass should not be allowed to contact metal parts. True or False?

33. On hardtop models, the front door glass should be adjusted _____ the rear door glass.

34. The rubber runs on framed doors can be lubricated with _____ spray.

35. If the glass in a hardtop door does not fit after the regulator has been adjusted, the door may require repositioning. True or False?

Activities–Chapter 13

1. Remove the interior panel and trim from a door of a vehicle with manually operated windows. Examine the window regulator mechanism carefully, and make two sketches: one with the window fully lowered and one with it fully raised. Label your sketches and all the parts of the assembly.

2. To confirm the growing use of glass in automobiles, locate two cars with approximately the same body size, one from the early 1980s and one from the early 1990s. For each car, determine the area of the glass (in square inches). Do so for each window by measuring its height and width, then multiplying one times the other. After all the car's windows are measured, add the totals together. Is the total for the 1990s car much larger?

3. Visit a specialty glass shop and observe the steps involved in removing and replacing windshields. Ask the manager if the shop does installation of many older-style rubber gasketed windshields, and if so, whether the process is easier or more difficult than installation with adhesives.

4. Talk to an insurance agent or adjuster about the frequency of windshield repair vs. replacement for stone damage. Find the answers to these questions: In what percentage of windshield damage is repair possible? Why do insurance companies encourage repair? What is the average repair cost? What is the average replacement cost? What percentage of vehicle owners choose repair over replacement? Write a short report or deliver an oral report to the class.

chapter 14

Electrical and Electronic Systems Repair

After studying this chapter, you will be able to:

☐ Define the terms current, voltage, and resistance.

☐ Identify electrical symbols used in automotive service manuals.

☐ Distinguish between series circuits and parallel circuits.

☐ Explain how to maintain, test, and charge a battery.

☐ Define closed, open, and short circuits.

☐ Describe the various tools used to test electrical systems.

☐ Explain methods for testing various electrical components.

Introduction

When repairing damaged vehicles, the auto body technician will often find it necessary to repair or replace various components in the **electrical system,** such as wires, switches, fuses, and lamps. See Figure 14-1. Today's vehicles are also equipped with complex **electronic systems**, such as computerized engine control systems and anti-lock brake systems. Expensive diagnostic equipment and a great deal of experience are required to repair these systems. Therefore, most body shops send *electronic system problems* to automotive service centers that specialize in this type repair. Minor electrical system repairs, on the other hand, require only a basic knowledge of electrical theory and inexpensive test equipment.

It is not practical to discuss all electrical theory or repair procedures in this text. Therefore, only the basic information necessary to troubleshoot and repair the most common *electrical system problems* will be presented in this chapter.

Electrical Vocabulary

To troubleshoot and repair electrical system problems, the technician must be familiar with the terms voltage, current, and resistance.

Voltage is the pressure that causes electricity to flow. Voltage is measured in units called **volts.** A **voltmeter** is used to measure voltage. Most automobiles operate on a 12-volt electrical system.

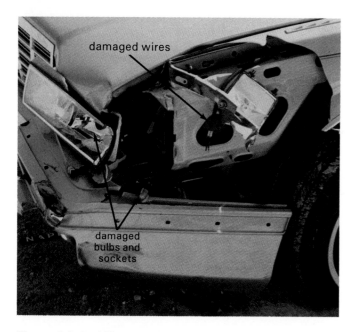

Figure 14-1 When correcting collision damage, the auto body technician must often make electrical system repairs. On this vehicle, damaged light bulbs must be replaced and broken wires must be repaired.

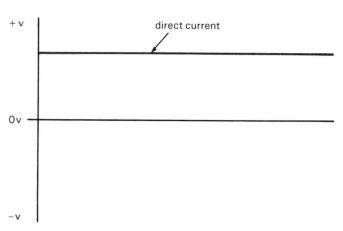

Figure 14-2 Direct current is produced by an automotive battery.

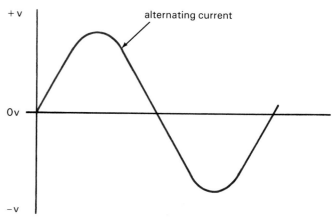

Figure 14-3 Alternating current changes direction several times a second.

The flow of electricity is called *current.* Current is measured in units called *amperes.* An *ammeter* is used to measure current. Current is produced in two forms: direct current and alternating current. *Direct current* (dc) travels in one direction, Figure 14-2. This is the type current that is produced by the car battery. *Alternating current* (ac), on the other hand, rapidly changes direction, Figure 14-3. A vehicle's alternator produces alternating current, which is rectified (changed to direct current) before it is used by the electrical system. This is accomplished by a rectifier circuit in the alternator. The rectifier circuit permits alternating current to leave the alternator in only one direction. See Figure 14-4.

Resistance is the opposition to the flow of electricity and is measured in units called *ohms.* An *ohmmeter* is used to take resistance measurements. All electrical components have some degree of resistance.

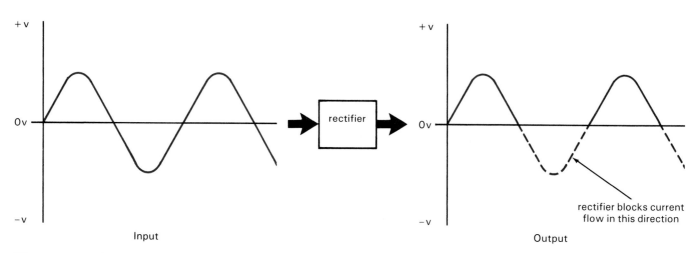

Figure 14-4 Current is rectified before being used in the automotive electrical system. Note that the negative current is not allowed to pass the rectifier.

Service Manuals

Service manuals are essential when diagnosing and repairing modern electrical systems. These manuals contain **wiring diagrams,** which are used to help isolate and trace electrical problems. See Figure 14-5. Wiring diagrams often show where wires are routed and how components are arranged. Symbols are generally used to represent various components (switches, lights, etc.) in wiring diagrams. Common electrical symbols are shown in Figure 14-6. Numerous electrical abbreviations are also used in service manuals. Common electrical abbreviations are shown in Figure 14-7. Many wiring diagrams contain wire code numbers that specify the size, application, and color of various wires. See Figure 14-8.

Electrical Circuits

Today's vehicles have many complex electrical circuits. An electrical circuit has three major parts:

☐ **Conductors** (materials that allow the flow of electricity through the circuit).

☐ **Power source** (source of electrical energy).

☐ **Load** (component that uses electrical energy).

A complete circuit requires one conductor to carry electricity from the source to the load and another conductor to carry electricity from the load back to the source. On vehicles with metal bodies, the body can serve as a common conductor. In most service manuals,

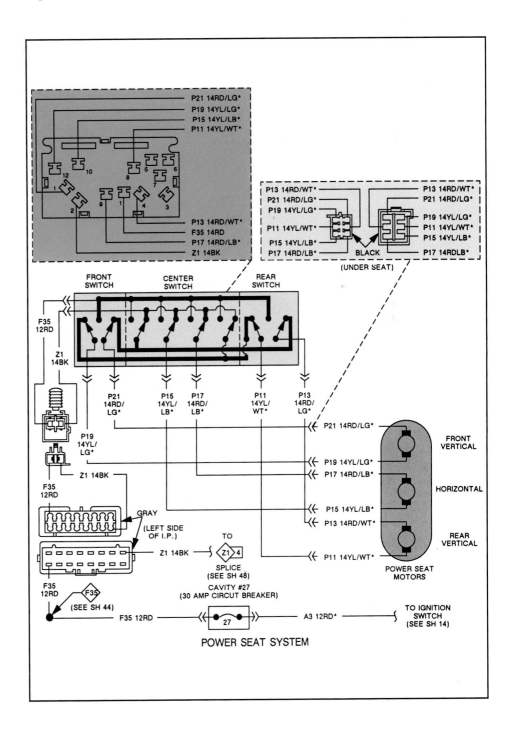

Figure 14-5 Wiring diagram for a power seat system. (Chrysler)

LEGEND OF SYMBOLS USED ON WIRING DIAGRAMS			
+	POSITIVE		CONNECTOR
−	NEGATIVE		MALE CONNECTOR
	GROUND		FEMALE CONNECTOR
	FUSE		DENOTES WIRE CONTINUES ELSEWHERE
	GANG FUSES WITH BUSS BAR		DENOTES WIRE GOES TO ONE OF TWO CIRCUITS
	CIRCUIT BREAKER		SPLICE
	CAPACITOR		SPLICE IDENTIFICATION
Ω	OHMS		THERMAL ELEMENT
	RESISTOR	TIMER	TIMER
	VARIABLE RESISTOR		MULTIPLE CONNECTOR
	SERIES RESISTOR		OPTIONAL WIRING WITH / WIRING WITHOUT
	COIL		"Y" WINDINGS
	STEP UP COIL	88:88	DIGITAL READOUT
	OPEN CONTACT		SINGLE FILAMENT LAMP
	CLOSED CONTACT		DUAL FILAMENT LAMP
	CLOSED SWITCH		L.E.D. — LIGHT EMITTING DIODE
	OPEN SWITCH		THERMISTOR
	CLOSED GANGED SWITCH		GAUGE
	OPEN GANGED SWITCH		SENSOR
	TWO POLE SINGLE THROW SWITCH		FUEL INJECTOR
	PRESSURE SWITCH		DENOTES WIRE GOES THROUGH BULKHEAD DISCONNECT
	SOLENOID SWITCH	STRG COLUMN	DENOTES WIRE GOES THROUGH STEERING COLUMN CONNECTOR
	MERCURY SWITCH	INST PANEL	DENOTES WIRE GOES THROUGH INSTRUMENT PANEL CONNECTOR
	DIODE OR RECTIFIER	ENG	DENOTES WIRE GOES THROUGH GROMMET TO ENGINE COMPARTMENT
	BY-DIRECTIONAL ZENER DIODE		DENOTES WIRE GOES THROUGH GROMMET
	MOTOR		HEATED GRID ELEMENTS
	ARMATURE AND BRUSHES		

Figure 14-6 Common automobile electrical symbols.

COMMON ELECTRICAL ABBREVIATIONS			
A	Ampere	POS	positive
ac	alternating current	PRES	pressure
ACC	accessory	SOL	solenoid
BAT	battery	SPDT	single-pole double-throw
C/B	circuit breaker	SPST	single-pole single-throw
dc	direct current	TEMP	temperature
DPDT	double-pole double-throw	TOG	toggle (switch)
MOM	momentary	V	Volt
MOT	motor	W	Watt
(n)	none	−	negative
NC	(nc) normally closed	Ω	Ohm
NEG	negative	+	positive
NO	(no) normally open	±	plus or minus
PB	push button	%	percent

Figure 14-7 Common electrical abbreviations.

CAV	WIRE CODE	INSTRUMENT PANEL CIRCUITS	SHEET
1	A3 12RD/WT*	IGNITION SWITCH FEED (BATTERY FEED)	5,7
2	A6 12RD/BK*	BATTERY FEED - PARK LAMPS	5,7
3	A18 14RD/PK*	VAN CONVERSION (BATTERY SUPPLY)	91
4	G19 20LG/BK*	ABS WARNING LAMP	72
5	—	—	—
6	L3 14RD/OR*	HEADLAMP HIGH BEAM	41
7	V30 22DB/RD*	SPEED CONTROL	43
8	V31 20BR/RD*	SPEED CONTROL	43
9	V33 20WT/LG*	SPEED CONTROL	43
10	V32 20YL/RD*	SPEED CONTROL	43
	V32 20YL/RD*	SPEED CONTROL	43
11	D2 18WT/BK*	CCD BUS (−)	56
12	D1 18VT/BR*	CCD BUS (+)	56
13	L43 20VT	FUSE 10 LT HEADLAMP	42
14	L44 20VT/RD*	FUSE TO RT HEADLAMP	41
15	G24 22GY/PK*	EMISS MAINT REMINDER LAMP	72
16	G34 16RD/BK*	DAYTIME RUNNING LIGHT MODULE TO HI-BM IND	72
17	G20 22VT/YL*	TEMPERATURE SEND	38, 39,40
18	G6 22GY	OIL PRESSURE LAMP	38, 39,40
19	G60 22GY/YL*	OIL PRESSURE SEND	38, 39,40
20	L39 18LB	FUSED FOG LAMP FEED	69
21	L61 18LG	LEFT TURN SIGNAL LAMP	54
22	L60 18TN	RIGHT TURN SIGNAL LAMP	54
23	A15 14PK	HAZARD FLASHER	54
24	V4 18RD/YL*	WIPER MOTOR HIGH SPEED	46
25	V3 18BR/WT*	WIPER MOTOR LOW SPEED	46
26	L7 18BK/YL*	PARKING LAMPS	42
27	F20 18WT	BACK-UP LAMP SWITCH FEED	89
28	L1 18VT/BK*	BACK-UP LAMP	89
29	V10 18BR	WINDSHIELD WASHER MOTOR	45
30	G29 22BK/TN*	LOW WASHER FLUID	46
31	A41 14YL	IGNITION START	11
32	X2 18DG/RD*	HORNS	44
33	C21 18DB/OR*	AIR CONDITIONING	27, 29
34	G4 20GY/BK*	BRAKE WARNING LAMP	104
35	V5 18DG	WINDSHIELD WIPER SWITCH	46
36	V6 18DB	WINDSHIELD WIPER MOTOR	46
	V6 18DB	WINDSHIELD WIPER MOTOR	46
37	B3 20LG/DB*	LEFT RR WHEEL SENSOR	34
38	B4 20LG	LEFT RR WHEEL SENSOR	34
39	B1 20YL/DB*	RIGHT RR WHEEL SENSOR	34
40	B2 20YL	RIGHT RR WHEEL SENSOR	34
41	K29 20WT/PK*	BRAKE SENSE	43
42	L50 18WT/OR*	SPEED SENSOR	89
43	D11 20WT/VT*	DIAG. ANTI-LOCK BRAKES	37
44	D12 20OR	DIAG. ANTI-LOCK BRAKES	37
45	A61 14DG/BK*	FUEL PUMP FEED	88, 100
46	L20 14LG/WT*	BATTERY FEED	50
47	A21 14DB	IGNITION RUN/START	4
48	A4 12BK/RD*	HEATED REAR WINDOW	4, 6
49	A1 12RD	IGNITION SWITCH FEED	7
50	A2 12PK/BK*	IGNITION SWITCH FEED	5, 7

TERMINAL END OF DISCONNECT

SMALL INDEX

LARGE INDEX

Figure 14-8 A connector showing wire codes. (Chrysler)

Figure 14-9 Wiring diagram for a common ground circuit. Note that the body serves as a common conductor.

this arrangement is referred to as a common ground and is represented with a ground symbol. See Figure 14-9. Good conductors offer little resistance to the flow of electricity. Plastic body panels and other plastic components are poor conductors and, therefore, cannot be used as common conductors. In most vehicles, current leaves the source from the negative terminal, travels through a load (motor, lamp, etc.), and returns to the source through the positive terminal connection.

Series circuits contain one or more loads that are connected so the current has only a single path to follow. See Figure 14-10. *Parallel circuits* contain two or more loads that are connected so that current will flow through all of the loads at any given time, Figure 14-11. It is important to note, however, that the amount of current flowing through each of the loads in a parallel circuit depends on the resistance of the individual loads included in the circuit.

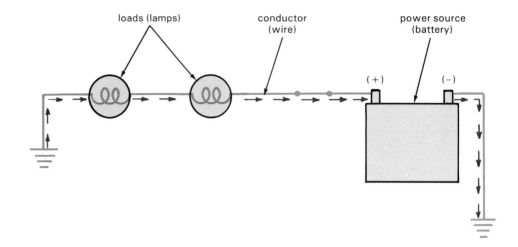

Figure 14-10 Series circuit.
The arrows indicate the
direction of current flow.

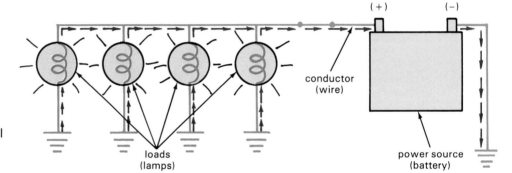

Figure 14-11 Typical parallel
circuit. Note that current will
flow through all four loads.

Wires

Wires are used in the automobile to carry electrical energy between a source and a load. Wiring is commonly routed under carpets, inside pillars, and behind fenders. Wires are often color coded to assist in assembly and repair. Typical color codes and their abbreviations are given in Figure 14-12. Some wires will have a base color and a colored strip or **tracer.** See Figure 14-13. The color codes for wires with tracers are generally represented by two letters in service manuals. The first letter represents the base color and the second letter represents the tracer color. Always mark or number wire connections during disassembly. This will save time and prevent damage during reassembly.

Terminals and Connectors

Various terminals and connectors are used to aid in the rapid assembly and repair of electrical circuits. **Terminals** are mechanical fasteners that are attached to wire ends. *Solderless terminals* are simply crimped to a wire. Other terminals are designed to be soldered to the wire. Several wire terminals are shown in Figure 14-14.

Connectors are used to make quick connections of two or more wires. Most connectors are designed with male and female halves, which are forced together. When numerous connections are to be made at one time, a *harmonica connector* can be used. The openings in a

COMMON WIRE COLOR CODES		
Color	**Abbreviations**	
Aluminum	AL	
Black	BLK	BK	B
Blue (Dark)	BLU DK	DB	DK BLU
Blue (Light)	BLU LT	LB	LT BLU
Brown	BRN	BR	BN
Glazed	GLZ	GL	
Gray	GRA	GR	G
Green (Dark)	GRN DK	DG	DK GRN
Green (Light)	GRN	LG	LT GRN
Maroon	MAR	M	
Natural	NAT	N	
Orange	ORN	O	ORG
Pink	PNK	PK	P
Purple	PPL	PR	
Red	RED	R	RD
Tan	TAN	T	TN
Violet	VLT	V	
White	WHT	W	WH
Yellow	YEL	Y	YL

Figure 14-12 Common wire color codes.
These codes are used to make wire
identification easier.

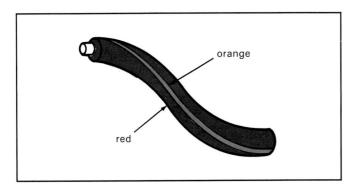

Figure 14-13 This wire has a colored tracer on the insulation.

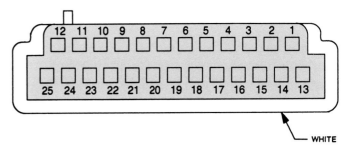

WHITE

CAV	CIRCUIT	DESCRIPTION	SHEET
1	G74 18TN/RD*	DOOR AJAR SWITCH RT FRONT DOOR	105
2	G78 18TN/BK*	LIFTGATE/DECK LID AJAR SWITCH	105
3	—	NOT USED	—
4	G9 20GY/BK*	BRAKE WARNING	104
5	—	NOT USED	—
6	—	NOT USED	—
7	L60 18TN	RT FRONT TURN SIGNAL	104
8	—	NOT USED	—
9	D14 18LB	DECODE - HIGH INST CLUSTER	104
10	P35 18 OR/VT*	POWER DOOR LOCK B+ LOCK	105
11	G60 22GY/YL*	OIL PRESSURE SENDING UNIT	104
12	D13 18OR/DB*	DECODE - LOW INST CLUSTER	104
13	—	NOT USED	—
14	G76 18TN/YL*	DOOR AJAR SWITCH REAR DOOR	105
15	G42 20DB/YL*	SIGNAL GROUND	105
16	—	NOT USED	—
17	G11 20WT/BK*	PARK BRAKE SWITCH	105
18	—	NOT USED	—
19	L61 18LG	LT FRONT TURN SIGNAL	104
20	L94 20OR/WT*	LO BEAM RELAY COIL	104
21	L2 16LG	HEADLAMP DIMMER SWITCH FEED	104
22	Q33 20BR/LB*	SP - SENSE - GND FROM LIFT GATE	105
23	G6 20GY	LOW OIL PRESSURE WARNING	104
24	—	NOT USED	—
25	G20 22VT/YL*	WATER TEMP SENDING UNIT	104

Figure 14-15 Harmonica connector. Note that each hole in the connector serves a specific circuit. (Chrysler)

PRIMARY TYPES OF SOLDERLESS TERMINALS

Ring Tongue	Hook Tongue
Spade Tongue	Flanged Spade Tongue
Butt or Parallel Connectors	Male and Female Quick Connects
Large Ring Tongue	Snap Terminal

Figure 14-14 Common solderless terminals.

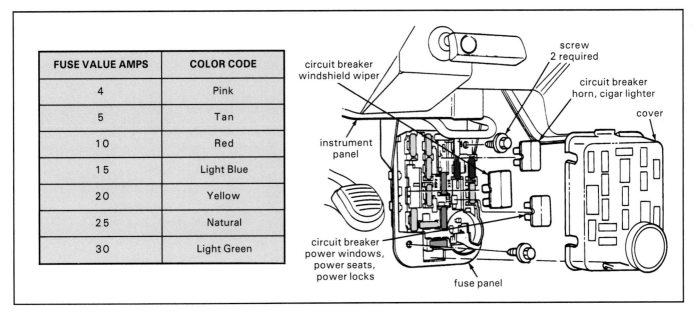

FUSE VALUE AMPS	COLOR CODE
4	Pink
5	Tan
10	Red
15	Light Blue
20	Yellow
25	Natural
30	Light Green

screw
2 required

circuit breaker
windshield wiper

circuit breaker
horn, cigar lighter

cover

instrument
panel

circuit breaker
power windows,
power seats,
power locks

fuse panel

Figure 14-16 Typical fuse block or panel. Note the various ''size'' fuses in this panel.

harmonica connector resemble the openings in a common harmonica. These connectors are sometimes used to attach diagnostic computers or scan tools when troubleshooting automotive electronic and computer circuits. In Figure 14-15, a body computer harmonica connector is shown. Note the descriptions associated with each pin number (opening) in the harmonica connector.

Circuit Protection

Fuses, circuit breakers, and/or fusible links are used to protect electrical circuits against short circuits and overloads. All of these components are normally closed (conduct electricity), but they open if excessive current passes through them. Most fuses and breakers are held in a block or panel. A typical fuse block is shown in Figure 14-16.

Fuses protect electrical circuits from damage caused by excessive current. See Figure 14-17. A fuse is wired in series in a circuit and will "blow" when excessive current is present. The current melts a conductor in the fuse, and the flow of electricity stops. See Figure 14-18. A blown fuse will often be slightly discolored (brown). Fuses are rated in amperes. The *fuse rating* represents the maximum amount of current that can pass through a fuse without causing it to "blow." A replacement fuse should have the same amperage rating as the original fuse.

Circuit breakers contain a bimetallic strip and a set of contact points. See Figure 14-19. If excessive current heats the strip, it will bend and the contact points will separate. This causes an open circuit. When the strip cools, it resumes its original shape and the contact points close. Some circuit breakers must be manually reset.

Fusible links are specially designed wire joints. Excessive current or overload conditions cause the joint to melt. An open circuit is created when the joint melts. Never attempt to repair a fusible link. An open fusible link must be replaced.

Batteries

Vehicles depend on a battery to produce electrical energy. Although it is commonly called a **storage battery**, the battery does not actually "store" electricity. As a battery charges, it converts electrical energy to chemical energy. During use, the battery converts the chemical energy back into electrical energy. The battery is a vehicle's only source of electricity when the engine is not running. It must contain enough energy to start the engine and to operate various electrical components when the vehicle is not being used. For example, late-model vehicles depend on the battery to keep clocks, computers, alarms, and other electronic systems functioning during storage. If the vehicle is parked for an extended period of time, the battery may be drained of all electrical energy. The alternator is the component that keeps the battery charged when the engine is running.

Figure 14-17 Fuses are available in a variety of configurations.

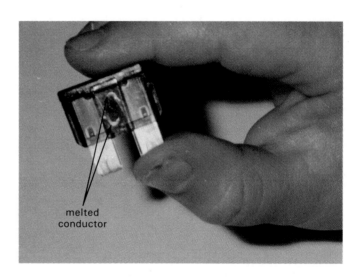

Figure 14-18 Excessive current caused this fuse to blow.

melted conductor

Figure 14-19 Circuit breakers are used to protect circuits from excessive voltage.

Battery Service

WARNING: Before working near a battery, remove all rings, bracelets, and wristwatches. Because most batteries are rated at only 12 volts, there is no danger of electrocution. However, metal jewelry is a good conductor (low resistance) and will allow a high rate of current to flow. This current may cause the jewelry to become red hot and produce serious burns.

Always remember to disconnect the battery ground cable when a vehicle is in the shop. This will prevent damage to electronic components during the repair procedures. It will also stop the drain on the battery and eliminate the possibility of an electrical fire. Never disconnect the battery when the ignition switch is in the ''on'' position. This practice may damage *electronic* components. When disconnecting cables from top posts, use a cable puller to avoid breaking the posts. Be very careful not to overtighten the cables on side-terminal batteries.

If battery terminals are corroded, they can be cleaned with a solution of baking soda and water. The hold-down clamps and battery box (when used) can also be cleaned with this solution. Replace the battery if its case is cracked or leaking. The capacity of the replacement battery should equal or exceed the capacity of the original battery.

Testing batteries. A 12-volt automotive battery contains six cells. Each cell produces 2.13 volts of electricity when fully charged. A *voltmeter* can be used to test a battery. A fully charged battery should produce a voltmeter reading of more than 12 volts (across the battery terminals) when it is at rest and the engine is off. A voltmeter reading of about 9.6 volts is normal when battery is energizing the starter.

Special testing instruments are often used to more accurately measure the condition of the battery. A *hydrometer* can be used to determine the state of charge in a battery. This instrument measures the specific gravity (relative density) of the electrolyte. *Specific gravity* is the ratio of the density of the electrolyte to the density of water. A battery with a full charge should have a specific gravity reading of 1.280. Fully discharged batteries will have a specific gravity of 1.110. Figure 14-20 illustrates the relationship between the specific gravity reading and the state of charge.

Many maintenance-free batteries have a built-in, eye-type hydrometer. The color of the built-in eye changes as the specific gravity of the electrolyte changes. A bright green eye indicates that the battery is at least 75% charged. A dark or black eye indicates that the battery needs to be charged. A yellow eye indicates that the electrolyte is low (usually below the plates).

Never charge a battery unless all plates are covered with electrolyte.

A *load tester* is the most accurate instrument used to determine the condition of a battery. This tester checks the battery under a full load. The load tester is simply placed across the terminals of the battery (observing polarity) and adjusted according to the manufacturer's instructions. A good battery should produce a tester reading of more than 9.6 volts when it is under load. Many electronic fuel-injected vehicles require adequate cranking speed in order to activate the computerized fuel system. A good battery is critical to the proper operation of these systems.

Recharging batteries. In some cases, batteries may become completely discharged. When this occurs, it may be necessary to recharge the battery with a *battery charger.* A battery will accept a charge when a voltage that is higher than terminal voltage is applied to its terminals. Batteries can be charged by a *constant-current charger* or a *constant-voltage charger*. Both types can be used to provide a *high-rate charge*, or a *low-rate charge* (trickle charge). The fastest method for charging a battery involves the use of a constant-voltage, high-rate charger. However, rapid charging may overheat and damage the battery. Rapid charging also accelerates the chemical action that deteriorates the electrodes in the battery. If time permits, a low-rate charge should be applied to a discharged battery. A low-rate charge (less than 4 amperes) at 12-14 volts will provide the best battery charge and will not cause damage. To eliminate the chances of damaging electronic or electrical components, it is best to remove the battery before applying a charge.

If possible, check the electrolyte (water) level to see that all battery plates are covered. Add distilled water or electrolyte if needed. Never charge or jump start a battery with a low electrolyte level. Generally, the electrolyte level in *maintenance-free batteries* (low water loss batteries) cannot be checked. These batteries are designed to operate for their full service life (about 5 years) without requiring additional electrolyte. All batteries are

From	To	State of Charge
1.260	1.280	100% charged
1.230	1.250	75% charged
1.200	1.220	50% charged
1.170	1.190	25% charged
1.140	1.160	very little useful capacity
1.110	1.130	discharged

Figure 14-20 Specific gravities.

Battery Capacity (Reserve Minutes)	Slow Charge	Fast Charge
80 minutes or less	10 hours @ 5 amps 5 hours @ 10 amps	2.5 hours @ 20 amps 1.5 hours @ 30 amps
Above 80, to 125 minutes	15 hours @ 5 amps 7.5 hours @ 10 amps	3.75 hours @ 20 amps 1.5 hours @ 50 amps
Above 125, to 170 minutes	20 hours @ 5 amps 10 hours @ 10 amps	5 hours @ 20 amps 2 hours @ 50 amps
Above 170, to 250 minutes	30 hours @ 5 amps 15 hours @ 10 amps	7.5 hours @ 20 amps 3 hours @ 50 amps

Figure 14-21 Charging guide for a 12-volt maintenance-free battery.

equipped with vent holes, which allow the hydrogen gas generated during charging to escape. A charging guide for 12-volt, maintenance-free batteries is shown in Figure 14-21.

To use a battery charger, connect the positive charger cable to positive battery terminal. Then attach the negative charger cable to the negative terminal of the battery. After connecting the cables, set the charger for the recommended charging rate and time. After the battery is recharged, shut off the charger and disconnect the cables.

Jump starting. *Jump starting* a disabled vehicle from another vehicle or battery is commonly performed instead of using a battery charger. To prevent damage to electronic components, the ignition switch must be in the "off" position when making jumper cable connections. Connect the cables in the order illustrated in Figure 14-22. The final connection (negative cable) should always be made to a common ground, such as a bracket, a bolt, or the frame.

After starting the disabled vehicle, remove the negative jumper cable from the common ground first. If there is a spark when the cable is removed, there is little danger of a hydrogen gas explosion. Do not allow sparks or open flames near the charging area.

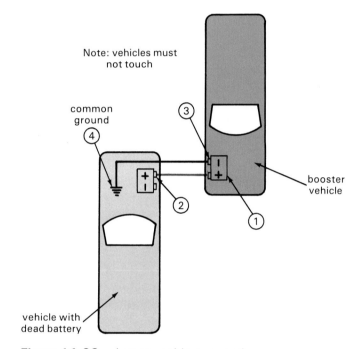

Figure 14-22 Jumper cable connections. The numbers represent the proper connection sequence.

WARNING: If hydrogen gas ignites and the battery explodes, electrolyte (acid) will shoot violently from the battery case. Although safety glasses or goggles should protect the eyes, the acid will damage clothes, skin, and paint. Wash affected areas with water immediately. Seek medical assistance if electrolyte contacts your skin or eyes. A solution of baking soda and water can be used to clean under the hood and other areas.

Lights

After body repairs are made, lights may need to be replaced, repaired, or adjusted. Poor ground contacts or defective light sockets are very common in damaged vehicles. *Light bulbs* are used throughout most late-model

vehicles. These bulbs may contain one or more filaments. Filaments are the internal elements that glow when a bulb is energized. A *one-filament bulb* requires only one electrical terminal, a *two-filament bulb* requires two terminals, and a *three-filament bulb* requires three terminals. In most cases, the bulb's base completes the electrical circuit for the filament.

Back-up lights and most interior lights have a single filament. Taillight and most headlight bulbs have more than one filament. Three-filament bulbs, commonly called "three-bulbs," are often used on each side of the rear of a vehicle (one filament for the turn signals, one for the brake lights, and one for the running lights). All vehicles produced since 1986 must have collision avoidance lights located at eye level.

Many late-model vehicles have *composite head-lights,* Figure 14-23. A composite light has a separate bulb, lens, and connector. These headlights generally

A

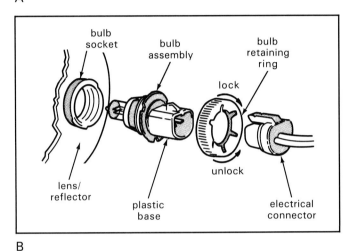

B

Figure 14-23 A–Composite headlight housing.
B–Bulb installation details for a composite
headlight assembly.

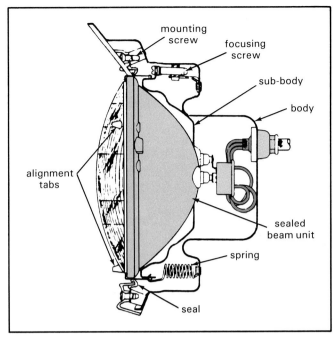

Figure 14-24 Sealed beam lamp assembly.
Note the alignment tabs on the glass lens.

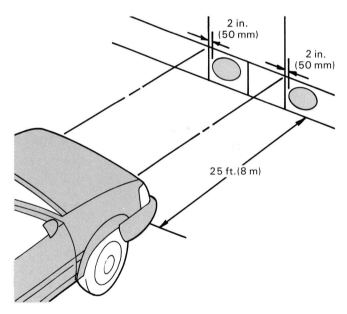

Figure 14-25 The headlight beam should be adjusted
to fall below the centerline and slightly toward
the right side of the vehicle.

have three focusing (adjustment) screws on the back
mounting. Use a clean cloth when handling the bulbs
used in composite headlights. Do not touch the bulbs
with your fingers. Oil from fingers may reduce bulb life.

Some vehicles have **sealed-beam headlights**. In
these lights, the filament, reflector, and lens are fused
into a single airtight unit. The focusing (adjustment)
screws, mounts, and socket for a sealed-beam headlight
are shown in Figure 14-24.

Most headlights are adjusted with a headlight alignment instrument. The light's focusing screws are adjusted until the proper reading is indicated in the
alignment instrument. If an alignment instrument is not
available, headlights can be adjusted by focusing them
on a wall. The wall should be 25 feet (7.6 m) from the
headlights. The high beam should be adjusted to the horizontal centerline of wall. The low beam should be adjusted to fall below the centerline and to the right of the
vehicle. Check the appropriate service manual for the
exact specifications. See Figure 14-25.

A two-headlight system is shown in Figure 14-26.
A dim filament and a bright filament must be used in each

of the lights. Some vehicles have four headlights, Figure
14-27. Each light in this system has only one filament.

A simple turn signal (directional) light circuit is
shown in Figure 14-28. A **flasher unit** is used to flash the
turn signal and the hazard lights. Contact points inside
these units are rapidly opened and closed as a quickly
expanding metal strip heats and cools.

Flasher units are designed to work in circuits that
contain a specific number of bulbs. If one bulb in the turn

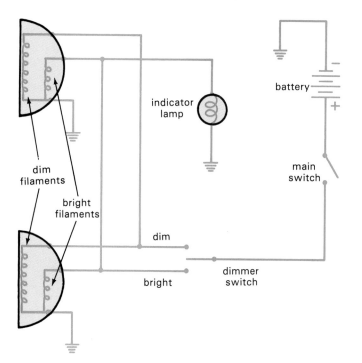

Figure 14-26   Two-headlight system. Each light in this system contains two filaments.

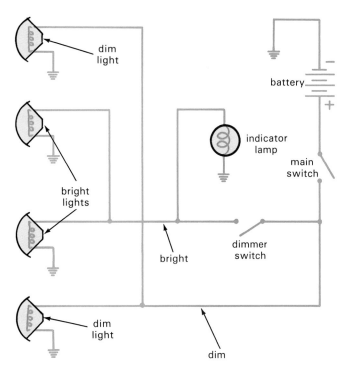

Figure 14-27   Each bulb in a four-headlight system contains one filament.

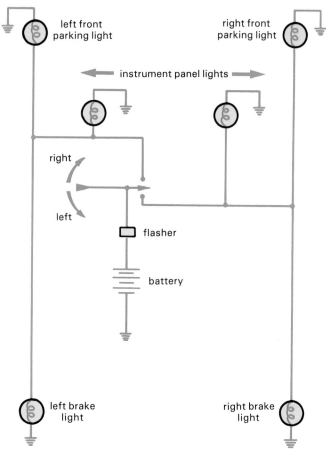

Figure 14-28   Simple turn signal schematic. Note the location of the flasher unit.

A simple brake and taillight circuit is shown in Figure 14-30. Most brake and taillights have two or three filaments. It is common for only one of the filaments to burn out (open). Movement of the mechanical brake linkage activates a brake light switch, which controls the lights. The brake light switch is adjustable to accommodate the travel of the brake linkage.

Dome lights illuminate the interior of the vehicle. They are turned on and off with switches in the door pillars and on the instrument panel. When problems occur with dome lights, check the bulb and the switches.

Indicator lamps (and indicator gauges) are used to signal problems with oil pressure, engine temperature, fuel level, and alternator output. When troubleshooting indicator lamps and other instruments, always begin by checking the appropriate fuses or breakers.

Electronic displays have replaced conventional instrument panels in many late-model vehicles. See Figure 14-31. Many of these displays are equipped with flexible circuits. Flexible circuits consist of a flexible plastic film upon which circuit components (wires, connectors, microswitches, etc.) are attached. Three types of electronic displays are used in modern vehicles: light-emitting diode displays (LEDs), liquid crystal displays (LCDs), and vacuum fluorescent displays. Electronic displays are very sensitive and costly! Take precautions to prevent

signal circuit is burned out, the flasher will not work. If all of the bulbs in a turn signal circuit will light but not flash, check the flasher unit for proper operation. If the hazard lights flash but the turn signals do not work, check the flasher unit and the turn signal switch. A turn signal diagnosis chart is shown in Figure 14-29.

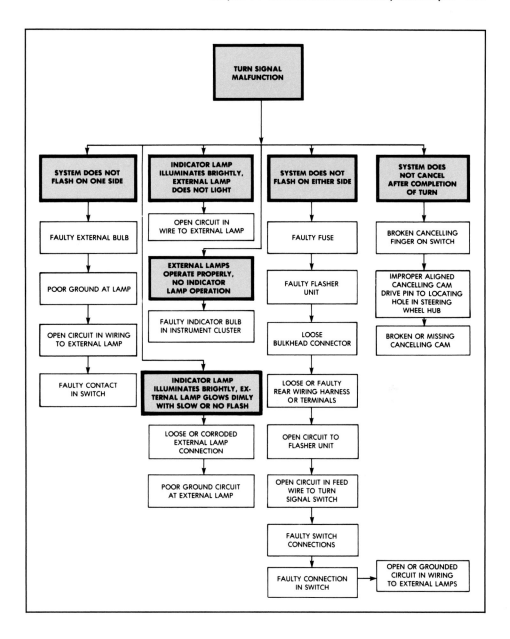

Figure 14-29 Turn signal flasher diagnosis chart. (Chrysler)

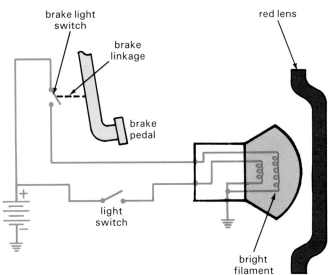

Figure 14-30 Typical brake light circuit. The brake linkage activates the brake light switch.

damaging these displays during the repair process. Repairs to electronic displays are not easily made in the shop. When damaged, these displays are generally replaced.

Electrical System Problems

Most electrical system problems fall into one of three categories: open circuits, short circuits, and faulty components.

Closed and Open Circuits

When current flows from a source to the load, a **closed circuit** exists. If a circuit is broken and the current cannot flow, an **open circuit** is created. Continuity does not exist in an open circuit. Open circuits occur when a switch is in the ''off'' position, when a wire is broken, or when a fuse, circuit breaker, or fusible link is open. See

A short circuit often occurs when electrical current leaks from the source to the vehicle's frame or body sheet metal. The current then flows directly back to the negative terminal of the power source without reaching the load. This type of short always opens a circuit breaker, blows a fuse, or melts a fusible link.

Most wires are covered with an insulator to help prevent short circuits. **Insulators** are materials that oppose the flow of electricity. In other words, insulators have very high resistance. Common insulators include plastic, rubber, and paper.

Short circuits often occur when insulation is pinched, cut, or worn. Vibrations often cause a wire's insulation to wear through. The intermittent operation of a load (radio, motor, or lamp) may indicate a short circuit or an intermittent open circuit caused by poor connections. When a short circuit occurs, the battery may be slowly drained.

Faulty Components

Faulty electrical components can cause a number of electrical system problems. The battery is a common cause of system problems. Check for dirty, broken, or frayed cables. If necessary, clean the battery posts and cable ends.

If a light does not work, an open filament in the bulb is the most likely problem. However, water vapor behind a lens cover may cause a corrosion problem that results in a short circuit (blown fuse). This problem can be remedied by cleaning the corroded terminals, repairing the leak around the lens cover, and replacing the fuse.

Switches generally wear with use. Any component that works intermittently may be the result of a dirty switch or worn contact. Dirt and corrosion commonly cause a switch to malfunction. Contacts within a switch can sometimes be cleaned with an aerosol contact cleaner and lubricant.

Figure 14-31 Electronic instrument display. (Buick)

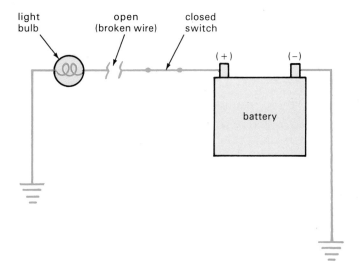

Figure 14-32 This open circuit will not conduct electricity.

Figure 14-32. Poor connections, faulty grounds, and burned-out lamps are also common open-circuit problems. In some cases, a bad connection will reduce the flow of electricity without stopping it completely. When this occurs, there is high resistance in the circuit. High resistance may cause bulbs to glow dimly and other components to operate slowly.

Short Circuits

Electrical leakage between two conductors is called a *short circuit* (short). If a conductor is placed directly across the terminals of a battery or an alternator, a short circuit is produced. Because there is little resistance in the conductor (load), the rate of current flow will be very high. This will cause the conductor to become hot and may cause the source (battery or alternator) to burn out. See Figure 14-33.

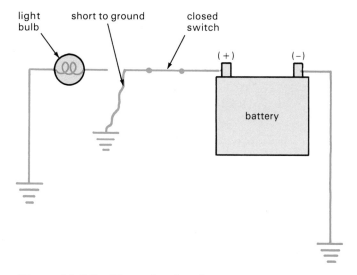

Figure 14-33 Short circuits often cause excessive current flow.

Electrical System Testing Equipment

In order to troubleshoot electrical systems, a few pieces of inexpensive test equipment are essential. Three of the most common instruments used for troubleshooting electrical systems include a test light, a continuity tester, and a multimeter. A jumper wire is also useful for troubleshooting electrical components.

A *test light* is equipped with a lamp that will light when voltage is present in a circuit, Figure 14-34. The probes of the test light can be connected in parallel to any electrical device, Figure 14-35. The tester will light if voltage is present in the circuit. In a similar test, one probe of the tester can be connected to ground, and the other probe can be moved to various points in the circuit. If the tester lights, there is power at the point where the probe is placed. Remember, test lights can only be used to check for voltage in ''live'' circuits.

A *jumper wire* can be used to bypass switches and relays. The wire can also be used to connect a component directly to the voltage source. Some jumper wires contain an in-line fuse to help prevent circuit damage. See Figures 14-36 and 14-37.

Continuity testers can be used to test light bulbs, fuses, switches, and other electrical items. These devices are used to verify a complete or closed circuit. If the circuit being tested is closed, a bulb will light in the tester. A small battery supplies the electrical power in the tester. See Figure 14-38. Never use a battery-powered continuity tester in an energized circuit. Additionally, a battery-powered tester should never be used when troubleshooting an air bag system. Improper testing procedures may trigger the system.

A *multimeter* is an extremely valuable tool in the auto body shop. See Figure 14-39. This instrument can be used to measure resistance, voltage, and amperage. It can also be used in place of a test light and a continuity tester. Both analog and digital multimeters are available. A high-impedance digital multimeter is essential when

Figure 14-34 This test light will glow when voltage is present.

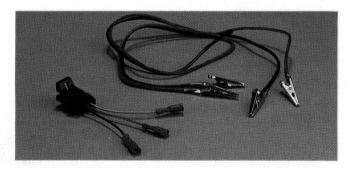

Figure 14-36 Jumper wires are commonly used to help isolate circuit problems. The jumper on the left was fabricated from a terminal cut from the wiring harness of a scrap vehicle.

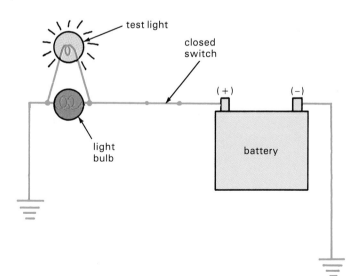

Figure 14-35 A test light is connected in parallel to check for voltage in a component.

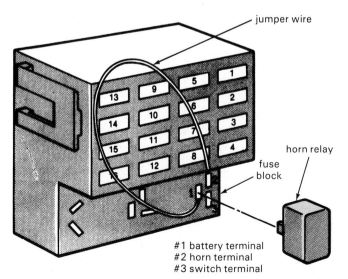

Figure 14-37 A jumper wire is used on this fuse block to test for an open circuit. (Chrysler)

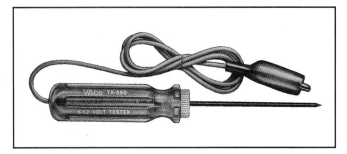

Figure 14-38   This continuity tester instantly detects shorts and broken circuits. (VACO Products)

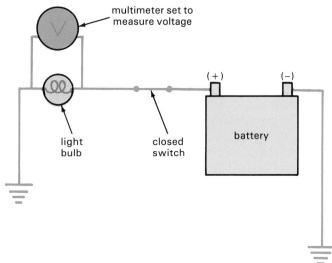

Figure 14-40   A multimeter is connected in parallel to measure voltage.

leads to the component's terminals. In some cases, there may be several filament or switch terminals to be tested. Test each terminal or filament independently. If a circuit is open (no continuity), the meter reading will indicate "infinite resistance." If there is a complete circuit, a very small amount of resistance will be shown on the meter. See Figure 14-41. Never test a "live" circuit when checking for continuity or measuring resistance with a multimeter. Testing a "live" circuit may damage the meter.

To measure current, the meter's probe should be connected in series with the component being tested and the meter should be set to the amperes position. See Figure 14-42. The amount of current flowing through the component will be shown on the meter.

Figure 14-39   This multimeter can be used to measure dc current, voltage, and resistance. (Fluke)

working on late-model vehicles. This type of meter is easy to read and will not damage sensitive components.

When measuring voltage, the meter is set to the voltage position and connected in parallel with the component being tested. See Figure 14-40. The amount of voltage across the connections of the component being tested will be displayed directly on the instrument. In most cases, using the multimeter to take voltage measurements eliminates the need for a test light.

Using the multimeter to test for resistance eliminates the need for a separate continuity tester. To use a multimeter to test for resistance, remove or disconnect the component to be tested from the circuit. Set the meter to the resistance position and connect the meter

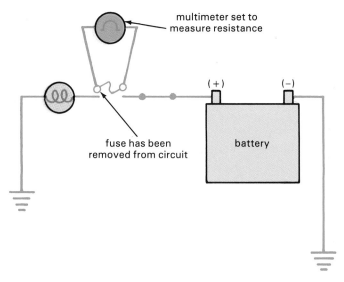

Figure 14-41   This multimeter is set to measure resistance. Note that the component has been removed from the circuit.

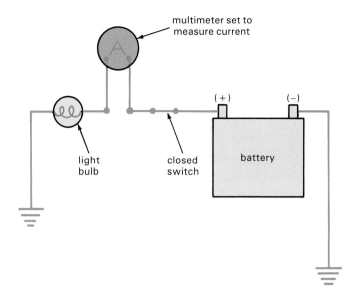

Figure 14-42 A multimeter can be connected in series to measure current.

Troubleshooting Electrical Systems

When troubleshooting electrical system problems, check for the most probable causes before using testers and meters. Look for blown fuses and burned-out bulbs.

Most late-model vehicles are equipped with computer systems that have self-diagnostic capabilities. In these systems, the performance of related solenoids, sensors, switches, and relays is constantly monitored and compared to factory specifications. If these components are not operating within specifications, trouble codes will be placed in the computer's memory. These codes represent specific computer system problems. In some systems, trouble codes can be accessed and displayed on the vehicle's instrument panel. In other systems, an electronic scan tool must be used to extract the codes from the computer. The manufacturer's service manual contains information on accessing and interpreting trouble codes.

Collision damage may break components or cause shorts between wires and the body ground. Without a sufficient load (resistance) from a component, an excessive amount of current will flow through a circuit. This current will blow fuses or trip circuit breakers if it exceeds the fuse amperage rating. Shorted wires or components may become hot enough to melt!

Connections often become loose as a result of a collision. This may result in an open circuit, short circuit, or an intermittent connection.

Testing for Open Circuits

A battery powered continuity tester is often used to check circuits and components for an open condition. As previously mentioned, all power in the circuit must be off when this instrument is used. With the tester leads connected across the component or circuit in question, the

tester should light up if voltage is present. The component (or circuit) may be defective if the tester does not light.

A non-powered test light can be used to check for an open condition between body ground and a component in a live circuit. To use the test light to check for an open circuit, connect one lead to ground and place the other lead on the component connection. If current is flowing through the component, the test light should glow. If there is no light, an open circuit may exist between the battery and the component.

Testing Fuses and Circuit Breakers

All electrical system checks should start at the fuse box. Remove the fuse and perform a continuity check to determine if it is good. If the fuse is good (has continuity), check for continuity in the rest of the circuit. To test fuses in a live circuit, simply touch one probe of a multimeter or a test light to the load side of the fuse and the other probe to ground. The meter should display voltage or the test light should glow if the fuse is good. See Figure 14-43. Circuit breakers can be tested in a similar manner.

Testing Switches

Switches are often tested with a non-powered test light. After the tester's probes are connected, the test light should glow only when the switch is closed. See Figure 14-44. If the tester does not glow in any switch position, the switch may be defective.

A multimeter set to measure resistance (ohms) can also be used to test for continuity in a switch. Disconnect (isolate) the switch from the circuit, and place the meter's leads across the terminals of the switch. There should be zero resistance when the switch is in the closed position and infinite resistance when it is in the

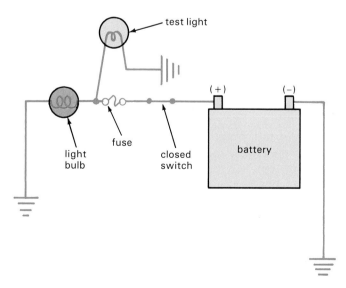

Figure 14-43 A fuse in a "live" circuit can be checked with a test light.

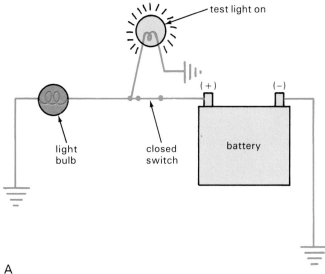

A

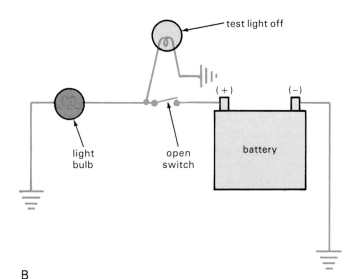

B

Figure 14-44 A test light can be used to check a switch for proper operation. A–Light should glow when switch is closed. B–Light will not glow when switch is open.

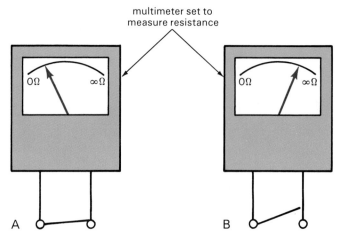

Figure 14-45 A multimeter that is set to measure resistance can be used to test a switch. A–Resistance should be very low when the switch is closed. B–When the switch is open, the meter should register infinite resistance.

Figure 14-46 A light bulb can be tested with a multimeter. The meter is set to measure resistance. One meter probe is touched to the bulb's base and the other probe is touched to the bulb's terminal(s).

open position, Figure 14-45. Switches that measure infinite resistance in both positions are defective (open) and must be replaced.

Testing Light Bulbs

As previously mentioned, lighting circuits contain various bulbs. Always check for proper connections when a faulty bulb is suspected. Dirty, oxidized connections may stop the flow of electricity to the bulb. To test a bulb, a multimeter set to the resistance position can be used. Place one meter lead on the bulb's base and the other lead to one of the bulb's filament terminals. The meter should indicate some resistance at the terminal. If it does not, the filament connected to the terminal is open and the bulb must be replaced. Repeat the test for all the bulb's terminals. See Figure 14-46.

Testing Miscellaneous Electrical Components

Power seats, power windows, windshield wipers, horns, and other components can be quickly checked using the test equipment and testing procedures previously mentioned.

If there is no voltage at an electrical component, check for broken wires, blown fuses, faulty connections, and malfunctioning switches. Use test equipment to check for open and short circuits. If components operate dimly or slowly, use a multimeter to check for excessive resistance in the related circuit.

Know These Terms

Electrical system, Electronic systems, Voltage, Volts, Voltmeter, Current, Amperes, Ammeter, Direct current, Alternating current, Resistance, Ohms, Ohmmeter, Wiring diagrams, Conductors, Power source, Load, Series circuits, Parallel circuits, Tracer, Terminals, Connectors, Fuses, Circuit breakers, Fusible links, Storage battery, Hydrometer, Specific gravity, Load tester, Battery charger, Maintenance-free batteries, Jump starting, Light bulbs, Composite headlights, Sealed-beam headlights, Flasher unit, Dome lights, Indicator lamps, Electronic displays, Closed circuit, Open circuit, Short circuit, Insulators, Test light, Jumper wire, Continuity testers, Multimeter.

Summary

Electrical systems are often repaired in the auto body shop. However, electronic system problems are complex and are generally sent to shops that specialize in repairing these systems.

There are several electrical terms that the auto body technician should know. Voltage is the pressure that causes electricity to flow. Voltage is measured in units called volts. The flow of electricity is called current. Current is measured in amperes. Resistance is the opposition to the flow of electricity. Resistance is measured in ohms.

Service manuals should be used when troubleshooting electrical systems. These manuals contain wiring diagrams, which show where wires are routed and how electrical components are arranged.

There are three major parts in all electrical circuits: a power source, a load, and conductors. In some vehicles, the metal body can serve as a conductor. Series circuits have one or more loads that are connected so that current has only one path to follow. Parallel circuits contain two or more loads that are connected so that current will flow through all of the loads at once.

Wires are used as conductors to carry electrical energy from a source to a load. The wires used in automotive electrical systems are often color coded to assist in assembly and repair. Terminals and connectors are also used to aid in the assembly and repair of electrical circuits.

Fuses, circuit breakers, and fusible links are used to protect circuits for overloads and shorts. These items will not conduct electricity if excessive current is passed through them.

A battery produces the electrical energy used by a vehicle. It must produce enough energy to start the vehicle and operate various components when the vehicle is not running. Batteries can be tested for proper operation with a voltmeter, a hydrometer, or a load tester. If necessary, batteries can be recharged with a battery charger. In many cases, a vehicle with a discharged battery can be jump started from another vehicle or battery.

Lights often require repair or adjustment. One-, two-, and three-filament light bulbs are used throughout most vehicles. Headlights are available in two designs: composite headlights and sealed-beam headlights. A flasher unit is used to flash turn signal and hazard lights. Dome lights illuminate the interior of a vehicle. Indicator lamps are used to signal problems with oil pressure, engine temperature, fuel level, and alternator output. Electronic displays have replaced conventional instrument panels in some late-model vehicles. When these displays are damaged, they are generally replaced.

Most electrical system problems fall into one of three categories: open circuits, short circuits, and faulty components. An open circuit exists when a circuit is broken and current cannot flow. A short circuit is present when there is electrical leakage between two conductors. Faulty electrical components can cause many electrical problems.

A few inexpensive instruments can be used to troubleshoot the electrical system, including a test light, a continuity tester, and a multimeter. A test light will glow when voltage is present in a circuit. It can only be used when checking "live" circuits. Continuity testers are used to verify a complete circuit. Continuity testers should never be used on an energized circuit. A multimeter can be used to measure resistance, voltage, and current. It is often used in place of a test light and/or a continuity tester.

Always check for the most probable problems when troubleshooting an electrical system. Check for blown fuses or burned-out light bulbs. Many late-model vehicles have self-diagnostic capabilities, which simplify troubleshooting procedures. Collision damage may break electrical components or cause short circuits. Collisions often loosen connections. If necessary, individual components and circuits can be checked for voltage, continuity, shorts, etc., with the appropriate test equipment.

Review Questions–Chapter 14

1. The electronic systems found on late-model vehicles can be repaired by most auto body technicians. True or False?

2. The pressure that causes electricity to flow is called _____.

3. Current is measured in units called _____.

4. Resistance is the _____ to the flow of electricity.

5. What type of instrument is used to measure resistance?
   a. Ammeter.
   b. Ohmmeter.
   c. Voltmeter.
   d. None of the above.

6. Poor conductors offer little resistance to the flow of current. True or False?

7. _____ circuits contain one or more loads that are connected so the current has only one path to follow.

8. In most vehicles, the metal chassis or body serves as a common conductor. True or False?

9. Wires are often _____ coded to facilitate assembly and repair.

10. Solderless terminals are usually screwed to a wire. True or False?

11. To protect against overloads, some electrical circuits are equipped with:
    a. fusible links.
    b. capacitors.
    c. resistors.
    d. all of the above.

12. Fuses are wired in _____ with a circuit.

13. Most circuit breakers must be replaced after they are exposed to excessive current. True or False?

14. The battery is a vehicle's only source of _____ when the engine is not running.

15. When disconnecting a battery, the ignition switch should be in the ''on'' position. True or False?

16. A _____ can be used to determine a battery's state of charge.

17. The ratio of the density of electrolyte to the density of water is called:
    a. relative volume.
    b. specific gravity.
    c. viscosity.
    d. none of the above.

18. If possible, a _____-_____ charge should be applied to a discharged battery.

19. When connecting jumper cables, the last connection should be made to a positive terminal. True or False?

20. Composite headlights are used on many late-model vehicles. True or False?

21. A _____ unit is used in turn signal and hazard light circuits.

22. Indicator lamps are often used to signal problems with:
    a. oil pressure.
    b. fuel level.
    c. engine temperature.
    d. all of the above.

23. Electronic displays can generally be repaired in the auto body shop. True or False?

24. An excessive amount of current flows through an open circuit. True or False?

25. A _____ _____ exists when electricity leaks between a source and a vehicle's frame or body.

26. The _____ is a component that frequently causes electrical system problems.

27. A test light can be used to determine if resistance is present in a circuit. True or False?

28. A continuity tester will light if the circuit being tested is _____.

29. Continuity testers should always be used in a ''live'' circuit. True or False?

30. A multimeter can be used to check for:
    a. voltage.
    b. continuity.
    c. current.
    d. all of the above.

31. The first step in troubleshooting electrical systems is to use a multimeter to establish a voltage reading. True or False?

32. Many late-model computer systems have _____-_____ capabilities.

33. A _____ test can be used to determine if a fuse is good.

34. A test light can be used to test a switch for proper operation. True or False?

35. When testing light bulbs, a multimeter can be used to measure _____ at each of the bulb's terminals.

Activities–Chapter 14

1. Do some research to find out about Ohm's Law (the formula that describes electrical relationships) and the ''pie'' diagram that is used to help remember it. Write a short report about the ways Ohm's Law can be used to find different electrical values.

2. If you have access to a computer with a drawing (CAD) program, use it to draw a series circuit with a single load, and a parallel circuit with three loads. Draw the loads as lamps and the power source as a battery. Use arrows to indicate the flow of current. Output your drawings to a printer, then make overhead transparencies. Explain the two types of circuits to the class.

3. Use a ''point-and-shoot'' camera to take step-by-step pictures of making the connections to jump-start a car with a dead battery. When the film is developed, arrange the prints in order on a sheet of poster board to make a display. Write a brief description under each picture.

# chapter 15

Mechanical Component Repairs

After reading this chapter, you will be able to:

☐ Identify damage to mechanical components.

☐ Explain the principles of operation for suspension and steering systems.

☐ Describe the importance of wheel alignment.

☐ Describe the importance of exhaust and emission systems.

☐ Check the cooling and air conditioning systems for damage.

Introduction

Auto body technicians must be able to diagnose and analyze mechanical component damage. The customer depends on the professional auto body technician for safe, reliable vehicle repair. It is the ethical responsibility of the technician to restore damaged vehicles to factory specifications. Auto body technicians must be concerned about their professional reputation and the legal liability of their services. A poorly repaired vehicle will ruin reputations. Improperly installed air bags or undetected damage to a steering mechanism may result in injury or death.

Analyzing Damage

Although the auto body technician may not perform the necessary mechanical repairs, it is essential that all structural and mechanical damage be properly assessed before starting auto body repairs. In many instances, the repair of mechanical parts must be done as the body panels are being repaired. At other times, body panel damage and frame damage must be corrected (aligned) before mechanical components can be repaired.

Many mechanical components are repaired by technicians who specialize in servicing mechanical systems. These technicians have the skill and equipment needed to properly service mechanical components.

Mechanical Systems

There are seven basic systems that should be checked and, if necessary, repaired when a vehicle suffers collision damage, including the:

- ☐ Drivetrain systems.
- ☐ Suspension systems.
- ☐ Steering systems.
- ☐ Brake systems.
- ☐ Exhaust and emission systems.
- ☐ Heating and cooling systems.
- ☐ Air conditioning system.

In addition to checking these systems, an overall inspection of a vehicle's safety features should be performed. See Figure 15-1.

Drivetrain Systems

For the purposes of this text, the term *drivetrain* will be used when referring to the engine and all of the components that transfer engine power to a vehicle's wheels. In addition to the engine, the drivetrain in rear-wheel drive vehicles includes the transmission, driveshaft, differential, and rear axles. In front-wheel drive designs, the drivetrain includes the engine, transaxle, and drive axles.

The sudden impact of a collision may damage the engine, transmission (or transaxle), or other drivetrain components. Major drivetrain parts are often mounted directly to structural body panels in unibody vehicles. Mountings can be torn or bent out of alignment in severe collisions. This may affect control linkages to the transmission or cause the vehicle to vibrate when driven. Misaligned or damaged drivetrain components may also produce unusual noises. If a noise changes in relation to engine speed, check for engine-related problems. If the noise changes in relation to vehicle speed, inspect the transmission, driveshaft, and axles for damage. A bent driveshaft (or drive axle) can sound and behave like an improperly balanced tire.

On front-wheel drive vehicles, check the rubber boots on the drive axles for cracks, splits, or tears. C-V joints are special universal joints used on front-wheel drive vehicles to compensate for the steering action. Dirt and moisture entering a damaged boot will quickly destroy these joints. Study the C-V joints for wear or damage. If service is required, refer to the appropriate service manual. Never attempt to service a drive axle without referring to a manual.

Modern engine compartments are crowded with components. This makes repair difficult. Even a minor impact can cause damage to mechanical and electronic components in a late-model vehicle.

In some cases, the drivetrain must be removed from a unibody vehicle before repairs are made. When this is necessary, carefully follow the car manufacturer's instructions for removal, repair, and re-assembly.

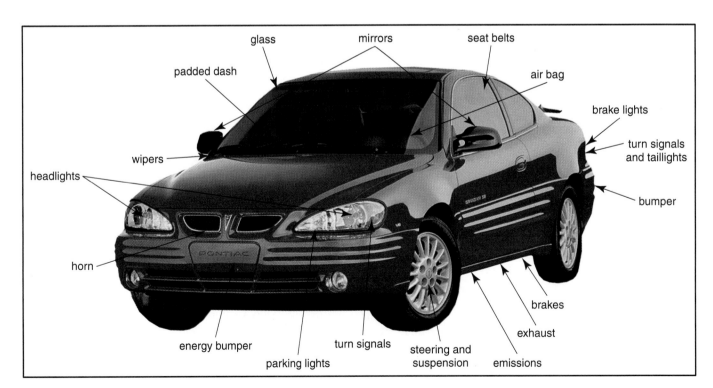

Figure 15-1 Important safety components or systems that must be checked or repaired to OEM condition before returning a vehicle to its owner. (Pontiac)

Suspension Systems

The proper operation of the *suspension system* is critical to safe vehicle operation. If this system is not repaired properly, customers may experience handling problems and suspension noise. Additionally, suspension system defects may affect fuel economy and passenger comfort. See Figure 15-2.

Strut assemblies are commonly used in unibody suspension systems. See Figure 15-3. When repairing unibody vehicles, the body and the suspension must be corrected as a unit. Before checking suspension parts on unibody vehicles, inspect the strut towers for bends and creases. If the towers are damaged, they must be repaired before performing other suspension system repairs. See Chapters 10 and 11 for information on repairing structural damage. Assuming that there are no bends or creases in the strut towers, check the shock or the shock assembly (strut damper assembly) for damage. The rear suspension must also be checked for broken or worn parts. Bounce the car on each of the four corners and observe the damping action of the shocks. If the vehicle does not recover from a bounce immediately, new shocks may be needed. If there are signs of a fluid leak around a shock, it must be replaced.

In some systems, *torsion bars* are used in place of coil springs. See Figure 15-4. Torsion bars are often bent as the result of a collision. Additionally, torsion bar supports and anchor brackets are sometimes bent or torn from the frame. Damaged torsion bars and related brackets or supports should be replaced. Torsion bars cannot be repaired.

Stabilizer bars are used in many suspension systems to reduce the tendency of a vehicle to lean in corners. Bent stabilizer bars and torn bushings must be replaced. Do not attempt to heat or straighten a stabilizer bar.

Coil spring suspensions are commonly used on trucks, vans, body-over-frame vehicles, and rear-wheel drive vehicles. Coil and leaf springs are used on vehicles with nonindependent rear suspension. Broken or worn springs can cause a vehicle to lean. Use a tape measure

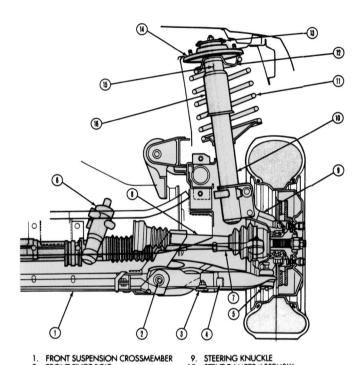

1. FRONT SUSPENSION CROSSMEMBER
2. FRONT PIVOT BOLT
3. LOWER CONTROL ARM
4. SWAY ELIMINATOR SHAFT ASSEMBLY
5. LOWER ARM BALL JOINT ASSEMBLY
6. STEERING GEAR
7. TIE ROD ASSEMBLY
8. DRIVESHAFT
9. STEERING KNUCKLE
10. STRUT DAMPER ASSEMBLY
11. COIL SPRING
12. UPPER SPRING SEAT
13. REBOUND STOP
14. UPPER MOUNT ASSEMBLY
15. JOUNCE BUMPER
16. DUST SHIELD

Figure 15-3 Typical front suspension detail. Note the arrangement of the components. (Nissan)

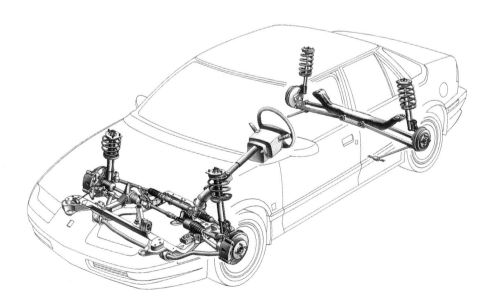

Figure 15-2 Typical suspension system for a late-model vehicle. (Saturn)

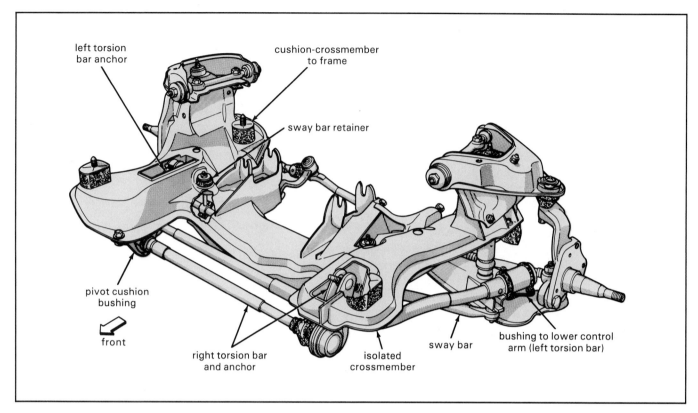

left torsion
bar anchor

cushion-crossmember
to frame

sway bar retainer

pivot cushion
bushing

front

right torsion bar
and anchor

isolated
crossmember

sway bar

bushing to lower control
arm (left torsion bar)

Figure 15-4 One type of torsion bar suspension. Coil springs are not used in torsion bar systems. (Chrysler)

or ruler to check distances from the bumper to the ground. Since vehicles are symmetrical (same), bumpers or body panels on the left side should be the same distance from the ground as the bumpers and panels on the right side. This quick check is to be used only to help detect damaged or broken springs. Remember, a vehicle cannot be satisfactorily repaired unless all of the major control points are returned to the manufacturers's specifications. On unibody vehicles, some of the suspension geometry is built into the mounting design.

Active suspension systems are growing in popularity. These systems automatically compensate for road and driving conditions. Most active suspension systems utilize sensors to monitor these conditions. The sensors send signals to a control module, which operates hydraulic or pneumatic actuators as necessary to improve handling and produce a comfortable ride. The actuators are used in place of struts, shock absorbers, and springs.

Electronic-air suspensions are found on a few cars. In these systems, a small compressor supplies air to four air springs. Height sensors, which are located at the corners of the vehicle, monitor the position (height) of each corner independently. When the vehicle's engine is running, any imbalance in weight distribution should be compensated for within 30 seconds. Leaky hoses, defective compressors, or improperly adjusted height sensors are common problems in these systems. Follow the manufacturer's instructions when troubleshooting and repairing active and electronic-air suspension systems.

Steering Systems

Steering system condition is also critical to safe vehicle operation. Parallelogram steering systems are found in many rear-wheel drive vehicles. These systems utilize tie rods, pitman arms, and other steering linkages to help guide the front wheels. Rack-and-pinion steering systems are used extensively on late-model cars. The rack-and-pinion assembly consists of a pinion gear, which is attached to the steering column, and a rack that moves the steering knuckle. When the pinion gear rotates, the rack moves (left or right). Rack-and-pinion gear systems have fewer parts to wear and are generally more reliable than linkage steering systems. See Figure 15-5.

Four-wheel steering systems continue to grow in popularity. In these systems, all four wheels pivot when the steering wheel is turned. Refer to an appropriate service manual when troubleshooting any steering system.

When servicing steering systems, check the tie rods and other steering linkages for damage. If a rod end is loose (excessive play), it must be replaced. Bent components are more difficult to detect than worn joints. Bends from a collision often look similar to factory bends. It may be necessary to align the wheels to detect bent steering components. Check an appropriate service manual before performing alignment adjustments. Many shops prefer to send wheel alignment work to specialty alignment shops.

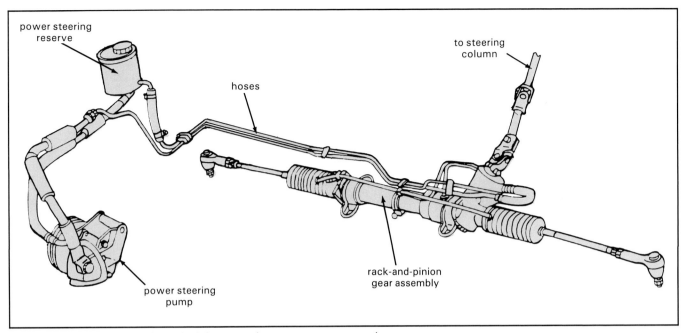

power steering
reserve

to steering
column

hoses

power steering
pump

rack-and-pinion
gear assembly

Figure 15-5   Power rack-and-pinion steering systems are used on many late-model vehicles.

Power steering systems use hydraulic pressure to facilitate steering action. An engine-driven pump is used to produce this pressure. If there is a noticeable loss of power assistance in a power steering system, check the fluid level and make certain that the pump is working properly. Check the system for worn drive belts, misaligned pullies, and pump or hose leaks. Damaged components should be serviced immediately.

Wheel Alignment

Wheel alignment is the key to proper steering control, safe handling, and maximum tire life. Alignment is often upset during a collision. More than 80% of today's vehicles have independent rear suspension. In these systems, both front and rear wheel alignment must be checked. When correcting alignment, reliable, accurate equipment should be used to aid in making critical checks and adjustments. In this text, no attempt will be made to describe the various types of alignment equipment available. Only general diagnostic and troubleshooting details will be presented. Some common causes of steering problems are shown in Figure 15-6.

Proper wheel alignment is so closely tied to the condition of the steering and suspension systems that many preliminary checks and adjustments are generally required before aligning a vehicle. These checks may lead to the replacement and/or repair of various parts. Common causes of steering, suspension, and alignment troubles include worn ball joints or tie rod ends; unbalanced or bent wheels; weak or inoperative shock absorbers; unlike tread patterns; different degrees of tread wear; improperly adjusted steering linkages; and improperly inflated tires. Unusual tire wear patterns are signs of incorrect tire pressure, chassis problems, or alignment problems.

Although there are many control angles that can be verified when checking alignment, the three most important are caster, camber, and toe.

Caster.   *Caster* is the steering angle that utilizes the mass (weight) and momentum of a vehicle to lead the front wheels in a straight path. Caster is determined by the backward or forward tilt of the steering axis (centerline of the steering knuckle) as observed from the side of the wheel and is generally measured in inches (millimeters) or degrees. See Figure 15-7.

Incorrect caster can cause a vehicle to pull to one side. *Positive caster* is produced when the top of the steering knuckle is tilted toward the rear of the car. Similarly, *negative caster* occurs when the top of the steering knuckle tilts toward the front of the vehicle. Caster can be adjusted to the manufacturer's specifications with shims, strut rods, eccentric bolts, bushings, pins, or oversize bolt holes. Caster adjustments are usually not provided on strut suspension systems. In these systems, the strut tower may need to be physically bent to achieve proper caster.

Camber.   *Camber* is the outward or inward tilt of the wheels at the top, Figure 15-8. Camber is measured in degrees. A small amount of positive (outward) camber is set into the front wheels of most cars. If camber is incorrect, the tire tread will not contact the road properly and the vehicle may pull to one side. Incorrect camber can also cause bearing and ball joint wear. Excessive camber causes one side of a tire to wear more than the other. Shims, eccentric bolts, bushings, pins, or oversize bolt holes are generally used to adjust camber. Some

TROUBLE SHOOTING	
Causes of steering difficulties include:	

HARD STEERING 　Lack of lubrication. 　Under-inflated tires. 　Maladjustment of steering gear. 　Incorrect front wheel alignment. 　Bent frame. 　Sagged front spring. LOOSE STEERING 　Maladjustment of steering gear. 　Defective front wheel bearings. 　Worn steering knuckle ball joints. 　Worn pitman shaft bushings. 　Worn steering linkage. 　Loose gear assembly at frame. 　Worn control arm bushings. SHIMMY 　Unbalanced front wheels. 　Faulty front wheel bearings. 　Loose wheel nuts. 　Defective front brakes. 　Worn steering linkage. 　Defective shock absorbers. 　Bent wheels. 　Low tire pressure. 　Incorrect caster. 　Incorrect toe-in. 　Worn steering knuckle bushings. 　Defective ball joints. 　Worn control arm bushings. 　Inoperative stabilizer. WHEEL TRAMP 　Unbalanced wheel assemblies. 　Defective shock absorbers. 　Inoperative stabilizer. ROAD WANDER 　Under-inflated tires. 　Maladjustment of steering gear. 　Defective front wheel bearings. 　Worn steering linkage. 　Worn steering knuckle bushings. 　Worn ball joints. 　Incorrect wheel alignment. 　Shifted rear axle. 　Worn steering gear. 　Binding upper or lower control arm shaft.	CAR PULLS TO ONE SIDE 　Low or uneven tire pressure. 　Incorrect caster or camber. 　Uneven car height at front. 　Bent frame. 　Shifted rear axle. 　Incorrect toe-in. 　Broken or weak rear springs. 　Bent steering knuckle or knuckle support. 　Inoperative shock absorber. 　One brake dragging SIDE WEAR ON TIRES 　Outside wear. 　Excessive positive camber. 　Inside: Excessive negative camber. 　Outside and Inside: Under-inflated tires or vehicle overloaded. CENTER RIB WEAR OF TIRES 　Over inflation. SHARP RIB EDGES ON TIRES 　Inside: Excessive toe-in. 　Outside: Excessive toe-out. 　Inside on one tire, outside on opposite tire: 　　Bent arm or steering knuckle. TIRE THUMP, TRAMP, SQUEAL 　Damaged fabric. 　Unbalanced condition. 　Incorrect air pressure. 　Incorrect wheel alignment. ABRASIVE ROUGHNESS 　Incorrect tow-in. 　Driving on rough finished concrete. HEEL AND TOE WEAR 　High speed driving. 　Excessive use of brakes. UNIFORM SPOTTY WEAR 　Lack of tire rotation. UNEVEN SPOTTY WEAR 　Unusual driving habits. 　Worn or loose parts. 　Incorrect wheel alignment.

Figure 15-6   Troubleshooting steering difficulties.

manufacturers provide a camber adjustment at the spindle assembly. There may not be a camber adjustment on some strut suspension systems.

　Camber is closely related to ***steering axis inclination*** (SAI). Steering axis inclination is the inward tilt of the steering knuckle. It is commonly represented by the angle between true vertical and an imaginary line from the lower ball joint through the top of the strut (or through the upper and lower ball joints). If a vehicle has a SAI of 0°, the lower ball joint will be located directly below the top of the strut. Steering axis inclination is not adjustable.

　Steering axis inclination and camber share a common side (the vertical axis of the wheel) and form what is known as the ***included angle.*** The included angle places the turning point of the wheel at the center of the tire-to-road contact area. See Figure 15-9.

　Toe.　***Toe*** is the difference in the distance (inches or millimeters) between the front edge and the back edge of the front or rear wheels. Toe is generally measured at hub height. ***Toe-in*** is present when a vehicle's wheels are "pigeon-toed," or closer together in the front than at the rear. A small amount of toe-in keeps the front wheels

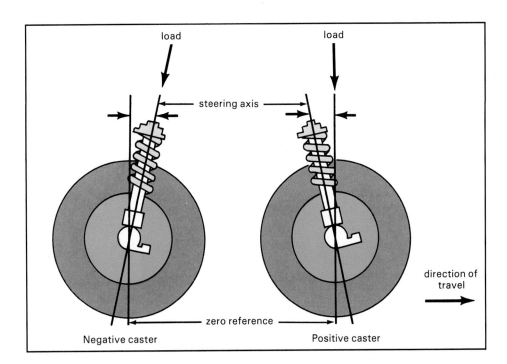

Figure 15-7 Negative and positive caster. Positive caster increases the stability of a vehicle by resisting the tendency to wander.

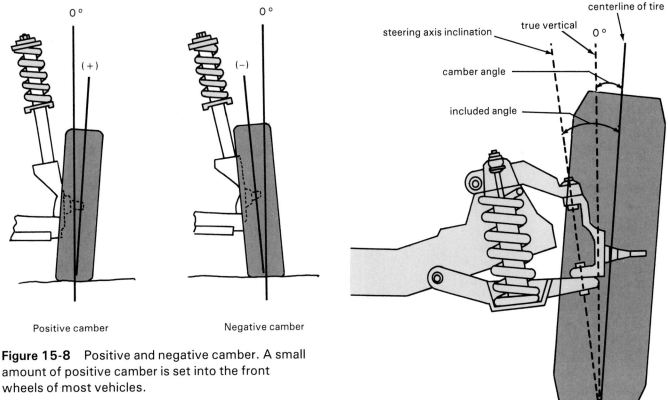

Figure 15-8 Positive and negative camber. A small amount of positive camber is set into the front wheels of most vehicles.

Figure 15-9 The included angle consists of the camber angle and the steering axis inclination.

running parallel by offsetting the forces that tend to spread them apart. It also prevents the tires from slipping and scuffing on the road. Toe-in is adjusted by turning the tie-rod ends to shorten or lengthen the tie-rods. On some vehicles, tie-rod adjustments are made with adjusting sleeves on the tie rod ends, Figure 15-10.

As a vehicle turns, the front wheels tend to experience **toe-out.** When this occurs, the front edge of the wheels are farther apart than the back edge. See Figure

15-11. In turns, the outside wheel is approximately 5 ft. (1.5 m) from the point about which the car is turning. Therefore, the outside wheel must swing through a larger arc and turn at a smaller angle than the inside wheel. Consequently, the inside wheel requires a

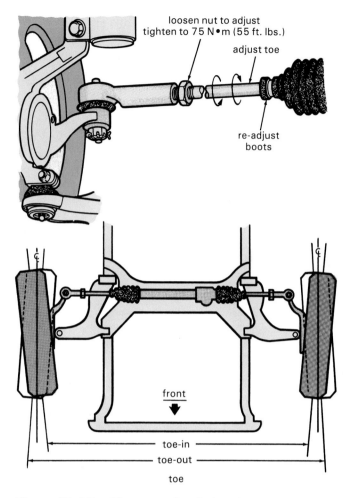

Figure 15-10   Alignment detail showing toe and toe adjustment. (Nissan)

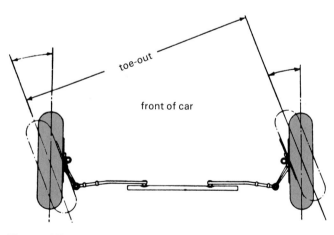

Figure 15-11   The front wheels on most vehicles toe-out on turns.

different turning radius than the outside wheel to prevent the tire from slipping or scuffing. To accomplish this, the spindles are designed to angle several degrees inside the parallel position. This serves to speed the action of the arm on the inside of the turn as it moves toward the centerline of the wheel spindle. This action slows the outside

wheel to obtain true rolling contact of the tires and to prevent slipping or scuffing.

Although the amount of toe-out on turns is not adjustable, it is controlled by the angle of the wheel spindle. Bent steering arms can affect toe-out. Never attempt to straighten spindles or steering arms. Bent steering components must be replaced.

Specially designed computerized alignment racks produce graphic displays that show alignment technicians how to measure and adjust a vehicle to obtain factory alignment tolerances, Figure 15-12.

Tracking.   Proper *tracking* occurs when the rear wheels follow directly behind the front wheels. In order to track correctly, a vehicle's *thrust line* must be parallel to its centerline and its rear axle must be perpendicular to the direction of travel. See Figure 15-13. The thrust line is an imaginary line that is parallel with a vehicle's rear wheels.

It is essential that all four wheels are adjusted correctly to achieve proper tracking. If rear wheels are not at right angles to the axle and parallel to the vehicle's geometric centerline, the rear of the vehicle will travel in the direction of the thrust line, rather than straight ahead. Tracking problems cannot be remedied simply by checking the wheel base and repositioning an axle. It is essential that toe be checked on all four wheels. Rear toe may not be adjustable in all cars. It may be necessary to replace axles, axle housings, cross members, or other parts to correct tracking problems.

Brake Systems

The auto body technician must be able to diagnosis *brake system* problems. Normal wear and major mechanical problems are generally repaired by brake specialists. However, brake line damage is a common problem encountered in the auto body shop. During a collision, steel and flexible brake lines are sometimes crimped, cut, or kinked. Damaged brake lines must be replaced. If brakes are not working properly, check the fluid level in the master cylinder. Modern vehicles are protected against brake system failure by a dual master cylinder, which divides the brake system into two hydraulic systems. These systems are commonly separated from front to rear or diagonally. When brake components are replaced (wheel cylinder, brake line, etc.), it is generally necessary to bleed the hydraulic system. This allows trapped air bubbles to escape from the system. When bleeding the hydraulic system, always follow the manufacturer's recommendations.

Power brake systems utilize a power booster (vacuum assist) to activate the master cylinder. Vacuum hoses and other connections to the booster should be carefully inspected after a collision. Leaks or poor connections will dramatically affect braking power.

The brake pads on many late-model vehicles are equipped with wear indicators. As pads wear, these

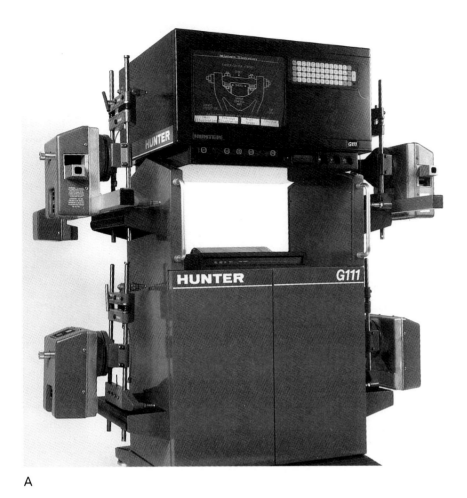

A

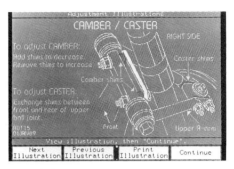

B

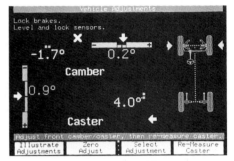

C

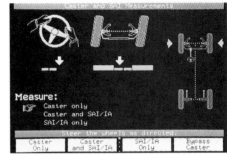

D

Figure 15-12 Computerized alignment equipment.
A–Computer with sensors. B–Adjustment illustrations.
C–Vehicle adjustments. D–Caster and SAI measurements.
(Hunter Engineering)

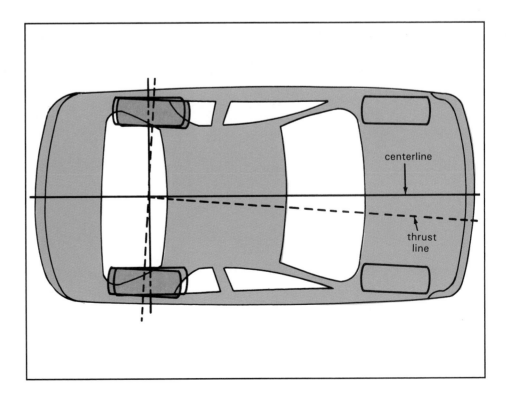

Figure 15-13 If the thrust
line is not parallel with the
vehicle's centerline, the
wheels will not track correctly.

indicators contact the brake disc and show through the pads. When the indicators are visible, the brake pads should be replaced.

Anti-Lock Brake Systems

Many late-model vehicles are equipped with **anti-lock brake systems.** These systems use wheel speed sensors, a hydraulic actuator/modulator, and an electronic control unit to prevent wheels from locking up during periods of hard braking. See Figure 15-14.

The most important components in an anti-lock brake system are the wheel speed sensors. These sensors are located at each wheel or at the front wheels and in the rear axle housing. Wheel speed sensors send information on wheel rotation to the control module. The module signals the actuator to pulsate hydraulic pressure to the brakes at the wheel or wheels that are locking up. Some vehicles have anti-lock brakes only on the rear wheels.

If an anti-lock brake system's warning lamp is activated, visually inspect the system for problems. Bent sensor brackets are common problems in anti-lock brake systems. If a visual inspection does not turn up a problem, a scan tool can be used to extract trouble codes from the system's electronic control unit. The trouble codes will provide information on the source of the problem.

WARNING: Be careful when servicing or working near anti-lock brake systems. These systems operate and store fluid at very high pressures. Carefully follow the manufacturer's diagnostic and repair procedures. Although all systems are similar, each has unique features and service precautions.

Exhaust and Emission Control Systems

A properly functioning **exhaust system** is essential for the proper operation of the engine and the health of the vehicle's occupants. Exhaust fumes (carbon monoxide) are deadly. The exhaust system includes the exhaust manifold(s), exhaust pipe, catalytic converter, muffler, and tail pipe. See Figure 15-15.

Inspect the entire system for holes, corrosion, dents, and signs of leakage. Collisions may cause hanger brackets or clamps to bend, resulting in a misaligned muffler, converter, or pipes. The impact from a collision also tends to loosen exhaust joints. When replacing any

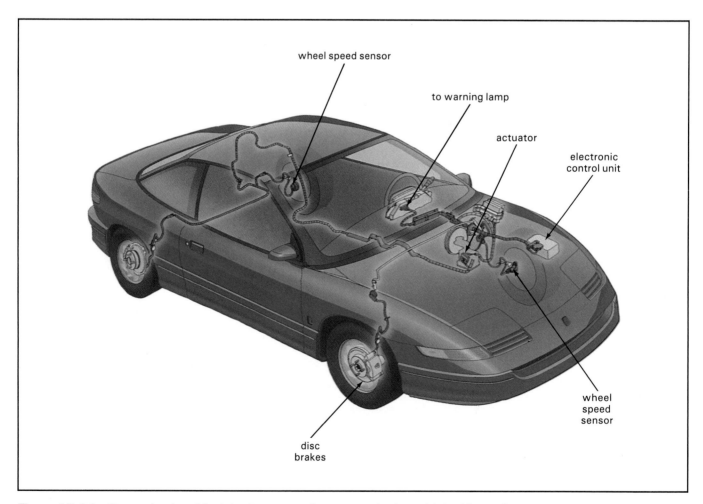

Figure 15-14 Four-wheel anti-lock brake system for one particular vehicle. (Saturn)

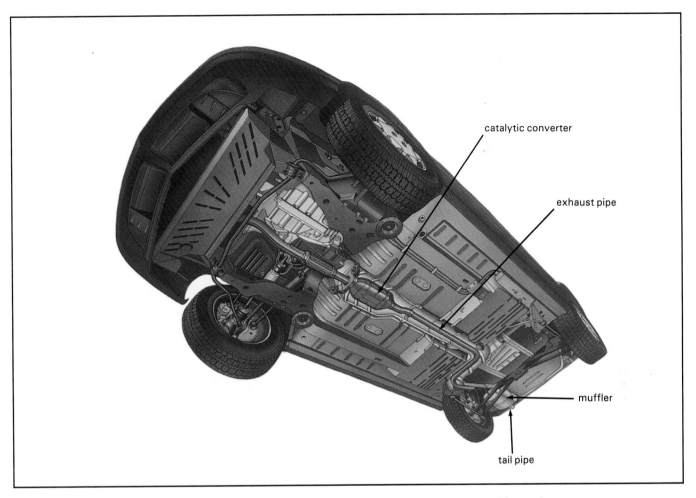

Figure 15-15 Typical exhaust system. Note the arrangement of the components. (Saturn)

exhaust component, make certain it meets the manufacturer's specifications.

Federal law requires technicians to restore **emission control systems** to the manufacturer's specifications. A collision may damage the PVC (positive crankcase ventilation) valve, EGR (exhaust gas recirculation) valve, air filter, catalytic converter, or vacuum lines. All of these items can affect engine performance and/or emissions. Therefore, repair procedures and replacement parts must comply with the manufacturer's specifications.

Heating and Cooling Systems

Heating and cooling systems generally include a radiator (with shroud), water pump, fan, heater core, drive belts, hoses, and switches. See Figure 15-16.

The radiator is the heart of the heating/cooling system. A water pump circulates coolant through hoses from the engine to the radiator. The radiator acts as a heat exchanger. As hot coolant flows through the radiator, the fan draws cool air over the hot radiator core. The cool air helps to remove heat from the coolant before it is returned to the engine. This prevents the engine (and automatic transmission) from overheating. Most late-model vehicles have electric fans rather than belt-driven

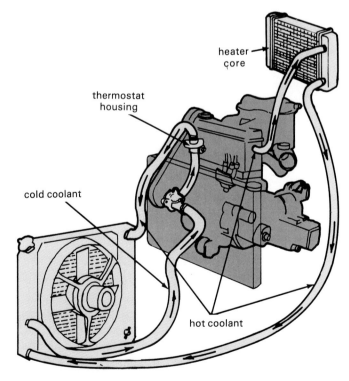

Figure 15-16 Typical heating system. Note that hot coolant flows from the engine to the heater core.

fans. Electric fans are activated by a coolant sensor, which triggers the fan motor when the engine coolant reaches a certain temperature. A *fan shroud* is generally mounted on the radiator to help direct and concentrate air movement. Never operate the engine without the shroud. Cracked or broken shrouds may be repaired.

To warm a vehicle's passenger compartment, heated water flows from the engine block to a heater core. A plenum assembly directs inside or outside air to the heater core. A small electric fan forces the air through the core. The air is heated in the core before it is distributed through various ducts in the passenger compartment.

Inspect the radiator and hose connections for leaks. Check the coolant level in the coolant reservoir or the radiator. If coolant is lost, it must be replaced. Make certain that the coolant will provide adequate protection in freezing temperatures. An inexpensive *hydrometer* can be used to determine if protection is adequate. Bubbles or discoloration in the coolant may indicate a leak in head, manifold, or transmission gaskets. Check the transmission lines and cooler section for visible damage or leaks. The loss of transmission fluid or the presence of water in the engine oil may indicate internal leakage between the cooling and lubrication system. After repairs are made, always refill the cooling system with a 50-50 mixture of antifreeze and water.

A V-belt is used to turn the water pump in the cooling system. The belt runs between the crankshaft pulley and the pump. A tension gauge is necessary for checking cogged or ribbed belts. The gauge is placed over the belt and provides a reading that can be compared with manufacturer's specifications. A conventional V-belt can be quickly checked by pressing on the middle of the belt span with your finger. These belts should have no more than 1/2 in. (12 mm) of give. If belts are too loose, the water pump (and other components driven by the belt) may not operate properly.

The cooling fan commonly causes considerable damage to the radiator core during a collision. Never attempt to straighten fan blades. Fan balance is critical. Damaged fans should always be replaced.

Air dams are essential parts of the cooling system. They are mounted under the front portion of a vehicle and are designed to direct air over the engine. See Figure 15-17. When air dams are damaged, they must be repaired or replaced. Missing or damaged air dams may contribute to engine overheating.

Air Conditioning Systems

Air conditioning systems consist of a condenser, compressor, receiver-dehydrator, evaporator, switches, lines, and other miscellaneous components. See Figure 15-18. The condenser, which is located in front of the radiator, is commonly damaged in front-end collisions. Air conditioning lines frequently break or leak refrigerant as the result of a collision. In some systems, a sight

glass, which is built into a line near or on top of the receiver-dehydrator, can be used to check for proper charge. The presence of bubbles or foam in the sight glass indicates that the system is low on refrigerant and must be recharged.

For many years, R-12, a chlorofluorocarbon, was the only refrigerant used in automotive air conditioning systems. In recent years, however, a great deal of emphasis has been placed on eliminating products containing

Figure 15-17 Air dams help prevent overheating.

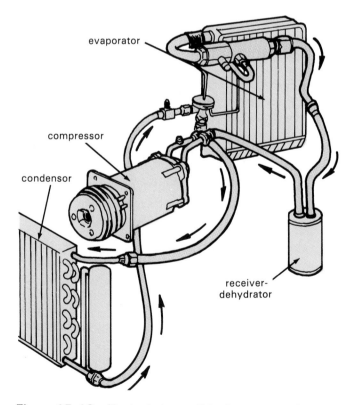

Figure 15-18 Typical air conditioning system. Note the orientation of the various components.

Figure 15-19 Typical refrigerant recovery and recycling unit. (Kent-Moore)

chlorofluorocarbons (CFCs). Chlorofluorocarbons have a detrimental effect on the earth's ozone layer. In 1991, regulations were imposed that require R-12 to be recycled. The regulations also require technicians who service mobile air conditioning systems to be certified in refrigerant recycling. Certification is offered through the several EPA-approved testing organizations. Businesses servicing mobile air conditioning systems must prove to the EPA that they use UL-approved recycling equipment and employ certified technicians. See Figure 15-19.

Late-model vehicles use R-134a refrigerant instead of R-12. This refrigerant does not contain CFCs. Because the chemical makeup of R-134a is radically different from R-12, R-134a must never be added to systems that contain R-12. Additionally, special service equipment is needed when working on R-134a systems. The conversion to environmentally safe R-134a is a major step toward reducing the amount of CFCs released into the atmosphere. However, over 150 million vehicles with R-12 air conditioning systems are still in use.

Many auto body shops send their air conditioning work to specialists. These specialists have the recycling, charging, and diagnostic equipment needed to service modern air conditioning systems.

Know These Terms

Suspension system, Steering system, Wheel alignment, Caster, Positive caster, Negative caster, Camber, Steering axis inclination, Included angle, Toe, Toe-in, Toe-out, Tracking, Thrust line, Brake system, Anti-lock brake systems, Exhaust system, Emission control systems, Heating and cooling systems, Air conditioning systems, Chlorofluorocarbons.

Summary

Auto body technicians must be able to diagnose and analyze mechanical component damage. Mechanical damage must be identified before body repairs can be made. In many cases mechanical repairs must be made as the body is being repaired. Most mechanical work is sent to shops that specialize in mechanical repairs.

The seven systems that must be checked and repaired when a vehicle suffers collision damage include the drivetrain, suspension, steering, brake, exhaust and emission, heating and cooling, and air conditioning systems. Additionally, the vehicle's safety systems should be checked before it is returned to its owner.

The drivetrain consists of the engine and all components that transfer engine power to the wheels. A collision may damage the engine, transmission, or other drivetrain components. In some unibody vehicles, the drivetrain must be removed before body repairs are made.

Proper operation of the suspension system is critical to safe vehicle operation. Suspension damage may affect handling, fuel economy, and comfort.

Steering linkage condition and alignment are also important to safe operation. Parallelogram steering systems, rack-and-pinion steering systems, and four-wheel independent steering systems are found on late-model vehicles.

Wheel alignment is commonly upset during a collision. There are several control angles that should be verified when checking alignment, including caster, camber, and toe. Tracking should also be checked.

Although most brake repairs are sent to brake specialists, the auto body technician should check for brake system problems. Special precautions should be taken when working near anti-lock brake systems. These systems operate at extremely high pressures.

Properly functioning exhaust and emission systems are important to proper vehicle operation and the health of the vehicle's occupants. Always repair these systems to the manufacturer's specifications.

A vehicle's heating and cooling system consists of a radiator, water pump, fan, heater core, drive belts, hoses, and switches. Inspect this system for loose connections, loose hoses, and diluted coolant. If necessary, replace coolant with a 50-50 mixture of antifreeze and water.

The major parts on an air conditioning system include the condenser, compressor, receiver-dehydrator, evaporator, switches, and lines. Air conditioning lines often break or leak as the result of a collision. Air conditioning systems must be serviced by certified technicians using approved recycling equipment. Late-model vehicles are equipped with air conditioning systems that utilize R-134a as a refrigerant. This refrigerant does not contain chlorofluorocarbons.

Review Questions–Chapter 15

1. Improperly repaired mechanical components may cause a vehicle to be unsafe. True or False?

2. Most major mechanical system problems are repaired by auto body technicians. True or False?

3. The systems that should be checked when a vehicle suffers collision damage include the:
   a. suspension system.
   b. air conditioning system.
   c. brake system.
   d. all of the above.

4. The _____ includes the engine and all components that transfer engine power to a vehicle's wheels.

5. Engine-related noises change in relation to vehicle speed. True or False?

6. C-V joints are used on _____-_____ drive vehicles to compensate for steering action.

7. A minor impact can damage mechanical components on a late-model vehicle. True or False?

8. An improperly repaired suspension system can cause _____ problems.

9. The body and suspension must be repaired as a unit on:
   a. body-over-frame vehicles.
   b. unibody vehicles.
   c. all vehicles.
   d. none of the above.

10. Torsion and stabilizer bars can be straightened by applying heat to the damaged areas. True or False?

11. Active suspension systems use _____ to monitor driving conditions.

12. Most rear-wheel drive vehicles are equipped with:
    a. four-wheel steering systems.
    b. parallelogram steering systems.
    c. rack-and-pinion steering systems.
    d. none of the above.

13. Rack-and-pinion steering systems are used extensively on late-model vehicles. True or False?

14. Bent steering linkages are easy to detect. True or False?

15. Most power steering systems operate on _____ pressure.

16. Wheel alignment affects:
    a. steering control.
    b. handling.
    c. tire life.
    d. all of the above.

17. Wheel alignment is dependent on the condition of _____ and _____ components.

18. The steering angle that utilizes the weight and momentum of a vehicle to lead the wheels in a straight path is called:
    a. toe.
    b. camber.
    c. caster.
    d. none of the above.

19. Steering axis inclination can be adjusted by changing the position of tie rod ends. True or False?

20. Modern vehicles are protected against brake system failure by a dual _____ _____.

21. When brake components are replaced, it is often necessary to bleed the system. True or False?

22. In an anti-lock brake system, wheel _____ _____ send information on wheel rotation to a control module.

23. A vehicle's emission system must be repaired to the manufacturer's specifications. True or False?

24. The heating and cooling system of a vehicle generally includes a:
    a. water pump.
    b. radiator.
    c. fan.
    d. all of the above.

25. A _____ can be used to determine the condition of engine coolant.

26. Water found in the engine oil may indicate leakage between the cooling system and the _____ system.

27. The air conditioning system component that is commonly damaged in frontal collisions is the:
    a. evaporator.
    b. compressor.
    c. condenser.
    d. none of the above.

28. Chlorofluorocarbons have a detrimental effect on the earth's _____ layer.

29. When servicing air conditioning systems, R-12 refrigerant must be recycled. True or False?

30. R-134a refrigerant can be added to R-12 systems when recharging is necessary. True or False?

Activities–Chapter 15

1. Using cardboard tubes and other scrap materials, make a cutaway model of a typical shock absorber. Mount it on a board for display, with all major parts identified.

2. Go to local car dealerships and gather sales brochures from two manufacturers – one domestic and one foreign. For each manufacturer's line, make a grid, with car models listed down the left side, and three columns across the top: steering, front-wheel drive, rear-wheel drive. In the steering column, write R/P for rack and pinion, C for conventional (parallelogram). Place an X in the appropriate column for front-wheel or rear-wheel drive. When your grids are completed, analyze them to answer the following questions:

   ☐ What type of steering is most common?

   ☐ Is front-wheel or rear-wheel drive used more often?

   ☐ Does there seem to be any relationship between the type of drive and the type of steering?

   ☐ Is there much difference between the answers to the preceding questions when domestic and foreign lines are compared?

3. Visit a shop specializing in muffler and exhaust system replacement and observe the operation. If possible, discuss with the manager or a technician the signs that indicate a component should be replaced, and special safety precautions that workers must observe when removing or installing exhaust system components.

4. Demonstrate the use of a pressure tester in checking a cooling system for leaks, and describe the necessary repair for any leaks discovered. Also demonstrate the use and interpretation of a simple hydrometer for determining the specific gravity (and thus the amount of protection) of an antifreeze solution.

Finishing materials and processes have changed significantly over the years. Early-model vehicles were painted with single-stage lacquer or enamel finishes. Late-model vehicles are painted with multi-stage finishes. (Buick)

chapter 16

Refinishing Materials

After studying this chapter, you will be able to:

- ☐ Describe the role of solvents, vehicle, binder, and other paint additives.

- ☐ Discuss how to safely use paints, additives, and other refinishing materials.

- ☐ Explain when to use primers, sealers, topcoats, and undercoats.

- ☐ Explain the advantages of various types of topcoat finishes.

- ☐ Describe the process of tinting paint to match an existing finish.

Refinishing Material Ingredients

Automotive refinishing materials have changed dramatically in the last decade. There are many brands and types of automotive paints on the market. As a result, the auto body technician must learn to apply various types of automotive finishes.

The terms *paint* and *finish* have broad meanings. These terms are used to describe many different finishing materials. They are most commonly used when referring to the outside layer or topcoat on metal or plastic components. This topcoat is generally about 0.004 in. (0.10 mm) thick.

All paints contain three basic ingredients: binders, solvents, and pigments. Special additives are also used in some paints to alter their properties and characteristics.

Binders

Binders are the resinous, film-forming ingredients that adhere to the surface being painted (substrate). Binders determine the physical and chemical characteristics of the paint, but do not provide any significant color. They are generally honey-like in consistency and appearance. Although nitrocellulose lacquer binders were popular at one time, they are rarely used today. They have been replaced by acrylic lacquer binders. Some of the more popular plastic resin binder systems used today include polymethyl methacrylate (acrylics), alkyd, polyvinyl chloride, and polyurethane binders.

All aftermarket repair finishes consist of a lacquer- or enamel-based binder. OEM finish formulations require baking to dry and cure properly. Aftermarket paints, on the other hand, cure by evaporation or by chemical action. Nevertheless, evaporation and cure can be accelerated with heat lamps.

Solvents

Solvents or *vehicles* are added to paint so that it can be more easily applied. Solvents essentially thin the paint pigments and binders so they are in a sprayable (liquid) form. Solvents are sometimes called *volatiles* because they easily vaporize and evaporate.

As solvents evaporate, they release many volatile organic compounds (VOCs) into the air. VOCs contribute to environmental air pollution and pose health hazards. Waterborne paints are currently used by a few manufacturers and will eventually be used in repair shops. These paints must be baked at very high temperatures and are then covered with polyurethane clearcoats. Because waterborne paint systems use water as the carrier instead of solvents, there are few VOCs released when applying these systems. Although harmful solvents do not evaporate into the atmosphere, small quantities of pigments and other additives are released into the air during the application (atomization) of waterborne paint systems.

Solvents are added by the paint manufacturer to help dissolve the binder. If additional solvent is required to dilute the paint before it is applied, a thinner or reducer is added by the technician.

It is important to note the difference between thinners and reducers. *Thinners* are used only with lacquer-based finishes. They cannot be used with enamels. *Reducers,* on the other hand, should be used only with enamel-based finishes. It is important to understand that enamels *set* or *cure* after the reducers have evaporated.

Never mix thinners and reducers. If enamel reducer is used in lacquer-based finishes, it will usually curdle the material. Both thinners and reducers are classified and sold according to their evaporation rate (slow, medium, or fast). As a rule, temperature and humidity are the main factors in choosing a thinner or reducer. A slow thinner or reducer will allow the paint to flow and level out before it evaporates or cures. A slow thinner or reducer is generally used when the temperature in the finishing area is above 75 °F (24 °C). On a cold wet day, a fast drying thinner or reducer should be used. Paint may absorb moisture and blush if a fast thinner is not used. *Blush* is a milky white haze that appears on the surface of the paint as it dries. Thinning rates are generally given in percentages, as shown in Figure 16-1.

Various types of thinners and reducers are produced for use with specific paints. For example, acrylic lacquer thinner is different from nitrocellulose lacquer thinner. Similarly, acrylic enamel reducers, synthetic enamel reducers, and polyurethane enamel reducers are different. See Figure 16-2.

Reduction Percentage	Proportions of Thinner to Paint
25%	1 part thinner to 4 parts paint
33%	1 part thinner to 3 parts paint
50%	1 part thinner to 2 parts paint
75%	3 parts thinner to 4 parts paint
100%	1 part thinner to 1 part paint
125%	5 parts thinner to 4 parts paint
150%	3 parts thinner to 2 parts paint
200%	2 parts thinner to 1 part paint
250%	5 parts thinner to 2 parts paint
300%	3 parts thinner to 1 part paint

Figure 16-1   Thinning percentages.

Figure 16-2   The type of reducer used for enamel-based finishes will vary with the type of enamel used.

Never use wash thinners (bulk thinners) or universal thinners to reduce or thin finishes. **Wash thinners** are low-cost solvents used to clean spray guns and other equipment. **Universal thinners** are used to thin lacquers *and* reduce enamels. Nevertheless, these materials are not recommended for reliable, quality work.

Pigments

Pigments are added to give the paint color. The amount and type of pigments added will also alter the durability, adhesion, flow, and other characteristics of the paint.

Both lacquers and enamels are available in a variety of colors and appear to have the same color value regardless of the angle from which they are viewed (nonmetallics). To give a finish a luminous quality, small *metallic flakes* are often mixed with paint. These flakes may vary in size. Paints that contain metallic flakes are known as **metallics**. When metallics are viewed from various angles, their color shade seems to change. The reason for the apparent variation in shade is that the metallic flakes reflect light differently when viewed at different angles.

To provide a **pearlescent** look, mica particles coated with titanium dioxide are added to paint. With each succeeding coat of this finish, additional ''pearlescent'' layers are applied. There is a color change from white, to gold, to red, to blue, and finally to green as the paint film thickness is increased. There is also a marked color change when these finishes are viewed from different angles.

In some paints, metal and mica flakes have been replaced with Mylar (polyester) plastic flakes. These flakes can be produced in a variety of colors and sizes. Paints with plastic flakes are also known as metallics.

Mica, metal, or plastic flakes can be used in the basecoat or in intermediate coats. Metallic paints are very popular, but they present a problem to the painter when attempting to match the shade and reflective quality during the repair procedure.

Additives

A number of **additives** are used in paint to alter its properties and characteristics. Always follow the manufacturer's instructions when mixing additives.

Additives that speed up cure are called **hardeners**. Those that slow cure are called **retarders**. **Flatteners** are added to paint to lower its gloss. Other additives are used to add flexibility. **Flex-agents** can be used in acrylic lacquers when finishing interior vinyl trim. They can also be added to enamels when painting exterior vinyl tops, bumpers, or composite body panels. **Fisheye eliminator** is use to eliminate fisheyes. **Fisheyes** are small round spots over which the paint will not flow. These spots are generally caused by a speck of silicone left on the substrate. Automotive paint protectants are often loaded with silicone additives, which are used to ward off the

effects of elements. Many ''miracle'' protectants penetrate the paint. This results in small, round spots of silicone on the substrate. As previously mentioned, paint will not adhere to these spots. Additives are also available to prevent blushing and to improve the chemical resistance of the finish.

Texturing agents are added to paint to produce a bumpy texture. Texture is controlled by the amount of agent used and the application technique. **Adhesion promoters** are sometimes added to acrylic polyurethane clearcoats. These products help to ensure adequate adhesion of the clearcoat to OEM (original equipment manufacturer's) finishes and to new basecoat colors. Many OEM finishes are so hard that new paint does not bond well to them. Sanding and the use of adhesion promoters or primers will help eliminate this problem.

Identifying Original Finish

Before a finish is applied, it may be necessary to determine what type paint is currently on the vehicle. This is especially true if spot repairs have been made or if a vehicle has been completely refinished. One method for testing the paint is to apply lacquer thinner to a rag and rub it over an inconspicuous spot. If the paint colors the rag, the finish is lacquer. Lacquer thinners will generally curdle or wrinkle enamel finishes.

To determine if a clearcoat finish has been used, sand a small paint spot with #800 grit sandpaper. If white sanding dust is created, a basecoat/clearcoat system was used. If colored dust is produced, a clearcoat finish was not used.

Another method for identifying finish types is to apply one of the compounds manufactured specifically for identification purposes. These compounds will dissolve lacquer but will not harm enamel finishes. If identification cannot be made, a sealer must be used before a new finish can be applied. Sealers will be covered later in this chapter.

Undercoats

Before a color coat or finish coat can be applied, the bare metal or plastic surface must be properly prepared. After sanding and cleaning, an **undercoat** should be applied. There are three types of undercoats used for auto body repair: primers (prepcoats), primer-surfacers, and sealers. See Figure 16-3.

Primers

Primers are designed to improve paint adhesion on plastic and metal surfaces. Primers are sometimes called *prepcoats.* The term prepcoat implies that the substrate is being prepared for a final coating. These materials may

Figure 16-3 Various undercoats are used in the refinishing process.

be formulated to prevent rust and corrosion or to improve adhesion. An appropriate primer is extremely important when refinishing plastics. See Figure 16-4.

There are two basic types of primers: lacquer-based primers and enamel-based primers. Many technicians prefer enamel-based primers because they are more durable and have slightly better adhesion properties than lacquer-based primers. Lacquer-based primers, on the other hand, dry faster than enamel primers.

In an effort to minimize the release of volatile organic compounds (VOCs), several paint companies have developed low-VOC primers. These heavy bodied primers are designed to be applied with rollers and brushes to minimize overspray and the release of VOCs.

Primers are intended for improving adhesion and will not fill most imperfections. When metal or plastic surfaces require filling, a primer-surfacer should be used.

To maximize adhesion, a three-step process should be followed. Before applying the primer, clean the surface to remove oil, wax, and polish. A metal conditioner is then used to remove any rust or corrosion. Finally, apply a conversion coat to improve adhesion.

When refinishing plastic or fiberglass, isopropyl alcohol

Topcoat
Undercoat
Substrate

Figure 16-4 Primers are used to prepare the substrate to receive the topcoat. (Du Pont)

is used to clean the surfaces. The alcohol prevents static electricity and removes lingering traces of silicone. It also assists in drying body surfaces. Moisture tends to creep along glass reinforcement fibers in these materials.

There are a number of special primers used on plastics and metals. All improve adhesion and prepare the substrate for surfacers, sealers, or color topcoats.

Epoxy-chromate primers have excellent adhesion and corrosion resistant properties. These primers are easy to apply and cure quickly. Once mixed with a hardener (catalyst), epoxy-chromate primers must be used immediately. Any type of topcoat can be applied over an epoxy primer.

A *zinc-chromate primer* or epoxy primer can be used as an undercoat when painting aluminum. Some of these primers have formulations that react chemically with topcoats. See Figure 16-5.

Weld-through primers are zinc-rich materials used to protect weld joints. They are applied to the joint area before the weld is made. All zinc-rich primers will provide galvanic protection.

Plastic primers are formulated to improve adhesion to plastic parts. All plastic parts must be primed before a topcoat is applied. Paint will chip and peel from unprimed plastic surfaces. See Chapter 9.

Wash-primers improve corrosion resistance by protecting the bare metal from the environment. This vinyl-based material contains an acid to "etch" into the metal for superior adhesion. A special reducer and a catalyst are required when using these primers.

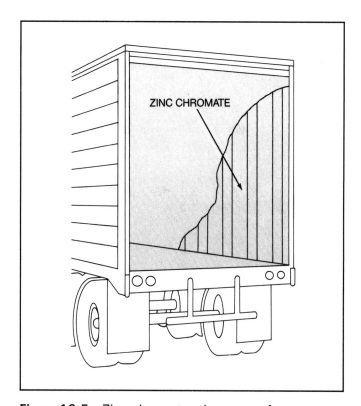

Figure 16-5 Zinc-chromate primers are often used on the aluminum surfaces of commercial vehicles.

Chip-resistant primers are sometimes applied to lower body sections to improve corrosion resistance and protect against gravel/stone impact damage. Specially formulated flex-additives add impact strength to these primers.

Primer-Surfacers

Before the color or finish coat is applied to a bare substrate, a ***primer-surfacer*** is often applied. Primer-surfacers fill imperfections, improve adhesion, and prevent rust and corrosion. See Figure 16-6. Several coats of this material can be quickly applied. Primer-surfacers will dry in about 20-30 minutes. When thoroughly dry, the primer-surfacer is sanded to provide a smooth, flat surface. Some primer-surfacers can be wet sanded; others are not water resistant and should not be subjected to moisture. Primers that are not water resistant may absorb water. Any moisture trapped in the primer-surfacer will eventually rust the metal substrate.

There are three general types of primer-surfacers: lacquer-based primer-surfacers, enamel-based primer-surfacers, and two-component primer-surfacers.

A *lacquer-based primer-surfacer* is used as an undercoat for lacquer-based paints. Acrylic lacquer-based primer-surfacers have replaced nitrocellulose-based surfacers in most shops. Acrylic primer-surfacers dry quickly, adhere properly, fill well, sand easily, and provide good hold-out. ***Hold-out*** is the property that prevents the topcoat from sinking into the primer-surfacer.

Before applying enamel topcoats, an *enamel-based primer-surfacer* is recommended. Enamel primer-surfacers must not be placed between an old lacquer-based finish and a new lacquer topcoat. Enamel primer-surfacers are designed to ''prime and surface'' large areas. They provide better adhesion, corrosion resistance, and flexibility than lacquer-based primer-surfacers.

Alkyd or *synthetic enamel primer-surfacers* are tough and flexible. They also provide good adhesion and excellent coverage. The major drawback to these materials is that they take about two hours to dry.

Acrylic polyurethane primer-surfacers are two-component systems that offer excellent coverage, hold-out, and adhesion. However, they cure slowly and produce a sticky overspray. *Polyester primer-surfacers* build-up rapidly, cure quickly, and can be used under most topcoats.

Primer-surfacers are made in several colors. A light-colored primer-surfacer is recommended for light topcoats. For best adhesion and finish, primer-surfacers must be sanded before sealers or topcoats are applied. Always follow the manufacturer's instructions. Use a primer-surfacer that is recommended for the type of color coat (or sealer) to be used.

Sealers

Sealers (primer-sealers) are used to prevent topcoat solvents from penetrating primer-surfacers. See Figure 16-7. In other words, they improve hold-out. Sealers are often used when recoating enamel or lacquer finishes. They are also used to seal sanding scratches. This helps reduce *sand-scratch swelling,* which occurs when solvents soften and swell the edges of sanding scratches. Sealers are not to be used as a primer. Sealers are applied over primer-surfacers (or original finishes) before the new topcoat is applied.

Most manufacturers provide two different formulations of sealers, *sanding sealers* and *non-sanding sealers.* A sanding sealer will have more pigment than a non-sanding sealer and can be sanded to improve surface quality. Non-sanding sealers are used in areas that are difficult to sand, such as the inside of hoods and door jams. Lacquer-, enamel-, and water-based sealers are available.

Any time lacquer is to be applied over enamel, a sealer should be used. Special sealers are used to seal reds, maroons, and other dark colors if a new light topcoat is to be applied. These materials help prevent the old color from *bleeding* through to the new topcoat. Sealers do not fill imperfections or adhere well to bare metal.

Some manufacturers offer *universal sealers*, which can be used under any type of topcoat. Nevertheless, it is recommended that products (paint, solvent, sealer, etc.) from one manufacturer be used.

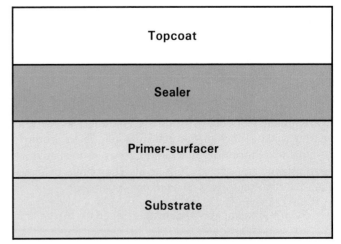

Figure 16-7 Sealers prevent the topcoat from penetrating the primer-surfacer.

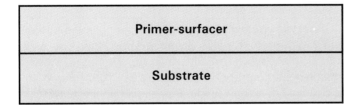

Figure 16-6 Primer-surfacers fill imperfections in the substrate.

Topcoats

There are three basic types of exterior topcoat finishes: lacquer topcoats, enamel topcoats, and waterborne topcoats. The term **topcoat** is used to indicate the color coat or the top layers of paint. Some manufacturers are using two-, three-, and four-stage paint systems. With multistage paint systems, several coats of highly pigmented enamel (acrylic) are covered with several coats of clear acrylic. These systems, which are called *basecoat/clearcoat systems,* will be discussed later in this chapter.

Temperature, humidity, solvents, and various additives affect the drying/curing time for all finishes. High temperatures generally accelerate evaporation and the chemical reaction of curing. Some shops use heat lamps or drying booths to speed drying time.

Lacquer

Lacquer topcoats dry as their solvents evaporate. Lacquer finishes dry from the outside in. Chemical hardeners or isocyanates are not used with these finishes. Lacquer finishes are popular because they dry quickly. Since lacquer remains more or less soluble, a new coat of acrylic lacquer will bond or unite with an old lacquer finish.

Acrylic lacquer is considered a general purpose finish since it can be used for spot repairs on both acrylic lacquer and baked enamel finishes. It can also be used for panel repairs and complete paint jobs.

Lacquer finishes are not used extensively today. These finishes do not flow out to fill or cover imperfections well. Lacquers require **color sanding** (wet sanding with #1200 grit abrasive), compounding, and polishing to produce a smooth, shiny finish.

Slow thinners are commonly used on the final coat of lacquer to eliminate **orange peel** and reduce the need for color sanding. Orange peel is a dry, bumpy surface that resembles the surface of an orange. This condition is caused by the fast evaporation of thinners. Most acrylic lacquers are thinned by 100-150%. The final coat may be thinned even more to improve flow-out.

Enamel

At one time, original equipment manufacturers (OEMs) used a specially formulated lacquer, which was heated (baked) in high-temperature ovens to promote drying and curing. However, lacquer-based finishes have been phased out at the OEM level. They have been replaced by various types of **enamels,** including:

☐ *Single-stage systems* (finish is baked on the vehicle with no clearcoat).

☐ *Two-stage systems* (colored basecoat is covered with a clearcoat).

☐ *Three-stage systems* (base color is covered with mica or metallic coat and a final clearcoat).

☐ *Waterborne systems* (color coat is baked and then covered with a clearcoat).

The most common OEM system used today is the two-stage basecoat/clearcoat system. Aftermarket three-stage systems (tri-coats) are composed of a colored basecoat, a particle-containing midcoat, and a top clearcoat. These systems may use an acrylic/enamel clearcoat (over acrylic enamel basecoat) or a polyurethane/enamel clearcoat (over lacquer or acrylic urethane basecoat).

Enamels dry in two stages: through the evaporation of their solvents and by the oxidation of their binder. Oxidation is the change in the binder that occurs when it combines with oxygen in the air. Although acrylic enamels dry to the touch in about 30 minutes, the finish continues to oxidize and harden for several weeks. Baking the finish accelerates drying.

Alkyd Enamel

Alkyd enamel has been a popular refinishing material for over 40 years. It is the least expensive of the enamels and usually covers in only two coats. It is sometimes known as *synthetic enamel* because the alkyd resin is made from petroleum rather than natural sources. Today, all automotive finishing materials are synthetic.

Alkyd enamels dry to a lustrous, high-gloss finish. Because they cure slowly, flow-out is excellent. Although hardener is not required, it can be added to shorten cure time. If hardener is not added, alkyd enamel finishes require at least 24 hours for proper curing.

Alkyd enamels are easily marred and have low chemical resistance for the first few days. Banks of infrared heat lamps are sometimes used to bake the finish at about 150 °F (65 °C) for one hour. This speeds drying and minimizes the possibility of finish contamination. When baking is used to achieve rapid drying, the finish is sometimes known as **baked enamel.**

Alkyd enamels are not as durable as many of the newer finishes. They also produce a great deal of wet overspray and are slow drying. Nevertheless, a few auto body technicians still prefer these finishes. Alkyd enamel remains a popular finish for trucks, buses, and industrial equipment.

Acrylic Enamel

Acrylic enamel consists of a solvent blend of binder and pigment materials. Because they flow out well, these finishes tend to fill small imperfections. Acrylic enamels are commonly reduced by 10-30% prior to application. These paints must be applied in a totally dust-free environment and take a long time to dry. When properly applied, acrylic enamels do not require compounding or polishing.

Acrylic enamels have several advantages over alkyd enamels. Acrylic enamels do not require compounding or polishing, are available in a variety of brilliant colors; can be used for spot repair of both lacquer and enamel original finishes; and have excellent flow characteristics, weatherability, and gloss retention.

Acrylic enamels and acrylic urethane enamels are preferred for polychromatic (metallic) colors. When compared to metallic polyurethane colors (covered later in this chapter), acrylic urethane enamel metallic colors are twice as durable. Remember, there is a pot life with all two-component materials. Always follow the manufacturer's instructions. A clearcoat can be applied after the color coat application. The clearcoat gives the basecoat and subsequent midcoats (when used) maximum depth, color, durability, and gloss retention. See Figure 16-8. Acrylic enamels can be recoated (or two-toned) within six hours of the initial application.

Special thermosetting acrylic enamels are used by manufacturers. These enamels are baked in ovens to dry and cure to a tough finish.

Polyurethane Enamel

The **polyurethane enamels** used for automotive refinishing provide a hard, tile-like finish; high gloss; excellent flow-out and appearance; good adhesion; and flexibility. These finishes have been used on aircraft, off-road equipment, fleet trucks, and automobiles. Polyurethane enamels are popular because they produce a ''wet-look'' finish.

There are several formulations of polyurethane enamels. Polyester-alkyd enamels cure by evaporation of solvents and through the chemical reaction of the two-part paint system. These finishes are normally mixed with equal parts of catalyst (hardener) and reducer.

WARNING: Polyurethane enamels contain isocyanates, which are extremely toxic. Respiratory protection is required when working with these products.

All polyurethane systems cure faster under heat. Most are cured at 150 °F (65 °C) for about thirty minutes. After curing, they can be wet sanded. Wet sanding affects the clearcoat and leaves the color basecoat untouched.

Acrylic-Polyurethane Enamels

Acrylic-polyurethane enamels have outstanding weatherability and generally provide higher gloss and greater durability than other polyurethane enamels. Like all two-part finishes, they must be applied immediately after they are mixed (activated). Acrylic-polyurethane enamels are commonly reduced by 20-50%.

Most acrylic-polyurethane enamels contain isocyanates. In Du Pont's Cronar™, however, the isocyanates have been replaced with polyoxithane without sacrificing quality. Although there is no isocyanate danger, toxic catalysts and fumes are still present in this paint.

Waterborne Acrylic Enamel

Some vehicles are being painted with waterborne acrylic enamels. These finishes are baked at more than 300 °F (150 °C) and then covered with a polyurethane clearcoat. Currently, this process is not practical for repair shops because most do not have baking ovens. Waterborne enamels also present additional problems. For example, acrylic lacquers can be used over water-based

Figure 16-8 Various types of clearcoats are used over modern finishes. Note the hardeners on the bottom shelf.

coats, but a sealer must be used first. Additionally, color matching may require the application of numerous color coats to match the existing finish.

Selecting the Topcoat

An important part of painting is the selection and preparation of the paint. Selecting the correct color is particularly important when repainting only a panel or a portion of a panel. Any variation in the color, hue, or shade will be easily detected.

Color Identification

To aid the auto body technician, each type and color of paint is given an identifying number (code). This number appears on a plate or tag on the vehicle's door frame, firewall, cowl, or other location, Figure 16-9. These plates are commonly called *vehicle identification plates* (VIPs).

Information on a vehicle's color, with identifying names and code numbers, is published by the paint manufacturer. These names and code numbers are commonly listed in a *paint chip book* or *color reference book*. Colored chips in these books are used to help identify the correct paint to be used when refinishing a vehicle. See

Figure 16-10. Keep in mind that age, environment, and care will affect the color of the original finish.

It is always a good idea to compare paint chips with protected or unexposed areas of the painted vehicle. Paint in door openings or under emblems will be close to the original color. If necessary, rubbing compound may be used to help clean oxides from painted areas. Although the technician is attempting to match the *current* condition or color of the paint, it is essential to correctly identify the original paint color.

Many people have color vision deficiencies, which make it difficult to match colors correctly. It is always a good idea to seek assistance from another technician when verifying a color match.

Topcoat Mixes

There are two ways that topcoats can be purchased commercially:

☐ Factory-mixed (packaged) topcoats.

☐ Custom-mixed topcoats.

Factory-mixed topcoats (factory-packaged) are carefully proportioned at the factory to achieve the desired color. Although not original formulations, these paints are designed to match the color and gloss of the "factory finish."

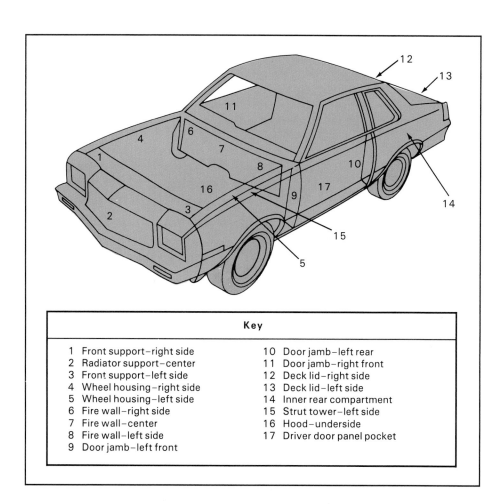

Figure 16-9 Identification plate locations will vary. Common locations are shown. (Du Pont)

Key	
1 Front support–right side	10 Door jamb–left rear
2 Radiator support–center	11 Door jamb–right front
3 Front support–left side	12 Deck lid–right side
4 Wheel housing–right side	13 Deck lid–left side
5 Wheel housing–left side	14 Inner rear compartment
6 Fire wall–right side	15 Strut tower–left side
7 Fire wall–center	16 Hood–underside
8 Fire wall–left side	17 Driver door panel pocket
9 Door jamb–left front	

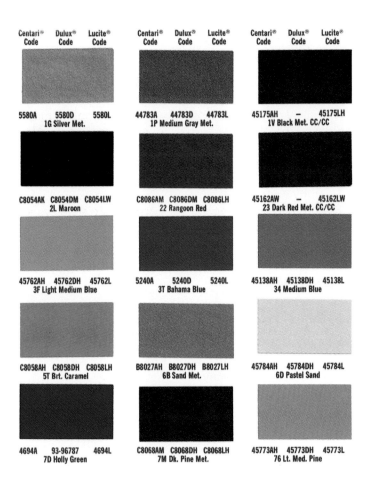

Centari® Code	Dulux® Code	Lucite® Code	Centari® Code	Dulux® Code	Lucite® Code	Centari® Code	Dulux® Code	Lucite® Code
5580A	5580D	5580L	44783A	44783D	44783L	45175AH	–	45175LH
	1G Silver Met.			1P Medium Gray Met.			1V Black Met. CC/CC	
C8054AK	C8054DM	C8054LW	C8086AM	C8086DM	C8086LH	45162AW	–	45162LW
	2L Maroon			22 Rangoon Red			23 Dark Red Met. CC/CC	
45762AH	45762DH	45762L	5240A	5240D	5240L	45138AH	45138DH	45138L
	3F Light Medium Blue			3T Bahama Blue			34 Medium Blue	
C8058AH	C8058DH	C8058LH	B8027AH	B8027DH	B8027LH	45784AH	45784DH	45784L
	5T Brt. Caramel			6B Sand Met.			6D Pastel Sand	
4694A	93-96787	4694L	C8068AM	C8068DH	C8068LH	45773AH	45773DH	45773L
	7D Holly Green			7M Dk. Pine Met.			76 Lt. Med. Pine	

Figure 16-10 Typical page from a color reference book.

Custom-mixed topcoats (intermix) are often used when attempting to match a badly oxidized or faded finish. They are also used when a customer wants a color that is not available as a factory mix. After about five years, paint manufacturers begin to phase out colors. When this occurs, a paint store or supply house will custom mix or blend colors to match original paint formulas. Custom mix equipment carefully measures the color pigments (by weight) added to a base color. This equipment is similar to the systems used to blend custom house paints.

Preparing Topcoats

Many paint failures are caused by improper mixing of the paint before spraying. Heavy pigments give color, opacity, and specific performance properties to paint. Some pigments weigh seven to eight times more than the liquid part of the paint. Consequently, pigments settle to the bottom of the paint container. This is particularly true of whites, chrome yellows, oranges, greens, reds, and yellow iron oxides. Metallic particles also tend to settle quickly.

The consistency or viscosity of the liquid part of the paint has a great deal to do with the rate of pigment settling. If paint has a high viscosity (thick consistency), the rate of settling will be relatively slow. Many paints are mixed and shipped at a high viscosity to reduce settling. Thinners or reducers are added to these paints to obtain a viscosity that can be properly sprayed. Each manufacturer has specific recommendations about the amount of thinner or reducer to be added before spraying. This amount may vary with specific colors. Always follow the manufacturer's instructions for the product at hand. Only thin enough material to do the job. Discard any prepared paint that is not used.

Paint that is allowed to stand for 10 minutes without being stirred will settle enough to be off-color when it is sprayed. This is especially true when applying metallics. If metallic flakes are allowed to settle for only a few minutes, the color will not match the previously applied finish.

If a paint has been in inventory (shop or supply house) for an extended period, most of its pigment will have settled. When this occurs, mix the paint thoroughly with a spatula and then with a power paint shaker. A pneumatic paint shaker is shown in Figure 16-11.

Figure 16-11 This pneumatic mixer can be used to thoroughly mix paint. (Broncorp Mfg. Co.)

Be certain to replace caps and lids immediately after using paint. This will prevent accidental spills and evaporation of the solvent. Several small holes can be poked through the groove around the top of a paint can. This will allow paint to flow back into the can rather than accumulating in the groove. Place a shop rag over the can lid before tapping it into place. This will prevent the paint that remains in the groove from splattering.

The technician must rely on calibrated mixing sticks to mix accurate ratios of paint, solvent, and catalyst (if used). See Figure 16-12. *Single-component paint systems* often require the mixing of solvents with the paint. *Two-component systems* require that solvents *and* catalysts be mixed with the paint. Mixing sticks for single-component systems have two columns. Paint is added to the appropriate line in the first column of the stick, and thinner or reducer is added to the corresponding line in the second column of the stick. In two-component paint systems, the mixing stick will have three columns. The first column is for paint, the second is for hardener, and the third column is for thinner or reducer. See Figure 16-13.

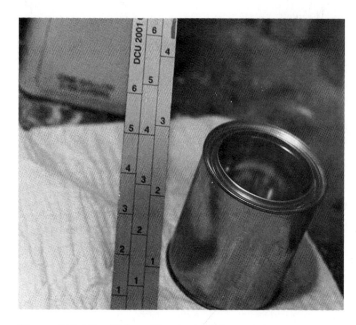

Figure 16-12   This calibrated mixing stick is used to mix accurate amounts of paint, solvent, and catalyst.

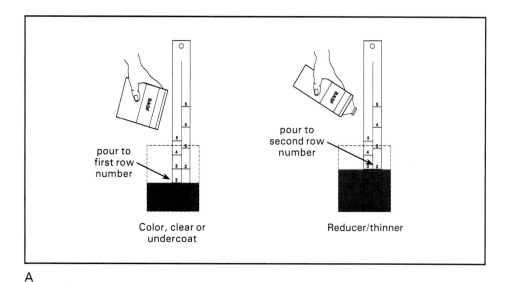

A

Figure 16-13   A—Using a calibrated mixing stick for single-component paint systems. Note that the stick has two columns. B—A mixing stick with three columns is used to mix two-component systems.

B

Color	If color too strong add	If color too light add	If color too green add	If color too red add	If color too yellow add	If color too blue add	If color too "dirty" add
Gray	White	Black	Mix white and oxide red	Medium green	Mix white and touch of indo blue	Mix medium yellow and either cadmium red or oxide red	Mix white and either blue toner or indo blue
Blue	White	Blue or blue toner or indo blue	Deep maroon	Medium green	Deep maroon	Mix medium yellow and either cadmium red or oxide red	Mix white and blue toner
Green	White or yellow	Medium green or blue or blue toner		Mix blue toner and med. yellow and med. green	Blue toner	Mix medium yellow and either cadmium red or oxide red	Mix medium yellow and blue toner
Red	Mix white and cadmium red	Oxide red or light maroon			Light maroon	Oxide red	Mix light maroon and touch of white
Maroon	Light maroon or cadmium red	Deep maroon			Deep maroon	Light maroon or oxide red or medium yellow	Mix deep maroon and touch of white
Yellow	White or medium yellow	Ferrite yellow or medium yellow	Mix white and touch of cadmium red	Mix white and light green	White		Mix white and medium yellow
Orange	Medium yellow	Cadmium red or orange	Mix cadmium red and medium yellow	Medium yellow	Cadmium red or toluidine red		Mix medium yellow and either cadmium red or toluidine red
Ivory	White	Ferrite yellow or medium yellow	Orange or touch of cadmium red	Mix white and light green	White		Mix white and touch of either ferrite yellow or medium yellow
Brown	Mix white and either orange or burnt sienna	Mix black and medium yellow and oxide red	Oxide red or burnt sienna	Mix light green and burnt sienna (add white if necessary)	Mix oxide red and black		Mix ferrite yellow and oxide red and touch of either orange or burnt sienna
Cream	White	Ferrite yellow or medium yellow	Mix white and either orange or cadmium red	Mix medium yellow and white (add light green if necessary)	White		Mix white and touch of either ferrite yellow or med. yellow
Tan	White	Burnt sienna or mix ferrite yellow and black	Cadmium red or toluidine red (add white if necessary)	Mix white and touch of light green	Mix white and either cadmium red or toluidine red		Mix white and either oxide red or ferrite yellow

Glamour color	If color too green add	If color too blue add	If color too "dirty" add	
Blue	Indo blue or deep maroon	Green toner	Blue toner and touch of white	CAUTION: A few drops of shading color may be enough, especially when the fresh color is too yellow, blue, green or red. Occasionally, two shading steps are needed for an accurate match. Glamour colors are very sensitive. Be very careful toning colors with these bases: Old gold toner, Blue toner, Green toner, Indo blue.
Green	Blue toner	Old gold	Touch of white	
Brown	Burnt sienna and light maroon	Old gold or burnt sienna	Burnt sienna or old gold	If the color contains not more than 20 parts of the glamour color base, use the regular tinting instructions. If the color contains more than 20 parts of the glamour color base, follow the instructions in the small chart.
Maroon		Burnt sienna or light maroon	Cadmium red	If necessary, add polychrome base, a very small amount at a time, to maintain brilliance.

Figure 16-14 Color tinting chart.

Color Matching

Color matching is a difficult job. If an entire vehicle is to be repainted, color matching is not a problem. In many cases, however, only small areas or individual panels of a vehicle are to be painted. When making spot repairs, matching the new color to the existing finish becomes very important.

Every color weathers differently, depending on pigment composition and exposure to the environment. Some colors fade lighter, while others become darker as they weather. In order to satisfy the customer, many paint shops tint colors to match the weathered color on a car.

Tinting Paint

The art of tinting colors requires a great deal of practice and experience. Each color has a mass tone and a tint tone. The **mass tone** can be determined by observing a color as it appears in the can or on the painted panel. The **tint tone** of a color is a shade that results when a small amount of the color is mixed with a large amount of white. A dark green mass tone, for example, will often produce a blue tint tone when it is added to white. Some maroon mass tones have a violet or purple tint tone. Small additions of a color will change base colors according to its tint tone. Large additions of a color will influence base colors according to its mass tone. The chart in Figure 16-14 can be used as a guide when tinting colors.

Remember that a color's tone will change as it dries. When tinting, a color should generally be kept on the light side until a final dried match is determined. Always check color in the daylight as well as under artificial light.

The terms value, hue, and chroma are commonly used to describe the color characteristics of paint. **Value** refers to the darkness or lightness of a color. Gray is in the middle of the value scale. The size and amount of metallic particles (if used) will also affect the value of a color.

Hue is the characteristic of a color that provides a red, yellow, blue, or green cast. In some cases, a finish will have an undesirable hue. When this occurs, a ''kill chart'' can be used to help correct hue. For example, adding a small amount of green to blue will ''kill'' (reduce) a red hue. The term shade is sometimes used to describe the visual transition of changing from one color to another. See Figure 16-15.

Chroma (color) is used to describe the purity and saturation (intensity) of a color. Intense colors have high chroma, while dull colors or those closer to gray have less chroma. Metallics tend to darken colors or make paint appear more gray. There will be more chroma (color) when a lower ratio of metallics is used. The terms clean and muddy are sometimes used to describe sharp contrasts between deep, bright color and gray or dirty looking colors.

Polychromatic (metallic) finishes are particularly difficult to tint because they often have what is known as *flop* (flip-flop). Flop is the condition that makes a color look different at an angle than it does straight on. When looking directly into a color (face value), the tint tones have the greatest effect. The mass tones have the greatest effect when a color is viewed at an angle. The flakes in metallic finishes act like small mirrors that reflect light in different directions. See Figure 16-16. Solid colors do not possess this effect.

Matching Colors with the Spray Gun

It is important to remember that the strength or tone of a color is affected by the manner in which it is applied. Spraying techniques can change a color considerably. This is particularly true with metallics.

METHODS OF CHANGING CASTS		
Color	**Add**	**Cast**
Blue	Green	to kill	Red
Blue	Red	to kill	Green
Green	Yellow	to kill	Blue
Green	Blue	to kill	Yellow
Red	Yellow	to kill	Blue
Red	Blue	to kill	Yellow
Gold	Yellow	to kill	Red
Gold	Red	to kill	Yellow
Maroon	Yellow	to kill	Blue
Maroon	Blue	to kill	Yellow
Bronze	Yellow	to kill	Red
Bronze	Red	to kill	Yellow
Orange	Yellow	to kill	Red
Orange	Red	to kill	Yellow
Yellow	Green	to kill	Red
Yellow	Red	to kill	Green
White	White	to kill	Blue
White	White	to kill	Yellow
Beige	Green	to kill	Red
Beige	Red	to kill	Green
Purple	Blue	to kill	Red
Purple	Red	to kill	Blue
Aqua	Blue	to kill	Green
Aqua	Green	to kill	Blue

Figure 16-15 Typical kill chart.

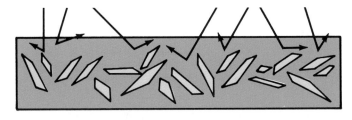

Figure 16-16 In metallic finishes, light is reflected by the metal flakes to produce the desired effect.

Flop results from the quantity, size, orientation, and depth of the flake-like particles in the paint film. Full, wet coats of metallic paint tend to be darker than light, dry coats. This occurs because lightweight pigments float toward the surface and metallics have time to settle in the wet paint film. Thin flash coats tend to trap the metallics relatively close to the top of the paint film, producing a lighter effect. See Figure 16-17.

The type of thinner or reducer used will affect the color. Each manufacturer formulates its paints to be used with a specific solvent. The solvent must have sufficient power to dissolve the binder portion of the paint. The solvent's rate of evaporation may also impact gloss.

The number of coats applied will also affect the color. By spraying an excessive number of coats, most colors—particularly pastels—will produce a lighter shade. Darker shades will be the result if fewer coats are applied. As a general rule, the undercoat and topcoat will each be about 0.002 in. (0.05 mm) thick. To obtain a good color match, the film thickness of the new paint should be approximately the same as the original finish. Several of the techniques used to correct solid color change and metallic flop are listed in Figure 16-18.

Verifying Color Match

Before applying a new finish, technicians should check for differences in color between the old finish and the new paint. Some technicians prepare and coat a small piece of metal. The metal is then placed on the vehicle and compared to the original finish.

As an alternate method, a small spot on the surface of the vehicle can be painted. Clean an original area to be refinished with rubbing compound. Then wash the area with a wax and grease remover to eliminate traces of oil, wax, or silicone. Cut a 2 in. (50 mm) hole in the center of

To lighten a color:

- Increase air pressure during application.
- Add more thinner or reducer.
- Close the fluid control valve on the spray gun more.
- Increase the distance from the spray gun to the surface.
- Use a faster thinner or reducer.
- Increase the size of the gun's fan pattern.
- Increase stroke speed.
- Allow conplete flash-off between coats.

To darken a color:

- Reduce air pressure during application.
- Decrease the amount of thinner or reducer used.
- Reduce the distance between the gun and the surface.
- Open the gun's fluid valve more.
- Reduce the size of the fan pattern.
- Use a slower thinner or reducer.
- Use medium coats instead of full, wet coats.
- Slow stroke speed.

Figure 16-18 Color correction techniques.

a 20 in. (500 mm) square piece of masking paper. Place the hole over the clean area and hold the masking paper in position with masking tape, Figure 16-19.

Using the new color, spray the 2 in. (50 mm) hole in the normal manner. Remove the masking paper and allow the sprayed area to dry. The newly finished area can then be accurately compared with the original finish.

Because there will be a difference in gloss between the compounded area and the newly sprayed test patch, it may be desirable to wet the entire area with thinner. If there is a color difference between the original finish and the test patch, you must determine which way the color is off. The color may have the wrong hue and will need to be redder, bluer, etc. The color may also need to be adjusted to a lighter or darker tint. Be careful when tinting with white. A little white goes a long way.

If in doubt as to which way the tinting should progress, take a small amount of the reduced color and an

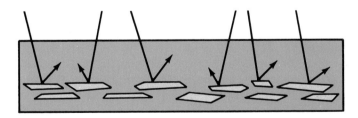

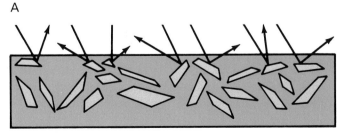

Figure 16-17 A—Wet coats allow metallic particles to settle in the film. B—Dry coats trap metallics close to the top of the film. (Du Pont)

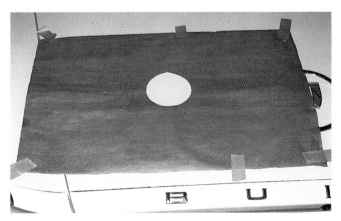

Figure 16-19 Spraying a restricted area helps determine the accuracy of the paint match.

appropriate amount of a tinting color. Note the result. Remember that contrasting shades will change the color more quickly than colors of a close shade.

Note: It is always a good idea to start by working with a small amount of reduced color. Any time one color is added in excess, it throws the entire color formula out of balance.

The tinted paint can be sprayed next to (slightly overlapping) the first test patch. If the tinted paint does not match, this process can be repeated until an exact match is obtained. Remember a clearcoat will add gloss to the finish. After the problem has been solved, the proper color can be used to tint the balance of the new paint.

In general, metallic colors can be tested in the same manner as solid colors. Nevertheless, the metallic effect must be taken into account when matching metallic colors. These colors must be viewed from different angles when checking the test patches. This will ensure achieving the proper light reflection quality from the metallic particles in the paint film. When comparing a metallic patch to the original finish, look directly into the test patch. If it appears too dark, it needs more metallic tinting material. If the patch is too light, it has too much metallic and needs more of the colors used in formulating the shade.

Many late-model vehicles have paint formulations with a high content of transparent materials to make the metallic particles more easily seen (reflective). These formulations make it difficult to determine what kind of color or how much color and metallic are needed for a better match. Medium metallics tend to lighten a color face-on (face value), but have little effect on the angle view. Fine metallics lighten a color face-on and from the angle view. Coarse metallics lighten a color faces on, but less than medium or fine metallics. Coarse metallic particles have fewer reflective surfaces on which to refract or reflect light. They may appear bright from only one viewpoint. If too many particles are applied, the base color may be obscured. A cloudy effect will be seen.

With many coats of tinted clear material being applied in three- and four-stage paints, color matching is even more difficult. These finishes are reminiscent of the old (1950s) custom *candy-apple finishes*. In these finishes, an amazing appearance of depth was obtained by spraying many coats of clear material over a metallic basecoat. Brass metallics were popular in candy-apple finishes. See Chapter 20 for more information on custom finishes.

Know These Terms

Paint, Finish, Binders, Solvents, Vehicles, Volatiles, Thinners, Reducers, Set, Cure, Blush, Wash thinners, Universal thinners, Pigments, Metallics, Pearlescent, Additives, Hardeners, Retarders, Flatteners, Flex-agents, Fisheye eliminator, Fisheyes, Texturing agents, Adhesion promoters, Undercoat, Primers, Primer-surfacer, Hold-out, Sealers, Topcoat, Lacquer, Color sanding, Orange peel, Enamels, Alkyd enamel, Baked enamel, Acrylic enamel, Polyurethane enamels, Acrylic-polyurethane enamels, Vehicle identification plates, Factory-mixed topcoats, Custom-mixed topcoats, Mass tone, Tint tone, Value, Hue, Chroma.

Summary

Refinishing materials have changed drastically over the past several years. Therefore, the auto body technician must be able to apply several types of finish.

All paints contain three basic ingredients: binders, solvents, and pigments. Various additives are also used to speed or slow cure, reduce gloss, or increase flexibility. Binders are the film-forming ingredients in paint that adhere to the substrate. Solvents thin paint so that it can be easily applied. Thinners are solvents used with lacquer finishes. Reducers are solvents used when thinning enamel finishes. Pigments are the materials that give paint color. Pigments can also alter the durability, adhesion, and flow of the paint.

In many cases, it is necessary to determine the type of original finish that is on a vehicle before a new finish is applied. This can be accomplished by testing the finish with lacquer thinner, sanding the finish, or applying a special compound to the surface. When identification cannot be made, a sealer should be used before the new finish is applied.

Before a finish coat of paint is applied, an undercoat must be applied to bare surfaces. The three common undercoats used for auto body repair include primers, primer-surfacers, and sealers. Primers improve paint adhesion on plastic and metal surfaces. Primer-surfacers fill small imperfections and improve adhesion. Sealers are applied to improve hold-out and seal sanding scratches. When a lacquer finish is applied over enamel, a sealer should be used.

There are three types of exterior topcoat finishes: lacquer topcoats, enamel topcoats, and waterborne topcoats. The topcoat is the color coat or the top layer of paint.

Lacquer topcoats dry as their solvents evaporate. These finishes dry quickly. Acrylic lacquer can be used for spot repairs on both lacquer and baked-enamel finishes. Lacquer finishes require color sanding.

Enamels have replaced lacquers for most applications. A two-stage enamel system is commonly used by manufacturers. Common enamels used for auto body refinishing include alkyd enamels, acrylic enamels, polyurethane enamels, and acrylic-polyurethane enamels. Polyurethane enamels contain isocyanates, which are extremely toxic.

An important part of painting is the selection and preparation of the paint. Information on a vehicle's color can be found in an identifying number on the vehicle identification plate.

Topcoats can be purchased in two ways. Factory-mixed topcoats are designed to match the color and gloss of the factory finish. Custom-mixed topcoats are blended to match badly oxidized or faded finishes.

Many paint failures are caused by improper mixing of the finish before spraying. Paint pigments tend to settle to the bottom of the container. In some cases, thinner or reducer must be added to paint before it is sprayed. Calibrated mixing sticks can be used to determine the amount of thinner, reducer, or catalyst (if necessary) that must be added to paint.

When small areas or individual panels are to be refinished, the new color must match the original finish. Therefore, colors must often be tinted to match the weathered finish of the vehicle. Tinting requires a great deal of practice and experience.

The terms value, hue, and chroma are used to describe the color characteristics of paint. Value refers to the darkness or lightness of a color. Hue provides a red, yellow, blue, or green cast. Chroma is used to describe the purity and saturation of a color.

Polychromatic colors are difficult to tint because the have flop. Flop results from the quantity, size, orientation, and depth of the flake-like particles in these finishes.

Spraying techniques can also alter a color. This is particularly true with metallic finishes. A dry spray will tend to lighten metallic colors, while a wet spray will darken colors. Spraying an excessive number of coats will tend to lighten many colors.

Before applying a finish (when making spot or panel repairs), the new paint should be checked for proper color. In some cases, a small piece of metal is painted and compared to the original finishes. In other cases, a small spot is painted on the surface to be refinished. If paint does not match, it should be tinted and retested. When checking the match of metallic colors, they should be viewed from several angles.

Review Questions–Chapter 16

1. All paints contain:
   a. pigments.
   b. additives.
   c. hardeners.
   d. all of the above.

2. _____ are the resinous, film-forming ingredients that adhere to the substrate.

3. Solvents are added to paints so that they can be easily applied. True or False?

4. _____ _____ _____ are released into the air as solvents evaporate.

5. Thinners are only used with enamel-based finishes. True or False?

6. In addition to giving color to paints, pigments can also alter:
   a. adhesion.
   b. flow
   c. durability.
   d. all of the above.

7. _____ are often added to paint to change its characteristics.

8. Flex-agents can be used when painting composite body panels. True or False?

9. Common undercoats used for auto body refinishing include:
   a. sealers.
   b. primer-surfacers.
   c. prepcoats.
   d. all of the above.

10. Primers are commonly used to fill small imperfections in the substrate. True or False?

11. _____ are used to improve hold-out.

12. The term _____ is used when referring to the top layers of paint.

13. Cure time is affected by:
   a. solvents.
   b. temperature.
   c. additives.
   d. all of the above.

14. Lacquers dry as their solvents evaporate. True or False?

15. _____ _____ is a bumpy paint surface that is caused by the fast evaporation of thinners.

16. Enamel-based finishes are used extensively by original equipment manufacturers. True or False?

17. Oxidation is the change in a binder that occurs when it combines with _____.

18. Acrylic enamels generally require compounding and polishing. True or False?

19. _____ enamels provide a ''wet-look'' finish.

20. Waterborne enamels are commonly used in repair shops. True or False?

21. Paints are generally assigned an _____ _____ to aid in color identification.

22. When attempting to match a paint chip to an original finish, it is best to compare the chip to a protected area of the finish. True or False?

23. _____-_____ topcoats are proportioned at the factory to match the color and gloss of the factory finish.

24. Paint failures are often caused by improper mixing. True or False?

25. _____ can weigh seven to eight times more than the liquid part of the paint.

26. The _____ of paint affects the rate of settling.

27. Calibrated _____ _____ can be used to determine the correct amount of paint, solvent, and catalyst to be mixed.

28. Paints are often tinted to match the weathered finish on a car. True or False?

29. The shade that results when a small amount of color is mixed with a large amount of white is called the:
    a. value.
    b. mass tone.
    c. hue.
    d. none of the above.

30. _____ is the term used to describe the purity and intensity of a color.

31. The condition that causes a metallic color to look different at an angle than it does straight on is called:
    a. face value.
    b. flop.
    c. wavering.
    d. none of the above.

32. Wet coats of metallic paints tend to be _____ than light, dry coats.

33. Color can be affected by the type of thinner or reducer used. True or False?

34. To obtain a proper color match, the _____ of the new paint film should be about the same as the original finish.

35. When attempting to match metallic colors, the metallic effect must be taken into account. True or False?

Activities—Chapter 16

1. Contact the fire prevention officer of your local fire department, and ask for information on safety in body shops and paint spray booths. Study the information provided, then make a safety inspection of your school body shop. Write down any problems you find and submit the information to your instructor.

2. Visit a paint store specializing in automotive finishes and gather literature on different preparation and finishing materials. Make an informative display using the materials.

3. Ask a paint technician at a body shop to discuss and demonstrate how he or she achieves a color match with an existing finish. Videotape the discussion and demonstration and show it to the entire class.

chapter 17

Refinishing Equipment

After studying this chapter, you will be able to:

☐ Describe the operation of three types of spray guns.

☐ Describe the care of paint spray guns.

☐ Explain the procedure for selecting the correct air compressor for painting.

☐ Describe the function of spray booths.

Refinishing Equipment

In order to achieve professional results when refinishing vehicles, top-quality equipment is essential. Refinishing equipment may include a spray gun, air compressor, air transformer, spray booth, dryers, protective gear, and other miscellaneous tools and pieces of equipment.

Spray Gun

The *spray gun* is a device that uses air pressure or fluid pressure to atomize sprayable material and apply it to a surface. Material is atomized when it is broken into very small particles to produce a fine spray. The spray gun is considered by many to be the most important piece of refinishing equipment in the shop. Many paint technicians have one gun for applying basecoats, one for clearcoats, one for primers, and one for other products. See Chapter 19 for information on applying finishes.

Gun Types

Spray guns can be classified as siphon-feed (suction-feed) guns, pressure-feed guns, or gravity-feed guns. See Figure 17-1.

Siphon-feed guns use a stream of compressed air to create a vacuum. The vacuum draws paint from an attached container into the gun. This type of gun is usually equipped with a one quart container or cup. Siphon-feed guns work best when applying finish to vertical surfaces. When the gun is tipped, the paint in the container may

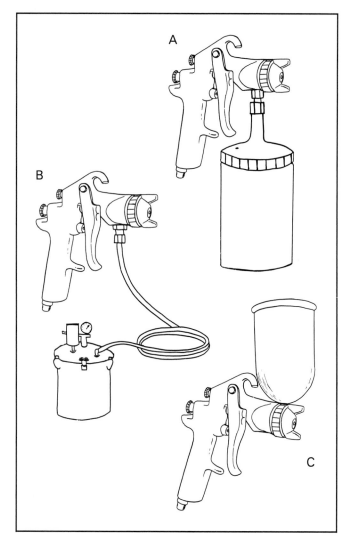

Figure 17-1   Three classes of spray guns.
A–Siphon-feed. B–Pressure-feed.
C–Gravity-feed.

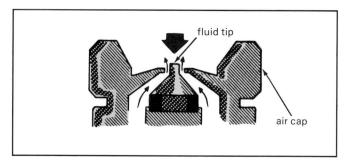

Figure 17-2   The fluid tip for a siphon-feed gun extends beyond the air cap.

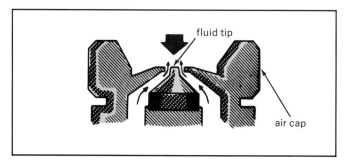

Figure 17-3   The fluid tip for a pressure-feed gun is flush with the air cap.

Figure 17-4   This pressure-feed spray gun has a separate paint container.

not be drawn into the paint tube. Tipping can also plug the vent in the gun's lid. This vent must be open to allow material to be drawn into the gun. A siphon-feed gun can be identified by the configuration of its air cap and fluid tip. The fluid tip of a siphon-feed gun extends slightly beyond the air cap, Figure 17-2.

Pressure-feed guns have a fluid tip that is generally flush with the air cap, Figure 17-3. Air pressure forces material into the gun from a cup, tank, or pot. A high-pressure pump is used to force the paint to the gun in airless pressure-feed systems. In all pressure-feed systems, the paint flows through a hose to the gun. This type of system is used extensively when large amounts of a single color are to be sprayed. Pressure-feed guns may be operated in any position because the paint is forced into the gun. Material is atomized by a pressure-feed gun in the same manner as it is in a siphon-feed gun. However, the pressure-feed gun is not dependent upon atomization air pressure to control paint flow. Paint flow can be adjusted with the fluid adjusting screw without

changing atomization air pressure. Since the paint container is not attached to the gun in these systems, the gun is lighter than siphon-feed guns and can be moved more freely. See Figure 17-4. More paint can be applied in the same amount of time with a pressure-feed system than with a siphon-feed system. More skill is also required to use a pressure-feed system.

Gravity-feed guns are used primarily for spot painting and custom work. A small container (500 mL) is attached to the top of the gun. Paint is fed into the gun by gravity. Gravity-feed guns are similar to siphon-feed guns in function and use. See Figure 17-5.

Suction-feed, pressure-feed, and gravity-feed guns can be further divided into bleeder, nonbleeder, external-mix, and internal-mix designs. *Bleeder guns* are seldom used in professional auto body shops. In this design, air passes through the gun at all times, preventing pressure buildup in the supply lines. Bleeder guns are used with small air compressors (limited capacity). There is no air pressure control on the bleeder gun. The gun's trigger controls only the flow of paint.

Nonbleeder guns are equipped with an air valve that shuts off the airflow when the trigger is released. The trigger on these guns controls both the flow of air and the flow of paint.

A spray gun that atomizes paint outside the air cap is known as an *external-mix gun.* See Figure 17-6. This type of gun is best suited for spraying fast-drying materials, such as professional automotive finishes.

An *internal-mix gun* atomizes material inside the cap before expelling them, Figure 17-7. This type of gun is best suited for spraying flat house paint. Internal-mix guns are not recommended for automotive painting.

Other spray guns, which are available for various types of production finishing, are usually variations of the previously described guns.

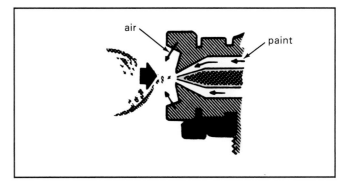

Figure 17-6 External-mix guns atomize paint outside the air cap.

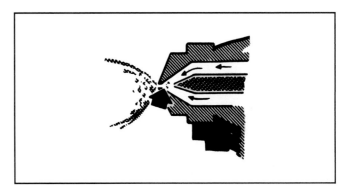

Figure 17-7 Internal-mix guns atomize material inside the air cap.

High-volume, low-pressure (HVLP) spray guns atomize paint into low-speed particles. Although HVLP guns look similar to conventional spray guns, they are specially designed for use in HVLP systems. HVLP systems are also known as *high-solids systems*. These systems apply more paint to a surface than other systems. There are fewer volatile organic compounds released and overspray can be reduced by 75-80% when using HVLP systems. Standard paint guns are about 25% efficient. This means that only about 25% of the material sprayed stays on the surface being painted.

Some high-volume, low-pressure (HVLP) systems use a special turbine that delivers a high volume of air at low pressure to the gun. See Figure 17-8. These turbines deliver air to the gun through a large hose.

Air conversion units are available to heat, clean, and control the pressure and volume of air from conventional air compressors. These units allow HVLP guns to be used with standard compressors.

Several HVLP guns are designed to hook directly to a conventional air compressor. These guns do not require the use of a conversion unit or a turbine. See Figure 17-9.

Spraying techniques for HVLP systems are similar to those used in conventional spray gun operations. The gun is held about 8 in. (203 mm) from the surface to be painted. A dry, rough finish will result if the gun is held too far from the surface. There is no ''blast'' of pressur-

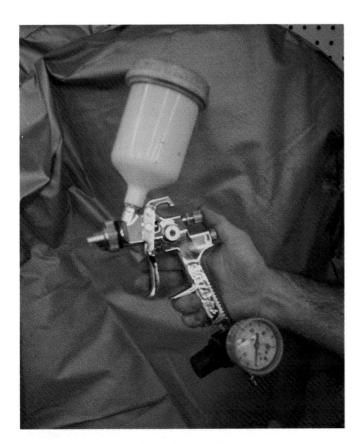

Figure 17-5 Typical gravity-feed spray gun.

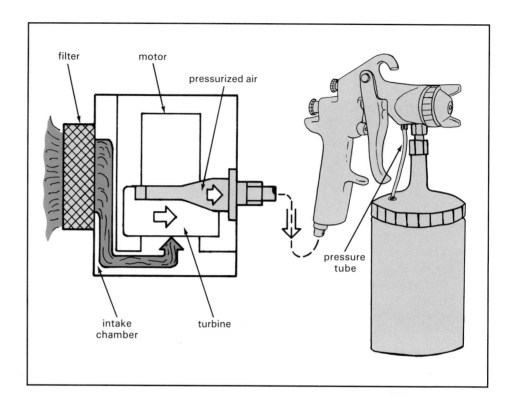

Figure 17-8   HVLP spray system that uses a turbine to supply the necessary air pressure.

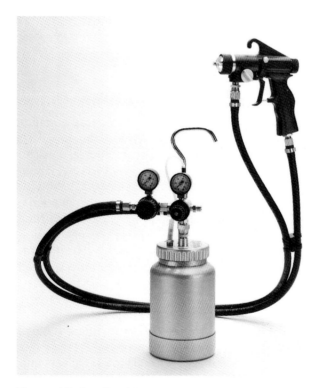

Figure 17-9   This HVLP spray system can be connected directly to a regulated air source. (Mattson Spray Equipment)

ized air to atomize the paint in HVLP systems. Consequently, most of the warm paint particles stick to the surface instead of bouncing back or blowing around. Paint film thickness builds up quickly. Expect to find a 40-50% savings in the amount of finish consumed. Al-

though HVLP systems are not well suited for the application of pearls or metallic paints, all medium viscosity materials, including waterborne paints, may be used in these systems. With increased environmental concerns and legislation limiting the amount of volatile organic compounds released into the environment, HVLP systems are becoming more common.

Spray Gun Construction

Typical spray guns are shown in Figures 17-10 and 17-11. The principal parts of a gun include the air cap, fluid tip, fluid needle, trigger, fluid adjustment screw, air valve, pattern adjustment valve, and the gun body.

Air Cap.   The *air cap* is located at the front of the gun and directs compressed air into the material stream. The air atomizes the material to form the spray. See Figure 17-12. The cross section of the spray is called the *spray pattern.* There are various caps that produce different sizes and shapes of patterns for all applications.

Fluid Tip.   The nozzle directly behind the air cap is known as the *fluid tip.* It meters the paint and directs it into the air stream. The fluid tip forms a seat for the *fluid needle,* which shuts off the flow of material. Fluid tips are available in a variety of nozzle (opening) sizes. The larger the nozzle, the greater the amount of material that can be sprayed. Tip sizes ranging from 0.041 to 0.070 in. (1.0-1.8 mm) are frequently used in the body shop.

Pattern Adjustment Valve.   To control the flow of air through the nozzles in the air cap, a *pattern adjustment valve* is provided. The size and shape of the spray

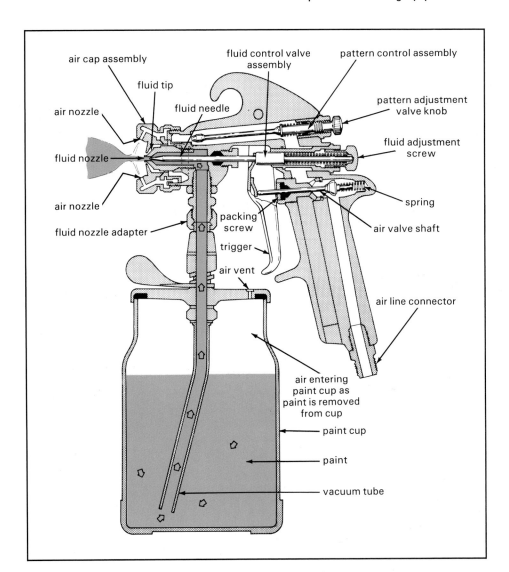

Figure 17-10 A typical siphon-feed spray gun and its parts. This type of gun is often used for auto body refinishing. (DeVilbiss Company)

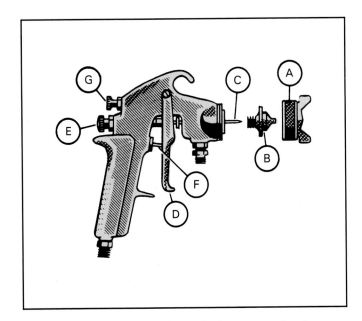

Figure 17-11 Details of a typical pressure-feed spray gun. A–Air cap. B–Fluid tip. C–Fluid needle. D–Trigger. E–Fluid adjustment screw. F–Air valve. G–Pattern adjustment valve.

Figure 17-12 Shape of spray from a spray gun.

pattern is controlled by this valve. When the valve is closed (turned in), a round pattern is produced by the gun. Opening the valve results in an oval spray pattern. See Figure 17-13.

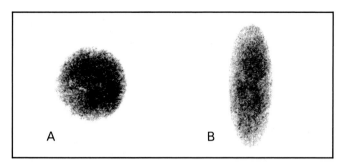

Figure 17-13   A–When the pattern adjustment valve is fully closed, a round pattern results. B–When the valve is opened, the pattern becomes oval.

Fluid Adjustment Screw.   The *fluid adjustment screw* controls the travel of the fluid needle. This screw determines the amount of material passing through the fluid tip as the trigger is fully depressed.

Trigger and Air Valve.   When the trigger is partially depressed (about half way) on a suction-feed gun, it pushes on the air valve, which releases only compressed air. This helps keep the air nozzle clean and can be used to dust unwanted particles from a surface before painting. When the trigger is fully depressed, the fluid needle opens, creating a partial vacuum at the fluid tip. Paint is sucked from the cup and out through the fluid nozzle opening.

Gun Body.   The gun body is a specially designed, aluminum alloy casting with various threaded holes and projections. The air inlet is in the bottom section of the body. The fluid inlet opening and the air cap mounting threads are located in the front of the body.

Spray Gun Care

Spray guns should be cleaned immediately after each use. If this is not done, paint will dry or cure in the nozzles and the container. Guns will not perform properly with clogged or restricted jets and passageways. Meticulous care must be given to spray guns if they are expected to perform properly.

The first step in cleaning a siphon-feed gun is to loosen the cup from the gun. While the paint tube is still in the cup, unscrew the air cap about two or three turns. Hold a cloth over the air cap and pull the gun's trigger. Air diverted into the fluid passageways will force material in the gun back into the cup, Figure 17-14.

Empty the cup of material and refill it with a small quantity of clean solvent. Spray the solvent through the gun to flush out the fluid passages, Figure 17-15. Wipe off the exterior of the gun with a solvent-soaked rag and remove the air cap. Clean the cap by immersing it in fresh solvent and then dry it with compressed air. If the small holes in the cap become clogged, soak it again in solvent and, if necessary, use a wooden toothpick to dislodge stubborn material. Never use a wire or nail to clean small

Figure 17-14   When a cloth is held over the air cap and the trigger is pulled, material is forced back into the paint container.

Figure 17-15   Solvent is being sprayed through a gun to flush out fluid passages.

passages. These items may enlarge holes, causing permanent damage to the cap.

WARNING: Finishing materials can be hazardous. Store or dispose of the excess paint properly. See Chapter 2 for more information on disposing of hazardous materials.

To clean a pressure-feed system, back off the regulator adjusting screw and release the pressure from the tank by triggering the relief valve or the safety valve. Loosen the spray gun's air cap approximately three turns. Hold a cloth over the air cap and pull the gun's trigger to force material back into tank.

Remove the fluid hose from the gun and attach it to a hose cleaner, Figure 17-16. The hose cleaner forces air

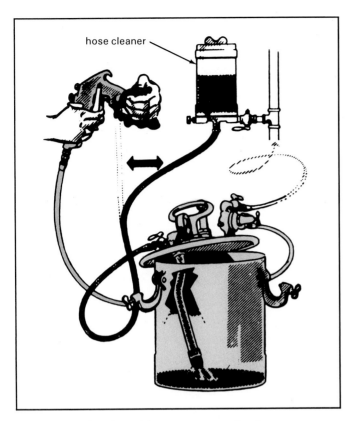

Figure 17-16 Attaching a pressure-feed system to a hose cleaner.

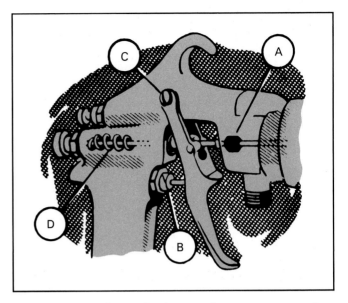

Figure 17-17 Several points on the spray gun require lubrication. A–Fluid needle packing. B–Air valve packing. C–Trigger bearing screw.

and solvent through the hose and the fluid tube, cleaning them of paint residue. This device can also be used to force air and solvent through the gun. After the gun, fluid tube, and hose are clean, dry the hose with compressed air. Clean the air cap as described in the section on cleaning siphon-feed guns. Clean out the tank and reassemble the system for future use.

Some states require the use of spray gun cleaning machines. These machines reduce the amount of solvent released into the air. Most cleaning machines filter and recycle the cleaning solvents. To use these machines, tanks, cups, strainers and other painting equipment are placed in the cleaning cabinet, and the lid is closed. Air and solvents are circulated in the machine to clean the equipment.

Spray guns should never be immersed in solvent. This practice allows sludge and dirt to collect in the air passages of the gun. Solvents also remove lubricants and dry out seals. Caustic alkaline solutions should never be used to clean spray guns. They will corrode aluminum and die cast parts.

Spray guns require occasional lubrication. Many manufacturers recommend that guns be lubricated at the end of each work day. The fluid needle packing, air valve packing, and the trigger bearing screw require a drop or two of light oil. See Figure 17-17. The fluid needle should be lubricated with petroleum jelly. Follow the manufacturer's recommendations for lubrication, inspection, and replacement of parts.

Compressors

Air compressors are available in single-stage designs and two-stage designs. Two-stage compressors are preferred in the body shop. In two-stage designs, air is compressed in a large cylinder and then compressed further in a small cylinder before being fed to the storage tank. See Figure 17-18.

Some HVLP systems rely on a high-speed turbine to supply air pressure. The turbine, which draws air through a replaceable filter, produces dry, heated air at high volume and low pressure. The turbine should draw air from a relatively clean air supply, not from a spray booth environment. The clean, warm air from the turbine travels through a hose to the gun at about 60 cfm at 5-10 psi.

Compressor Size

Compressors must be large enough to supply all of the shop's air consumption requirements. If the air compressor is for the paint department only, the consumption requirements will include air for the spray guns, pneumatic lifts, vacuum cleaners, etc. If the same compressor is to be used to supply air for the entire shop, the air consumption for all of the tools and equipment in the shop must be taken into account. The amount of air needed to operate various shop tools and equipment can be determined using the chart in Figure 17-19.

There are two important compressor ratings: **pressure** and **free air capacity** (volume). Free air capacity is the actual amount of air that is available at the compressor's working pressure. Pressure is expressed as the force (pounds per square inch) of the air delivered to the gun. Pressure is needed to atomize the paint. Capacity is needed to evenly distribute the paint.

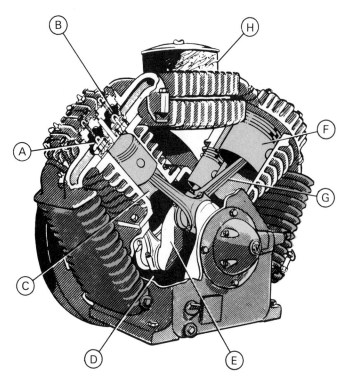

Figure 17-18   Details of a two-stage, four-cylinder air compressor. Each large cylinder is connected to a small cylinder by twin intercoolers. A–Outlet valve. B–Inlet valve. C–High-pressure cylinder. D–Crankcase. E–Crankshaft. F–Piston. G–Connecting rod. H–Air filter (mounted on top of twin intercooler).

Type device	Air pressure range	Average free air capacity
Air filter cleaner	70-100	3.0
Air hammer	70-100	16.5
Body polisher	70-100	2.0
Body sander	70-100	5.0
Brake tester	70-100	3.5
Carbon remover	70-100	3.0
Car rocker	120-150	5.75
Car washer	70-100	8.5
Dusting gun (blow gun)	70-100	2.5
Engine cleaner	70-100	5.0
Fender hammer	70-100	8.75
Grease gun (high pressure)	120-150	3.0
Hoist (one ton)	70-100	1.0
Hydraulic lift *	145-170	5.25
Paint spray gun (production)	70-100	8.5
Paint spray gun (touch-up)	70-100	2.25
Pneu. garage door	120-150	2.0
Radiator tester	70-100	1.0
Rim stripper	120-150	6.0
Spark plug cleaner	70-100	5.0
Spark plug tester	70-100	.5
Spray gun (undercoating)	70-100	19.0
Spring oiler	70-100	3.75
Tire changer	120-150	1.0
Tire inflation line	120-150	1.5
Tire spreader	120-150	1.0
Trans. and diff. flusher	70-100	3.0
Vacuum cleaner	120-150	6.5

* For 8000 lbs. capacity. Add .65 cfm for each additional 1000 lbs. capacity.

Figure 17-19   Average free air capacity for various pneumatic tools.

To operate properly, most spray guns require a free air capacity of about 8.5 cfm (0.004 cubic meters per second). If three guns are used, the total requirement will be three times 8.5 cfm or 25.5 cfm (0.012 cubic meters per second). After all of the shop's free air capacity needs have been totaled, note the highest pressure required to operate any one tool or piece of equipment. This is the shop's maximum pressure requirement. Use the chart in Figure 17-20 to select the pressure range capable of meeting the maximum pressure requirement. Within that range, locate the line that contains a compressor capacity that meets the shop's free air capacity requirement. Note that as pressure drops, so does air volume. The minimum compressor size required (in horsepower) is listed in the next column on the same line.

Siphon-feed guns require a free air capacity of 8.5 cfm (0.004 cubic meters per second). For pressure-feed guns, free air capacity should be 14 cfm (0.0065 cubic meters per second). As a rule of thumb, a one horsepower compressor will provide 5 cfm. Many shops have a ten horsepower compressor, which is adequate if the spray gun is used intermittently. The compressor will have time to cool when it is not in use. When the spraying operation is continuous, the compressor capacity should be 1/3 larger than the minimum recommendation.

Compressor Care

Always refer to the manufacturer's recommendations when servicing an air compressor. The crankcase of the compressor should be filled to the proper level with the lubricant recommended by the manufacturer. The oil level should be checked at least once a week, and the oil should be changed every three months.

Belt tension should be maintained so that belts do not slip. Cooling fins on the compressor and the intercooler should be kept clean and free of dust. The air cleaner on the compressor's intake should be cleaned weekly (more often if the compressor is located in a dusty area). The drain cock on the storage tank should be opened monthly to drain condensed moisture that may be present. To ensure the operation of the tank's safety valve, it should be operated by hand each week.

Air for Painting

To produce smooth, defect-free painted surfaces, the compressed air supply must be free from dirt, moisture, and oil. Additionally, constant air pressure must be maintained during painting operations.

Pressure Range (PSI)	Continuous Operation Free Air Consumption Cubic Feet per Minute of Total Equipment	Compressor Horsepower
80-100	3.1- 3.9 4.0- 5.8 5.9- 7.6 7.7-13.2	1 1-1/2 2 3
100-125	13.3-20.0 20.1-29.2 29.3-40.0 40.1-50.0	5 7-1/2 10 15
120-150	up to-1.1 1.2-2.1 2.2-2.9 3.0-4.3 4.4-5.7	1/2 3/4 1 1-1/2 2
140-175	up to- 3.4 3.5- 5.3 5.4- 6.9 7.0-10.4 10.5-17.0 17.1-26.4 26.5-35.3 35.4-48.0	1 1-1/2 2 3 5 7-1/2 10 15

Figure 17-20 Air capacity and pressure range must be determined to calculate compressor size.

In order to supply clean air, some shops use a separate compressor for painting. The system is generally equipped with an air transformer and/or oil and moisture separators. Some systems have an air drying unit, which removes all moisture from the air. See Figure 17-21.

Air Transformer

The air transformer, Figure 17-22, is used to maintain the pressure of the air supply and to prevent oil, dirt, and water from entering the air lines.

A high-quality air transformer will maintain air pressure within .75 psi (0.5 kPa) for each 10 psi (6.9 kPa) in the main air line. The gauges on the transformer indicate air pressure, and the valves provide outlets for hoses.

Various types of filter elements are used in transformers to remove foreign matter from the air lines. These elements are generally equipped with drain cocks so that oil, sludge, and moisture can be easily drained from the system. Air transformers without filters are also available.

Locating Compressors/Transformers

It is advisable to place the air compressor as close to the paint spray booth as possible. This practice ensures that the air lines will be kept short, reducing the amount of moisture condensing in the lines.

Figure 17-21 Typical aftercooler and dryer.

Figure 17-22 One type of transformer or regulator.

An air transformer should be installed in the paint booth for convenience in reading the gauges and operating the valves. Additionally, the transformer should be installed at least 25 ft. (7.5 m) from the compressor.

Piping should be as direct as possible. Piping from the compressor to the transformer must be the correct size for the volume of air used. Pipe size recommenda-

MINIMUM PIPE SIZE RECOMMENDATIONS			
Compressing Outfit		Main Air Line	
Size	Capacity	Length	Size
1–1/2 & 2 H.P.	6 to 9 cfm	over 50 ft.	3/4''
3 & 5 H.P.	12 to 20 cfm	up to 200 ft. over 200 ft.	3/4'' 1''
5 to 10 H.P.	20 to 40 cfm	up to 100 ft. over 100 to 200 ft. over 200 ft.	3/4'' 1'' 1-1/4''
10 to 15 H.P.	40 to 60 cfm	up to 100 ft. over 100 to 200 ft. over 200 ft.	1'' 1-1/4'' 1-1/2''

Figure 17-23   Minimum pipe size recommendations.

tions are shown in Figure 17-23. If a large number of fittings are installed, a large diameter pipe should be used to help overcome excessive pressure drop. The take-off from the transformer should be from the top of the line as shown at C in Figure 17-24. If possible, piping should slope toward the compressor. If the pipe slopes away from the compressor, a drain leg should be installed at the end of the air line or at the end of each branch. This will provide a means for draining moisture from the lines.

Valves at the lower end of the drain leg should be opened at the beginning of each work day to allow accumulated condensation to escape.

Hose Size

It is important to use hoses of adequate size when connecting the spray gun to the air transformer. Resistance to airflow (or paint flow) increases rapidly as the hose diameter decreases.

For automotive refinishing, a 3/8 in. (9.5 mm) inside diameter (I.D.) hose is generally used for large guns. For smaller guns, a 5/16 in. (8 mm) I.D. hose can be used. HVLP guns require 1 in. (25 mm) I.D. hose for proper operation.

Pressure Drop

Pressure drop is the loss of air pressure between the source of air and point of use. Pressure drop can become serious, particularly on long hose and piping runs or when a small-diameter hose is used. The chart in Figure 17-25 can be used to determine pressure drop when locating the compressor and the transformer or when purchasing hose.

The I.D. of couplers should be equal to the I.D. of the piping or hose used. Make certain that 3/8 in. I.D. (9.5 mm) couplers are used on 3/8 in. I.D. hose. Quick couplers and other connectors will restrict airflow. Pressure loss will be equal to the diameter of the smallest passage in the pipe or hose.

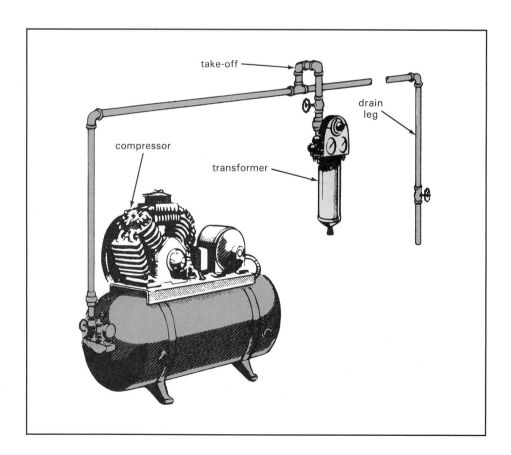

Figure 17-24   Air piping should be direct, and take-offs (connections) should be made from the top of the line.

AIR PRESSURE DROP AT SPRAY GUN						
Size of air hose inside diameter	5-foot length	10-foot length	15-foot length	20-foot length	25-foot length	50-foot length
1/4-inch	lbs.	lbs.	lbs.	lbs.	lbs.	lbs.
At 40 lbs. pressure	6	8	9-1/2	11	12-3/4	24
At 50 lbs. pressure	7-1/2	10	12	14	16	28
At 60 lbs. pressure	9	12-1/2	14-1/2	16-3/4	19	31
At 70 lbs. pressure	10-3/4	14-1/2	17	19-1/2	22-1/2	34
At 80 lbs. pressure	12-1/4	16-1/2	19-1/2	22-1/2	25-1/2	37
At 90 lbs. pressure	14	18-3/4	22	25-1/4	29	39-1/2
5/16-inch	lbs.	lbs.	lbs.	lbs.	lbs.	lbs.
At 40 lbs. pressure	2-1/4	2-3/4	3-1/4	3-1/2	4	8-1/2
At 50 lbs. pressure	3	3-1/2	4	4-1/2	5	10
At 60 lbs. pressure	3-3/4	4-1/2	5	5-1/2	6	11-1/2
At 70 lbs. pressure	4-1/2	5-1/4	6	6-3/4	7-1/4	13
At 80 lbs. pressure	5-1/2	6-1/4	7	8	8-3/4	14-1/2
At 90 lbs. pressure	6-1/2	7-1/2	8-1/2	9-1/2	10-1/2	16

Figure 17-25 Air pressure drops.

Spray Booths

A spray booth is a fireproof compartment, room, or enclosure, which is designed to filter incoming air and to confine and exhaust overspray or fumes that result from the painting process. The spray booth must comply with federal, state, and local safety codes. Some communities require that automatic fire extinguishers be installed in spray booths.

There are two major reasons for placing vehicles in a spray booth when they are being painted:

1. Dust is excluded from the painting area and, therefore, will not settle on the fresh paint.

2. Exhaust fans in the booth draw out overspray and paint fumes. This reduces fire hazards and improves the working conditions for the painter.

WARNING: Operators/refinishers should never inhale paint fumes or allow overspray to contact the skin. Full-head respirators are recommended when applying paint. Painting materials and fumes are highly flammable. When spraying is done on the open shop floor, sparks may ignite fumes.

Booth Designs

There are several spray booth designs available. A spray booth must have adequate lighting to eliminate all shadows. It must also be equipped with an exhaust fan capable of maintaining air movement of 100 linear feet per minute (30 linear meters per minute) throughout the booth area. The exhaust system should completely change the volume of air in the booth every 20-30 minutes. A filtered air intake and exhaust system is essential. This type of system prevents contamination (dust, insects, etc.) of the newly painted vehicle and removes overspray particles from the exhausted air. In winter months, it may be necessary to use a *temperature make-up system.* This system filters and warms air before it enters the booth.

There are several types of *air make-up systems.* Air make-up refers to the system's ability to replace air as it is exhausted from the spray booth. Both wet and dry booth designs have been utilized. In wet designs, air is drawn through a series of water curtains and baffles to remove solids from the overspray before it is exhausted. Remember, the fumes that are exhausted are often regulated by state and local codes.

Dry booth systems are the most common. In dry, flow-through designs, filtered air is moved from front-to-back or from side-to-side in the booth. Most dry booth designs use disposable filters (similar to household furnace filters) to remove solids from the air. These filters can be replaced as needed.

The most popular dry booth system is the downdraft booth. See Figures 17-26 and 17-27. This system allows filtered air to enter overhead and exit through vents in the floor. The downdraft design pulls overspray away from the freshly painted vehicle and quickly removes fumes from the work area.

Paint Drying Equipment

Various drying equipment is used to hasten the drying and curing of finishes. Drying equipment ranges from single, bulb-type units to large ovens, Figure 17-28. The

Figure 17-26 Typical downdraft booth. The lines in the photo represent airflow. (DeVilbiss Company)

the oven. Baking ovens cannot duplicate an OEM finishing system. Some manufacturers use waterborne paints, which are baked at 320 °F (160 °C) and then covered with a clearcoat. This paint system is not practical for use in repair shops. An automobile's glass, plastic, and upholstery cannot withstand the heat necessary to cure waterborne paints. See Figure 17-29.

Paint drying (curing) equipment is generally used with enamels. There are two basic types of drying equipment: radiant-drying equipment and convection drying equipment. The convection drying equipment heats the

drying or curing equipment is occasionally installed in the spray booth. In some shops, a baking oven or tunnel is placed at the end of the spray booth. These ovens generally operate at temperatures under 165 °F (75 °C). As soon as the spraying is complete, the vehicle is rolled into

Figure 17-28 A portable infrared unit is used for spot or panel drying. (John J. Fannon Co.)

Figure 17-27 A downdraft spray booth and drying oven system. (DeVilbiss Company)

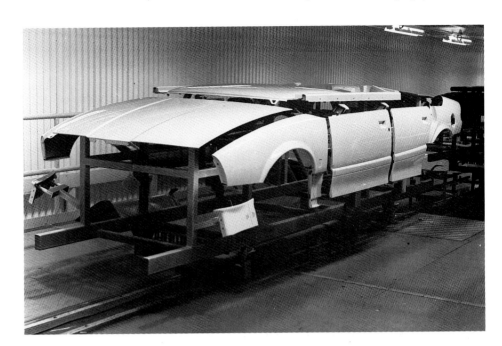

Figure 17-29 A waterborne paint system is used to provide a lustrous finish on these body panels. Note that the panels are painted "in position." (Saturn Corp)

surface with hot air. These systems are similar to the forced-air furnaces used in homes.

Radiant-drying equipment heats the painted surface with electrically powered infrared or ceramic heating units. When infrared heating units are used, consideration must be given to the fact that darker colors absorb more heat than lighter colors. Excessive heat may cause loss of gloss, discoloration, blistering, and wrinkling. See Figure 17-30.

Before putting a vehicle in the baking oven, 10-15 minutes should elapse to provide time for the solvent to "flash off" or evaporate. Heavy layers of putty or numerous coats of surfacer have a tendency to blister when exposed to heat.

Figure 17-30 This infrared heating unit is used when an entire vehicle has been repainted.

Protective Wear

Paint fumes are toxic, particularly if inhaled. A respirator that covers the nose and mouth must be worn to prevent inhalation of toxic particles or vapors. Hood-type respirators, which also protect the eyes and face, are recommended in the paint booth.

Replaceable cartridge-type respirators are used to absorb organic vapors. They also remove dust particles.

WARNING: Some respirators are satisfactory for removing dust, but do not remove toxic fumes or vapors. Check OSHA/NIOSH regulations. See Chapter 1 for more information on choosing respirators.

A paint jacket will provide some protection from overspray and paint. Neoprene (or nitrile latex) gloves will prevent solvents and other paint chemicals from contacting hands. Note that the technician in Figure 17-31 is wearing gloves, a protective suit, and a respirator.

Other Equipment/Tools

Every body shop must have some method to hold or hang components. A couple inexpensive *sawhorses* are very useful. Work can be placed on these horses during repair or refinishing. Some shops have hanger stands to aid in refinishing. See Figure 17-32. Hooks that are suspended from the ceiling of the paint room or booth are also very helpful. Small parts are simply suspended from the hooks.

In order to thoroughly mix and agitate finishes (especially metallics), a *paint shaker* is commonly used. See Chapter 4. If the finish is not thoroughly mixed, pigments or metallics may not be properly suspended in the paint solvents. Remember, pigments and other particles are heavier than the solvents. They quickly settle to the bottom of the container or paint cup. It is impossible to produce an even coat or match an existing color if the finish is not mixed properly.

All paint should be strained into the spray cup or pressure pot before it is used. *Strainers* remove small lumps, dirt, or other debris from the paint. If this is not done, a poor finish or a plugged gun may result. See Figure 17-33.

Figure 17-32   Special stands can be used to hold panels during repair or refinishing.

Figure 17-31   Protective wear should be used when mixing paint.

Figure 17-33   A paint strainer is used to help remove unwanted lumps and debris from paint.

For safety and convenience, paints, thinners, and other chemicals should be stored in a *paint cabinet*. Check local building and fire codes for proper cabinet designs and the amount of finish that may be safely stored in the cabinets.

A small workbench is commonly placed in the spray booth or paint room. The bench provides a convenient place to mix paint and store extra finish, strainers, containers, rags, and solvents needed during refinishing. A generous supply of rags or paper toweling is needed to clean surfaces and to apply solvents or polishes.

Know These Terms

Spray gun, Siphon-feed guns, Pressure-feed guns, Gravity-feed guns, Bleeder guns, Nonbleeder guns, External-mix guns, Internal-mix guns, High-volume, low-pressure guns, High-solids systems, Air cap, Spray pattern, Fluid tip, Fluid needle, Pattern adjustment valve, Fluid adjustment screw, Pressure, Free air capacity, Pressure drop, Temperature make-up system, Air make-up systems, Paint shaker, Strainers, Paint cabinet.

Summary

Refinishing equipment used in the shop includes a spray gun, air compressor, air transformer, spray booth, and various other pieces of equipment.

The spray gun uses paint or air pressure to atomize paint and apply it to a surface. Siphon-feed guns use compressed air to create a vacuum, which draws the paint into the gun from an attached container. In pressure-feed guns, air pressure forces material into the gun from a cup, tank, or pot. Airless spray systems use a pump to force paint from a container to a gun. Gravity-feed guns are generally used for spot repair. In these systems, paint is fed into the gun by the force of gravity.

Paint guns can be divided into bleeder, nonbleeder, external-mix, and internal-mix designs. Bleeder guns allow air to travel through the gun at all times and are seldom used for auto body repair. Airflow through non-bleeder guns is stopped when the trigger is released. External-mix guns atomize paint outside the air cap, and internal-mix guns atomize paint inside the air cap.

High-volume, low-pressure spray systems atomize paint into low-speed particles. These systems greatly reduce overspray. HVLP spraying techniques are similar to those used in conventional spray gun operations. However, these systems are not well suited for the application of pearls or metallics.

To prevent clogged or restricted passageways, spray guns should be cleaned after each use. If necessary, the holes in the air cap can be cleaned with a wooden toothpick. Never use a wire to clean small passages. In some cases, a spray gun cleaning machine can be used to clean painting equipment. However, the spray gun should never be immersed in solvent. Some guns require lubrication after use.

Two-stage compressors are preferred for body shop work. The compressor must be large enough to supply all of a shop's air consumption requirements. The two most important compressor ratings are air pressure and free air capacity. Pressure is needed to atomize paint. Capacity is needed to evenly distribute the paint.

The compressed air used for painting must be free from dirt, moisture, and oil. Constant air pressure must be maintained during painting operations. Air transformers are commonly used to maintain pressure and to remove oil, dirt, and water from the air.

Compressors should be located close to the spray booth. This keeps the length of the air lines to a minimum. For convenience, the transformer should be installed in the booth.

Piping from the compressor to the transformer should be as direct as possible. It must also be the correct size for the volume of air used. When possible, the piping should slope toward the compressor.

Hoses between the spray gun and the transformer must also be the correct size. Resistance to airflow increases as hose diameter decreases.

Spray booths are fireproof enclosures designed to confine and exhaust overspray and fumes that result from the painting process. They also help exclude dust from the painting area. There are several spray booth designs available. All booths should have adequate lighting. A temperature make-up system filters and warms air before it enters the booth. Air make-up systems replace air as it is exhausted from the booth.

Drying equipment is often used to speed drying and curing. There are two basic types of drying equipment: radiant-drying equipment and convection drying equipment. Radiant-drying equipment uses infrared or ceramic heating units to heat the painted surface. Convection equipment heats the painted surface with hot air.

Proper protective equipment should be worn when applying finishes. A respirator that covers the nose and mouth will help prevent inhalation of toxic particles. A paint jacket will provide protection from overspray, and gloves will protect hands from chemicals.

There should be some method to hold or hang components in the painting area. Special hanger stands are designed for this purpose. A paint shaker should be used to thoroughly agitate finishes. Strainers should be used to remove lumps and debris from paint as it is poured into a cup or tank. Thinners, paint, and other chemicals should be stored in a paint cabinet.

Review Questions–Chapter 17

1. Material is _____ when it is broken into small particles to produce a fine spray.

2. Siphon-feed spray guns use compressed air to create a _____ in the gun.

3. When using a pressure-feed spray system, paint flow is adjusted by changing atomization air pressure. True or False?

4. Gravity-feed guns are generally used for _____ painting.

5. Bleeder guns are commonly used in the body shop. True or False?

6. In external-mix guns, paint is atomized outside the _____ _____.

7. Paint systems that atomize paints into low-speed particles are called:
   a. internal-mix systems.
   b. nonbleeder systems.
   c. HVLP systems.
   d. none of the above.

8. High-volume, low-pressure spray systems are ideal for applying metallic finishes. True or False?

9. The _____ _____ is located at the front of the spray gun and directs compressed air into the material stream.

10. The fluid tip forms a seat for the:
    a. fluid valve.
    b. air valve.
    c. fluid needle.
    d. all of the above.

11. The _____ adjustment valve controls air to the air cap.

12. The fluid adjustment screw controls the travel of the _____ _____.

13. When a nonbleeder gun's trigger is partially depressed, the gun will only release air. True or False?

14. Spray guns should be cleaned:
    a. at the end of each week.
    b. after each use.
    c. after each work day.
    d. none of the above.

15. A clogged air cap can be cleaned with _____ _____.

16. A spray gun should not be immersed in solvent for more than 30 minutes. True or False?

17. _____-_____ compressors are commonly used in the body shop.

18. Compressors must be able to supply all of a shop's _____ _____ requirements.

19. In order to produce a defect-free painted surface, compressed air must be free from:
    a. dirt.
    b. oil.
    c. moisture.
    d. all of the above.

20. If possible, piping should slope _____ the compressor.

21. As hose size increases, resistance to airflow:
    a. increases.
    b. decreases.
    c. stays the same.
    d. none of the above.

22. _____ _____ is the loss of air pressure between the source and the point of use.

23. The key function of a spray booth is to:
    a. provide a fireproof enclosure for painting.
    b. exhaust paint fumes and overspray.
    c. filter incoming air.
    d. all of the above.

24. A temperature make-up system _____ and _____ air as it enters the spray booth.

25. In downdraft spray booths, air enters through floor vents and exits overhead. True or False?

26. Drying equipment is generally used with _____ finishes.

27. Light colors tend to absorb more heat than dark colors. True or False?

28. Cartridge-type respirators are designed to absorb _____ vapors.

29. If paints are not mixed thoroughly, _____ may not be suspended in the solvents properly.

30. Before use, paint should be used _____ to remove lumps, dirt, and other debris.

Activities–Chapter 17

1. With your instructor's permission, disassemble a pressure-feed spray gun and either a siphon-feed or gravity feed spray gun. How are they alike? How do they differ?

2. Learn how to clean a pressure-feed spray gun, then conduct a demonstration for a small group or the entire class. If your state or school requires use of a spray gun cleaning machine, demonstrate the proper steps for its operation.

3. Your shop is expanding its finishing operation, and wants a system capable of providing compressed air to five spray guns at one time. Each spray gun requires a free air capacity of 8.5 cfm at a maximum pressure of 60 psi. Calculate the total air volume needed, then use the chart shown in Fig. 17-20 of the text to determine the compressor size required.

chapter 18

Surface Preparation

After studying this chapter, you will be able to:

- [ ] Describe how to remove and sand paint in preparation for refinishing.
- [ ] Describe three methods of removing deteriorated paint.
- [ ] Explain how to properly mask a vehicle.

Surface Preparation

Before applying paint to a vehicle, its surfaces must be prepared properly. All surface preparation should begin with a thorough cleaning. After washing the vehicle with soap and water, it should be cleaned with a wax and silicone remover. See Figure 18-1. Thinners or reducers should never be used to clean surfaces in preparation for refinishing. When applying cleaning solvents, always use new, clean rags. Rags that have been laundered often contain small amounts of grease, detergents, or other materials that will prevent the paint from adhering properly. The cleaning solvents are simply wiped on the surface with one rag and removed with a clean rag. See Figure 18-2. All old wax, silicone, and other contaminants must be removed from an old finish before deciding whether to sand or remove the paint. It has been estimated that 80% of all new paint problems are related to improper preparation of the old finish.

After cleaning, it is essential to detect any deterioration of the original paint or substrate. Make sure that the paint film adheres to the substrate properly. If areas of a panel have low gloss or display signs of checking, cracking, or blistering, sand through the finish in a small area and taper the edges between the bare panel and the paint. See Figure 18-3. If the thin edge of the paint along the tapered area does not crumble or break, it is reasonable to assume there is no rust under the area. If paint bubbles are evident, determine whether they are caused by surface rust or rust through. Bubbles commonly occur along the lower edge of the doors and rocker panels.

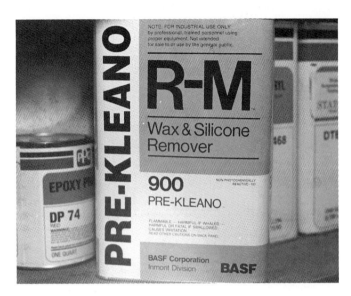

Figure 18-1   Typical cleaning solvent used during refinishing preparations.

Figure 18-2   This technician is carefully wiping the surface with cleaning solvent.

Paint Removal

If the original finish is in good condition, it is not necessary to remove the paint before refinishing. However, it may be necessary to remove the original paint if it is in poor condition (pits, rust, poor adhesion, flaking, etc.). Usually, paint must only be removed from a small portion of a vehicle, such as the hood or door.

There are several methods used to remove paint, including power sanding, sandblasting, and chemical removal. The method used depends on the quantity of paint to be removed and personal preference. If there are

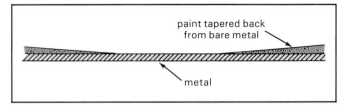

Figure 18-3   Note that the edge of the paint is tapered back.

a number of panels requiring paint removal, sandblasting or chemical paint removers can be used. If only a portion of the vehicle's paint is to be removed, power sanding is often preferred.

Power Sanding

Power sanding is accomplished using a disk sander, Figure 18-4. This is the fastest and most popular method of removing paint. Old finish can be removed with a #16 grit open-coat abrasive. The exposed metal should be sanded with a #50 grit abrasive and then finished with a #220 grit abrasive. If only a portion of the panel is to be refinished, all edges of the paint film should be tapered as shown in Figure 18-5. This tapering procedure is known as *feathering*. The finish adjoining the surface to be sprayed is sanded carefully to eliminate sharp edges. To do this, start with a #320 grit abrasive and finish with #400 grit abrasive. It is often best to feather by hand using a sanding block. Water can be used to help provide an extremely smooth surface. Wet sanding will be covered in detail later in this chapter.

Sandblasting

Sandblasting is a process that uses air pressure to direct a stream of abrasive particles (sand or other abrasives) against the painted surface of a vehicle. The abra-

Figure 18-4   A power sander can be used to quickly remove paint.

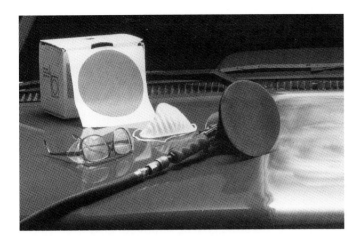

Figure 18-5 Resin paper (adhesive backed) was used to sand this hood and feather the paint. (Carborundum Abrasives Co.)

Figure 18-6 A sandblaster is used to remove paint, rust, and scale from an auto body prior to refinishing. (Clements National Co.)

sive particles chip or blast the paint from the surface, leaving metal bare. The abrasive particles make tiny indentations in the surface of the metal, which generally improve undercoat adhesion. See Figure 18-6.

Sandblasting leaves metal panels exposed. Unless the metal is painted (treated and given an undercoating) promptly, it will rust. All bare metal surfaces should be cleaned with a metal conditioner and conversion coat to ensure proper primer adhesion.

Sandblasting should be performed in an area where the dust created by the process cannot get to the rest of the shop. Plastic covers are commonly used to protect the engine compartment and other areas from dust accumulation.

WARNING: Sandblasting procedures create a great deal of dust. Therefore, respirators, goggles, and other protective wear should be worn when sandblasting.

Chemical Remover

Paint removers or **strippers** chemically loosen paint. They are relatively easy to use, but are costly and create potential health hazards.

WARNING: Always use paint removers in well-ventilated areas. Wear eye protection and gloves when working with paint removers.

Before applying a paint remover, read the label carefully. Aluminum, chrome, and plastic parts may be damaged by exposure to these chemicals. Some parts may have to be removed or carefully masked. Polyethylene plastic is commonly placed under the work area. Any

remover or paint residue that falls on the plastic can be easily discarded when the job is done.

Removers are generally applied to a small area at a time with a gun or brush. The solution should remain liquid on the paint for about 15 minutes. Be sure to apply enough remover and do not rush the process. After the remover works on the surface for a sufficient length of time, the paint will be loose. It can then be easily scraped off with a putty knife. All traces of the remover must be cleaned from the surface before the car is painted. Wash the car and use a **neutralizer** recommended by the manufacturer on the bare metal. Take special care to remove all traces of the paint remover in cracks and joints. After cleaning off the remover, sand the surface with a #60 grit abrasive and before priming.

Preparing a Painted Surface For Refinishing

Although it may not be necessary to completely remove old paint, the finish should be sanded thoroughly to remove oxides and contamination not removed by washing. Sanding also smooths out the paint film and provides a slightly rough surface for better adhesion of the new paint film. Surface preparation occurs in two phases: preliminary sanding and finish sanding.

Preliminary Sanding

Dual-action or orbital (jitterbug) sanders are commonly used for the preliminary sanding of most surfaces. An abrasive grade of no more than #320 grit should be used in this step. Never use a disk sander (grinder) for preliminary sanding. Remember to keep power sanders away from moldings and high-crown areas.

Power sanding should be followed by hand sanding. Sand a small area at a time with a straight, back-and-forth motion. Always use a sanding block when wet sanding, sanding large flat surfaces, sanding body filler, or sanding thick layers of primer-surfacer. A half sheet of abrasive paper is commonly wrapped around a sanding block to smooth the old finish. A half sheet of sandpaper that is folded into thirds can be used by hand to reach areas that are not accessible with the sanding block. See Figure 18-7. Be careful to spread the force of your fingers over the entire surface of the folded sandpaper. This will prevent sanding shallow grooves in the paint.

After preliminary sanding procedures, the old paint should be smooth and have a dull appearance. Use your hand to feel for small imperfections. Chips, bumps, or scratches will generally show up when the topcoat is applied. If imperfections are found, cleaning solvent should be used to remove wax from the area around the defect. Wet sand the area and feather it to a smooth taper. Spot putty may be used to fill small nicks and scratches. For deep imperfections, feather the damaged area and apply several coats of primer-surfacer.

Carefully sand along joints, moldings, and ridges. It is easy to sand through the paint on a ridge or edge. If the paint film is sanded to bare metal, apply a primer-surfacer to the metal surface. Lightly sand all spot repairs before applying the topcoat. Depressions in the paint caused by sanding in one spot will be easily seen when the topcoat is applied.

Liquid sandpaper is sometimes used in door jambs, under the trunk lid or hood, and in other areas that are difficult to sand using conventional methods. Liquid sandpaper cleans and etches the paint. Flexible sanding pads, which consist of abrasive-coated, interwoven fibers, can be used to sand any contour. These pads come in coarse, medium, and fine abrasive grades.

Finish Sanding

Finish sanding is the last stage in preparing an old finish for repainting. Finish sanding is accomplished by hand using #400 grit sandpaper. A sanding block or pad should be used when possible. Always sand with long, straight strokes. Sand along the length of the panels and follow the body lines.

Wet sanding procedures are often used in the finish sanding stage. **Wet sanding** requires the use of a wet-or-dry abrasive. When wet sanding, a wet sponge or controlled water hose is used to keep the sanding area wet. See Figure 18-8. Water prevents the paper from becoming clogged by washing away old paint and debris. This keeps the abrasive clean and sharp. A squeegee can be used to periodically wipe away the water. Water often fills scratches and makes it difficult to judge sanding progress. Wash out the abrasive paper periodically and change the paper when it does not cut properly.

Although wet sanding is slower then dry sanding, it produces a much smoother surface. It also reduces sanding effort, dust, and the amount of paper consumed.

Guide Coat Sanding

A **guide coat** is often applied to a panel to help detect high or low spots. The guide coat consists of a thin contrasting color coat that is sprayed over the primer-surfacer. After the guide coat has dried, the surface is block sanded. Low and high spots will become evident as the abrasive paper cuts through the guide coat in high spots and leaves color in low areas. See Figures 18-9 and 18-10.

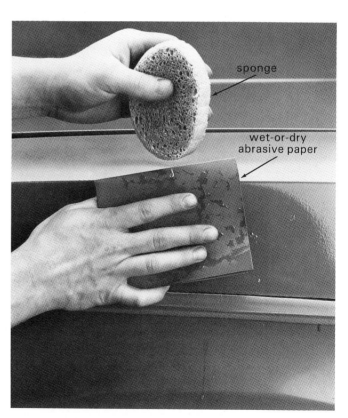

Figure 18-8   Wet sanding. Note that a sponge is used to keep the sanding surface wet. (Carborundum Abrasives Co.)

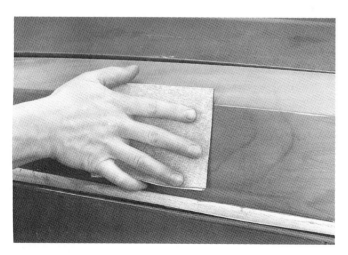

Figure 18-7   Sanding an old finish by hand. Note that the side molding has been taped to prevent damage. (Carborundum Abrasives Co.)

Figure 18-9 A guide coat has been sprayed over the primer-surfacer on this panel.

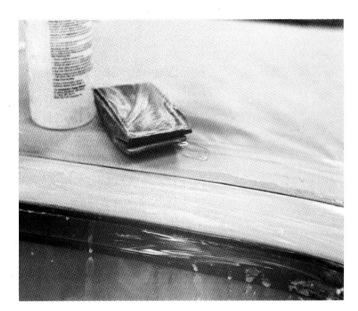

Figure 18-10 A sanding block is used to wet sand the guide coat on the primer-surfacer.

Masking

Once a surface has been cleaned and sanded, the vehicle should be washed with water or wax-and-grease remover one final time. Use compressed air to blow dust out of cracks and crevices. Make every effort to keep the surface clean. Avoid touching the prepared surface if possible.

After the surface is dry, it is ready for *masking.* Masking techniques will vary slightly in every shop. Proper masking is critical because it reflects the quality of workmanship.

Before painting, it is important to protect various areas from paint overspray. Areas to be protected are often covered with *masking paper*. Do not use newspa-

per for this purpose. It is too porous and will allow wet paint to bleed through. Quality masking paper will not permit paint to penetrate or seep through to the panel it is protecting. Masking paper is attached to the vehicle with *masking tape*. If necessary, large areas of a vehicle can be covered with sheets of plastic.

Masking tape must adhere easily to painted and unpainted surfaces, such as plastic, chrome, aluminum, glass, steel, and other materials. Additionally, none of the tape's adhesive should remain on the surface after the tape is removed. Quality tape will retain its adherent qualities when it is drenched during wet sanding operations.

There are two general types of masking tape. One type used with air-drying or curing paints, and the other type is designed to withstand paint baking temperatures.

Masking tape and masking paper come in several widths. Narrow tape is easier to form around curves. Wide tape and paper are used to cover large areas quickly. Special dispensers are available that speed up masking preparation. See Figures 18-11 and 18-12. As the masking paper is pulled from the dispenser, the tape is automatically applied to its edge. Half the width of the tape is applied to the edge of the paper. The remaining half is free to hold the paper in position on the vehicle.

Figure 18-11 This stand is designed to speed the dispensing of masking paper.

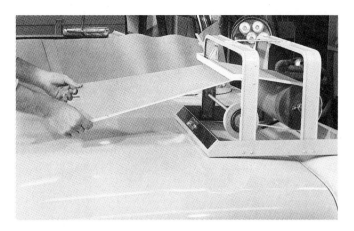

Figure 18-12 Pulling off a sheet of masking paper to mask the windshield.

Masking Precautions

Masking tape should be applied only to surfaces that are free from water, silicones, lubricants, dust, rust, etc. Unless you are masking curved surfaces, tape should not be stretched. Simply lay the tape on the surface and press it firmly in place. Make sure that the edges of the tape adhere to the surface. If the tape does not adhere properly, water from sanding operations or paint will seep under the tape and will free it from the panel. It is best to cut the tape instead of tearing it. Tearing creates an irregular edge and usually stretches (deforms) the tape. In many cases, the thumbnail can be used to cut masking tape.

Tape manufacturers caution against applying or removing tape at temperatures below 50°F (10°C). Masking paper and tape should not be removed until the newly applied paint is dry. When removing tape, it should be pulled directly outward at 90° to the painted surface. Remove the tape from the vehicle as soon as possible. The longer tape remains on a vehicle, the harder it will be to remove. Masking tape should be stored in a cool location and should never be placed on a hot surface. Over time, tape will dry out. Make certain that masking tape is fresh before applying it to a vehicle.

Masking Trim and Hardware

Extreme care must be taken when masking trim and hardware components. If masking is not perfect, the unprotected areas will be painted. This is a sure sign of careless workmanship.

When masking trim, paper is not required. Select a tape that is wide enough to cover the trim components as completely as possible. In Figure 18-13, a 1 in. (25 mm) wide piece of tape is being applied to a door handle. In this instance, the tape was applied to the upper area of the handle first. A second piece was then used to cover the lower side of the handle and, at the same time, slightly overlap the first piece.

Chrome beading, molding, and similar trim pieces can be quickly and effectively masked using tape of the correct width. By using the correct width, the entire surface can be masked with a single strip of tape. Figure 18-14 shows the taping operation being performed on a front door molding strip. This is typical of the procedure used on other moldings.

In Figure 18-15, masking tape is being applied to weatherstripping on a door. Clean the weatherstripping with lacquer thinner to help the masking tape stick better.

A decorative emblem is being masked in Figure 18-16. The base of the emblem is covered with tape, and then the front and back faces are covered. Finally, tape is placed around the perimeter of the emblem. This helps seal the edges of the tape on the front and rear emblem faces.

To mask a side-view mirror, some shops use a small plastic bag. The bag is placed over the mirror. Tape is used to secure the bag and to cover the base of the mirror.

Figure 18-13 One method for masking door handles.

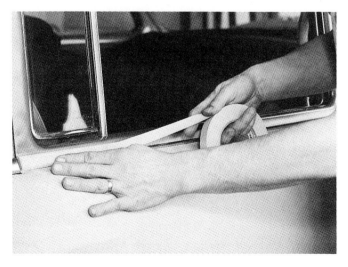

Figure 18-14 Chrome trim strips are easily masked.

Figure 18-15 When the correct tape width is selected, the job of masking weatherstripping is quick and easy.

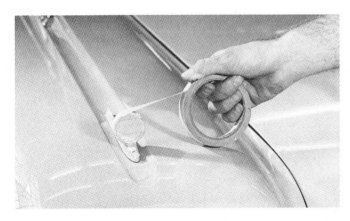

Figure 18-16 Masking the perimeter of a decorative emblem.

A radio antenna can be quickly masked by slipping a length of cardboard tubing over it. The tubing can be taped around the base of the antenna. An alternate method is to simply tape both sides of the antenna with long strips of tape and then cover the base of the antenna. See Figure 18-17. If possible, the antenna should be removed and the hole should be covered from the inside of the panel.

Figure 18-17 This radio antenna has been covered with two strips of masking paper.

When masking bumpers, 12 in. (300 mm) wide masking paper will do an effective job. A similar procedure can be used on grilles. When masking grille openings, extend the masking paper or a drop cloth well inside the engine compartment to prevent overspray from reaching the radiator, engine, etc.

Letters and emblems often present a problem that is easily solved with narrow widths (1/4 in.) of masking tape. When possible, it is best to remove emblems. The emblems on many late-model vehicles are attached with double-faced tape. Adhesive removers can be used to soften the tape adhesive. Hot air guns can also be used to soften the adhesive on emblems and other trim components. Many taillights can be masked using 3-6 in. (75-150 mm) wide masking paper and tape.

Masking Windshields

Two sheets of masking paper are generally needed to successfully mask the windshield on a modern car. The number of sheets depends on the height of the windshield and the width of the paper. Begin the masking operation by running a strip of tape around the windshield trim or the glass itself. Attach masking paper to the lower portion of the windshield. Then apply a top piece of masking paper that overlaps the bottom piece. Figure 18-18 illustrates the masking procedure. After the windshield is completely covered, apply tape along the seam between the top and bottom pieces. When the windshield is masked in this way, water or debris (overspray, paint, dust) will run down over the masking paper and will not reach the covered area. Other large areas can be masked using this technique.

Figure 18-18   Masking a windshield is completed by covering the lapped edges of masking paper with tape.

Masking Windows

The procedure for masking a window is shown in Figure 18-19. Apply paper to the lower area and then to the upper area. When the two sheets are in position, run a length of tape on the overlapping edge to form a complete seal.

Masking a Panel

When masking a panel for a two-tone paint job, as in Figure 18-20, select paper that is slightly wider than the area to be covered. Attach tape to one edge of the paper, and apply the taped edge to the car body. Then fold the paper to the required width and tape it in position.

For spot repairs, *reverse masking* techniques are used to help blend the paint and make the transition less

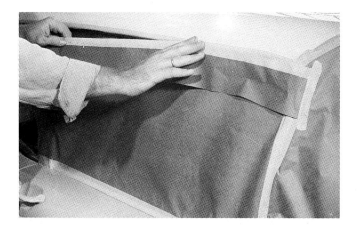

Figure 18-19   When masking a window, the lower area is covered before the upper area.

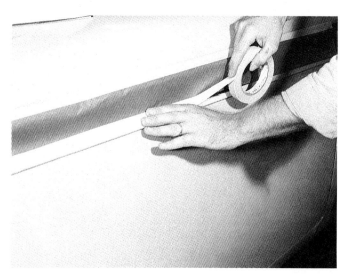

Figure 18-20   Masking a panel with paper and tape.

noticeable. Tape a piece of paper (along top edge only) over the area to be painted. Then lift the paper, pulling back about 2/3 of the tape width. Tape the paper loosely in place, leaving a small portion of the sticky side of the tape exposed. This will create a curved surface along the tape line. See Figure 18-21.

Reverse masking techniques will help prevent paint from building up and creating a ridge (line between old and new paint). Reverse masking also helps reduce solvent and paint bleeding (bleed-through) along the taped edge. **Bleed-through** will make it difficult to match and blend spot repairs. Try to locate breaks for spot repairs along moldings, high-crown areas, sharp seams and beads, or other natural break lines. This will make new paint more difficult to detect.

Masking Upholstery

If a complete color change is planned, the door jambs and other parts must be painted. When painting the inside of a door jamb, it is necessary to protect the upholstery from overspray. Starting at the outside lower corner, place a narrow strip of masking paper around the door jamb in a single operation. Follow the same procedure on the door frame. Then use large pieces of masking paper to cover the remainder of the door opening and the interior trim panel. Remember to mask all of the weatherstripping around the door and door jamb. See Figure 18-22. In some cases, a drop cloth can be used to cover seats, carpets, and other upholstery items.

Masking the Trunk Area and Engine Compartment

Some technicians remove the hood and deck lid when painting the underside of these panels. Once dry, these components can be reinstalled and the remainder of the vehicle can be painted.

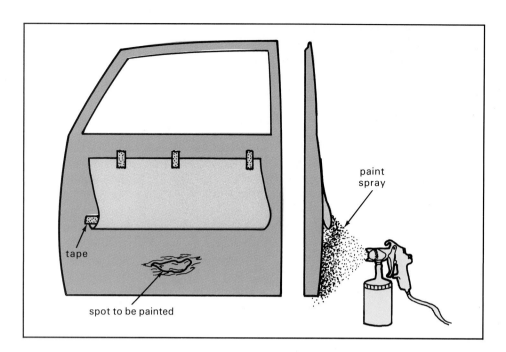

Figure 18-21 Reverse masking techniques are used to help blend paint and make the paint transition less noticeable.

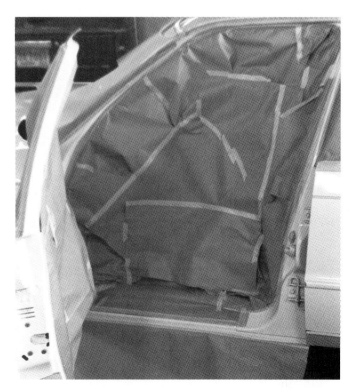

Figure 18-22 One method of masking a door and a door frame. Note that masking paper is used to cover the entire door opening.

An alternative to removing the hood is to carefully mask the perimeter of the hood opening. Mask the inside edges of the fenders and the cowl. A drop cloth can be used to protect most of the engine compartment from overspray. Allow the paper to overlap the drop cloth. Some shops remove the black (unpainted) fender bolts before painting. The bolts are reinstalled after the paint dries.

If the deck lid is not removed, the trunk area can be treated like the engine compartment. Overspray should not be allowed to enter the trunk area. The rubber weatherstripping around the trunk opening should also be carefully masked.

Masking Headlights

Headlights vary in shape and size, but the basic masking procedure is the same for all types. Usually, 6-8 in. (150-200 mm) wide masking paper is all that is needed to protect the lights.

Cut a piece of masking paper that will go approximately three quarters of the way around the light. Tape the paper to one side of the light. Then, apply a second piece so that a ''cone'' of paper surrounds the light, Figure 18-23. Fold the paper over the front of the light and hold it in position with strips of masking tape. See Figure 18-24. Molded plastic covers are available for some lights. These covers are simply pressed over the light. See Figure 18-25.

Small areas, such as safety marker lights on the side of fenders, are easily masked using various widths of tape. In most cases, 2 in. (50 mm) wide tape is used to cover marker lights.

Masking Wheels

When it is necessary to mask wheels, pleating an apron of masking paper will make it easier to follow the curved contour of the wheel and will prevent the paper from bunching or wrinkling. Cut a piece of masking paper to the desired length. Fold 1/4 in. (6 mm) deep pleats in the paper by crimping both edges. The pleats should extend the full width of the paper. Place a pleat every 4 in. (100 mm) along the entire length of the paper. Apply the

Figure 18-23   After taping one piece of masking paper around the headlights, overlap it with a second piece to form a cone.

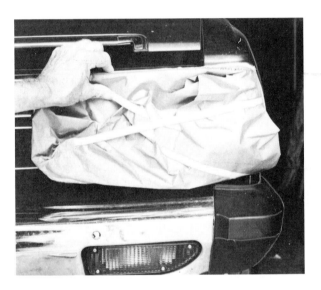

Figure 18-24   Complete headlight masking by folding paper over the lights and taping it in place.

Figure 18-25   Plastic headlight maskers. (Lenco, Inc.)

pleated paper to the wheel. After the paper is securely taped in place, fold the untaped edge so it will catch the overspray. See Figure 18-26. This pleating technique can be used on all circular surfaces.

Masking the Front End

Masking a car with large areas of chrome or plastic on the front end can be quickly accomplished by using wide paper. Each car requires different treatment. See Figure 18-27. In Figure 18-28, the area around a plastic fascia is masked before painting. A flex additive is added to the paint used on plastic components. This additive causes the paint to be flexible. Paint that contains a flex additive must not contact metal panels.

Masking Partial Panels

In some cases, only a portion of a panel is refinished. In Figure 18-29, only the top section of a door panel is

Figure 18-26   Masking a tire before painting the wheel.

Figure 18-27   This technician is masking the grille, bumper, and headlights.

Figure 18-28 The front panels on this vehicle were masked before the bumper was painted.

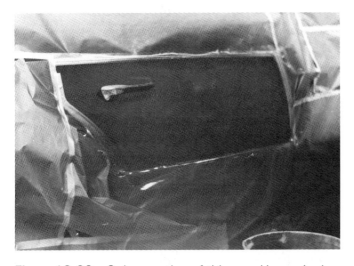

Figure 18-29 Only a portion of this panel is masked.

being wet sanded in preparation for repainting. To prevent the accumulation of sanding particles and overspray, the bottom of the door panel and the adjacent panels are masked.

Masking Other Areas

Overspray on exhaust pipes, tires, fender wells, splash shields, engine compartments, etc., is an obvious sign of careless masking. Drop cloths, masking paper, and masking tape should be used to protect these areas during the painting process. Remember to remove or mask rubber stops and seals. Vehicles waiting to be repaired can be protected with a sheet of plastic as shown in Figure 18-30.

Know These Terms

Feathering, Sandblasting, Paint removers, Strippers, Neutralizer, Liquid sandpaper, Finish sanding, Wet sanding, Guide coat, Masking, Masking paper, Masking tape, Reverse masking, Bleed-through.

Summary

Surface preparation should always begin with a thorough cleaning to remove dirt, wax, silicone, and other contaminates. After cleaning, the original surface should be studied for signs of deterioration.

If the original finish is in good condition, it does not require removal. However, it may be necessary to remove paint that is in poor condition. There are several methods used to remove paint, including power sanding, sandblasting, and chemical removal.

Power sanding with a disk sander is the fastest method of paint removal. This technique is used when

Figure 18-30 Large areas can be protected with plastic film.

only a portion of a vehicle's paint is to be removed. Sandblasting is a process that uses air pressure to direct a stream of abrasive particles against a painted surface. The particles blast the paint from the surface. Paint removers chemically loosen paint.

If old paint is not removed, it must be thoroughly sanded to remove oxides and other contamination. Sanding occurs in two phases: preliminary sanding and finish sanding. Preliminary sanding is accomplished using a dual-action or orbital sander and a #320 grit abrasive. Power sanding is followed by hand sanding. After preliminary sanding procedures, the old paint should be smooth and dull. If necessary, liquid sandpaper can be used in door jambs and other areas that are difficult to sand.

Finish sanding is the last stage in preparing an old finish for repainting. A #400 grit abrasive should be used in this step. Wet sanding procedures are commonly used in the finish sanding stage.

A guide coat is often applied to help detect high or low spots on panels. After the coat has dried, the surface is block sanded. Paint will be sanded away in high spots and will remain intact in low areas.

Before painting, various areas must be protected from overspray. These areas are often covered with masking paper. Masking tape is used to attach the paper to the vehicle. Make sure that surfaces are free from water, silicones, lubricants, etc., before applying the tape.

When masking most trim pieces, masking paper is not required. By using the correct width of masking tape, the entire surface of a trim piece can generally be covered with a single strip of tape.

When masking windshields, run a strip of tape around the trim or around the glass itself. Attach the masking paper to the lower half of the windshield. Then apply a piece of masking paper to the top half of the windshield that overlaps the bottom piece. Make sure that all edges are taped down to form a complete seal. Windows are masked in a similar manner.

When making spot repairs, reverse masking techniques can be used to help blend the repair. Reverse masking also helps reduce solvent and paint bleeding along taped edges.

If door jambs are to be painted, it is necessary to protect the interior from overspray. Rubber seals around the door and door jamb must also be masked. When painting the underside of the hood and deck lid, the engine and trunk compartment must be protected from overspray. A drop cloth is commonly used for this purpose.

Headlights are usually masked with 6-8 in. masking paper. Molded plastic covers are available for some lights. Safety marker lights are easily masked with tape.

When masking wheels, the masking paper should be pleated to prevent bunching and wrinkling. After the paper is taped in place, the untaped edges should be folded to catch overspray.

The procedures for masking the front of a vehicle vary. Wide masking paper is commonly used to cover large areas of chrome or plastic.

In some cases, only a portion of a panel is repaired. When this occurs, the rest of the panel (and surrounding areas) is covered to prevent the accumulation of overspray.

Drop cloths, masking paper, and masking tape should be used to protect exhaust pipes, tires, fender wells, etc., from paint. Overspray on these items is an obvious sign of careless masking.

Review Questions—Chapter 18

1. All surface preparation should begin with a thorough _____.

2. Laundered rags are recommended for applying cleaning solvents. True or False?

3. After cleaning, a surface should be checked for _____.

4. Chemical paint removers are commonly used when a small portion of a vehicle's paint must be removed. True or False?

5. Tapering the edge between a painted surface and a bare panel is called:
   a. smoothing.
   b. feathering.
   c. leveling.
   d. none of the above.

6. _____ is a process that directs a stream of abrasive particles against a painted surface.

7. Chemical removers may damage aluminum, chrome, and plastic parts. True or False?

8. If old paint is not removed, it should be thoroughly _____.

9. A disk sander should be used for preliminary sanding procedures. True or False?

10. A sanding block should be used when:
    a. wet sanding.
    b. sanding thick layers or primer-surfacer.
    c. sanding large, flat surfaces.
    d. all of the above.

11. _____ _____ can often be used in areas that are difficult to sand using conventional techniques.

12. A #320 grit abrasive should be used for finish sanding. True or False?

13. Wet sanding produces a _____ finish than dry sanding.

14. A _____ _____ is commonly applied to help detect high and low spots.

15. Newspapers can be used when masking large areas. True or False?

16. Masking tape should only be stretched when taping _____ surfaces.

17. Masking tape should not be applied or removed when the temperature is below ____ °F.

18. Masking paper is generally not necessary when masking trim. True or False?

19. When two pieces of paper are needed to mask a windshield, the bottom piece should be applied _____.

20. When masking spot repairs, _____ _____ techniques can be used to help blend the paint and make the transition less noticeable.

21. A drop cloth is commonly used to protect the _____ from overspray.
    a. engine compartment
    b. upholstery
    c. trunk area
    d. all of the above

22. Some technicians _____ the hood and deck lid when painting the underside of these components.

23. The rubber weatherstripping around the trunk opening should be carefully taped before painting. True or False?

24. Before masking wheels, the masking paper should be _____.

25. Paints that contain flex additives can be used on metal surfaces. True or False?

Activities–Chapter 18

1. Identify at least three shop safety items (such as a warning to wear eye protection when sanding or grinding) and make posters that could be hung in the shop. Posters should be approximately 11″ x 17″ in size.

2. Make a demonstration panel showing the stages of preparing a painted surface for refinishing. A section of scrapped panel about 12″ x 36″, such as part of an old door skin, will work well. From left to right, the panel should show an area of surface before preparation, an area that has been machine-sanded, an area with hand sanding following the machine, an area that has been finish-sanded with the wet sanding method, and finally, a finish-sanded area that has been cleaned with wax-and-grease remover and is ready for finish application.

3. Demonstrate for the class the proper procedure for masking a windshield on an automobile. Use two pieces of masking paper, so that the upper piece overlaps the lower for the most complete protection.

Before applying finish, a vehicle must be thoroughly masked. This technician is applying masking paper to a windshield in preparation for painting. (Oatey)

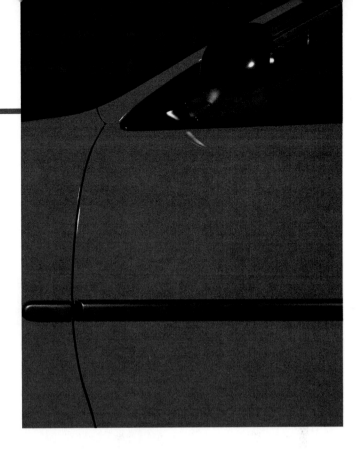

chapter 19

Applying Finish

After studying this chapter, you will be able to:

☐ List steps in finishing a vehicle.

☐ Describe how to properly adjust and use a spray gun.

☐ Identify various painting problems and explain how to remedy them.

☐ Describe the procedures for applying various finishes to metal and plastic substrates.

Applying Finish

The quality of a finish is determined by many factors. One of the most important factors is *cleanliness*. Any residue, dust, moisture, etc., left on the substrate will cause finish problems. Surface imperfections will be magnified in basecoat/clearcoat systems. The condition of the painting area (booth) and equipment is also important. It is not possible to apply a quality finish with poorly maintained equipment.

Regular equipment maintenance will prevent many problems. Dust problems can be controlled by using a paint booth, changing filters, washing down the paint area, wiping off hoses and other equipment, and making certain that the paint area is accessible only to authorized personnel.

Using a Spray Gun

A production-type spray gun is required to obtain the proper atomization and to apply paint in a minimum amount of time. See Figure 19-1.

For siphon-feed gun work, a suitable air cap and fluid tip are needed. A 0.070 in. (1.8 mm) diameter fluid tip is normally used for these guns. For faster paint application or when applying more viscous (thicker) materials, a 0.086 in. (2 mm) diameter tip can be used. For pressure-feed work, a 0.0425-0.0460 in. (1.0-1.1 mm) diameter fluid tip should be used.

Both siphon-feed and pressure-feed spray guns have two manual adjustments: the pattern control valve and the fluid control valve. See Figure 19-2. Similar controls are used on high-volume, low-pressure guns. See Figure 19-3.

When the ***pattern control valve*** is fully closed, it shuts off air to the horns on the air cap assembly, resulting in a round spray pattern. As the valve is gradually opened, air is emitted from the air cap and the spray pattern changes from round to oval. See Figure 19-4. This adjustment allows the operator to select a pattern width to suit the job at hand. For touch-up work and spot repairs, a round spray pattern can be used. When painting panels and other large areas, the gun is adjusted to a wide, oval pattern.

The ***fluid control valve*** determines the amount of paint coming from the gun. When the valve is fully closed, paint is not sprayed through the gun. When the

Figure 19-1 Typical spray gun used for automotive refinishing.

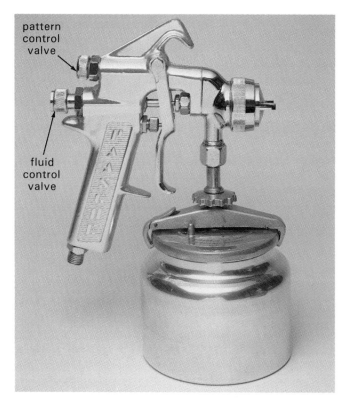

Figure 19-2 A typical siphon-feed spray gun. Note the location of the pattern control valve and the fluid control valve. (The Eastwood Co.)

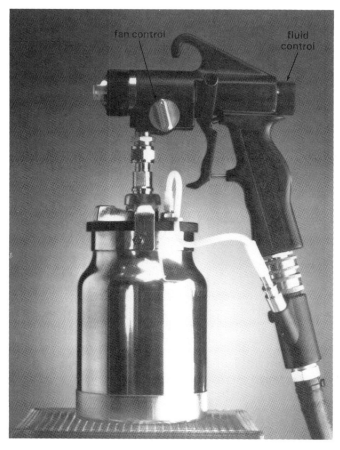

Figure 19-3 A high-volume, low-pressure (HVLP) spray gun. Note the location of the adjustment valves. (Mattson Spray Equipment)

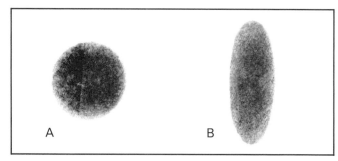

Figure 19-4 A—When the pattern control valve is fully closed, a round pattern is produced. B—When the valve is opened, the pattern becomes oval.

fluid control valve is fully open, maximum paint flow is provided. This adjustment permits the operator to choose a setting that will furnish the proper paint flow for the job. For spot work, minimum paint flow is used. When painting large areas, maximum flow is preferred.

The air pressure used at the gun to atomize the paint will vary with the viscosity and type of material being applied. As previously mentioned, the length and diameter of the air hose will affect the pressure at the gun. Air pressures are generally lower for modern multiple-stage finishing systems than for conventional one-step finishes. Gun air pressure is usually adjusted and controlled with the air regulator, which is part of the air transformer. See Figure 19-5. For added control, a pressure gauge and a regulator are sometimes attached to the gun.

The ability to choose the correct pressure for painting is gained through experience. The proper pressure is arrived at by applying a series of test patterns, Figure 19-6. The size and shape of the pattern are important. Varying the pattern shape is accomplished by changing the setting of the pattern control valve. This adjustment is important to reducing material costs. Select the setting most suitable to the size and contour of the panel being refinished. Never use a pattern that is wider than the surface being painted.

Low air pressure will result in under-atomized paint. This condition will produce a heavy, rough coat. Pressure that is too high will result in a dry spray. It may also cause *orange peel* due to the lack of proper flow-out. Generally, the atomizing pressure at the gun will range from 30-60 psi (205-410 kPa), depending on the type of finish applied. A pressure-feed gun will ordinarily require less air pressure than a siphon-feed gun. HVLP guns operate at about 5 psi (35 kPa).

Figure 19-5   One type of transformer or regulator.

The first step in operating a spray gun is to adjust the air pressure until the desired pattern and atomization are obtained. Test the spray pattern on a piece of paper or a scrap panel. If the air cap or tip is dirty or worn, an unsatisfactory pattern will result. In general, the height of the

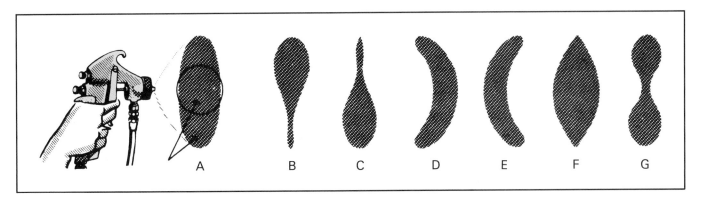

Figure 19-6   Spray pattern detail. A–Spray guns can be adjusted to either round or oval patterns. B–Top-heavy pattern caused by air cap holes partly clogged, obstruction on the top of the fluid tip, dirt on the air cap seat or the fluid tip seat. C–Bottom-heavy pattern caused by air cap holes partly clogged, obstruction on the bottom side of the fluid tip, dirt on the air cap seat or the fluid tip seat. D–Heavy right side pattern caused by right side air cap holes partly clogged or dirt on the right side of the fluid tip. E–Heavy left side pattern caused by left side air cap holes partly clogged or dirt on left side of the fluid tip. F–Heavy center pattern caused by a low setting of the spreader adjustment valve, low atomization pressure or paint too thick (siphon-feed system), excessive paint pressure for the atomization air being used or the material flow is in excess of the normal capacity of the cap (pressure-feed system), improper nozzle size. G–Split pattern caused by improperly balanced air and paint. Reduce width of spray pattern by means of spreader adjustment valve or increase fluid pressure.

oval should be about 6 in. (150 mm) and the width should be about 2 in. (50 mm). To correct pattern distortions, clean the air cap and fluid tip thoroughly.

Spitting is a condition caused by a dried-out packing around the fluid needle valve that permits air to get into fluid passageways. To eliminate this problem, loosen the nut on the air valve and lubricate the packing with machine oil. Spitting may also be caused by dirt between the fluid nozzle seat and the gun body, a loosely installed fluid nozzle, or a defective swivel nut on the siphon cup or material hose.

When applying paint, it is important to hold the gun at the correct distance from the work surface. For synthetic enamels, the gun should be held approximately 8-10 in. (200-250 mm) from the surface. The correct distance for lacquers is about 6-8 in. (150-200 mm). If the gun is too close to the work surface, the paint film will be too heavy and will tend to sag. If the gun is too far from the work, there will be excessive dusting and a sandy finish will be produced. See Figures 19-7 and 19-8.

It is important to remember that the gun should be held at the correct distance through the *entire length* of the stroke. Always keep the gun perpendicular to the surface being painted. Never use a fanning or a whipping motion when finishing a panel. See Figure 19-9. When the gun is held at an angle to the surface, more material is applied on one side of the spray pattern than the other. This results in streaks, sags, runs, and wasted paint.

Start painting at the top of a panel and work down. Use steady, horizontal strokes from one side of the panel to the other. The gun's trigger should be pulled when the gun is directly over the edge of the panel, Figure 19-10. The spray gun is then moved to the other side of the panel and the trigger is released. The stroke is continued for a few inches before reversing direction for the next stroke. Proper triggering is an important part of the spraying technique. It helps maintain full coverage, with a minimum of overspray. When proper triggering is achieved, the quality of the paint job is improved and little paint is wasted.

In another method of painting, the ends of the panel are **banded** before the face of the panel is sprayed, Figure

19-11. This technique allows the operator to begin each stroke and then pull the trigger. Additionally, the trigger can be released before completing the stroke. A smooth, complete coating will result and overspray will be minimized when using this system.

When the edges have been banded, the habit of fanning or whipping the gun is more easily controlled. Whipping the gun wastes energy and material. The banded surfaces also serve as a signal to trigger the gun at exactly the correct moment.

Each stroke must be smooth, allowing enough time for sufficient material to be applied to the surface. However, they must be fast enough to prevent too much material from being applied. Strokes should overlap each other by approximately 50%. See Figure 19-12.

To ensure even coverage on candies, pearls, and metallics, the second coat is often applied vertically (gun passed from top to bottom and bottom to top). All other coats are applied horizontally.

When spraying a hood, roof, or other wide horizontal surface, always start at the near side and work toward the far side. This is particularly important when lacquer

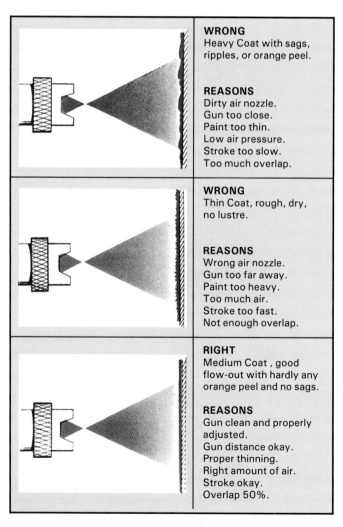

	WRONG Heavy Coat with sags, ripples, or orange peel.
	REASONS Dirty air nozzle. Gun too close. Paint too thin. Low air pressure. Stroke too slow. Too much overlap.
	WRONG Thin Coat, rough, dry, no lustre.
	REASONS Wrong air nozzle. Gun too far away. Paint too heavy. Too much air. Stroke too fast. Not enough overlap.
	RIGHT Medium Coat, good flow-out with hardly any orange peel and no sags.
	REASONS Gun clean and properly adjusted. Gun distance okay. Proper thinning. Right amount of air. Stroke okay. Overlap 50%.

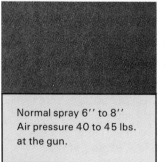
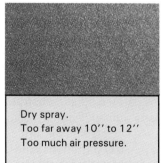

Normal spray 6'' to 8''
Air pressure 40 to 45 lbs.
at the gun.

Dry spray.
Too far away 10'' to 12''
Too much air pressure.

Figure 19-7 Note how excessive air pressure and holding the spray gun too far from the surface affect the color of paint.

Figure 19-8 Proper and improper methods of applying paint.

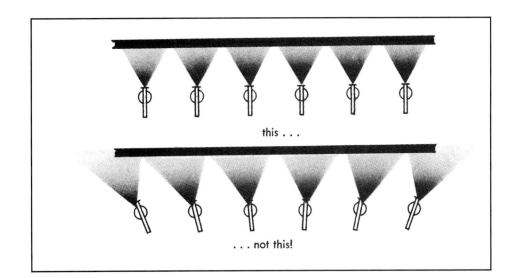

Figure 19-9 For even paint distribution and film thickness, always hold the gun perpendicular to the surface of the panel.

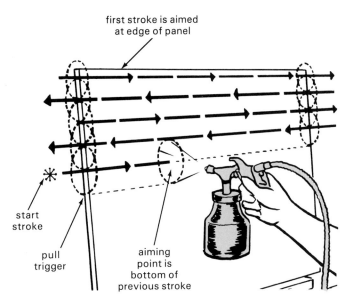

Figure 19-10 In this method of spraying, the gun is triggered at the edge of the panel.

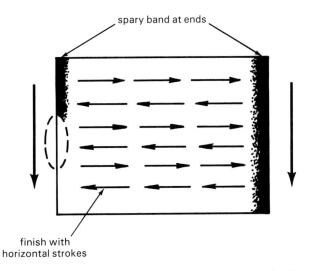

Figure 19-11 The sides of this panel are banded before the rest of the panel is coated.

is being sprayed. See Figure 19-13. When using this technique, overspray will land on a dry (tack-free) surface. Overspray landing on a wet surface will result in a sandy surface. If a pressure gun is not used, a siphon-feed gun should be tilted slightly when painting horizontal surfaces. Caution: There is always the danger of paint leaking from the vent port when a siphon-feed gun is tipped!

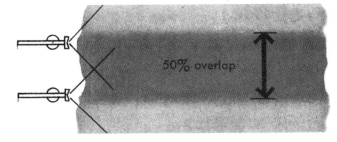

Figure 19-12 A 50% overlap should be allowed with each pass of the gun.

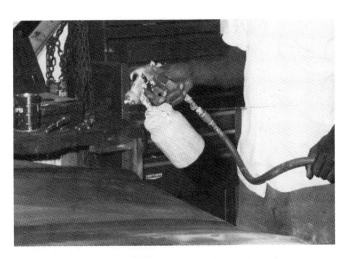

Figure 19-13 When spraying horizontal surfaces, start at the near side of the panel and work toward the far side.

PROBLEM	CAUSES	REPAIR
Lifting: A swelling of wet film. 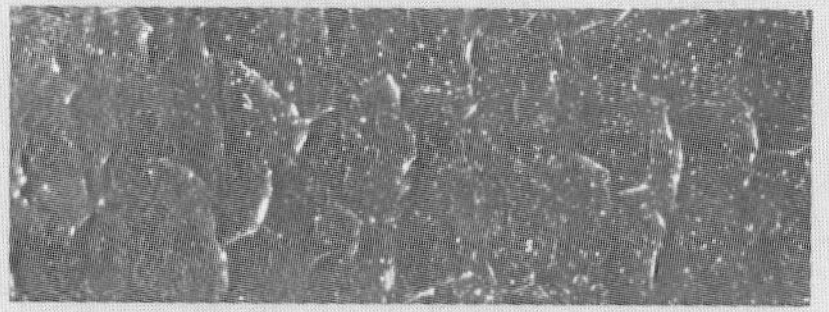	CAUSES: Recoating improperly cured enamel; improper drying of previous coat; spraying over a surface that has not been properly cleaned; using acrylic lacquer over enamel or acrylic enamel undercoats.	REPAIR: Material must be removed and the surface must be refinished.
Peeling: A film separation occurring between two layers of finish. 	CAUSES: Improper cleaning; poor surface preparation; incompatibility of one coat to the other.	REPAIR: Remove old finish from an area larger than the affected zone. Properly clean and treat the surface, then refinish. For materials other than steel, use recommended primers.
Orange peel: Finish that looks like the surface of an orange. 	CAUSES: Excessive air pressure; gun fanning before paint droplets have a chance to flow; color coats not reduced enough to permit proper atomization; improper thinning or reducing; spray equipment not properly adjusted; gun held too far away; shop temperatures too high.	REPAIR: On enamel, use a fine compound to rub out orange peel. On lacquer, sand or use rubbing compound. If necessary, remove paint and refinish.
Fish eyes: Small, crater-like openings in the finish. 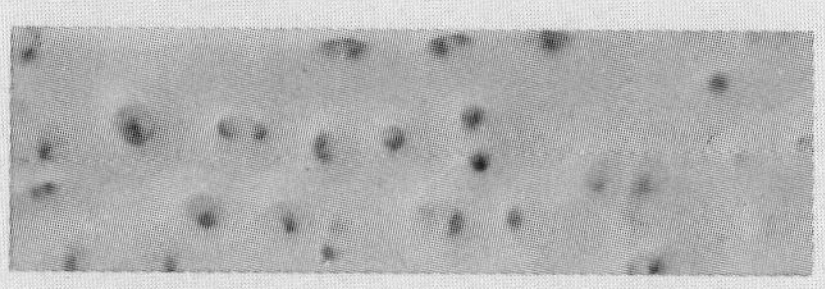	CAUSES: Spraying over silicone; improperly cleaned substrate.	REPAIR: If the finish is still wet, wash off paint. Thoroughly clean surfaces and refinish.
Wrinkling: A shriveling of the finish. 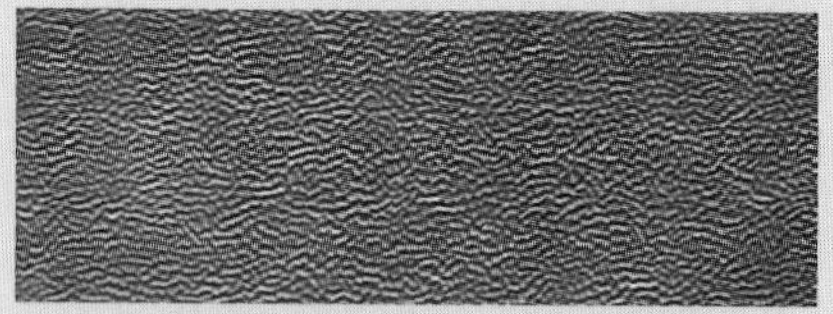	CAUSES: Excessively heavy enamel color coats; extremely high temperature or humidity conditions; enamel sprayed in hot sun; freshly painted surface exposed to sunlight; enamel finish coats reduced with lacquer or acrylic lacquer thinner instead of enamel reducer.	REPAIR: Remove finish and recoat.
Water spotting: Spotty appearance and dulling of gloss in spots. 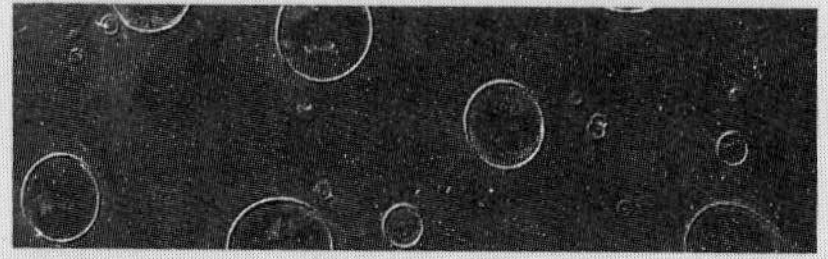	CAUSES: Finish is exposed to water before being completely dry; alternate exposure to sun and rain.	REPAIR: Use fine rubbing compound and rub lightly with a damp cloth. If polishing fails, refinish. To prevent recurrence, keep car out of rain and do not wash until paint is completely dry.
Rust: Raised section of the finish; blistering. 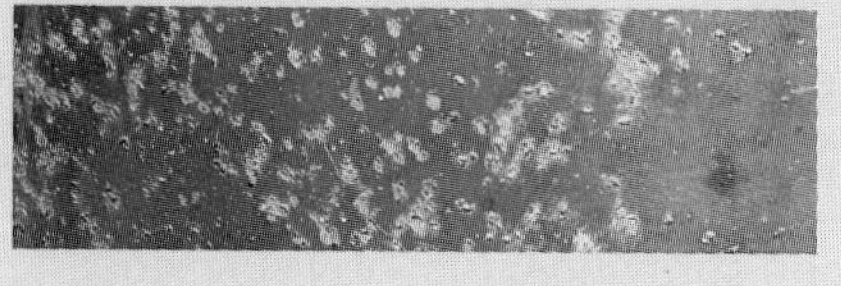	CAUSES: Poor penetration; improper cleaning of surface.	REPAIR: Sand surface, treat surface with rust remover, and refinish.

Figure 19-14 Typical paint defects.

PROBLEM	CAUSES	REPAIR
Pitting: Finish distortions.	CAUSES: Oil or moisture escaping through the air line.	REPAIR: Sand down to smooth surface and refinish. Overhaul compressor and separator to correct trouble.
Blistering: Bubbly or swollen appearance. 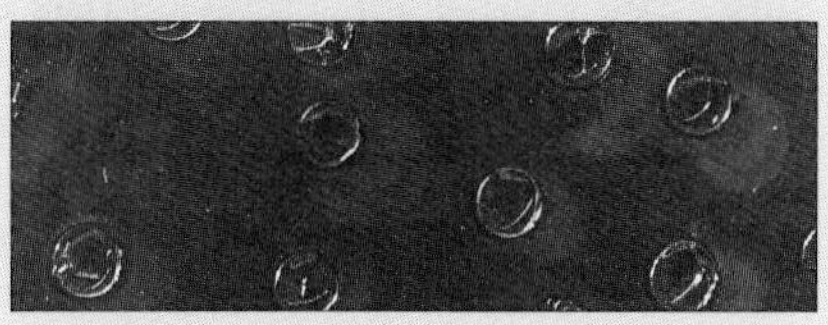	CAUSES: Trapped solvents; painting over grease or oil; rust under surface; moisture in spray lines; prolonged exposure of film to high humidity.	REPAIR: Remove all blisters by sanding. If necessary, sand to bare metal. After sanding, refinish the surface. To prevent blistering, clean and treat metal thoroughly; allow ample drying time between coats; and drain water from air lines. If temperature and humidity are high, use overly fast thinners.
Pin point blistering: Small broken blisters that have the appearance of pits. 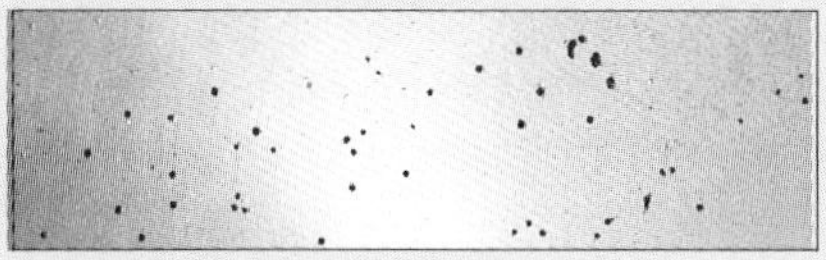	CAUSES: Trapped solvents; painting over grease or oil; rust under the surface; moisture in the spray lines; prolonged exposure of film to high humidity.	Sand down to bare metal and refinish.
Mottled surface: Blotchy, uneven appearance. 	CAUSES: Paint applied on surface that has been treated with silicone type polish.	REPAIR: Sand down to bare metal, remove all traces of polish, and refinish.
Checking: Deep cracks. 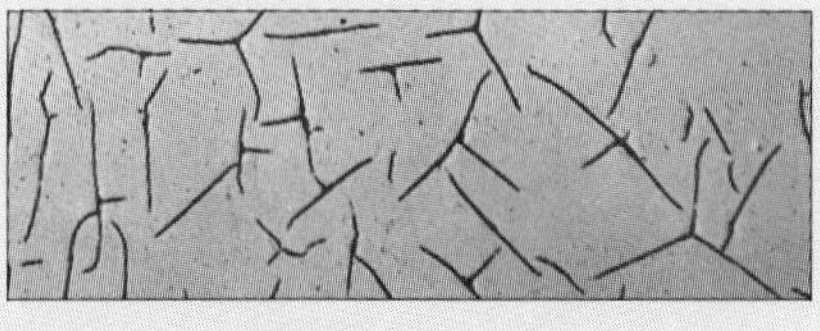	CAUSES: Spraying a new finish over previously cracked finish; spraying an excessively thick finish coat over undercoats; spraying improperly mixed topcoats; heavy application of finish coat with insufficient time between coats.	REPAIR: Sand down to smooth finish. If necessary, sand to bare metal. Avoid extreme temperatures, spray uniform coats, and allow proper drying time between coats.
Chalking: Dulling and powdering of the paint film.	CAUSES: Excessive weathering and sunlight.	REPAIR: Apply paste cleaner, followed by polish. In extreme cases, complete refinishing is necessary.
Runs or sags: Failure of coating to adhere uniformly over the surface. 	CAUSES: Slow thinner or reducer; over-reduced color coats; too little air pressure when applying color coats; color coats sprayed over wax, oil, or grease; excessively heavy finishing coats; refinishing materials or work surface that is too hot or cold.	REPAIR: If the finish is wet, use a fine camel hair brush to brush out the sag and recoat the surface. If the finish coat is completely dry, remove excess paint by sanding with a fine grit abrasive paper. Compound, polish, or refinish as required.

Figure 19-14 Typical paint defects. (Continued)

Examples of paint that has been improperly applied or applied to poorly prepared surfaces are shown in Figure 19-14.

Film Thickness

Some paint manufacturers specify the thickness of the paint film. Film thickness affects the gloss, tendency to sag, and durability of the paint. Recommended thicknesses vary with the type of finish and the manufacturer. The topcoat on a new vehicle generally ranges from 0.003-0.005 in. (0.075-0.120 mm) thick. New color coats should not exceed 0.004 in. (0.10 mm). Specialized equipment is available for measuring paint film thickness.

There are several techniques used when applying finishes. A *tack coat* is a light dusting coat that is allowed to flash or become tacky before a full, wet coat is applied. A tack coat allows wet coats to be applied without running or sagging. A *full, wet coat* is a heavy application of finish. It is used to thoroughly cover the substrate. A *mist coat* is a greatly reduced topcoat. This finish will have little or no color (clear) and is generally used to help level and blend the topcoat.

Paint Temperature

The paint temperature should be checked as the material is put into the pressure pot or cup. If the material is too cold, it becomes thick and heavy bodied. When paint is overheated, the viscosity drops and the material becomes more liquid. The chemical action of hardeners or other additives is also affected by changes in temperature.

Always store paint materials and equipment at temperatures between 70-85 °F (20-30 °C). If stored and applied at higher or lower temperatures, a poor paint job may result. Remember, putting paint in a hot or cold container will affect the temperature of the material. Never attempt to paint a vehicle that has been standing in the sun or in an extremely cold area.

Viscosity

A viscometer is a device that is used to measure a material's viscosity. A typical viscometer used in the paint shop is the Zahn cup. A *Zahn cup* (dip cup) is simply a cup with a hole in the bottom. The time (in seconds) it takes for a finish to flow out of the cup is an indication of the material's viscosity. See Figure 19-15. As a rule of thumb, paint viscosity should be about 20 seconds in a *#2 Zahn cup.* Mist or blend coats are generally a lower viscosity (18 sec.), while full, wet coats may be a slightly higher viscosity.

Basic Refinishing Techniques

It is not possible to provide detailed instructions for every refinishing technique. Procedures will vary with each job and finishing material. Keep in mind that the paint manufacturer's refinishing instructions should be carefully followed.

WARNING: It is extremely important to wear gloves, goggles, and proper respiratory protection during refinishing procedures. Many product labels list the NIOSH-approved respirator suggested for use. See Figure 19-16.

Before painting, the surface must be cleaned to remove all debris, wax, and polish. All surfaces must be

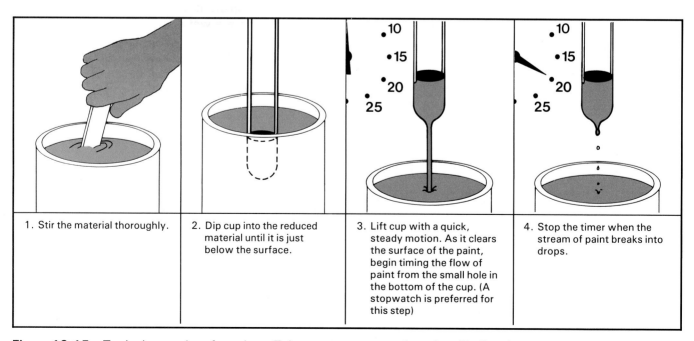

| 1. Stir the material thoroughly. | 2. Dip cup into the reduced material until it is just below the surface. | 3. Lift cup with a quick, steady motion. As it clears the surface of the paint, begin timing the flow of paint from the small hole in the bottom of the cup. (A stopwatch is preferred for this step) | 4. Stop the timer when the stream of paint breaks into drops. |

Figure 19-15   Typical procedure for using a Zahn cup to measure viscosity. (Du Pont)

Figure 19-16   NIOSH-approved paint spray mask. (3-M Company)

Figure 19-17   A tack rag is used to clean off dust particles before the final finish is applied.

smooth and free from minor imperfections. Remember, primer-surfacers are capable of filling some fine scratches and will improve adhesion. Select the primer-surfacer that is compatible with the color coat. Applying heavy coats of primer-surfacer with one pass of the gun is not recommended. When applied in this manner, primer-surfacers usually have a surface hardness, but do not dry next to the metal for some time. Heavy coats of primer-surfacer can also lead to difficult sanding, poor adhesion, pin holes, and other film defects. It is best to apply thin, wet coats of primer-surfacer and to allow adequate *flash time* between coats.

The time required for primer-surfacer to dry will depend on the thickness of the coat, the type of thinner, and the environmental conditions. After the primer-surfacer has dried, putty can be applied to any rough areas.

After the putty is dry, sand the entire surface. To prevent sand scratches and obtain a smooth surface, use #600 grit (or finer) abrasive. If you accidentally sand through the primer-surfacer, it will be necessary to recoat the surface. After the sanding is complete, wash the sanded area with water to remove dust. After allowing the surface to dry thoroughly, blow out crevices and moldings with compressed air.

Before applying the color coat, the surface must be cleaned with an appropriate solvent (Prep-Sol). Use a clean rag to apply the solvent and a second rag to dry the clean panel. Once again, use the blow gun to remove remaining dust from cracks and crevices. Make certain that the surface is completely dry before applying the final finish.

A tack rag should be used to wipe the surface immediately before the final finish is applied. See Figure 19-17. The **tack rag** is a resin-impregnated cheesecloth that is used to pick up small particles on the surface. Gently wipe the surface with the rag. If the tack rag becomes dirty, discard it. Never leave the tack rag on a

painted surface. It may leave a resin residue or soften the paint.

When painting an entire vehicle, a planned pattern should be followed that allows the painter to keep a wet edge while minimizing overspray. Although there is no "correct" pattern, two suggested spray painting sequences are shown in Figure 19-18. The sequence used depends on the spray booth design. The first step to refinishing a vehicle is to paint the hidden edges, door jambs, and areas under the deck lid and hood. When spraying door jambs, use air pressure of 20 psi (140 kPa), then increase pressure per the manufacturer's instructions. Leave the doors slightly ajar to prevent sticking and to permit proper drying. Then proceed to paint the exterior of the car. Many painters prefer to do half of the top and complete it as they work around the car. Always work from a wet edge. At no time should you spray or lap into a semi-dry area. This may cause air streaks in the finished paint job.

To obtain an extremely smooth finish and a high gloss from acrylic paints, the final finish can be sanded with #1200 grit (or finer) wet-or-dry sandpaper. This technique is called **color sanding**. Color sanding helps remove orange peel and other imperfections. A bucket of water and a rubber squeegee are commonly used when color sanding. The sandpaper is dipped in the water periodically to clean and wet the paper. This is important because the abrasives on the paper are close together and are easily clogged with paint particles. In some cases, a sponge is used to keep the work surface wet at all times. The squeegee is used to wipe water from the surface to help determine sanding progress. Obviously, it is important to avoid sanding through the paint film.

On some finishes, the next-to-last coat is carefully color sanded before a final coat is applied. On other finishes, only the final coat is color sanded. See Figure 19-19.

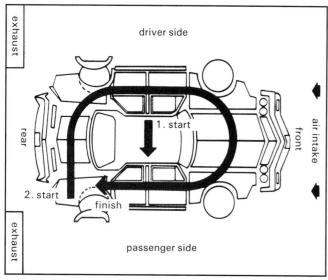

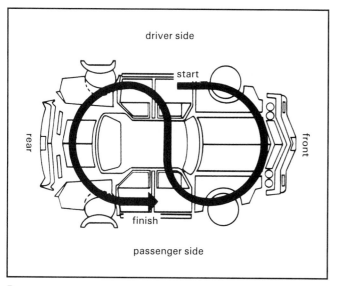

Figure 19-18 Recommended spraying sequence.
A–Sequence for crossdraft booth. B–Sequence
for downdraft booth. (Du Pont)

Color sanding is followed by machine and hand polishing to achieve a high gloss. Before machine polishing, wash the work surface to remove any residue and perform a final check of the paint.

Rubbing compounds are fine, paste-like abrasives. *Hand rubbing compounds* differ from *machine compounds.* Hand rubbing compounds must not be used with a power polisher/buffer. The abrasives (pumice) in hand rubbing compounds are fairly coarse and will scratch the surface if applied with a machine. Machine compounds contain very fine abrasives and can be safely used with a power buffer. See Figure 19-20.

Remember that rubbing compounds are designed to remove paint. Hand rubbing compounds are applied with a soft rag and are rubbed on the paint surface to remove

Figure 19-19 Color sanding with #1200 grit sandpaper to achieve a glass-smooth finish with basecoat/clearcoat systems. (Carborundum Abrasives Co.)

all sanding marks. When using compounds on spot repairs, make every attempt to start on the new paint and rub toward the original finish. This will minimize the danger of causing a dull appearance in the blend area. After hand compounding, wash the surface with water to remove all rubbing compound and other debris.

A clean rag is used to apply machine compound to the surface, and a buffer (with soft bonnet) is used to smooth the surface. Keep the buffer moving at all times and watch the paint surface closely. Be careful when compounding near a corner or sharp edge. The machine can easily burn (cut) off the paint in these areas. Lift the machine so that the only part of the wheel (bonnet area) touching the surface is the half that is turning *toward* the edge.

After machine compounding, wash (clean) the surface to remove all compounds. Swirl marks will generally be left from the machine compounding. These marks can

Figure 19-20 This technician is polishing a finish to improve luster.

be removed by using a **polishing cream** or a **swirl remover.** Apply the polishing cream directly from the bottle and use a clean, damp cheesecloth to work it into a small area. Allow the cream to dry and wipe it off with a clean cheesecloth. See Figure 19-21.

Applying Acrylic Lacquer

Many paint manufacturers recommend that one or two coats of sealer be applied before applying acrylic lacquer. When the sealer is dry, three or four wet, double coats of acrylic lacquer (thinned according to the manufacturer's instructions) should be applied. Allow each double coat of finish to flash before applying succeeding coats. Most acrylic lacquers are thinned by 125-150% and applied with air pressures between 35 and 45 psi (240-310 kPa). In hot weather, a retarder can be added to the thinner to aid leveling and to prevent blushing.

When spraying acrylic lacquers at temperatures below 60 °F (15 °C), crazing (mesh of fine cracks) may result. Crazing can be prevented by heating the area with an infrared light and applying the sealer while the surface is still warm. If the temperature is low, always allow at least 24 hours drying time before compounding acrylic lacquers.

When spot repairing acrylic lacquer finishes, extend each color coat a little beyond the previous coat to blend into surrounding finish. Progressively thinner layers of new paint are applied farther from the repair. This technique is called **blending** or **drifting.** It is essentially an attempt to create an optical illusion. Finally, spray a mist coat of retarder and thinner over the repair to increase the gloss (leveling) and reduce the amount of compounding required. This step will also level overspray roughness.

Figure 19-21 Swirl remover can be used to eliminate marks made by power compounding.

For most brands of acrylic lacquer, allow at least four hours for air drying (preferably overnight) before sanding or compounding. If the finish is force dried with infrared lights or an oven, heat the finish area for least 30 minutes at about 165 °F (175 °C). Then process the repair area by color sanding, compounding, and polishing. Wax should not be applied to the finish for at least 60 days to allow the acrylic to harden. Acrylic may lose some of its original luster if it is not thoroughly dry before compounding and polishing. If this occurs, the luster can be restored by lightly buffing the finish after the paint has aged for about ten days.

Applying Acrylic Enamels

Before applying an acrylic enamel color coat, a sealer may be applied. Be certain that the finish is mixed properly. Chemical hardeners can be added to acrylic enamel to improve gloss (flow-out) and eliminate the recoat period. When performing spot repairs, spray a full, wet coat that is reduced by about 50% (slow drying reducer) at an air pressure between 30-40 psi (205-275 kPa). After allowing 15-20 minutes of flash time, apply a second and third wet coat.

Catalyzed acrylic enamels (polyurethane catalyst) are commonly used in *three-coat systems.* These systems consist of a base mist coat, a transparent color or metallic coat, and a clearcoat. Wet (color) sanding affects the clearcoat and leaves the color basecoat untouched. *Two-coat* systems utilize a base color coat that is covered with a few layers of clearcoat. Matching multiple-coat system paints is difficult. Some painters use test panels (old panels) in an attempt to check painting procedures and colors. These test panels are compared with the original finish.

For solid acrylic enamels, apply one medium, wet coat. Allow the finish to flash for at least 10 minutes and then spray a second coat. Metallic colors will produce the best effect by applying a full, wet coat and then applying a light coat. If a mottled appearance occurs after second coat, apply a mist coat to produce a uniform appearance.

Metallics tend to darken when applied in full, wet coats. A faster reducer, increased air pressure, or a greater distance between the gun and the surface (about 12-18 in. or 300-450 mm) will lighten metallic colors. See Chapter 16 for more information on color matching.

Clear acrylic lacquer may be applied over acrylic metallic or solid color coats to provide a high gloss. The gloss level is influenced by the number of clearcoats applied. Color sanding and buffing are sometimes performed on the color coats and clearcoats.

Applying Synthetic Enamels

Pressure for spraying synthetic enamels is usually between 55 and 65 psi (380-450 kPa) when using a siphon-feed gun. Less pressure is used with a pressure-feed gun. Hold the gun about 10 in. (250 mm) from the surface of the panel. The greatest error in spraying enamel is putting too much paint on the substrate. A thick film of enamel is no more durable than a film of normal thickness. In some cases, a thick film is actually less durable. Two coats of a quality enamel will usually hide any color. Solid colors spray easiest by applying a medium coat first. After allowing this coat to get tacky, spray a full, wet coat of paint.

Some manufacturers recommend spraying one panel at a time when applying synthetic enamels. This is done by applying two medium coats to each panel, one immediately following the other.

The cure time of synthetic (alkyd) enamels varies among manufacturers. Temperature, humidity, and additives also impact cure time. Special reducers can be added to compensate for shop temperatures. Most synthetic enamels are reduced by 20-30%.

Applying Polyurethane Enamels

Polyurethane enamel finishes are applied like synthetic enamels. They are normally mixed with equal parts of catalyst and reducer. Two wet coats of this type of finish are normally sufficient. Always allow a flash time of at least 15 minutes between coats. For metallics, apply a tack coat and allow it to set for about 20 minutes before applying the topcoat. If desired, a reduced topcoat or mist coat may be applied. Air pressure should be set between 50-60 psi (345-410 kPa) when applying this type of finish.

WARNING: Remember to wear a respirator when working with polyurethane finishes. Polyurethanes contain isocyanates, which are extremely toxic.

Applying Acrylic Polyurethane Enamels

Acrylic polyurethane enamels are mixed with equal parts of catalyst. Solid colors are commonly reduced by more than 25% (one part reducer to four parts of catalyzed color). Most metallic polyurethane enamels are reduced by 50%. Gun air pressure should be set between 50 and 60 psi (345-410 kPa). Two or three double, wet coats with flash time between double coats is common. Remember to clean the equipment immediately after use.

Clearcoats. To obtain the basecoat/clearcoat gloss and wet look of factory finishes, clear acrylic polyurethane is commonly applied over color coats (solid or metallic). Catalyst (hardener or initiator) is added to the clearcoat according to the manufacturer's instructions. Two wet coats of this finish are normally sufficient. Clearcoats are reduced by as much as 150-200% and applied with air pressure of 50 psi (345 kPa). Some manufacturers recommend that a mist coat be applied at lower air pressure to aid in basecoat blending. If sanding and buffing are planned for blending a repair, a third coat of finish may be needed. Allow the finish to cure for at least 24 hours before compounding.

Clearcoat polyurethane enamels and acrylic polyurethane enamels are sometimes used in custom work to provide additional protection over stripes and graphic designs.

Minor Spot Repairs

Many small chips can be repaired by carefully cleaning the chip and applying a small drop of finish in the chip depression. A toothpick or a small brush is used to apply the paint. Do not attempt to brush out the paint. Many **touch-up paints** are available for this purpose. Color sanding is generally not necessary when making this type of repair. See Figure 19-22.

When repairing defects that protrude from the surface, a sharp razor blade can be used to cut off the defect, Figure 19-23. Color sanding and polishing will restore gloss to the damaged surface.

Refinishing Plastics

With the extensive use of plastics in late-model vehicles, every auto body technician must know how to repair and refinish plastic components. Simplified plastic repairs were discussed in Chapter 9. There are two major

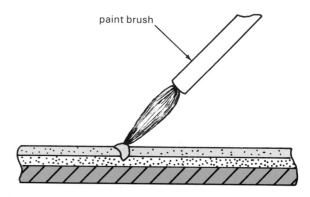

Figure 19-22 A small brush is used to place paint directly on the chip depression.

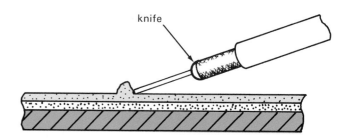

Figure 19-23 A sharp blade is used to cut off the imperfection. The spot can then be wet sanded and polished.

concerns that must be addressed when refinishing plastic materials: adhesion and flexibility. Anytime paint is applied to a late-model vehicle, plastics are being coated.

Plastic components are normally painted before installation. Many new parts come pre-primed. If necessary, damage must be repaired and an appropriate undercoat must be applied before the topcoat is applied. Polypropylene and other polyolefins should be primed with a special polycarbonate primer. Polystyrene, ABS, and other styrene-containing plastics should be carefully primed. Most solvents (lacquer thinners and reducers) "eat" into these materials. Carefully follow the instructions provided by the manufacturer.

As a rule, plastic components can be given a topcoat using acrylic lacquer, acrylic enamel, polyurethane enamel, or polyvinyl chloride paint. Other formulations are sometimes used. Painting procedures for SMC, fiberglass, and most rigid plastics are similar to those for steel.

Before finishing flexible plastic parts, a flex additive should be added to the paint. Some of the finishes for fabric vinyls and vinyl-coated leathers (polyvinyl chloride lacquers) come pre-mixed with a flex additive. Others require that the additive be inserted before application. If the part is to be painted on the vehicle, carefully mask the vehicle's finish. Paint with flex additives must not be allowed to contact metal surfaces. See Figure 19-24. In some cases, an adhesion promoter is added to the paint system.

Stone Protection

To protect the lower body and rocker panels from being marred by flying stones, an abrasion-resistant coating is commonly applied. A polyvinyl chloride coat-

Figure 19-24 A flex additive was added to the paint before coating this plastic bumper.

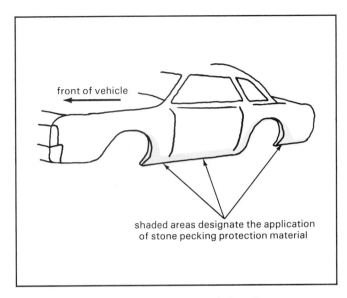

Figure 19-25 Typical locations of abrasive-resistant coating.

ing may be sprayed on these areas. The areas can also be covered with a pressure-sensitive PVC film. This abrasion-resistant coating (stone-guard, gravel protector) has been popular for about a decade. See Figure 19-25.

Know These Terms

Pattern control valve; Fluid control valve; Spitting; Banded; Tack coat; Full, wet coat; Mist coat; Zahn cup; Tack rag; Color sanding; Rubbing compounds; Hand rubbing compounds; Machine compounds; Polishing cream; Swirl remover; Blending; Drifting; Touch-up paints.

Summary

The quality of a finish depends on many factors. The substrate must be perfectly clean. The condition of the painting area and the equipment are also important. It is impossible to apply a quality finish with poorly maintained equipment.

Siphon-feed and pressure-feed spray guns have two manual adjustments: the pattern control valve and the fluid control valve. HVLP guns have similar adjustments. The pattern control valve regulates airflow to control the shape of the spray pattern. The fluid control valve determines the amount of paint coming from the gun.

The air pressure used at the gun will vary with the viscosity and type of finish being applied. The proper pressure is determined by applying a series of test patterns. Low pressure will result in under-atomized paint. Excessive pressure will lead to a dry spray.

When applying paint, the gun must be held the correct distance from the work surface. This distance must be maintained through the entire stroke. Start at the top of the panel and work down. The gun's trigger should be pulled when the gun is directly over the edge of the panel. Proper triggering is an important part of the spraying technique. In some cases, the edges of a panel are banded before the face is sprayed. When a panel is banded, the tendency of fanning the gun is more easily controlled. A siphon-feed gun must be tipped slightly when applying paint to horizontal surfaces.

Paint film thickness affects the gloss, tendency to sag, and durability of paint. Equipment is available for measuring film thickness. Paint temperature should be checked when the material is put into a cup or container. Paint should be stored at temperatures between 70 and 85°F (20-30°C). A paint's viscosity should also be checked. For most finishes, viscosity should be about 20 sec. in a #2 Zahn cup.

Procedures for refinishing vary with each job. Before painting, the surface should be cleaned, primed, and sanded. After sanding, clean the surface with solvent and blow dust from cracks and crevices. Wipe the surface with a tack rag immediately before applying the finish. After the paint is applied, color sanding techniques are used to produce a smooth surface and a high gloss. Color sanding can be followed by machine buffing and hand polishing.

When spraying an entire vehicle, a planned sequence should be followed that allows the painter to keep a wet edge while minimizing overspray. Spraying into a semi-dry area may cause air streaks in the paint job.

Many manufacturers recommend the use of a sealer before applying acrylic lacquer. When the sealer is dry, three or four wet, double coats of the finish should be applied. Allow at least four hours for air drying before sanding or compounding acrylic lacquer finishes.

Before applying an acrylic enamel color coat, a sealer should be used. Then apply one medium, wet coat of the finish. After allowing an adequate flash time, a second coat can be applied.

When applying synthetic enamels, the gun should be held approximately 10 in. from the work surface. Apply a medium coat of finish first. After allowing the finish to become tacky, apply a full, wet coat to thoroughly cover the surface.

Polyurethane enamels are applied like synthetic enamels, but are mixed with equal parts of catalyst and reducer. Remember to wear a respirator when working with polyurethane finishes.

Solid color acrylic polyurethane enamels are commonly reduced by more than 25%. Metallic acrylic polyurethane enamels are reduced by 50%. Two or three double coats of this material are generally sufficient. Be sure to allow flash time between double coats.

Clear acrylic polyurethane is commonly applied over color coats to obtain the gloss of factory finishes. Two wet coats of this finish are generally applied. Allow the finish to cure for 24 hours before compounding.

Chips in a painted surface can be repaired by applying a drop of finish in the chip depression with a small brush. To repair defects that protrude from a surface, use a sharp razor blade to cut off the defect.

When repairing plastics, adhesion and flexibility must be taken into account. Flex additives are often added to paints when finishing flexible parts. In some cases, an adhesion promoter can be added to paint.

To protect rocker panels and the lower body from stone and gravel chips, abrasion-resistant coatings are commonly applied. These coatings have been popular for about ten years.

Review Questions–Chapter 19

1. Regular equipment maintenance will help to eliminate finishing problems. True or False?

2. A _____-type spray gun is needed to obtain proper atomization and apply finish in a minimum amount of time.

3. The pattern control valve controls airflow to the _____ _____.

4. The fluid control valve should be closed when painting large areas. True or False?

5. The _____ and _____ of the air hose will affect air pressure at the gun.

6. Recommended air pressures are generally _____ for multiple-stage finishes than for one-step finishes.

7. Excessive air pressure commonly results in a _____ spray.

8. The first step in operating a spray gun is to:
   a. clean the air cap and fluid tip.
   b. adjust the fluid control valve to obtain desired material flow.
   c. adjust air pressure to obtain the proper spray pattern.
   d. none of the above.

9. When spraying lacquers, the gun should be held 4-5 in. from the work surface. True or False?

10. Under normal circumstances, paint strokes should overlap by approximately:
    a. 50%.
    b. 75%.
    c. 20%.
    d. 65%.

11. When spraying a _____ surface, work should start at the near side and progress toward the far side.

12. Paint film thickness affects:
    a. tendency to sag.
    b. durability.
    c. gloss.
    d. all of the above.

13. A tack coat is generally applied before a full, wet coat. True or False?

14. A mist coat is used to help _____ and _____ the topcoat.

15. The chemical action of hardeners can be affected by changes in temperature. True or False?

16. A _____ cup is used to measure a material's viscosity.

17. A _____ _____ should be used to wipe off a surface immediately before applying the final finish.

18. When painting an entire vehicle, a pattern should be followed that allows the painter to keep a _____ edge.

19. Spraying into a semi-dry area may cause:
    a. air streaks.
    b. blistering.
    c. peeling.
    d. none of the above.

20. Color sanding with a #_____ grit abrasive will help remove orange peel and other imperfections.

21. Hand rubbing compounds can be used with a power buffer. True or False?

22. Acrylic lacquers are commonly thinned by _____-_____%.

23. When making spot repairs, the process of progressively extending each layer of color coat beyond the previous layer is called:
    a. mixing.
    b. drifting.
    c. shading.
    d. none of the above.

24. Sealers should not be used before applying acrylic enamels. True or False?

25. When spraying _____ enamels, some manufacturers recommend applying finish to one panel at a time.

26. Acrylic polyurethane _____ can be reduced by as much as 200%.

27. After painting a small chip, the repair should be color sanded and compounded. True or False?

28. _____ and _____ must be taken into account when refinishing plastic components.

29. Solvents will not affect polystyrene and ABS plastics. True or False?

30. A _____ _____ is commonly added to paints when refinishing flexible parts.

Activities–Chapter 19

1. Make a series of test patterns showing the different shapes and sizes of paint patterns resulting from changes in the pattern control valve and air pressure settings. Make note of the settings that produce each pattern.

2. Videotape several students using spray guns as an aid to analyzing and improving their painting skills. Use a wide angle of view to show the full painting stroke and the paint coverage as applied. The persons videotaped can view the tape as a group to analyze each other's technique and make suggestions.

3. Demonstrate the technique used for determining paint viscosity, using a No. 2 Zahn cup and a watch.

Custom bodies are often constructed for prototype vehicles. These designers
are preparing a clay model of a concept car. (Pontiac)

chapter 20

Custom Painting and Body Designs

After studying this chapter, you will be able to:

- ☐ Describe wet and dry methods of applying overlays.
- ☐ List the supplies, tools, and equipment needed for custom painting and designs.
- ☐ Describe how to produce various custom paint finishes.
- ☐ Describe how to install decals and adhesive pinstripes.
- ☐ Describe several ways to produce custom body designs.

Custom Painting

The term **custom painting** is used to describe refinishing and/or decorating a vehicle in a personalized manner. Custom painting may involve landscapes, animals, geometric designs (stripes, flames, etc.), names, numbers, or unusual paint colors and patterns. See Figure 20-1.

This type of work requires considerable experience and skill. There are a number of commercially available designs and patterns that may assist the technician. Always lay out full-size patterns on paper first. This will provide a chance to see how the design will fit and look on the vehicle. Although this is considerable work, it saves time in the long run. Removing a design is expensive!

Tools and Equipment

Customized effects are obtained using spray guns, striping tools, brushes, masking tape, and other equipment.

In custom painting, the conventional spray gun is used primarily for spraying large areas with undercoats, color coats, and clearcoats. A **touch-up gun** is similar to a conventional spray gun in operation, but is lighter and has a smaller capacity, Figure 20-2. It is designed for general touch-up work and for small detail work.

An **air brush** is used for fine detailing, fish scaling, and similar work. It does not have a spray pattern control. The fluid volume control and air pressure determine material flow in the air brush. The small physical size allows great flexibility of movement. See Figure 20-3.

Figure 20-1 This vehicle has been given a custom paint job.

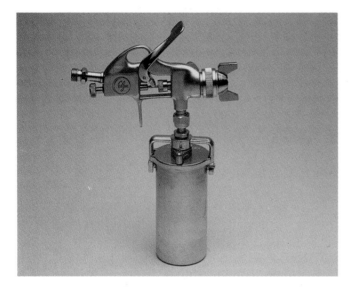

Figure 20-2 A touch-up gun is commonly used for spot repairs. Note the size of the paint container. (The Eastwood Co.)

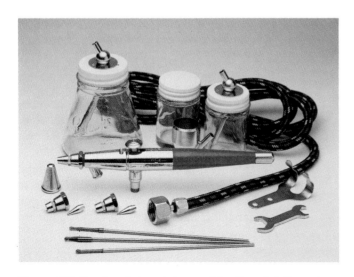

Figure 20-3 An air brush is used for fine detail work. This tool does not have a spray pattern control. (The Eastwood Co.)

A *striping tool* or *roller gun* consists of a small container for paint and a brass applicator wheel. See Figure 20-4. Gravity forces paint from the container to the wheel as the tool is pulled along the surface.

Striping brushes and other small brushes are used to apply pinstripes and other designs by hand. Sable or camel's hair dagger brushes are commonly used for striping. See Figure 20-5.

Materials

Regular and special masking tapes, accent tapes, decals, metallic flakes, custom colors, markers, and other materials are needed for custom work. In Figure 20-6, masking tape is used to help create a custom design.

Specialty Finishes

While almost any type of paint can be used for custom painting, acrylic lacquers are popular for design work. They may be worked rapidly in successive coats. These materials can be applied with a conventional spray gun, touch-up gun, air brush, or an aerosol can. Each method has advantages, depending largely on the design and area to be covered.

Polychromatic finishes are used extensively for custom work. Three- and four-part paint systems are sometimes used. *Candy-apple, pearlescent,* and *metal flake paints* are generally considered specialty finishes.

Candy-apple finishes are three-part paint systems. They begin with a metallic basecoat (generally silver or gold). Several transparent color coats are applied over the basecoat, and are followed by a clearcoat. Acrylics or polyurethanes are used for this process.

Pearlescent finishes are three-part systems. They usually begin with a color basecoat. A clear topcoat containing pearlescent powders (fine Mylar metallics) is then applied. This topcoat is covered by a clearcoat.

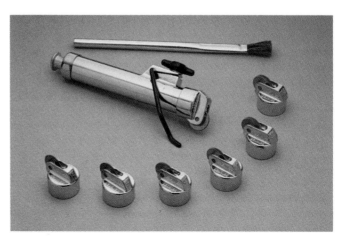

Figure 20-4 This striping tool is used when painting pinstripes. (The Eastwood Co.)

Figure 20-5 A typical brush used for applying painted pinstripes. (The Eastwood Co.)

Metal flake finishes utilize various sizes, shapes, and colors of metal or Mylar flakes. A basecoat is applied and is followed by a clear topcoat containing the metal or Mylar flakes. A clearcoat is then applied to provide protection and give depth to the finish.

It is advisable to paint a test panel before actually spraying pearlescent or metal flake finishes onto a vehicle. It is impossible to know what effects will result unless the finish is seen on a surface. Air pressure, distance to the surface, amount of metallics, thinning, and other variables will change the visual appearance of the custom finish.

Custom Techniques

Custom painting starts with a careful preparation of the surface. The surface should be cleaned, sanded, and cleaned again to remove any traces of silicone or other debris.

White or black China markers or colored Sharpie permanent markers work well for outlining designs on the car finish. China Markers are easy to erase with a soft cloth. Isopropyl alcohol will remove Sharpie marks.

Masking is the most important part of custom painting. A variety of widths are needed. When outlining sharp curves or other intricate designs, a 1/8 in. (3 mm) tape is used. One frequently used custom painting technique is called *endless line,* Figure 20-7. After the surface has been prepared in the usual manner, 1/8 tape is applied in the desired design. Several coats of acrylic lacquer are then sprayed on the surface. Each coat must be allowed to dry thoroughly. The tape is then removed, and the surface is carefully wet sanded. Finally, a clearcoat is applied to level and protect the surface.

Painted *pinstripes* may be applied with *technical pens*, *roller guns,* or *pinstriping brushes.* These tools are also useful in making irregularly shaped or curved stripes. A strip of masking tape is sometimes used to assist in drawing straight lines. A special masking tape can be used for painting pinstripes. When this pre-cut tape has been placed on the surface, a clear film is peeled off to leave evenly spaced pieces of masking tape.

Plastic pinstripes (accent stripes) are adhesive backed tapes. These stripes come in a variety of colors, widths, and designs. They are applied in the same manner as overlays and decals described later. No wetting solutions are needed. See Figure 20-8.

Figure 20-6 Using masking tape to produce a special design.

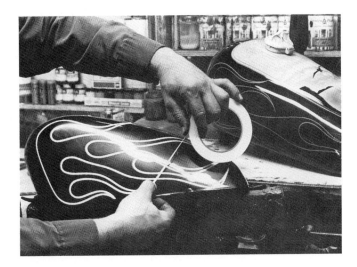

Figure 20-7 Applying endless line tape as a means of customizing.

Figure 20-8 Plastic pinstripes being applied to this vehicle. (Spartan International)

Flame designs are also popular, Figure 20-9. The flame-like design is produced using *stencils* and paint. Stencils are impervious materials (paper, cardboard, tape, plastic, frisket, etc.) in which designs have been cut. See Figure 20-10. Paint only strikes the surface through the openings in the stencil. Make certain that the stencil material is held securely against the surface if a sharp design is desired.

Once the flame design is painted on the surface, the stencil can be removed. An air brush can provide further color blending of the flame edge. Several customizing stencil designs are shown in Figure 20-11. In some cases, a *spray mask* can be applied to a surface. Once the mask dries, the design may be carefully cut (razor or X-Acto knife) through the mask film. The cut portion of the film is removed, and the paint is applied over the masked area.

Frisket paper or other adhesive-backed (shelf paper, tape) materials are often used as stencils. The protective backing paper is removed, and the paper or plastic is

Figure 20-11   Some popular forms of customizing stencils.

Figure 20-9   This vehicle has a custom flame design.

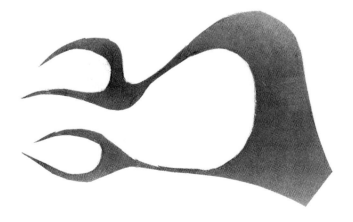

Figure 20-10   A special stencil is cut to form a flame.

applied to the surface. The design is then cut through the material as described in the section on spray masks. In some cases, the frisket material can be cut before it is applied to the surface. This technique in not practical on designs with many ''islands,'' such as letters.

Lace painting is a stencil technique in which various fabric lace designs are carefully stretched over the surface to be painted. Paint is then sprayed through the lace openings. After drying, the surface is wet sanded and a clearcoat is applied.

Spider webbing is an unusual custom painting technique. It is produced by forcing acrylic lacquer from the spray gun in the form of a fibrous thread. A base color coat is applied and followed by the spider web layer (fibrous thread). This layer is wet sanded, and a clearcoat is applied.

Shading is one of the most popular custom painting techniques. Shading is also known as *card masking.* Careful masking is very important when shading, since most of the material being sprayed will fall on the masking, not on the work area. A number of card shapes (squares, rounds, etc.) are arranged in the form of a fan, Figure 20-12. The outer edges may be even or staggered. The fan is held a few inches from the work surface, and the color is applied in a light fog around the edge of the masked surface. Most of the color will fall on the masked surface, and the overspray will create the shading effect. This step should be followed by wet sanding and the application of a clearcoat. Special templates can be used to produce shell, swirl, and quilt designs.

Figure 20-12 A card fan used to produce a zigzag design.

Overlays

Many late-model vehicles have overlays, transfers, decorative tapes, or protective moldings, which add a ''custom'' look. Some overlays provide a function, such as corrosion or abrasion protection.

Overlays are thin plastic layer(s) of material that are applied to various parts of the vehicle. They may have a wood-grain pattern, a multicolor design, or a solid stripe. Transparent (clear) polyurethane and polyvinyl overlays are sometimes placed on the lower body panels for abrasion and corrosion protection. Pressure-sensitive adhesives (dry tapes) and water- or alcohol-activated adhesives (wet) are used to apply these films. These ''dry'' and ''wet'' methods of installation are also used on other types of overlays.

Overlay Removal

If an old overlay material is to be removed, wood-grain remover and/or heat may be used. Remove the appropriate reveal moldings and mask off areas to be protected from the chemical remover. Spray on the wood-grain remover and allow the chemical to stand for about 10-15 minutes. A second application may be necessary to remove stubborn spots. With the aid of a putty knife or a plastic squeegee, begin peeling the film from the surface. Additional remover may be used to remove residual adhesive. Once the old overlay has been removed and the surface has been washed, sanded, and cleaned with solvent, a new overlay may be applied. Heat can be used to remove pressure-sensitive overlays.

Overlay Application

Before applying an overlay, make certain that the surface is smooth and clean. Small imperfections will show through the overlay. Always follow instructions for application provided by the manufacturer!

Application temperature should be between 70° and 90 °F (20-32 °C). Use heat lamps to warm the surface if necessary. Pieces of masking tape and paper can be used to help protect and guide the placement of the overlay.

Wet Method of Installation

It is important to pull the backing paper from the overlay. If the overlay is pulled from the backing paper, it may stretch or tear. It is best to remove the backing paper during the installation process.

Cut the overlay 1/2 in. (12 mm) larger than the area to be covered. Lay the overlay on a clean flat surface with the backing paper facing up. Hold the overlay firmly and remove the backing paper in a smooth motion. Under hot, humid conditions, a slight jerking motion may aid in removing the backing paper.

Thoroughly mix two or three level teaspoons (10-15 mL) of mild powdered household detergent in a gallon (4 L) of clean, warm water. This solution (wetting solution) will be used to help hold the overlay in place during installation.

Thoroughly wet the application surfaces (body and adhesive surface) with the wetting solution. Immediately apply the overlay (pattern out) to the vehicle. Adjust the overlay so that 1/2 in. (12 mm) of material shows beyond all edges. Apply the wetting solution to the outer surface of overlay. A spray bottle works well for this purpose.

Use a soft rubber or plastic squeegee to press on all flat surfaces with firm, over-lapping strokes. This will help to ensure proper adhesion and remove bubbles and wrinkles. See Figure 20-13. On vertical surfaces, work the entire top edge before progressing toward the bottom.

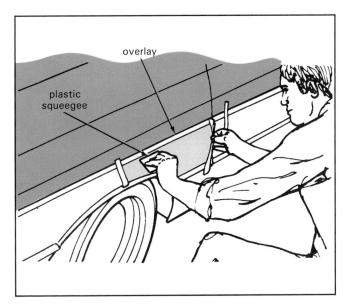

Figure 20-13 This technician is using a squeegee to smooth an overlay. (Ford)

On horizontal surfaces, start at the center and work toward the edges. Do not apply pressure to edges that will be wrapped around doors, fenders, gas cap areas, or to compound curve areas.

On flanges, brush a vinyl adhesive on the entire flange area. Avoid a lumpy build-up of adhesive under the transfer. Note in Figure 20-14, Section A-A is the break between the front fender and the front door; Section B-B is the break between the doors; and Section C-C is the break between the rear door and the rear fender.

Warm the unapplied overlay with a heat lamp and wrap it around the flange area. Avoid trapping air between the overlay and the panel when wrapping the overlay around the flange. Press the edge firmly with your fingers, making sure overlay overlaps the flange. Use a single-edge razor blade to trim off all material extending beyond the flange.

Press the flange area with a rubber roller or squeegee to be sure the overlay is well adhered to the metal surface.

For contoured areas, warm the unapplied overlay with a heat lamp. Working on a small area at a time, press and level off the small warm area. Repeat warming and pressing until the entire contoured surface adheres properly and is free of bubbles and wrinkles.

During application, inspect for blisters caused by trapped air or water. All blisters should be worked out with a squeegee or punctured with a sharp pin. See Figure 20-15. Do not run over a wrinkle with the squeegee. Try to realign or lift the section and remove the wrinkle. It is likely that a number of small bubbles will be trapped under the film. These bubbles are easily removed. Make certain that all edges are secured properly.

Finally, remove the pre-mask (if used) by pulling at 180° angle and again inspect the overlay for bubbles. The pre-mask is a protective covering on the outside surface of the overlay.

To install large decals by wet method, position the decal on the area to be decorated. Secure it with masking tape and mark the position with a pen or marker.

Mix a teaspoon of standard dish washing detergent in one gallon of water and fill a spray bottle with the solution. Remove the decal from the vehicle and lay it on a flat area with the backing paper facing up. Completely remove the backing paper from the decal.

Using the wetting solution (detergent and water), wet the adhesive side of the decal and the area of vehicle to be decorated. Position the decal on the vehicle and use a squeegee to apply a firm, overlapping pressure. See Figure 20-16. Begin at the center of the decal and squeegee toward the sides. If air bubbles appear, lift the decal

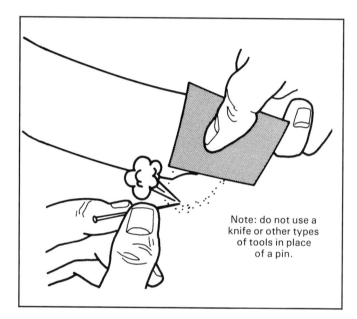

Note: do not use a knife or other types of tools in place of a pin.

Figure 20-15 A pin should be used when repairing an air bubble or blister. (Ford)

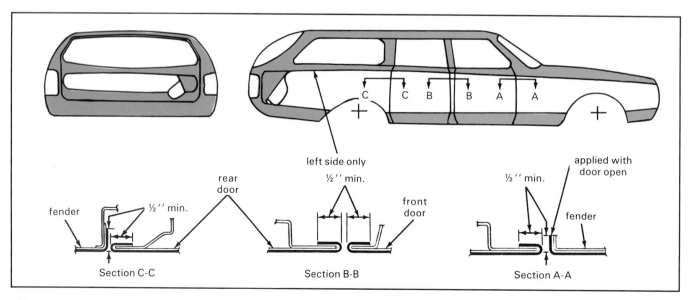

Figure 20-14 Application of wood-grain overlay.

Figure 20-16 This decal is being applied by the wet method. (Spartan International)

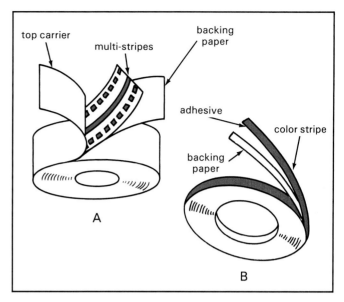

Figure 20-17 A–Multiple pinstripe tape shown with top carrier and backing paper. B–Single pinstripe tape with backing paper.

and reapply it. After the decal is in place, remove the pre-mask if necessary. Use a heat gun to mold the decal into recessed areas.

Dry Method of Installation

Small decals and pinstripes are often installed using the dry method. However, pinstripes that are more than 2 in. (50 mm) wide are more easily applied using the wet method of installation.

There are two basic types of pinstripe tape. One has a top carrier paper or layer and the other does not. See Figure 20-17. Both types are applied in a similar manner. The only difference is that the top carrier is removed after the stripe is firmly in place.

After cleaning the painted surface, align the pinstripe tape with the contour of the vehicle. Use masking tape to hold stripe in place. Grease pens are sometimes used to help mark the alignment position. After marking the pinstripe's position and cutting it to length, remove the stripe from the vehicle. Remove a few inches of backing paper from the pinstripe and apply the stripe to the vehicle with your fingers. The backing paper is removed by sharply bending the edge of pinstripe with your fingernail and peeling the paper from the stripe. Avoid touching the tape adhesive or the application area. Continue to remove the backing and apply the stripe along the guide marks. It is best to apply the tape in long lengths to achieve straight lines. Gently realign the tape as needed. See Figure 20-18.

Using a squeegee or rag, start from the center of the panel and press (burnish) the striping in place, working toward the end of the panel. Do not use your hands or fingers to smooth the pinstripe. This may create creases and air bubbles. See Figure 20-19.

Figure 20-18 This adhesive-backed stripe is being carefully applied to a vehicle. (Spartan International)

Figure 20-19 Note the use of a squeegee to rub the pinstripe in place. (Spartan International)

For pinstripe tapes with a top carrier, the carrier is removed and the striping is rubbed again with a squeegee or soft rag. Remove the top carrier by pulling at a 180° angle away from the stripe.

Small nicks or scratches in decals and pinstripes can be repaired with touch-up paints. To repair blisters or air bubbles, pierce them with sharp pin or needle. Work the trapped air out through the pinhole with your fingers. At the same time, press the decal firmly against the panel. If necessary, preheat the panel slightly to soften the adhesive and to remove wrinkles. Mold decals and striping in recessed areas using 750°F (400°C) heat gun and a soft, clean cloth.

Arrowheads or other designs may be made to end a stripe if desired. A razor blade or X-Acto knife is used to cut through the tape. Avoid cutting into the paint! See Figure 20-20.

Various aftermarket protective moldings are applied in a similar manner. They are sold in rolls of various widths and have an adhesive backing. The technician in Figure 20-21 is applying a special protective molding.

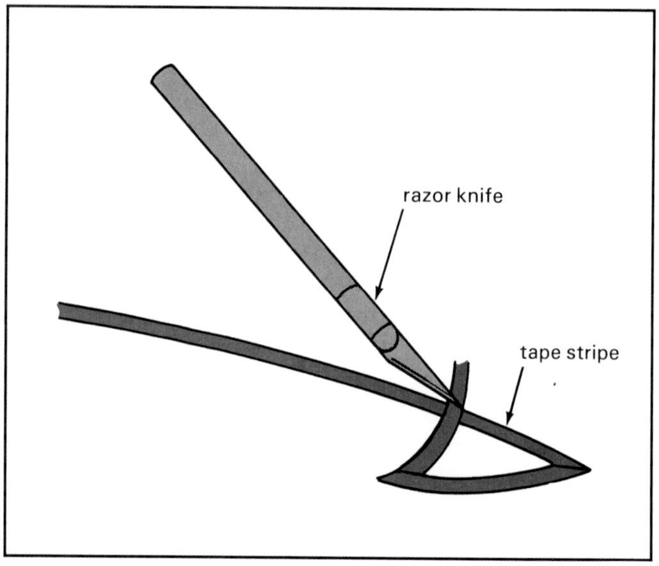

Figure 20-20 An arrowhead design is made by trimming a single pinstripe with a knife. The knife must not penetrate the finish.

Customizing Vehicle Bodies

Customizing bodies may include removing or adding moldings, sectioning a portion of the body, changing the basic shape of panels. In some cases, a complete body is constructed.

Customizing or altering the lines of automobile bodies can be accomplished by using epoxy resins and fiberglass. This work can range from simply filling in joints between panels to providing new body or panel lines.

When altering the lines of a body, the basic procedure is to first build a frame of wire mesh, polyurethane foam, polystyrene, cardboard, or other materials. The purpose of the wire mesh frame is to provide a form for a reinforced lay-up. Any material that is easily shaped and can withstand the chemicals of the resin system may be used for this purpose. Polyester resins will attack polystyrene foams. Wire mesh is easily shaped and can be welded, soldered, or held in position with screws. An epoxy resin and fiberglass reinforcement are then applied over the frame. When cured, the surface is sanded smooth and painted.

When **hooding** headlights or performing other tasks where custom parts are required for both sides of a vehicle, it is essential that the pieces be identical. This can be accomplished by making a male form. This form must be the exact shape desired.

The surface of the form should be sealed with a clear lacquer. When the lacquer is dry, the form should be coated with a parting agent or mold release. Polyvinyl alcohol and silicone-based waxes are commonly used for this purpose. The next step is to place a couple of laminations or layers of fiberglass material (mat) over the

Figure 20-21 This technician is applying a protective side molding.

form. When this has hardened, it can be lifted from the form and used as a mold. Make certain that sufficient layers of resin and reinforcement have been used to provide a stable, strong mold. This mold can be used to make as many identical lamp hoods, tail fins, wind scoops, etc., as desired.

Although the use of molds is preferred, many shops simply form fiberglass-reinforced custom parts directly on the vehicle.

Some shops specialize in sectioning and chopping vehicles. The term **chopping** describes the process of lowering a vehicle's profile. In this process, all pillars are shortened to lower the roof line. See Figure 20-22. In some designs, the body is lengthened or shortened. In others, a door is removed or different panels are used. In many vans, windows or observation ports are added.

Constructing Custom Bodies

Complete bodies are constructed in some shops. Most are metal or fiberglass ''shells'' that are placed on a chassis. Metal bodies (aluminum and mild steel) are generally fabricated and formed by hand. Fiberglass bodies can be made on a frame (form). The frame may be made by shaping wire, plaster, clay, plastic foam, or wood. This frame is then used to make a female mold. The female mold is used to produce the body. If a male part is made on a frame, the outside surface will be rough and the surface next to the mold will be smooth. If a female mold is used to make a male part, the outside (side next to mold) will be smooth and the inside will be rough. This is desirable because less finishing is required on the surface and additional reinforcements can be placed on the underside (rough) of the body.

Figure 20-23 shows the first step of making a frame. This frame consists of a series of plywood panels. The edge shapes are used to help form the basic design contour. The frame is covered with mesh or other materials to build the final contours. See Figure 20-24. The surface is carefully prepared and coated with a parting agent. See Figure 20-25. A female mold can be made from this frame. However, many choose to simply use the frame to achieve the final body shape. Several futuristic or stylized automobiles are shown in Figure 20-26.

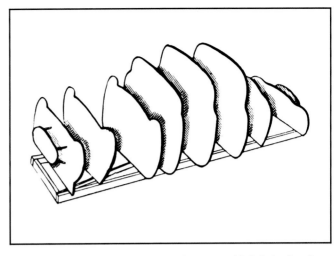

Figure 20-23 This skeleton frame, which is built of plywood, will be used as the basis for building a fiberglass body.

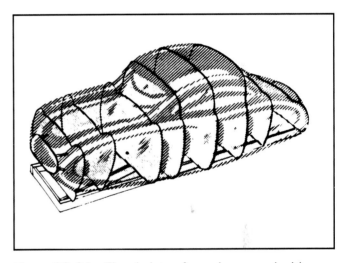

Figure 20-24 The skeleton frame is covered with chicken wire prior to the application of fiberglass.

Figure 20-22 The roof line of this vehicle has been lowered by removing a portion of the pillars.

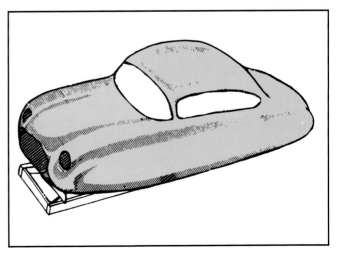

Figure 20-25 The completed body after application of fiberglass and preliminary sanding.

Figure 20-26 Futuristic or stylized automobiles. (Ford)

Know These Terms

Custom painting, Touch-up gun, Air brush, Striping tool, Roller gun, Striping brushes, Endless line, Pinstripes, Technical pens, Roller guns, Pinstriping brushes, Flame, Stencils, Spray mask, Frisket paper, Lace painting, Spider webbing, Shading, Card masking, Overlays, Hooding, Chopping.

Summary

Custom painting is the process of finishing or decorating a vehicle in a personalized manner. This type of work requires considerable experience and skill.

Spray guns, striping tools, brushes, tapes, transfers, and other equipment are used for custom painting. A touch-up gun is smaller than a conventional spray gun and is designed for general touch-up and small detail work. An air brush is very small and is used for fine detailing. Striping tools and striping brushes are used to apply pinstripes and other designs.

Although most finishes can be used for custom painting, acrylic lacquers are the most popular for design work. Polychromatic finishes are used extensively for design work. Common polychromatic finishes include candy-apple, pearlescent, and metal flake paints.

Custom painting should always start with careful surface preparation. White or black markers can be used to outline designs on the car's finish. Masking tape is commonly used in custom painting.

Painted pinstripes can be applied with technical pens, roller guns, or pinstriping brushes. A special masking tape is available to aid in painting pinstripes.

Plastic pinstripes are adhesive-backed tapes and are available in a variety of designs. Flame designs can be produced using stencils and paint. After the flame has been painted on a surface, an air brush can be used to blend the flame edge. In some cases, spray masks or frisket paper can be used as a stencil.

Lace painting involves stretching lace fabric over the surface to be painted. The lace serves as a stencil, and paint is sprayed through the lace openings. Spider webbing involves applying acrylic lacquer in the form of a fibrous thread. Shading is a technique the involves holding a masking card in front of the surface to be painted and allowing overspray from the gun to create the effect.

Many vehicles are equipped with overlays. Some overlays provide corrosion or abrasion protection. Old overlays can be removed with wood-grain remover or heat. Before applying a new overlay, make sure the surface is smooth and clean. The overlay should be cut 1 in. larger than the area to be covered. The application surfaces should be covered with a wetting solution, and the overlay should be applied. A soft squeegee can be used to work out air bubbles and ensure proper adhesion. A vinyl adhesive should be applied to the flange areas before applying the overlay. Heat can be used to help form the overlay around flanges.

Small decals and pinstripes are positioned using the dry method of installation. After cleaning the painted surface, align the pinstripe along the vehicle's contour. Secure the stripe with tape and mark its position with a grease pen. After cutting the pinstripe to length, remove a few inches of backing paper and apply the tape to the panel. After the stripe is applied, use a squeegee to press it in place.

Vehicle bodies are commonly customized by adding or removing moldings, sectioning a portion of the body, changing the basic shape of body panels. In some cases, a complete body can be constructed.

When altering the lines of a body, a frame is often covered with an epoxy resin and fiberglass reinforcement. When the fiberglass and epoxy cure, the surface can be sanded and painted. In cases where identical pieces must be constructed (lamp hoods, tail fins, etc.), a mold can be made to simplify the process. Although the use of molds is preferred, many shops simply form fiberglass-reinforced shapes directly on the vehicle.

Some shops specialize in sectioning and chopping vehicles. Chopping is the process of lowering a vehicle's profile. Some shops construct complete custom bodies. Metal bodies are generally fabricated by hand. Fiberglass bodies are often made on a frame. If desired, a frame can also be used to make a female mold. The mold is then used to create the final body. This method is desirable because it produces a relatively smooth outside surface.

Review Questions–Chapter 20

1. Custom painting may involve:
   a. animals.
   b. landscapes.
   c. geometric designs.
   d. all of the above.

2. A conventional spray gun is used for small detail work. True or False?

3. An _____ _____ has no spray pattern control.

4. Compressed air forces paint over the applicator wheel in a striping tool. True or False?

5. Acrylic enamels are the most popular finish used for custom design work. True or False?

6. Candy-apple and pearlescent finishes are types of _____-_____ paint systems.

7. When outlining intricate designs, 1/2 in. wide masking tape should be used. True or False?

8. Painted pinstripes can be applied with:
   a. roller guns.
   b. technical pens.
   c. pinstriping brushes.
   d. all of the above.

9. Thin plastic pinstripes are applied with a wetting solution. True or False?

10. Flame designs are commonly produced using:
    a. permanent markers.
    b. brushes.
    c. stencils.
    d. none of the above.

11. Overlays are thin layers of _____ material.

12. Old overlays can be removed by applying a special chemical remover. True or False?

13. After an overlay is applied, a soft _____ should be used to help remove bubbles and ensure proper adhesion.

14. Heat can be used to help place an overlay in a contoured area. True or False?

15. The protective covering on the outside surface of an overlay is called the:
    a. outer shield.
    b. barrier.
    c. pre-mask.
    d. none of the above.

16. Some stripe tapes have a _____ _____ paper, which must be removed after the tape is firmly in place.

17. Pinstripe tape should be applied in short lengths to achieve straight lines. True or False?

18. Customizing a car body may include:
    a. changing the shape of a panel.
    b. sectioning a portion of the body.
    c. removing moldings.
    d. all of the above.

19. Chopping is the process of raising a vehicle's profile. True or False?

20. Fiberglass bodies are commonly constructed on a _____.

Activities–Chapter 20

1. Attend a custom car show in your area and take photographs of cars customized with some of the techniques discussed in this chapter. Make a bulletin board display of your pictures, with the custom techniques identified.

2. Obtain stencil material, then design and cut a pattern for stencil application. Test your design on a scrap panel or a sheet of smooth cardboard.

3. Explore career opportunities in vehicle customizing and custom painting by interviewing one or more local shop operators who do such work. If such persons are not readily available to interview, do library research. Specialty automotive magazines frequently carry articles about, or interviews with, successful customizers.

4. Use drafting tools or a computer drawing program to develop a full-sized pattern that could be executed in striping tape on a car hood or trunk lid.

When a vehicle is involved in an accident, a police report is often required before the insurance company wil! process the claim. (Jack Klasey)

chapter 21

Estimating

After studying this chapter, you will be able to:

☐ List several kinds of estimates.

☐ Explain the differences between types of insurance claims.

☐ Outline the steps in making an estimate.

☐ Prepare a written estimate.

The Estimate

When a vehicle is damaged, the owner and any insurance companies that are involved may want to have an estimate of damages. The **estimate** will let the concerned parties know how much the repair will cost. Estimates may be for body repairs, glass replacement, refinishing, or other services.

The person who prepares the estimate, or the **estimator**, must have a thorough knowledge of vehicle construction and be experienced in auto body repair and refinishing. In addition, an estimator should have good interpersonal skills. He or she must deal directly with customers and insurance company representatives and must be able to maintain good working relationships with these people, Figure 21-1.

Normally, one person does the estimating for a body shop. It is vitally important that estimates be accurate, honest, and fair. The accuracy of the estimate determines the profit or loss for the shop. If the estimate is too high, it is likely that the shop will not get the job. Repair work will be taken to another shop. If an estimate is too low, the shop will have to absorb a loss. In other words, it will cost the shop more to do the job than it will receive in from the customer.

Figure 21-1 A customer is being greeted by the shop estimator.

Types of Estimates

There are four types of estimates made by the estimator, including:

☐ Visual estimates.

☐ Courtesy estimates.

☐ Noncompetitive estimates.

☐ Competitive estimates.

Visual Estimates

Visual estimates are simply experienced guesses by an estimator about the cost of repairing damage. An experienced estimator will normally be fairly close to the actual cost of repair. Visual estimates are not presented in written form and, therefore, are not *firm estimates*. This means that the auto body shop is under no obligation to perform the work for the amount estimated. Visual estimates may help customers decide about having damage repaired or decide about submitting a claim to the insurance company.

Courtesy Estimates

Courtesy estimates are more accurate than visual estimates and are presented to the customer in written form. The estimator uses various estimating aids to assist in arriving at material, labor, and other costs when preparing courtesy estimates.

As an example, an insurance company may ask a body shop to provide a courtesy estimate to verify that a vehicle is economically beyond repair. As another example, a customer may request a courtesy estimate to provide evidence to another party of how much it should cost to repair a certain damaged vehicle.

In general, a courtesy estimate is for record keeping purposes; a customer does not use it as a basis for deciding to proceed with a shop's services. Courtesy estimates are prepared without incentive to offer the best price, as the estimator will know in advance whether or not they will be doing the repair job. Generally, work does not come about from the courtesy estimate. Since the estimator may spend several hours writing a detailed estimate, repair shops often charge for courtesy estimates.

Noncompetitive Estimates

Noncompetitive estimates are usually done for minor damage. A customer is considering having the shop do the work. No claims are to be filed with an insurance company. Noncompetitive estimates are detailed and accurate. They are prepared with the help of various estimating aids.

As an example, a noncompetitive estimate may be requested for the cost of additional work not covered by an insurance policy. An insurance company, for instance, may be willing to pay for painting of damaged areas only and not for the entire vehicle. Some customers would like to have the whole car painted rather than a spot repair. In this case, a noncompetitive estimate would be given to the customer. It would be in writing. It would describe the work to be done and would present the total cost to be paid by the customer.

Competitive Estimates

This type of estimate is the most common. Often, an insurance company will ask that three written estimates be obtained for a damage claim. These **competitive estimates** are so named because different shops are independently competing for the work. The shop estimator knows that the detailed estimate has been requested by an insurance company and that it will be compared to others. The estimator tries to offer the most favorable terms. In Figure 21-2, the shop estimator is examining damage and making an estimate for repair.

Some insurance companies will have one of their own representatives help determine if estimates are accurate. This person is called an **adjuster** (appraiser). The adjuster's job is to approve collision repairs and see that the customer's vehicle is being repaired to pre-collision condition.

Adjusters sometimes alter, or *adjust*, estimates to negotiate a final cost that is acceptable to the insurance company. For example, it may be felt that used parts

Figure 21-2 An estimator examines a damaged vehicle.

would be more appropriate than new ones or that too much labor has been charged to repair a panel. The adjuster may discover that the markup on parts is too great and may seek an adjustment. **Markup** is the amount that the shop adds to its costs to determine selling price. It is *gross profit*, which covers *overhead expenses*, such items as rent and supplies, and provides *net profit.*

Insurance

Much of the work of an auto body shop is done for insurance companies. Experienced estimators will be knowledgeable in many of the operations of insurance companies. Although the estimators are not concerned with who was at fault, they should be familiar with the basic types of insurance coverage.

Types of Insurance Coverage

There are four broad types of *vehicle* insurance coverage that specifically cover damage to personal property resulting from an accident involving one or more vehicles. These are categorized according to who owns the vehicle and who or what was at fault. The coverage types are:

☐ Liability.

☐ Collision.

☐ Comprehensive.

☐ No-fault.

Liability Insurance

Automotive **liability insurance** covers the policyholder, or *insured*, on damages to personal property of others, not the insured's. The insurance company will pay up to a certain amount of money to the other party to repair or replace the damaged property. It pays for damage repair on the other vehicle, or if the insured's vehicle runs into a building, for example, it pays the cost of having the building repaired.

Collision Insurance

Collision insurance covers property damages sustained by the insured as a result of a collision. Thus, it pays for damage repair on the insured's vehicle. Most policies have a stated **deductible**. Deductible amounts vary from $100–$500. The insured pays the amount of the deductible. The insurance company, then, pays all repair charges exceeding the amount of the deductible that are covered by the policy.

Comprehensive Insurance

Comprehensive insurance covers damages not covered by liability or collision insurance policies, such as hail or other storm damage. In addition, fire and theft coverage is included as part of some comprehensive options.

No-Fault Insurance

In coverages discussed thus far, damage repairs are paid by the insurance company of the driver who was at fault. For example, if driver B was at fault, any damage to driver A's vehicle is paid for by driver B's liability coverage. It is not paid for by driver A's collision coverage. (Driver A's *uninsured motorist* coverage would pay if driver B had no insurance.)

Some states now require **no-fault insurance**. This type of insurance covers the insured's vehicle (and/or personal injury) *only*, regardless of who caused the accident. The insurance company does not pay for damages sustained by the other driver. The other driver must carry his or her own no-fault insurance to be covered in the event of an accident.

Making an Estimate

There are a number of steps that are used to complete an estimate. They include the following:

1. Before making a written estimate, the estimator must obtain some preliminary information about the owner (name, address, phone number, insurance company, etc.) and about the vehicle (make, model, VIN, etc.). The estimator must not become involved in who was at fault or what caused the accident. This is between the insured and the insurance

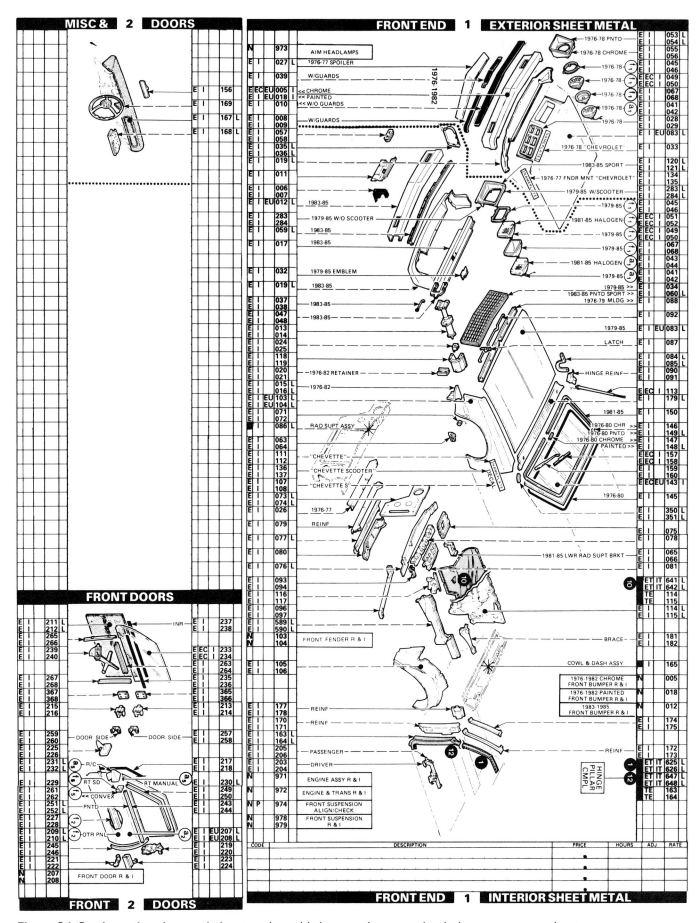

Figure 21-3   An estimating worksheet such as this is sometimes used to help prepare an estimate. (Automatic Data Processing, Collision Service Division)

company. This is a good time to inquire about insurance coverage and how deductible or full payment will be made.

2. Thoroughly analyze the damage. It is essential that the estimator does not overlook **secondary damage**, which is damage that occurs at areas other than the primary impact zone. Secondary damage is often hidden. Check to see if a dent in the rear panel, for example, was a result of the front-end collision. If it is determined to be unrelated to the accident, insurance will not pay for this repair.

   In the analyzing process, the question is asked whether or not the vehicle is worth fixing. A severely damaged vehicle may be declared a **total loss**. When this occurs, the vehicle is often said to be *totaled*. This means repair will be very close to or exceed the value of the vehicle. In general, older vehicles are more likely to be declared a total loss. They have reduced value, and parts are more difficult to find.

   To determine whether a car should be repaired or whether it should be declared a total loss, it will be necessary to determine the value of a similar vehicle. The **average retail value** is commonly used for this purpose. Determining a fair and realistic value requires honest research into recent vehicle sales.

   Several sources can be used to determine the value of a vehicle, including local newspapers, car dealers, and used car price guides. Latest average retail values based on actual sales reports from car dealers are published in used car price guides. One such guide is *NADA Official Used Car Guide*, commonly referred to as the *Blue Book*. In helping to determine average retail value, such guides take into consideration the make, year, model, mileage, options, and condition of a vehicle.

3. If the decision is made to fix the car, a detailed inspection must be conducted, taking note of all damage, and a written estimate must be prepared. Carefully list all the parts that are needed. This might include new panels, emblems, molding, and glass. Group components together by zone.

   Use a sequential inspection system. Check the primary impact zone first, then, proceed around the vehicle. Take note of door, fender, and panel alignment. Doors that do not close properly or uneven gaps between panels may indicate hidden damage. Check the underside of the vehicle for possible damage to frame or drivetrain. It may be necessary to **sublet**, or have other shops do, alignment or mechanical repairs. Next, inspect the engine compartment and the passenger compartment. See if energy-absorbing bumpers, air bags, or other safety features are working. If the vehicle is drivable, check to see that steering system, brake system, and other mechanical systems are operating properly.

Some estimators use a commercial collision service form or worksheet when examining damage. This type of worksheet helps identify construction details and individual components. See Figure 21-3.

Sometimes, hidden damage may be suspected, but it cannot be verified until the repair work is underway. In such cases, it may be necessary to indicate on the estimate that the final cost of repair (bid) is to be left open. This is referred to as an **open bid**. This indicates to the insurance company that it may be necessary to replace a part, but it cannot be determined until the actual repair begins.

Insurance companies prefer to have a **closed bid** rather than leave the final cost undetermined. With an open bid, if a replacement part becomes required during repair, the cost must be added to the original estimate. Insurance companies refer to this unveiled damage and the additional charge as **overage.**

4. Carefully determine the cost, part number, and source of each part. Used parts may be used when appropriate. Be certain that part shipping and handling charges are included. Determine the standard labor hours, or **flat-rate time**, which includes time for replacement, repair, and refinishing. Information should be accurately recorded on the estimate form.

   Collision manuals (crash manuals) are valuable sources of information. These and other estimating aids may indicate replacement cost of parts. (Part prices are normally very similar.) These aids also give guidelines on how long it will take to repair or replace a part. A typical page from a collision manual is shown in Figure 21-4. Be careful in your efforts. Any mistakes here can make the difference between profit and loss.

   There are several frequently used terms concerning labor hours that are encountered when using collision manuals. The estimator must be familiar with them and their abbreviations. These commonly used terms include:

   ☐ **Remove and reinstall (R&I).** This means an item must be removed to gain access to another part and is later reinstalled. As an example, a listing for *R&I door* might be given at 1.5 hours. This indicates the total amount of time required to remove a door and to reinstall it.

   ☐ **Remove and repair (R&R).** This means damaged parts are removed, repaired, and reinstalled. Old parts are removed, salvageable items are transferred to a new part, and the new part is installed.

   ☐ **Overhaul (O/H).** This means an assembly is removed, cleaned, and inspected. Damaged portions of the assembly are replaced, and the assembly is reinstalled.

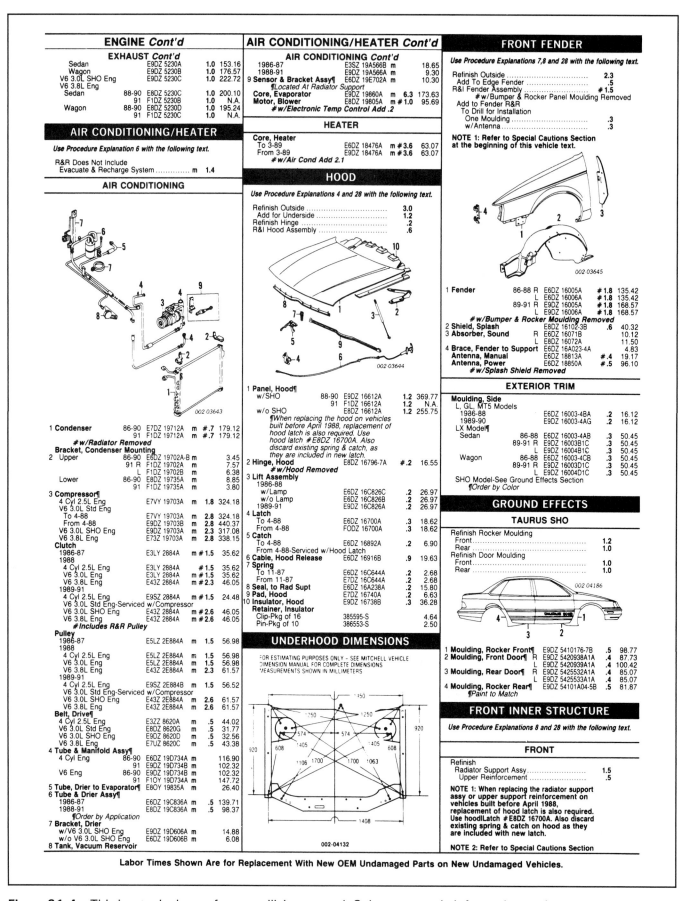

ENGINE Cont'd

EXHAUST Cont'd

Sedan	E9DZ 5230A		1.0	153.16
Wagon	E9DZ 5230B		1.0	176.57
V6 3.0L SHO Eng	E9DZ 5230C		1.0	222.72
V6 3.8L Eng				
Sedan 88-90	E8DZ 5230C		1.0	200.10
91	F1DZ 5230B		1.0	N.A.
Wagon 88-90	E8DZ 5230D		1.0	195.24
91	F1DZ 5230C		1.0	N.A.

AIR CONDITIONING/HEATER

Use Procedure Explanation 6 with the following text.

R&R Does Not Include
  Evacuate & Recharge System .... m **1.4**

AIR CONDITIONING

1 Condenser 86-90	E7DZ 19712A	m	**#.7**	179.12
91	F1DZ 19712A	m	**#.7**	179.12
# w/Radiator Removed				
Bracket, Condenser Mounting				
2 Upper 86-90	E6DZ 19702A-B	m		3.45
91	F1DZ 19702A	m		7.57
L	F1DZ 19702B			6.38
Lower 86-90	E8DZ 19735A	m		8.85
91	F1DZ 19735A	m		3.80
3 Compressor¶				
4 Cyl 2.5L Eng	E7VY 19703A	m	**1.8**	324.18
V6 3.0L Std Eng				
To 4-88	E7VY 19703A	m	**2.8**	324.18
From 4-88	E9DZ 19703B	m	**2.8**	440.37
V6 3.0L SHO Eng	E9DZ 19703A	m	**2.3**	317.08
V6 3.8L Eng	E73Z 19703A	m	**2.8**	338.15
Clutch				
1986-87	E3LY 2884A	m	**1.5**	35.62
1988				
4 Cyl 2.5L Eng	E3LY 2884A		**#1.5**	35.62
V6 3.0L Eng	E3LY 2884A	m	**#1.5**	35.62
V6 3.8L Eng	E43Z 2884A	m	**#2.3**	46.05
1989-91				
4 Cyl 2.5L Eng	E9SZ 2884A	m	**#1.5**	24.48
V6 3.0L Std Eng-Serviced w/Compressor				
V6 3.0L SHO Eng	E43Z 2884A	m	**#2.6**	46.05
V6 3.8L Eng	E43Z 2884A	m	**#2.6**	46.05
# Includes R&R Pulley				
Pulley				
1986-87	E5LZ 2E884A		**1.5**	56.98
1988				
4 Cyl 2.5L Eng	E5LZ 2E884A	m	**1.5**	56.98
V6 3.0L Eng	E5LZ 2E884A	m	**1.5**	56.98
V6 3.8L Eng	E43Z 2E884A	m	**2.3**	61.57
1989-91				
4 Cyl 2.5L Eng	E9SZ 2E884B	m	**1.5**	56.52
V6 3.0L Std Eng-Serviced w/Compressor				
V6 3.0L SHO Eng	E43Z 2E884A	m	**2.6**	61.57
V6 3.8L Eng	E43Z 2E884A	m	**2.6**	61.57
Belt, Drive¶				
4 Cyl 2.5L Eng	E3ZZ 8620A	m	**.5**	44.02
V6 3.0L Std Eng	E8DZ 8620G		**.5**	31.77
V6 3.0L SHO Eng	E9DZ 8620D	m	**.5**	32.56
V6 3.8L Eng	E7UZ 8620C		**.5**	43.38
4 Tube & Manifold Assy¶				
4 Cyl Eng 86-90	E6DZ 19D734A	m		116.90
91	E9DZ 19D734B	m		102.32
V6 Eng 86-90	E9DZ 19D734B	m		102.32
91	F1OY 19D734A	m		147.72
5 Tube, Drier to Evaporator¶	E8OY 19835A	m		26.40
6 Tube & Drier Assy¶				
1986-87	E6DZ 19C836A	m	**.5**	139.71
1988-91	E8DZ 19C836A	m	**.5**	98.37
¶Order by Application				
7 Bracket, Drier				
w/V6 3.0L SHO Eng	E9DZ 19D606A	m		14.88
w/o V6 3.0L SHO Eng	E6DZ 19D606B	m		6.08
8 Tank, Vacuum Reservoir				

AIR CONDITIONING/HEATER Cont'd

AIR CONDITIONING Cont'd

1986-87	E3SZ 19A566B	m		18.65
1988-91	E9DZ 19A566A	m		9.30
9 Sensor & Bracket Assy¶	E6DZ 19E702A	m		10.30
¶Located At Radiator Support				
Core, Evaporator	E9DZ 19860A	m	**6.3**	173.63
Motor, Blower	E8DZ 19805A	m	**#1.0**	95.69
# w/Electronic Temp Control Add .2				

HEATER

Core, Heater				
To 3-89	E6DZ 18476A	m	**#3.6**	63.07
From 3-89	E9DZ 18476A	m	**#3.6**	63.07
# w/Air Cond Add 2.1				

HOOD

Use Procedure Explanations 4 and 28 with the following text.

Refinish Outside	**3.0**
Add for Underside	**1.2**
Refinish Hinge	**.2**
R&I Hood Assembly	**.6**

002-03644

1 Panel, Hood¶					
w/SHO	88-90	E9DZ 16612A		1.2	369.77
	91	F1DZ 16612A		1.2	N.A.
w/o SHO		E8DZ 16612A		1.2	255.75

¶When replacing the hood on vehicles built before April 1988, replacement of hood latch is also required. Use hood latch #E8DZ 16700A. Also discard existing spring & catch, as they are included in new latch.

2 Hinge, Hood		E8DZ 16796-7A		**#.2**	16.55
# w/Hood Removed					
3 Lift Assembly					
1986-88					
w/Lamp		E6DZ 16C826C		.2	26.97
w/o Lamp		E6DZ 16C826B		.2	26.97
1989-91		E6DZ 16C826A		.2	26.97
4 Latch					
To 4-88		E6DZ 16700A		.3	18.62
From 4-88		FODZ 16700A		.3	18.62
5 Catch					
To 4-88		E6DZ 16892A		.2	6.90
From 4-88-Serviced w/Hood Latch					
6 Cable, Hood Release		E6DZ 16916B		.9	19.63
7 Spring					
To 11-87		E6DZ 16C644A		.2	2.68
From 11-87		E7DZ 16C644A		.2	2.68
8 Seal, to Rad Supt		E6DZ 16A238A		.2	15.80
9 Pad, Hood		E7DZ 16740A		.2	6.63
10 Insulator, Hood		E9DZ 16738B		.5	36.28
Retainer, Insulator					
Clip-Pkg of 16		385595-S			4.64
Pin-Pkg of 10		386553-S			2.50

UNDERHOOD DIMENSIONS

FOR ESTIMATING PURPOSES ONLY – SEE MITCHELL VEHICLE DIMENSION MANUAL FOR COMPLETE DIMENSIONS MEASUREMENTS SHOWN IN MILLIMETERS

002-04132

FRONT FENDER

Use Procedure Explanations 7,8 and 28 with the following text.

Refinish Outside	**2.3**
Add To Edge Fender	**.5**
R&I Fender Assembly	**# 1.5**
# w/Bumper & Rocker Panel Moulding Removed	
Add to Fender R&R	
To Drill for Installation	
One Moulding	**.3**
w/Antenna	**.3**

NOTE 1: Refer to Special Cautions Section at the beginning of this vehicle text.

002-03645

1 Fender	86-88	R	E6DZ 16005A	**#1.8**	135.42
		L	E6DZ 16006A	**#1.8**	135.42
	89-91	R	E9DZ 16005A	**#1.8**	168.57
		L	E9DZ 16006A	**#1.8**	168.57
# w/Bumper & Rocker Moulding Removed					
2 Shield, Splash			E8DZ 16102-3B	**.6**	40.32
3 Absorber, Sound		R	E6DZ 16071B		10.12
		L	E8DZ 16072A		11.50
4 Brace, Fender to Support			E6DZ 16A023-4A		4.83
Antenna, Manual			E6DZ 18813A	**#.4**	19.17
Antenna, Power			E8DZ 18850A	**#.5**	96.10
# w/Splash Shield Removed					

EXTERIOR TRIM

Moulding, Side					
L, GL, MT5 Models					
1986-88			E6DZ 16003-4BA	.2	16.12
1989-90			E9DZ 16003-4AG	.2	16.12
LX Model¶					
Sedan	86-88		E6DZ 16003-4AB	.3	50.45
	89-91		E9DZ 16003B1C	.3	50.45
		L	E9DZ 16004B1C	.3	50.45
Wagon	86-88		E6DZ 16003-4CB	.3	50.45
	89-91	R	E9DZ 16003D1C	.3	50.45
		L	E9DZ 16004D1C	.3	50.45

SHO Model-See Ground Effects Section
¶Order by Color

GROUND EFFECTS

TAURUS SHO

Refinish Rocker Moulding	
Front	**1.2**
Rear	**1.0**
Refinish Door Moulding	
Front	**1.0**
Rear	**1.0**

002-04186

1 Moulding, Rocker Front¶			E9DZ 5410176-7B	**.5**	98.77
2 Moulding, Front Door¶		R	E9DZ 5420938A1A	**.4**	87.73
		L	E9DZ 5420939A1A	**.4**	100.42
3 Moulding, Rear Door¶		R	E9DZ 5425532A1A	**.4**	85.07
		L	E9DZ 5425533A1A	**.4**	85.07
4 Moulding, Rocker Rear¶			E9DZ 54101A04-5B	**.5**	81.87
¶Paint to Match					

FRONT INNER STRUCTURE

Use Procedure Explanations 8 and 28 with the following text.

FRONT

Refinish	
Radiator Support Assy..............	**1.5**
Upper Reinforcement	**.5**

NOTE 1: When replacing the radiator support assy or upper support reinforcement on vehicles built before April 1988, replacement of hood latch is also required. Use hood latch #E8DZ 16700A. Also discard existing spring & catch on hood as they are included with new latch.

NOTE 2: Refer to Special Cautions Section

Labor Times Shown Are for Replacement With New OEM Undamaged Parts on New Undamaged Vehicles.

Figure 21-4 This is a typical page from a collision manual. Columns contain information such as part numbers, labor hours (boldface type), and part costs. Illustrations of car parts help in part number identification. (Mitchell International)

In addition to collision *manuals*, some shops keep current pricing data on *microfilm* or *microfiche*. These reference aids keep information on film rather than on paper. Since information is stored on a reduced scale, pages of information are contained on a single roll or small sheet of film. Film readers are used to enlarge the contents of the microfilm or microfiche so that the information may be read. See Figure 21-5.

Computerized information systems have replaced manuals and microfilm in many shops. Computers are fast and easy to use, and they result in fewer errors. Software is available to add applicable sales taxes, list the parts and numbers, calculate labor, and note other vital information. Information for the specific job is entered into the computer. The computer performs all required calculations and determines the total cost. A printout of the completed estimate is obtained, and information concerning the particular estimate is stored in the computer for future reference.

Various companies offer specialized computer systems that capture, integrate, and transmit detailed color photographs of vehicle damage to support a computerized estimate. The estimator or technician can send the digital photographs of the damage, as well as the estimated cost of parts and labor, directly to major insurance companies. This saves time, minimizes errors, and helps document damage. Insurance companies can quickly respond to the estimator's electronic transmission of the damage and estimate. Electronic approval or further communications for clarification can be made quickly. This greatly improves the speed with which estimators and technicians turn out their work.

Estimates must reflect current pricing information. All systems must be updated periodically. New models, price increases, availability of parts, and other relevant information must be kept current. If it is not, the estimator may lose the repair job for the shop by overbidding. Perhaps even more likely, the estimator will cause the shop to lose money by underbidding the job.

5. Adjust labor hours. Estimated labor hours for any given task will most likely vary between shops; adjust labor hours for specific shop conditions. The labor times given in Figure 21-4 are for replacement with new OEM, undamaged parts. Experience, number of skilled workers, and availability of modern repair equipment are all factors that will influence the labor hours required. Undetected damage and new parts versus used parts will also affect the flat-rate times.

Note that some used parts have rust, previous repairs, or other damage that may require additional labor charges. The estimator should factor in additional time for labor if used parts are estimated. The condition of used parts is of utmost importance, and parts managers must seek used parts in the best possible condition to minimize labor costs.

Labor hours determined on part-by-part basis result in some **overlap**, or unnecessary duplication of tasks. As a result, estimated times will be higher than actual installation times. Labor hours should be reduced to account for overlap; if not, the estimate may be out of line with the competing estimates. As an example, consider removal and repair of a fender and a wheel house. A deduction should be taken for overlap because many of the bolts that secure the fender, also hold the wheel house in place. The time allotted for the bolting task should reflect this.

Indicate labor hours for **customer-requested (C/R)** repairs, to differentiate them from repairs that the insurance company will authorize. Insurance companies normally do not pay for C/R repairs. C/R repairs frequently include rust repair, two-tone finish, or refinishing an entire vehicle (rather than a spot repair).

6. Once all necessary adjustments have been made to labor hours, the *cost* for labor is calculated. Various hourly rates are multiplied by the number of hours for specific tasks. For example, straightening may be charged at a rate of $25 per hour. Finishing, installing glass, and welding may be charged at a rate of $30 per hour. In addition, an overhead and miscellaneous expense allowance may be charged to the job. Generally, this allowance is calculated by multiplying some flat rate per hour by the total estimated hours.

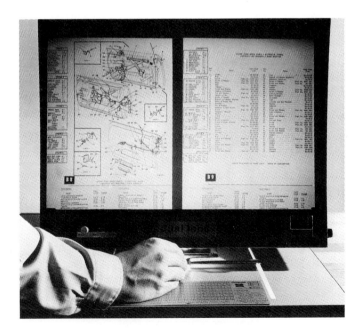

Figure 21-5 A film reader is being used to obtain pricing information stored on microfiche. (Chrysler)

THORNRIDGE MOTORS

"WE MEET BY ACCIDENT"

NAME Joe Smith	ADDRESS 123 Maple St.		PHONE 555-0604	DATE
YEAR 93	MAKE Escort	MODEL 4dr. HB	LICENSE No. 456 555	SPEEDOMETER 12,059

MTR No.
SER No. 1FAPP9596LK1171378

INSURANCE CARRIER New American Ins.	ADJUSTER George	PHONE 555-1466	CAR LOCATED AT Town Garage

OPERATIONS	PART No.	PARTS	LABOR
Replace rear bumper (w/strip)	0473J	494 06	3 7
Replace rear bumper chrome strip	0473J-A	36 35	
Repair rt. rear ¼ panel and wheelhouse panel			12 3
Replace rt. rear ¼ panel strip (paint on)			4
Repair rt. rear door			5 5
Replace rt. rear wheel cover	1574C2	64 98	
Repair rt. rear door lower side molding (reglue)			3
Repair corrosion protection		12 00	5
Paint		114 80	
Shop supplies		28 70	
overlap on refinish			(-) 4
			22 3
Labor 22.3 hours @ $28.00 per hour			

INSURED PAYS $ 250   INS. CO. PAYS 1250.45   R. O. No. _____

INS. CHECK PAYABLE TO Thornridge Motors

The above is an estimate, based on our inspection, and does not cover additional parts or labor which may be required after the work has been opened up. Occasionally, after work has started, worn, broken or damaged parts are discovered which are not evident on first inspection. Quotations on parts and labor are current and subject to change.

EST. MADE BY Mike Johnson

AUTHORIZATION FOR REPAIR. You are hereby authorized to make the above specified repairs to the car described herein

SIGNED Joe Smith _____ DATE _____

	PARTS	LABOR
TOTALS	752 89	624 40
WRECKER SERVICE		25 00
TAX	52 70	45 46
	805 59	694 86
TOTAL OF ESTIMATE	1500	45

Figure 21-6 Example of an estimate.

Rather than having a rate for different jobs such as straightening, frame alignment, etc., many shops charge a *flat labor rate*. This combines all different pay rates into a single hourly rate. Usually, the flat labor rate includes an overhead allowance to cover rags, sandpaper, equipment maintenance, utilities, etc. It also has profit built in. The flat labor rate is multiplied by the total hours to determine the total labor cost.

Some body shops sublet portions of the work. When this occurs, it should be clearly indicated on the estimate form and figured into the cost of the job.

7. Total the dollar amount of the estimate for parts, labor, and other expenses. Include a part discount when appropriate. Do not forget to include taxes. Accurately recalculate all computations and total the estimate. Do this work before the adjuster arrives. An estimate is shown in Figure 21-6.

8. The estimator must sign and date the estimate. Normally, estimates are honored for 30 days. A copy of the estimate is then given to the customer or insurance company, and one copy is kept on file in the office.

9. No matter who pays for the repair—owner or insurance company—make certain that authorization is made in writing before the parts are ordered. Make it clear to the customer that it is his or her responsibility to see that the bill is paid in full.

Summary

When a vehicle is damaged, the customer and/or any insurance companies that are involved may want to have an estimate of damages. The estimate will let the concerned parties know how much the repair will cost.

The estimator must have a thorough knowledge of vehicle construction and be experienced in auto body repair and refinishing. In addition, an estimator should have good interpersonal skills. The accuracy of the estimate determines the profit or loss for the shop.

There are four types of estimates. Visual estimates are experienced guesses by an estimator about the cost of repairing damage. These are the least accurate. In general, a courtesy estimate is for record keeping purposes; a customer does not use it as a basis for deciding to proceed with a shop's services. Noncompetitive estimates are prepared for customers in need of minor damage repair, where an insurance company will not be involved. Competitive estimates are prepared for insurance companies, where competing body shops try to offer the most favorable terms in order to be awarded the repair job.

Adjusters are insurance company representatives. They work with estimators in trying to negotiate a final cost that is acceptable to the insurance company.

Before making a written estimate, an estimator must obtain preliminary information about the owner, vehicle, and insurance company. The damage is then thoroughly analyzed, and it is determined if it is economically feasible to repair the damage. A severely damaged vehicle may be totaled. This means repair will be very close to or exceed the value of the vehicle.

If the decision is made to fix the car, a detailed inspection must be conducted, and a written estimate must be prepared. Use a sequential inspection system. Check the primary impact zone first, then, proceed around the vehicle. Do not overlook secondary damage. Carefully list all the parts that are needed.

Determine the cost, part number, and source of each part. Also, determine the flat-rate time. Collision manuals are valuable sources of information. These and other estimating aids may indicate replacement cost of parts and give guidelines on how long it will take to repair or replace a part. Labor hours must be adjusted for specific shop conditions and other circumstances, such as for use of used parts and for overlap.

Once all necessary adjustments have been made to labor hours, the cost for labor is calculated. Many shops charge a flat labor rate, which combines all different pay rates into a single hourly rate and also includes overhead and profit. The flat labor rate is multiplied by the total hours to determine the total labor cost.

Total the dollar amount of the estimate for parts, labor, and any other expenses, such as subcontract work. Do not forget to include taxes. The estimator must sign and date the estimate, give a copy to the customer or insurance company, and keep one on file in the office.

No matter who pays for the repair, make certain that authorization is made in writing before the parts are ordered. Make it clear to the customer that it is his or her responsibility to see that the bill is paid in full.

Know These Terms

Estimate, Estimator, Visual estimate, Courtesy estimate, Noncompetitive estimate, Competitive estimate, Adjuster, Markup, Liability insurance, Collision insurance, Deductible, Comprehensive insurance, No-fault insurance, Secondary damage, Total loss, Average retail value, Sublet, Open bid, Closed bid, Overage, Flat-rate time, Collision manuals, Remove and reinstall (R&I), Remove and repair (R&R), Overhaul (O/H), Overlap, Customer requested (C/R), Flat labor rate.

Review Questions–Chapter 21

1. Estimators need not have strong interpersonal skills because they work strictly with numbers. True or False?

2. Estimates must be accurate since they affect an auto body shop's profit and loss. True or False?

3. The insurance _____ approves collision repairs and sees that the customer's vehicle is being repaired to pre-collision condition.

4. _____ estimates are simply experienced guesses.

5. When an insurance company asks the insured to obtain three estimates, it is asking for:
   a. definitive estimates.
   b. courtesy estimates.
   c. noncompetitive estimates.
   d. competitive estimates.

6. The first step in making an estimate is to carefully determine the cost, part number, installation time, and source of each part. True or False?

7. When analyzing vehicle damage, it is important to look for hidden damage. True or False?

8. A car is _____ when estimated cost of the repair exceeds the value of the vehicle.

9. The chief advantage of using a computer to do estimating is that estimated total costs are always equal to actual costs at job completion. True or False?

10. Experience and availability of modern repair equipment will most likely affect:
   a. material cost.
   b. labor cost.
   c. overlap.
   d. average retail cost.

Activities—Chapter 21

1. Check an insurance bill for your automobile (or your parents') to determine the kinds of coverage being paid for. Often, the different coverages (liability, un-insured motorist, road service) are shown as letter codes. The codes may be explained on the back of the bill or in the policy itself.

2. Select two cars of different makes but approximately the same size (sub-compact, compact, mid-size) as examples. Use a collision manual to determine the cost of parts and the approximate time it would take to replace the rear bumper on each of the cars. Also determine cost and time to replace a damaged headlight assembly (lenses, trim, reflector, bulb—assume no damage to adjoining panels). Compare the costs for the two cars in both instances. Are they fairly similar, or is there considerable difference? If costs are different, what do you feel is the reason?

3. Videotape an estimator as he or she works, showing the damage and the filling out of the estimating form. Ask the estimator to discuss what he or she is doing while performing the action. Show the tape to the class.

chapter 22

Career Opportunities

After studying this chapter, you will be able to:

☐ List various job opportunities in the auto body field.

☐ Explain the duties of some of the positions in auto body repair.

☐ List several advantages and disadvantages of working in a body shop.

☐ List several ways in which body shop personnel are paid.

☐ Cite the advantages and disadvantages of entrepreneurship.

Body Shop Personnel

There are many vehicles on the road today that need auto body repair. The number of vehicles continues to increase each year. Generally, vehicle owners cannot have their cars fixed immediately. Many auto body shops are booked a month in advance. Some shops have difficulty finding qualified auto body technicians. These situations show a great need for additional auto body technicians and related personnel.

There are a variety of jobs associated with auto body repair and refinishing. Not all of these jobs are in the auto body shop. Job or career opportunities in the auto body field include:

☐ Apprentice.

☐ Auto body technician.

☐ Alignment specialist.

☐ Glass installer.

☐ Upholsterer.

☐ Paint technician.

☐ Parts manager.

☐ Estimator.

☐ Manager.

☐ Insurance adjuster.

☐ Sales representative.

☐ Instructor.

Apprentice

An **apprentice** learns a trade by working under the supervision of a skilled technician while also receiving classroom training. Auto body skills may be learned by working at a local body shop or through vocational/technical school programs.

The apprentice in a body and paint shop usually starts by sweeping the floor, assisting in removing and installing parts, sanding, and masking. This affords a priceless opportunity for observing how work progresses in restoring vehicles to their proper condition.

The apprentice is commonly asked to bring needed tools to the job. An alert apprentice is soon able to anticipate the need for a special item. Competently doing these simple jobs is the basis for advancement to more challenging work.

Generally, three to four years of on-the-job training are required to become a fully qualified auto body technician. **On-the-job training** occurs when the worker learns the trade from experienced technicians while partaking in the repair process. During this time, the tasks the apprentice must complete progressively become more difficult. In addition, the apprentice is expected to accumulate hand tools while gaining experience. See Figure 22-1.

The experience gained as an apprentice makes the technician more marketable. With technical skills, a pleasant personality, and a good work ethic, apprentices can easily find good jobs when they finish their training.

Auto Body Technician

The auto body technician must be capable of doing many jobs well. The job of the **body technician** includes removing dents, replacing badly damaged parts, welding metal, sectioning, filing, and sanding, Figure 22-2. Each vehicle brought in for repair presents a different problem. Therefore, a broad knowledge of automobile construction and repair techniques is essential.

Many repair jobs begin with simple dolly and hammer work to straighten minor damage. This work is not difficult, but it requires skill and practice. To return the vehicle to its proper appearance, hammer and dolly work must be performed correctly.

Sanding the surface of a panel is another very important task, Figure 22-3. The appearance of the completed job depends on how well the sanding was performed. Fillers and finishing materials will not stick well to a panel that has been poorly sanded. Care and experience are necessary to do a satisfactory job. Carelessness or lack of attention can result in deep scratches and gouges in a panel's surface. As a result, additional sanding will be required.

Auto body technicians must analyze damaged vehicles and make necessary corrections by bracing, pushing, pulling, and spreading the damaged components.

There are many different types of power equipment available, each with certain advantages. These units utilize hydraulic and/or pneumatic power to straighten bent and twisted vehicles.

To use power equipment successfully, the technician must be familiar with the basic structure of the vehicle and know where to apply the straightening force so the damage can be fixed, Figure 22-4. In many cases, the

Figure 22-1 A portion of this car is being masked in preparation for refinishing. This work is commonly done by an apprentice. (Du Pont)

Figure 22-2 This technician is installing new trim around a headlight.

Figure 22-3 A good sanding job is necessary to finish a job correctly. This technician is wet sanding the body panel.

Figure 22-4 This technician carefully corrects damage to a unibody vehicle. Power equipment is used to straighten the metal.

force must be applied at several points and in several directions at the same time. Obviously, work of this scope requires care and skill in execution.

Power equipment work involves more than straightening sheet metal panels. In a damaged vehicle, the frame or unitized body may be bent. This may require the use of special body and frame alignment equipment.

Alignment Specialist

Alignment specialists are needed in auto body repair because steering linkages are often damaged in a collision. Although damaged steering parts are generally replaced, alignment work involves the correction of the steering geometry.

Alignment specialists align and balance wheels using special alignment equipment and wheel balancing machines. They also repair steering mechanisms and suspension systems.

Glass Installer

Windshield and door glass replacement is an important body shop job. In unibody cars, the glass is vital in maintaining the structural integrity of the vehicle. Small body shops may send glass work to specialists. Large shops make glass replacement an important part of the services offered.

Windshield replacement usually involves two people, an experienced *glass installer* and a helper. This work requires special handling techniques and tools for removing and replacing windshield glass. The glass installer must also be familiar with many different regulator designs.

Upholsterer

The *upholsterer* repairs or replaces both interior and exterior materials. Areas of work include headlinings, seat covers, door panels, carpets, convertible tops, and vinyl tops.

In many shops, the upholsterer must be skilled in the repair and adjustment of power seat and window mechanisms. In addition, knowledge of convertible top and tail gate mechanisms may be required.

Paint Technician

There is a great deal more to being a *paint technician* than pointing the spray gun at a panel and pulling the trigger. Painting requires patience and practice.

A necessary and important job is masking the parts and areas that are not to be painted. Masking is done by covering these surfaces with masking paper and masking tape. In large shops, this is often done by an apprentice or assistant painter. In small shops, the painter will generally do the masking.

Many factors are involved in painting an automobile. The surface to be painted must be smooth and clean. The temperature of the vehicle and paint should be within specified limits. The paint must be thoroughly mixed, and the color should be accurately matched. The spray gun and air adjustments must be correct, and the proper application technique must be followed. See Figure 22-5. Paint technicians must have a thorough knowledge of primers, sealers, solvents, and other painting materials.

Custom painting, striping, and sign lettering are sometimes requested. This requires considerable artistic and technical skill, Figure 22-6. Sometimes, artists are employed to paint intricate scenes or designs.

Parts Manager

The job of the *parts managers* in large auto body shops or dealerships is to maintain a sizable stock of replacement parts. Because it is impossible to carry a complete inventory of parts, slow-moving items are not stocked and are generally ordered from warehouses. It is the job of the parts manager to see that the correct parts are ordered and inventoried, Figure 22-7.

Estimator

One of the most important jobs in an auto body shop is estimating the cost of a repair. The *estimator* examines the damaged vehicle and then determines how much the repair will cost, Figure 22-8.

The cost of most repair work, such as brake jobs, tune-ups, and transmission overhauls, can be obtained from a book. This is not as easily done with collision damage. No two repair jobs are alike. Various estimating aids are used to help determine the cost of parts and labor.

The work of the estimator is vital to the success of the shop. If an estimator overestimates the cost of repairs, the job will go to another shop. If an estimator consistently underestimates repairs, the shop will lose money.

When making an estimate, the estimator must take into account the capabilities of the shop and its employees. Many estimators gain experience by working at various positions in the shop. In some shops, the owner does the estimating.

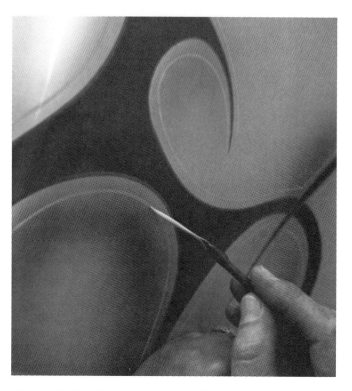

Figure 22-6 Custom painting allows the painter to be creative.

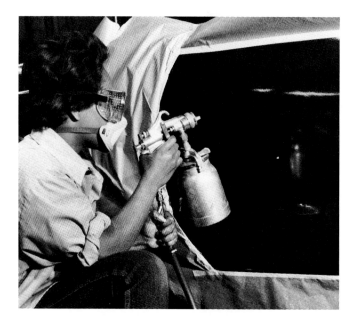

Figure 22-5 A great deal of practice has given this technician considerable skill in applying finish.

Figure 22-7 Computers have made the parts manager's job much easier.

Figure 22-8 This estimator is carefully examining a damaged vehicle. An accurate estimate is an important part of the repair process.

Manager

The *manager* (supervisor) usually controls all business matters. See Figure 22-9. This person often assumes full control of shop operations. Managers hire, train, promote, and fire personnel. They also deal directly with customers, explaining repair procedures and selling products and services.

It is the job of the manager to hire enough workers to handle the volume of business and to see that safe working conditions exist.

In many shops, some or all of the managerial work is performed by the owner. In large shops, however, the owner often hires a manager to oversee the operation.

The shop manager handles business relations with suppliers, associates, and union representatives. It is the manager's responsibility to see that company ledgers are kept accurately and that employees are paid appropriately. Managers may also decide what type of advertising or promotions should be used to stimulate business.

Most auto body businesses that fail do so because of poor management, not because of poor repair skills.

Insurance Adjuster

Insurance adjusters do not work for auto body shops. They work for insurance companies. The job of the *insurance adjuster* is to estimate the extent of damage a vehicle has sustained and decide how much the insurance company should pay for the repair.

Insurance adjusters are among the highest paid workers in the field of auto body repair. They must have vast experience in body repair and a thorough knowledge of vehicle construction.

Some companies require adjusters to have legal training. Adjusters meet with estimators and customers, so they also need good social skills.

Figure 22-9 Heading up a large auto body and paint shop are the owner and shop manager. Almost invariably, they have gained experience through years of work in the shop.

Sales

Auto body equipment and supplies must be sold to shops all over the country. *Sales representatives* are needed to sell various products or services to repair shops. Sales can be very rewarding, but it does require excellent interpersonal skills. Some experienced auto body technicians sell insurance, cars, or related automotive supplies.

Instructor

Experienced auto body technicians are often needed as *instructors.* In addition to trade experience, instructors must have educational training. These professionals teach other people the trade of auto body repair and refinishing. Training programs are offered through public and private trade schools and vocational-technical schools. Many manufacturers, associations, colleges, federal agencies, and organizations also offer training in various aspects of auto body repair and refinishing.

Career Advantages and Disadvantages

All jobs have advantages and disadvantages. In many instances, an aspect of a job that one person considers an advantage will be perceived as a disadvantage by somebody else. Not all people view each situation in the same way. Personality, experience, maturity, and ambition play a significant role in job preference.

Advantages of Careers in Auto Body Repair

Repair jobs are often very satisfying. It gives many people a sense of accomplishment and pride to have repaired a badly damaged vehicle. In addition, customers are grateful for a professional repair.

Most auto body work is done during daylight hours. There is little travel or after-hour work. Most work is done indoors, away from foul weather.

Experienced technicians have excellent employability skills. They can find work in nearly any part of the country. Pay in the auto body repair business is average to above average for the service trades.

Disadvantages of Careers in Auto Body Repair

Auto body repair work can be physically demanding. The work is generally done on concrete, which may complicate back and leg problems. This type of work requires a great deal of bending and squatting. The hands and arms are used constantly. Auto body and paint tech-

nicians are exposed to various chemicals. Many of these chemicals are toxic and pose health hazards.

Careers in auto body repair also require a significant time commitment. Several years of training and experience are required to become a competent body technician.

Financial Rewards

Most auto body technicians work between 40 and 48 hours per week. Technicians can be compensated for their efforts in one of three ways, including:

☐ Commission.

☐ Salary or wages.

☐ Salary plus commission.

Commission

When workers are paid on a *commission* basis, they receive a percentage of the total labor charge for each repair job. Commission may run from 40-60% of the total labor charge.

Commission in auto repair is similar to commission in sales. The more work that is done, the more commission that is earned.

Salary or Wages

A *salary* is a fixed amount paid to a worker on a weekly, monthly, or yearly basis. A salaried person does not get paid for overtime.

Wages are paid to workers on an hourly basis. This is preferred by some because they are paid for each hour they work and they may receive overtime. Wages vary with experience and skill level.

Salary Plus Commission

Like all businesses, the auto body repair industry experiences slow periods. This can cause financial difficulties for employees who work on straight commission. Workers may be paid a base salary plus a small commission on each job completed. This method of compensation combines the incentive of a commission with the stability of a salary.

Entrepreneurship

It is the dream of many auto body technicians to own their own shop. People who attempt to start their own business are known as *entrepreneurs.* Entrepreneurs put up a great deal of time, effort, and money to get their enterprise on its feet. The risks are great, but the rewards can be even greater.

Starting a body shop is not easy. Entrepreneurs need a thorough knowledge of the financial, managerial, and technical aspects of the auto body business. They will have to put in long hours for the first several years. Entrepreneurs also take a great financial risk. Any money they put in the business can be lost if it is not successful.

Nevertheless, a successful business is worth the risk to many. Owners have the authority to run the business as they choose. They can grow as they see fit. The earning potential of an owner is only bounded by the earning potential of the shop. In addition, many people get a great deal of personal satisfaction out of watching a business they have created become a success.

Summary

There is currently a great need for trained personnel in the field of collision repair. There are several positions available to suit the strengths and desires of different people.

Positions range from beginning apprentices to the skilled technicians and estimators. Some jobs demand hands-on mechanical skills, while others require organizational and interpersonal skills. Some jobs in the auto body shop will require skills in both areas.

There are several methods by which employees are paid: commission, salary or wages, and salary plus commission. Entrepreneurs are limited in their earning only by the earnings of their business.

Careers in the auto body field have their strengths and weaknesses. Individuals must decide what features they are looking for in their career. Once they have succeeded in doing that, they can decide if a career in auto body repair is right for them.

Know These Terms

Apprentice, On-the-job training, Body technician, Alignment specialist, Glass installer, Upholsterer, Paint technician, Parts manager, Estimator, Manager, Insurance adjuster, Sales representative, Instructor, Commission, Salary, Wages, Entrepreneur.

Review Questions–Chapter 22

1. The auto body field has many openings for trained personnel. True or False?

2. List five technical jobs you can work at in an auto body shop.

3. _____ attend classes while learning a trade from experienced workers.

4. People training to become auto body technicians are expected to acquire their own _____.

5. The person who determines how much it will cost to fix a vehicle is called the:
   a. apprentice.
   b. estimator.
   c. power equipment operator.
   d. entrepreneur.

6. The person with the most control in a body shop is the _____.

7. Most businesses that fail do so because of poor _____ skills.

8. List several careers in the auto body field that do not require physical repair work on a vehicle.

9. When workers are paid a salary, they receive a certain amount of money for each hour they work. True or False?

10. Entrepreneurs face few risks when starting a business. True or False?

Activities–Chapter 22

1. Visit the Reference section of your school or community library and locate the *Occupational Outlook Handbook*. This thick volume has information on many different types of jobs, the training needed to qualify for them, and the expected demand by employers for people with such training or experience. Check on the outlook for several of the jobs associated with auto body repair that were listed in this chapter.

2. Interview the owners of several small body shops, if possible, on the advantages and disadvantages of owning your own business. Also try to determine what kind of investment, in equipment and operating capital, would be needed to start a properly equipped shop today. Report to the class on what you have found out.

3. Which method of pay would be best for you? Assume that you worked 48 hours last week to complete a repair and refinishing job on a customer's car. You normally are paid $9.00 per hour, with overtime pay (1.5 times your hourly rate, or "time-and-a-half") for any hours over 40. Would you make more money on this job if you were paid a commission of 40 percent of the $1200 labor charge on the customer's bill? Or would you be better off if you were a salaried worker at $450 per week (no extra pay for overtime)? Which of the three methods of pay would give you the largest paycheck?

Cutaway view of a late-model vehicle illustrating many of the systems and components that must be taken into account when repairing collision damage. (Saturn)

Appendix

COMMON ABBREVIATIONS			
U.S. Customary		**Metric**	
Unit	Abbreviation	Unit	Symbol
inch	in	kilometer	km
feet	ft	hectometer	hm
yard	yd	dekameter	dam
mile	mi	meter	m
grain	gr	decimeter	dm
ounce	oz	centimeter	cm
pound	lb	millimeter	mm
teaspoon	tsp	cubic centimeter	cm^3
tablespoon	tbsp	kilogram	kg
fluid ounce	fl oz	hectogram	hg
cup	c	dekagram	dag
pint	pt	gram	g
quart	qt	decigram	dg
gallon	gal	centigram	cg
cubic inch	in^3	milligram	mg
cubic foot	ft^3	kiloliter	kl
cubic yard	yd^3	hectoliter	hl
square inch	in^2	dekaliter	dal
square foot	ft^2	liter	L
square yard	yd^2	centiliter	cl
square mile	mi^2	milliliter	ml
Fahrenheit	F	dekasteer	das
barrel	bbl	square kilometer	km^2
fluid dram	fl dr	hectare	ha
board foot	bd ft	are	a
rod	rd	centare	ca
dram	dr	tonne	t
bushel	bu	Celsius	C

MEASUREMENT SYSTEMS

U.S. CUSTOMARY   METRIC

LENGTH

U.S. Customary	Metric
12 inches = 1 foot	1 kilometer = 1000 meters
36 inches = 1 yard	1 hectometer = 100 meters
3 feet = 1 yard	1 dekameter = 10 meters
5,280 feet = 1 mile	1 meter = 1 meter
16.5 feet = 1 rod	1 decimeter = 0.1 meter
320 rods = 1 mile	1 centimeter = 0.01 meter
6 feet = 1 fathom	1 millimeter = 0.001 meter

WEIGHT

U.S. Customary	Metric
27.34 grains = 1 dram	1 tonne = 1,000,000 grams
438 grains = 1 ounce	1 kilogram = 1000 grams
16 drams = 1 ounce	1 hectogram = 100 grams
16 ounces = 1 pound	1 dekagram = 10 grams
2000 pounds = 1 short ton	1 gram = 1 gram
2240 pounds = 1 long ton	1 decigram = 0.1 gram
25 pounds = 1 quarter	1 centigram = 0.01 gram
4 quarters = 1 cwt	1 milligram = 0.001 gram

VOLUME

U.S. Customary	Metric
8 ounces = 1 cup	1 hectoliter = 100 liters
16 ounces = 1 pint	1 dekaliter = 10 liters
32 ounces = 1 quart	1 liter = 1 liter
2 cups = 1 pint	1 deciliter = 0.1 liter
2 pints = 1 quart	1 centiliter = 0.01 liter
4 quarts = 1 gallon	1 milliliter = 0.001 liter
8 pints = 1 gallon	1000 milliliters = 1 liter

AREA

U.S. Customary	Metric
144 sq. inches = 1 sq. foot	100 sq. millimeters = 1 sq. centimeter
9 sq. feet = 1 sq. yard	100 sq. centimeters = 1 sq. decimeter
43,560 sq. ft. = 160 sq. rods	100 sq. decimeters = 1 sq. meter
160 sq. rods = 1 acre	10,000 sq. meters = 1 hectare
640 acres = 1 sq. mile	

TEMPERATURE

FAHRENHEIT		CELSIUS
32 degrees F	Water freezes	0 degree C
68 degrees F	Reasonable room temperature	20 degrees C
98.6 degrees F	Normal body temperature	37 degrees C
173 degrees F	Alcohol boils	78.34 degrees C
212 degrees F	Water boils	100 degrees C

USEFUL CONVERSIONS

WHEN YOU KNOW:	MULTIPLY BY:	TO FIND:

TORQUE		
Pound - inch	0.11298	newton-meters (N-m)
Pound - foot	1.3558	newton-meters
LIGHT		
Footcandles	1.0764	lumens/meters^2 (lm/m^2)
FUEL PERFORMANCE		
Miles/gallon	0.4251	kilometers/liter (km/L)
SPEED		
Miles/hour	1.6093	kilometers/hr (km/h)
FORCE		
kilogram	9.807	newtons (n)
ounce	0.278	newtons
pound	4.448	newtons
POWER		
Horsepower	0.746	kilowatts (kw)
PRESSURE OR STRESS		
Inches of water	0.2491	kilopascals (kPa)
Pounds/sq. in.	6.895	kilopascals
ENERGY OR WORK		
BTU	1055.0	joules (J)
Foot - pound	1.3558	joules
Kilowatt-hour	3600000.0	joules (J = one W/s)

CONVERSION TABLE
METRIC TO U.S. CUSTOMARY

WHEN YOU KNOW ▼	MULTIPLY BY: * = Exact		TO FIND ▼
	VERY ACCURATE	APPROXIMATE	
LENGTH			
millimeters	0.0393701	0.04	inches
centimeters	0.3937008	0.4	inches
meters	3.280840	3.3	feet
meters	1.093613	1.1	yards
kilometers	0.621371	0.6	miles
WEIGHT			
grains	0.00228571	0.0023	ounces
grams	0.03527396	0.035	ounces
kilograms	2.204623	2.2	pounds
tonnes	1.1023113	1.1	short tons
VOLUME			
milliliters		0.2	teaspoons
milliliters	0.06667	0.067	tablespoons
milliliters	0.03381402	0.03	fluid ounces
liters	61.02374	61.024	cubic inches
liters	2.113376	2.1	pints
liters	1.056688	1.06	quarts
liters	0.26417205	0.26	gallons
liters	0.03531467	0.035	cubic feet
cubic meters	61023.74	61023.7	cubic inches
cubic meters	35.31467	35.0	cubic feet
cubic meters	1.3079506	1.3	cubic yards
cubic meters	264.17205	264.0	gallons
AREA			
square centimeters	0.1550003	0.16	square inches
square centimeters	0.00107639	0.001	square feet
square meters	10.76391	10.8	square feet
square meters	1.195990	1.2	square yards
square kilometers		0.4	square miles
hectares	2.471054	2.5	acres
TEMPERATURE			
Celsius	*9/5 (then add 32)		Fahrenheit

CONVERSION TABLE
U.S. CUSTOMARY TO METRIC

WHEN YOU KNOW	MULTIPLY BY: * = EXACT		TO FIND
	VERY ACCURATE	APPROXIMATE	
LENGTH			
inches	* 25.4		millimeters
inches	* 2.54		centimeters
feet	* 0.3048		meters
feet	* 30.48		centimeters
yards	* 0.9144	0.9	meters
miles	* 1.609344	1.6	kilometers
WEIGHT			
grains	15.43236	15.4	grams
ounces	* 28.349523125	28.0	grams
ounces	* 0.028349523125	.028	kilograms
pounds	* 0.45359237	0.45	kilograms
short ton	* 0.90718474	0.9	tonnes
VOLUME			
teaspoons		5.0	milliliters
tablespoons		15.0	milliliters
fluid ounces	29.57353	30.0	milliliters
cups		0.24	liters
pints	* 0.473176473	0.47	liters
quarts	* 0.946352946	0.95	liters
gallons	* 3.785411784	3.8	liters
cubic inches	* 0.016387064	0.02	liters
cubic feet	* 0.028316846592	0.03	cubic meters
cubic yards	* 0.764554857984	0.76	cubic meters
AREA			
square inches	* 6.4516	6.5	square centimeters
square feet	* 0.09290304	0.09	square meters
square yards	* 0.83612736	0.8	square meters
square miles		2.6	square kilometers
acres	* 0.40468564224	0.4	hectares
TEMPERATURE			
Fahrenheit	* 5/9 (after subtracting 32)		Celsius

METRIC–INCH EQUIVALENTS

INCHES FRACTIONS	DECIMALS	MILLIMETERS	INCHES FRACTIONS	DECIMALS	MILLIMETERS
	.00394	.1	15/32	.46875	11.9063
	.00787	.2		.47244	12.00
	.01181	.3	31/64	.484375	12.3031
1/64	.015625	.3969	1/2	.5000	12.70
	.01575	.4		.51181	13.00
	.01969	.5	33/64	.515625	13.0969
	.02362	.6	17/32	.53125	13.4938
	.02756	.7	35/64	.546875	13.8907
1/32	.03125	.7938		.55118	14.00
	.0315	.8	9/16	.5625	14.2875
	.03543	.9	37/64	.578125	14.6844
	.03937	1.00		.59055	15.00
3/64	.046875	1.1906	19/32	.59375	15.0813
1/16	.0625	1.5875	39/64	.609375	15.4782
5/64	.078125	1.9844	5/8	.625	15.875
	.07874	2.00		.62992	16.00
3/32	.09375	2.3813	41/64	.640625	16.2719
7/64	.109375	2.7781	21/32	.65625	16.6688
	.11811	3.00		.66929	17.00
1/8	.125	3.175	43/64	.671875	17.0657
9/64	.140625	3.5719	11/16	.6875	17.4625
5/32	.15625	3.9688	45/64	.703125	17.8594
	.15748	4.00		.70866	18.00
11/64	.171875	4.3656	23/32	.71875	18.2563
3/16	.1875	4.7625	47/64	.734375	18.6532
	.19685	5.00		.74803	19.00
13/64	.203125	5.1594	3/4	.7500	19.05
7/32	.21875	5.5563	49/64	.765625	19.4469
15/64	.234375	5.9531	25/32	.78125	19.8438
	.23622	6.00		.7874	20.00
1/4	.2500	6.35	51/64	.796875	20.2407
17/64	.265625	6.7469	13/16	.8125	20.6375
	.27559	7.00		.82677	21.00
9/32	.28125	7.1438	53/64	.828125	21.0344
19/64	.296875	7.5406	27/32	.84375	21.4313
5/16	.3125	7.9375	55/64	.859375	21.8282
	.31496	8.00		.86614	22.00
21/64	.328125	8.3344	7/8	.875	22.225
11/32	.34375	8.7313	57/64	.890625	22.6219
	.35433	9.00		.90551	23.00
23/64	.359375	9.1281	29/32	.90625	23.0188
3/8	.375	9.525	59/64	.921875	23.4157
25/64	.390625	9.9219	15/16	.9375	23.8125
	.3937	10.00		.94488	24.00
13/32	.40625	10.3188	61/64	.953125	24.2094
27/64	.421875	10.7156	31/32	.96875	24.6063
	.43307	11.00		.98425	25.00
7/16	.4375	11.1125	63/64	.984375	25.0032
29/64	.453125	11.5094	1	1.0000	25.4001

Dictionary of Technical Terms

A

Abrasive: A gritty substance used for wearing away a surface by friction or rubbing.

Abrasive coatings: In closed coating paper, the complete surface of the paper is covered with abrasive; no adhesive is exposed. In open coating, adhesive is exposed between the grains of abrasive.

Accent stripes: Lines applied to a vehicle to add a decorative, customized look.

Access holes: Openings that permit a technician to reach fasteners and other components inside a door.

Accessible area: An area that can be reached without having to remove parts from the vehicle.

Accessories: Items not essential to the operation of a vehicle (such as the radio, luggage rack, or heater).

Acetylene: A gas used in flame welding and cutting.

Acid core: A type of solder in tubular wire form, containing an acid flux paste.

Acrylic: A thermoplastic synthetic resin used in both emulsion- and solvent-based paints. Available as a lacquer or enamel.

Acrylic enamel: A type of finish that contains polyurethane and acrylic additives.

Acrylic-polyurethane enamels: Materials with outstanding weatherability that generally provide higher gloss and greater durability than other polyurethane enamels.

Active restraints: Seat belts that the occupants of a vehicle must fasten.

Additives: Chemicals added to a substance (such as paint) in relatively small quantities to impart desirable properties.

Adhesion: The ability of a substance to stick to another.

Adhesion promoters: Chemicals that react with the adhesive and plastic surfaces to form a stronger bond.

Adhesive: A substance used to bond two surfaces together.

Adhesive-backed moldings: Trim pieces provided with an adhesive back coating to simplify installation.

Adhesive bonding: A mechanical bonding between the adhesive and the surfaces being joined.

Adhesive caulk: A substance used to seal or join seams. Used extensively to install windshields and rear window glass.

Adhesive compounds: Non-hardening caulk-type materials used to hold fixed glass in place in today's vehicles.

Adhesive joining: Assembly of components with chemical bonding agents.

Adhesive primer/hardener: Material brushed on the mirror support and on the glass before applying mirror-mounting adhesive.

Adjusters: Insurance company personnel authorized to determine amount of payment on a damage claim.

Adjusting slots: Elongated holes on the mounting brackets and the bumper shock absorbers to permit alignment during installation.

Adjustment: Bringing parts into alignment or to proper dimensions. Many body parts are attached with fasteners that permit some movement for adjustment.

Aftermarket: Parts installed after original manufacture of the vehicle. Parts may be new, or may be used components salvaged for repair of damaged vehicles.

Aging: Allowing paint to cure or dry.

Aiming screws: Adjusting screws used to adjust the aim of a headlight.

Air bag system: A passive restraint system that deploys a balloon-like bag in front of the driver or passenger as a result of impact on the vehicle.

Air brush: Small spraying device used for fine detailing, fish scaling, and similar paint work.

Air cap: Component located at the front of the gun that directs compressed air into the material stream.

Air compressor: Equipment used to supply pressurized (compressed) air to operate shop equipment and tools.

Air conditioning systems: Compressor, evaporator, condenser, and associated components that cool the air in the passenger compartment.

Air dams: Structures mounted under the front portion of a vehicle and designed to direct air over the engine.

Air dry: Term for process of allowing paint to dry at ordinary room temperatures.

Air filter: A device used to trap or screen out dirt particles or other debris in an air line.

Air gun: See Blowgun.

Airless spraying: A paint spray system in which the material is atomized by forcing it under high pressure through a small opening (orifice).

Air line: A hose or pipe used to transport compressed air.

Air make-up system: Method used to replace air as it is exhausted from the spray booth.

Air-over-hydraulic systems: Those that utilize a pneumatic motor to drive the hydraulic pump.

Air pressure: The force exerted on a container by air that has been compressed.

Air-purifying respirators: Filtered breathing aids used to clean or purify the surrounding air.

Air suspension: Vehicle suspension system that makes use of pneumatic cylinders to replace or supplement mechanical springs.

Air transformer: A pneumatic control device used to filter and control air delivered by a compressor.

Align: To adjust a part for proper spacing or relative position. Specified tolerances may apply to doors, panels, frames, or wheels.

Alignment: Term used to refer to the arrangement of a vehicle's basic structural components in relation to each other.

Alignment gap: The specified space between components, such as a door and pillar or fender and hood.

Alkyd: A polymer resin used as the base for some enamel paints. It is tough, flexible, and has excellent adhesion.

Alkyd enamel: The least expensive of the enamels.

Alligatoring: A paint finish defect in which the finish resembling the pattern of an alligator's skin.

Alloy: A mixture of two or more metals.

Alternating current: Current that rapidly changes direction (alternates).

Alternator: A device used to generate alternating current. It is rectified into direct current for use in the vehicle's electrical system.

Aluminum: A light, strong, and corrosion-resistant metal.

Aluminum oxide: An abrasive that is extremely tough. It is highly resistant to fracturing and capable of penetrating hard surfaces without dulling.

Ambient temperature: Temperature that exists in the shop or around the vehicle.

Ammeter: An instrument used to measure electrical current (amperage).

Ampere: The electrical unit for current. Abbreviated A or amps.

Antenna wire circuit: Circuit either placed between the layers of glass or printed on the interior surface of the glass.

Antilacerative glass: A form of laminated glass that has an additional layer of plastic on the occupant side to contain glass fragments in case of breakage.

A-pillar: The windshield post.

Appraisal: The act or result of setting a value on a vehicle or repair of a vehicle.

Appraisers: Persons who estimate the cost of repair or replacement of a damaged vehicle.

Apprentice: Person who learns a trade working under the supervision of a skilled technician concurrent with classroom training.

Arc spot welding: Process of making spot welds with the heat of an arc, rather than resistance heating, used primarily in areas that are not accessible with resistance spot welders.

Arc welding: A welding (joining) technique that uses an electrical arc as the heat source.

ASE: National Institute for Automotive Service Excellence.

Assembly: Two or more parts joined together (by mechanical fastening, an adhesive, or welding) to form a single unit.

Assembly drawings: Those used by the manufacturer when assembling a vehicle.

Atmosphere-supplied respirators: Systems that employ a blower or a special compressor to supply outside air to a face mask or hood.

Atomization: The degree to which air pressure at the nozzle of a paint spray gun breaks up the paint and solvent into fine particles.

Atomize: To break up a liquid, such as paint, into very fine airborne particles.

Attachments: Special-purpose tools or parts that are attached to base tools.

Automatic cutoff: A safety device used to shut off the air compressor at a pre-set pressure.

Average retail price: Value of a like vehicle, based on actual sales reports from new and used car dealers.

B

Backfire: Small explosion that causes a sharp popping sound in oxygen-acetylene welding equipment.

Baked enamel: Finish achieved when heat is used to achieve rapid drying.

Baked-on finish: Paint that has been cured (hardened) by heating after application.

Banding: Spray painting around the edges of a panel or door being painted.

Bankruptcy: Situation that occurs when a company does not have sufficient assets to pay its debts.

Barrier creams: Hand creams that provide some protection and soothe the skin when working with irritating materials.

Base: The resin component of paint to which color pigments and other components are added.

Base coat: The layer (undercoat) of paint upon which the final coats will be applied. Base coats are highly pigmented and may have metallic flakes.

Base metal: Sometimes referred to as parent metal. Refers to any metal to be welded or cut.

Bathtub clip: Small plastic attachment pieces that are pressed into holes in the vehicle body. Moldings are then attached to these clips.

Battery charger: Device that recharges a vehicle battery.

Bead: The amount of filler metal or plastic material deposited in a joint when welding two pieces together.

Bearing plate: A plastic spacer that reduces friction between the door handle and the trim panel.

Belt line: The horizontal molding or crown along the side of a vehicle.

Belt trim support retainers: Parts that hold the window glass in position and prevent it from wobbling.

Bench grinder: Tool for sharpening or metal removal that is bolted to a workbench and driven by an electric motor.

Bench system: An alignment method using equipment that allows the vehicle to be set on preadjusted pins to check factory specifications for damage.

Bench vises: Heavy, adjustable holding tool that is mounted to a bench or other support.

Bend: Any change in a part from its original shape.

Bezel: The trim ring that surrounds a lamp (headlight) or gauge.

Binder: The component of paint that binds or cements the pigment particles together.

Binders: The resinous, film-forming ingredients that adhere to the surface being painted (substrate).

Bleeder guns: Gun design that allows air to pass through the gun at all times, preventing pressure buildup in the supply lines.

Bleeding: Situation in which the old base color shows through the new topcoat of paint. Red and maroon colors are most likely to ''bleed.'' Also, in hydraulic systems, the process of removing trapped air from hydraulic lines.

Bleedthrough: See Bleeding.

Blending: Mixing two or more paint colors together to achieve the desired color. Also, technique used in spot repairing acrylic lacquer finishes, extending each color coat a little beyond the previous coat to blend into surrounding finish.

Blistering: Formation of bubbles on the surface of paint, usually caused by moisture or dirt.

Block sanding: Using a flat object (block of wood) and sandpaper to obtain a flat surface.

Bloom: Clouded appearance on finish paint coat.

Blowguns: Devices that use blasts of compressed air to help clean and dry work surfaces.

Blush: A milky white haze that appears on the surface of the paint as it dries.

Bodied cements: Syrupy solvent cements that are composed of solvents and a small quantity of compatible plastics.

Body: On a vehicle, the enclosures for passengers, engine, and luggage. Also, the thickness (viscosity) of a fluid.

Body code plate: Manufacturer-mounted plate on an auto giving body type and other information.

Body files: Flat or half-round designed to be pushed across the work surface in the direction of the cutting teeth.

Body fillers: Plastic and solder materials used to fill holes and low spots prior to finishing.

Body hammers: Specialized hammers used to reshape damaged sheet metal.

Body hardware: Appearance and functional parts (such as handles) on the interior and exterior of a vehicle.

Body mounting: Method by which a vehicle body is placed onto a chassis. To reduce noise and transmission of vibration, rubber mounting pads are used where the components touch.

Body-over-frame construction: One in which the automobile's body is bolted to a separate frame.

Body panels: Large sheets of metal or plastic shaped to form a portion of the vehicle's exterior.

Body pull rods: See Pull rods.

Body saw: A special saw, equipped with an abrasive blade, used to cut floor sections or panels.

Body solder: An alloy of tin and lead, used to fill dents and other body defects.

Body spoon: See Spoon.

Body technician: Person who performs such basic repair tasks as removing dents, replacing badly damaged parts, welding metal, sectioning, filing, and sanding.

Body trim: Materials used to finish the interior of the passenger and trunk compartments. Sometimes used to refer to the rubber and metal moldings on the exterior of vehicles.

Bolt-through glass: Glass held to the regulator mechanism with mechanical fasteners, such as bolts or rivets.

Bonding strips: Strips of aluminum or fiberglass used to patch holes in vehicle bodies. Aluminum or stainless steel tape is sometimes used. Fiberglass cloth or mat is used to reinforce and patch the underside or surface of plastic vehicle bodies.

B-pillar: The pillar between the belt line and roof between the front and rear doors on four-door and station wagon models.

Brackets: A part used to attach components to one another or to the body and frame.

Brazing: A joining process in which the filler (rod) metal is an alloy of brass. The filler rod melts at a temperature lower than the base metal.

Bronzing: A metallic-appearing haze on a paint film.

Brushes: Tool with bristles of wire or synthetic material, used for cleaning tasks.

Buckles: Distortion (ridges or high places) on metal body parts as a result of collision damage.

Buffers: Tools that resemble disk sanders, but run at a higher speed and use a polishing bonnet to buff the final coat of paint.

Buffing compound: Abrasive paste or cake used with cloth or sheepskin pads to remove fine scratches and polish lacquer finishes.

Bulge: A dent with a high crown or area of stretched metal.

Bumping: The process of smoothing the damaged area further, following roughing.

Bumping files: Tools with a spoon-like shape and serrated surfaces, used to slap down and shrink high spots.

Bumping hammer: A hammer used to roughly pound out a dent.

Bumping spoons: Spoons that are often used as pry bars.

Burnishing: Hand-rubbing a finish with mild abrasive or special compounds to improve the gloss.

Butt weld: A weld where the pieces are joined edge-to-edge, without overlapping.

Butyl adhesive: A rubber-like compound used to bond fixed glass in place.

Butyl tape: Tape used with a separate adhesive to bond fixed glass in place.

C

Caged plate assemblies: A threaded (tapped) plate inside a sheet metal box spot welded to the inside of a door or pillar. The plate accepts hinge bolts, striker bolts, etc., and is moved in the cage during adjustment.

Calibrate: Process of checking equipment to see that it meets test specifications, and that the settings of the equipment are correct.

Camber: The outward or inward tilt of the wheels at the top.

Canisters: Containers of chemicals designed to remove specific vapors and gases from breathing air.

Carbonizing flame: A welding flame with excess acetylene, which will introduce carbon into the molten metal.

Carbon monoxide: A deadly gas created by the incomplete burning of fuel. Even a small amount can be fatal.

Card masking: See Shading.

Carnauba wax: A hard wax obtained from a species of palm tree and used in some body polishing materials.

Carpets: Floor coverings used in passenger vehicles.

Caster: Backward or forward tilt of the king pin or wheel spindle support arm at the top.

Casting: A process of molding materials using only atmospheric pressure. Also, a part produced by that process.

Catalyst: Chemical that causes plastic body filler, polyester resin, or other resin systems to harden. The catalyst does not become part of the chemical reaction.

Catalytic converter: A device used to reduce harmful exhaust gases through a chemical reaction between a catalyst and the pollutant gases.

Caulking compound: A flexible sealer used to fill cracks, seams, joints, and to eliminate water or air leaks and rattles.

C-clamps: C-shaped devices with threaded posts, used to hold parts together during assembly.

Centerline strut gauge: Device used to detect misalignment of strut towers in relation to the center plane and the datum plane.

Center pillar: The box-like column that separates the front and rear doors on a four-door vehicle. This reinforced piece holds the front door striker/lock and the rear door hinges. Sometimes called the hinge pillar.

Center plane: Imaginary centerline running lengthwise along the datum plane.

Center punches: Hammered tool with a pointed, tapered shaft, used to make ''starting dents'' for drilling.

Centimeter: A unit of linear measurement in the SI Metric system. There are 100 centimeter in one meter.

Ceramic mask: Opaque black mask baked directly on the perimeter of the glass to help hide the black polyurethane adhesive and the butyl tape.

Cerium-oxide powder: Extremely fine abrasive used to polish out scratches on glass.

Chalking: The decomposition of paint film into a dull powder on the surface.

Channel: See Window channel.

Chassis: The frame plus major operating components attached to it, such as the engine, drive train, and running gear. Generally considered to include everything except the vehicle body.

Checking: A paint defect exhibiting numerous short narrow cracks in the film surface. It is caused by shrinkage of the topcoat due to oxidation or extreme cold. Cracks may assume many patterns, but the usual ones resemble the print of a bird's foot or small squares.

Checking blocks: See Glass spacers.

Check valve: A special valve that allows passage of air or fluid in one direction.

Chipping: Condition in which small segments of topcoat break away from the finish, usually as a result of being struck with small stones. Also know as a ''stone bruise.''

Chlorofluorocarbons: Chemicals from refrigerants that have a detrimental effect on the earth's ozone layer.

Chopping: Term that describes lowering the vehicle profile.

Chroma: The term used to describe the purity and saturation (intensity) of a color.

Circuit: A path for electricity. The circuit must be complete (a closed path) before any current will flow.

Circuit breakers: Devices with a bimetallic strip and a set of contact points that are opened if excessive current heats the strip and makes it bend.

Claimant: The person who files a claim with an insurance company.

Clamp saw: Saw used to cut through spot welds. It cuts through only the top layer of material.

Clearance: Space between moving or stationary parts .

Clearance specifications: Required space left between adjoining parts (such as a door and fender).

Clearcoat: A clear finish sprayed over the color coat. Also called topcoat.

Clip: A mechanical fastener used to hold moldings to a panel. Also, a section of a salvaged vehicle.

Clip removal tools: Special hand tools for removing the mechanical fasteners used to attach door handles and trim.

Closed bid: One in which the final cost has been determined.

Closed-coat abrasive: One in which the abrasive grains are as close together as possible.

Closed sections: See Closed structural members.

Closed structural members: Rails, pillars, and other boxed-in vehicle parts accessible only from the outside.

Coated abrasives: A combination of abrasive grains, backing materials, and bonding agents. Sandpaper is a common example.

Cohesive bonding: Joining process that involves using solvent cements to melt plastic materials together.

Cold knife: Device used to cut through adhesive securing fixed glass or other components.

Cold shrinking: Reducing the surface area of metal by using a shrinking hammer and shrinking dolly.

Cold working: Working metal without applying heat.

Collision insurance: Insurance that covers property damages sustained by the insured as a result of a collision.

Color sanding: Wet sanding with #1200 grit abrasive.

Commission: Payment to a worker on the basis of a percentage of the total labor for a repair job. Commissions may run from 40-60 percent.

Compatibility: Term that refers to the ease with which a weld is made and the soundness of the finished joint and surrounding area.

Competitive estimate: An estimate which can be used to compare costs with the estimates made by other body shops.

Composite: Term used to describe any plastic formed by combining two or more materials, such as a polymer resin (matrix) and a reinforcement material.

Composite headlights: Those with a separate bulb, lens, and connector.

Compounding: Term used to describe applying a paste-like abrasive (rubbing compound) by hand or machine in a circular motion to improve gloss.

Comprehensive insurance: Insurance that covers damages not covered by liability or collision insurance policies.

Compression resistance spot welding: Method that uses clamping force and resistance heating to form two-sided spot welds.

Compressor: See Air compressor.

Concave: Curved inward, like a dent.

Condensation: Liquid formed on a surface by a material changing from a gaseous state.

Conductors: Materials that allow the flow of electricity.

Connectors: Devices with male and female halves, which are forced together to join wires.

Contaminants: Anything material that gets into paint or the finish and adversely affects it.

Contamination: Presence of dirt or other impurities in an area to be welded; one of the leading causes of weld failure.

Continuity testers: Devices that are used to test light bulbs, fuses, switches, and other electrical items, and to verify a complete (closed) circuit.

Continuous sanders: Sanders that use an abrasive belt to remove paint and to sand body filler.

Contract: An agreement, usually in the form of a written legal document, between two or more people.

Control points: Designated reference points used to position panels and other vehicle components during manufacture. These points are also used to verify correct dimensions during repair.

Conventional frame: Type of construction in which the vehicle engine and body are bolted to a separate frame.

Conventional points: Points on the unibody used as references when making a repair. See Control points.

Conversion coatings: Metal treatments that improve paint adhesion and corrosion resistance.

Convertible top fabric: Originally, tops were made from canvas, but today, synthetic fabric and vinyl are used.

Convex: Curved outward, like a bump.

Cordless tools: Tools that use a battery (cell) as the power supply, instead of electricity from a wall outlet.

Core: The group of tubes that form coolant passages in a radiator (heat exchanger).

Corporate Average Fuel Economy: A goal of 40 mpg is to be realized by the year 2000 by each automaker.

Corporation: A business that has many owners. Shares of the corporation, which are called ownership stocks, are sold to raise capital for the business.

Corrosion: Break down of a metal caused by chemical action. Rust is an example.

Courtesy estimate: A written estimate primarily for recordkeeping purposes; a customer does not use it as a basis for deciding to proceed with a shop's services.

Coverage: The area that a given amount of paint will cover when applied according to manufacturer's directions.

Coveralls: See Jump suits.

Cowl: The part of the vehicle that supports the instrument panel and other controls.

Cowl cut: A nose or front end that is cut behind the cowl or firewall.

C-pillar: The pillar connecting the roof to the rear quarter panel.

Cracking: A defect consisting of breaks in the paint film that generally extend down to the undercoat or metal. Cracking is generally caused by insufficient drying time for primer or applying too much topcoat with insufficient flash drying between layers.

Crane: Portable device that can be used to lift or move heavy objects, such as a vehicle engine.

Cratering: Holes in the paint film, usually caused by surface contamination.

Crazing: Paint defect consisting of minute interlacing cracks or splits on the surface of a finish.

Creeper: A low platform with four caster rollers, used by a mechanic for mobility when working under a vehicle.

Creeping: A condition in which paint seeps underneath masking tape.

Crossmembers: Reinforcing pieces that connect the side rails of a vehicle frame.

Crown: A convex curve or line on a body panel.

Crush zones: Crinkled (pleated), dimpled, or convoluted areas that allow the rails to collapse on impact to absorb energy.

Cubic centimeter: A unit of volume equal to one milliliter.

Cure: See Set.

Curing: The final drying stage in which a paint reaches complete strength and dryness as the result of chemical change or solvent loss. Also, the hardening of plastic resins used in filler or fiberglass repair kits.

Current: The flow of electrons in a circuit.

Customer requested: Repairs the customer wishes to have done, even though they will not be covered by insurance.

Customizing: Altering a vehicle to meet individual specifications.

Custom-mixed topcoats: Special blends that are often used when attempting to match a badly oxidized or faded finish.

Custom painting: Term used to describe refinishing or decorating a vehicle in a personalized manner.

Cyanoacrylate adhesive systems: Two-part adhesives that form an extremely strong bond on hard plastics and similar materials.

D

Datum plane: The horizontal plane or line used to determine correct frame measurements. Self-centering gauges are used, in conjunction with the datum plane, to check manufacturer's specifications.

Decals: Paint films in the form of pictures or letters which can be transferred from a temporary paper mounting to other surfaces. Also known as decalcomania.

Deductible: The amount of a claim that the vehicle owner must pay, with the remainder paid by the insurance company.

Defroster circuits: Narrow bands of a conductive coating that are printed on the interior surface of the glass.

Depreciation: Loss of value of a vehicle or other property due to age, wear, or damage.

Depression: A concave (inward) dent.

Diamond: Damage resulting from a collision in which the frame and/or body is out-of-square (diamond-shaped).

Die: A cutting tool used to make external threads or to restore damaged threads.

Dinging: The process of using a body hammer and a dolly to remove minor dents.

Dinging hammer: A special hammer used for removal of dents. Heavier heads are used for preliminary straightening processes.

Direct current: Current that travels in only one direction.

Direct damage: Damage that occurred at the point of impact.

Disassemble: To take apart.

Disk grinder: An electric or pneumatic tool used with abrasive wheels for heavy-duty grinding, deburring, and smoothing welds.

Disk sanders: Rotary power tools commonly used to remove paint and locate low spots in panels.

Distortion: Condition in which a component is bent, twisted, or stretched out of its original shape.

Doghouse: The front-end assembly of a vehicle.

Dog tracking: Situation in which the rear wheels of a vehicle do not follow the front wheels. They are off-center.

Dolly block: An anvil-like, metal hand tool held on one side of a dented panel while the other side is struck with a dinging hammer. Also called simply a ''dolly.''

Domestic: Classification for any vehicle that has more than 75% of its parts manufactured in the United States.

Door hinge wrench: A specially shaped wrench used to remove or install the retaining bolts on door hinges.

Door lock assembly: The assembly that makes up the door lock.

Door lock striker: The part of a door lock that is engaged by the latching mechanism when the door is closed.

Door skins: Term for the outer door panel.

Double coat: Paint applied horizontally as a first coat, immediately followed by a second, vertically applied coat.

Drain holes: Holes in the bottom of doors, rocker panels, and other components to allow water to drain.

Drier: A chemical added to paint to reduce drying or cure time.

Drifting: See Blending.

Drift punches: Tools that have long tapered shafts with flat tips, used to align holes.

Drill press: Floor- or bench-mounted, electric drill used to drill holes in various objects.

Drills: Power tools with interchangeable cutting bits that are used to bore holes.

Drip molding: Metal molding that serves as a rain gutter over doors. Sometimes called a drip cap.

Drivetrain: Group of connected mechanisms (engine, transmission, differential) used to cause a vehicle to move.

Droplight: A portable light source attached to a long electrical cord, used to illuminate the work area.

Drying time: The time required to cure paint or allow solvents to evaporate from a paint coat.

Dry sanding: A technique used to sand finishes without use of a liquid. See Wet sanding.

Dry spray: Condition in which a small amount of paint is used in relation to the spray gun air pressure, resulting in a rough, dull-appearing finish.

Dual-action sanders: Sanders that combine the merits of circular and orbital-motion devices.

Ductility: The property that permits metal deformation under tension.

E

Early-model: Term used to describe automobiles that are more than 15 years old.

Eccentric: Offset section on a shaft, used to convert rotary to reciprocating motion. Also called a cam.

E-coat: A cathodic electrodeposition coating process that produces a tough epoxy primer.

Elastic deformation: Condition that occurs when a material is not stretched beyond its elastic limit.

Elasticity: Term that describes a material's ability to be stretched and then return to its original shape.

Elastic limit: Point at which a material will not return to its original shape after being stretched.

Elastomer: A material that can be stretched to at least twice its original length (at room temperature) and return to its original size when released.

Electrical system: The alternator, wires, switches, fuses, and lamps used in a vehicle.

Electric convertible top: One that uses an electric motor and actuator assembly for raising and lowering.

Electric-over-hydraulic systems: Those that use an electric motor to drive the hydraulic pump.

Electric tools: Those that operate on electrical power.

Electrode: Metal rod, used in arc welding, that melts to help join the pieces to be welded.

Electronic displays: Those incorporating light-emitting diodes (LEDs) and other devices to provide vehicle information.

Electronic systems: Computerized vehicle controls such as engine control systems and anti-lock brake systems.

Enamel: A finishing material that dries by oxidation and evaporation of its reducers.

Endless line: Custom painting technique in which narrow tape is applied in the desired design. The tape is then removed after several coats of acrylic lacquer have been sprayed over it.

Energy reserve module: An alternate source of power for an air bag system if battery voltage is lost during a collision.

Entrepreneur: People who attempt to start their own business.

Epoxy: A tough, hard, resin-based finish. Also, a strong two-part adhesive.

Epoxy fiberglass fillers: Waterproof, fiberglass reinforced material used for minor rustout repair.

Estimate: A statement of the approximate cost for repair of damage.

Estimator: Person who examines the damaged vehicle and determines how long the repair will take and how much it will cost.

Ethylene dichloride: Chemical commonly used as a solvent to cement plastic joints.

Ethylene glycol: The chemical base used for permanent antifreeze.

Evaporation: Change of a paint solvent from liquid to gaseous state, allowing it to escape to the air.

Expansion tank: Small tank used to hold excess fuel or coolant as it expands when heated.

Extended method: Complete replacement of the adhesive material when installing new fixed glass.

Extension rods: Arms used to connect the lock cylinder to the locking mechanism on the door latch assembly.

Exterior door handles: Devices that permit opening of car doors from the outside.

Exterior locks: Those used on front doors and on trunk lids or hatches.

Exterior trim pieces: Moldings and other components applied to the outside of the vehicle.

External-mix guns: Those that mix and atomize air and paint outside the air cap.

Eye bath: Device that can be used to flood the eyes with water in case of accidental contact with a chemical or other hazardous substance.

F

Face bar: A bare bumper, with no hardware attached.

Face shield: Device worn to protect the face and eyes from airborne hazards and chemical splashes.

Factory-mixed topcoats: Paints carefully proportioned at the factory to achieve the desired color and match the original ''factory finish.''

Factory specifications: Specific measurements used during original manufacture of a vehicle. This data is used during repair.

Fading: A general lightening of an original color, resulting from weathering and exposure to sunlight.

Fan shroud: The plastic or metal enclosure placed around an engine fan used to direct air and improve fan action.

Feather: The tapered edge between the bare panel and the paint.

Feathering: The process of using sandpaper to taper the paint surface around a damaged area, from the base metal to topcoat.

Fiberglass: Fine-spun filaments of glass used as insulation, and (in mat or cloth form) for reinforcement of a resin binder when repairing vehicle bodies.

Fiberglass cloth: Relatively heavy woven reinforcement that provides the greatest physical strength of all the fibrous mats.

Fibrous composites: Material composed of fiber reinforcements in a resin base. Also referred to as reinforced plastics or fiber reinforced plastics.

Fibrous mats: Reinforcing material consisting of nondirectional strands of chopped glass held together by a resinous binder.

Fibrous pads: Pads of resinated fiber or fiberglass that are used on the inside of the hood, and other areas to help deaden sound and provide thermal insulation.

Files: Tools with hardened ridges or teeth cut across their surfaces, used for metal removal and smoothing.

Filler: A material used to level (fill) concave damaged areas.

Filler metal: Metal added when making a weld.

Filler panel: A panel placed between the body and the bumper.

Filler strip: Strip included in windshield installation kits to be used in the antenna lead area.

Finish: See Paint.

Finish coat: Last coat of finish material applied to a vehicle.

Finishing hammer: A hand tool used to hammer metal back into its original contour.

Finish sanding: The last stage in hand sanding the old finish or primer-surfacer, using #400 grit or finer sandpaper.

Fisheye eliminator: Additive that makes paint less likely to show fisheyes.

Fisheyes: Circular blemishes in the finish coat, usually of an opalescent character. Typically caused by failure to remove all traces of silicone polish prior to painting.

Fixed glass: Glass that is not designed to move, such as a windshield.

Fixed pricing: Prices for performing a service or repair that do not change.

Flaking: Paint defect in which small pieces of paint film detach themselves from the finish.

Flames: Flame-like design is produced by the use of stencils and paint.

Flash: The rapid evaporation of thinner or other solvents, during which the high gloss of the finish turns dull. Also known as flash-off.

Flashback: Condition in which the oxygen-acetylene mixture burns back into the body of the welding torch.

Flasher unit: Device used to flash the turn signal and hazard lights.

Flash time: The time needed for the solvents in the finish to evaporate.

Flat boy: A term sometimes used to describe a speed file.

Flat chisels: Hammered tools designed for shearing steel, including such tasks as removing bolt heats or rivets. Also called cold chisels.

Flat labor rate: A rate, used by some shops, that combines all different pay rates into a single hourly rate, with overhead and profit built in.

Flat-rate time: Standard labor hours for a specific task.

Flatteners: Additives that flatten (lower) the gloss of finishing materials.

Flex-additives: Material added to topcoats to make them flexible.

Floor jack: A portable piece of equipment used to lift a vehicle.

Floor pan: The main underbody assembly forming the floor of the passenger compartment.

Flow: The ability of particles of paint spray to merge together to form a smooth surface. Also known as flow-out.

Fluid adjustment screw: Control that regulates the amount of material passing through the fluid tip of the spray gun as the trigger is depressed.

Fluid control valve: Manual adjustment that determines the amount of paint coming from the gun.

Fluid needle: Valve component that shuts off the flow of material through a spray gun.

Fluid tip: Nozzle that meters the paint and directs it into the air stream.

Fog coat: A thin, highly atomized paint coat used to minimize penetration of the thinner into the old finish.

Foreign: Classification for any vehicle that has less than 75% of its parts manufactured in the United States.

Frame: The assembly of components or parts that supports the vehicle engine and body.

Frame alignment: The act of straightening a damaged frame to original manufacturer's specifications.

Frame-and-panel straighteners: Portable or stationary hydraulically powered devices used to repair damaged sheet metal and correct slight frame damage.

Framed doors: Design in which the door frame surrounds and supports the glass.

Frame gauges: Special gauges hung from the car frame to check its alignment.

Frame systems: A heavy frame assembly upon which various attachments, designed to match a manufacturer's control points, are mounted.

Free air capacity: The actual amount of air that is available at the compressor's working pressure.

Frisket paper: Adhesive-backed paper used as a stencil material.

Front body hinge pillar: Pillar to which front door hinges are attached.

Full-body sectioning: Procedure in which a salvaged rear half is joined to the undamaged front half of a vehicle.

Full cut-out method: Complete replacement of the adhesive material when installing new fixed glass.

Full-wet coat: A heavy application of finish used to thoroughly cover the substrate.

Fuse block: Holder for fuses protecting the vehicle's electrical circuits.

Fuses: Protective devices with a soft metal element that will melt and open an electrical circuit if more that the rated amount of current flows through it.

Fusibility: The measure of a material's ability to join another while in a liquid state.

Fusible link: A specially designed wire joint that melts and opens the circuit if too much current flows.

Fusion welding: Joining operation that involves melting of two pieces of metal together.

G

Gap: The opening or distance between two pieces.

Garnish moldings: Decorative or finish moldings around the inside of glass.

Gaskets: Rubber strips used extensively to secure fixed glass on early-model vehicles.

Gas metal arc welding: See Metal inert gas welding.

Gauge: Refers to a measure of the thickness of sheet metal. Also spelled gage.

General-purpose files: Flat, round, and half-round shapes used to remove burrs and sharp edges from metal parts.

General-purpose hammers: Those used for striking tools or tasks other than shaping sheet metal.

General-purpose tools: Those hand tools that are common to any shop performing automotive service or repair.

Glass installer: Technician responsible for windshield and door glass replacement.

Glass run channels: See Window channels.

Glass spacers: Rubber pieces used to position or align glass.

Glazing putty: Paste-like material used to fill small surface pits or flaws.

Gloss: The shine, luster or sheen of light reflected off a dried paint film.

Grain pattern: The surface appearance and color variation of vinyl fabric.

Grater file: Special file used to shape (cut) body filler before it completely hardens.

Gravity-feed guns: Guns into which paint is fed by gravity.

Greenhouse: The passenger portion of a vehicle body.

Grit: The abrasive grains used on sandpaper or discs.

Grommet: A donut-shaped rubber device used to surround wires or hoses for protection where they pass through holes in sheet metal.

Ground-return system: In metal-framed vehicles, the frame is part of the electrical circuit, so only one wire is needed to complete the circuit. Composite or plastic bodies require two wires.

Guide coat: Thin, contrasting color coat of finish applied to a panel, then sanded, to help detect high or low spots.

Gutter: See Drip molding.

H

Hacksaws: Hand saws used to cut metal.

Hand rubbing compounds: Those designed for manual use only.

Hardeners: Additives that speed up the curing of finishing materials.

Hard-faced hammers: Those used to strike tools or to bend or straighten metal parts.

Hard hat: Metal or plastic headgear worn to help protect the head from abrasions, hot sparks, and chemical sprays.

Hardtop: Automobile body style that does not have a roof-supporting center pillar.

Hardtop doors: Door design without a frame around the glass. The glass rests against the top and sides of the door opening and the weatherstripping.

Harness: Electrical wires and cables tied together as a unit.

Hazardous materials: Any material that can cause serious physical harm or pose a risk to the environment.

Hazardous substances: A subset of hazardous materials that poses a threat to waterways and the environment.

Hazardous waste: Material that can endanger human health if handled or disposed of improperly.

Headlining: Fabric used to cover the overhead interior of a vehicle.

Heat gun: An electric hand tool that blows heated air to soften plastic parts or speed drying.

Heat shrinking: Heating with a torch, then using a hammer and dolly to flatten the panel, and finally quenching with water to shrink the metal.

Hem flange: Flange at the bottom of a door panel.

Hemming tool: Pneumatic tool used to create a hem seam.

Hem seam: Door-bottom seam formed by bending the outer panel hem flange over the inner panel flange with a hammer and a dolly.

High-solids systems: Those that use high-volume low-pressure spray guns.

High-strength low alloy: A type of steel used in the manufacture of unibody designs.

High-strength steel: A type of steel used in the manufacture of car body frames. This steel is much stronger than cold-rolled steels.

High-volume low-pressure guns: Systems that atomize paint into low-speed particles.

Hinge pillar: See Center pillar.

Hold-out: The ability of the undercoat to keep the top-coat from penetrating or sinking into the undercoat. This greatly aids rapid buildup of coats.

Hood: The body part that covers the engine compartment.

Hooding: Applying a cover or hood, built up from epoxy resin and fiberglass reinforcement, to the headlight area.

Hot gas welding: Using air or inert gas, heated by a specially designed torch, to melt and fuse some thermoplastics and plastic filler rods together.

Hot glue gun: Electrically heated device used to melt and apply adhesive to plastics and other materials.

Hot knife: An electrically heated tool for cutting the polyurethane adhesive used to secure windshields.

Hue: The characteristic of a color that provides a red, yellow, blue, or green cast.

Humidity: The percentage of moisture in the air.

Hydraulic-electric convertible tops: Systems that employ hydraulic cylinders and electric motors to raise and lower the top.

Hydraulic presses: A press typically consists of a hydraulic jack that is held overhead in a heavy frame and used for pressing, straightening, assembling, and disassembling various components.

Hydraulics: Term for the use of a liquid or fluid under pressure to do work.

Hydraulic tools: Tools equipped with a pump system that forces hydraulic fluid into a cylinder to either push or pull a ram.

Hydrometer: An instrument used to measure the relative density (specific gravity) of a liquid. Commonly used to check battery electrolyte and engine coolant.

I

I-CAR: The Inter-Industry Conference on Auto Collision Repair.

Impact chisel: Electrically or pneumatically driven tool that creates a hammering, reciprocating action on a chisel bit to cut metal.

Impact tool: Electric or pneumatic tool used to tighten or loosen bolts or nuts.

Impact wrenches: Electrically or pneumatically driven tool used to tighten or loosen nuts and bolts.

Impurities: Paint, rust, and other contaminates that can substantially weaken a weld joint.

Included angle: Angle that places the turning point of the wheel at the center of the tire-to-road contact area.

Independent shop: May be a proprietorship or a partnership. The name stems from the characteristics of individual owners who desire some degree of independence when making business decisions.

Independent suspension: System in which wheels and related suspension assemblies are allowed to act individually or independently.

Indicator lamps: Lights used to signal problems with oil pressure, engine temperature, fuel level, or alternator output.

Indirect damage: Damage that occurs away from the point of impact.

Infrared dryers: Electrical heating elements that emit radiant energy to speed drying or curing of finishes.

Inner panels: Body components that add strength and rigidity to the outer panels.

Install: To apply or attach a part or component to a vehicle.

Instructor: Professional who teaches other people the trade of autobody repair and refinishing.

Insulation: Material commonly applied to muffle excessive noise, reduce vibration, and provide thermal insulation (prevent unwanted heat transfer).

Insulators: Materials that oppose the flow of electricity.

Insurance adjuster: Insurance company employee or independent contractor who estimates the extent of damage a vehicle has sustained and decides how much the insurance company should pay for repairs.

Insurance adjustment: An agreement among the vehicle owner, insurance company, and the body shop about what repairs will be made and who will pay for them.

Integrally welded: Term describing two or more parts that have been welded together to make one unit.

Interchangeability: Ability of new or replacement parts to fit just as well as the originally manufactured part.

Interior door trim assemblies: The coverings and hardware on the passenger-compartment surface of a door.

Interior locks: A mechanical knob or button attached to a rod, which is connected to the lock portion of the latch assembly.

Interior trim: The upholstery and moldings used on the inside of the vehicle.

Internal-mix guns: Spray gun that mixes air and material inside the cap before expelling them.

Internal rust-out: Rust damage caused by oxidization (rusting) from the inside to the outside.

Isopropyl alcohol: Solvent that will dissolve grease, oil, and wax, but will not harm paint finishes or plastic surfaces.

J

Jacks: Lifting devices usually operated with a manual pump.

Jack stand: See Safety stand.

Jig: Device used to hold a workpiece and to keep it from distorting or getting out of the desired alignment. A jig may also be used for checking dimensions.

Jumper wire: Test component used to connect a component directly to the voltage source.

Jump starting: Connecting a vehicle with a dead battery to a good battery, so that enough current will flow to start the engine.

Jump suits: Specially made, lint-free garments that resist paint absorption, provide full-body protection, and can be worn over other clothing.

K

Kerf: The space or gap left after metal has been removed by cutting with a saw or torch.

Keyless lock systems: Those that operate the lock through use of a numeric keypad on which a code is entered, or a radio transmission from a small transmitter.

Kick pad or panel: The piece that fits between the cowl and front door openings.

Kicks over: Term sometimes used to indicate that a plastic filler has hardened.

Kilogram: A base unit for measuring mass (weight) in the SI Metric system.

Kilometer: A unit of linear measure in the SI Metric system, equal to 1000 meters.

Kink: A bend of more than 90° in a distance of less than 3mm.

Kinking: A variation of cold shrinking, accomplished by using a pick hammer and a dolly to create a series of pleats (kinks) in the bulged area.

L

Labor: Work. Also, the cost of the time spent by personnel performing work.

Lace painting: A stencil technique in which paint is sprayed over fabric lace designs stretched across the surface to be decorated.

Lacquer: Topcoat that dries quickly as its solvents evaporate.

Ladder frames: Design in which the frame rails were nearly straight and several crossmembers were used to stiffen the structure.

Laminar composites: Layers of reinforcing materials held together by a resin matrix.

Laminated glass: Glass with plastic film sandwiched between glass layers. Sometimes called safety glass.

Lamination: Process in which layers of materials are joined together. Also, one of the layers.

Laser measuring systems: Systems that use one or more light beams to measure vehicle alignment.

Latch: A mechanism inside a panel, or on an adjacent panel, that grasps and holds a striker plate. Latches hold doors, hoods, and trunk lids closed.

Latch assemblies: Power-operated handle mechanisms for the trunk or the hatch.

Late-model: Term used to describe vehicles manufactured in the last 15 years.

Leader hose: Short length of air hose with quick coupler connections, use to connect pneumatic tools to the shop air supply.

Leading: Term used for applying lead-based solder body filler.

Liability: Legal responsibility for business decisions and actions.

Liability insurance: Insurance that covers the policyholder on damages to the personal property of others.

Lift channels: Channels in which window glass is supported as it is raised and lowered.

Lifting: Finish defect that occurs when new coats of paint are applied and the solvents in them cause loss of adhesion and ''lift'' the base coat. Paint surface may resemble a shriveled prune skin.

Lifts: Hydraulic mechanisms that are designed to raise a vehicle off the floor, allowing the technician to inspect and/or work under it.

Light bulbs: Devices with filaments (internal elements) that glow when electrical energy is supplied.

Liquid sandpaper: Chemical that cleans and etches the paint surface.

Liquid vinyl: A specially formulated paint that consists of vinyl in an organic solvent. A vinyl coating is left on the painted surface.

Liquid vinyl: Material sometimes used to repair holes or tears in vinyl upholstery or similar applications.

Liquid vinyl patching compound: A thick material applied to severely damaged areas of vinyl.

Listings: Small pockets in the headlining that hold support rods.

Liter: A measure of volume in the SI Metric system.

Load: Component that uses electrical energy.

Load tester: The most accurate instrument used to determine the condition of a battery.

Lock: A mechanism that prevents a latch assembly from operating.

Lock cylinder: In mechanical lock systems, the mechanism operated with a key.

Locking cord: See Locking strip.

Locking strip: A strip that fits into the gasket groove between the glass and pinch-weld flange to secure the glass in the body gasket.

Lock-out tools: Specialized devices used to open the door if a door latch is inoperative or the keys are lost.

Lock pillar: The vertical door post containing the lock striker.

Longitudinal: Term used to identify engines positioned so the crankshaft is perpendicular to the vehicle's axles.

Lord Fusor: Body panel repair adhesive recommended for bonding panels to space frames.

Low crown: Damage with a slightly convex (outward) curve.

Lower glass supports: Supports placed at the bottom edge of the window opening.

Low spots: Small concave (inward) dents.

M

Machine guards: Devices used to prevent personnel from coming into contact with moving parts of a machine.

Machine rubbing compounds: Compounds with very fine abrasive particles, suitable for machine application.

MacPherson strut: A type of independent suspension including a coil spring and a shock-absorber.

Maintenance-free batteries: Batteries designed to operate for their full service life without requiring additional electrolyte.

Major damage: Term for damage that includes severely bent body panels and damaged frame or underbody components.

Malleability: The property that allows metal deformation under compression.

Manager/Supervisor: Person who usually has full control of shop operations and of the hiring, training, promotion, and firing of personnel.

Manual convertible top systems: Those that are raised and lowered by hand.

Manually operated seats: Seats that are adjusted back and forth on a track manually.

Markup: The amount that a shop adds to its costs to determine selling price.

Marred: Term describing part or component that has been damaged or scratched.

Mash: Damage (buckling and shortening) to a vehicle frame as a result of a front- or rear-end collision.

Masking: Using paper and tape to cover and protect glass, trim, or other areas from paint during spraying.

Masking paper: Special paper that will not permit paint to bleed through. Usually attached with masking tape.

Masking tape: Adhesive-coated paper tape used to protect parts from spray paint. Also used to attach masking paper.

Mass tone: Color of paint as it appears in the can or on the painted panel.

Material safety data sheets: Sheets are available from paint and chemical manufacturers for every substance they produce. They cover chemical identification, hazardous ingredients, physical data, fire and explosion data, health hazards, reactivity data, storage and disposal procedures, spills and leaks, protective equipment, and other miscellaneous information.

Matting: Glass-fiber materials loosely held together and used with a resin to make repairs to some vehicle bodies.

Mechanical fasteners: Devices such as screws, nuts, bolts, rivets, and spring clips, that allow for convenient adjustment and replacement of assemblies or components.

Mechanical joining: Techniques for holding components together through use of fasteners, folded metal joints, or other techniques.

Mechanical measuring systems: Systems that utilize a precision bridge (beam) and a series of tram-like adjustable pointers to verify dimensions.

Mechanism: Working parts of an assembly.

Metal conditioner: Chemical preparation applied to unfinished metal to prevent rust formation and slightly etch the surface.

Metal inert gas welding (MIG): Welding technique that uses an inert gas to shield the arc and filler electrode from atmospheric oxygen. Also known as gas metal-arc welding (GMAW).

Metal inserts: Components used to help strengthen and secure the repair when sectioning rocker panels.

Metallic paint: Finishes that include flakes of metal (commonly aluminum) in addition to the pigment.

Metallics: Term for paints that contain metallic flakes.

Metallurgy: The study of metals and the technology of metals.

Metal snips: Scissor-like hand tool used to cut thin metal.

Meter: An instrument used to make measurements. Also, a base unit of measurement in the SI Metric system.

MIG spot welding: Technique often used to tack panels in place before welding with continuous MIG welds or compression resistance spot welds.

Mill-and-drill pads: Attachment points used when sectioning plastic body panels.

Millimeter: A unit of linear metric measurement equal to 1/1000 part of a meter.

Mineral spirits: A petroleum product with about the same evaporation rate as gum turpentine. Sometimes used as a liquid for wet sanding and to clean spray guns.

Minor damage: Term for repairs that require relatively little time and skill to complete.

Mirror bracket adhesive: Strong bonding material used to mount mirror on inside of windshield.

Misaligned: Term describing the failure of parts or components that do not fit properly or which have uneven gaps between body panels.

Miscible: Capable of being mixed.

Mist coat: Finish coat achieved by overthinning the color and spraying very wet. Usually the final coat for lacquer or acrylic polychromatic colors.

Mold core method: Procedure commonly used to repair curved or irregularly shaped sections.

Molding clips: Mechanical fasteners used to secure automotive trim. Sometimes called retaining clips.

Motorized seat belt system: One designed to automatically apply the shoulder belts to the front-seat passengers.

Mottling: Paint defect in which metallic flakes float to the surface if the coat is too wet. It results in a spotty or dappled effect in metallic finishes.

Movable glass: Windows designed to be moved up and down or to be opened and closed.

Movable sections: Components held in position by mechanical fasteners.

Mud: Slang term for plastic filler that is ready for use.

Multimeter: Instrument that can be used to measure resistance, voltage, and amperage.

Music wire: Steel wire with wood handles, used for cutting through adhesives.

N

Negative caster: Condition produced when the top of the steering knuckle is tilted toward the front of the car.

Negligent: Careless or irresponsible.

Net: The amount of money left after paying all the bills. Also known as profit.

Neutral flame: Flame of an oxyacetylene torch that has been adjusted to eliminate all of the acetylene feather at the inner cone.

Neutralizer: Material used to chemically eliminate traces of paint remover before finishing begins.

Nibbler: A power tool used to cut small bites or nibbles out of sheet metal.

Nitrile gloves: Protective gloves commonly used when working with paints, solvents, catalysts, and fillers.

No-fault insurance: A type of insurance covers only the insured's vehicle (and/or personal injury) *only*, regardless of who caused the accident.

Noise intensity: Loudness of noise. Too great an intensity can be harmful.

Nonbleeder guns: Spray guns equipped with a valve that shuts off the airflow when the trigger is released.

Noncompetitive estimate: Detailed and accurate estimates, usually done for minor damage where no claims are to be filed with an insurance company.

Nose: The front body section ahead of the doors. Includes finders, hood, grille, bumpers, radiator, and radiator support.

Nozzle: See Fluid tip.

O

Office staff: People who perform such office duties as billing, receiving payment and making deposits, ordering parts, and paying bills.

Off-the-dolly dinging: A technique where the dolly is held away from the raised areas being hit by the hammer.

Ohmmeter: Device used to measure resistance.

Ohms: Unit of measure for resistance.

One-wire system: Electrical wiring for vehicles that use the chassis as an electrical path to ground. This eliminates the necessity for a second wire to complete the circuit.

On-the-dolly dinging: A technique where the dolly is held directly under the area where the hammer is used.

On-the-job training: Method in which the worker learns the trade from experienced technicians while taking part in the repair process.

Open bid: In an estimate, a situation in which a part may be suspected of needing repair, but the bid price for that part cannot be established until the damage repair is started.

Open circuit: A circuit in which a break or interruption halts the flow of current.

Open-coat abrasives: Those in which the abrasive grains are widely separated.

Orange peel: Paint defect with a nubby surface looking like the skin on an orange. It may or may not have a good gloss.

Orbital sander: Power sanding tool that operates in an elliptical or oval pattern.

Orifice: A small hole or opening.

Original finish: The paint applied at the factory by the vehicle manufacturer.

Outer-belt weatherstripping: Material located between the door panel and the window glass to prevent dirt, air, and moisture from entering the door cavity.

Outside surface rust: Rust that begins from the outside of a panel.

Overage: Added charge for damage discovered after the original estimate.

Overhaul: Situation in which an assembly is removed, cleaned, and inspected. Damaged portions are replaced and the assembly is reinstalled.

Overhead dome lights: Those that illuminate the interior of the vehicle.

Overlap: Spray pattern that covers part of the previous stroke. Also, unnecessary duplication of tasks when labor hours are determined on part-by-part basis.

Overlays: Thin layers of plastic material, often with designs or patterns, that are applied to various parts of the vehicle.

Overpulling: Situation in which metal has been stretched (pulled) too much during repair.

Overspray: An overlap of dry spray (finish) particles on areas where they are not wanted.

Oxidation: Chemical combination of oxygen from the air with the paint film. This process dries and continues to harden paint for a period of time. Chalking of a paint film due to age is also a form of oxidation.

Oxidizing flame: An oxyacetylene welding flame produced by too much oxygen. The inner cone of the flame is pointed.

Oxyacetylene welding: A joining process that fuses metal with heat produced by burning oxygen and acetylene gases.

Ozone: The primary component of smog.

P

Package paint: Paint that is not mixed in the shop, but is factory-matched.

Package shelf panel: The horizontal panel located between the rear seat and the back window.

Padding: Unethical practice of adding unjustified costs to a repair bill.

Paint: Finishing material containing three basic ingredients: binders, solvents, and pigments.

Paint cabinet: Metal cabinet designed for the safe storage of finish materials.

Paint code plate: Metal tag or label providing codes used to identify the type and color of finish used on a vehicle.

Paint film: The thickness of the paint on the surface.

Paint removers: Chemicals that soften paint for easy removal.

Paint shakers: Mechanical devices for thoroughly mixing paint.

Paint technician: Specialist who handles the masking and painting of vehicles after repair.

Panel crimper: See Pneumatic flange tool.

Panel spot welders: Equipment used in body shops to weld patches and replacement panels in place.

Parallel circuits: Circuits containing two or more loads that are connected so that current will flow through all of the loads at once.

Partial cut-out method: Partial replacement of the adhesive material when installing new fixed glass.

Partnership: Form of business in which two or more people share the legal responsibilities of operating a shop.

Parts manager: Person responsible for maintaining inventory and ordering needed parts.

Passive restraints: Safety features that do not require action from the occupants to make them functional.

Pattern adjustment valve: Valve that controls the size and shape of the spray pattern.

Pattern control valve: Manual adjustment that allows the operator to select a spray pattern width to suit the job at hand.

Pearlescent: A luster similar to that of a pearl, achieved by multiple coats of finish with mica particles coated with titanium dioxide added to them.

Peeling: Paint defect in which the film is detached in relatively large pieces. Paint applied to a damp or unclean surface usually peels.

Penetration: The depth of fusion achieved during a welding operation.

Perimeter frame: Type that is still used for most vans and pickup trucks.

Pick hammer: A hammer with a pointed shank on one end of the head and a flat face on the other.

Picks: Metal-shaping tools used to push against low spots located in confined spaces that cannot be reached with a pick hammer.

Pigment: Material (usually a powder) used to impart color, opacity, and other effects to paint.

Pillar: A strong structural post that is used to separate glass areas or doors.

Pinch weld: Refers to joints (usually right-angle flanges) made by resistance spot welding.

Pinholes: Any small, unwanted holes in plastic filler, caused by improper mixing or application.

Pinholing: Paint defect consisting of small holes that form in the topcoat or undercoat.

Pin punches: Hammered tools with long straight shafts and flat tips, used to drive out pins and stubborn bolts.

Pin stripes: Adhesive-backed plastic tapes used to make accent stripes on a vehicle.

Pinstriping brushes: See Striping brushes.

Plasma arc cutting: A system in which hot (ionized) gas heats the metal, and the molten material is blown away by nitrogen or compressed air.

Plastic alloy: Material formed when two or more different polymers are physically mixed together.

Plastic deformation: The use of compressive or tensile force to change the shape of metal.

Plastic filler: Special compounds used to fill dents and cracks in panels before applying finishes.

Plasticity: The property that allows metal to be shaped.

Plasticizers: Softening additives in vinyl fabric.

Plastic-resin mixture: Material developed to fill chips and pits on a windshield.

Plastics: Manufactured lightweight materials now being used extensively in automobile construction.

Platform frame: A frame that consists of a floor pan and a central tunnel that runs down the middle to provide strength.

Pliers: Hand tools designed for gripping objects .

Pliogrip: Body panel repair adhesive recommended for bonding panels to space frames.

Plug weld: Welding method in which filler metal is placed in a hole in the first layer to bond top and bottom pieces together.

Pneumatic flange tool: Tool that forms an offset crimp along the joint edge of a panel to permit a flush, professional lap joint.

Pneumatic tools: Tools powered by compressed air. Such tools are used extensively in the body shop.

Polishers: See Buffers.

Polishing compound: A fine abrasive paste used for smoothing and polishing a finish.

Polishing cream: Extremely fine abrasive used for manual removal of swirl marks left after machine compounding.

Polyblends: Plastics that have been modified by the addition of an elastomer.

Polyester resin: A thermosetting plastic used as a finish and matrix binder with reinforcing materials (usually glass fibers).

Polyethylene: A very common thermoplastic used for interior applications.

Polypropylene: A thermoplastic material used for interior and some under hood applications. It is less common than polyethylene.

Polyurethane: A thermosetting plastic used for exterior and interior body panels. Also a base resin for some finishes.

Polyurethane adhesive: A plastic compound used with butyl tape to bond fixed glass in place.

Polyurethane enamels: Refinishing material that provides a hard, tile-like finish.

Polyurethane foam: Plastic material used to fill pillars and other cavities. It adds strength, rigidity, and sound insulation.

Polyurethane primer: Material brushed onto the areas where the adhesive will be applied to hold glass in place.

Polyvinyl chloride: A thermoplastic material used in pipes, fabrics, and other upholstery materials.

Pool: Term for the molten metal area that is created by the heat of the welding process.

Poor drying: Condition in which a finish stays soft and does not dry or cure as quickly as the technician would like.

Pop rivet guns: Hand-held tool designed to place rivets into blind holes.

Porosity: Holes or gas pockets are present in the weld.

Portable alignment systems: Systems designed for correcting slight frame and body damage.

Portable grinder: See Disc grinder.

Positive caster: Condition produced when the top of the steering knuckle is tilted toward the rear of the car.

Positive post: The positive terminal of a battery.

Pot system: A variation of the rail alignment system that uses portable hydraulic units anchored to attachment holes in the floor.

Power rams: Hydraulic body jacks often used to correct severe damage.

Power ratchets: Electrically or pneumatically powered tools that are not as heavy-duty as impact wrenches.

Power seats: Seats that are adjusted vertically and horizontally with electric motors.

Power source: Source of electrical energy.

Power tool: Tools that use electrical, hydraulic, or pneumatic energy as their source of power, rather than human muscle power.

Power washer: Cleaning device that uses a high-pressure spray of water to dislodge stubborn debris.

Press fit: A joining technique in which one part is forced into the other with a mechanical device (press).

Pressure: The force (measured in pounds per square inch) of the air delivered to a spray gun.

Pressure drop: The loss of air pressure between the source of air and point of use.

Pressure-feed guns: Spray guns in which air pressure or a high-pressure pump force the paint to the gun.

Pressure pot: Paint spray system in which the paint is fed to the spay gun by air pressure.

Pressurize: To apply greater-than-atmospheric pressure to a gas or liquid.

Primary damage: Local damage at the point of impact.

Prime coat: Coat of material applied to bare metal to obtain adhesion. See Primer.

Primer: The undercoat that is placed on bare metal or older paint to promote good adhesion and provide a smooth surface for the topcoat.

Primer-sealer or sealer: A primer coating used to improve adhesion and seal the old topcoat.

Primer surfacer: A base-coating material used to improve adhesion and fill minor surface imperfections on bare metal surfaces.

Proprietorship: A company or shop that is owned and operated by one person.

Pullers: Tools used from the front side of a panel to pull out dents.

Pull rods: Tools that allow repair work to be performed from the outside of the damaged panel. Holes are drilled in the deepest part (creased area) of the damaged area. The hooked ends of the pull rods are placed in the holes. A pulling force is exerted on the handles.

Pull tabs: Metal tabs welded to a damaged panel to allow use of a slide hammer.

Putty: A dense, thick material used to fill flaws that are too large to be filled by primer surfacer.

Q

Quarter panel: The exterior covering which extends from the door to the rear bumper, so-called because it usually is one-quarter of the total length of a vehicle.

Quench: To cool quickly.

R

Rails: The major members that form the box-like support in unibody construction.

Rail systems: Systems consisting of specially designed steel members set into the shop floor to provide a firm anchorage for the pushing and pulling equipment used when repairing body or frame damage.

Reaction injection molding: Process that involves injecting reactive polyurethane or a similar resin onto a mold.

Rear clip: The entire rear portion of the car with part of the roof attached.

Rear compartment lid: The trunk door or panel and reinforcement that covers the luggage compartment.

Rear-engine: Term used to identify engines positioned directly above or slightly in front of the vehicle's rear axle.

Rechrome: To replate a part, such as a bumpers, with chrome.

Reciprocating sanders: Power sander with a sanding surface designed to reciprocate (move in small circles) while moving in a straight line.

Reducers: Solvents used only with enamel-based finishes.

Regulator: A mechanism used to raise or open glass in a vehicle door. Also, a device that controls pressure of liquids or gases.

Reinforced reaction injection molding: Process that involves injecting reactive polyurethane, polyurea, or dicyclopentadiene resin into a mold that contains a pre-formed glass mat.

Reinforcement pieces: Sheet metal welded in place along a joint to strengthen critical sections.

Reinforcements: Braces and other structural parts used to strengthen panels.

Relative density: The mass (weight) of a given volume of a substance compared to the same volume of water at the same temperature. Commonly called specific gravity.

Relief valve: A safety valve designed to open at a specified pressure.

Remove and reinstall: Term for work that involves removing an item to gain access to another part, then reinstalling the item.

Remove and repair: Term for work in which parts are removed, repaired, and reinstalled.

Replacement panels: Complete body panel used to replace a damaged one.

Resin: Common term used to refer to polyester or epoxy resin systems used in autobody repair. Catalyst is added to cause the resin to cure.

Resistance: Opposition to the flow of electricity.

Resistance spot welder: Electric welding equipment used to heat and fuse together a small spot to join two or more pieces of metal.

Resource Conservation and Recovery Act: Law passed to enable the EPA to control and manage hazardous waste generators.

Respirator: A protective mask-type device designed to filter harmful particles out of the air so that they do not reach the lungs.

Retaining clip: Spring device used to secure one component to another and allow disassembly.

Retaining strips: Strips sewn into the headlining and attached to T-slots on the inner roof panel to help support the headlining.

Retarders: Additives that slow down the curing of finishing materials.

Reveal files: Curved files used to shape tight curves or rounded panels.

Reveal moldings: Exterior trim pieces that accent glass openings.

Reverse masking: Spot repair technique used to help blend the paint and make the transition less noticeable.

Reverse polarity: Connecting the MIG welding gun to the positive terminal of the DC welder to provide greater penetration.

Right-to-know law: Law that requires employers to inform their employees about the hazardous materials used in the shop and teach them to take the proper safety precautions when using such products.

Rocker panel: The narrow panel located under the doors of a vehicle.

Roller gun: See Striping tool.

Roughing out: The preliminary work of bringing the damaged sheet metal back to approximately the original contour.

Rubber stops: Adjustable hood bumpers used to make minor alignment adjustments and to keep the hood from fluttering or squeaking.

Rubbing compounds: Fine, paste-like abrasives designed for controlled removal of paint.

Run or running: A condition in which paint is applied too heavily, or has been reduced too much, and drips down vertical surfaces.

Rust inhibitor: A chemical applied to steel to slow down rusting or oxidation.

Rust-out: Condition that occurs when rust is allowed to eat through a metal panel.

S

Safety glasses: Protective eyewear.

Safety shoes: Well-constructed, metal-toed shoes to protect feet from dropped objects and other hazards.

Safety stand: A metal support placed under a raised vehicle. Also called a jack stand.

Sag: Defect caused by too much paint, so that the paint film drips or runs.

Salary: A fixed amount paid a worker per week, month, or year.

Sales personnel: Manufacturers' or equipment suppliers' representatives who sell various products or services to repair shops.

Salvage: The remaining value of a wrecked vehicle that has been declared beyond repair.

Sandblasters: Devices that shoot a high-pressure stream of air and abrasive particles to remove paint and rust.

Sandblasting: Process that uses air pressure to direct a stream of abrasive particles against the surface of a vehicle to remove paint.

Sander: Electric or pneumatic tool used to sand auto bodies with reciprocal, orbital, or rotary action.

Sanding block: A piece of wood or hard rubber with a flat surface, used with sandpaper in hand sanding.

Sand scratches: Marks made in metal or old finish by an abrasive. Term is also used for scratches showing in the finish coat due to lack of paint fill or sealing.

Saturate: To fill an absorbent material with a liquid.

Scrapers: Edged tools used to scrape away paint or other surface materials.

Scratch awls: Pointed tool useful for marking (scratching) and piercing sheet metal.

Screwdrivers: Hand or electrically powered tools used to tighten or loosen screw-type fasteners.

Sealant: A compound used to caulk or seal body joints.

Sealed-beam headlights: Lights in which the filament, reflector, and lens are fused into a single airtight unit.

Sealer: A liquid coating applied between the topcoat and the primer or old finish to prevent previous coatings from bleeding through.

Sealing strips: Strips inside doors that prevent dust from entering the drain holes, but allow water to drain.

Seat belts: Restraints that hold passengers in their seats during a collision to help prevent injury.

Secondary damage: Damage in areas other than the primary impact area.

Sectioning: Splicing together of panels during vehicle repair.

Self-centering gauges: Devices designed to show general misalignment.

Self-contained respirators: Compressed air cylinder-equipped devices that provide excellent protection and added mobility over atmosphere-supplied respirators.

Self-etching primers: Primers containing an agent that ''bites'' into the metal for improved adhesion.

Series circuits: Circuits with one or more loads that are wired so the current has only one path to follow.

Service manuals: Annual guides printed by vehicle manufacturers, listing specifications and service procedures for each model. Also called shop manuals.

Set: Term for the curing of enamels after the reducers have evaporated.

Setting time: The time it takes solvents to evaporate or resins to cure or become firm.

Shaded glass: Glass with a dark color band across its top. It may also have a light color tint in the remaining area.

Shading: A popular custom painting method created by holding a mask or card in place and overspraying the surrounding panel.

Sheet molding compounds: Thermoset composites that can be formed into strong and stiff body components.

Shelf life: The maximum length of time the manufacturer recommends that a material can be kept before use. Many resins will harden in the container if kept beyond their shelf life.

Shims: Thin pieces of metal used behind hinges or fasteners to match heights of body components.

Shop layout: The arrangement of work areas, storage, aisles, office, and other spaces in a shop.

Shop manuals: See Service manuals.

Shop tools: Tools that the shop owner normally provides.

Short circuit: Sympton of electrical leakage between two conductors.

Short method: Partial replacement of the adhesive material when installing new fixed glass.

Shrinking: Removing a bulge from metal by hammering with a special hammer and dolly, with or without heat.

Shrinking dollies: Tool designed to reduce the surface area of metal without using heat. Used with a shrinking hammer.

Shrinking hammers: Tool designed to reduce the surface area of metal without using heat. Used with a shrinking dolly.

Sidesway: Collision damage that occurs when an impact to the side of a vehicle causes the frame to bend or wrinkle.

Silicon carbide: Abrasive used in sanding or grinding grit.

Silicone: An ingredient in waxes and polishes that makes them sleek to the touch and improves the appearance of the finish coat. Silicone residues must be removed before painting or fisheyes will occur.

Silicone adhesives: Adhesive used to repair torn vinyl trim and upholstery.

Silicone-treated graining paper: Special paper used to create the final grain pattern in vinyl during upholstery repair.

Simulated seam tape: Tape used to provide the appearance of seams in a spray-on vinyl roof covering.

Single coat: Defined as passing once over the surface to be painted, with each stroke overlapping the previous coat 50 percent.

Siphon feed gun: A type of spray gun in which the paint is drawn out of the container (cup) by vacuum action, then mixes with the air.

Skin: Refers to the outer panel.

Slide caliper rule: Rule used to measure inside or outside dimensions and the depth of holes.

Slide hammer: A device with a hammer head that is slid along a rod and against a stop, so that it pulls against the object to which the rod has been fastened.

Snap fits: Joining technique in which parts are forced over a lip or into an undercut retaining ring.

Sodium hydroxide powder: Powder that is produced when the sodium azide pellets in an air bag system are activated.

Soft-faced hammer: General-purpose hammer with a head of plastic, wood, or other soft material, used to minimize damage to the surfaces being struck.

Solder: A mixture of tin and lead, melted to fill dents and cracks in metal.

Soldering: Joining process in which the base metal is heated enough to allow the solder to melt and make an adhesive bond.

Solder paddle: Wooden tool designed for applying and spreading body solder.

Solids: The part of the paint that does not evaporate, but remains on the surface.

Solvent: A liquid capable of dissolving or diluting a material. Reducers and thinners are considered solvents.

Solvent cements: Thin liquids that partly dissolve plastic materials and bond them together.

Sound-deadening materials: Pads or sheets of plastic material that absorb sound.

Space frame: A variation of unitized body construction in which molded plastic panels are bonded (with adhesive or mechanical fasteners) to a specially designed space frame.

Spanner sockets: Specialty tools with 2-4 prongs, designed to aid in the removal of antennas, mirrors, and radio trim nuts.

Specialty shops: Those that specialize in frame straightening, wheel alignment, upholstering, or custom painting operations.

Specific gravity: See Relative density.

Speed file: Long metal or wooden holder used with strips of coarse sandpaper to smooth a work area.

Spider webbing: An unusual custom painting effect produced by forcing acrylic lacquer from the spray gun in the form of fibrous thread.

Spitting: Spray gun problem caused by dried-out packing around the fluid needle valve that permits air to get into fluid passageways.

Spoon: A tool used in much the same manner as a dolly, but designed for use in confined areas. Also used to pry panels back into position.

Spot cutter bit: Tool used to cut through the welds on a panel being replaced.

Spot putty: Fast-drying material used to fill small imperfections before painting.

Spot welds: Fusion by localized heat of two or more metal components in a small area (spot).

Spray gun: Device that uses air pressure or paint pressure to atomize sprayable material and apply it to a surface.

Spray mask: A film that is sprayed on the surface to be decorated. The design is cut through the film, the desired portions removed, and paint is applied.

Spray-on roof coverings: Vinyl coverings sprayed into place, in contrast to a cut-and-fitted fabric covering.

Spray pattern: The cross section of the spray.

Spreaders: Rigid, rectangular pieces of plastic used to spread body filler over dented areas.

Spread rams: A spread ram has two jaws that are forced apart when the tool is activated.

Squeegee: A flexible rubber or plastic tool used to apply body putty or filler.

Stationary rack systems: Systems that can be used to repair extensive collision damage.

Stationary sections: Permanent assemblies or components of the vehicle that cannot be moved.

Steering alignment specialist: Technicians who align and balance wheels, as well as repairing steering mechanisms and suspension systems.

Steering axis inclination: The inward tilt of the steering knuckle.

Stencils: Impervious materials into which designs have been cut. The paint is then allowed to strike the surface through these openings.

Stitch welding: Process that limits heat buildup (and thus distortion of metal) by utilizing a series of short overlapping welds.

Stools: Low seats, sometimes equipped with wheels, that allow a technician to work from a seated position rather than kneeling.

Stops: Check blocks or spacers used in movable glass installations.

Storage battery: Device that converts chemical energy into electrical energy.

Strainers: Fine mesh screens used to remove small lumps of paint, dirt, or other debris from paint.

Stress lines: Low areas in a damaged panel that usually start at the actual point of impact and travel outward.

Stretching: Deformation of metal under tension.

Striker pin: A bolt that can be adjusted laterally and vertically, as well as fore and aft, to achieve proper door clearance and alignment.

Striker plate: The portion of a door lock that is mounted on the body pillar and is engaged by the latch when the door is closed.

Stringer beads: Welds are made by moving the electrode in a straight continuous line.

Striping brushes: Small brushes are used to apply stripes and other designs by hand.

Striping tool: Device with a small container for paint and a brass applicator wheel that applies paint as the tool is pulled along the surface.

Strippers: See Paint removers.

Stripping: Removing old finish or other material to expose bare metal.

Structural adhesive: Strong, flexible thermosetting adhesive.

Structural integrity: A vehicle's body strength and ability to remain in one piece.

Structural member: A primary load-bearing component of the body structure.

Stub frame: A unibody with no center rail portions but with front and rear stub sections.

Stud: A headless bolt that is threaded on one or both ends.

Subassembly: An assembled unit composed of several other parts or units.

Subframe: In some unibody designs, a pair of short rails that is fastened to the car.

Sublet: Work sent out to other shops.

Submembers: Box- or channel-like reinforcements welded to the vehicle floor.

Substrate: The base material upon which paint or other substances can be placed.

Suction cups: Rubber or plastic cups that can be used to hold and position large pieces of glass, such as a windshield.

Sun roof: An adjustable roof panel that slides backwards and forward on guide tracks.

Sun roof panels: Transparent sections of the roof that can be removed or slid into a recess for ventilation.

Support rods: Metal rods used to support the headlining in a vehicle.

Surface rust: Rust on the outside of a panel that has not penetrated the steel.

Surface-scratching method: Scratching an arc welding electrode across the work to form the arc.

Surfacing mat: Very thin fiberglass mat that is used as the top or outermost layer when making repairs.

Surform: A surface forming file with open, rasp-like teeth that was originally manufactured by the Stanley Tool Company. Also known as a grater file.

Swirl remover: See Polishing cream.

Syntactic foams: Resin and catalyst systems that contain small glass or plastic spheres, and are used to fill rusted areas in door sills and rocker panels.

T

Tack coat: A light dusting coat that is allowed to flash or become tacky before the next coat is applied.

Tack rag: A resin-impregnated cheesecloth, which is used to pick up small particles on the surface before finishing.

Tack welds: Small, temporary welds that hold parts in place during final welding operations.

Tap: Device for cutting internal threads on metal.

Tape measures: Retractable steel measuring tools.

Tapping technique: Touching an arc welding electrode to the work as a means of beginning or striking an arc.

Taps and dies: Tools used to cut new threads or restore damaged threads.

Technical pens: Specialized pens used to draw pinstripes by hand on vehicles.

Temperature-indicating crayons: Crayons used to make marks across a weld area to monitor temperature. The marks will disappear as the metal reaches the specified temperature.

Temperature make-up system: A system that filters and warms air before it enters a spray booth.

Tempered glass: Glass that has been heat-treated, so that it crumbles into small pieces upon impact.

Terminals: Mechanical fasteners that are attached to wire ends.

Test light: Device equipped with a lamp that will light when voltage is present in a circuit.

Texturing agents: Material added to paint to produce a bumpy texture.

Thermoplastic: A plastic material that will soften when heated and harden when cooled.

Thermosetting plastic: Resin that does not melt when heated. Thermosetting plastics, such as polyester and epoxy, must be catalyzed to cause the resin to set.

Thinner: Solvent used to thin lacquers and acrylic to proper viscosity for spraying.

Thrust line: An imaginary line that is parallel with the rear wheels.

Tinning: Melting a soldering paste and flux onto an area to be filled with solder.

Tinted glass: Glass with a color tint added.

Tint tone: Shade that results when a small amount of a color is mixed with a large amount of white.

Toe: The difference in the distance between the front edge and the back edge of the front or rear wheels.

Toe-in: Wheel alignment so that the front of the wheels are closer together than the back of the wheels.

Toe-out: Condition that occurs when a vehicle turns, so that the front edges of the front wheels are farther apart than the back edges.

Tolerances: Allowable limits or deviation from a standard.

Topcoat: The final finish coat of a paint system.

Torque box: Specially designed structural component engineered to allow some twisting as a means of absorbing road and collision impact shock.

Torsion bars: Metal bars that are twisted as a lid is closed, providing the spring tension necessary to ''pop'' the lid open when the latch is released.

Total loss: A situation in which the cost of repair will likely be very close to or exceed the value of the vehicle.

Touch-up gun: Spray gun that is similar to a conventional spray gun, but with a smaller capacity. It is used for touch-up work, stenciling, and small detail work.

Touch-up paints: Small containers of paint, matched to factory colors, that are used to fill small chips in a vehicle finish.

Tower: The upright portions of frame-straightening systems.

Tower cut: Same as a nose, but including a portion of the inner structure known as the shock tower or strut tower.

Toxic fumes: Fumes that can cause illness or death.

Tracer: Colored strip on a wire to make it possible to trace electricity flow through a circuit.

Tracking: The ability of the rear wheels of a vehicle to follow the front wheels.

Tracking gauges: Devices used to detect misalignment of front and rear wheels.

Track moldings: Trim pieces that consist of a metal track and a plastic insert.

Tram gauge: Instrument used to measure vehicle damage and check alignment and dimensions against factory specifications.

Transmitter/receiver lock system: System in which a signal is sent from a small, key ring transmitter to a receiver located in the door, activating the locking mechanism.

Transverse: Term used to identify engines positioned so the crankshaft is parallel to the vehicle's axles.

Trim: Moldings, upholstery, or bright decorative components of a vehicle.

Trim cement: Special adhesive used to attach upholstery and selected trim.

Twist: Damage that distorts the cross members of a frame.

Two-component epoxy primers: Material with two components that react after being mixed together.

Two-tone: Use of two different colors on a single paint job.

U

Underbody: The lower portion of the vehicle, containing the floor pan, trunk floor, and structural reinforcements.

Undercoating: The second coat in a three-coat finish; the first coat in repainting. Also, the coating or sealer on the underside of panels to help prevent rust and deaden sound.

Unibody construction: A vehicle type in which the body and underbody form an integral structural unit.

Universal measuring system: An adjustable measuring device which is mounted on a frame (beam) and used to measure the dimensions of vehicles. It may utilize mechanical or laser measuring devices.

Universal thinners: Solvents that can be used both to thin lacquers and to reduce enamels.

Upholsterer: Person whose responsibility is the repair or replacement of interior surface materials.

Upholstery ring pliers: Specialty pliers used to remove or install upholstery rings.

Upsetting: Deformation of metal under compression.

Up-stops: Components that limit the upward travel of the lift channel.

Urethane: Short for polyurethane, a tough, flexible material used in paint finishes, and for some molded body parts.

Utility knives: Cutting tools that often have replaceable, retractable blades.

V

Vacuum: A condition of negative pressure, as compared to atmospheric pressure.

Vacuum cleaner: Portable suction device used to clean glass, dirt, and other debris from vehicle interiors.

Vacuum cup puller: Dent puller using a large suction cup.

Vacuum patch: Device placed over a glass repair area to withdraw all air and ensure that all voids are filled with resin.

Value: The darkness or lightness of a color.

Vapor: Any substance in a gaseous state.

Vehicle: A term used to refer to all the liquid components of a finishing material. Also, a means of conveyance such as an automobile, bus, or truck.

Vehicle identification number (VIN): The number assigned by the manufacturer to each vehicle during fabrication.

Vehicles: See Solvents.

Veil: See Surfacing mat.

Ventilation fan: A device used to remove vapors and fine particles from work areas.

Vibrating knife: Knife with a rapidly moving blade that gently cuts through polyurethane adhesives.

Vinyl: Term used to refer to polyvinyl chloride products or plastics.

Vinyl-coated fabrics: Material with a plastic protective or decorative layer bonded to a fabric base that provides strength.

Vinyl paint: Material applied to a vinyl top to restore color.

Viscosity: Refers to how easily a material will pour or flow. Viscosity determination is important for paints and lubricants.

Visual estimate: Experienced guess by an estimator about the cost of repairing damage.

Volatile organic compounds: Hydrocarbons that readily evaporate into the air and are extremely flammable.

Volatiles: Another name for solvents, since they vaporize easily.

Voltage: The pressure that causes electricity to flow.

Voltmeter: Device used to measure voltage.

Volts: The unit of measure of electrical pressure or potential difference.

W

Wages: Amount paid to workers, computed on a ''per hour'' basis.

Warpage: Distortion of a panel during heat shrinking.

Wash thinners: Low-cost solvents used to clean spray guns and other equipment.

Water/air shield: A deflector built into a vehicle door.

Waterproof sandpaper: Any sandpaper that may be used with water.

Water spotting: Marring of a finish by water droplets, snow, or dew before it has become completely dry.

Weathering: Change or failure in a paint film, caused by exposure to weather.

Weatherstripping: Rubber gasket used to keep dirt, air, and moisture out of the passenger or trunk compartments of a vehicle.

Weave bead: Wider weld bead made by moving the electrode back and forth in a weaving motion.

Welding: Joining method that involves melting and fusing two pieces of material together to form a permanent joint.

Weld-through primers: Primers applied to joints before welding to help prevent galvanic corrosion.

Wetcoat: A heavy coat of paint.

Wet sanding: The act of using a liquid (usually water) during the sanding operation to help keep the sandpaper from clogging.

Wheel alignment: The process of making certain all wheels are properly positioned according to manufacturer's specifications.

Wheelhouse: Term for the inner body housing over the rear wheel.

Whipping: Improper movement of the spray gun that wastes energy and material.

Wind lace or wind cord: Rope-like trim placed around doors to help seal and decorate the openings.

Window channel: The grooves, guides, or slots in which the glass slides up and down.

Window regulator: Door-mounted mechanism that provides a means of cranking the window up and down.

Window stop: Device inside door used to limit maximum glass height and depth.

Window tools: Those required to properly remove and install glass.

Windshield pillar: The structural member that attaches the body to the roof panel.

Wiring diagrams: Plans that show where wires are routed and how components are arranged.

Wiring harness: A number of electrical wires gathered in a bundle.

Wood-grain transfer films: Plastic sheet materials used to simulate wood, usually on the sides of vehicles.

Work-hardened: Term for metal that has become stiffer and harder in the stretched areas due to permanent stresses.

Wrenches: Hand tools designed to fit over and turn various fasteners.

Wrinkling: Paint defect caused by skinning-over a heavy coat of paint before the underpart of the film has properly dried.

X

X-checking: The process of taking measurements and comparing them to corresponding dimensions on the opposite side of the vehicle to reveal damage.

X-frame: Frame design that does not rely on the floor pan (underbody area) for torsional rigidity.

Z

Zahn cup: A cup with a hole in the bottom that is used to measure a material's viscosity.

Zebra effect: A streaky looking metallic finish, usually caused by uneven application.

Zero planes: Planes that divide the datum plane into front, middle, and rear sections.

Zinc chromate: A common primer for aluminum and other nonferrous metals.

Zoning ordinances: Laws that limit the types of businesses allowed in a particular area or zone.

Index